Business Law for the CPA Candidate

CPA Problems

Eighth Edition

Mark E. Roszkowski
Professor of Business Law
University of Illinois at Urbana-Champaign

Stipes Publishing L.L.C.
202 W. University Avenue
Champaign, Illinois 61820

BUSINESS LAW FOR THE CPA CANDIDATE: CPA PROBLEMS (EIGHTH EDITION)

PREFACE

This book is a study aid to be used in conjunction with a comprehensive course preparing the student for the business law coverage on the *Regulation* and *Business Environment and Concepts* portions of the Uniform Certified Public Accountant Examination. It is organized to be used in conjunction with my textbook *Business Law: Principles, Cases, and Policy*, which covers in detail all topics tested on the exam. This book may, however, also be used to supplement a CPA review manual or any current, comprehensive business law text having substantial Uniform Commercial Code coverage.

The book includes an edited selection of questions appearing on the business law portion of the CPA examination from May 1974 to November 1995 (the last disclosed examination). It also includes questions released by the AICPA from the May 1996 to the November 2003 exams. These are indicated by the letter R and year of the exam, for example (R98). Also included are the AICPA unofficial answers to all questions. To facilitate self-testing, these answers are located at the end of the book. Answer to essay questions are in brackets ([) immediately following the facts and requirements of the question.

This book organizes hundreds of past exam questions into outlines covering all business law CPA examination topics (for example, contracts, negotiable instruments, accountants' liability). Thus, the book allows the student to examine a number of CPA questions testing a particular topic while studying the law governing that topic.

Before 1996, the questions and unofficial answers for each CPA examination were released to the public within a few months after the examination was administered. These questions provided an ideal resource for CPA candidates, who could use past questions as a detailed guide to the scope and depth of the coverage. They also allowed candidates continually to test their understanding of specific subjects in the context of actual CPA exam questions.

Beginning in 1996, the AICPA stopped releasing past exam questions to the public. Instead, it now releases only a handful of selected questions each year. This nondisclosure practice magnifies the importance of pre-1996 exam questions as a tool for serious exam preparation for two reasons. First, the hundreds of questions involved (for example, substantial portions of 44 disclosed exams are included in this book), when organized by topic, create a comprehensive and detailed study outline for the entire exam. Second, the old questions continue to be relevant because the content specification outlines for the exam are virtually unchanged over the last thirty years. For example, the Information for Uniform CPA Examination Candidates booklet for 1975 lists the following as the business law topics to be tested:

> Accountant's Legal Responsibility
> Antitrust
> Bankruptcy
> Commercial Paper (Negotiable Instruments)
> Contracts
> Estates and Trusts

Federal Securities Regulation
Forms of Business Organization (includes Agency)
Insurance
Real Property
Regulation of the Employer-Employee Relationship
Sales
Secured Transactions
Suretyship

With the exception of estates and trusts, the above topics are also those tested on the computer-based exam that commenced in 2004. Business organizations (unincorporated business associations and corporations) is tested on the *Business Environment and Concepts* section, and agency and the remaining topics appear in the *Regulation* section of the exam.

Finally, I would like to thank Carol Nelson, who typed the manuscript, for her patience and cooperation in this project.

Mark Edward Roszkowski
Champaign, Illinois

January, 2005

Summary of Contents

DETAILED TABLES OF CONTENTS FOR EACH TOPIC
ARE CONTAINED ON THE PAGES INDICATED ABOVE

---

*Based on "Uniform CPA Examination Content Specifications—Effective upon the Launch of the Computer-based Uniform CPA Examination," June 14, 2002.

Summary of Contents

PART I – PROFESSIONAL AND LEGAL RESPONSIBILITIES AND LIABILITIES OF ACCOUNTANTS

TABLE OF CONTENTS

PART I

PROFESSIONAL AND LEGAL RESPONSIBILITIES
AND LIABILITIES OF ACCOUNTANTS

I. Common Law Liability

6 (May 89)

When CPAs fail in their duty to carry out their contracts for services, liability to clients may be based on

	Breach of contract	Strict liability
a.	Yes	Yes
b.	Yes	No
c.	No	No
d.	No	Yes

4 (November 86)

Ritz Corp. wished to acquire the stock of Stale, Inc. In conjunction with its plan of acquisition Ritz hired Fein, CPA, to audit the financial statements of Stale. Based on the audited financial statements and Fein's unqualified opinion, Ritz acquired Stale. Within six months, it was discovered that the inventory of Stale had been overstated by $500,000. Ritz commenced an action against Fein. Ritz believes that Fein failed to exercise the knowledge, skill, and judgment commonly possessed by CPAs in the locality, but is not able to prove that Fein either intentionally deceived it or showed a reckless disregard for the truth. Ritz also is unable to prove that Fein had any knowledge that the inventory was overstated. Which of the following two causes of action would provide Ritz with proper bases upon which Ritz would most likely prevail?
  a. Negligence and breach of contract.
  b. Negligence and gross negligence.
  c. Negligence and fraud
  d. Gross negligence and breach of contract.

A. Negligence
1. Standard of Negligence

1 (November 93)

Beckler & Associates, CPAs, audited and gave an unqualified opinion on the financial statements of Queen Co. The financial statements contained misstatements that resulted in a material overstatement of Queen's net worth. Queen provided the audited financial statements to Mac Bank in connection with a loan made by Mac to Queen. Beckler knew that the financial statements would be provided to Mac. Queen defaulted on the loan. Mac sued Beckler to recover for its losses associated with Queen's default. Which of the following must Mac prove in order to recover?
  I. Beckler was negligent in conducting the audit.
  II. Mac relied on the financial statements.
  a. I only.
  b. II only.
  c. Both I and II.
  d. Neither I nor II.

Professional and Legal Responsibilities and Liabilities of Accountants

2 (November 93)

Which of the following statements best describes whether a CPA has met the required standard of care in conducting an audit of a client's financial statements?

a. The client's expectations with regard to the accuracy of audited financial statements.

b. The accuracy of the financial statements and whether the statements conform to generally accepted accounting principles.

c. Whether the CPA conducted the audit with the same skill and care expected of an ordinarily prudent CPA under the circumstances.

d. Whether the audit was conducted to investigate and discover all acts of fraud.

1 (May 93)

Sun Corp. approved a merger plan with Cord Corp. One of the determining factors in approving the merger was the financial statements of Cord that were audited by Frank & Co., CPAs. Sun had engaged Frank to audit Cord's financial statements. While performing the audit, Frank failed to discover certain irregularities that later caused Sun to suffer substantial losses. For Frank to be liable under common law negligence, Sun at a minimum must prove that Frank

a. Knew of the irregularities.

b. Failed to exercise due care.

c. Was grossly negligent.

d. Acted with scienter.

1 (November 91)

Cable Corp. orally engaged Drake & Co., CPAs, to audit its financial statements. Cable's management informed Drake that it suspected the accounts receivable were materially overstated. Though the financial statements Drake audited included a materially overstated accounts receivable balance, Drake issued an unqualified opinion. Cable used the financial statements to obtain a loan to expand its operations. Cable defaulted on the loan and incurred a substantial loss.

If Cable sues Drake for negligence in failing to discover the overstatement, Drake's best defense would be that Drake did **not**

a. Have privity of contract with Cable.

b. Sign an engagement letter.

c. Perform the audit recklessly or with an intent to deceive.

d. Violate generally accepted auditing standards in performing the audit.

2 (November 91)

When performing an audit, a CPA

a. Must exercise the level of care, skill, and judgment expected of a reasonably prudent CPA under the circumstances.

b. Must strictly adhere to generally accepted accounting principles.

c. Is strictly liable for failing to discover client fraud.

d. Is **not** liable unless the CPA commits gross negligence or intentionally disregards generally accepted auditing standards.

28 (November 87)

One of the elements necessary to hold a CPA liable to a client for conducting an audit negligently is that the CPA

a. Acted with scienter or guilty knowledge.

b. Was a fiduciary of the client.

c. Failed to exercise due care.

d. Executed an engagement letter.

4 (November 83)

In an action for negligence against a CPA, "the custom of the profession" standard is used at least to some extent in determining whether the CPA is negligent. Which of the following statements describes how this standard is applied?

a. If the CPA proves he literally followed GAAP and GAAS, it will be conclusively presumed that the CPA was **not** negligent.

b. The custom of the profession argument may only be raised by the defendant.

    c.   Despite a CPA's adherence to the custom of the profession, negligence may nevertheless be present.

    d.   Failure to satisfy the custom of the profession is equivalent to gross negligence.

2 (November 78)

Magnus Enterprises engaged a CPA firm to perform the annual examination of its financial statements. Which of the following is a correct statement with respect to the CPA firm's liability to Magnus for negligence?

    a.   Such liability can <u>not</u> be varied by agreement of the parties.

    b.   The CPA firm will be liable for any fraudulent scheme it does <u>not</u> detect.

    c.   The CPA firm will <u>not</u> be liable if it can show that it exercised the ordinary care and skill of a reasonable man in the conduct of his own affairs.

    d.   The CPA firm must <u>not</u> only exercise reasonable care in what it does, but also must possess at least that degree of accounting knowledge and skill expected of a CPA.

1 (November 76)

Martin Corporation orally engaged Humm & Dawson to audit its year-end financial statements. The engagement was to be completed within two months after the close of Martin's fiscal year for a fixed fee of $2,500. Under these circumstances, what obligation is assumed by Humm & Dawson?

    a.   None, because the contract is unenforceable since it is <u>not</u> in writing.

    b.   An implied promise to exercise reasonable standards of competence and care.

    c.   An implied obligation to take extraordinary steps to discover all defalcations.

    d.   The obligation of an insurer of its work which is liable without fault.

21 (November 75)

Martinson is a duly licensed CPA. One of his clients is suing him for negligence alleging that he failed to meet generally accepted auditing standards in the current year's audit thereby failing to discover large thefts of inventory. Under the circumstances

    a.   Martinson is <u>not</u> bound by generally accepted auditing standards unless he is a member of the AICPA.

    b.   Martinson's failure to meet generally accepted auditing standards would result in liability.

    c.   Generally accepted auditing standards do <u>not</u> currently cover the procedures which must be used in verifying inventory for balance sheet purposes.

    d.   If Martinson failed to meet generally accepted auditing standards, he would undoubtedly be found to have committed the tort of fraud.

23 (November 75)

Walters & Whitlow, CPAs, failed to discover a fraudulent scheme used by Davis Corporation's head cashier to embezzle corporate funds during the past five years. Walters & Whitlow would have discovered the embezzlements promptly if they had <u>not</u> been negligent in their annual audits. Under the circumstances, Walters & Whitlow will normally <u>not</u> be liable for

    a.   Punitive damages.

    b.   The fees charged for the years in question.

    c.   Losses occurring after the time the fraudulent scheme should have been detected.

    d.   Losses occurring prior to the time the fraudulent scheme should have been detected and which could have been recovered had it been so detected.

2B (May 79)

The CPA firm of Blank, Miller & Tage prepares a significant number of individual and corporate income tax returns. Jones is a newly hired junior accountant. This is Jones' first job since graduation from school. Jones' initial assignment is to work with the tax department in the preparation of clients' 1978 income tax returns.

Required: Answer the following, setting forth reasons for any conclusions stated.

1. What is the principal legal basis for potential liability of the CPA firm and Jones to clients in connection with the preparation of income tax returns?

2. Give some examples of performance which would result in such liability?

3. What is the basis for determining the amount of damages to be awarded?

1. The principal legal basis for liability of the firm and Jones is negligence. Jones, acting as an agent of the firm, is personally liable to clients for his negligent preparation of their tax returns. The firm, as principal, is responsible for the acts of its agents.

2. Some common examples of negligence are--
    - Failure to timely prepare and submit tax returns to the client for filing as agreed.
    - Erroneous application of the law to facts submitted.
    - Failure to recommend timely elections.
    - Failure to review performance of, supervise, and train employees.
    - Lack of awareness or understanding of the law essential to the proper preparation of returns.

3. The amount of damages to be awarded to the client because of negligent preparation of tax returns is typically the amount of penalties assessed, interest assessed, no-longer-recoverable taxes erroneously paid by the client, and other costs directly resulting from negligence depending upon the specific circumstances (e.g., fee paid to another tax return preparer for an amended return). In cases of gross negligence, punitive damages may also be awarded.

7A (May 76)

Jackson was a junior staff member of an accounting firm. He began the audit of the Bosco Corporation which manufactured and sold expensive watches. In the middle of the audit he quit. The accounting firm hired another person to continue the audit of Bosco. Due to the changeover and the time pressure to finish the audit, the firm violated certain generally accepted auditing standards when they did not follow adequate procedures with respect to the physical inventory. Had the proper procedures been used during the examination they would have discovered that watches worth more than $20,000 were missing. The employee who was stealing the watches was able to steal an additional $30,000 worth before the thefts were discovered six months after the completion of the audit.

Required: Discuss the legal problems of the accounting firm as a result of the above facts.

The firm is undoubtedly liable for negligence. The failure to follow generally accepted auditing standards indicates negligence in the conduct of the audit. Although the courts do not always recognize adherence to the custom of the profession (generally accepted auditing standards) as a defense, they invariably hold that the failure to follow customary practice constitutes negligence. The fact that Jackson left in the middle of the audit and caused a problem for the firm is of no consequence. The firm, by reason of the negligence of its agents, will be liable for the actual loss up to at least the $30,000 worth of watches stolen after the completion of the audit. This loss would not have occurred if the audit had been conducted properly. In addition, the firm may also be liable on the initial $20,000 of thefts to the extent that prompt discovery in the course of the audit would have permitted recovery of this loss.

2. Parties to Whom Liable

1 (R97)

Which of the following statements is generally correct regarding the liability of a CPA who negligently gives an opinion on an audit of a client's financial statements?

a. The CPA is only liable to those third parties who are in privity of contract with the CPA.

b. The CPA is only liable to the client.

c. The CPA is liable to anyone in a class of third parties who the CPA knows will rely on the opinion.

d. The CPA is liable to all possible foreseeable users of the CPA's opinion.

8 (November 95)

Under the "Ultramares" rule, to which of the following parties will an accountant be liable for negligence?

	Parties in privity	Foreseen parties
a.	Yes	Yes
b.	Yes	No
c.	No	Yes
d.	No	No

4 (November 91)

Hark, CPA, failed to follow generally accepted auditing standards in auditing Long Corp.'s financial statements. Long's management had told Hark that the audited statements would be submitted to several banks to obtain financing. Relying on the statements, Third Bank gave Long a loan. Long defaulted on the loan. In a jurisdiction applying the Ultramares decision, if Third sues Hark, Hark will

   a. Win because there was no privity of contract between Hark and Third.
   b. Lose because Hark knew that banks would be relying on the financial statements.
   c. Win because Third was contributorily negligent in granting the loan.
   d. Lose because Hark was negligent in performing the audit.

29 (November 87)

In general, the third party (primary) beneficiary rule as applied to a CPA's legal liability in conducting an audit is relevant to which of the following causes of action against a CPA?

	Fraud	Constructive fraud	Negligence
a.	Yes	Yes	No
b.	Yes	No	No
c.	No	Yes	Yes
d.	No	No	Yes

1 (November 83)

Locke, CPA, was engaged by Hall, Inc. to audit Willow Company. Hall purchased Willow after receiving Willow's audited financial statements, which included Locke's unqualified auditor's opinion. Locke was negligent in the performance of the Willow audit engagement. As a result of Locke's negligence, Hall suffered damages of $75,000. Hall appears to have grounds to sue Locke for

	Breach of contract	Negligence
a.	Yes	Yes
b.	Yes	No
c.	No	Yes
d.	No	No

18 (November 75)

The traditional common law rules regarding accountants' liability to third parties for negligence
   a. Remain substantially unchanged since their inception.
   b. Were more stringent than the rules currently applicable.
   c. Are of relatively minor importance to the accountant.
   d. Have been substantially changed at both the federal and state levels.

Professional and Legal Responsibilities and Liabilities of Accountants

5 (November 88)

In order to expand its operations, Dark Corp. raised $4 million by making a private interstate offering of $2 million in common stock and negotiating a $2 million loan from Safe Bank. The common stock was properly offered pursuant to Rule 505 of Regulation D.

In connection with this financing, Dark engaged Crea & Co., CPAs, to audit Dark's financial statements. Crea knew that the sole purpose for the audit was so that Dark would have audited financial statements to provide to Safe and the purchasers of the common stock. Although Crea conducted the audit in conformity with its audit program, Crea failed to detect material acts of embezzlement committed by Dark's president. Crea did not detect the embezzlement because of its inadvertent failure to exercise due care in designing its audit program for this engagement.

After completing the audit, Crea rendered an unqualified opinion on Dark's financial statements. The financial statements were relied upon by the purchasers of the common stock in deciding to purchase the shares. In addition, Safe approved the loan to Dark based on the audited financial statements.

Within 60 days after the sale of the common stock and the making of the loan by Safe, Dark was involuntarily petitioned into bankruptcy. Because of the president's embezzlement, Dark became insolvent and defaulted on its loan to Safe. Its common stock became virtually worthless. Actions have been commenced against Crea by:

- The purchasers of the common stock who have asserted that Crea is liable for damages under Section 10(b) and Rule 10b-5 of the Securities Exchange Act of 1934.
- Safe, based upon Crea's negligence.

Required: In separate paragraphs, discuss the merits of the actions commenced against Crea, indicating the likely outcomes and the reasons therefor.

Crea will not be liable to the purchasers of the common stock. Although an offering of securities made pursuant to Regulation D is exempt from the registration requirements of the Securities Act of 1933, the antifraud provisions of the federal securities acts continue to apply. In order to establish a cause of action under Section 10(b) and Rule 10b-5 of the Securities Exchange Act of 1934, the purchasers generally must show that: Crea made a material misrepresentation or omission in connection with the purchase or sale of a security; Crea acted with some element of scienter (intentional or willful conduct); Crea's wrongful conduct was material; the purchasers relied on Crea's wrongful conduct; and that there was a sufficient causal connection between the purchaser's loss and Crea's wrongful conduct.

Under the facts of this case, Crea's inadvertent failure to exercise due care, which resulted in Crea's not detecting the president's embezzlement, will not be sufficient to satisfy the scienter element because such conduct amounts merely to negligence. Therefore, Crea will not be liable for damages under Section 10(b) and Rule 10b-5 of the Securities Exchange Act of 1934.

Crea is likely to be held liable to Safe Bank based on Crea's negligence despite the fact that Safe is not in privity of contract with Crea. In general, a CPA will not be liable for negligence to creditors if its auditor's report was primarily for the benefit of the client, for use in the development of the client's business, and only incidentally or collaterally for the use of those to whom the client might show the financial statements. However, a CPA is generally liable for ordinary negligence to third parties if the audit report is for the identified third party's primary benefit.

In order to establish Crea's negligence, Safe must show that: Crea had a legal duty to protect Safe from unreasonable risk; Crea failed to perform the audit with the due care or competence expected of members of its profession; there was a causal relationship between Safe's loss and Crea's failure to exercise due care; actual damage or loss resulting from Crea's failure to exercise due care. On the facts of this case, Crea will be liable based on negligence since the audited financial statement reports were for the primary benefit of Safe, an identified third party, and Crea failed to exercise due care in detecting the president's embezzlement, which resulted in Safe's loss, i.e., Dark's default in repaying the loan to Safe.

2 (May 84)

Perfect Products Co. applied for a substantial bank loan from Capitol City Bank. In connection with its application, Perfect engaged William & Co., CPAs, to audit its financial statements. William completed the audit and rendered an unqualified opinion. On the basis of the financial statements and William's opinion, Capitol granted Perfect a loan of $500,000.

Within three months after the loan was granted, Perfect filed for bankruptcy. Capitol promptly brought suit against William for damages, claiming that it had relied to its detriment on misleading financial statements and the unqualified opinion of William.

William's audit workpapers reveal negligence and possible other misconduct in the performance of the audit. Nevertheless, William believes it can defend against liability to Capitol based on the privity defense.

Required: Answer the following, setting forth reasons for any conclusions stated.
1. Explain the privity defense and evaluate its application to William.
2. What exceptions to the privity defense might Capitol argue?

1. Privity is an early common law concept that was adopted by the courts to prevent third parties from bringing a legal action based upon a contract to which they were not parties. William was in privity of contract with Perfect, its audit client, but William had no contractual relationship with Capitol despite Capitol's reliance upon the statements audited by William. Moreover, Capitol gave no consideration to William. Therefore, under strict application of the privity rule, Capitol lacks the standing to sue for breach of contract or negligence since Capitol is not in a direct contractual relationship with William.

Privity has been the subject of much critical reevaluation, and the courts have frequently narrowed or rejected it. However, in a landmark opinion (Ultramares), privity was retained to some extent in an action against a CPA firm based partially upon negligence. Some court decisions, however, have directly overruled the privity defense in actions against CPAs, particularly when the third party was contemplated as a user of the financial statements, as in this case.

2. The first major exception to the privity requirement is fraud. Although a CPA may generally avoid liability for ordinary negligence based upon privity, where the action is for fraud, an injured third party has the requisite standing to sue. However, in order to recover based on fraud, the third party (Capitol) must prove scienter or guilty knowledge on the part of the CPA.

The second exception to the privity defense is constructive fraud. Constructive fraud is generally defined as a false representation of a material fact with lack of reasonable ground for belief and with an expectation of reliance by another, and, in fact, there is reasonable reliance resulting in damage. Constructive fraud may also be inferred from evidence of gross negligence or recklessness, although they are not necessarily constructive fraud in and of themselves. The dividing line between what actions will meet the scienter requirement for actual fraud and what is necessary to evoke the constructive fraud doctrine is not clear.

The third exception to the privity defense is gross negligence. Gross negligence represents an extreme, flagrant, or reckless departure from standards of due care. For example, a knowing failure to follow GAAS on a material matter might be held by a jury to be gross negligence. The jury might then find that the defendant's conduct was so gross as to satisfy the scienter requirement.

In addition to fraud and its various offshoots, one may avoid the privity barrier if it can be established by the third party that it was the party that the contract was intended to benefit. Thus, if a third party plaintiff suing a CPA can establish that the audit was for his benefit, then the injured third party may have standing to sue. He is a third party beneficiary of the contract and privity will not bar him from recovery. Recovery under this theory has been significantly expanded. It has recently been held that liability extends to those in a fixed, definable, and contemplated group whose conduct is to be governed by the contract's performance.

3B (May 82)

Pelham & James, CPAs, were retained by Tom Stone, sole proprietor of Stone Housebuilders, to compile Stone's financial statements. Stone advised Pelham & James that the financial statements would be used in connection with a possible incorporation of the business and sale of stock to friends. Prior to undertaking the engagement, Pelham & James were also advised to pay particular attention to the trade accounts payable. They agreed to use every reasonable means to determine the correct amount.

At the time Pelham & James were engaged, the books and records were in total disarray. Pelham & James proceeded with the engagement applying all applicable procedures for compiling financial statements. They failed however, to detect and disclose in the financial statements Stone's liability for certain unpaid bills. Documentation concerning those bills was available for Pelham & James' inspection had they looked. This omission led to a material understatement ($60,000) of the trade accounts payable.

Pelham & James delivered the compiled financial statements to Tom Stone with their compilation report which indicated that they did not express an opinion or any other assurance regarding the financial statements. Tom Stone met with two prospective investors, Dickerson and Nichols. At the meeting, Pelham & James stated that they were confident that the trade accounts payable balance was accurate to within $8,000.

Stone Housebuilders was incorporated. Dickerson and Nichols, relying on the financial statements, became stockholders along with Tom Stone. Shortly thereafter, the understatement of trade accounts payable was detected. As a result, Dickerson and Nichols discovered that they had paid substantially more for the stock than it was worth at the time of purchase.

Required: Answer the following, setting forth reasons for any conclusions stated.
Will Pelham & James be found liable to Dickerson and Nichols in a common law action for their damages?

Yes. Pelham & James will be found liable to Dickerson and Nichols based on their negligent misrepresentation that the trade accounts payable balance was accurate within $8,000, when in fact it was materially understated. The understatement was due to the firm's failure to detect certain unpaid bills that were available for their inspection.

It should be recognized that Pelham & James will be liable to Dickerson and Nichols even though they are third-party users of the financial statements and not in privity of contract with Pelham & James. Dickerson's and Nichols' reliance, both on the financial statements and on Pelham & James' oral representations, was specifically known, and thus, Pelham & James owed them a duty of due care. Moreover, Pelham & James' compilation report, which disclaimed any opinion or other assurances, will not release them from liability.

3. Specific Situations

9 (November 95)
When performing an audit, a CPA will most likely be considered negligent when the CPA fails to
a. Detect all of a client's fraudulent activities.
b. Include a negligence disclaimer in the client engagement letter.
c. Warn a client of known internal control weaknesses.
d. Warn a client's customers of embezzlement by the client's employees.

2 (May 93)
A CPA will most likely be negligent when the CPA fails to
a. Correct errors discovered in the CPA's previously issued audit reports.
b. Detect all of a client's fraudulent activities.
c. Include a negligence disclaimer in the CPA's engagement letter.
d. Warn a client's customers of embezzlement by the client's employees.

4 (May 93)
A CPA's duty of due care to a client most likely will be breached when a CPA
a. Gives a client an oral instead of written report.
b. Gives a client incorrect advice based on an honest error of judgment.
c. Fails to give tax advice that saves the client money.
d. Fails to follow generally accepted auditing standards.

5 (November 90)
Mix and Associates, CPAs, issued an unqualified opinion on the financial statements of Glass Corp. for the year ended December 31, 1989. It was determined later that Glass' treasurer had embezzled $300,000 from Glass during 1989. Glass sued Mix because of Mix's failure to discover the embezzlement. Mix was unaware of the embezzlement. Which of the following is Mix's best defense?
a. The audit was performed in accordance with GAAS.
b. The treasurer was Glass' agent and, therefore, Glass was responsible for preventing the embezzlement.
c. The financial statements were presented in conformity with GAAP.
d. Mix had no actual knowledge of the embezzlement.

1 (May 89)
Krim, President and CEO of United Co., engaged Smith, CPA, to audit United's financial statements so that United could secure a loan from First Bank. Smith issued an unqualified opinion on May 20, 1988, but the loan was delayed. On

August 5, 1988, on inquiry to Smith by First Bank, Smith, relying on Krim's representation, made assurances that there was no material change in United's financial status. Krim's representation was untrue because of a material change which took place after May 20, 1988. First relied on Smith's assurances of no change. Shortly thereafter, United became insolvent. If First sues Smith for negligent representation, Smith will be found

    a. Not liable, because Krim misled Smith, and a CPA is <u>not</u> responsible for a client's untrue representations.

    b. Liable, because Smith should have undertaken sufficient auditing procedures to verify the status of United.

    c. Not liable, because Smith's opinion only covers the period up to May 20.

    d. Liable, because Smith should have contacted the chief financial officer rather than the chief executive officer.

9 (May 89)

Nast Corp. orally engaged Baker & Co., CPAs, to audit its financial statements. The management of Nast informed Baker that it suspected the accounts receivable were materially overstated. Although the financial statements audited by Baker did, in fact, include a materially overstated accounts receivable balance, Baker issued an unqualified opinion. Nast relied on the financial statements in deciding to obtain a loan from Century Bank to expand its operations. Nast has defaulted on the loan and has incurred a substantial loss.

If Nast sues Baker for negligence in failing to discover the overstatement, Baker's best defense would be that

    a. Baker did <u>not</u> perform the audit recklessly or with an intent to deceive.

    b. Baker was <u>not</u> in privity of contract with Nast.

    c. The audit was performed by Baker in accordance with generally accepted auditing standards.

    d. No engagement letter had been signed by Baker.

1 (May 81)

DMO Enterprises, Inc. engaged the accounting firm of Martin, Seals & Anderson to perform its annual audit. The firm performed the audit in a competent, non-negligent manner and billed DMO for $16,000, the agreed fee. Shortly after delivery of the audited financial statements, Hightower, the assistant controller, disappeared, taking with him $28,000 of DMO's funds. It was then discovered that Hightower had been engaged in a highly sophisticated, novel defalcation scheme during the past year. He had previously embezzled $35,000 of DMO funds. DMO has refused to pay the accounting firm's fee and is seeking to recover the $63,000 that was stolen by Hightower. Which of the following is correct?

    a. The accountants can <u>not</u> recover their fee and are liable for $63,000.

    b. The accountants are entitled to collect their fee and are <u>not</u> liable for $63,000.

    c. DMO is entitled to rescind the audit contract and thus is <u>not</u> liable for the $16,000 fee, but it can <u>not</u> recover damages.

    d. DMO is entitled to recover the $28,000 defalcation, and it is <u>not</u> liable for the $16,000 fee.

3 (November 78)

The Apex Surety Company wrote a general fidelity bond covering defalcations by the employees of Watson, Inc. Thereafter, Grand, an employee of Watson, embezzled $18,900 of company funds. When his activities were discovered, Apex paid Watson the full amount in accordance with the terms of the fidelity bond, and then sought recovery against Watson's auditors, Kane & Dobbs, CPAs. Which of the following would be Kane & Dobbs' best defense?

    a. Apex is <u>not</u> in privity of contract.

    b. The shortages were the result of clever forgeries and collusive fraud which would <u>not</u> be detected in an examination made in accordance with generally accepted auditing standards.

    c. Kane & Dobbs were <u>not</u> guilty either of gross negligence or fraud.

    d. Kane & Dobbs were <u>not</u> aware of the Apex-Watson surety relationship.

3 (November 76)

Winslow Manufacturing, Inc. sought a $200,000 loan from National Lending Corporation. National Lending insisted that audited financial statements be submitted before it would extend credit. Winslow agreed to this and also agreed to pay the audit fee. An audit was performed by an independent CPA who submitted his report to Winslow to be used solely for the purpose of negotiating a loan from National. National, upon reviewing the audited financial statements, decided in good faith <u>not</u> to extend the credit desired. Certain ratios, which as a matter of policy were used by National in reaching its decision, were deemed too low. Winslow used copies of the audited financial statements to obtain credit elsewhere. It was subsequently learned that the CPA, despite the exercise of reasonable care, had failed to discover a sophisticated embezzlement scheme by Winslow's chief accountant. Under these circumstances, what liability does the CPA have?

    a.   The CPA is liable to third parties who extended credit to Winslow based upon the audited financial statements.

    b.   The CPA is liable to Winslow to repay the audit fee because credit was not extended by National.

    c.   The CPA is liable to Winslow for any losses Winslow suffered as a result of failure to discover the embezzlement.

    d.   The CPA is not liable to any of the parties.

3A (November 81)

Herbert McCoy is the chief executive officer of McCoy Forging Corporation, a small but rapidly growing manufacturing company. For the past several years, Donovan & Company, CPAs, had been engaged to do compilation work, a systems improvement study, and to prepare the company's federal and state income tax returns. In 1980, McCoy decided that due to the growth of the company and requests from bankers it would be desirable to have an audit. Moreover, McCoy had recently received a disturbing anonymous letter which stated: "Beware you have a viper in your nest. The money is literally disappearing before your very eyes! Signed: A friend."

McCoy believed that the audit was entirely necessary and easily justifiable on the basis of the growth and credit factors mentioned above. He decided he would keep the anonymous letter to himself.

Therefore, McCoy on behalf of McCoy Forging engaged Donovan & Company, CPAs, to render an opinion on the financial statements for the year ended June 30, 1981. He told Donovan he wanted to verify that the financial statements were "accurate and proper." He did not mention the anonymous letter. The usual engagement letter providing for an audit in accordance with generally accepted auditing standards (GAAS) was drafted by Donovan & Company and signed by both parties.

The audit was performed in accordance with GAAS. The audit did not reveal a clever defalcation plan by which Harper, the assistant treasurer, was siphoning off substantial amounts of McCoy Forging's money. The defalcations occurred both before and after the audit. Harper's embezzlement was discovered in October 1981. Although the scheme was fairly sophisticated, it could have been detected had additional checks and procedures been performed by Donovan & Company. McCoy Forging demands reimbursement from Donovan for the entire amount of the embezzlement, some $20,000 of which occurred before the audit and $25,000 after. Donovan has denied any liability and refuses to pay.

Required: Answer the following, setting forth reasons for any conclusions stated.

    1.   In the event McCoy Forging sues Donovan & Company, will it prevail in whole or in part?

    2.   Might there by any liability to McCoy Forging on McCoy's part and if so, under what theory?

1. No. Although the normal or typical audit may very well detect defalcations, an auditor's duty to detect fraud is limited to that which can be detected in the course of a GAAS audit. Nor does the engagement encompass taking the additional steps necessary that might detect a defalcation, unless this is specifically agreed. The engagement in the instant case in no way indicated that it was intended to discover defalcations. Even if McCoy had told Donovan of the anonymous letter, it is doubtful that liability would attach unless there was a negligently performed audit or a specific engagement to detect defalcations that was not properly performed. The fact that McCoy thought the usual audit would automatically include procedures to specifically detect defalcations would not affect the outcome of the case in the absence of additional facts--for example, if Donovan knew of McCoy's belief. Even assuming negligence on Donovan's part, recovery by McCoy Forging would be limited to the amount of damages caused by the negligent failure to discover the defalcation. In effect, recovery would be limited to defalcations subsequent to the audit.

2. Yes. The facts raise the question of whether or not McCoy acted as a reasonably prudent person in light of the circumstances. The theory applicable is negligence. McCoy owed the corporation a duty of due care in the performance of his duties as chief executive officer of McCoy Forging. Either the corporation or a shareholder suing derivatively could proceed against McCoy under the negligence theory for failing to disclose the letter and take appropriate action.

3B (November 81)

Arm Watchbank Company manufactures a full line of expansion watch bands, including platinum, gold, and a medium-priced silver. With the skyrocketing prices of precious metal and booming sales, Arm is bursting at the seams with cash and extremely valuable inventory. Dutch, the controller of Arm, noted some irregularities which aroused his suspicion that there might be some embezzlement of company funds. He therefore instituted a full-fledged internal audit of the company's books and records, examined all accounting procedures, and took other appropriate steps necessary to assure himself that nothing was amiss. The only thing unearthed by this was a $300 discrepancy in petty cash which had apparently been stolen.

Dutch talked to Wheeler, the president of Arm and told him his fears. He also suggested that in addition to the regular annual audit performed by Rice & Campbell, CPAs, that they be engaged to perform a full-fledged defalcation audit. This was authorized by Wheeler, and the engagement letter for the audit in question clearly reflected this understanding.

Rice & Campbell performed the normal annual audit in their usual competent, non-negligent manner. The special defalcation audit revealed additional shortages in petty cash. The method was determined and the culprit was exposed and dismissed. Nothing else was revealed despite the fact that the customary procedures for such an audit were followed. Ten months later, Schultz, the warehouse supervisor, was caught by another employee substituting inexpensive copies of watchbands for the genuine Arm items. The copies were remarkably similar to the originals in appearance. In fact, it would take a precious metals expert to tell the difference based upon a careful visual examination. The packaging was the same since Schultz had access to the packaging materials including the seals which were used in an attempt to provide greater security and detect theft. Schultz always placed the boxes of the copies at the bottom of the inventory supplies. Despite this fact one such carton had been shipped to a leading department store several months ago, but the substitution of copies for the originals had not been detected.

Required: Answer the following, setting forth reasons for any conclusions stated.

Would Rice & Campbell be liable for failure to detect the defalcation scheme in question?

No. A CPA who engaged in a defalcation audit is not an insurer. Liability, if any, must be predicated on fault based on the failure to exercise the care of a reasonable person under the circumstances and in accordance with the special skill or training of that person. As indicated, recovery for negligence is predicated on fault and, consequently, where there is a defalcation that cannot be discovered even with the exercise of the special care required in the performance of a defalcation audit, there is no liability. This certainly appears to be the case here. Furthermore, the difficulty of detection of the particular scheme is evidenced by the failure of the internal audit to detect anything and by the failure of the company to detect anything until Schultz was caught in the act, even though the company had continuous control of the inventory.

Finally, the excellence of the copies, the near impossibility of detection by physical examination except by an expert, and the identical repackaging, all seem to indicate that the defalcation was such that it would not have been detected even by a carefully and competently executed defalcation audit.

B. Fraud Liability

2 (R99)

Which of the following statements is (are) correct regarding the common law elements that must be proven to support a finding of constructive fraud against a CPA?

     I. The plaintiff has justifiably relied on the CPA's misrepresentation.

    II. The CPA has acted in a grossly negligent manner.

  a. I only.

  b. II only.

  c. Both I and II.

  d. Neither I nor II.

10 (November 95)

Which of the following is the best defense a CPA firm can assert in a suit for common law fraud based on its unqualified opinion on materially false financial statements?

  a. Contributory negligence on the part of the client.

  b. A disclaimer contained in the engagement letter.

  c. Lack of privity.

  d. Lack of scienter.

Professional and Legal Responsibilities and Liabilities of Accountants

10 (November 94)

Under common law, which of the following statements most accurately reflects the liability of a CPA who fraudulently gives an opinion on an audit of a client's financial statements?
   a. The CPA is liable only to third parties in privity of contract with the CPA.
   b. The CPA is liable only to known users of the financial statements.
   c. The CPA probably is liable to any person who suffered a loss as a result of the fraud.
   d. The CPA probably is liable to the client even if the client was aware of the fraud and did not rely on the opinion.

9 (May 94)

If a CPA recklessly departs from the standards of due care when conducting an audit, the CPA will be liable to third parties who are unknown to the CPA based on
   a. Negligence.
   b. Gross negligence.
   c. Strict liability.
   d. Criminal deceit.

3 (May 93)

Which of the following elements, if present, would support a finding of constructive fraud on the part of a CPA?
   a   Gross negligence in applying generally accepted auditing standards.
   b. Ordinary negligence in applying generally accepted accounting principles.
   c. Identified third party users.
   d. Scienter.

3 (November 91)

Ford & Co., CPAs, issued an unqualified opinion on Owens Corp.'s financial statements. Relying on these financial statements, Century Bank lent Owens $750,000. Ford was unaware that Century would receive a copy of the financial statements or that Owens would use them to obtain a loan. Owens defaulted on the loan.

To succeed in a common law fraud action against Ford, Century must prove, in addition to other elements, that Century was
   a. Free from contributory negligence.
   b. In privity of contract with Ford.
   c. Justified in relying on the financial statements.
   d. In privity of contract with Owens.

5 (November 91)

A CPA who fraudulently performs an audit of a corporation's financial statements will
   a. Probably be liable to any person who suffered a loss as a result of the fraud.
   b. Be liable only to the corporation and to third parties who are members of a class of intended users of the financial statements.
   c. Probably be liable to the corporation even though its management was aware of the fraud and did not rely on the financial statements.
   d. Be liable only to third parties in privity of contract with the CPA.

1 (November 90)

A CPA firm issues an unqualified opinion on financial statements not prepared in accordance with GAAP. The CPA firm will have acted with scienter in all the following circumstances except where the firm
   a. Intentionally disregards the truth.
   b. Has actual knowledge of fraud.
   c. Negligently performs auditing procedures.
   d. Intends to gain monetarily by concealing fraud.

2 (May 89)

If a stockholder sues a CPA for common law fraud based on false statements contained in the financial statements audited by the CPA, which of the following, if present, would be the CPA's best defense?

a. The stockholder lacks privity to sue.
b. The false statements were immaterial.
c. The CPA did not financially benefit from the alleged fraud.
d. The contributory negligence of the client.

7 (May 89)

Which one of the following, if present, would support a finding of constructive fraud on the part of a CPA?

a. Privity of contract.
b. Intent to deceive.
c. Reckless disregard.
d. Ordinary negligence.

Items 26 and 27 are based on the following information:

Brown & Co., CPAs, issued an unqualified opinion on the financial statements of its client, King Corp. Based on the strength of King's financial statements, Safe Bank loaned King $500,000. Brown was unaware that Safe would receive a copy of the financial statements or that they would be used in obtaining a loan by King. King defaulted on the loan.

26 (November 87)

If Safe commences an action for negligence against Brown, and Brown is able to prove that it conducted the audit in conformity with GAAs, Brown will

a. Be liable to Safe because Safe relied on the financial statements.
b. Be liable to Safe because the Statute of Frauds has been satisfied.
c. Not be liable to Safe because there is a conclusive presumption that following GAAS is the equivalent of acting reasonably and with due care.
d. Not be liable to Safe because there was a lack of privity of contract.

27 (November 87)

If Safe commences an action for common law fraud against Brown, then to be successful, Safe must prove in addition to other elements that it

a. Was in privity of contract with Brown.
b. Was not contributorily negligent.
c. Was in privity of contract with King.
d. Justifiably relied on the financial statements.

2(b) (R96)

Dredge Corp. engaged Crew, a CPA licensed by a state board of accountancy, to perform an audit of Dredge's financial statements so that Dredge could obtain a large capital improvement loan. During the audit, Bold, Dredge's CFO, asked Crew to accept a consulting engagement to assist Dredge with the installation of a new computerized accounting system. Crew accepted the consulting engagement and performed it simultaneously with the audit.

While performing the audit, Crew discovered material misstatements in Dredge's financial statements resulting from management fraud committed by Bold. Crew notified Bold of the discovery and was told to disregard it or Crew would lose the consulting engagement. Believing that the consulting engagement would be lost, Crew intentionally did not notify Dredge's audit committee of the fraud, and rendered an unqualified opinion on Dredge's financial statements.

Dredge submitted to Ocean Bank the materially misstated financial statements together with Crew's auditor's report. Ocean relied on the opinion in agreeing to finance Dredge's capital improvement.

While performing the consulting engagement, Crew failed to discover that Dredge's new computerized accounting system had insufficient control procedures because Crew omitted steps in order to complete the engagement on time. The insufficient control procedures had allowed and were allowing employees to steal from the corporation.

As a result of Bold's fraud, Dredge defaulted on the Ocean loan and was petitioned into bankruptcy under Chapter 11 of the Federal Bankruptcy Code.

Professional and Legal Responsibilities and Liabilities of Accountants

The following events resulted from the above situation:
- Dredge Corp. reported Crew's actions to the state board of accountancy that licensed Crew.
- Dredge Corp. sued Crew for negligence in performing the consulting engagement.
- Ocean Bank sued Crew for common law fraud for giving an unqualified opinion on Dredge's financial statements.

Required:

1. State the outcome of Dredge Corp.'s suit against Crew for negligence in performing the consulting engagement, and give the reasons for your conclusion.

2. State the outcome of Ocean Bank's suit against Crew for common law fraud for giving an unqualified opinion on Dredge's financial statements, and give the reasons for your conclusion.

1. Dredge Corp. will be successful in its negligence suit against Crew. Crew owed a duty of care to Dredge to perform the consulting engagement according to the standards of the profession. Crew breached that duty by failing to discover that there were insufficient control procedures in Dredge's new computerized accounting system. Dredge was damaged by Crew's breach of duty because the insufficient control procedures had allowed and were continuing to allow employees to steal.

2. Ocean Bank will be successful in its common law fraud suit against Crew. Crew intentionally issued an unqualified opinion on Dredge's materially misstated financial statements. The financial statements and Crew's accountant's report were submitted to Ocean. Ocean justifiably relied on Crew's unqualified opinion in agreeing to finance Dredge's capital improvement. Ocean was damaged as a result of Dredge's default on the loan, which was caused by the fraud.

4 (May 95)

Verge Associates, CPAs, were retained to perform a consulting service engagement by Stone Corp. Verge contracted to advise Stone on the proper computers to purchase. Verge was also to design computer software that would allow for more efficient collection of Stone's accounts receivable. Verge prepared the software programs in a manner that allowed some of Stone's accounts receivable to be erroneously deleted from Stone's records. As a result, Stone's expense to collect these accounts was increased greatly.

During the course of the engagement, a Verge partner learned from a computer salesperson that the computers Verge was recommending to Stone would be obsolete within a year. The salesperson suggested that Verge recommend a newer, less expensive model that was more efficient. Verge intentionally recommended, and Stone purchased, the more expensive model. Verge received a commission from the computer company for inducing Stone to purchase that computer.

Stone sued Verge for negligence and common law fraud.

Required:

a. State whether Stone will be successful in its negligence suit against Verge and describe the elements of negligence shown in the above situation that Stone should argue.

b. State whether Stone will be successful in its fraud suit against Verge and describe the elements of fraud shown in the above situation that Stone should argue.

a. Stone will be successful in its negligence suit against Verge. The elements of negligence are as follows:
- duty of care owed
- breach of the duty
- loss caused by the breach of duty

Verge Associates, CPAs owed a duty to its client, Stone Corp., to perform the consulting services engagement in a competent manner with the expertise necessary to perform the engagement. Verge breached this duty by incompetently preparing the computer software programs. As a result of the breach, Stone sustained damages through increased accounts receivable collection costs.

b. Stone will be successful in its fraud suit against Verge. The elements of fraud are as follows:
- false representation of a material fact
- done intentionally or with gross negligence
- justifiable reliance by the plaintiff
- resultant damages sustained by the plaintiff

Verge Associates falsely represented that it was recommending the best possible computer to Stone when, in fact, it was recommending an inferior product. The computer to be purchased was material to the entire engagement. Verge made its recommendation knowing that a better, less expensive computer was available. Stone, as Verge's client, justifiably relied on Verge's recommendation. Stone was damaged because it spent more money for an inferior computer.

3 (November 89)

Astor, Inc. purchased the assets of Bell Corp. A condition of the purchase agreement required Bell to retain a CPA to audit Bell's financial statements. The purpose of the audit was to determine whether the unaudited financial statements furnished to Astor fairly presented Bell's financial position. Bell retained Salam & Co., CPAs, to perform the audit.

While performing the audit, Salam discovered that Bell's bookkeeper had embezzled $500. Salam had some evidence of other embezzlements by the bookkeeper. However, Salam decided that the $500 was immaterial and that the other suspected embezzlements did not require further investigation. Salam did not discuss the matter with Bell's management. Unknown to Salam, the bookkeeper had, in fact, embezzled large sums of cash from Bell. In addition, the accounts receivable were significantly overstated. Salam did not detect the overstatement because of Salam's inadvertent failure to follow its audit program.

Despite the foregoing, Salam issued an unqualified opinion on Bell's financial statements and furnished a copy of the audited financial statements to Astor. Unknown to Salam, Astor required financing to purchase Bell's assets and furnished a copy of Bell's audited financial statements to City Bank to obtain approval of the loan. Based on Bell's audited financial statements, City loaned Astor $600,000.

Astor paid Bell $750,000 to purchase Bell's assets. Within six months, Astor began experiencing financial difficulties resulting from the undiscovered embezzlements and overstated accounts receivable. Astor later defaulted on the City loan.

City has commenced a lawsuit against Salam based on the following causes of action:

- Constructive fraud
- Negligence

Required: In separate paragraphs, discuss whether City is likely to prevail on the causes of action it has raised, setting forth reasons for each conclusion.

City is likely to prevail against Salam based on constructive fraud. To establish a cause of action for constructive fraud, City must prove that:

- Salam made a materially false statement of fact.
- Salam lacked a reasonable ground for belief that the statement was true. Constructive fraud may be inferred from evidence of gross negligence or recklessness.
- Salam intended another to rely on the false statement.
- City justifiably relied on the false statement.
- Such reliance resulted in damages or injury.

Under the facts of this case, Salam is likely to be liable to City based on constructive fraud. Salam made a materially false statement of fact by rendering an unqualified opinion on Bell's financial statements. Salam lacked a reasonable ground for belief that the financial statements were fairly presented by recklessly departing from the standards of due care in that it failed to investigate other embezzlements, despite having knowledge of at least one embezzlement, and did not notify Bell's management of the matter. Salam intended that others rely on the audited financial statements in deciding to loan Astor $600,000 and damages resulted evidenced by Astor's default on the City loan.

City is not likely to prevail against Salam based on negligence. In order to establish a cause of action for negligence against Salam, City must prove that:

- Salam owed a legal duty to protect Clay.
- Salam breached that legal duty by failing to perform the audit with the due care or competence expected of members of the profession.
- City suffered actual losses or damages.
- Salam's failure to exercise due care proximately caused City to suffer damages.

The facts of this case establish that Salam was negligent by not detecting the overstatement of accounts receivable because of its inadvertent failure to follow its audit program. However, Salam will not be liable to City for negligence because Salam owed no duty to City. This is the case because Salam was not in privity of contract with City, and the financial statements were neither audited by Salam for the primary benefit of City, nor was City within a known and intended class of third party beneficiaries who were to receive the audited financial statements.

2 (May 86)

Tyler Corp. is insolvent. It has defaulted on the payment of its debts and does not have assets sufficient to satisfy its unsecured creditors. Slade, a supplier of raw materials, is Tyler's largest unsecured creditor and is suing Tyler's auditors, Field & Co., CPAs. Slade had extended $2 million of credit to Tyler based on the strength of Tyler's audited financial statements. Slade's complaint alleges that the auditors were either (1) negligent in failing to discover and disclose fictitious accounts receivable created by management or (2) committed fraud in connection therewith. Field believes that the financial statements of Tyler were prepared in accordance with GAAP and, therefore, its opinion was proper. Slade has established that:

- The accounts receivable were overstated by $10 million.
- Total assets were reported as $24 million of which accounts receivable were $16 million.
- The auditors did not follow their own audit program which required that confirmation requests be sent to an audit sample representing 80% of the total dollar amount of outstanding receivables. Confirmation requests were sent to only 45%.
- The responses which were received represented only 20% of the total dollar amount of outstanding receivables. This was the poorest response in the history of the firm, the next lowest being 60%. The manager in charge of the engagement concluded that further inquiry was necessary. This recommendation was rejected by the partner in charge.
- Field had determined that a $300,000 account receivable from Dion Corp. was nonexistent. Tyler's explanation was that Dion had reneged on a purchase contract before any products had been shipped. At Field's request Tyler made a reversing entry to eliminate this overstatement. However, Field accepted Tyler's explanation as to this and several similar discrepancies without further inquiry.

Slade asserts that Field is liable:
- As a result of negligence in conducting the audit.
- As a result of fraud in conducting the audit.

Required: Answer the following, setting forth reasons for any conclusions stated.
Discuss Slade's assertions and the defenses which might be raised by Field.

The facts reveal negligence on Field's part in that it did not follow its own audit program nor did it make a proper investigation into the many irregularities and suspicious circumstances. Compliance with GAAP is of some evidentiary value to Field if it in fact complied with the principles set forth therein. However, the courts do not invariably accept GAAP as the conclusive test to disprove negligence. Furthermore, even if assuming GAAP were followed literally, GAAS certainly were not under the facts stated.

Field will undoubtedly rely upon the privity defense to avoid liability to Slade, a third party to the Field-Tyler contract. However, most jurisdictions recognize the standing of a third party beneficiary to sue. Therefore, Slade would assert such status. In a majority of jurisdictions Slade would be regarded as a third party beneficiary if it is within a known and intended class of beneficiaries. Other jurisdictions have gone even further in recognizing a duty is owed to those whom the CPA should reasonably foresee as recipients of the financial statements for authorized business purposes. There are insufficient facts to determine whether Field knew that Tyler intended to use the audited financial statements to secure credit from Slade. Therefore, it is not possible to determine whether the privity defense will bar recovery.

Fraud does not require that the party suing be in privity of contract with the defendant. However, the most significant problem in proceeding based upon fraud is that fraud requires a knowledge of falsity (scienter) or a recognized substitute therefor. Based upon the facts, Field did not actually know of management's fraud. However, it may be guilty of conduct which may be deemed to be reckless disregard for the truth. The courts also resort to the constructive fraud theory where the facts are compelling, i.e., a shutting of one's eyes to the obvious. Sometimes, the conduct is labeled gross negligence, and an inference of fraud may be drawn from this by the trier of fact.

18

II. Liability Under Federal Securities Law
A. Liability Under § 11 of the 1933 Act

1 (R00)

Under the liability provisions of Section 11 of the Securities Act of 1933, which of the following must a plaintiff prove to hold a CPA liable?

    I. The misstatements contained in the financial statements certified by the CPA were material.

    II. The plaintiff relied on the CPA's unqualified opinion.

a. I only.
b. II only.
c. Both I and II.
d. Neither I nor II.

3 (R99)

Under the liability provisions of Section 11 of the Securities Act of 1933, an auditor may help to establish the defense of due diligence if

    I. The auditor performed an additional review of the audited statements to ensure that the statements were accurate as of the effective date of a registration statement.

    II. The auditor complied with GAAS.

a. I only.
b. II only.
c. Both I and II.
d. Neither I nor II.

12 (November 95)

Under Section 11 of the Securities Act of 1933, which of the following standards may a CPA use as a defense?

	Generally accepted accounting principles	Generally accepted fraud detection standards
a.	Yes	Yes
b.	Yes	No
c.	No	Yes
d.	No	No

Items 12 and 13 are based on the following:

Under the liability provisions of Section 11 of the Securities Act of 1933, a CPA may be liable to any purchaser of a security for certifying materially misstated financial statements that are included in the security's registration statement.

12 (November 94)

Under Section 11, a CPA usually will not be liable to the purchaser

a. If the purchaser is contributorily negligent.
b. If the CPA can prove due diligence.
c. Unless the purchaser can prove privity with the CPA.
d. Unless the purchaser can prove scienter on the part of the CPA.

13 (November 94)

Under Section 11, which of the following must be proven by a purchaser of the security?

	Reliance on the financial statements	Fraud by the CPA
a.	Yes	Yes
b.	Yes	No
c.	No	Yes
d.	No	No

Items 3 through 5 are based on the following:

While conducting an audit, Larson Associates, CPAs, failed to detect material misstatements included in its client's financial statements. Larson's unqualified opinion was included with the financial statements in a registration statement and prospectus for a public offering of securities made by the client. Larson knew that its opinion and the financial statements would be used for this purpose.

3 (November 93)

Which of the following statements is correct with regard to a suit against Larson and the client by a purchaser of the securities under Section 11 of the Securities Act of 1933?
  a. The purchaser must prove that Larson was negligent in conducting the audit.
  b. The purchaser must prove that Larson knew of the material misstatements.
  c. Larson will <u>not</u> be liable if it had reasonable grounds to believe the financial statements were accurate.
  d. Larson will be liable unless the purchaser did <u>not</u> rely on the financial statements.

4 (November 93)

In a suit by a purchaser against Larson for common law negligence, Larson's best defense would be that the
  a. Audit was conducted in accordance with generally accepted auditing standards.
  b. Client was aware of the misstatements.
  c. Purchaser was <u>not</u> in privity of contract with Larson.
  d. Identity of the purchaser was <u>not</u> known to Larson at the time of the audit.

5 (November 93)

In a suit by a purchaser against Larson for common law fraud, Larson's best defense would be that
  a. Larson did <u>not</u> have actual or constructive knowledge of the misstatements.
  b. Larson's client knew or should have known of the misstatements.
  c. Larson did <u>not</u> have actual knowledge that the purchaser was an intended beneficiary of the audit.
  d. Larson was <u>not</u> in privity of contract with its client.

6 (November 91)

Quincy bought Teal Corp. common stock in an offering registered under the Securities Act of 1933. Worth & Co., CPAs, gave an unqualified opinion on Teal's financial statements that were included in the registration statement filed with the SEC. Quincy sued Worth under the provisions of the 1933 Act that deal with omission of facts required to be in the registration statement. Quincy must prove that
  a. There was fraudulent activity by Worth.
  b. There was a material misstatement in the financial statements.
  c. Quincy relied on Worth's opinion.
  d. Quincy was in privity with Worth.

8 (November 91)

Jay, CPA, gave an unqualified opinion on Nast Power Co.'s financial statements. Larkin bought Nast bonds in a public offering subject to the Securities Act of 1933. The registration statement filed with the SEC included Nast's financial statements. Larkin sued Jay for misstatements contained in the financial statements under the provisions of Section 11 of the Securities Act of 1933. To prevail, Lark must prove

	Scienter	Reliance
a.	Yes	No
b.	Yes	Yes
c.	No	No
d.	No	Yes

6 (November 90)

Holly Corp. engaged Yost & Co., CPAs, to audit the financial statements to be included in a registration statement Holly was required to file under the provisions of the Securities Act of 1933. Yost failed to exercise due diligence and did not discover the omission of a fact material to the statements. A purchaser of Holly's securities may recover from Yost under Section 11 of the Securities Act of 1933 only if the purchaser

    a.   Brings a civil action within one year of the discovery of the omission and within three years of the offering date.
    b.   Proves that the registration statement was relied on to make the purchase.
    c.   Proves that Yost was negligent.
    d.   Establishes privity of contract with Yost.

Items 7 and 8 are based on the following:

Petty Corp. made a public offering subject to the Securities Act of 1933. In connection with the offering, Ward & Co., CPAs, rendered an unqualified opinion on Petty's financial statements included in the SEC registration statement. Huff purchased 500 of the offered shares. Huff has brought an action against Ward under Section 11 of the Securities Act of 1933 for losses resulting from misstatements of facts in the financial statements included in the registration statement.

7 (November 90)

To succeed, Huff must prove that

    a.   Ward performed the audit negligently.
    b.   The misstatements were material.
    c.   Ward rendered its opinion with knowledge of material misstatements.
    d.   Huff relied on the financial statements included in the registration statement.

8 (November 90)

Ward's weakest defense would be that

    a.   Huff knew of the misstatements when Huff purchased the stock.
    b.   Huff's losses were _not_ caused by the misstatements.
    c.   Ward was _not_ in privity of contract with Huff.
    d.   Ward conducted the audit in accordance with GAAS.

7 (November 86)

On July 1, 1986, Kent purchased common stock of Salem Corp. in an offering subject to the Securities Act of 1933. Mane & Co., CPAs, rendered an unqualified opinion on the financial statements of Salem which were included in Salem's registration statement filed with the SEC on March 1, 1986. Kent has commenced an action against Mane based on the Securities Act of 1933 provisions dealing with omissions of facts required to be stated in the registration statement. Which of the following elements of a cause of action under the Securities Act of 1933 must be proved by Kent?

    a.   Kent relied upon Mane's opinion.
    b.   Kent was the initial purchaser of the stock and gave value for it.
    c.   Mane's omission was material.
    d.   Mane acted negligently or fraudulently.

5 (November 84)

Hall purchased Eon Corp. bonds in a public offering subject to the Securities Act of 1933. Kosson and Co., CPAs, rendered an unqualified opinion on Eon's financial statements, which were included in Eon's registration statement. Kosson is being sued by Hall based upon misstatements contained in the financial statements. In order to be successful, Hall must prove

	Damages	Materiality of the misstatement	Kosson's scienter
a.	Yes	Yes	Yes
b.	Yes	Yes	No
c.	Yes	No	No
d.	No	Yes	Yes

5 (November 83)

Lewis & Clark, CPAs, rendered an unqualified opinion on the financial statements of a company that sold common stock in a public offering subject to the Securities Act of 1933. Based on a false statement in the financial statements, Lewis & Clark are being sued by an investor who purchased shares of this public offering. Which of the following represents a viable defense?
   a.   The investor has not met the burden of proving fraud or negligence by Lewis & Clark.
   b.   The investor did not actually rely upon the false statement.
   c.   Detection of the false statement by Lewis & Clark occurred after their examination date.
   d.   The false statement is immaterial in the overall context of the financial statements.

3 (May 81)

Major, Major & Sharpe, CPAs, are the auditors of MacLain Industries. In connection with the public offering of $10 million of MacLain securities, Major expressed an unqualified opinion as to the financial statements. Subsequent to the offering, certain misstatements and omissions were revealed. Major has been sued by the purchasers of the stock offered pursuant to the registration statement which included the financial statements audited by Major. In the ensuing lawsuit by the MacLain investors, Major will be able to avoid liability if
   a.   The errors and omissions were caused primarily by MacLain.
   b   .It can be shown that at least some of the investors did not actually read the audited financial statements.
   c.   It can prove due diligence in the audit of the financial statements of MacLain.
   d.   MacLain had expressly assumed any liability in connection with the public offering.

29 (November 79)

Under the Securities Act of 1933, an accountant may be held liable for any materially false or misleading financial statements, including an omission of a material fact therefrom, provided the purchaser
   a.   Proves reliance on the registration statement or prospectus.
   b.   Proves negligence or fraud on the part of the accountant.
   c.   Brings suit within four years after the security is offered to the public.
   d.   Proves a false statement or omission existed and the specific securities were the ones offered through the registration statement.

1 (November 77)

A CPA is subject to criminal liability if the CPA
   a.   Refuses to turn over the working papers to the client.
   b.   Performs an audit in a negligent manner.
   c.   Willfully omits a material fact required to be stated in a registration statement.
   d.   Willfully breaches the contract with the client.

4 (November 76)

An investor seeking to recover stock market losses from a CPA firm, based upon an unqualified opinion on financial statements which accompanied a registration statement, must establish that
   a.   There was a false statement or omission of material fact contained in the audited financial statements.
   b.   He relied upon the financial statements.
   c.   The CPA firm did not act in good faith.
   d.   The CPA firm would have discovered the false statement or omission if it had exercised due care in its examination.

4B (November 80)

Jackson is a sophisticated investor. As such, she was initially a member of a small group who was going to participate in a private placement of $1 million of common stock of Clarion Corporation. Numerous meetings were held among management and the investor group. Detailed financial and other information was supplied to the participants. Upon the eve of completion of the placement, it was aborted when one major investor withdrew. Clarion then decided to offer $2.5 million of Clarion common stock to the public pursuant to the registration requirements of the Securities Act of 1933. Jackson subscribed to $300,000 of the Clarion public stock offering. Nine months later, Clarion's earnings dropped significantly and as a result the stock dropped 20% beneath the offering price. In addition, the Dow Jones Industrial Average was down 10% from the time of the offering.

Jackson has sold her shares at a loss of $60,000 and seeks to hold all parties liable who participated in the public offering including Allen, Dunn, and Rose, Clarion's CPA firm. Although the audit was performed in conformity with generally accepted auditing standards, there were some relatively minor irregularities. The financial statements of Clarion Corporation, which were part of the registration statement, contained minor misleading facts. It is believed by Clarion and Allen, Dunn, and Rose, that Jackson's asserted claim is without merit.

Required: Answer the following, setting forth reasons for any conclusions stated.
1. Assuming Jackson sues under the Securities Act of 1933, what will be the basis of her claim?
2. What are the probable defenses which might be asserted by Allen, Dunn, and Rose in light of these facts?

1. The basis of Jackson's claim will be that she sustained a loss based upon misleading financial statements. Specifically, she will rely upon § 11(a) of the Securities Act of 1933, which provides the following:

> In case any part of the registration statement, when such part became effective, contained an untrue statement of a material fact or omitted to state a material fact required to be stated therein or necessary to make the statements therein not misleading, any person acquiring such security (unless it is proved that at the time of such acquisition he knew of such untruth or omission) may, either at law or in equity, in any court of competent jurisdiction, sue . . . every accountant . . . who has with his consent been named as having prepared or certified any part of the registration statement. . . .

To the extent that the relatively minor irregularities resulted in the certification of materially false or misleading financial statements, there is potential liability. Jackson's case is based on the assertion of such an untrue statement or omission coupled with an allegation of damages. Jackson does not have to prove reliance on the statements nor the company's or auditor's negligence in order to recover the damages. The burden is placed on the defendant to provide defenses that will enable it to avoid liability.

2. The first defense that could be asserted is that Jackson knew of the untruth or omission in audited financial statements included in the registration statement. The Act provides that the plaintiff may not recover if it can be proved that at the time of such acquisition she knew of such "untruth or omission."

Since Jackson was a member of the private placement group and presumably privy to the type of information that would be contained in a registration statement, plus any other information requested by the group, she may have had sufficient knowledge of the facts claimed to be untrue or omitted. If this be the case, then she would not be relying on the certified financial statements but upon her own knowledge.

The next defense assertable would be that the untrue statement or omission was not material. The SEC has defined the term as meaning matters about which an average prudent investor ought to be reasonably informed before purchasing the registered security. For § 11 purposes, this has been construed as meaning a fact that, had it been correctly stated or disclosed, would have deterred or tended to deter the average prudent investor from purchasing the security in question.

Allen, Dunn, and Rose would also assert that the loss in question was not due to the false statement or omission; that is, that the false statement was not the cause of the price drop. It would appear that the general decline in the stock market would account for at least a part of the loss. Additionally, if the decline in earnings was not factually connected with the false statement or omission, the defendants have another basis for refuting the causal connection between their wrongdoing and the resultant drop in the stock's price.

Finally, the accountants will claim that their departure from generally accepted auditing standards was too minor to be considered a violation of the standard of due diligence required by the Act.

B. 1934 Act Liability

11 (November 95)

Under the anti-fraud provisions of Section 10(b) of the Securities Exchange Act of 1934, a CPA may be liable if the CPA acted
- a. Negligently.
- b. With independence.
- c. Without due diligence.
- d. Without good faith.

13 (November 95)

Ocean and Associates, CPAs, audited the financial statements of Drain Corporation. As a result of Ocean's negligence in conducting the audit, the financial statements included material misstatements. Ocean was unaware of this fact. The financial statements and Ocean's unqualified opinion were included in a registration statement and prospectus for an original public offering of stock by Drain. Sharp purchased shares in the offering. Sharp received a copy of the prospectus prior to the purchase but did not read it. The shares declined in value as a result of the misstatements in Drain's financial statements becoming known. Under which of the following Acts is Sharp most likely to prevail in a lawsuit against Ocean?

	Securities Exchange Act of 1934, Section 10(b), Rule 10b-5	Securities Act of 1933, Section 11
a.	Yes	Yes
b.	Yes	No
c.	No	Yes
d.	No	No

11 (November 94)

Under the provisions of Section 10(b) and Rule 10b-5 of the Securities Exchange Act of 1934, which of the following activities must be proven by a stock purchaser in a suit against a CPA?
  I.   Intentional conduct by the CPA designed to deceive investors.
  II. Negligence by the CPA.
- a. I only.
- b. II only.
- c. Both I and II.
- d. Neither I nor II.

6 (November 93)

Jay and Co., CPAs, audited the financial statements of Maco Corp. Jay intentionally gave an unqualified opinion on the financial statements even though material misstatements were discovered. The financial statements and Jay's unqualified opinion were included in a registration statement and prospectus for an original public offering of Maco stock. Which of the following statements is correct regarding Jay's liability to a purchaser of the offering under Section 10(b) and Rule 10b-5 of the Securities Exchange Act of 1934?
- a. Jay will be liable if the purchaser relied on Jay's unqualified opinion on the financial statements.
- b. Jay will be liable if Jay was negligent in conducting the audit.
- c. Jay will not be liable if the purchaser's loss was under $500.
- d. Jay will not be liable if the misstatement resulted from an omission of a material fact by Jay.

Items 2 through 5 are based on the following:

Dart Corp. engaged Jay Associates, CPAs, to assist in a public stock offering. Jay audited Dart's financial statements and gave an unqualified opinion, despite knowing that the financial statements contained misstatements. Jay's opinion was included in Dart's registration statement. Larson purchased shares in the offering and suffered a loss when the stock declined in value after the misstatements became known.

2 (May 92)

In a suit against Jay and Dart under the Section 11 liability provisions of the Securities Act of 1933, Larson must prove that

a. Jay knew of the misstatements.
b. Jay was negligent.
c. The misstatements contained in Dart's financial statements were material
d. The unqualified opinion contained in the registration statement was relied on by Larson.

3 (May 92)

If Larson succeeds in the Section 11 suit against Dart, Larson would be entitled to

a. Damages of three times the original public offering price.
b. Rescind the transaction.
c. Monetary damages only.
d. Damages, but only if the shares were resold before the suit was started.

4 (May 92)

In a suit against Jay under the anti-fraud provisions of Section 10(b) and Rule 10b-5 of the Securities Exchange Act of 1934, Larson must prove all of the following except

a. Larson was an intended user of the false registration statement.
b. Larson relied on the false registration statement.
c. The transaction involved some form of interstate commerce.
d. Jay acted with intentional disregard of the truth.

5 (May 92)

If Larson succeeds in the Section 10(b) and Rule 10b-5 suit, Larson would be entitled to

a. Only recover the original public offering price.
b. Only rescind the transaction.
c. The amount of any loss caused by the fraud.
d. Punitive damages.

7 (November 91)

For a CPA to be liable for damages under the anti-fraud provisions of Section 10(b) and Rule 10b-5 of the Securities Exchange Act of 1934, a plaintiff must prove all of the following except that

a. The plaintiff relied on the financial statements audited by the CPA.
b. The CPA violated generally accepted auditing standards.
c. There was a material misrepresentation of fact in the financial statements audited by the CPA.
d. The CPA acted with scienter.

8 (May 89)

Burt, CPA, issued an unqualified opinion on the financial statements of Midwest Corp. These financial statements were included in Midwest's annual report and Form 10-K filed with the SEC. As a result of Burt's reckless disregard for GAAS, material misstatements in the financial statements were not detected. Subsequently, Davis purchased stock in Midwest in the secondary market without ever seeing Midwest's annual report or Form 10-K. Shortly thereafter, Midwest became insolvent and the price of the stock declined drastically. Davis sued Burt for damages based on Section 10(b) and Rule 10b-5 of the Securities Exchange Act of 1934. Burt's best defense is that

a. There has been no subsequent sale for which a loss can be computed.
b. Davis did not purchase the stock as part of an initial offering.
c. Davis did not rely on the financial statements or Form 10-K.
d. Davis was not in privity with Burt.

8 (May 88)

West & Co., CPAs, was engaged by Sand Corp. to audit its financial statements. West issued an unqualified opinion on Sand's financial statements. Sand has been accused of making negligent misrepresentations in the financial statements, which Reed relied upon when purchasing Sand stock. West was not aware of the misrepresentations nor was it negligent in performing the audit. If Reed sues West for damages based upon Section 10(b) and Rule 10b-5 of the Securities Exchange Act of 1934, West will

    a. Lose, because Reed relied upon the financial statements.
    b. Lose, because the statements contained negligent misrepresentations.
    c. Prevail, because some element of scienter must be proved.
    d. Prevail, because Reed was <u>not</u> privity of contract with West.

2 (May 94)

Items 61 through 66 are based on the following:

    Under Section 11 of the Securities Act of 1933 and Section 10(b), Rule 10b-5 of the Securities Exchange Act of 1934, a CPA may be sued by a purchaser of registered securities.

Required: Items 61 through 66 relate to what a plaintiff who purchased securities must prove in a civil liability suit against a CPA. For each item determine whether the statement must be proven under Section 11 of the Securities Act of 1933, under Section 10(b), Rule 10b-5 of the Securities Exchange Act of 1934, both Acts, or neither Act.

- If the item must be proven <u>only</u> under Section 11 of the Securities Act of 1933, choose A.
- If the item must be proven <u>only</u> under Section 10(b), Rule 10b-5, of the Securities Exchange Act of 1934, choose B.
- If the item must be proven under <u>both</u> Acts, choose C.
- If the item must be proven under <u>neither</u> of the Acts, choose D.

<u>Only Section 11</u>	<u>Only Section 10(b)</u>	<u>Both</u>	<u>Neither</u>
<u>A</u>	<u>B</u>	<u>C</u>	<u>D</u>

The plaintiff security purchaser must allege or prove:

61. Material misstatements were included in a filed document.
62. A monetary loss occurred.
63. Lack of due diligence by the CPA.
64. Privity with the CPA.
65. Reliance on the document.
66. The CPA had scienter.

5 (May 91)

    Sleek Corp. is a public corporation whose stock is traded on a national securities exchange. Sleek hired Garson Associates, CPAs, to audit Sleek's financial statements. Sleek needed the audit to obtain bank loans and to make a public stock offering so that Sleek could undertake a business expansion program.

    Before the engagement, Fred Hedge, Sleek's president, told Garson's managing partner that the audited financial statements would be submitted to Sleek's banks to obtain the necessary loans.

    During the course of the audit, Garson's managing partner found that Hedge and other Sleek officers had embezzled substantial amounts of money from the corporation. These embezzlements threatened Sleek's financial stability. When these findings were brought to Hedge's attention, Hedge promised that the money would be repaid and begged that the audit not disclose the embezzlements.

    Hedge also told Garson's managing partner that several friends and relatives of Sleek's officers had been advised about the projected business expansion and proposed stock offering, and had purchased significant amounts of Sleek's stock based on this information.

    Garson submitted an unqualified opinion on Sleek's financial statements, which did not include adjustments for or disclosures about the embezzlements and insider stock transactions. The financial statements and audit report were submitted to Sleek's regular banks including Knox Bank. Knox, relying the financial statements and Garson's report, gave Sleek a $2,000,000 loan.

Sleek's audited financial statements were also incorporated in a registration statement prepared under the provisions of the Securities Act of 1933. The registration statement was filed with the SEC in conjunction with Sleek's public offering of 100,000 shares of its common stock at $100 per share.

An SEC investigation of Sleek disclosed the embezzlements and the insider trading. Trading in Sleek's stock was suspended and Sleek defaulted on the Knox loan.

As a result, the following legal actions were taken:
- Knox sued Garson.
- The general public purchasers of Sleek's stock offering sued Garson.

Required: Answer the following questions and give the reasons for your conclusions.
- a. Would Knox recover from Garson for fraud?
- b. Would the general public purchasers of Sleek's stock offerings recover from Garson
  1. Under the liability provisions of Section 11 of the Securities Act of 1933?
  2. Under the anti-fraud provisions of Rule 10b-5 of the Securities Exchange Act of 1934?

a. Knox would recover from Garson for fraud. The elements of fraud are: the misrepresentation of a material fact (because Garson issued an unqualified opinion on misleading financial statements. Garson's opinion did not include adjustments for or disclosures about the embezzlements and insider stock transactions); with knowledge or scienter (because Garson was aware of the embezzlements and insider stock transactions); and a loss sustained by Knox (because of Sleek's default on the loan).

b. 1. The general public purchasers of Sleek's stock offerings would recover from Garson under the liability provisions of Section 11 of the Securities Act of 1933. Section 11 of the Act provides that anyone, such as an accountant, who submits or contributes to a registration statement or allows material misrepresentations or omissions to appear in a registration statement is liable to anyone purchasing the security who sustains a loss. Under the facts presented, Garson could not establish a "due diligence" defense to a Section 11 action because it knew that the registration statement failed to disclose material facts.

b. 2. The general public purchasers of Sleek's stock offerings would also recover from Garson under the anti-fraud provisions of Section 10(b) and Rule 10b-5 of the Securities Exchange Act of 1934. Under Rule 10b-5, Garson's knowledge that the registration statement failed to disclose a material fact, such as the insider trading and the embezzlements, is considered a fraudulent action. The omission was material. Garson's action was intentional or, at a minimum, a result of gross negligence or recklessness (scienter). These purchasers relied on Garson's opinion on the financial statements and incurred a loss.

2A (November 82)

James Danforth, CPA, audited the financial statements of the Blair Corporation for the year ended December 31, 1981. Danforth rendered an unqualified opinion on February 6, 1982. The financial statements were incorporated into Form 10-K and filed with the Securities and Exchange Commission. Blair's financial statements included as an asset a previously sold certificate of deposit (CD) in the amount of $250,000. Blair had purchased the CD on December 29, 1981, and sold it on December 30, 1981, to a third party who paid Blair that day. Blair did not deliver the CD to the buyer until January 8, 1982. Blair deliberately recorded the sale as an increase in cash and other revenue thereby significantly overstating working capital, stockholders' equity, and net income. Danforth confirmed Blair's purchase of the CD with the seller and physically observed the CD on January 5, 1982.

Assume that on January 18, 1982, while auditing other revenue, Danforth discovered that the CD had been sold. Further assume that Danforth agreed that in exchange for an additional audit fee of $20,000, he would render an unqualified opinion on Blair's financial statements (including the previously sold CD).

Required: Answer the following, setting forth reasons for any conclusions stated.
1. The SEC charges Danforth with criminal violations of the Securities Exchange Act of 1934. Will the SEC prevail? Include in your discussion what the SEC must establish in this action.
2. Assume the SEC discovers and makes immediate public disclosure of Blair's action with the result that no one relies to his detriment upon the audit report and financial statements. Under these circumstances, will the SEC prevail in its criminal action against Danforth?

1. Yes. Section 32(a) of the Securities Exchange Act of 1934 provides that any person who "willfully" violates a substantive provision of the 1934 Act or any person who "willfully and knowingly" makes, or causes to be made, false or misleading statements in reports required to be filed with the SEC shall be subject to criminal sanctions. The elements of the government's case would be (1) falsity, that is, the false information included in the Form 10-K; (2) of a "material" fact, satisfied here based on the facts; and (3) criminal intent, as evidenced by the acceptance of the additional $20,000 fee by Danforth as payment for not mentioning the CD in his report. To prove criminal intent, it need only be established that Danforth rendered his opinion knowing that the financial statements were false.

2. Yes. The fact that Danforth can establish that no one was damaged will not be a valid defense to the criminal action. The reason is that such damage is not an element of proof in criminal proceedings.

III. Accountant-Client Privilege

4 (R01)

Which of the following statements is correct regarding an accountant's working papers?
a. The accountant owns the working papers and generally may disclose them as the accountant sees fit.
b. The client owns the working papers but the accountant has custody of them until the accountant's bill is paid in full.
c. The accountant owns the working papers but generally may <u>not</u> disclose them without the client's consent or a court order.
d. The client owns the working papers but, in the absence of the accountant's consent, may <u>not</u> disclose them without a court order.

2 (R00)

To which of the following parties may a CPA partnership provide its working papers without either the client's consent or a lawful subpoena?

	The IRS	The FASB
a.	Yes	Yes
b.	Yes	No
c.	No	Yes
d.	No	No

14 (November 95)

Which of the following statements is correct regarding a CPA's working papers? The working papers must be
a. Transferred to another accountant purchasing the CPA's practice even if the client hasn't given permission.
b. Transferred permanently to the client if demanded.
c. Turned over to any government agency that requests them.
d. Turned over pursuant to a valid federal court subpoena.

15 (November 95)

Thorp, CPA, was engaged to audit Ivor Co.'s financial statements. During the audit, Thorp discovered that Ivor's inventory contained stolen goods. Ivor was indicted and Thorp was subpoenaed to testify at the criminal trial. Ivor claimed accountant-client privilege to prevent Thorp from testifying. Which of the following statements is correct regarding Ivor's claim?
a. Ivor can claim an accountant-client privilege only in states that have enacted a statute creating such a privilege.
b. Ivor can claim an accountant-client privilege only in federal courts.
c. The accountant-client privilege can be claimed only in civil suits.
d. The accountant-client privilege can be claimed only to limit testimony to audit subject matter.

5 (May 95)

A CPA is permitted to disclose confidential client information without the consent of the client to
    I.   Another CPA firm if the information concerns suspected tax return irregularities.
    II. A state CPA society voluntary quality control review board.
a.   I only.
b.   II only.
c.   Both I and II.
d.   Neither I nor II.

14 (November 94)

Which of the following statements concerning an accountant's disclosure of confidential client data is generally correct?
a.   Disclosure may be made to any state agency without subpoena.
b.   Disclosure may be made to any party on consent of the client.
c.   Disclosure may be made to comply with an IRS audit request.
d   Disclosure may be made to comply with Generally Accepted Accounting Principles.

15 (November 94)

To which of the following parties may a CPA partnership provide its working papers, without being lawfully subpoenaed or without the client's consent?
a.   The IRS.
b.   The FASB.
c.   Any surviving partner(s) on the death of a partner.
d.   A CPA before purchasing a partnership interest in the firm.

10 (May 94)

Which of the following statements is correct with respect to ownership, possession, or access to a CPA firm's audit working papers?
a.   Working papers may <u>never</u> be obtained by third parties unless the client consents.
b.   Working papers are <u>not</u> transferable to a purchaser of a CPA practice unless the client consents.
c.   Working papers are subject to the privileged communication rule which, in most jurisdictions, prevents any third-party access to the working papers.
d.   Working papers are the client's exclusive property.

10 (November 93)

A CPA's working papers
a.   Need <u>not</u> be disclosed under a federal court subpoena.
b.   Must be disclosed under an IRS administrative subpoena.
c.   Must be disclosed to another accountant purchasing the CPA's practice even if the client hasn't given permission.
d.   Need <u>not</u> be disclosed to a state CPA society quality review team.

6 (May 93)

A CPA is permitted to disclose confidential client information without the consent of the client to
    I.   Another CPA who has purchased the CPA's tax practice.
    II. Another CPA firm if the information concerns suspected tax return irregularities.
    III. A state CPA society voluntary quality control review board.
a.   I and III only.
b.   II and III only.
c.   II only.
d.   III only.

Professional and Legal Responsibilities and Liabilities of Accountants

9 (May 93)

Pym, CPA, was engaged to audit Silo Co.'s financial statements. During the audit Pym discovered that Silo's inventory contained stolen goods. Silo was indicted and Pym was subpoenaed to testify at the criminal trial. Silo claimed accountant-client privilege to prevent Pym from testifying. Silo will be able to prevent Pym from testifying

    a.   If the action is brought in a federal court.

    b.   About the nature of the work performed in the audit.

    c.   Due to the common law in the majority of the states.

    d.   Where a state statute has been enacted creating such a privilege.

1 (May 92)

In a jurisdiction having an accountant-client privilege statute, to whom may a CPA turn over workpapers without a client's permission?

    a.   Purchaser of the CPA's practice.

    b.   State tax authorities.

    c.   State court.

    d.   State CPA society quality control panel.

3 (November 90)

Mell Corp. engaged Davis & Co., CPAs, to audit Mell's financial statements. Mell's management informed Davis it suspected that the accounts receivable were materially overstated. Although the financial statements did include a materially overstated accounts receivable balance, Davis issued an unqualified opinion. Mell relied on the financial statements in deciding to obtain a loan from County Bank to expand its operations. County relied on the financial statements in making the loan to Mell. As a result of the overstated accounts receivable balance, Mell has defaulted on the loan and has incurred a substantial loss.

If County sues Davis for fraud, must Davis furnish County with the audit working papers?

    a.   Yes, if the working papers are lawfully subpoenaed into court.

    b.   Yes, provided that Mell does _not_ object.

    c.   No, because of the privileged communication rule, which is recognized in a majority of jurisdictions.

    d.   No, because County was _not_ in privity of contract with Davis.

9 (November 90)

Locke, CPA, was engaged to perform an audit for Vorst Co. During the audit, Locke discovered that Vorst's inventory contained stolen goods. Vorst was indicted and Locke was validly subpoenaed to testify at the criminal trial. Vorst has claimed accountant-client privilege to prevent Locke from testifying. Locke may be compelled to testify

    a.   Only with Vorst's consent.

    b.   In any federal court located in the 50 states.

    c.   In any state court.

    d.   Only about the nature of the work performed in the audit.

Items 1 through 3 are based on the following information:

Mead Corp. orally engaged Dex & Co., CPAs, to audit its financial statements. The management of Mead informed Dex that it suspected that the accounts receivable were materially overstated. Although the financial statements audited by Dex did, in fact, include a materially overstated accounts receivable balance, Dex issued an unqualified opinion. Mead relied on the financial statements in deciding to obtain a loan from City Bank to expand its operations. City relied on the financial statements in making the loan to Mead. As a result of the overstated accounts receivable balance, Mead has defaulted on the loan and has incurred a substantial loss.

1 (May 88)

If Mead sues Dex for negligence in failing to discover the overstatement, Dex's best defense would be that

    a.   No engagement letter had been signed by Dex.

    b.   The audit was performed by Dex in accordance with generally accepted auditing standards.

    c.   Dex was _not_ in privity of contract with Mead.

    d.   Dex did _not_ perform the audit recklessly or with an intent to deceive.

2 (May 88)

   If City sues Dex for fraud, Dex would most likely avoid liability if it could prove that
   a. Dex was <u>not</u> in privity of contract with City.
   b. Dex did <u>not</u> perform the audit recklessly or with an intent to deceive.
   c. Mead should have provided more specific information concerning its suspicions.
   d. Mead was contributorily negligent.

3 (May 88)

   If City sues Dex for fraud, could Dex be compelled to furnish City with the audit working papers?
   a. No, because of the privileged communication rule, which is recognized in a majority of jurisdictions.
   b. No, because City was <u>not</u> in privity of contract with Dex.
   c. Yes, if the working papers are relevant to the action.
   d. Yes, provided that Mead does <u>not</u> object.

9 (November 86)

   In general, which of the following statements is correct with respect to ownership, possession, or access to workpapers prepared by a CPA firm in connection with an audit?
   a. The workpapers may be obtained by third parties where they appear to be relevant to issues raised in litigation.
   b. The workpapers are subject to the privileged communication rule which, in a majority of jurisdictions, prevents third-party access to the workpapers.
   c. The workpapers are the property of the client after the client pays the fee.
   d. The workpapers must be retained by the CPA firm for a period of ten years.

10 (November 86)

   The accountant-client privilege is recognized
   a. Only if the action involved is in federal court.
   b. Where a state statute has been enacted creating such a privilege.
   c. By virtue of the common law in the majority of states.
   d. In the majority of states as a result of legislative enactment and court adoption.

9 (November 83)

   With respect to privileged communications of accountants, which of the following is correct?
   a. A state statutory privilege will be recognized in a case being tried in a federal court involving a federal question.
   b. Most courts recognize a common-law privilege between an accountant and the client.
   c. As a result of legislative enactment and court adoption, the client-accountant privilege is recognized in the majority of jurisdictions.
   d. The privilege will be lost if the party asserting the privilege voluntarily submits part of the privileged communications into evidence.

10 (November 83)

   Working papers prepared by a CPA in connection with an audit engagement are owned by the CPA, subject to certain limitations. The rationale for this rule is to
   a. Protect the working papers from being subpoenaed.
   b. Provide the basis for excluding admission of the working papers as evidence because of the privileged communication rule.
   c. Provide the CPA with evidence and documentation which may be helpful in the event of a lawsuit.
   d. Establish a continuity of relationship with the client whereby indiscriminate replacement of CPAs is discouraged.

2 (May 81)

The CPA firm of Knox & Knox has been subpoenaed to testify and produce its correspondence and workpapers in connection with a lawsuit brought by a third party against one of their clients. Knox considers the subpoenaed documents to be privileged communication and therefore seeks to avoid admission of such evidence in the lawsuit. Which of the following is correct?

a. Federal law recognizes such a privilege if the accountant is a Certified Public Accountant.
b. The privilege is available regarding the working papers since the CPA is deemed to own them.
c. The privileged communication rule as it applies to the CPA-client relationship is the same as that of attorney-client.
d In the absence of a specific statutory provision, the law does <u>not</u> recognize the existence of the privileged communication rule between a CPA and his client.

3 (May 87)

Dill Corp. was one of three major suppliers who sold raw materials to Fogg & Co. on credit. Dill became concerned over Fogg's ability to pay its debts. Payments had been consistently late and some checks had been returned, marked "insufficient funds." In addition, there were rumors concerning Fogg's solvency. Dill decided it would make no further sales to Fogg on credit unless it received a copy of Fogg's current, audited financial statements. It also required Fogg to assign its accounts receivable to Dill to provide security for the sales to Fogg on credit.

Clark & Wall, CPAs, was engaged by Fogg to perform an examination of Fogg's financial statements upon which they subsequently issued an unqualified opinion. Several months later, Fogg defaulted on its obligations to Dill. At this point Dill was owed $240,000 by Fogg. Subsequently, Dill discovered that only $60,000 of the accounts receivable that Fogg had assigned to Dill as collateral was collectible.

Dill has commenced a lawsuit against Clark & Wall. The complaint alleges that Dill has incurred a $180,000 loss as a result of negligent or fraudulent misrepresentations contained in the audited financial statements of Fogg. Specifically, it alleges negligence, gross negligence, and actual and/or constructive fraud on the part of Clark & Wall in the conduct of the audit and the issuance of an unqualified opinion.

State law applicable to this action follows the majority rule with respect to the accountant's liability to third parties for negligence. In addition, there is no applicable state statute which creates an accountant-client privilege. Dill demanded to be provided a copy of the Fogg workpapers from Clark & Wall who refused to comply with the request claiming that they are privileged documents. Clark & Wall has asserted that the entire action should be dismissed because Dill has no standing to sue the firm because of the absence of any contractual relationship with it, i.e., a lack of privity.

Required: Answer the following, setting forth reasons for any conclusions stated.
a. Will Clark & Wall be able to avoid production of the Fogg workpapers upon the assertion that they represent privileged communications?
b. What elements must be established by Dill to show negligence on the part of Clark & Wall?
c. What is the significance of compliance with GAAS in determining whether the audit was performed negligently?
d. What elements must be established by Dill to show actual or constructive fraud on the part of Clark & Wall?

a. No. Since there is no accountant-client privilege recognized at common law and there is no applicable state statute which creates an accountant-client privilege, Clark & Wall will be required to produce its workpapers. Furthermore, the right to assert the accountant-client privilege generally rests with the client and not with the accountant.

b. The elements necessary to establish a cause of action for negligence against Clark & Wall are:
- A legal duty to protect the plaintiff (Dill) from unreasonable risk.
- A failure by the defendant (Clark & Wall) to perform or report on an engagement with the due care or competence expected of members of its profession.
- A causal relationship, i.e., that the failure to exercise due care resulted in the plaintiff's loss.
- Actual damage or loss resulting from the failure to exercise due care.

In addition to the foregoing, Dill must be able to establish that it is within a known and intended class of third party beneficiaries in order to recover damages from Clark & Wall for negligence. This is necessary because Clark & Wall has asserted that it is not in privity of contract with Dill.

c. The primary standards against which the accountant's conduct will be tested are GAAS. Such standards are generally known as "the custom of the industry." Failure by Clark & Wall to meet the standards of the profession will undoubtedly result in a finding of negligence. However, meeting the standard of the profession will not be conclusive evidence that Clark & Wall was not negligent, although it is of significant evidentiary value.

d. The requirements to establish actual or constructive fraud on the part of Clark & Wall are:

1. A false representation of fact by the defendant (Clark & Wall).

2. For actual fraud, knowledge by the defendant (Clark & Wall) that the statement is false (scienter) or that the statement is made without belief that it is truthful. Constructive fraud may be inferred from gross negligence or a reckless disregard for the truth.

3. An intention to have the plaintiff (Dill) rely upon the false statement.

4. "Justifiable" reliance upon the false statement.

5. Damage resulting from said reliance.

3B (May 78)

A CPA firm has been named as a defendant in a class action by purchasers of the shares of stock of the Newly Corporation. The offering was a public offering of securities within the meaning of the Securities Act of 1933. The plaintiffs alleged that the firm was either negligent or fraudulent in connection with the preparation of the audited financial statements which accompanied the registration statement filed with the SEC. Specifically, they allege that the CPA firm either intentionally disregarded, or failed to exercise reasonable care to discover, material facts which occurred subsequent to January 31, 1978, the date of the auditor's report. The securities were sold to the public on March 16, 1978. The plaintiffs have subpoenaed copies of the CPA firm's working papers. The CPA firm is considering refusing to relinquish the papers, asserting that they contain privileged communication between the CPA firm and its client. The CPA firm will, of course, defend on the merits irrespective of the questions regarding the working papers.

Required: Answer the following, setting forth reasons for any conclusions stated.

1. Can the CPA firm rightfully refuse to surrender its working papers?

2. Discuss the liability of the CPA firm in respect to events which occur in the period between the date of the auditor's report and the effective date of the public offering of the securities.

1. No. Neither federal nor common law recognizes the validity of the privilege rule insofar as accountants are concerned. Furthermore, even where the privilege rule is applicable, it can only be claimed by the client. Only a limited number of jurisdictions recognize the rule, and these jurisdictions have by statute overridden the common law rule which does not consider such communications to be within the privilege rule. The privilege rule applies principally to the attorney-client and doctor-patient relationships.

2. The Securities Act of 1933 requires a review by the auditor who reported on the financial statements accompanying the registration statement of events in the period between the date of the auditor's report and the date of the public sale of the securities. The auditors must show that they made a reasonable investigation, had a reasonable basis for their belief, and they did believe the financial statements were true as of the time the registration statement became effective. The auditor defendants have the burden of proving that the requisite standard was met. Therefore, unless the auditors can satisfy the foregoing tests, they will be liable.

Professional and Legal Responsibilities and Liabilities of Accountants

IV. Tax Return Preparation Liability

4 (May 95)

Kopel was engaged to prepare Raff's 1994 federal income tax return. During the tax preparation interview, Raff told Kopel that he paid $3,000 in property taxes in 1994. Actually, Raff's property taxes amounted to only $600. Based on Raff's word, Kopel deducted the $3,000 on Raff's return, resulting in an understatement of Raff's tax liability. Kopel had no reason to believe that the information was incorrect. Kopel did not request underlying documentation and was reasonably satisfied by Raff's representation that Raff had adequate records to support the deduction. Which of the following statements is correct?

a. To avoid the preparer penalty for willful understatement of tax liability, Kopel was obligated to examine the underlying documentation for the deduction.

b. To avoid the preparer penalty for willful understatement of tax liability, Kopel would be required to obtain Raff's representation in writing.

c. Kopel is <u>not</u> subject to the preparer penalty for willful understatement of tax liability because the deduction that was claimed was more than 25% of the actual amount that should have been deducted.

d. Kopel is <u>not</u> subject to the preparer penalty for willful understatement of tax liability because Kopel was justified in relying on Raff's representation.

7 (May 94)

According to the profession's ethical standards, a CPA preparing a client's tax return may rely on unsupported information furnished by the client, without examining underlying information, unless the information

a. Is derived from a pass-through entity.

b. Appears to be incomplete on its face.

c. Concerns dividends received.

d. Lists charitable contributions.

8 (May 94)

Which of the following acts by a CPA will <u>not</u> result in a CPA incurring an IRS penalty?

a. Failing, without reasonable cause, to provide the client with a copy of an income tax return.

b. Failing, without reasonable cause, to sign a client's tax return as preparer.

c. Understating a client's tax liability as a result of an error in calculation.

d. Negotiating a client's tax refund check when the CPA prepared the tax return.

9 (November 93)

Clark, a professional tax return preparer, prepared and signed a client's 1992 federal income tax return that resulted in a $600 refund. Which one of the following statements is correct with regard to an Internal Revenue Code penalty Clark may be subject to for indorsing and cashing the client's refund check?

a. Clark will be subject to the penalty if Clark indorses and cashes the check.

b. Clark may indorse and cash the check, without penalty, if Clark is enrolled to practice before the Internal Revenue Service.

c. Clark may <u>not</u> indorse and cash the check, without penalty, because the check is for more than $500.

d. Clark may indorse and cash the check, without penalty, if the amount does <u>not</u> exceed Clark's fee for preparation of the return.

7 (May 93)

A CPA will be liable to a tax client for damages resulting from all of the following actions <u>except</u>

a. Failing to timely file a client's return.

b. Failing to advise a client of certain tax elections.

c. Refusing to a sign a client's request for a filing extension.

d. Neglecting to evaluate the option of preparing joint or separate returns that would have resulted in a substantial tax savings for a married client.

8 (May 93)

Starr, CPA, prepared and signed Cox's 1992 federal income tax return. Cox informed Starr that Cox had paid doctors' bills of $20,000 although Cox actually had paid only $7,000 in doctors' bills during 1992. Based on Cox's representations, Starr computed the medical expense deduction that resulted in an understatement of tax liability. Starr had no reason to doubt the accuracy of Cox's figures and Starr did not ask Cox to submit documentation of the expenses claimed. Cox orally assured Starr that sufficient evidence of the expenses existed. In connection with the preparation of Cox's 1992 return, Starr is

a. Liable to Cox for interest on the underpayment of tax.
b. Liable to the IRS for negligently preparing the return.
c. Not liable to the IRS for any penalty or interest.
d. Not liable to the IRS for any penalty, but is liable to the IRS for interest on the underpayment of tax.

9 (November 91)

A CPA who prepares clients' federal income tax returns for a fee must

a. File certain required notices and powers of attorney with the IRS before preparing any returns.
b. Keep a completed copy of each return for a specified period of time.
c. Receive client documentation supporting all travel and entertainment expenses deducted on the return.
d. Indicate the CPA's federal identification number on a tax return only if the return reflects tax due from the taxpayer.

3 (May 89)

Tax preparers who aid and abet federal tax evasion are subject to

	Injunction to be prohibited from acting as tax preparers	General federal criminal prosecution
a.	No	No
b.	Yes	No
c.	No	Yes
d.	Yes	Yes

33 (November 87)

In preparing Watt's 1986 individual income tax return, Stark, CPA, took a deduction contrary to a Tax Court decision that had disallowed a similar deduction. Stark's position was adopted in good faith and with a reasonable belief that the Tax Court decision failed to conform to the Internal Revenue Code. Under the circumstances, Stark will

a. Not be liable for a preparer penalty unless the understatement of taxes is at least 25% of Watt's tax liability.
b. Not be liable for a preparer penalty if Stark exercised due diligence.
c. Be liable for the preparer's negligence penalty.
d. Be liable for the preparer's penalty because of Stark's intentional disregard of the Tax Court decision.

34 (November 87)

In preparing Tint's 1986 individual income tax return, Boe, CPA, took a $3,000 deduction for unreimbursed travel and entertainment expenses, which Tint stated he paid in 1986. Boe has no reason to believe that documentation of the travel and entertainment expenses is inadequate or non-existent. In order to avoid the preparer's negligence penalty, Boe

a. May rely solely on Tint's statement as to the amount of the deduction.
b. Must be advised by Tint that the documentation exists.
c. Must examine the documentation.
d. Must maintain copies of the documentation in its file.

Professional and Legal Responsibilities and Liabilities of Accountants

8 (November 86)

Lee, CPA, prepared Sly's 1985 federal income tax return. Sly gave Lee a list of purported 1985 contributions to various recognized charities, totaling $18,000. In fact, Sly had actually contributed only $2,000 to charities during 1985. Based on Sly's list, Lee deducted $18,000 for contributions in Sly's 1985 return, resulting in a tax understatement of about $8,000. Sly's total tax liability shown on the return was $65,000. Lee had no reason to doubt the accuracy of Sly's figures, although Lee did not request supporting documentation. In connection with Lee's preparation of Sly's 1985 return, Lee is subject to

a. An automatic IRS penalty of $100.
b. An automatic IRS penalty of $500.
c. A 5% negligence penalty.
d. No IRS penalty.

6 (November 83)

The Internal Revenue Code provisions dealing with tax return preparation

a. Require tax return preparers who are neither attorneys nor CPAs to pass a basic qualifying examination.
b. Apply to all tax return preparers whether they are compensated or uncompensated.
c. Apply to a CPA who prepares the tax returns of the president of a corporation the CPA audits, without charging the president.
d. Only apply to preparers of individual tax returns.

V. Professional Responsibilities

(R03)

Which of the following is (are) a correct definition of professional standards?
    I. Procedures used by an auditor to gather evidence on which to base an opinion.
    II. Measures of the quality of the auditor's performance.

a. I only.
b. II only.
c. Both I and II.
d. Neither I nor II.

(R03)

Which of the following fee arrangements generally would not be permitted under the ethical standards of the profession?

a. A referral fee paid by a CPA to obtain a client.
b. A commission for compiling a client's internal-use financial statements.
c. A contingent fee for preparing a client's income tax return.
d. A contingent fee for representing a client in tax court.

3 (R01)

Which of the following statements is (are) correct regarding a CPA employee of a CPA firm taking copies of information contained in client files when the CPA leaves the firm?
    I. A CPA leaving a firm may take copies of information contained in client files to assist another firm in serving that client.
    II. A CPA leaving a firm may take copies of information contained in client files as a method of gaining technical expertise.

a. I only.
b. II only.
c. Both I and II.
d. Neither I nor II.

1 (R99)

Which of the following services is a CPA generally required to perform when conducting a personal financial planning engagement?
- a. Assisting the client to identify tasks that are essential in order to act on planning decisions.
- b. Assisting the client to take action on planning decisions.
- c. Monitoring progress in achieving goals.
- d. Updating recommendations and revising planning decisions.

1 (R98)

According to the standards of the profession, which of the following would be considered a part of a consulting services engagement?
- I. Expressing a conclusion about the reliability of a client's financial statements.
- II. Reviewing and commenting on a client-prepared business plan.

a. I only.
b. II only.
c. Both I and II.
d. Neither I nor II.

1 (R96)

Which of the following services may a CPA perform in carrying out a consulting service engagement for a client?
- I. Review of the client-prepared business plan.
- II. Preparation of information for obtaining financing.

a. I only.
b. II only.
c. Both I and II.
d. Neither I nor II.

2 (R96)

Which of the following bodies ordinarily would have the authority to suspend or revoke a CPA's license to practice public accounting?
a. The SEC.
b. The AICPA.
c. A state CPA society.
d. A state board of accountancy.

1 (November 95)

According to the ethical standards of the profession, which of the following acts is generally prohibited?
a. Purchasing a product from a third party and reselling it to a client.
b. Writing a financial management newsletter promoted and sold by a publishing company.
c. Accepting a commission for recommending a product to an audit client.
d. Accepting engagements obtained through the efforts of third parties.

2 (November 95)

According to the ethical standards of the profession, which of the following acts is generally prohibited?
a. Issuing a modified report explaining a failure to follow a governmental regulatory agency's standards when conducting an attest service for a client.
b. Revealing confidential client information during a quality review of a professional practice by a team from the state CPA society.
c. Accepting a contingent fee for representing a client in an examination of the client's federal tax return by an IRS agent.
d. Retaining client records after an engagement is terminated prior to completion and the client has demanded their return.

Professional and Legal Responsibilities and Liabilities of Accountants

3 (November 95)

According to the standards of the profession, which of the following activities may be required in exercising due care?

	Consulting with experts	Obtaining specialty accreditation
a.	Yes	Yes
b.	Yes	No
c.	No	Yes
d.	No	No

5 (November 95)

Under the Statements on Standards for Consulting Services, which of the following statements best reflects a CPA's responsibility when undertaking a consulting services engagement? The CPA must
a. Not seek to modify any agreement made with the client.
b. Not perform any attest services for the client.
c. Inform the client of significant reservations concerning the benefits of the engagement.
d. Obtain a written understanding with the client concerning the time for completion of the engagement.

6 (November 95)

According to the standards of the profession, which of the following sources of information should a CPA consider before signing a client's tax return?
    I. Information actually known to the CPA from the tax return of another client.
    II. Information provided by the client that appears to be correct based on the client's returns from prior years.
a. I only.
b. II only.
c. Both I and II.
d. Neither I nor II.

7 (November 95)

According to the standards of the profession, which of the following statements is (are) correct regarding the action to be taken by a CPA who discovers an error in a client's previously filed tax return?
    I. Advise the client of the error and recommend the measures to be taken.
    II. Withdraw from the professional relationship regardless of whether or not the client corrects the error.
a. I only.
b. II only.
c. Both I and II.
d. Neither I nor II.

2 (May 95)

Which of the following best describes what is meant by the term generally accepted auditing standards?
a. Rules acknowledged by the accounting profession because of their universal application.
b. Pronouncements issued by the Auditing Standards Board.
c. Measures of the quality of the auditor's performance.
d. Procedures to be used to gather evidence to support financial statements.

3 (May 95)

According to the standards of the profession, which of the following events would require a CPA performing a consulting services engagement for a nonaudit client to withdraw from the engagement?
    I. The CPA has a conflict of interest that is disclosed to the client and the client consents to the CPA continuing the engagement.
    II. The CPA fails to obtain a written understanding from the client concerning the scope of the engagement.

a. I only.
b. II only.
c. Both I and II.
d. Neither I nor II.

1 (November 94)

The profession's ethical standards most likely would be considered to have been violated when a CPA represents that specific consulting services will be performed for a stated fee and it is apparent at the time of the representation that the

a. Actual fee would be substantially higher.
b. Actual fee would be substantially lower than the fees charged by other CPAs for comparable services.
c. CPA would not be independent.
d. Fee was a competitive bid.

2 (November 94)

According to the profession's ethical standards, which of the following events may justify a departure from a Statement of Financial Accounting Standards?

	New legislation	Evolution of a new form of business transaction
a.	No	Yes
b.	Yes	No
c.	Yes	Yes
d.	No	No

3 (November 94)

To exercise due professional care an auditor should

a. Critically review the judgment exercised by those assisting in the audit.
b. Examine all available corroborating evidence supporting management's assertions.
c. Design the audit to detect all instances of illegal acts.
d. Attain the proper balance of professional experience and formal education.

5 (November 94)

According to the profession's standards, which of the following is not required of a CPA performing a consulting engagement?

a. Complying with Statements on Standards for Consulting Services.
b. Obtaining an understanding of the nature, scope, and limitations of the engagement.
c. Supervising staff who are assigned to the engagement.
d. Maintaining independence from the client.

6 (November 94)

According to the profession's standards, which of the following would be considered consulting services?

	Advisory services	Implementation services	Product services
a.	Yes	Yes	Yes
b.	Yes	Yes	No
c.	Yes	No	Yes
d.	No	Yes	Yes

Professional and Legal Responsibilities and Liabilities of Accountants

7 (November 94)

According to the profession's standards, which of the following statements is correct regarding the standards a CPA should follow when recommending tax return positions and preparing tax returns?

a. A CPA may recommend a position that the CPA concludes is frivolous as long as the position is adequately disclosed on the return.

b. A CPA may recommend a position in which the CPA has a good faith belief that the position has a realistic possibility of being sustained if challenged.

c. A CPA will usually <u>not</u> advise the client of the potential penalty consequences of the recommended tax return position.

d. A CPA may sign a tax return as preparer knowing that the return takes a position that will <u>not</u> be sustained if challenged.

1 (May 94)

Which of the following actions by a CPA most likely violates the profession's ethical standards?

a. Arranging with a financial institution to collect notes issued by a client in payment of fees due.

b. Compiling the financial statements of a client that employed the CPA's spouse as a bookkeeper.

c. Retaining client records after the client has demanded their return.

d. Purchasing a segment of an insurance company's business that performs actuarial services for employee benefit plans.

2 (May 94)

Which of the following statements best explains why the CPA profession has found it essential to promulgate ethical standards and to establish means for ensuring their observance?

a. A distinguishing mark of a profession is its acceptance of responsibility to the public.

b. A requirement for a profession is to establish ethical standards that stress primary responsibility to clients and colleagues.

c. Ethical standards that emphasize excellence in performance over material rewards establish a reputation for competence and character.

d. Vigorous enforcement of an established code of ethics is the best way to prevent unscrupulous acts.

5 (May 94)

Which of the following services may a CPA perform in carrying out a consulting service for a client?

      I. Analysis of the client's accounting system.
     II. Review of the client's prepared business plan.
    III. Preparation of information for obtaining financing.

a. I and II only.

b. I and III only.

c. II and III only.

d. I, II, and III.

6 (May 94)

Nile, CPA, on completing an audit, was asked by the client to provide technical assistance in implementing a new EDP system. The set of pronouncements designed to guide Nile in this engagement is the Statement(s) on

a. Quality Control Standards.

b. Auditing Standards.

c. Standards for Accountants' EDP Services.

d. Standards for Consulting Services.

PART II -- AGENCY

TABLE OF CONTENTS

PART II

AGENCY

I. Introduction to Agency
A. General Principles of Agency
1. Definitions; Creation and Formality; Capacity of Parties

6 (May 95)

Trent was retained, in writing, to act as Post's agent for the sale of Post's memorabilia collection. Which of the following statements is correct?

        I. To be an agent, Trent must be at least 21 years of age.

        II. Post would be liable to Trent if the collection was destroyed before Trent found a purchaser.

a. I only.
b. II only.
c. Both I and II.
d. Neither I nor II.

16 (November 94)

Which of the following actions requires an agent for a corporation to have a written agency agreement?

a. Purchasing office supplies for the principal's business.
b. Purchasing an interest in undeveloped land for the principal.
c. Hiring an independent general contractor to renovate the principal's office building.
d. Retaining an attorney to collect a business debt owed the principal.

11 (November 93)

Noll gives Carr a written power of attorney. Which of the following statements is correct regarding this power of attorney?

a. It must be signed by both Noll and Carr.
b. It must be for a definite period of time.
c. It may continue in existence after Noll's death.
d. It may limit Carr's authority to specific transactions.

6 (May 92)

A principal and agent relationship requires a

a. Written agreement.
b. Power of attorney.
c. Meeting of the minds and consent to act.
d. Specified consideration.

11 (November 91)

Forming an agency relationship requires that

a. The agreement between the principal and agent be supported by consideration.
b. The principal and agent not be minors.
c. Both the principal and agent consent to the agency.
d. The agent's authority be limited to the express grant of authority in the agency agreement.

Agency

13 (November 91)

Orr gives North power of attorney. In general, the power of attorney
a. Will be valid only if North is a licensed attorney at law.
b. May continue in existence after Orr's death.
c. May limit North's authority to specific transactions.
d. Must be signed by both Orr and North.

1 (May 85)

Wok Corp. has decided to expand the scope of its business. In this connection, it contemplates engaging several agents. Which of the following agency relationships is within the Statute of Frauds and thus should be contained in the signed writing?
a. A sales agency where the agent normally will sell goods which have a value in excess of $500.
b. An irrevocable agency.
c. An agency which is of indefinite duration but which is terminable upon one month's notice.
d. An agency for the forthcoming calendar year which is entered into in mid-December of the prior year.

22 (November 84)

Jim entered into an oral agency agreement with Sally whereby he authorized Sally to sell his interest in a parcel of real estate, Blueacre. Within seven days Sally sold Blueacre to Dan, signing the real estate contract on behalf of Jim. Dan failed to record the real estate contract within a reasonable time. Which of the following is correct?
a. Dan may enforce the real estate contract against Jim since it satisfied the Statute of Frauds.
b. Dan may enforce the real estate contract against Jim since Sally signed the contract as Jim's agent.
c. The real estate contract is unenforceable against Jim since Sally's authority to sell Blueacre was oral.
d. The real estate contract is unenforceable against Jim since Dan failed to record the contract within a reasonable time.

12 (November 81)

Which of the following is not an essential element of an agency relationship?
a. It must be created by contract.
b. The agent must be subject to the principal's control.
c. The agent is a fiduciary in respect to the principal.
d. The agent acts on behalf of another and not himself.

26 (November 80)

A power of attorney is a useful method of creation of an agency relationship. The power of attorney
a. Must be signed by both the principal and the agent.
b. Exclusively determines the purpose and powers of the agent.
c. Is the written authorization of the agent to act on the principal's behalf.
d. Is used primarily in the creation of the attorney-client relationship.

4 (May 78)

Winter is a sales agent for Magnum Enterprises. Winter has assumed an obligation to indemnify Magnum if any of Winter's customers fail to pay. Under these circumstances, which of the following is correct?
a. Winter's engagement must be in writing regardless of its duration.
b. Upon default, Magnum must first proceed against the delinquent purchaser-debtor.
c. The above facts describe a del credere agency relationship and Winter will be liable in the event his customers fail to pay Magnum.
d. There is no fiduciary relationship on either Winter's or Magnum's part.

5 (May 78)

Gladstone has been engaged as sales agent for the Doremus Corporation. Under which of the following circumstances may Gladstone delegate his duties to another?

a. Where an emergency arises and the delegation is necessary to meet the emergency.
b. Where it is convenient for Gladstone to do so.
c. Only with the express consent of Doremus.
d. If Doremus sells its business to another.

2. Duties of Principal and Agent to Each Other

6 (R01)

Blue, a used car dealer, appointed Gage as an agent to sell Blue's cars. Gage was authorized by Blue to appoint subagents to assist in the sale of the cars. Vond was appointed as a subagent. To whom does Vond owe a fiduciary duty?
   a. Gage only.
   b. Blue only.
   c. Both Blue and Gage.
   d. Neither Blue nor Gage.

3 (R00)

Which of the following is (are) available to a principal when an agent fraudulently breaches a fiduciary duty?

	Termination of the agency	Constructive trust
a.	Yes	Yes
b.	Yes	No
c.	No	Yes
d.	No	No

3 (R96)

Which of the following statements represent(s) a principal's duty to an agent who works on a commission basis?
   I. The principal is required to maintain pertinent records, account to the agent, and pay the agent according to the terms of their agreement.
   II. The principal is required to reimburse the agent for all authorized expenses incurred unless the agreement calls for the agent to pay expenses out of the commission.
   a. I only.
   b. II only.
   c. Both I and II.
   d. Neither I nor II.

9 (May 95)

Young Corp. hired Wilson as a sales representative for six months at a salary of $5,000 per month plus 6% of sales. Which of the following statements is correct?
   a. Young does not have the power to dismiss Wilson during the six-month period without cause.
   b. Wilson is obligated to act solely in Young's interest in matters concerning Young's business.
   c. The agreement between Young and Wilson is not enforceable unless it is in writing and signed by Wilson.
   d. The agreement between Young and Wilson formed an agency coupled with an interest.

30 (May 81)

Moderne Fabrics, Inc. hired Franklin as an assistant vice president of sales at $2,000 a month. The employment had no fixed duration. In light of their relationship to each other, which of the following is correct?
   a. Franklin has a legal duty to reveal any interest adverse to that of Moderne in matters concerning his employment.
   b. If Franklin voluntarily terminates his employment with Moderne after working for it for several years, he can not work for a competitor for a reasonable period after termination.

    c.   Moderne can dismiss Franklin only for cause.

    d.   The employment contract between the parties must be in writing.

45 (May 79)

What fiduciary duty, if any, exists in an agency relationship?

    a.   The principal owes a fiduciary duty to his agent.

    b.   The agent owes a fiduciary duty to third parties he deals with for and on behalf of his principal.

    c.   The agent owes a fiduciary duty to his principal.

    d.   There is <u>no</u> fiduciary duty in an agency relationship.

3 (May 78)

Smith has been engaged as a general sales agent for the Victory Medical Supply Company. Victory, as Smith's principal, owes Smith several duties which are implied as a matter of law. Which of the following duties is owed by Victory to Smith?

    a.   <u>Not</u> to compete.

    b.   To reimburse Smith for all expenditures as long as they are remotely related to Smith's employment and <u>not</u> specifically prohibited.

    c.   <u>Not</u> to dismiss Smith without cause for one year from the making of the contract if the duration of the contract is indefinite.

    d.   To indemnify Smith for liability for acts done in good faith upon Victory's orders.

B. Agency and Contracts
1. General Principles of Contract Liability

7 (May 92)

Young was a purchasing agent for Wilson, a sole proprietor. Young had the express authority to place purchase orders with Wilson's suppliers. Young conducted business through the mail and had little contact with Wilson. Young placed an order with Vanguard, Inc. on Wilson's behalf after Wilson was declared incompetent in a judicial proceeding. Young was aware of Wilson's incapacity. With regard to the contract with Vanguard, Wilson (or Wilson's legal representative) will

    a.   Not be liable because Vanguard dealt only with Young.

    b.   Not be liable because Young did <u>not</u> have authority to enter into the contract.

    c.   Be liable because Vanguard was unaware of Wilson's incapacity.

    d.   Be liable because Young acted with express authority.

3 (May 91)

Frost's accountant and business manager has the authority to

    a.   Mortgage Frost's business property.

    b.   Obtain bank loans for Frost.

    c.   Insure Frost's property against fire loss.

    d.   Sell Frost's business.

5 (May 90)

Ace engages Butler to manage Ace's retail business. Butler has the implied authority to do all of the following, <u>except</u>

    a.   Purchase inventory for Ace's business.

    b.   Sell Ace's business fixtures.

    c.   Pay Ace's business debts.

    d.   Hire or discharge Ace's business employees.

33 (November 79)

Wanamaker, Inc. engaged Anderson as its agent to purchase original oil paintings for resale by Wanamaker. Anderson's express authority was specifically limited to a maximum purchase price of $25,000 for any collection provided it contained a minimum of five oil paintings. Anderson purchased a seven-picture collection on Wanamaker's behalf for $30,000. Based upon these facts, which of the following is a correct legal conclusion?

    a. The express limitation on Anderson's authority negates any apparent authority.

    b. Wanamaker can not ratify the contract since Anderson's actions were clearly in violation of his contract.

    c. If Wanamaker rightfully disaffirms the unauthorized contract, Anderson is personally liable to the seller.

    d. Neither Wanamaker nor Anderson is liable on the contract since the seller was obligated to ascertain Anderson's authority.

29 (November 76)

Under which of the following circumstances will an agent acting on behalf of a disclosed principal not be liable to a third party for his action?

    a. He signs a negotiable instrument in his own name and does not indicate his agency capacity.

    b. He commits a tort in the course of discharging his duties.

    c. He is acting for a non-existent principal which subsequently comes into existence after the time of the agent's actions on the principal's behalf.

    d. He lacks specific express authority but is acting within the scope of his implied authority.

15 (November 75)

Farley Farms, Inc. shipped 100 bales of hops to Burton Brewing Corporation. The agreement specified that the hops were to be of a certain grade. Upon examining the hops, Burton claimed that they were not of that grade. Farley's general sales agent who made the sale to Burton agreed to relieve Burton of liability and to have the hops shipped elsewhere. This was done, and the hops were sold at a price less than Burton was to have paid. Farley refused to accede to the agent's acts and sued Burton for the amount of its loss. Under these circumstances

    a. Farley will prevail only if the action by its agent was expressly authorized.

    b. Even if Farley's agent had authority to make such an adjustment, it would not be enforceable against Farley unless ratified in writing by Farley.

    c. Because the hops were sold at a loss in respect to the price Burton had agreed to pay, Burton would be liable for the loss involved.

    d. Farley is bound because its agent expressly, impliedly, or apparently had the authority to make such an adjustment.

31 (May 75)

Normally a principal will not be liable to a third party

    a. On a contract signed on his behalf by an agent who was expressly forbidden by the principal to make it and where the third party was unaware of the agent's limitation.

    b. On a contract made by his agent and the principal is not disclosed, unless the principal ratifies it.

    c. For torts committed by an independent contractor if they are within the scope of the contract.

    d. On a negotiable instrument signed by the agent in his own name without revealing he signed in his agency capacity.

9 (November 74)

Badger Corporation engaged Donald Keller as one of its sales representatives to sell automotive parts. Keller signed an employment contract which required him to obtain home-office approval on any contract in excess of $500 entered into by Keller on Badger's behalf. The industry custom and most of Badger's agents had authority to make such contracts if they did not exceed $1,000. Keller signed a contract on Badger's behalf with Zolar Garages, Inc., for $850. Badger rejected the contract and promptly notified Zolar of its decision. Under these circumstances

    a. Keller is a del credere agent.

    b. Keller did not have express authority to make the Zolar contract.

    c. Keller had the implied authority to make the contract.

    d. Badger's prompt disaffirmance of Keller's action retroactively terminated any liability it might have had.

2. Contract Liability--Undisclosed Principals

4 (R99)

Which of the following statements is (are) correct regarding the relationship between an agent and a nondisclosed principal?

        I. The principal is required to indemnify the agent for any contract entered into by the agent within the scope of the agency agreement.

        II. The agent has the same actual authority as if the principal had been disclosed.

a. I only.
b. II only.
c. Both I and II.
d. Neither I nor II.

8 (May 95)

When a valid contract is entered into by an agent on the principal's behalf, in a nondisclosed principal situation, which of the following statements concerning the principal's liability is correct?

	The principal may be held liable once disclosed	The principal must ratify the contract to be held liable
a.	Yes	Yes
b.	Yes	No
c.	No	Yes
d.	No	No

18 (November 94)

Easy Corp. is a real estate developer and regularly engages real estate brokers to act on its behalf in acquiring parcels of land. The brokers are authorized to enter into such contracts, but are instructed to do so in their own names without disclosing Easy's identity or relationship to the transaction. If a broker enters into a contract with a seller on Easy's behalf,

a. The broker will have the same actual authority as if Easy's identity had been disclosed.
b. Easy will be bound by the contract because of the broker's apparent authority.
c. Easy will <u>not</u> be liable for any negligent acts committed by the broker while acting on Easy's behalf.
d. The broker will <u>not</u> be personally bound by the contract because the broker has express authority to act.

19 (November 94)

An agent will usually be liable under a contract made with a third party when the agent is acting on behalf of a(an)

	Disclosed principal	Undisclosed principal
a.	Yes	Yes
b.	Yes	No
c.	No	Yes
d.	No	No

14 (November 93)

Which of the following rights will a third party be entitled to after validly contracting with an agent representing an undisclosed principal?

a. Disclosure of the principal by the agent.
b. Ratification of the contract by the principal.
c. Performance of the contract by the agent.
d. Election to void the contract after disclosure of the principal.

4 (May 90)

Able, as agent for Baker, an undisclosed principal, contracted with Safe to purchase an antique car. In payment, Able issued his personal check to Safe. Able could not cover the check but expected Baker to give him cash to deposit before the check was presented for payment. Baker did not do so and the check was dishonored. Baker's identity became known to Safe. Safe may <u>not</u> recover from

a. Baker individually on the contract.
b. Able individually on the contract.
c. Baker individually on the check.
d. Able individually on the check.

3 (November 89)

Parc contracted with Furn Brothers Corp. to buy hotel furniture and fixtures on behalf of Global Motor House, a motel chain. Global instructed Parc to use Parc's own name and not to disclose to Furn that Parc was acting on Global's behalf. Who is liable to Furn on this contract?

	Parc	Global
a.	Yes	No
b.	No	Yes
c.	Yes	Yes
d.	No	No

Items 23 and 24 are based on the following information:

Frey entered into a contract with Cara Corp. to purchase televisions on behalf of Lux, Inc. Lux authorized Frey to enter into the contract in Frey's name without disclosing that Frey was acting on behalf of Lux.

23 (November 87)

If Lux repudiates the contract, Cara may

a. Obtain specific performance, compelling Lux to perform on the contract.
b. Hold Frey liable on the contract whether or not Cara discovers that Lux is the principal.
c. Hold Frey liable on the contract but only if Cara fails to discover that Lux was the principal.
d. Not hold Lux liable because proof that Lux was the principal will be barred by the parol evidence rule.

24 (November 87)

If Cara repudiates the contract, which of the following statements concerning liability on the contract is <u>not</u> correct?

a. Frey may hold Cara liable and obtain money damages.
b. Frey may hold Cara liable and obtain specific performance.
c. Lux may hold Cara liable upon disclosing the agency relationship with Frey.
d. Cara will be free from liability to Lux if Frey fraudulently stated that he was acting on his own behalf.

60 (May 86)

Cox engaged Datz as her agent. It was mutually agreed that Datz would <u>not</u> disclose that he was acting as Cox's agent. Instead he was to deal with prospective customers as if he were a principal acting on his own behalf. This he did and made several contracts for Cox. Assuming Cox, Datz or the customer seeks to avoid liability on one of the contracts involved, which of the following statements is correct?

    a.   Cox must ratify the Datz contracts in order to be held liable.

    b.   Datz has <u>no</u> liability once he discloses that Cox was the real principal.

    c.   The third party can avoid liability because he believed he was dealing with Datz as a principal.

    d.   The third party may choose to hold either Datz or Cox liable.

4 (May 84)

Jim, an undisclosed principal, authorized Rick to act as his agent in securing a contract for the purchase of some plain white paper. Rick, without informing Sam that he was acting on behalf of a principal, entered into a contract with Sam to purchase the paper. If Jim repudiates the contract with Sam, which of the following is correct?

    a.   Rick will be released from his contractual obligations to Sam if he discloses Jim's identity.

    b.   Upon learning that Jim is the principal, Sam may elect to hold either Jim or Rick liable on the contract.

    c.   Rick may <u>not</u> enforce the contract against Sam.

    d.   Sam may obtain specific performance, compelling Jim to perform on the contract.

14 (November 83)

Steel has been engaged by Lux to act as the agent for Lux, an undisclosed principal. As a result of this relationship

    a.   Steel has the same implied powers as an agent engaged by a disclosed principal.

    b.   Lux can <u>not</u> be held liable for any torts committed by Steel in the course of carrying out the engagement.

    c.   Steel will be free from personal liability on authorized contracts for Lux when it is revealed that Steel was acting as an agent.

    d.   Lux must file the appropriate form in the proper state office under the fictitious business name statute.

7 (November 82)

Davidson is the agent of Myers, a fuel dealer. Myers is an undisclosed principal. Davidson contracts with Wallop to purchase 30,000 tons of coal at $20 per ton. Which of the following is correct?

    a.   If Davidson acts outside the scope of his authority in entering into this contract, Myers can <u>not</u> ratify the contract.

    b.   Wallop is bound to this contract only if Davidson acts within the scope of his authority.

    c   .If Davidson acts within the scope of his authority, Wallop can <u>not</u> hold Davidson personally liable on the contract.

    d.   Should Davidson refuse to accept delivery of the coal, Wallop will become an agent of Myers by substitution.

29 (May 81)

Barton, a wealthy art collector, orally engaged Deiter to obtain a rare and beautiful painting from Cumbers, a third party. Cumbers did not know that Barton had engaged Deiter to obtain the painting for Barton because as Barton told Deiter "that would cause the price to skyrocket." Regarding the liability of the parties if a contract is made or purported to be made, which of the following is correct?

    a.   Since the appointment of Deiter was oral, no agency exists, and any contract made by Deiter on Barton's behalf is invalid.

    b.   Because Barton specifically told Deiter <u>not</u> to reveal for whom he (Deiter) was buying the painting, Deiter can <u>not</u> be personally liable on the contract made on Barton's behalf.

    c.   If Deiter makes a contract with Cumbers which Deiter breaches, Cumbers may, after learning of the agreement between Barton and Deiter, elect to recover from either Barton or Deiter.

    d.   If Deiter makes a contract to purchase the painting, without revealing he is Barton's agent, Cumbers had entered into a contract which is voidable at his election.

34 (May 81)

Jason Manufacturing Company wishes to acquire a site for a warehouse. Knowing that if it negotiated directly for the purchase of the property the price would be substantially increased, it employed Kent, an agent, to secure lots without disclosing that he was acting for Jason. Kent's authority was evidenced by a writing signed by the proper officers of Jason. Kent entered into a contract in his own name to purchase Peter's lot, giving Peter a negotiable note for $1,000 signed by Kent as first payment. Jason wrote Kent acknowledging the purchase. Jason also disclosed its identity as Kent's principal to Peter. In respect to the rights and liabilities of the parties, which of the following is a correct statement?

  a. Peter is <u>not</u> bound on the contract since Kent's failure to disclose he was Jason's agent was fraudulent.
  b. Jason, Kent and Peter are potentially liable on the contract.
  c. Unless Peter formally ratifies the substitution of Jason for Kent, he is <u>not</u> liable.
  d. Kent has <u>no</u> liability since he was acting for and on behalf of an existing principal.

31 (November 79)

Magnus Real Estate Developers, Inc. wanted to acquire certain tracts of land in Marshall Township in order to build a shopping center complex. To accomplish this goal, Magnus engaged Dexter, a sophisticated real estate dealer, to represent them in the purchase of the necessary land without revealing the existence of the agency. Dexter began to slowly but steadily acquire the requisite land. However, Dexter made the mistake of purchasing one tract outside the description of the land needed. Which of the following is correct under these circumstances?

  a. The use of an agent by Magnus, an undisclosed principal, is manifestly illegal.
  b. Either Magnus or Dexter may be held liable on the contracts for the land, including the land that was <u>not</u> within the scope of the proposed shopping center.
  c. An undisclosed principal such as Magnus can have <u>no</u> liability under the contract since the third party believed he was dealing with Dexter as a principal.
  d. An agent for an undisclosed principal assumes <u>no</u> liability as long as he registers his relationship to the principal with the clerk of the proper county having jurisdiction.

20 (November 76)

Wishing to acquire a site for its factory without provoking a rise in price, Peter Corporation engaged Argus Realty Company to purchase land without disclosing Peter's name. Argus did so and signed a contract in its own name with Tyrone to purchase Tyrone's land. Under these circumstances

  a. The transaction is fraudulent.
  b. Argus is not personally liable on the contract.
  c. Peter Corporation must formally ratify the contract if it is to hold Tyrone liable.
  d. Tyrone may obtain recourse against either Peter or Argus if the contract is <u>not</u> performed.

48 (May 76)

If an agent makes a contract for his undisclosed principal

  a. As between the principal and his agent, the agent has <u>no</u> implied authority.
  b. The principal has committed a fraud upon any and all third parties with whom the agent deals.
  c. The agent is personally liable on the contract if the third party sues him.
  d. The contract between the undisclosed principal and his agent must be in writing, witnessed, and duly notarized to be valid.

22 (May 75)

Filmore hired Stillwell as his agent to acquire Dobbs' land at a price <u>not</u> to exceed $50,000; the land is badly needed to provide additional parking space for Filmore's shopping center. In order to prevent Dobbs from asking for an exorbitant price, Filmore told Stillwell <u>not</u> to disclose his principal. Stillwell subsequently purchased the land for $45,000. Under these circumstances

  a. Stillwell and Filmore committed fraud when they did <u>not</u> disclose the fact that Stillwell was Filmore's agent.
  b. Absent an agreement regarding the compensation to be paid Stillwell, he is entitled to the difference between the $50,000 limitation and the $45,000 he paid for the land; i.e., $5,000 based upon quasi contract.
  c. Dobbs may rescind the contract upon his learning the truth as long as the conveyance has <u>not</u> been accomplished.
  d. Dobbs may sue either Filmore or Stillwell on the contract in the event of default by Filmore.

Agency

10 (November 74)

An agent for an undisclosed principal

a. Has less express authority than would be the case if he were acting as an agent for a disclosed principal.
b. Has liability on a contract he made with a third party, if the third party elects to hold him liable thereon.
c. Must derive whatever authority he may have from a written power of attorney.
d. Must disclose his principal's identity prior to performance.

5 (November 77)

Duval was the agent for Sunshine Pools, Inc. He sold pools, related equipment, and accessories for Sunshine. Holmes, president of Tilden Sporting Equipment, Inc., approached Duval and offered him an excellent deal on a commission basis if he would secretly sell their brand of diving boards and platforms instead of the Sunshine products. Duval agreed. The arrangement which was worked out between them was to have Duval continue to act as a general sales agent for Sunshine and concurrently act as the agent for an "undisclosed" principal in respect to Tilden diving boards. He could then sell both lines to new pool customers and go back to prior customers to solicit sales of the Tilden boards. Duval was not to mention his relationship with Tilden to the prospective customers, and of course, no mention of these facts would be made to Sunshine. Duval was told to use his discretion insofar as effectively misleading the prospective customers about whose diving boards they were purchasing.

Things went smoothing for the first several months until Tilden began to manufacture and ship defective diving boards. Subsequently, Tilden became insolvent, and Holmes absconded with advance payments made by purchasers including those who had purchased from Duval.

Required: Answer the following, setting forth reasons for any conclusions stated.
a. What are the rights of the various customers against Duval?
b. What are the rights of the various customers against Tilden and/or Holmes?
c. What rights does Sunshine have against Duval?
d. What rights does Sunshine have against Tilden and/or Holmes?

a. Duval has potential liability based upon two separate legal theories: the undisclosed principal doctrine and the theory of fraud. Duval led the customers to believe that the diving boards were Sunshine products. Thus, at a minimum, he would not be disclosing his true principal, or he may have been intentionally misstating the facts so as to make it appear that the purchaser was obtaining all Sunshine products. The rule is clear that an agent is personally liable on the contracts when acting for an undisclosed principal. Thus, the customers can sue Duval and recover on this basis. Alternatively, fraud may be asserted, and if proved, liability will attach in that the agent is responsible for his torts even though committed to an agency capacity.

b. Tilden, an undisclosed principal, is liable for the contracts made for and on its behalf even though its identity was not initially disclosed. Furthermore, Tilden would be liable for the tort of conversion committed by Holmes who absconded with advance payments made by purchasers. Tilden also would be liable for breach of warranty with respect to defective goods delivered to the various customers. Finally, Holmes would be personally liable for the conversion of the customers' advance payments.

c. Duval has breached his fiduciary duty by selling a competing item without his principal's knowledge and consent. Therefore, he can be dismissed, and he can be required to account for any profits he has realized as a result of his breach of contract and trust.

d. Sunshine could proceed against Tilden based upon Tilden's intentional interference with a contractual relationship. This well-recognized tort occurs, as it did here, when a party intends to induce the breach of a contract or interfere with the performance of a contract (here the Sunshine-Duval contract) with the knowledge of the existence of that contract and the belief that such breach or interference will follow. In addition, Sunshine would have an action against Holmes personally as a result of his tortious conduct even though Holmes acted in his capacity as president of Tilden.

3. Ratification

6 (May 87)

Starr is an agent of a disclosed principal, Maple. On May 1, Starr entered into an agreement with King Corp. on behalf of Maple that exceeded Starr's authority as Maple's agent. On May 5, King learned of Starr's lack of authority and immediately notified Maple and Starr that it was withdrawing from the May 1 agreement. On May 7, Maple ratified the May 1 agreement in its entirety. If King refuses to honor the agreement and Maple brings an action for breach of contract, Maple will

    a.   Prevail since the agreement of May 1 was ratified in its entirety.

    b.   Prevail since Maple's capacity as a principal was known to Starr.

    c.   Lose since the May 1 agreement is void due to Starr's lack of authority.

    d.   Lose since King notified Starr and Maple of its withdrawal prior to Maple's ratification.

15 (November 84)

Sol, an agent for May, made a contract with Simon which exceeded Sol's authority. If May wishes to hold Simon to the contract, May must prove that

    a.   Sol was May's general agent even though Sol exceeded his authority.

    b.   Sol believed he was acting within the scope of his authority.

    c.   Sol was acting in the capacity of an agent for an undisclosed principal.

    d.   May ratified the contract before withdrawal from the contract by Simon.

3 (May 84)

Harp entered into a contract with Rex on behalf of Gold. By doing so, Harp acted outside the scope of his authority as Gold's agent. Gold may be held liable on the contract if

    a.   Gold retains the benefits of the contract.

    b.   Gold ratifies the entire contract after Rex withdraws from the contract.

    c.   Rex elects to hold Gold liable on the contract.

    d.   Rex was aware of the limitation on Harp's authority.

6 (May 82)

Harper Company appointed Doe as its agent. It was essential that Harper's identity be kept secret. Therefore, Doe was to act in the capacity of an agent for an undisclosed principal. The duration of the agency was for exactly one year commencing Wednesday of the following week. As a result of this agreement between Harper and Doe, Harper

    a.   Is <u>not</u> liable on the agency contract unless it is in writing.

    b.   Can <u>not</u> ratify the unauthorized acts of Doe.

    c.   Can rely upon the parol evidence rule to avoid liability to third parties if the contract is in writing.

    d.   Can <u>not</u> be held liable for torts committed by Doe while acting as an agent.

7 (May 82)

Mathews is an agent for Sears with the express authority to solicit orders from customers in a geographic area assigned by Sears. Mathews has no authority to grant discounts nor to collect payment on orders solicited. Mathews secured an order from Davidson for $1,000 less a 10% discount if Davidson makes immediate payment. Davidson had previously done business with Sears through Mathews but this was the first time that a discount-payment offer had been made. Davidson gave Mathews a check for $900 and thereafter Mathews turned in both the check and the order to Sears. The order clearly indicated that a 10% discount had been given by Mathews. Sears shipped the order and cashed the check. Later Sears attempted to collect $100 as the balance owed on the order from Davidson. Which of the following is correct?

    a.   Sears can collect the $100 from Davidson because Mathews contracted outside the scope of his express or implied authority.

    b.   Sears can <u>not</u> collect the $100 from Davidson because Mathews as an agent with express authority to solicit orders had implied authority to give discounts and collect.

   c. Sears can <u>not</u> collect the $100 from Davidson as Sears has ratified the discount granted and payment made to Mathews.

   d. Sears can <u>not</u> collect the $100 from Davidson because although Mathews had <u>no</u> express or implied authority to grant a discount and collect, Mathews had apparent authority to do so.

27 (November 80)

Agents sometimes have liability to third parties for their actions taken for and on behalf of the principal. An agent will <u>not</u> be personally liable in which of the following circumstances?

   a. If he makes a contract which he had no authority to make but which the principal ratifies.

   b. If he commits a tort while engaged in the principal's business.

   c .If he acts for a principal which he knows is nonexistent and the third party is unaware of this.

   d. If he acts for an undisclosed principal as long as the principal is subsequently disclosed.

40 (May 79)

Dolby was employed as an agent for the Ace Used Car Company to purchase newer model used cars. His authority was limited by a $3,000 maximum price for any car. A wholesaler showed him a 1938 classic car which was selling for $5,000. The wholesaler knew that Ace only dealt in newer model used cars and that Dolby had never paid more than $3,000 for any car. Dolby bought the car for Ace, convinced that it was worth at least $7,000. When he reported this to Williams, Ace's owner, Williams was furious but he nevertheless authorized processing of the automobile for resale. Williams also began pricing the car with antique car dealers who indicated that the current value of the car was $4,800. Williams called the wholesaler, told him that Dolby had exceeded his authority, that he was returning the car, and that he was demanding repayment of the purchase price. What is the wholesaler's <u>best</u> defense in the event of a lawsuit?

   a. Dolby had apparent authority to purchase the car.

   b. Dolby's purchase was effectively ratified by Ace.

   c. Dolby had express authority to purchase the car.

   d. Dolby had implied authority to purchase the car.

22 (November 76)

Walker made a contract for and on behalf of his principal which was legally unauthorized. What is the status of this contract?

   a. It is illegal.

   b. It can be ratified only by a written affirmation of the contract.

   c. It can <u>not</u> bind the third party regardless of the principal's subsequent action.

   d. It can be ratified by the principal by his silence and the receipt and retention of the benefits of the contract.

16 (November 75)

The ratification doctrine with respect to principal and agent

   a. Does <u>not</u> apply to real estate contracts.

   b. Requires that a written notice of ratification be sent to the third party and the agent in order to create an enforceable contract.

   c. Does <u>not</u> apply to torts committed by the agent.

   d. Requires that the agent or purported agent indicates to the third party that he is acting for and on behalf of person subsequently ratifying.

30 (May 75)

The ratification doctrine

    a.   Is <u>not</u> applicable to situations where the party claiming to act as the agent for another has <u>no</u> express or implied authority to do so.

    b.   Is designed to apply to situations where the principal was originally incompetent to have made the contract himself, but who, upon becoming competent, ratifies.

    c.   Requires the principal to ratify the entire act of the agent and the ratification is retroactive.

    d.   Applies only if the principal expressly ratifies in writing the contract made on his behalf within a reasonable time.

5A (May 80)

    Vogel, an assistant buyer for the Granite City Department Store, purchased metal art objects from Duval Reproductions. Vogel was totally without express or apparent authority to do so, but believed that his purchase was a brilliant move likely to get him a promotion. The head buyer of Granite was livid when he learned of Vogel's activities. However, after examining the merchandise and listening to Vogel's pitch, he reluctantly placed the merchandise in the storeroom and put a couple of pieces on display for a few days to see whether it was a "hot item" and a "sure thing" as Vogel claimed. The item was neither "hot" nor "sure" and when it didn't move at all, the head buyer ordered the display merchandise repacked and the entire order returned to Duval with a letter that stated the merchandise had been ordered by an assistant buyer who had absolutely no authority to make the purchase. Duval countered with a lawsuit for breach of contract.

    Required: Answer the following, setting forth reasons for any conclusions stated.
    Will Duval prevail?

    Yes. Despite the stated lack of express or apparent initial authority of Vogel, Granite City Department Store's agent, there would appear to be a ratification by the principal.

    It is clear from the facts stated that Granite would not have been liable on the Vogel contract if the head buyer had immediately notified Duval and returned the goods. Instead the head buyer retained the goods and placed some on display in an attempt to sell them. Had they proved to be a "hot" item, undoubtedly the art objects would have been gratefully kept by Granite. Granite wants to reject the goods if they don't sell but wants to have the benefits if they do sell. Such conduct is inconsistent with a repudiation based upon the agent's lack of express or apparent authority. The retention of the goods for the time indicated, the attempted sale of the goods, and a failure to notify Duval in a timely way, when taken together, constitute a ratification of the unauthorized contract.

4. Apparent Authority

13 (May 89)

    Simmons, an agent for Jensen, has the express authority to sell Jensen's goods. Simmons also has the express authority to grant discounts of up to 5% of list price. Simmons sold Hemple goods with a list price of $1,000 and granted Hemple a 10% discount. Hemple had not previously dealt with either Simmons or Jensen. Which of the following courses of action may Jensen properly take?

    a.   Seek to void the sale to Hemple.

    b.   Seek recovery of $50 from Hemple only.

    c.   Seek recovery of $50 from Simmons only.

    d.   Seek recovery of $50 from either Hemple or Simmons.

4 (May 88)

    Able, on behalf of Pix Corp., entered into a contract with Sky Corp., by which Sky agreed to sell computer equipment to Pix. Able disclosed to Sky that she was acting on behalf of Pix. However, Able had exceeded her actual authority by entering into the contract with Sky. If Pix does not want to honor the contract, it will nonetheless be held liable if Sky can prove that

a.   Able had apparent authority to bind Pix.
b.   Able believed she was acting within the scope of her authority.
c.   Able was an employee of Pix and <u>not</u> an independent contractor.
d.   The agency relationship between Pix and Able was formalized in a signed writing.

59 (May 86)

Borg is the vice-president of purchasing for Crater Corp. He has authority to enter into purchase contracts on behalf of Crater provided that the price under a contract does not exceed $2 million. Dent, who is the president of Crater, is required to approve any contract that exceeds $2 million. Borg entered into a $2.5 million purchase contract with Shady Corp. without Dent's approval. Shady was unaware that Borg exceeded his authority. Neither party substantially changed its position in reliance on the contract. What is the most likely result of this transaction?

a.   Crater will be bound because of Borg's apparent authority.
b.   Crater will <u>not</u> be bound because Borg exceeded his authority.
c.   Crater will only be bound up to $2 million, the amount of Borg's authority.
d.   Crater may avoid the contract since Shady has <u>not</u> relied on the contract to its detriment.

1 (May 84)

Dill is an agent for Mint, Inc. As such, Dill made a contract for and on behalf of Mint with Sky Co. which was not authorized and upon which Mint has disclaimed liability. Sky has sued Mint on the contract asserting that Dill had the apparent authority to make it. In considering the factors which will determine the scope of Dill's apparent authority, which of the following would <u>not</u> be important?

a.   The express limitations placed upon Dill's authority which were <u>not</u> known by Sky.
b.   The custom and usages of the business.
c.   The status of Dill's position in Mint.
d.   Previous acquiescence by the principal in similar contracts made by Dill.

2 (May 83)

Terrance has been Pauline's agent in the liquor business for ten years and has made numerous contracts on Pauline's behalf. Under which of the following situations could Terrance continue to have power to bind Pauline?

a.   The passage of a federal constitutional amendment making the sale or purchase of alcoholic beverages illegal.
b.   The death of Pauline without Terrance's knowledge.
c.   The bankruptcy of Pauline with Terrance's knowledge.
d.   The firing of Terrance by Pauline.

5 (November 82)

The apparent authority of an agent would <u>not</u> be determined by reference to

a.   Prior dealings between the parties.
b.   The types of activity engaged in by the agent.
c.   An undisclosed limitation on the agent's usual power.
d.   Industry custom.

31 (May 81)

Sly was a general agent of the Cute Cosmetics Company with authority to sell, make collections, and adjust disputes. Sly was caught padding his monthly expense account by substantial amounts and was dismissed. Cute hired another general agent, Ready, to replace Sly. Ready was slowly but steadily calling upon Sly's accounts to make sales and was informing them that Sly's services had been terminated. Cute also published a notice in the appropriate trade journals and the local newspaper announcing the replacement of Sly with Ready. Sly, after he was let go, called on all the customers who had outstanding accounts payable and quickly made whatever collections he could in cash and absconded. Which of the following statements is correct regarding Cute's legal right against the customers?

a. Cute can regain possession of the goods since title did <u>not</u> pass because Sly's actions constituted a fraud.

b. Cute can obtain payment from the customers despite Sly's wrongful acts since it had published a notice of Sly's dismissal.

c. Cute will have to absorb the loss since Sly had continuing implied authority to make collections.

d. Cute will have to absorb the loss unless Cute can prove the customers had actual notice of Sly's dismissal.

10 (May 78)

Futterman operated a cotton factory and employed Marra as a general purchasing agent to travel through the southern states to purchase cotton. Futterman telegraphed Marra instructions from day to day as to the price to be paid for cotton. Marra entered a cotton district in which she had not previously done business and represented that she was purchasing cotton for Futterman. Although directed by Futterman to pay no more than 25 cents a pound, Marra bought cotton from Anderson at 30 cents a pound, which was the prevailing offering price at that time. Futterman refused to take the cotton. Under these circumstances, which of the following is correct?

a. The negation of actual authority to make the purchase effectively eliminates any liability for Futterman.

b. Futterman is <u>not</u> liable on the contract.

c. Marra has <u>no</u> potential liability.

d. Futterman is liable on the contract.

23 (May 77)

Star Corporation dismissed Moon, its purchasing agent. Star published a notice in appropriate trade journals which stated: "This is to notify all parties concerned that Moon is no longer employed by Star Corporation, and the corporation assumes no further responsibility for his acts." Moon called on several of Star's suppliers with whom he had previously dealt, and when he found one who was unaware of his dismissal, he placed a substantial order for merchandise to be delivered to a warehouse in which Moon rented space. Star had rented space in the warehouse in the past when its storage facilities were crowded. Moon also called on several suppliers with whom Star had never dealt and made purchases from them on open account in the name of Star. The merchandise purchased by Moon was delivered to the warehouse. Moon then sold all the merchandise and absconded with the money. Which of the following most accurately describes the legal implications of this situation?

a. Moon had apparent authority to make contracts on Star's behalf with suppliers with whom Moon was currently dealing as Star's agent if they had <u>no</u> actual knowledge of his dismissal.

b. The suppliers who previously had <u>no</u> dealings with Star can enforce the contracts against Star if the suppliers had <u>no</u> actual knowledge of Moon's lack of authority.

c. Star is liable on the Moon contracts to all suppliers who had dealt with Moon in the past as Star's agent and who have <u>not</u> received personal notice, even though they had read the published notice.

d. Constructive notice by publication in the appropriate trade journals is an effective notice to all third parties regardless of whether they had previously dealt with Moon or read the notice.

27 (May 77)

Wilkinson is a car salesman employed by Fantastic Motors, Inc. Fantastic instructed Wilkinson <u>not</u> to sell a specially equipped and modified car owned by the company. Fantastic had decided to use this car as a "super" demonstrator to impress potential purchasers. The car had just arrived from Detroit, had been serviced, and was parked alongside another similar model. Barkus "fell in love" with the car and, after some negotiation with Wilkinson, signed a contract to purchase the car. Barkus gave Wilkinson a check for 20% of the purchase price and executed a note and a purchase money security agreement. Wilkinson forged Fantastic's name on the check and disappeared. Fantastic seeks to repossess the car from Barkus. What is the probable outcome based on the above facts?

a. Fantastic will be permitted to repossess the car but must compensate Barkus for any inconvenience.

b. Barkus will be permitted to keep the car if Barkus assumes the loss on the check given to Wilkinson.

c. Fantastic will be permitted to repossess the car because there was an express prohibition against the sale of this car.

d. Barkus will be permitted to keep the car because Wilkinson had the apparent authority to bind Fantastic to the contract of sale.

2 (November 95)
Items 61 through 65 are based on the following:

Lace Computer Sales Corp. orally contracted with Banks, an independent consultant, for Banks to work part-time as Lace's agent to perform Lace's customers' service calls. Banks, a computer programmer and software designer, was authorized to customize Lace's software to the customers' needs, on a commission basis, but was specifically told not to sell Lace's computers.

On September 15, Banks made a service call on Clear Co. to repair Clear's computer. Banks had previously called on Clear, customized Lace's software for Clear, and collected cash payments for the work performed. During the call, Banks convinced Clear to buy an upgraded Lace computer for a price much lower than Lace would normally charge. Clear had previously purchased computers from other Lace agents and had made substantial cash down payments to the agents. Clear had no knowledge that the price was lower than normal. Banks received a $1,000 cash down payment and promised to deliver the computer the next week. Banks never turned in the down payment and left town. When Clear called the following week to have the computer delivered, Lace refused to honor Clear's order.

Required: **Items 61 through 65** relate to the relationships between the parties. For each item, select from List I whether only statement I is correct, whether only statement II is correct, whether both statements I and II are correct, or whether neither statement I nor II is correct.

List I
A   I only.
B   II only.
C   Both I and II
D   Neither I nor II

61.   I.   Lace's agreement with Banks had to be in writing for it to be a valid agency agreement.
      II.   Lace's agreement with Banks empowered Banks to act as Lace's agent.

62.   I.   Clear was entitled to rely on Banks' implied authority to customize Lace's software.
      II.   Clear was entitled to rely on Banks' express authority when buying the computer.

63.   I.   Lace's agreement with Banks was automatically terminated by Banks' sale of the computer.
      II.   Lace must notify Clear before Banks' apparent authority to bind Lace will cease.

64.   I.   Lace is <u>not</u> bound by the agreement made by Banks with Clear.
      II.   Lace may unilaterally amend the agreement made by Banks to prevent a loss on the sale of the computer to Clear.

65.   I.   Lace, as a disclosed principal, is solely contractually liable to Clear.
      II.   Both Lace and Banks are contractually liable to Clear.

6A (May 74)
In examining the financial statements of Plover Corporation, you learn that Plover hired Amber to manage its farm and gave him authority to purchase seed up to a maximum of $500 per year. Amber was also given authority to hire employees to help operate the farm. Plover also gave Amber authority to buy for Plover a forty-acre tract, adjacent to the farm, if it became available, and to collect the monthly rental of a house located on the farm.

Amber purchased seed from Supplee as authorized but exceeded his authority by contracting in Plover's name with Supplee for fertilizer in the amount of $600. Amber hired Mans to operate a farm tractor. While operating the tractor in a negligent manner, Mans destroyed a boundary fence belonging to Naybor. Meanwhile, Amber had entered into a contract to purchase the forty acres from Honer, its owner, without revealing that he was purchasing for Plover.

Plover, on learning of the Mans incident, discharged Amber. Amber, who had been collecting the rents on the house, promptly collected the rent then due for the current month from the lessee and disappeared. The lessee did not know of Amber's discharge.

Required:
1. Discuss Plover's liability to Supplee on the order for fertilizer.
2. To what extent, if any, is Plover liable to Naybor for Mans' actions?
3. What are Plover's rights under the agreement for the forty acres?
4. Discuss Plover's liability on the contract for the purchase of the land if it wishes to avoid the obligation.
5. Discuss Plover's rights to recover from the tenant of the house for the last rental payment made to Amber.

1. Amber had actual authority to carry on major management duties in connection with the farm and would be deemed to have had apparent authority to purchase normal farming supplies. Supplee could reasonably believe that Amber, as farm manager, could contract for the fertilizer as well as the seed. The fact that the contract was in the amount of $600, or in excess of Amber's actual authority, would not permit Plover to avoid liability thereon because this would also reasonably appear to be within the scope of Amber's apparent authority.

2. Plover is probably liable to Naybor for the damage to Naybor's fence as a result of Mans negligence. Amber had authority to hire employees to help operate the farm, and Plover would be responsible for the act of his employee-agent acting within the scope of his employment.

3. Although Plover was an undisclosed principal, it has the right to enforce the contract made by its agent within the scope of the agent's authority.

4. The fact that Plover was an undisclosed principal gives it no right to avoid a contract made by its agent for the principal within the scope of the agent's authority.

5. The tenant, having made payment to Amber, is not liable to Plover. Plover, the principal, did not give the tenant notice that Amber's authority had been terminated. The tenant, having paid the rent to Amber on prior occasions and without notice of any lack of authority on the part of Amber to make the collection, is protected under the apparent authority doctrine, and payment to the agent is deemed effective payment to the principal.

6B (May 74)

Partridge entered into a written contract with Alder whereby Alder was to have an exclusive right for nine months to sell Partridge's farm. Alder was required to publish specified advertisements at his expense and was to be entitled to a commission of $10,000 upon sale. Alder advertised as required. One month later Partridge notified Alder that the right to sell was revoked. One day after receiving Partridge's revocation, Alder entered into a contract of sale of the farm to Tenney who had relied on the advertisement authorizing Alder to sell for Partridge.

Required:
1. What rights, if any, does Tenney have under the agreement with Alder?
2. What are the rights of
   a. Partridge against Alder?
   b. Alder against Partridge?

1. Tenney had the right to rely upon the apparent authority of Alder. He therefore has an action for breach of contract if Partridge refuses to perform and, in an appropriate case, a right to specific performance.

2.(a) Alder is subject to liability to Partridge for any damages resulting to Partridge as a result of the agreement with Tenney.

(b) Alder is not entitled to the commission specified in the contract because his agency was terminated. However, Partridge is subject to liability for damages to Alder for breach of his agreement with Alder in terminating Alder's rights under the agency agreement, and the relative claims may be offset against each other in an action between them.

C. Termination of Agency Powers
1. Termination of Actual and Apparent Authority

7 (May 95)

Thorp was a purchasing agent for Ogden, a sole proprietor, and had the express authority to place purchase orders with Ogden's suppliers. Thorp placed an order with Datz, Inc. on Ogden's behalf after Ogden was declared incompetent in a judicial proceeding. Thorp was aware of Ogden's incapacity. Which of the following statements is correct concerning Ogden's liability to Datz?

    a. Ogden will be liable because Datz was <u>not</u> informed of Ogden's incapacity.

    b. Ogden will be liable because Thorp acted with express authority.

    c. Ogden will <u>not</u> be liable because Thorp's agency ended when Ogden was declared incompetent.

    d. Ogden will <u>not</u> be liable because Ogden was a nondisclosed principal.

17 (November 94)

Bolt Corp. dismissed Ace as its general sales agent and notified all of Ace's known customers by letter. Young Corp., a retail outlet located outside of Ace's previously assigned sales territory, had never dealt with Ace. Young knew of Ace as a result of various business contacts. After his dismissal, Ace sold Young goods, to be delivered by Bolt, and received from Young a cash deposit for 20% of the purchase price. It was not unusual for an agent in Ace's previous position to receive cash deposits. In an action by Young against Bolt on the sales contract, Young will

    a. Lose, because Ace lacked any implied authority to make the contract.

    b. Lose, because Ace lacked any express authority to make the contract.

    c. Win, because Bolt's notice was inadequate to terminate Ace's apparent authority.

    d. Win, because a principal is an insurer of an agent's acts.

1 (May 90)

Generally, an agency relationship is terminated by operation of law in all of the following situations <u>except</u> the

    a. Principal's death.

    b. Principal's incapacity.

    c. Agent's renunciation of the agency.

    d. Agent's failure to acquire a necessary business license.

2 (November 88)

Harris is a purchasing agent for Elkin, a sole proprietor. Harris has the express authority to place purchase orders with Elkin's suppliers. Harris typically conducts business through the mail and has very little contact with Elkin. Elkin was incapacitated by a stroke and was declared incompetent in a judicial proceeding. Subsequently, Harris placed an order with Ajax, Inc. on behalf of Elkin. Neither Ajax nor Harris were aware of Elkin's incapacity. With regard to the contract with Ajax, Elkin (or Elkin's legal representative) will

    a. Not be liable because Harris was without authority to enter into the contract.

    b. Not be liable provided that Harris had placed orders with Ajax in the past.

    c. Be liable because Harris was acting within the scope of Harris' authority.

    d. Be liable because Ajax was unaware of Elkin's incapacity.

6 (May 88)

The apparent authority of a general agent for a disclosed principal will terminate without notice to third parties when the

    a. Principal dismisses the agent.

    b. Principal or agent dies.

    c. Purpose of the agency relationship has been fulfilled.

    d. Time period set forth in the agency agreement has expired.

4 (May 87)

A general agent's apparent authority to bind her principal to contracts with third parties will cease without notice to those third parties when the

    a.   Agent has fulfilled the purpose for which the agency relationship was created.

    b.   Time set forth in the agreement creating the agency relationship has expired.

    c.   Principal and agent have mutually agreed to end their relationship.

    d.   Principal has received a discharge in bankruptcy under the liquidation provisions of the Bankruptcy Code.

14 (November 84)

Dent is an agent for Wein pursuant to a written agreement with a three-year term. After two years of the term, Wein decides that he would like to terminate the relationship with Dent. Wein may terminate the relationship

    a.   Without cause, but may be held liable for breach of contract.

    b.   Even if Dent is an agent coupled with an interest.

    c.   Without cause, but may be held liable for the intentional interference with an existing contract.

    d.   Only if Dent breaches the fiduciary duties owed to Wein.

2 (May 84)

Notice to third parties is not required to terminate a disclosed general agent's apparent authority when the

    a.   Principal has died.

    b.   Principal revokes the agent's authority.

    c.   Agent renounces the agency relationship.

    d.   Agency relationship terminates as a result of the fulfillment of its purpose.

29 (November 80)

Park Manufacturing hired Stone as a traveling salesman to sell goods manufactured by Park. Stone also sold a line of products manufactured by a friend. He did not disclose this to Park. The relationship was unsatisfactory and Park finally fired Stone after learning of Stone's sales of the other manufacturer's goods. Stone, enraged at Park for firing him, continued to make contracts on Park's behalf with both new and old customers that were almost uniformly disadvantageous to Park. Park, upon learning of this, gave written notice of Stone's discharge to all parties with whom Stone had dealt. Which of the following is incorrect?

    a.   Park can bring an action against Stone to have him account for any secret profits.

    b.   Prior to notification, Stone retained some continued authority to bind Park despite termination of the agency relationship.

    c.   New customers who contracted with Stone for the first time could enforce the contracts against Park if they knew that Stone had been Park's salesman but were unaware that Stone was fired.

    d.   If Park had promptly published a notification of termination of Stone's employment in the local newspapers and in the trade publications, he would not be liable for any of Stone's contracts.

11 (November 74)

An agent's power to bind his principal to a contract is generally terminated

    a.   Automatically upon the commission of a tort by the agent.

    b.   Instantly upon the death of the principal.

    c.   Upon the bankruptcy of the agent.

    d.   Without further action by the principal upon the resignation of the agent.

2. Termination of a Power Given as Security (Agency Coupled with an Interest)

11 (May 89)

Pell is the principal and Astor is the agent in an agency coupled with an interest. In the absence of a contractual provision relating to the duration of the agency, who has the right to terminate the agency before the interest has expired?

	<u>Pell</u>	<u>Astor</u>
a.	Yes	Yes
b.	No	Yes
c.	No	No
d.	Yes	No

3 (May 85)

An agency coupled with an interest will be created by a written agreement which provides that a(an)

a. Borrower shall pledge securities to a lender which authorizes the lender to sell the securities and apply the proceeds to the loan in the event of default.

b. Employee is hired for a period of two years at $40,000 per annum plus 2% of net sales.

c. Broker is to receive a 5% sales commission out of the proceeds of the sale of a parcel of land.

d. Attorney is to receive 25% of a plaintiff's recovery for personal injuries.

34 (November 82)

Downtown Disco, Inc. engaged Charleston as club manager in a written agreement providing for a $20,000 salary, plus 2% of gross revenues, and exclusive management authority including entertainment bookings. The agreement is irrevocable by Downtown for three years but terminable by Charleston upon one month's written notice. The Downtown-Charleston arrangement is

a. An agency coupled with an interest.

b. A partnership between Downtown and Charleston.

c. Terminable at any time by Downtown despite the three-year irrevocability clause.

d. Enforceable by Charleston by an action for specific performance.

50 (November 79)

Ozgood is a principal and Flood is his agent. Ozgood is totally dissatisfied with the agency relationship and wishes to terminate it. In which of the following situations does Ozgood <u>not</u> have the power to terminate the relationship?

a. Ozgood and Flood have agreed that their agency is irrevocable.

b. Flood has been appointed as Ozgood's agent pursuant to a power of attorney.

c. Flood is an agent coupled with an interest.

d. The agency agreement is in writing and provides for a specific duration which has <u>not</u> elapsed.

25 (November 76)

Farber, a principal, engaged Waters for six months as his exclusive agent to sell specific antiques.

a. The creation of such an agency must be in writing.

b. If the principal sells the antiques through another agent, he will be liable to Waters for damages.

c. The principal does <u>not</u> have the legal power to terminate the agency since it is an agency coupled with an interest.

d. Waters has impliedly guaranteed that he will sell the antiques within the six month period.

II. Agency and Torts
A. Tort Liability of Principal and Agent

13 (November 93)

Generally, a disclosed principal will be liable to third parties for its agent's unauthorized misrepresentations if the agent is an

	Employee	Independent Contractor
a.	Yes	Yes
b.	Yes	No
c.	No	Yes
d.	No	No

2 (May 90)

Pine, an employee of Global Messenger Co., was hired to deliver highly secret corporate documents for Global's clients throughout the world. Unknown to Global, Pine carried a concealed pistol. While Pine was making a delivery, he suspected an attempt was being made to steal the package, drew his gun and shot Kent, an innocent passerby. Kent will <u>not</u> recover damages from Global if

a. Global discovered that Pine carried a weapon and did nothing about it.
b. Global instructed its messengers <u>not</u> to carry weapons.
c. Pine was correct and an attempt was being made to steal the package.
d. Pine's weapon was unlicensed and illegal.

2 (November 89)

A principal will <u>not</u> be liable to a third party for a tort committed by an agent

a. Unless the principal instructed the agent to commit the tort.
b. Unless the tort was committed within the scope of the agency relationship.
c. If the agency agreement limits the principal's liability for the agent's tort.
d. .If the tort is also regarded as a criminal act.

12 (May 89)

Neal, an employee of Jordan, was delivering merchandise to a customer. On the way, Neal's negligence caused a traffic accident that resulted in damages to a third party's automobile. Who is liable to the third party?

	Neal	Jordan
a.	No	No
b.	Yes	Yes
c.	Yes	No
d.	No	Yes

5 (May 87)

If an agent has, within the scope of the agency relationship, committed both negligent and intentional acts resulting in injury to third parties, the principal

a. May be liable even if the agent's acts were unauthorized.
b. May effectively limit its liability to those third parties if the agent has signed a disclaimer absolving the principal from liability.
c. Will be liable under the doctrine of respondeat superior only for the intentional acts.
d. Will <u>never</u> be criminally liable unless it actively participated in the acts.

12 (November 83)

Ivy Corp. engaged Jones as a sales representative and assigned him to a route in Southern Florida. Jones worked out of Ivy's main office and his duties, hours, and routes were carefully controlled. The employment contract contained a provision which stated: "I, <u>Jones</u>, do hereby promise to hold the corporation harmless from any and all tort liability to third parties which may arise in carrying out my duties as an employee." On a sales call, Jones negligently dropped a case of hammers on the foot of Devlin, the owner of Devlin's Hardware. Which of the following statements is correct?

a. Ivy has <u>no</u> liability to Devlin.

b. Although the exculpatory clause may be valid between Ivy and Jones, it does <u>not</u> affect Devlin's rights.

c. Ivy is <u>not</u> liable to Devlin in any event, since Jones is an independent contractor.

d. The exculpatory clause is totally invalid since it is against public policy.

13 (November 83)

Wall & Co. hired Carr to work as an agent in its collection department, reporting to the credit manager. Which of the following is correct?

a. Carr does <u>not</u> owe a fiduciary duty to Wall since he does not compete with the company.

b. Carr will be personally liable for any torts he commits even though they are committed in the course of his employment and pursuant to Wall's directions.

c. Carr has the implied authority to engage counsel and commence legal action against Wall's debtors.

d. Carr may commingle funds collected by him if this is convenient as long as he keeps proper records.

5 (May 82)

The liability of a principal to a third party for the torts of his agent

a. Can be effectively limited by agreement with the agent.

b. Can <u>not</u> extend to the inclusion of a criminal act committed by the agent.

c. Is less onerous if the agent is acting for an undisclosed principal.

d. Is an example of the imposition of liability without fault upon the principal.

14 (November 81)

Wilcox works as a welder for Miracle Muffler, Inc. He was specially trained by Miracle in the procedures and safety precautions applicable to installing replacement mufflers on automobiles. One rule of which he was aware involved a prohibition against installing a muffler on any auto which had heavily congealed oil or grease or which had any leaks. Wilcox disregarded this rule, and as a result an auto caught fire causing extensive property damage and injury to Wilcox. Which of the following statements is correct?

a. Miracle is <u>not</u> liable because its rule prohibited Wilcox from installing the muffler in question.

b. Miracle is <u>not</u> liable to Wilcox under the workmen's compensation laws.

c. Miracle is liable irrespective of its efforts to prevent such an occurrence and the fact that it exercised reasonable care.

d. Wilcox does <u>not</u> have any personal liability for the loss because he was acting for and on behalf of his employer.

15 (November 81)

The key characteristic of a servant is that

a. His physical conduct is controlled or subject to the right of control by the employer.

b. He is paid at an hourly rate as contrasted with the payment of a salary.

c. He is precluded from making contracts for and on behalf of his employer.

d. He lacks apparent authority to bind his employer.

16 (November 81)

Brian purchased an automobile from Robinson Auto Sales under a written contract by which Robinson obtained a security interest to secure payment of the purchase price. Robinson reserved the right to repossess the automobile if Brian failed to make any of the required ten payments. Ambrose, an employee of Robinson, was instructed to repossess the automobile on the ground that Brian had defaulted in making the third payment. Ambrose took possession of the automobile and delivered it to Robinson. It was then discovered that Brian was not in default. Which of the following is <u>incorrect</u>?

  a. Brian has the right to regain possession of the automobile and to collect damages.
  b. Brian may sue and collect from either Robinson or Ambrose.
  c. If Ambrose must pay in damages, he will be entitled to indemnification from Robinson.
  d. Ambrose is <u>not</u> liable for the wrongful repossession of the automobile since he was obeying the direct order of Robinson.

4 (November 77)

Gaspard & Devlin, a medium-sized CPA firm, employed Marshall as a staff accountant. Marshall was negligent in auditing several of the firm's clients. Under these circumstances, which of the following statements is true?

  a. Gaspard & Devlin is <u>not</u> liable for Marshall's negligence because CPAs are generally considered to be independent contractors.
  b. Gaspard & Devlin would <u>not</u> be liable for Marshall's negligence if Marshall disobeyed specific instructions in the performance of the audits.
  c. Gaspard & Devlin can recover against its insurer on its malpractice policy even if one of the partners was also negligent in reviewing Marshall's work.
  d. Marshall would have <u>no</u> personal liability for negligence.

21 (November 76)

Harper was employed as a carpenter by the Ace Construction Company. He negligently constructed a scaffold at one of Ace's construction sites. The scaffold collapsed and injured Dirks (a fellow employee), Franklin (a supplier), and Harper.

  a. Ace Construction Company is <u>not</u> liable to Franklin if Harper disobeyed specific instructions regarding construction of the scaffold.
  b. Ace Construction Company is liable to Franklin even though Harper was grossly negligent.
  c. Harper is <u>not</u> personally liable to Dirks or Franklin.
  d. Harper <u>cannot</u> obtain workmen's compensation.

45 (May 76)

Jackson is a junior staff member of Stutz & Harris, CPAs. He has been with the firm for one year working with the audit staff.

  a. If Jackson is injured while auditing one of the firm's clients, the client's workmen's compensation insurance will cover him.
  b. The federal wage and hour laws do <u>not</u> apply to Jackson.
  c. Stutz & Harris will be liable for the torts committed by Jackson within the scope of his employment.
  d. Clients will be liable for the torts committed by Jackson since he and his principal (Stutz & Harris) were engaged by them.

27 (May 75)

Head is a crane operator for Magnum Construction Corporation. One day while operating the crane he negligently swung the crane into another building, which caused extensive damage to the other building and the crane. The accident also resulted in fracturing Head's elbow and dislocating his hip. In this situation,

  a. Head is liable for the damages he caused to the crane and the building.
  b. Magnum's liability is limited to the damage to the building only if Head was acting within the scope of his authority.
  c. Magnum will <u>not</u> be liable for damage to the building if Head's negligence was in clear violation of Magnum's safety standards and rules regarding operation of the crane.
  d. Head is <u>not</u> entitled to workmen's compensation.

14 (November 74)

Joe Walters was employed by the Metropolitan Department Store as a driver of one of its delivery trucks. Under the terms of his employment he made deliveries daily along a designated route and brought the truck back to the store's garage for overnight storage. One day instead of returning to the garage as required, he drove the truck twenty miles north of the area he covered expecting to attend a social function unrelated to his employment or to his employer's affairs. Through his negligence in operating the truck while en route, Walters seriously injured Richard Bunt. Walters caused the accident and was solely at fault. Bunt entered suit in tort against the store for damages for personal injuries, alleging that the store, as principal, was responsible for the tortious acts of its agent. Under these circumstances

   a. Metropolitan is <u>not</u> liable because Walters was an independent contractor.
   b. Metropolitan is <u>not</u> liable because Walters had abandoned his employment and was engaged in an independent activity of his own.
   c. Metropolitan is liable based upon the doctrine of <u>respondeat superior</u>.
   d. Bunt can recover damages from both Walters and Metropolitan.

4 (November 92)

Exotic Pets, Inc. hired Peterson to be the manager of one of its stores. Exotic sells a wide variety of animals. Peterson was given considerable authority by Exotic to operate the store, including the right to buy inventory. Peterson was told that any inventory purchase exceeding $2,000 required the approval of Exotic's general manager.

On June 1, 1992, Peterson contracted with Creatures Corp. to buy snakes for $3,100. Peterson had regularly done business with Creatures on Exotic's behalf in the past, and on several occasions had bought $1,000 to $1,750 worth of snakes from Creatures. Creatures was unaware of the limitation on Peterson's authority to buy inventory.

Peterson occasionally would buy, for Exotic, a certain breed of dog from Premier Breeders, Inc., which was owned by Peterson's friend. Whenever Exotic bought dogs from Premier, Preier paid Peterson 5% of the purchase price as an incentive to do more business with Premier. Exotic's management was unaware of these payments to Peterson.

On June 20, 1992, Mathews went to the Exotic store managed by Peterson to buy a ferret. Peterson allowed Mathews to handle one of the ferrets. Peterson knew that this particular ferret had previously bitten one of the store's clerks. Mathews was bitten by the ferret and seriously injured.

On July 23, 1992, Peterson bought paint and brushes for $30 from Handy Hardware. Peterson charged the purchase to exotic's account at Handy. Peterson intended to use the paint and brushes to repaint the pet showroom. Exotic's management had never specifically discussed with Peterson whether Peterson had the authority to charge purchases at Handy. Although Exotic paid the Handy bill, Exotic's president believes Peterson is obligated to reimburse Exotic for the charges.

On August 1, 1992, Exotic's president learned of the Creatures contract and advised Creatures that Exotic would neither accept delivery of the snakes, nor pay for them, because Peterson did not have the authority to enter into the contract.

Exotic's president has also learned about the incentive payments Premier made to Peterson.

Exotic has taken the following positions:

   ▪ It is not liable to Creatures because Peterson entered into the contract without Exotic's consent.
   ▪ Peterson is obligated to reimburse Exotic for the charges incurred by Peterson at Handy Hardware.
   ▪ Peterson is liable to Exotic for the incentive payments received from Premier.

Mathews has sued both Peterson and Exotic for the injuries sustained from the ferret bite.

Required:
   a. State whether Exotic's positions are correct and give the reasons for your conclusions.
   b. State whether Mathews will prevail in the lawsuit against Exotic and Peterson and give the reasons for your conclusions.

a. Exotic's first position is incorrect. Although Peterson lacked actual authority to bind Exotic to the Creatures contract, from Creatures' perspective Peterson did have apparent authority to do so. Peterson was a store manager and had previously contracted with Creatures on Exotic's behalf. Creatures would not be bound by the limitation on Peterson's authority unless Creatures was aware of it.

Exotic's second position is incorrect. Although Peterson did not have express authority to charge purchases at Handy Hardware, Peterson had the implied authority as store manager to enter into contracts incidental to the express grant of authority to act as manager. Buying paint and brushes to improve Exotic's store would fall within Peterson's implied grant of authority.

Exotic's third position is correct. An agent owes a duty of loyalty to his or her principal. An agent may not benefit directly or indirectly from an agency relationship at the principal's expense. If an agent receives any profits from the principal/agent relationship without the consent of the principal, the agent must pay the profits to the principal. In this case, Peterson's incentive payments constituted a violation of Peterson's fiduciary duty to Exotic. Peterson must turn over all incentive payments to Exotic.

b. Peterson was negligent by allowing Mathews to handle a ferret that Peterson knew was dangerous. An employer is held liable for the torts of its employees if the tort occurs within the scope of employment and if the employee is subject to the employer's control. At the time of the accident, Peterson was acting within the scope of employment and subject to Exotic's control because this conduct occurred while on the job, during normal working hours, and with the intention of benefitting Exotic. Exotic, therefore, will be liable to Mathews because the accident occurred within the scope of Peterson's employment.

Peterson also will be liable to Mathews because all persons are liable for their own negligence.

3 (November 90)

Prime Cars, Inc. buys and sells used automobiles. Occasionally Prime has its salespeople purchase used cars from third parties without disclosing that the salesperson is in fact buying the Prime's used car inventory. Prime's management believes better prices can be negotiated using this procedure. One of Prime's salespeople, Peterson, entered into a contract with Hallow in accordance with instructions from Prime's sales manager. The car was to be delivered one week later. After entering into the contract with Hallow, and while driving back to Prime's place of business, Peterson was involved in an automobile accident with another vehicle. Peterson's negligence, and the resulting collision, injured Mathews, the driver of the other car involved in the accident.

Prime terminated Peterson's employment because of the accident. Following Prime's general business practices, Prime published an advertisement in several trade journals that gave notice that Peterson was no longer employed by Prime. Shortly thereafter, Peterson approached one of Prime's competitors, Bagley Autos, Inc., and contracted to sell Bagley several used cars in Prime's inventory. Bagley's sales manager, who frequently purchased cars out of Prime's inventory from Peterson, paid 25% of the total price to Peterson, with the balance to be paid ten days later when the cars were to be delivered. Bagley's sales manager was unaware of Peterson's termination. Prime refused to deliver the cars to Bagley or to repay Bagley's down payment, which Prime never received from Peterson.

Prime also refused to go through with the contract entered into by Peterson with Hallow. Mathews sued both Peterson and Prime for the injuries sustained in the automobile accident. Bagley sued Prime for failing to deliver the cars or return the down payment paid to Peterson.

Required: Answer each of the following questions, setting forth the reasons for your conclusions.
 a. What rights does Hallow have against Prime or Peterson?
 b. Will Mathews prevail in the lawsuit against Prime and Peterson?
 c. Will Bagley prevail in its lawsuit against Prime?

a. Peterson was acting for an undisclosed principal (Prime) with regard to the contract with Hallow. Peterson was acting with actual authority; therefore, Prime is liable to Hallow. Peterson is also liable to Hallow because agents acting on behalf of undisclosed principals are liable to the third parties on the contracts they enter into with such third parties on behalf of the principal. Hallow, however, cannot collect damages from both Peterson and Prime and must make an election between them.

b. At the time of the accident, Peterson was acting within the scope of employment because the conduct engaged in (that is, entering into a contract with Hallow) was authorized by Prime. Prime, therefore, will be liable to Mathews because the accident occurred within the scope of Peterson's employment.

Peterson will also be liable to Mathews because all persons are liable for their own negligence.

c. Peterson's actual authority to enter into contracts on Prime's behalf ceased on termination of employment by Prime. Peterson, however, continued to have apparent authority to bind Prime because:

- Peterson was acting ostensibly within the scope of authority as evidenced by past transactions with Bagley;
- Bagley was unaware of Peterson's termination.

The trade journal announcement was not effective notice to terminate Peterson's apparent authority in relation to Bagley because:

- Prime was obligated to give actual notice to Bagley that Peterson was no longer employed;
- Actual notice is required because of Bagley's past contact with Peterson while Peterson was employed by Prime.

3A (November 78)

Rapid Delivery Service, Inc. hired Dolson as one of its truck drivers. Dolson was carefully selected and trained by Rapid. He was specifically instructed to obey all traffic and parking rules and regulations. One day while making a local delivery, Dolson doubled parked and went into a nearby customer's store. In doing so, he prevented a car legally parked at the curb from leaving. The owner of the parked car, Charles, proceeded to blow the horn of the truck repeatedly. Charles was doing this when Dolson returned from his delivery. As a result of a combination of several factors, particularly Charles' telling him to "move it" and that he was "acting very selfishly and in an unreasonable manner," Dolson punched Charles in the nose, severely fracturing it. When Charles sought to restrain him, Dolson punched Charles again, this time fracturing his jaw. Charles has commenced legal action against Rapid.

Required: Answer the following, setting forth reasons for any conclusions stated.
1. Will Charles prevail?
2. What liability, if any, would Dolson have?

1. Probably yes. A master is liable for his servant's unauthorized tortious conduct within the scope of employment. This is true despite the fact that the master is in no way personally at fault or has forbidden the type of conduct engaged in by the servant. A servant is normally an employee who renders personal service to his employer and whose activities are subject to the control of the employer. A truck driver such as Dolson would clearly fall within such a description. Once this has been established, the question is whether the assaults committed upon Charles by Dolson were within the scope of his employment. When the intentional use of force is involved, the courts have taken an expansive view insofar as imposition of liability upon the employer. If the servant's action are predictable, there is likelihood that liability will be imposed upon the master. Where the servant deals with third persons in carrying out his job, the courts ask whether the wrongful act which occurred was likely to arise out of the performance of his job. Additionally, consideration is given to whether any part of his motive was the performance of his job, or if not, whether it was a normal reaction to a situation created by the job. Truck drivers using force in situations involving parking space or after a collision resulting in a dispute are not uncommon. The courts have usually imposed liability in cases such as this unless the assault was unrelated to the job, was solely personal, or was outrageous.

2. Dolson is liable to Charles for the tortious injury inflicted. The fact that Dolson may have been acting as a servant of Rapid and may impose liability upon his employer does not relieve him from liability.

3B (November 78)

Harold Watts was employed by Superior Sporting Goods as a route salesman. His territory, route, and customers were determined by Superior. He was expected to work from 9:00 AM to 5:00 PM, Monday through Friday. He received a weekly salary plus time and one-half for anything over 40 hours. He also received a small commission on sales which exceeded a stated volume. The customers consisted of sporting goods stores, department stores, athletic clubs, and large companies which had athletic programs or sponsored athletic teams. Watts used his personal car in making calls or, upon occasion, making a delivery where the customer was in a rush and the order was not large. Watts was reimbursed for the use of the car for company purposes. His instructions were to assume the customer is always right and to accommodate the customer where to do so would cost little and would build goodwill for the company and himself.

One afternoon while making a sales call and dropping off a case of softballs at the Valid Clock Company, the personnel director told Watts he was planning to watch the company's team play a game at a softball field located on the other side of town, but that his car would not start. Watts said, "Don't worry, it will be my pleasure to give you a lift and I would like to take in a few innings myself." Time was short and while on the way to the ballpark, Watts ran a light and collided with another car. The other car required $800 of repairs and the owner suffered serious bodily injury.

Required: Answer the following, setting forth reasons for any conclusions stated.
1. What is Superior's potential liability, if any, to the owner of the other car?
2. What is Valid's potential liability, if any, to the owner of the other car?

1. Superior Sporting Goods is liable for the negligence of its servant-agent Watts. The requisite control of his activities is apparent from the facts. Furthermore, based upon the instructions Watts received, it would appear that he was acting within the scope of his employment. In fact, one could conclude from the facts that Watts had express authority to make a trip such as the one he made when the accident occurred. He specifically was told to generally accommodate the customer where to do so would cost little and would build goodwill for the company and himself. This appears to be exactly what he did. Superior will undoubtedly attempt to assert the "independent frolic" doctrine and claim that Watts had abandoned his employment in order to pursue his own interest or pleasures. However, the deviation was not great, it took place during normal working hours, and, most importantly, was at the request of a customer and was a type of conduct Superior specifically encouraged.

2. Valid Clock Company has no liability. Its agent was not at fault, nor can it be reasonably argued that an agency relationship was created between itself and Watts because its personnel director accepted the ride offered by Watts. The requisite control of Watts' physical activities by Valid is not present.

B. Workers' Compensation

5 (R01)

Lee repairs high-speed looms for Sew Corp., a clothing manufacturer. Which of the following circumstances best indicates that Lee is an employee of Sew and **not** an independent contractor?
   a. Lee's work is not supervised by Sew personnel.
   b. Lee's tools are owned by Lee.
   c. Lee is paid weekly by Sew.
   d. Lee's work requires a high degree of technical skill.

16 (R01)

Which of the following parties generally is ineligible to collect workers' compensation benefits?
   a. Minors.
   b. Truck drivers.
   c. Union employees.
   d. Temporary office workers.

33 (November 95)

Which of the following claims is (are) generally covered under workers' compensation statutes?

	Occupational disease	Employment aggravated pre-existing disease
a.	Yes	Yes
b.	Yes	No
c.	No	Yes
d.	No	No

34 (November 95)

Generally, which of the following statements concerning workers' compensation laws is correct?
a. The amount of damages recoverable is based on comparative negligence.
b. Employers are strictly liable without regard to whether or not they are at fault.
c. Workers' compensation benefits are not available if the employee is negligent.
d. Workers' compensation awards are payable for life.

36 (November 94)

Which of the following provisions is basic to all workers' compensation systems?
a. The injured employee must prove the employer's negligence.
b. The employer may invoke the traditional defense of contributory negligence.
c. The employer's liability may be ameliorated by a co-employee's negligence under the fellow-servant rule.
d. The injured employee is allowed to recover on strict liability theory.

36 (November 93)

Which one of the following statements concerning workers' compensation laws is generally correct?
a. Employers are strictly liable without regard to whether or not they are at fault.
b. Workers' compensation benefits are not available if the employee is negligent.
c. Workers' compensation awards are not reviewable by the courts.
d. The amount of damages recoverable is based on comparative negligence.

28 (May 93)

Kroll, an employee of Acorn, Inc., was injured in the course of employment while operating a forklift manufactured and sold to Acorn by Trell Corp. The forklift was defectively designed by Trell. Under the state's mandatory workers' compensation statute, Kroll will be successful in

	Obtaining worker's compensation benefits	A negligence action against Acorn
a.	Yes	Yes
b.	Yes	No
c.	No	Yes
d.	No	No

38 (May 92)

Workers' Compensation Acts require an employer to
a. Provide coverage for all eligible employees.
b. Withhold employee contributions from the wages of eligible employees.
c. Pay an employee the difference between disability payments and full salary.
d. Contribute to a federal insurance fund.

34 (November 91)

Workers' Compensation laws provide for all of the following benefits <u>except</u>
a. Burial expenses.
b. Full pay during disability.
c. The cost of prosthetic devices.
d. Monthly payments to surviving dependent children.

38 (May 91)

The primary purpose for enacting Workers' Compensation statutes was to
a. Eliminate all employer-employee negligence lawsuits.
b. Enable employees to recover for injuries regardless of negligence.
c. Prevent employee negligence suits against third parties.
d. Allow employees to recover additional compensation for employer negligence.

38 (November 90)

If an employee is injured, full workers' compensation benefits are <u>not</u> payable if the employee
a. Was injured because of failing to abide by written safety procedures.
b. Was injured because of the acts of fellow employees.
c. Intentionally caused self-inflicted injury.
d. Brought a civil suit against a third party who caused the injury.

32 (November 89)

An employee will generally be precluded from collecting full worker's compensation benefits when the injury is caused by

	Noncompliance with the employer's rules	An intentional, self-inflicted action
a.	No	No
b.	Yes	Yes
c.	No	Yes
d.	Yes	No

44 (May 88)

Bing was employed as a taxi driver by Speedy, Inc. While acting in the scope and course of employment with Speedy, Bing collided with a van driven by Hart. Hart was an independent contractor making a delivery for Troy Corp. The collision was caused solely by Bing's negligence. As a result of the collision, both Bing and Hart suffered permanent injuries. Speedy and Troy were both in compliance with the state's workers' compensation statute. If Hart commences an action against Bing and Speedy for negligence, which of the following statements is correct?
a. Hart is entitled to recover damages from Bing or Speedy.
b. Bing will either be denied workers' compensation benefits or have his benefits reduced because of his negligence.
c. Hart's action for negligence will be dismissed because Hart is an independent contractor.
d. Hart is entitled to recover damages from Speedy's workers' compensation carrier to the extent <u>no</u> duplicate payment has been received by Hart.

15 (November 87)

In general, which of the following is <u>not</u> an available method of complying with a state's workers' compensation statute for a private employer?
a. Self-insurance by the employer.
b. Participation in the state insurance fund.
c. Participation in a federal insurance fund.
d. Purchase of insurance from a private insurer.

36 (May 87)

Nix, an employee of Fern, Inc., was injured in the course of employment while operating a drill press manufactured and sold to Fern by Jet Corp. It has been determined that Fern was negligent in supervising the operation of the drill press and that the drill press was defectively designed by Jet. If Fern has complied with the state's mandatory workers' compensation statute, Nix may
a. Not properly commence a products liability action against Jet.
b. Not obtain workers' compensation benefits.
c. Obtain workers' compensation benefits and properly maintain a products liability action against Jet.
d. Obtain workers' compensation benefits and properly maintain separate causes of action against Jet and Fern for negligence.

38 (November 86)

While in the course of employment with Marco, Inc., Payne was injured. Marco has complied with the state's mandatory workers' compensation statute. Marco's workers' compensation carrier has asserted the following defenses to Payne's claim for workers' compensation benefits:
    I. Marco was free from any wrongdoing.
    II. Payne assumed the risk by disregarding Marco's safety procedures.
    III. Payne's injury was intentionally self-inflicted.
Which defense(s) asserted by the workers' compensation carrier, if proven, will prevent Payne from recovering?
a. I only.
b. II only.
c. III only.
d. I or II.

17 (May 86)

Farr, an employee of Sand Corp., was involved in an accident with Wohl, an independent contractor. Wohl was making a delivery for Byrd Corp. when Farr negligently passed through a red light resulting in the accident and injuries to Wohl and Farr. The accident occurred during Farr's regular working hours and in the course of Farr's employment. If Sand and Byrd have complied with the state's workers' compensation laws, which of the following is correct?
a. Farr will either be denied workers' compensation benefits or have his benefits reduced due to his negligence.
b. Farr will be denied workers' compensation benefits since Sand was free from any wrongdoing.
c. Wohl will be denied workers' compensation benefits under Sand's or Byrd's workers' compensation policy.
d. Wohl will be denied workers' compensation benefits due to the fellow-servant rule.

21 (November 85)

Fred Gray, an employee of Gold Transport Corp., was injured when the corporate truck which he was driving struck a tree. The state in which Gold was incorporated and operated its business had a compulsory worker's compensation law. Gray will likely receive workers' compensation benefits despite the fact he
a. Was properly excluded from coverage under the compulsory workers' compensation law.
b. Was driving the truck outside the course of his employment at the time of the accident.
c. Intentionally drove the truck into the tree.
d. Was negligent by failing to adhere to Gold's safety procedures while operating the truck.

30 (May 85)

Silk was employed by Rosco Corp. as a chauffeur. While in the course of employment, Silk was involved in an automobile accident with Lake who was employed by Stone Corp. as a truck driver. While making a delivery for Stone, Lake negligently drove through a red light causing the accident with Silk. Both Silk and Lake have received workers' compensation benefits as a result of the accident. Silk

    a. Is precluded from suing Lake since both are covered under workers' compensation laws.

    b. Is precluded from suing Stone if Stone complied fully with the state's workers' compensation laws.

    c. Can recover in full against Lake only, but must reimburse the workers' compensation carrier to the extent the recovery duplicates benefits already obtained under workers' compensation laws.

    d. Can recover in full against Lake or Stone, but must reimburse the workers' compensation carrier to the extent the recovery duplicates benefits already obtained under workers' compensation laws.

39 (November 84)

Which of the following is required in order for an employee to recover under a compulsory state worker's compensation statute?

    a. The employee must be free from any wrongdoing.

    b. The injury must arise out of the negligence of the employer or fellow employee.

    c. The injury must arise out of and in the course of employment.

    d. The injury must occur while the employee is engaged in interstate commerce.

28 (May 84)

Wilk, an employee of Young Corp., was injured by the negligence of Quick, an independent contractor. The accident occurred during regular working hours and in the course of employment. If Young has complied with the state's workers' compensation laws, which of the following is correct?

    a. Wilk is barred from suing Young or Quick for negligence.

    b. Wilk will be denied workers' compensation if he was negligent in failing to adhere to the written safety procedures.

    c. The amount of damages Wilk will be allowed to recover from Young will be based on comparative fault.

    d. Wilk may obtain workers' compensation benefits and also properly maintain an action against Quick.

34 (May 83)

Fairfax was employed by Wexford Manufacturing Company as a salaried salesman. While Fairfax was driving a company car on a sales call, a truck owned and operated by Red Van Lines ran a stop light and collided with Fairfax's car. Fairfax applied for and received workers' compensation for the injuries sustained. As a result of receiving workers' compensation, Fairfax

    a. Must assign any negligence cause of action to Wexford pursuant to the doctrine of <u>respondeat superior</u>.

    b. Is precluded from suing Red for negligence because of the workers' compensation award.

    c. Can recover in full against Red for negligence, but must return any duplication of the workers' compensation award.

    d. Can recover in full against Red for negligence and retain the full amounts awarded under workers' compensation.

26 (November 82)

Which of the following regarding workers' compensation is correct?

    a. A purpose of workers' compensation is for the employer to assume a definite liability in exchange for the employee giving up his common law rights.

    b. It applies to workers engaged in or affecting interstate commerce only.

    c. It is optional in most jurisdictions.

    d. Once workers' compensation has been adopted by the employer, the amount of damages recoverable is based upon comparative negligence.

27 (November 82)

Which of the following would be the employer's best defense to a claim for workers' compensation by an injured route salesman?

    a.   A route salesman is automatically deemed to be an independent contractor, and therefore excluded from workers' compensation coverage.

    b.   The salesman was grossly negligent in carrying out the employment.

    c.   The salesman's injury was caused primarily by the negligence of an employee.

    d.   The salesman's injury did <u>not</u> arise out of and in the course of employment.

60 (May 81)

Musgrove Manufacturing Enterprises is subject to compulsory workers' compensation laws in the state in which it does business. It has complied with the state's workers' compensation provisions. State law provides that where there has been compliance, workers' compensation is normally an exclusive remedy. However, the remedy will <u>not</u> be exclusive if

    a.   The employee has been intentionally injured by the employer personally.

    b.   The employee dies as a result of his injuries.

    c.   The accident was entirely the fault of a fellow-servant of the employee.

    d.   The employer was only slightly negligent and the employee's conduct was grossly negligent.

48 (November 79)

Yeats Manufacturing is engaged in the manufacture and sale of convertible furniture in interstate commerce. Yeats' manufacturing facilities are located in a jurisdiction which has a compulsory workmen's compensation act. Hardwood, Yeats' president, decided that the company should, in light of its safety record, choose to ignore the requirement of providing workmen's compensation insurance. Instead, Hardwood indicated that a special account should be created to provide for such contingencies. Basset was severely injured as a result of his negligent operation of a lathe which accelerated and cut off his right arm. In assessing the potential liability of Yeats, which of the following is a correct answer?

    a.   Federal law applies since Yeats is engaged in interstate commerce.

    b.   Yeats has <u>no</u> liability, since Basset negligently operated the lathe.

    c.   Since Yeats did <u>not</u> provide workmen's compensation insurance, it can be sued by Basset and cannot resort to the usual common law defenses.

    d.   Yeats is a self-insurer, hence it has <u>no</u> liability beyond the amount of the money in the insurance fund.

47 (May 79)

Wilson was grossly negligent in the operation of a drill press. As a result he suffered permanent disability. His claim for workmen's compensation will be

    a.   Reduced by the percentage share attributable to his own fault.

    b.   Limited to medical benefits.

    c.   Denied.

    d.   Paid in full.

48 (May 78)

Jones has filed a claim with the appropriate Workmen's Compensation Board against the Atlas Metal & Magnet Company. Atlas denies liability under the State Workmen's Compensation Act. In which of the following situations will Jones recover from Atlas or its insurer?

    a.   Jones intentionally caused an injury to himself.

    b.   Jones is an independent contractor.

    c.   Jones is basing the claim upon a disease unrelated to the employment.

    d.   Jones and another employee of Atlas were grossly negligent in connection with their employment, resulting in injury to Jones.

14 (May 77)

The Jax Corporation owned and operated a modern, highly efficient sawmill. Forrester was one of its saw operators. Jax Corporation was subject to periodic inspections of its operations by both governmental and insurance company inspectors regarding its safety standards. It was agreed by virtually everyone involved in examining Jax's safety standards and equipment that they were outstanding and far above the minimum level which most other mills in the state met. Forrester was an employee of long standing and a man of firm convictions. He believed that many of the rules and required safety equipment were nothing more than a "bloody nuisance." Forrester repeatedly disregarded them when he could do so without being caught. Unfortunately, one day Forrester was seriously injured while using a power saw. He lost his left hand. Had he followed proper procedures and used the required safety equipment the injury would <u>not</u> have occurred. What circumstance described above would preclude Forrester from recovering under workmen's compensation?

   a. Forrester's gross negligence.
   b. Agreement by all inspectors that safety standards were outstanding and far above minimum levels.
   c. Forrester's disregard of safety standards only when he could do it without being caught.
   d. None of the circumstances described above would preclude Forrester's recovery under workmen's compensation.

48 (November 75)

Workmen's compensation laws are
   a. Governed by federal regulation.
   b. Applicable to all types of employment.
   c. Designed to eliminate the employer's defense of contributory negligence when an employee is injured on the job.
   d. <u>Not</u> applicable if the employee signs a waiver and consents to his noncoverage under workmen's compensation at the time he is hired.

35 (May 75)

Workmen's compensation laws
   a. Are uniform throughout the United States with the exception of Louisiana.
   b. Have <u>not</u> been adopted by all states except where required by federal law.
   c. Do <u>not</u> preclude an action against a third party who has caused an injury.
   d. Do <u>not</u> cover employees injured outside the jurisdiction.

44 (May 75)

Busby & Nelson, a general partnership, is a small furniture manufacturing company located in a southwestern state. It sells most of its products to fine furniture stores in Chicago, Los Angeles, and New York. It employs 50 skilled workmen and 10 other employees. Busby & Nelson has elected <u>not</u> to be covered under the state law which provides for elective workmen's compensation coverage because its safety standards are excellent, and there has <u>not</u> been a serious employee injury for several years. Busby & Nelson

   a. Would <u>not</u> be liable for workmen's compensation to an injured employee if the injury was due to the employee's negligence.
   b. Is obligated to pay workmen's compensation benefits to its employees even though such coverage was optional.
   c. Is subject to lawsuits for damages by injured employees and may <u>not</u> assert the common-law defenses such as contributory negligence.
   d. <u>Cannot</u> create any type of pension plan for the partners and its employees which will permit payments thereto to be deducted in whole or part for federal income tax purposes.

43 (May 74)

If an employer carried workmen's compensation coverage on his employees, an injured employee would
a. Probably be covered even if the injury was caused by a co-worker.
b. <u>Not</u> be covered if the injury was caused by grossly negligent maintenance by the employer.
c. Probably <u>not</u> be covered if the injury was due to a violation of plant rules in operating the machine.
d. Be covered if the employee was driving to work from his home.

46 (May 74)

An employee was injured while working on a machine in his employer's plant. The employer carried workmen's compensation with Ace Casualty as the carrier. In this circumstance
a. If the injury was the fault of a third person covered by insurance, contribution is the usual method of apportioning the effect of the injury.
b. The existence of workmen's compensation covering the injury precludes an action against the machine manufacturer if faulty design caused the injury.
c. If the injury was covered, the employee normally has <u>no</u> cause of action for damages against the employer.
d. Payment by the carrier usually subrogates the carrier to the injured worker's rights against a negligent employer.

3 (November 88)

Maple owns 75% of the common stock of Salam Exterminating, Inc. Maple is not an officer or employee of the corporation, and does not serve on its board of directors. Salam is in the business of providing exterminating services to residential and commercial customers.

Dodd performed exterminating services on behalf of Salam. Dodd suffered permanent injuries as a result of inhaling one of the chemicals used by Salam. This occurred after Dodd sprayed the chemical in a restaurant that Salam regularly services. Dodd was under the supervision of one of Salam's district managers and was trained by Salam to perform exterminating services following certain procedures, which he did. Later that day several patrons who ate at the restaurant also suffered permanent injuries as a result of inhaling the chemical. The chemical was manufactured by Ace Chemical Corp. and sold and delivered to Salam in a closed container. It was not altered by Salam. It has now been determined that the chemical was defectively manufactured and the injuries suffered by Dodd and the restaurant patrons were a direct result of the defect.

Salam has complied with an applicable compulsory workers' compensation statute by obtaining an insurance policy from Spear Insurance Co.

As a result of the foregoing, the following actions have been commenced:
- Dodd sued Spear to recover workers' compensation benefits.
- Dodd sued Salam based on negligence in training him.
- Dodd sued Ace based on strict liability in tort.
- The restaurant patrons sued Maple claiming negligence in not preventing Salam from using the chemical purchased from Ace.

Required: Discuss the merits of the actions commenced by Dodd and the restaurant patrons, indicating the likely outcomes and your reasons therefor.

Dodd is entitled to recover workers' compensation benefits from Spear because Dodd was an employee of Salam, the injury was accidental, and the injury occurred out of and in the course of his employment with Salam. Based on the facts of this case, Dodd would be considered an employee and not an independent contractor because Salam had control over the details of Dodd's work by training Dodd to perform the services in a specified manner and Dodd was subject to Salam's supervision.

Dodd will be unsuccessful in his action against Salam based on negligence in training him because Dodd is an employee of Salam and Salam has complied with the applicable compulsory workers' compensation statute by obtaining workers' compensation insurance. Under workers' compensation, an employee who receives workers' compensation benefits cannot successfully maintain an action for negligence against his employer seeking additional compensation. Therefore, whether Salam was negligent in training Dodd is irrelevant.

Dodd's action against Ace based on strict liability in tort will be successful. Generally, in order to establish a cause of action based on strict liability in tort, it must be shown that: the product was in defective condition when it left the possession or control of the seller; the product was unreasonably dangerous to the consumer or user; the cause of the consumer's or user's injury was the defect; the seller engaged in the business of selling such a product; the product was one which the seller expected to, and, did reach the consumer or user without substantial changes in the condition in which it was sold. Under the facts of this case, Ace will be liable based on strict liability in tort because all of the elements necessary to state such a cause of action have been met. The fact that Dodd is entitled to workers' compensation benefits does not preclude Dodd from recovering based on strict liability in tort from a third party (Ace).

Maple will not be liable to the restaurant patrons based on negligence, because shareholders of a corporation are insulated from personal liability for the negligence of the corporation or the corporation's employees. This rule would apply even though Maple owned a controlling interest in the common stock of Salam. Therefore, whether Salam or Dodd was negligent is irrelevant.

3C (November 78)

Eureka Enterprises, Inc. started doing business in July 1977. It manufactures electronic components and currently employs 35 individuals. In anticipation of future financing needs, Eureka has engaged a CPA firm to audit its financial statement. During the course of the examination, the CPA firm discovers that Eureka has no workmen's compensation insurance, which is in violation of state law, and so informs the president of Eurcka.

Required: Answer the following, setting forth reasons for any conclusions stated.
1. What is the purpose of a state workmen's compensation law?
2. What are the legal implications of not having workmen's compensation insurance?

1. Workmen's compensation laws provide a system of compensation for employees who are injured, disabled, or killed as a result of accidents or occupational diseases in the course of their employment. Benefits also extend to survivors or dependents of these employees.

2. In all but a distinct minority of jurisdictions, workmen's compensation coverage is mandatory. In those few jurisdictions that have elective workmen's compensation, employers who reject workmen's compensation coverage are subject to common law actions by injured employees and are precluded from asserting the defenses of fellow-servant, assumption of risk, and contributory negligence. The number of such jurisdictions having elective compensation coverage has been constantly diminishing. The penalty in these jurisdictions is the loss of forcgoing defenses.

The more common problem occurs in connection with the failure of an employer to secure compensation coverage even though he is obligated to do so in the majority of jurisdictions. The one uniform effect of such unwise conduct on the part of the employer is to deny him the use of the common law defenses mentioned above.

In addition to the foregoing, an increasing number of states have provided for the payment of workmen's compensation by the state to the injured employee of the uninsured employer. The state in turn proceeds against the employer to recover the compensation cost and to impose penalties that include fines and imprisonment. Other jurisdictions provide for a penalty in the form of additional compensation payments over and above the basic amounts, or they require an immediate lump-sum payment.

PART III -- CONTRACTS

TABLE OF CONTENTS

PART III

CONTRACTS

I. Introduction to Contracts
A. Introduction to Property and the Uniform Commercial Code; Code and Common Law Contracts

57 (May 95)
   Which of the following items is tangible personal property?
   a. Share of stock.
   b. Trademark.
   c. Promissory note.
   d. Oil painting.

50 (November 94)
   Under the Sales Article of the UCC, which of the following statements is correct?
   a. The obligations of the parties to the contract must be performed in good faith.
   b. Merchants and nonmerchants are treated alike.
   c. The contract must involve the sale of goods for a price of more than $500.
   d. None of the provisions of the UCC may be disclaimed by agreement.

42 (May 94)
   Under the UCC Sales Article, which of the following statements is correct concerning a contract involving a merchant seller and a non-merchant buyer?
   a. Whether the UCC Sales Article is applicable does <u>not</u> depend on the price of the goods involved.
   b. Only the seller is obligated to perform the contract in good faith.
   c. The contract will be either a sale or return or sale on approval contract.
   d. The contract may <u>not</u> involve the sale of personal property with a price of more than $500.

50 (November 93)
   Which of the following statements would <u>not</u> apply to a written contract governed by the provisions of the UCC Sales Article?
   a. The contract may involve the sale of personal property.
   b. The obligations of a non-merchant may be different from those of a merchant.
   c. The obligations of the parties must be performed in good faith.
   d. The contract must involve the sale of goods for a price of $500 or more.

43 (November 88)
   In general, the UCC Sales Article applies to the sale of
   a. Goods only if the seller is a merchant and the buyer is <u>not</u>.
   b. Goods only if the seller and buyer are both merchants.
   c. Consumer goods by a non-merchant.
   d. Real estate by a merchant for $500 or more.

34 (May 86)
   The UCC Sales Article applies
   a. To a contract for personal services.
   b. To the sale of patents.
   c. To the sale of goods only if the buyer and seller are merchants.
   d. To the sale of specially manufactured goods.

55 (May 84)

The UCC Sales Article applies
a.   Exclusively to the sale of goods between merchants.
b.   To the sale of real estate between merchants.
c.   To the sale of specially manufactured goods.
d.   To the sale of investment securities.

33 (November 76)

Which of the following contracts falls within common law rules and is <u>not</u> covered by the Uniform Commercial Code?
a.   A requirements contract for the purchase of fuel oil.
b.   A contract for the sale of 200 chess sets.
c.   A contract for the sale of goods which are manufactured according to the buyer's specifications.
d.   An employment contract which by its terms has a set period of eighteen months.

35 (November 76)

The distinction between contracts covered by the Uniform Commercial Code and contracts which are <u>not</u> covered by the code is
a.   Basically dependent upon whether the subject matter of the contract involves the purchase or sale of goods.
b.   Based upon the dollar amount of the contract.
c.   Dependent upon whether the Statute of Frauds is involved.
d.   Of relatively little or no importance to the CPA since the laws are invariably the same.

B. Basic Definitions and Concepts

11 (November 81)

Where a client accepts the services of an accountant without an agreement concerning payment there is
a.   An implied in fact contract.
b.   An implied in law contract.
c.   An express contract.
d.   No contract.

1 (May 76)

A contract is said to be executory when
a.   Any of the obligations thereunder remain to be performed.
b.   All of the obligations thereunder have been performed.
c.   It is in writing.
d.   It is informal.

II. Contract Formation--Agreement
A. The Offer
1. Basic Definitions and Concepts

19 (May 78)

Normally, the offer initiates the process by which a contract is created. Therefore, the offer is critical insofar as satisfying basic contract law requirements. Which of the following statements is <u>incorrect</u>?
a.   The offer may only be expressed in words.
b.   The offer must be communicated to the other party.
c.   The offer must be certain enough to determine the liability of the parties.
d.   The offer must be accepted by the other party.

2. Objective Theory of Contract; Intent and Definiteness

21 (May 92)

On September 10, Harris, Inc., a new car dealer, placed a newspaper advertisement stating that Harris would sell 10 cars at its showroom for a special discount only on September 12, 13, and 14. On September 12, King called Harris and expressed an interest in buying one of the advertised cars. King was told that five of the cars had been sold and to come to the showroom as soon as possible. On September 13, Harris made a televised announcement that the sale would end at 10:00 PM that night. King went to Harris' showroom on September 14 and demanded the right to buy a car at the special discount. Harris had sold the 10 cars and refused King's demand. King sued Harris for breach of contract. Harris' best defense to King's suit would be that Harris'

    a.   Offer was unenforceable.

    b.   Advertisement was <u>not</u> an offer.

    c.   Television announcement revoked the offer.

    d.   Offer had <u>not</u> been accepted.

25 (May 89)

To announce the grand opening of a new retail business, Hudson placed an advertisement in a local newspaper quoting sales prices on certain items in stock. The grand opening was so successful that Hudson was unable to totally satisfy customer demands. Which of the following statements is correct?

    a.   Hudson made an invitation seeking offers.

    b.   Hudson made an offer to the people who read the advertisement.

    c.   Anyone who tendered money for the items advertised was entitled to buy them.

    d.   The offer by Hudson was partially revocable as to an item once it was sold out.

15 (November 86)

Kraft Corp. published circulars containing price quotes and description of products which it would like to sell. Rice, a prospective customer, demands the right to purchase one of the products at the quoted price. Which of the following statements is correct under general contract law?

    a.   Kraft must sell the product which Rice demands at the quoted price.

    b.   Rice has accepted Kraft's firm offer to sell.

    c.   Kraft has made an offer.

    d.   Rice has made an offer.

7 (November 85)

Fenster Corp. requested Wein & Co., CPAs, to perform accounting services for it. Wein agreed to perform the services. Fenster and Wein had not discussed the amount of the fees. Which of the following is correct?

    a.   No contract was formed since the amount of the fees was <u>not</u> agreed upon.

    b.   A quasi contract was formed at the time Wein agreed to perform the services.

    c.   A unilateral contract was formed at the time of Fenster's request.

    d.   A bilateral contract was formed at the time of Wein's agreement to perform.

27 (November 83)

Flaxx, a sales representative of Dome Home Sites, Inc., escorted Mr. & Mrs. Grand through several acres of Dome's proposed subdivision and showed the Grands various one-acre lots for sale at $27,000 each. Upon conclusion of the tour, the Grands expressed interest in purchasing a lot in the near future. Flaxx urged them to show their good faith and sign a letter of intent, which stated: "We, the undersigned, having decided to purchase a lot from Dome Home Sites in the future, deliver to the corporation's agent one hundred dollars ($100) earnest money." This was signed by the Grands at the bottom of the form and the $100 was delivered to Flaxx by the Grands. Under the circumstances

    a.   The Grands have made an offer to buy a lot from Dome.

    b.   If all the lots are sold by Dome, the Grands have a cause of action for breach of contract.

    c.   If no deal is ever consummated, the Grands have the right to the return of the $100.

    d.   The $100 constitutes liquidated damages and will be forfeited in the event the Grands do not purchase a lot.

Contracts

6 (May 83)

In determining whether a bilateral contract has been created, the courts look primarily at
   a. The fairness to the parties.
   b. The objective intent of the parties.
   c. The subjective intent of the parties.
   d. The subjective intent of the offeror.

2 (November 82)

Harris wrote Douglas a letter which might be construed alternatively as an offer to sell land, an invitation to commence negotiations, or merely an invitation to Douglas to make an offer. Douglas claims that the communication was a bona fide offer which he has unequivocally accepted according to the terms set forth therein. In deciding the dispute in question, the court will
   a. Look to the subjective intent of Harris.
   b. Use an objective standard based on how a reasonably prudent businessman would have interpreted the letter to Douglas.
   c. Decide that an offer had not been made if any of the usual terms were omitted.
   d. Decide on the basis of what Douglas considered the writing to be.

7 (November 79)

Master Corporation, a radio and television manufacturer, invited Darling Discount Chain to examine several odd lots of discontinued models and make an offer for the entire lot. The odd lots were segregated from the regular inventory but inadvertently included 15 current models. Darling was unaware that Master did not intend to include the 15 current models in the group. Darling made Master an offer of $9,000 for the entire lot, which represented a large discount from the normal sales price. Unaware of the error, Master accepted the offer. Master would not have accepted had it known of the inclusion of the 15 current models. Upon learning of the error, Master alleged mistake as a defense and refused to perform. Darling sued for breach of contract. Under the circumstances, what is the status of the contract?
   a. There is no contract since Master did not intend to include the 15 current models in the group of radios to be sold.
   b. The contract is voidable because of a unilateral mistake.
   c. The contract is voidable because of a mutual mistake.
   d. There is a valid and binding contract which includes the 15 current model radios.

27 (November 78)

Martin Stores, Inc. decided to sell a portion of its eight-acre property. Consequently, the president of Martin wrote several prospective buyers the following letter:

Dear Sir: We are sending this notice to several prospective buyers because we are interested in selling four acres of our property located in downtown Metropolis. If you are interested, please communicate with me at the above address. Don't bother to reply unless you are thinking in terms of at least $100,000.

James Martin, President

Under the circumstances, which of the following is correct?
   a. The Statute of Frauds do not apply because the real property being sold is the division of an existing tract which had been properly recorded.
   b. Markus, a prospective buyer, who telegraphed Martin that he would buy at $100,000 and forwarded a $100,000 surety bond to guarantee his performance, has validly accepted.
   c. Martin must sell to the highest bidder.
   d. Martin's communication did not constitute an offer to sell.

3. Communication, Effectiveness, and Duration of the Offer

16 (May 88)

In order for an offer to confer the power to form a contract by acceptance, it must have all of the following elements <u>except</u>
- a. Be communicated to the offeree and the communication must be made or authorized by the offeror.
- b. Be sufficiently definite and certain.
- c. Be communicated by words to the offeree by the offeror.
- d. Manifest an intent to enter into a contract.

7 (November 81)

Water Works had a long-standing policy of offering employees $100 for suggestions actually used. Due to inflation and a decline in the level and quality of suggestions received, Water Works decided to increase the award to $500. Several suggestions were under consideration at that time. Two days prior to the public announcement of the increase to $500, a suggestion by Farber was accepted and put into use. Farber is seeking to collect $500. Farber is entitled to
- a. $500 because Water Works had decided to pay that amount.
- b. $500 because the suggestion submitted will be used during the period that Water Works indicated it would pay $500.
- c. $100 in accordance with the original offer.
- d. Nothing if Water Works chooses <u>not</u> to pay since the offer was gratuitous.

3 (May 76)

An offer is generally effective when it is
- a. Dispatched.
- b. Signed.
- c. Mailed.
- d. Received.

B. Termination of the Offer Before Acceptance
1. Termination by the Offeror--Revocation
a. In General; Effectiveness

13 (November 92)

On June 15, Peters orally offered to sell a used lawn mower to Mason for $125. Peters specified that Mason had until June 20 to accept the offer. On June 16, Peters received an offer to purchase the lawn mower for $150 from Bronson, Mason's neighbor. Peters accepted Bronson's offer. On June 17, Mason saw Bronson using the lawn mower and was told the mower had been sold to Bronson. Mason immediately wrote to Peters to accept the June 15 offer. Which of the following statements is correct?
- a. Mason's acceptance would be effective when received by Peters.
- b Mason's acceptance would be effective when mailed.
- c. Peters' offer had been revoked and Mason's acceptance was ineffective.
- d. Peters was obligated to keep the June 15 offer open until June 20.

10 (November 88)

The president of Deal Corp. wrote to Boyd, offering to sell the Deal factory for $300,000. The offer was sent by Deal on June 5 and was received by Boyd on June 9. The offer stated that it would remain open until December 20. The offer
- a. Constitutes an enforceable option.
- b. May be revoked by Deal any time prior to Boyd's acceptance.
- c. Is a firm offer under the UCC but will be irrevocable for only three months.
- d. Is a firm offer under the UCC because it is in writing.

3 (November 82)

Starbuck Corporation sent Crane Company an offer by a telegram to buy its patent on a calculator. The Starbuck telegram indicated that the offer would expire in ten days. The telegraph was sent on February 1, 1982, and received on February 2, 1982, by Crane. On February 8, 1982, Starbuck telephoned Crane and indicated it was withdrawing the offer. Crane telegraphed an acceptance on the 11th of February. Which of the following is correct?

    a.   Starbuck's withdrawal of the offer was ineffective because it was <u>not</u> in writing.

    b.   The offer was an irrevocable offer, but Crane's acceptance was too late.

    c.   No contract arose since Starbuck effectively revoked the offer on February 8, 1982.

    d.   Since Crane used the same means of communication, acceptance was both timely and effective.

10 (May 81)

On March 1, Wilkins wrote Conner a letter and offered to sell him his factory for $150,000. The offer stated that the acceptance must be received by him by April 1. Under the circumstances, Wilkins' offer

    a.   Will be validly accepted if Conner posts an acceptance on April 1.

    b.   May be withdrawn at any time prior to acceptance.

    c.   May <u>not</u> be withdrawn prior to April 1.

    d.   Could <u>not</u> be validly accepted since Wilkins could assert the Statute of Frauds.

17 (November 74)

An outstanding offer to sell a tract of real property is terminated at the time the

    a.   Buyer learns of the seller's death.

    b.   Seller posts his revocation if the original offer was made by mail.

    c.   Buyer posts a rejection of the offer if the original offer was received by mail.

    d.   Buyer learns of the sale of the property to a third party.

33 (May 74)

Ambrose undertook to stage a production of a well-known play. He wired Belle, a famous actress, offering her the lead at $1,000 per week (for six evening performances per week) for six weeks from the specific opening night, plus $1,000 for a week of rehearsal prior to opening. The telegram also said, "Offer ends in three days."

Assuming Belle's reply was received by Ambrose within the time limit, it would

    a.   Be an effective acceptance if she telephoned Ambrose and accepted within the three-day period and prior to receiving any indication of revocation of the offer even though Ambrose had previously dispatched a letter to Belle revoking the offer.

    b.   Be an effective acceptance only if she replied by telegram.

    c.   Be an effective acceptance if she replied immediately, "Fine if Howard is my leading man."

    d.   <u>Not</u> be an effective acceptance if she replied, "Fine, but I hope you will try to line up Howard as my leading man."

b. Situations in Which the Offeror Cannot Revoke--
     Option Contracts

24 (May 89)

Dye sent Hill a written offer to sell a tract of land located in Newtown for $60,000. The parties were engaged in a separate dispute. The offer stated that it would be irrevocable for 60 days if Hill would promise to refrain from suing Dye during this time. Hill promptly delivered a promise not to sue during the term of the offer and to forgo suit if Hill accepted the offer. Dye subsequently decided that the possible suit by Hill was groundless and therefore phoned Hill and revoked the offer 15 days after making it. Hill mailed an acceptance on the 20th day. Dye did not reply. Under the circumstances,

    a.   Dye's offer was supported by consideration and was <u>not</u> revocable when accepted.

    b.   Dye's written offer would be irrevocable even without consideration.

    c.   Dye's silence was an acceptance of Hill's promise.

    d.   Dye's revocation, <u>not</u> being in writing, was invalid.

19 (November 84)

On January 1, Lemon wrote Martin offering to sell Martin his ranch for $80,000 cash. Lemon's letter indicated that the offer would remain open until February 15 if Martin mailed $100 by January 10. On January 5, Martin mailed $100 to Lemon. On January 30, Martin telephoned Lemon stating that he would be willing to pay $60,000 for the ranch. Lemon refused to sell at that price and immediately placed the ranch on the open market. On February 6, Martin mailed Lemon a letter accepting the original offer to buy the ranch at $80,000. At that time the ranch was on the market for $100,000. Which of the following is correct?

    a.   Martin's mailing of $100 to Lemon on January 5 failed to create an option.

    b.   Martin's communication of January 30 automatically terminated Lemon's offer of January 1.

    c.   The placing of the ranch on the market by Lemon constituted an effective revocation of his offer of January 1.

    d.   Martin's letter of February 6 formed a binding contract based on the original terms of Lemon's January 1 letter.

28 (November 83)

Love granted Nelson a written option to buy a tract of land in an industrial park. The option stated that it was irrevocable for 11 days and was given for $20 and other valuable consideration. The $20 was not paid and there was no other valuable consideration. Which of the following is a correct statement regarding the option in question?

    a.   Since real property is involved, Nelson's acceptance must be contained in a signed writing if Nelson is to enforce it against Love.

    b.   It is an option contract enforceable for the 11-day period.

    c.   Acceptance must be received at Love's place of business before expiration of the 11 days.

    d.   It is unenforceable because it lacks consideration.

4 (November 81)

Which of the following offers for the sale of the Lazy L Ranch is enforceable?

    a.   Owner tells buyer she will sell the ranch for $35,000 and that the offer will be irrevocable for ten days.

    b.   Owner writes buyer offering to sell the ranch for $35,000 and stating that the offer will remain open for ten days.

    c.   Owner telegraphs buyer offering to sell the ranch for $35,000 and promises to hold the offer open for ten days.

    d.   Owner writes buyer offering to sell the ranch for $35,000 and stating that the offer will be irrevocable for ten days if buyer will pay $1.00. Buyer pays.

8 (May 76)

Vantage telephoned Breyer on December 19, 1975, and offered to sell a plot of land to Breyer for $5,000. Vantage promised to keep the offer open until December 27, 1975. Breyer said he was interested in the land but wanted to inspect it before making any commitment. Which of the following best describes the legal significance of these events?

    a.   Vantage may revoke the offer at will.

    b.   Vantage may not revoke the offer prior to December 27.

    c.   A contract was formed on December 18.

    d.   Breyer's response constituted a rejection and counteroffer.

10 (May 76)

A written option to buy land generally cannot be revoked before acceptance if the offer

    a.   Is supported by consideration from the offeree.

    b.   Allows a specific time for acceptance.

    c.   Is made exclusively to one person.

    d.   By its terms is not revocable before acceptance.

6 (May 75)

Gregor paid $100 to Henry for a thirty-day written option to purchase Henry's commercial real property for $75,000. Twenty days later Henry received an offer from Watson to purchase the property for $85,000. Henry promptly notified Gregor that the option price was now $85,000, or the option was revoked. Gregor said he would not pay a penny more than $75,000 and that he still had 10 days remaining on the option. On the 28th day of the option Gregor telephoned Henry that he had decided to exercise the option; he tendered his $75,000 check the next day which was to be held in escrow until delivery of the deed. Henry refused to accept the tender stating that he had decided not to sell and that he was going to retain the property for the present. Which of the following best describes the legal rights of the parties involved?

    a. Henry effectively revoked his offer to sell because he did this prior to Gregor's acceptance.

    b. Consideration given for the option is irrelevant because the option was in writing and signed by Henry.

    c. Because Gregor's acceptance was not in writing and signed, it is invalid according to the Statute of Frauds.

    d. Gregor's acceptance was valid, and in the event of default he may obtain the equitable remedy of specific performance.

c. Situations in Which the Offeror Cannot Revoke-- Firm Offers--UCC § 2-205

18 (R01)

Patch, a frequent shopper at Soon-Shop Stores, received a rain check for an advertised sale item after Soon-Shop's supply of the product ran out. The rain check was in writing and stated that the item would be offered to the customer at the advertised sale price for an unspecified period of time. A Soon-Shop employee signed the rain check. When Patch returned to the store one month later to purchase the item, the store refused to honor the rain check. Under the Sales Article of the UCC, will Patch win a suit to enforce the rain check?

    a. No, because one month is too long a period of time for a rain check to be effective.

    b. No, because the rain check did not state the effective time period necessary to keep the offer open.

    c. Yes, because Soon-Shop is required to have sufficient supplies of the sale item to satisfy all customers.

    d. Yes, because the rain check met the requirements of a merchant's firm offer even though no effective time period was stated.

41 (November 95)

Under the Sales Article of the UCC, a firm offer will be created only if the

    a. Offer states the time period during which it will remain open.

    b. Offer is made by a merchant in a signed writing.

    c. Offeree gives some form of consideration.

    d. Offeree is a merchant.

51 (November 83)

In order to have an irrevocable offer under the Uniform Commercial Code, the offer must

    a. Be made by a merchant to a merchant.

    b. Be contained in a signed writing which gives assurance that the offer will be held open.

    c. State the period of time for which it is irrevocable.

    d. Not be contained in a form supplied by the offeror.

38 (May 83)

A merchant's irrevocable written offer (firm offer) to sell goods

    a. Must be separately signed if the offeree supplies a form contract containing the offer.

    b Is valid for three months unless otherwise provided.

    c. Is nonassignable.

    d. Can not exceed a three-month duration even if consideration is given.

18 (May 81)

Doral Inc. wished to obtain an adequate supply of lumber for its factory extension which was to be constructed in the spring. It contacted Ace Lumber Company and obtained a 75-day written option (firm offer) to buy its estimated needs for the building. Doral supplied a form contract which included the option. Ace Lumber signed at the physical end of the contract but did not sign elsewhere. The price of lumber has risen drastically and Ace wishes to avoid its obligation. Which of the following is Ace's best defense against Doral's assertion that Ace is legally bound by the option?

    a.   Such an option is invalid if its duration is for more than two months.

    b.   The option is <u>not</u> supported by any consideration on Doral's part.

    c.   Doral is <u>not</u> a merchant.

    d.   The promise of irrevocability was contained in a form supplied by Doral and was <u>not</u> separately signed by Ace.

8 (November 75)

A merchant's offer to sell goods which states the offer will be held open is revocable during the time stated

    a.   In all situations.

    b.   Unless the offer is evidenced by a signed writing.

    c.   Unless the offer is oral and has a duration of 6 months or less.

    d.   Only if the goods are fungible.

39 (May 75)

A merchant made the following offer: "I offer you 100 cases of No. 3 macaroni at $13.50 per case. This offer is irrevocable for ten days." In which of the following situations would the offer be irrevocable because it is a "firm offer" or option contract under the Uniform Commercial Code?

    a.   The offer was made orally and admitted to in court by the seller.

    b.   The offer was written and signed by the seller.

    c.   The offer was written and signed by the seller, but the second sentence read: "Acceptance must be made within ten days."

    d.   Like all previous contracts for macaroni between the offeror and offeree, the offer was made by telephone.

5A (November 78)

Clauson Enterprises, Inc. was considering adding a new product line to its existing lines. The decision was contingent upon its being assured of a supply of an electronic component for the product at a certain price and a positive market study which clearly justified the investment in the venture.

Clauson's president approached Migrane Electronics and explained the situation to Migrane's president. After much negotiation, Migrane agreed to grant Clauson an option to purchase 12,000 of the necessary electronic components at $1.75 each or at the prevailing market price, whichever was lower. Clauson prepared the option below incorporating their understanding.

Option Agreement
Clauson Enterprises/Migrane Electronics

Migrane Electronics hereby offers to sell Clauson Enterprises 12,000 miniature solid state electronic breakers at $1.75 each or at the existing market price at the time of delivery, whichever is lower, delivery to be made in 12 equal monthly installments beginning one month after the exercise of this option. This option is irrevocable for six months from January 1, 1978.

Clauson Enterprises agrees to deliver to Migrane its market survey for the product line in which the component would be used if it elects not to exercise the option.

Both parties signed the option agreement and Migrane's president signed Migrane's corporate name alongside the last sentence of the first paragraph. On May 1, 1978, Migrane notified Clauson that it was revoking its offer. The market price for the components had increased to $1.85. On May 15, 1978, Clauson notified Migrane that it accepted the offer and that if Migrane did not perform, it would be sued and held liable for damages. Migrane replied that the offer was not binding and was revoked before Clauson accepted. Furthermore, even if it were binding, it was good for only three months as a matter of law.

Upon receipt of Migrane's reply, Clauson instituted suit for damages.

Required: Answer the following, setting forth reasons for any conclusions stated.

Who will prevail? Discuss all the issues and arguments raised by the fact situation.

Clauson Enterprises will prevail. The option in question is supported by consideration and consequently is a binding contract. The offer is definite and certain despite the fact that the pricing terms are not presently determinable. The Uniform Commercial Code is extremely liberal regarding satisfaction of the pricing terms.

Except for the presence of consideration in the form of the promise by Clauson to deliver the market survey to Migrane, the option would not have been binding beyond three months and Migrane would have prevailed. Section 2-205 of the Uniform Commercial Code provides as follows:

> An offer by a merchant to buy or sell goods in a signed writing which by its terms gives assurance that it will be held open is not revocable, for lack of consideration, during the time stated or if no time is stated for a reasonable time, but in no event may such period of irrevocability exceed three months; but any such term of assurance on a form supplied by the offeree must be separately signed by the offeror.

It is apparent from the wording of this section that the option was valid without consideration, but only for three months. It was an offer by a merchant contained in a signed writing and clearly stated its irrevocability. Furthermore, the separately signed requirement where the form is supplied by the offeree was satisfied. But the section is inapplicable to the facts of this case since bargained-for consideration was present. The Uniform Commercial Code's three-month limitation does not apply to options where consideration is present. Hence, Clauson's acceptance was valid, and if Migrane refuses to perform, Clauson will be entitled to damages.

2. Termination by the Offeree--Rejection
a. In General; Effectiveness

21 (May 89)

Martin wrote Dall and offered to sell Dall a building for $200,000. The offer stated it would expire 30 days from April 1. Martin changed his mind and does not wish to be bound by his offer. If a legal dispute arises between the parties regarding whether there has been a valid acceptance of the offer, which one of the following is correct?

a. The offer cannot be legally withdrawn for the stated period of time.

b. The offer will <u>not</u> expire before the 30 days even if Martin sells the property to a third person and notifies Dall.

c. If Dall categorically rejects the offer on April 10, Dall cannot validly accept within the remaining stated period of time.

d .If Dall phoned Martin on May 3, and unequivocally accepted the offer, a contract would be created, provided that Dall had <u>no</u> notice of withdrawal of the offer.

22 (May 89)

Which of the following statements concerning the effectiveness of an offeree's rejection and an offeror's revocation of an offer is generally correct?

	An offeree's rejection is effective when	An offeror's revocation is effective when
a.	Received by offeror	Sent by offeror
b.	Sent by offeree	Received by offeree
c.	Sent by offeree	Sent by offeror
d.	Received by offeror	Received by offeree

b. The "Mirror Image" Rule--Rejection by Counteroffer

11 (November 92)

On February 12, Harris sent Fresno a written offer to purchase Fresno's land. The offer included the following provision: "Acceptance of this offer must be by registered or certified mail, received by Harris no later than February 18 by 5:00 p.m. CST." On February 18, Fresno sent Harris a letter accepting the offer by private overnight delivery service. Harris received the letter on February 19. Which of the following statements is correct?

   a. A contract was formed on February 19.
   b. Fresno's letter constituted a counteroffer.
   c. Fresno's use of the overnight delivery service was an effective form of acceptance.
   d. A contract was formed on February 18 regardless of when Harris actually received Fresno's letter.

12 (May 90)

On September 27, Summers sent Fox a letter offering to sell Fox a vacation home for $150,000. On October 2, Fox replied by mail agreeing to buy the home for $145,000. Summers did not reply to Fox. Do Fox and Summers have a binding contract?

   a. No, because Fox failed to sign and return Summers' letter.
   b. No, because Fox's letter was a counteroffer.
   c. Yes, because Summers' offer was validly accepted.
   d. Yes, because Summers' silence is an implied acceptance of Fox's letter.

17 (May 88)

On July 1, Silk, Inc., sent Blue a telegram offering to sell Blue a building for $80,000. In the telegram, Silk stated that it would give Blue 30 days to accept the offer. On July 15, Blue sent Silk a telegram that included the following statement: "The price for your building seems too high. Would you consider taking $75,000?" This telegram was received by Silk on July 16. On July 19, Tint made an offer to Silk to purchase the building for $82,000. Upon learning of Tint's offer, Blue, on July 27, sent Silk a signed letter agreeing to purchase the building for $80,000. This letter was received by Silk on July 29. However, Silk now refuses to sell Blue the building. If Blue commences an action against Silk for breach of contract, Blue will

   a. Win, because Blue effectively accepted Silk's offer of July 1.
   b. Win, because Silk was obligated to keep the offer open for the 30-day period.
   c. Lose, because Blue sent the July 15 telegram.
   d. Lose, because Blue used an unauthorized means of communication.

1 (May 86)

Ted Marx sent Stahl & Co. a signed letter on January 3, 1986 offering to sell his warehouse for $95,000. The letter indicated that the offer would remain open until January 30, 1986. On January 26, Stahl wrote Marx that it would be willing to pay $88,000 for the warehouse. The letter was received by Marx on January 29. On January 28, Stahl was advised that a similar property had been sold for $99,000. Based on this information, Stahl telephoned Marx on January 28 and accepted the original offer of January 3. Marx refused to sell the warehouse to Stahl for $95,000. Which of the following statements is correct?

a. Stahl's acceptance on January 28 formed a contract which bound Marx to the terms of his original offer.
b. Marx's letter dated January 3 is a firm offer under the UCC.
c. Stahl is barred under the parol evidence rule from introducing evidence of its oral acceptance since it contradicts its letter dated January 26.
d. A contract was never formed since Stahl's letter of January 26 was a counteroffer which terminated Marx's offer when mailed.

9 (May 83)

Luxor wrote Harmon offering to sell Harmon Luxor's real estate business for $200,000. Harmon sent a telegram accepting the offer at $190,000. Later, learning that several other parties were interested in purchasing the business, Harmon telephoned Luxor and made an unqualified acceptance on Luxor's terms. The telegram arrived an hour after the phone call. Under the circumstances.
a. Harmon's telegram effectively terminated the offer.
b. Harmon's oral acceptance is voidable, because real estate is involved.
c. The offer was revoked as a result of Harmon's learning that others were interested in purchasing the business.
d. Harmon has made a valid contract at $200,000.

6 (May 76)

Baker Corporation sent a letter to Sampson Company in which Baker offered to purchase 10 acres of certain real estate from Sampson for $4,000. Sampson responded that it would sell 8 of these acres for that price. Baker and Sampson have created
a. A contract for sale of 8 acres for $4,000.
b. A contract for sale of 10 acres for $4,000.
c. A contract to sell 8 acres for $3,200.
d. No contract in this connection.

18 (November 74)

Donaldson Retailers engaged in lengthy negotiations for the purchase of an office building from Universal Real Estate, Inc. The parties reached an impasse on the price. Universal's written offer to sell was $150,000. Donaldson replied by telegram offering $140,000--"Take it or leave it." Universal filed the telegram away for future reference but did not respond. Donaldson then sent a letter stating that Universal was to disregard its prior communication and that it accepted the offer at $150,000. Universal wrote back stating, "The price is now $160,000--take it or leave it." Donaldson promptly telegraphed Universal that it held Universal to its original offer of $150,000. Under these circumstances
a. The purported contract is unenforceable in any event under the Statute of Frauds.
b. No contract was formed.
c. Since the same means of communication was not used throughout the transaction, there can be no contract.
d .Donaldson's reply offering $140,000 constituted a mere counter proposal which did not terminate the original offer.

c. UCC Change--§ 2-207

46 (November 89)

Cookie Co. offered to sell Distrib Markets 20,000 pounds of cookies at $1.00 per pound, subject to certain specified terms for delivery. Distrib replied in writing as follows:

"We accept your offer for 20,000 pounds of cookies at $1.00 per pound, weighing scale to have valid city certificate."

Under the UCC

    a.   A contract was formed between the parties.

    b.   A contract will be formed only if Cookie agrees to the weighing scale requirement.

    c.   No contract was formed because Distrib included the weighing scale requirement in its reply.

    d.   No contract was formed because Distrib's reply was a counteroffer.

53 (November 84)

Bizzy Corp. wrote Wang ordering 100 Wang radios for $2,500. Wang unequivocally accepted Bizzy's offer but in doing so Wang added a clause providing for interest on any overdue invoices pertaining to the sale, a practice which is common in the industry. If Wang and Bizzy are both merchants and there are <u>no</u> further communications between the parties, relating to the terms, then

    a.   Wang has made a counteroffer.

    b.   A contract can <u>not</u> be formed unless Bizzy expressly accepts the term added by Wang.

    c.   A contract is formed incorporating only the terms of Bizzy's offer.

    d.   A contract is formed with Wang's additional term becoming a part of the agreement.

53 (November 83)

On October 1, Baker, a wholesaler, sent Clark, a retailer, a written signed offer to sell 200 pinking shears at $9 each. The terms were F.O.B. Baker's warehouse, net 30, late payment subject to a 15% per annum interest charge. The offer indicated that it must be accepted no later than October 10, that acceptance would be effective upon receipt, and that the terms were not to be varied by the offeree. Clark sent a telegram which arrived on October 6, and accepted the offer expressly subject to a change of the payment terms to 2/10, net/30. Baker phoned Clark on October 7, rejecting the change of payment terms. Clark then indicated it would accept the October 1 offer in all respects, and expected delivery within 10 days. Baker did not accept Clark's oral acceptance of the original offer. Which of the following is a correct statement?

    a.   Baker's original offer is a firm offer, hence irrevocable.

    b.   There is <u>no</u> contract since Clark's modifications effectively rejected the October 1 offer, and Baker never accepted either of Clark's proposals.

    c.   Clark actually created a contract on October 6, since the modifications were merely proposals and did <u>not</u> preclude acceptance.

    d.   The Statute of Frauds would preclude the formation of a contract in any event.

4 (November 82)

Calvin Poultry Co. offered to sell Chickenshop 20,000 pounds of chicken at 40 cents per pound under specified delivery terms. Chickenshop accepted the offer as follows:

"We accept your offer for 20,000 pounds of chicken at 40 cents per pound per city scale weight certificate."

Which of the following is correct?

    a.   A contract was formed on Calvin's terms.

    b.   Chickenshop's reply constitutes a conditional acceptance, but <u>not</u> a counteroffer.

    c.   Chickenshop's reply constitutes a counteroffer and <u>no</u> contract was formed.

    d.   A contract was formed on Chickenshop's terms.

35 (May 79)

Almovar Electronics was closing out several lines of electronic parts which were becoming outdated. It sent a letter on March 8 to Conduit Sales & Service Company, one of its largest retail customers, offering the entire lot at a substantial reduction in price. The offer indicated that it was for "immediate acceptance." The terms were "cash, pick up by your carrier at our loading dock and <u>not</u> later than March 15." It also indicated that the terms of the offer were <u>not</u> subject to variance. The letter did <u>not</u> arrive until March 10 and Conduit's letter accepting the offer was <u>not</u> mailed until March 12. The letter of acceptance indicated that Conduit would take the entire lot, would pay in accordance with the usual terms (2/10, net/30), and would pick up the goods on March 16. Which of the following <u>best</u> describes the legal relationship of the parties?

a. The acceptance was not timely, hence no contract.
b. The different terms of the acceptance are to be construed as proposals for changes in the contract.
c. The different terms of the acceptance constituted a rejection of the offer.
d. Since both parties were merchants and the changes in the acceptance were not material, there is a valid contract.

36 (May 78)
Cutler sent Foster the following offer by mail:

"I offer you 150 Rex portable electric typewriters, model J-1, at $65 per typewriter, F.O.B. your truck at my warehouse, terms 2/10, net/30. I am closing out this model, hence the substantial discount. Accept all or none. (signed) Cutler"

Foster immediately wired back:

"I accept your offer re the Rex electric typewriters, but will use Blue Express Company for the pickup, at my expense of course. In addition, if possible, could you have the shipment ready for Tuesday at 10:00 A.M. because of the holidays? (signed) Foster"

Based on the above correspondence, what is the status of Foster's acceptance?
a. It is not valid because it states both additional and different terms than those contained in the offer.
b. It represents a counteroffer which will become a valid acceptance if not negated by Cutler within 10 days.
c. It is valid but will not be effective until received by Cutler.
d. It is valid upon dispatch despite the fact it states both additional and different terms than those contained in the offer.

1 (November 75)
With respect to a contract for the sale of goods, a definite and seasonable expression of acceptance sent within a reasonable time is effective as an acceptance even though it states minor additional terms to those offered, except in which of the following situations?
a. The acceptance was accompanied by a request that the goods be shipped by truck instead of by rail, if convenient.
b. The offer impliedly limits acceptance to its terms.
c. Acceptance is expressly conditional on assent to the additional terms.
d. The price is in excess of $500.

3. Termination by Operation of Law

14 (May 90)
Opal offered, in writing, to sell Larkin a parcel of land for $300,000. If Opal dies, the offer will
a. Terminate prior to Larkin's acceptance only if Larkin received notice of Opal's death.
b. Remain open for a reasonable period of time after Opal's death.
c. Automatically terminate despite Larkin's prior acceptance.
d. Automatically terminate prior to Larkin's acceptance.

23 (May 89)
An offer is not terminated by operation of law solely because the
a. Offeror dies.
b. Offeree is adjudicated insane.
c. Subject matter is destroyed.
d. Subject matter is sold to a third party.

34 (May 74)

Ambrose undertook to stage a production of a well-known play. He wired Belle, a famous actress, offering her the lead at $1,000 per week (for six evening performances per week) for six weeks from the specified opening night, plus $1,000 for a week of rehearsal prior to opening. The telegram also said, "Offer ends in three days."

Ambrose's death

a. Would <u>not</u> terminate the offer if it occurred after Belle sent a telegraphed acceptance but before receipt of the telegram at Ambrose's office.

b. Would terminate any contract previously made with Belle.

c. On the day of the offer would <u>not</u> prevent Belle from subsequently accepting within the three-day period.

d. Transforms the offer into an offer to enter into a unilateral contract.

C. Acceptance
1. Unilateral v. Bilateral Contracts

16 (May 91)

Kay, an art collector, promised Hammer, an art student, that if Hammer could obtain certain rare artifacts within two weeks, Kay would pay for Hammer's post-graduate education. At considerable effort and expense, Hammer obtained the specified artifacts within the two-week period. When Hammer requested payment, Kay refused. Kay claimed that there was no consideration for the promise. Hammer would prevail against Kay based on

a. Unilateral contract.

b. Unjust enrichment.

c. Public policy.

d. Quasi contract.

46 (May 90)

Jefferson Hardware ordered three hundred Ram hammers from Ajax Hardware. Ajax accepted the order in writing. On the final date allowed for delivery, Ajax discovered it did not have enough Ram hammers to fill the order. Instead, Ajax sent three hundred Strong hammers. Ajax stated on the invoice that the shipment was sent only as an accommodation. Which of the following statements is correct?

a. Ajax's note of accommodation cancels the contract between Jefferson and Ajax.

b. Jefferson's order can only be accepted by Ajax's shipment of the goods ordered.

c. Ajax's shipment of Strong hammers is a breach of contract.

d. Ajax's shipment of Strong hammers is a counteroffer and <u>no</u> contract exists between Jefferson and Ajax.

41 (May 85)

Taylor signed and mailed a letter to Peel which stated: "Ship promptly 600 dozen grade A eggs." Taylor's offer

a. May be accepted by Peel only by a prompt shipment.

b. May be accepted by Peel either by a prompt promise to ship or prompt shipment with notice.

c. Is invalid since the price terms were omitted.

d. Is invalid since the shipping terms were omitted.

8 (May 83)

Justin made an offer to pay Benson $1,000 if Benson would perform a certain act. Acceptance of Justin's offer occurs when Benson

a. Promises to complete the act.

b. Prepares to perform the act.

c. Promises to perform and begins preliminary performance.

d. Completes the act.

15 (November 80)

Joseph Manufacturing, Inc. received an order from Raulings Supply Company for certain valves it manufactured. The order called for prompt shipment. In respect to Joseph's options as to the manner of acceptance, which of the following is <u>incorrect</u>?

    a   Joseph can accept only by prompt shipment since this was the manner indicated in the order.

    b.   The order is construed as an offer to enter into either a unilateral or bilateral contract and Joseph may accept by a promise of or prompt shipment.

    c   .If Joseph promptly ships the goods, Raulings must be notified within a reasonable time.

    d.   Joseph may accept by mail, but he must make prompt shipment.

5 (November 79)

Which of the following represents the basic distinction between a bilateral contract and a unilateral contract?

    a.   Specific performance is available if the contract is unilateral whereas it is _not_ if the contract is bilateral.

    b.   There is only one promise involved if the contract is unilateral whereas there are two promises if the contract is bilateral.

    c.   The Statute of Frauds applies to a bilateral contract but _not_ to a unilateral contract.

    d.   The rights under a bilateral contract are assignable whereas rights under a unilateral contract are _not_ assignable.

9 (November 79)

Lally sent Queen Supply Company, Inc. a telegram ordering $700 of general merchandise. Lally's telegram indicated that immediate shipment was necessary. That same day Queen delivered the goods to the Red Freight Company. The shipment was delayed due to a breakdown of the truck which was transporting the goods. When the merchandise did _not_ arrive as promptly as expected, Lally notified Queen that it revoked the offer and was purchasing the goods elsewhere. Queen indicated to Lally that the merchandise had been shipped the same day Lally had ordered it and Lally's revocation was _not_ good. Which of the following statements _best_ describes the transaction?

    a.   The Statute of Frauds will be a defense on any action by Queen to enforce the contract.

    b.   Prompt shipment of the merchandise by Queen constituted an acceptance.

    c.   Lally's revocation of the offer was effective since Lally had _not_ received a notice of acceptance.

    d.   Lally's order was an offer to Queen to enter into a bilateral contract which could be accepted only by a promise.

5A (November 80)

Fennimore owned a ranch which was encumbered by a seven percent (7%) mortgage held by the Orange County Bank. As of July 31, 1980, the outstanding mortgage amount was $83,694. Fennimore decided to sell the ranch and engage in the grain storage business. During the time that he was negotiating the sale of the ranch, the bank sent out an offer to several mortgagors indicating a five percent (5%) discount on the mortgage if the mortgagors would pay the entire mortgage in cash or by certified check by July 31, 1980. The bank was doing this in order to liquidate older unprofitable mortgages which it had on the books. Anyone seeking to avail himself of the offer was required to present his payment at the Second Street branch on July 31, 1980. Fennimore, having obtained a buyer for his property, decided to take advantage of the offer since his buyer was arranging his own financing and was not interested in assuming the mortgage. Therefore, on July 15th he wrote the bank a letter which stated: "I accept your offer on my mortgage, see you on July 31, 1980, I'll have a certified check." Fennimore did not indicate that he was selling the ranch and would have to pay off the full amount in any event. On July 28, the bank sent Fennimore a letter by certified mail which was received by Fennimore on the 30th of July which stated: "We withdraw our offer. We are oversubscribed. Furthermore, we have learned that you are selling your property and the mortgage is not being assumed." Nevertheless, on July 31 at 9:05 in the morning when Fennimore walked in the door of the bank holding his certified check, Vogelspiel, a bank mortgage officer, approached him and stated firmly and clearly that the bank's offer had been revoked and that the bank would refuse to accept tender of payment. Dumbfounded by all this, Fennimore nevertheless tendered the check, which was refused.

Required: Answer the following, setting forth reasons for any conclusions stated.

In the eventual lawsuit that ensued, who will prevail?

Orange County Bank will prevail. The fact situation poses a classic illustration of a withdrawal of an offer to enter into a unilateral contract. The bank's offer to Fennimore called for the performance of an act (the actual paying of the mortgage), not a promise to pay it, as the means of acceptance. The language in the offer is clear and unambiguous, providing a 5 percent discount on a mortgage if the mortgagor would pay the entire mortgage in cash or by certified check by July 31, 1980, at the Second Street branch of the bank. Thus, the bank's letter was an offer to enter into a unilateral contract that required the performance of the act as the authorized and exclusive means of acceptance. Fennimore's promise to perform the act was ineffectual in creating a contract. Contract law generally provides that offers may be revoked at any time prior to acceptance; even if the bank revoked its offer the instant before the purported acceptance, it was a timely revocation and the acceptance was too late. The tender of performance would also be of no avail since notice of revocation had been received on the 30th.

In this situation, strict common law rules would deny the creation of a contract. Some states, in recognition of the hardship of such results, have adopted what is known as the Restatement of Contracts rule. This modification of the common law rule in respect to the unilateral contract rule holds that the unilateral promise in an offer calling for an act becomes binding as soon as part of the requested performance actually has been rendered or a proper tender of performance has been made. The courts have required substantial action on the part of the offeree, which does not appear to be present here.

The fact that Fennimore was selling his property and did not disclose the fact that he would have to pay the mortgage off in any event is immaterial. There was no material misrepresentation of fact made by him, hence his action was not fraudulent nor did he misrepresent. He was silent. Additionally, the fact that the bank was using the sale as a reason for terminating the offer was immaterial.

2. Bilateral Contracts; Mailbox Acceptance Rule

22 (May 92)

On April 1, Fine Corp. faxed Moss an offer to purchase Moss' warehouse for $500,000. The offer stated that it would remain open only until April 4 and that acceptance must be received to be effective. Moss sent an acceptance on April 4 by overnight mail and Fine received it on April 5. Which of the following statements is correct?

    a. No contract was formed because Moss sent the acceptance by an unauthorized method.

    b. No contract was formed because Fine received Moss' acceptance after April 4.

    c. A contract was formed when Moss sent the acceptance.

    d. A contract was formed when Fine received Moss' acceptance.

11 (May 91)

Nix sent Castor a letter offering to employ Castor as controller of Nix's automobile dealership. Castor received the letter on February 19. The letter provided that Castor would have until February 23 to consider the offer and, in the meantime, Nix would not withdraw it. On February 20, Nix, after reconsidering the offer to Castor, decided to offer the job to Vick, who accepted immediately. That same day, Nix called Castor and revoked the offer. Castor told Nix that an acceptance of Nix's offer was mailed on February 19. Under the circumstances,

    a. Nix's offer was irrevocable until February 23.

    b. No contract was formed between Nix and Castor because Nix revoked the offer before Nix received Castor's acceptance.

    c. Castor's acceptance was effective when mailed.

    d. Any revocation of the offer would have to be in writing because Nix's offer was in writing.

13 (May 90)

On November 1, Yost sent a telegram to Zen offering to sell a rare vase. The offer required that Zen's acceptance telegram be sent on or before 5:00 P.M. on November 2. On November 2, at 3:00 P.M., Zen sent an acceptance by overnight mail. It did not reach Yost until November 5. Yost refused to complete the sale to Zen. Is there an enforceable contract?

    a.   Yes, because the acceptance was made within the time specified.
    b.   Yes, because the acceptance was effective when sent.
    c.   No, because Zen did <u>not</u> accept by telegram.
    d.   No, because the offer required receipt of the acceptance within the time period.

9 (November 89)

The mailbox rule generally makes acceptance of an offer effective at the time the acceptance is dispatched. The mailbox rule does <u>not</u> apply if
    a.   Both the offeror and offeree are merchants.
    b.   The offer proposes a sale of real estate.
    c.   The offer provides that an acceptance shall <u>not</u> be effective until actually received.
    d.   The duration of the offer is <u>not</u> in excess of three months.

Items 11 and 12 are based on the following:

On April 2, Jet Co. wrote to Ard, offering to buy Ard's building for $350,000. The offer contained all of the essential terms to form a binding contract and was duly signed by Jet's president. It further provided that the offer would remain open until May 30 and an acceptance would not be effective until received by Jet. On April 10, Ard accepted Jet's offer by mail. The acceptance was received by Jet on April 14.

11 (November 88)

For this item only, assume that on April 11 Jet sent a telegram to Ard revoking its offer and that Ard received the telegram on April 12. Under the circumstances,
    a.   A contract was formed on April 10.
    b.   A contract was formed on April 14.
    c.   Jet's revocation effectively terminated its offer on April 12.
    d.   Jet's revocation effectively terminated its offer on April 11.

12 (November 88)

For this item only, assume that on April 13 Ard sent a telegram to Jet withdrawing the acceptance and rejecting Jet's offer and that Jet received the telegram on April 15. Under the circumstances,
    a.   A contract was formed on April 14.
    b.   A contract was formed on April 10.
    c.   Ard's rejection effectively terminated Jet's offer on April 13.
    d.   Ard's rejection effectively terminated Jet's offer on April 15.

11 (May 87)

On April 2, 1987, Bonn & Co., CPAs, mailed Marble Corp. a signed proposal to perform certain accounting services for Marble provided Marble accepts the proposal by April 30, 1987. Under the circumstances,
    a.   f Marble accepts by telephone on April 30, 1987, <u>no</u> contract will be formed between the parties.
    b.   Marble must accept the Bonn proposal in writing in order to form a contract.
    c.   A contract will be formed between the parties if Marble mails an acceptance to Bonn on April 29, 1987, even if it is <u>not</u> received by Bonn until May 3, 1987.
    d.   Bonn may <u>not</u> withdraw its proposal prior to May 1, 1987.

Items 15 and 16 are based on the following information:

On March 1, Mirk Corp. wrote to Carr offering to sell Carr its office building for $280,000. The offer stated that it would remain open until July 1. It further stated that acceptance must be by telegram and would be effective only upon receipt.

15 (May 87)

For this question only, assume that Carr telegrammed its acceptance on June 28 and that it was received by Mirk on July 2. Which of the following statements is correct?

a. A contract was formed when Carr telegrammed its acceptance.
b. A contract was formed when Mirk received Carr's acceptance.
c. No contract was formed because three months had elapsed since the offer was made.
d. No contract was formed since the acceptance was received after July 1.

16 (May 87)

For this question only, assume that on May 10, Mirk mailed a letter to Carr revoking its offer of March 1. Carr did not learn of Mirk's revocation until Carr received the letter on May 17. Carr had already sent a telegram of acceptance to Mirk on May 14, which was received by Mirk on May 16. Which of the following statements is correct?

a. Carr's telegram of acceptance was effective on May 16.
b. Mirk's offer of March 1 was irrevocable and therefore could <u>not</u> be withdrawn prior to July 1.
c. Mirk's letter of revocation effectively terminated its offer of March 1 when mailed.
d. Carr's telegram of acceptance was effective on May 14.

12 (November 86)

Stable Corp. offered in a signed writing to sell Mix an office building for $350,000. The offer, which was sent by Stable on April 1, indicated that it would remain open until July 9. On July 5, Mix mailed a letter rejecting Stable's offer. On July 6, Mix sent a telegram to Stable accepting the original offer. The letter of rejection was received by Stable on July 8 and the telegram of acceptance was received by Stable on July 7. Which of the following is correct?

a. Mix's telegram resulted in the formation of a valid contract.
b. Mix's letter of July 5 terminated Stable's offer when mailed.
c. Stable was <u>not</u> entitled to withdraw its offer until after July 9.
d. Although Stable's offer on April 1 was a firm offer under the UCC it will only remain open for three months.

24 (November 86)

Quick Corp. mailed a letter to Blue Co. on May 1, 1986, offering a three-year franchise dealership. The offer stated the terms in detail and at the bottom stated that the offer would not be withdrawn prior to June 5, 1986. Which of the following is correct?

a. The offer can <u>not</u> be assigned to another party by Blue if Blue chooses <u>not</u> to accept.
b. A letter of acceptance from Blue to Quick sent on June 5, 1986, and which was received by Quick on June 6, 1986, does <u>not</u> create a valid contract.
c. The offer is an irrevocable option which can <u>not</u> be withdrawn prior to June 5, 1986.
d. The Statute of Frauds does <u>not</u> apply to the proposed contract.

2 (May 86)

Able Sofa, Inc. sent Noll a letter offering to sell Noll a custom made sofa for $5,000. Noll immediately sent a telegram to Able purporting to accept the offer. However, the telegraph company erroneously delivered the telegram to Able Soda, Inc. Three days later, Able mailed a letter of revocation to sell Noll the sofa. Noll sued Able for breach of contract. Able

a. Would have been liable under the deposited acceptance rule only if Noll had accepted by mail.
b. Will avoid liability since it revoked its offer prior to receiving Noll's acceptance.
c. Will be liable for breach of contract.
d. Will avoid liability due to the telegraph company's error.

6 (November 85)

On May 1, Apple mailed a signed offer to sell an office building to Fein for $90,000. The offer indicated that it would remain open until May 10. On May 5, Fein assigned the offer to Boyd for $5,000. On May 8, Boyd orally accepted Apple's offer. Apple refused to sell the building to Boyd. Which of the following statements is correct?

a. Fein's assignment to Boyd was effective because an option contract was formed between Apple and Fein on May 1.

b. Fein's assignment to Boyd was effective against Apple because valid consideration was given.

c. Boyd's acceptance was ineffective because the offer could <u>not</u> be assigned.

d. Boyd's acceptance was ineffective against Apple because it was oral.

11 (November 85)

On April 1, Knox signed and mailed a letter containing an offer to sell Wax a warehouse for $75,000. The letter also indicated that the offer would expire on May 3. Which of the following is correct?

a. The offer is a firm offer under the UCC and can <u>not</u> be withdrawn by Knox prior to May 3.

b. Wax can benefit from the early acceptance rule <u>no</u> matter what means of communication he uses as long as the acceptance is sent on or before May 3.

c. If Wax purports to accept the offer on April 15 at $50,000 and Knox refuses to sell at that price, Wax nevertheless has the right to accept at $75,000 by May 3.

d. A telephone call by Wax to Knox on May 3, accepting the offer at $75,000, will effectively bind Knox.

18 (November 84)

The following conversation took place between Mary and Ed. Mary: "Ed, if you wanted to sell your table, what would you ask for it?" Ed: "I suppose $400 would be a fair price." Mary: "I'll take it, if you will have it refinished." Ed: "Sold." Thus

a. Ed's statement: "I suppose $400 would be a fair price" constituted an offer.

b. Mary's reply: "I'll take it, if you will have it refinished" was a conditional acceptance, terminating Ed's offer.

c. No contract resulted since Ed never stated he would actually sell the table for $400.

d. A contract was formed when Ed said: "Sold."

29 (November 83)

West sent a letter to Baker on October 18, 1983, offering to sell a tract of land for $70,000. The offer stated that it would expire on November 1, 1983. Baker sent a letter on October 25, indicating the price was too high and that he would be willing to pay $62,500. On the morning of October 26, upon learning that a comparable property had sold for $72,500, Baker telephoned West and made an unconditional acceptance of the offer of $70,000. West indicated that the price was now $73,000. Baker's letter offering $62,500 arrived the afternoon of October 26. Under the circumstances

a. West's letter was a firm offer as defined under the Uniform Commercial Code.

b. Baker validly accepted on the morning of October 26.

c. There is <u>no</u> contract since Baker's acceptance was not in a signed writing.

d. The parol evidence rule will preclude Baker from contradicting his written statements with oral testimony contra to his letter of October 25.

1 (November 82)

On October 1, 1982, Arthur mailed to Madison an offer to sell a tract of land located in Summerville for $13,000. Acceptance was to be not later than October 10. Madison posted his acceptance on the 6th of October. The acceptance arrived on October 7th. On October 4th, Arthur sold the tract in question to Larson and mailed to Madison notice of the sale. That latter arrived on the 6th of October, but after Madison had dispatched his letter of acceptance. Which of the following is correct?

a. There was a valid acceptance of the Arthur offer on the day Madison posted his acceptance.

b. Arthur's offer was effectively revoked by the sale of the tract of land to Larson on the 4th of October.

c. Arthur could <u>not</u> revoke the offer to sell the land until after October 10th.

d. Madison's acceptance was <u>not</u> valid since he was deemed to have notice of revocation prior to the acceptance.

15 (May 82)

On May 1st, Perry Boat Sales sent a letter to James offering to sell James a boat for $4,000. James received the offer the morning of May 3rd. That afternoon, James delivered an acceptance to the telegraph office. Due to an error by the telegraph company, the acceptance was never received by Perry. Which of the following is correct?

a. Perry is bound to a contract even though the telegram of acceptance was never received.
b. Perry is <u>not</u> bound to a contract because the telegraph company's error excused him of any responsibility.
c. Perry would be bound to a contract only if James had sent his acceptance by mail.
d. If Perry had sold the boat to Evans, without James' knowledge, before James delivered his acceptance to the telegraph office, Perry would <u>not</u> be bound in contract to James.

15 (May 78)

Milbank undertook to stage a production of a well-known play. He wired Lucia, a famous actress, offering her the lead in the play at $2,000 per week for six weeks from the specified opening night plus $1,000 for a week of rehearsal prior to opening. The telegram also said, "Offer ends in three days." Lucia wired an acceptance the same day she received it. The telegram acceptance was temporarily misplaced by the telegraph company and did not arrive until five days after its dispatch. Milbank, not hearing from Lucia, assumed she had declined and abandoned the production. Which of the following is correct if Lucia sues Milbank?
a. The contract was automatically terminated when Milbank decided <u>not</u> to proceed.
b. Lucia has entered into a valid contract and is entitled to recover damages if Milbank fails to honor it.
c. Lucia may <u>not</u> take any other engagement for the period involved if she wishes to recover.
d. Milbank is excused from any liability since his action was reasonable under the circumstances.

4 (May 76)

Unless the offer specifies otherwise, an acceptance is generally effective when it is
a. Signed by the offeree.
b. Received by the offeror.
c. Delivered by the communicating agency.
d. Dispatched by the offeree.

4 (November 89)

Anker Corp., a furniture retailer, engaged Best & Co., CPAs, to audit Anker's financial statements for the year ended December 31, 1988. While reviewing certain transactions entered into by Anker during 1988, Best became concerned with the proper reporting of the following transactions:

- On September 8, 1988, Crisp Corp., a furniture manufacturer, signed and mailed a letter offering to sell Anker 50 pieces of furniture for $9,500. The offer stated it would remain open until December 20, 1988. On December 5, 1988, Crisp mailed a letter revoking this offer. Anker received Crisp's revocation the following day. On December 12, 1988, Anker mailed its acceptance to Crisp, and Crisp received it on December 13, 1988.

- On December 6, 1988, Dix Corp. signed and mailed a letter offering to sell Anker a building for $75,000. The offer stated that acceptance could only be made by certified mail, return receipt requested. On December 10, 1988, Anker telephoned Dix requesting that Dix keep the offer open until December 20, 1988 because it was reviewing Dix's offer. On December 12, 1988, Dix signed and mailed a letter to Anker indicating that it would hold the offer open until December 20, 1988. On December 19, 1988, Anker sent its acceptance to Dix by a private express mail courier. Anker's acceptance was received by Dix on December 20, 1988.

After reviewing the documents concerning the foregoing transactions, Best spoke with Anker's president who made the following assertions:

- The September 8, 1988 offer by Crisp was irrevocable until December 20, 1988, and therefore a contract was formed by Anker's acceptance on December 12, 1988.
- Dix's letter dated December 12, 1988 formed an option contract with Anker.
- Anker's acceptance on December 19, 1988 formed a contract with Dix.

Required: In separate paragraphs, discuss the assertions made by Anker's president. Indicate whether the assertions are correct and the reasons therefor.

The president's assertion that the September 8, 1988 offer by Crisp was irrevocable until December 20, 1988, and that, therefore, a contract was formed by Anker's acceptance on December 12, 1988, is incorrect. Because the offer made by Crisp involves a transaction in goods, i.e., furniture, the UCC Sales Article applies. The UCC Sales Article provides that an offer by a merchant to buy or sell goods in a signed writing which by its terms gives assurance that it will be held open is not revocable, for lack of consideration, during the time stated or, if no time is stated, for a reasonable time, but in no event may such period of irrevocability exceed three months. Under the facts of this case, Crisp's offer was a firm offer that could not be revoked because the offer was made by Crisp, a merchant, concerning the kind of goods being sold (furniture); was in writing and signed by Crisp; and stated that it would remain open until December 20, 1988. Despite the provision that the offer will remain open until December 20, 1988, a firm offer remains irrevocable for a three-month period. Therefore, Crisp's letter of revocation on December 5, 1988 did not terminate the firm offer because the three-month period had not yet expired. The revocation was effective on December 8, 1988, when the three-month period expired. Therefore, Anker's attempted acceptance on December 12, 1988 did not form a contract with Crisp. Instead, Anker's attempted acceptance is likely to be treated as an offer.

The president's assertion that Dix's December 12, 1988 letter formed an option contract is incorrect. To form an option contract, where the subject matter is real estate, all of the elements necessary to form a contract must be met. In this case, Anker did not furnish any consideration in return for Dix's promise to keep the offer open until December 20, 1988; therefore, an option contract was not formed.

The president's assertion that Anker's acceptance on December 19, 1988 formed a contract with Dix is incorrect. In general, acceptance of an offer is effective when it is dispatched. If, however, an offer specifically stipulates the method of communication to be utilized by the offeree, the acceptance to be effective must conform to that method. Thus, an acceptance by another method of communication is ineffective and no contract is formed. Under the facts of this case, Anker's acceptance on December 19, 1988 by a private express mail courier is ineffective, despite Dix's receipt of the acceptance on December 20, 1988, because Dix's offer specifically stipulated that acceptance could only be made by certified mail, return receipt requested. Instead, Anker's attempted acceptance is likely to be treated as a counteroffer.

4 (November 87)

On April 1, Sam Stieb signed and mailed to Bold Corp. an offer to sell Bold a parcel of land for $175,000. On April 5, Bold called Stieb and requested that Stieb keep the offer open until June 1, by which time Bold would be able to determine whether financing for the purchase was available. That same day, Stieb signed and mailed a letter indicating that he would hold the offer open until June 1 if Bold mailed Stieb $100 by April 20.

On April 17, Stieb sent Bold a signed letter revoking his offers dated April 1 and April 5. Bold received that letter on April 19. However, Bold had already signed and mailed on April 18 its acceptance of Stieb's offer of April 5 along with a check for $100. Stieb received the check and letter of acceptance on April 20.

On May 15, Bold wrote Stieb stating that the $175,000 purchase price was too high but that it would be willing to purchase the land for $160,000. Upon receipt, Stieb immediately sent a telegram to Bold indicating that he had already revoked his offer and that even if his revocation was not effective he considered Bold's offer a counteroffer which he would not accept. Otherwise, Stieb did nothing as a result of Bold's May 15 letter.

On May 25, Bold executed and delivered the original contract of April 1 to Stieb without any variation of the original terms.

Stieb does not wish to sell the land to Bold because he has received another offer for $200,000. In order to avoid the sale to Bold for $175,000, Stieb asserts the following:

- Bold could not validly accept Stieb's offer dated April 5 because $100 was inadequate consideration to hold the offer open until April 20.
- Stieb's offer dated April 5 had terminated because he had revoked the offer prior to Bold's acceptance
- Even if his revocation was not effective, Bold's letter of May 15 was a counteroffer, which automatically terminated Bold's right to accept Stieb's offer of April 1.

Required: Discuss Stieb's assertions, indicating whether such assertions are correct or incorrect and setting forth the reasons for any conclusions stated.

Stieb's first assertion, that Bold could not validly accept his offer dated April 5 because $100 was inadequate consideration to hold the offer open, is incorrect. In general, the courts will not question the adequacy of consideration if the consideration has legal sufficiency and there is a bargained-for exchange. Adequacy of consideration has nothing to do with legal sufficiency. Thus the subject matter that the parties have exchanged need not have approximately the same value. Based upon the facts, Bold's payment of the $100 in exchange for Stieb's promise to keep the offer open was both legally sufficient and bargained for.

Stieb's second assertion, that his offer dated April 5 had terminated since he had revoked his offer prior to Bold's acceptance, is incorrect. An offer may be terminated by the offeror if a revocation is communicated to the offeree before the offeree accepts. In the majority of states revocation is effective upon receipt of the revocation by the offeree or the offeree's agent. On the other hand, acceptance will generally take effect at the time the acceptance is sent (dispatched) by an authorized means of communication. Bold used an authorized means of communication, i.e., the mail, which was the same method used by Stieb in making the offer. Therefore, Bold's acceptance and payment of $100 on April 18 was effective on that date and formed an option contract. Thus, Stieb's letter of revocation mailed on April 17 was not effective until Bold received the revocation on April 19 by which time an option contract had already been formed and the offer could not be revoked.

Stieb's third assertion, that even if his revocation was not effective, Bold's letter of May 15 was a counteroffer, which automatically terminated Bold's right to accept Stieb's offer of April 1, is incorrect. In general, the power of acceptance under an option contract is not terminated by a rejection or counteroffer made by the offeree, unless the requirements are met for the discharge of a contractual duty or the offeror changes its position to its detriment in reliance on such rejection or counteroffer. Although a rejection and/or counteroffer will terminate an offer when communicated, Bold's letter of May 15 will not terminate its right to exercise its option on the land because there was neither a discharge of a contractual duty nor reliance by Stieb to its detriment on the May 15 letter.

5B (November 80)

Austin wrote a letter and mailed it to Hernandez offering to sell Hernandez his tuna canning business for $125,000. Hernandez promptly mailed a reply acknowledging receipt of Austin's letter and expressing an interest in purchasing the cannery. However, Hernandez offered Austin only $110,000. Later Hernandez decided that the business was in fact worth at least the $125,000 that Austin was asking. He therefore decided to accept the original offer tendered to him at $125,000 and telegraphed Austin an unconditional acceptance at $125,000. The telegram reached Austin before Hernandez's prior letter, although the letter arrived later that day. Austin upon receipt of the telegram telegraphed Hernandez that as a result of further analysis as to the worth of the business, he was not willing to sell at less than $150,000. Hernandez claims a contract at $125,000 resulted from his telegram. Austin asserts either that there is no contract or that the purchase price is $150,000.

Required: Answer the following, setting forth reasons for any conclusions stated.

If the dispute goes to court, who will prevail?

Hernandez will prevail. An offer is not effective until communicated to the offeree. The same rule applies to counteroffers including a change in the price, as occurred here. Therefore, a counteroffer is not effective until received by Austin, the original offeror. Hernandez's counteroffer does not destroy the offer until it is received. Thus, Hernandez's telegram, which accepted Austin's offer and arrived ahead of Hernandez's letter containing the counteroffer, is effective in creating a binding contract.

This rule applies even if Hernandez had mailed a letter that unequivocally accepted Austin's offer and that would have been effective upon dispatch. The general rule that an acceptance is effective when dispatched is subject to an exception that is designed to prevent entrapment of an offeror who is misled to his disadvantage by an offeree who attempts to take two inconsistent positions. Thus, when an offeree first rejects an offer, then subsequently accepts it, the subsequent acceptance will be considered effective upon dispatch by an authorized means only if it arrives prior to the offeror's receipt of the rejection. If the rejection arrives first, the original offeror may treat the attempted acceptance as a counteroffer which he is free to accept or not. Were this not the rule, an offeror who, upon receipt of a rejection, in good faith changed his position (that is, sold the goods to another customer), could find himself having sold the same goods twice.

3B (May 80)

Jane Anderson offered to sell Richard Heinz a ten-acre tract of commercial property. Anderson's letter indicated the offer would expire on March 1, 1980, at 3:00 p.m. and that any acceptance must be received in her office by that time. On February 29, 1980, Heinz decided to accept the offer and posted an acceptance at 4:00 p.m. Heinz indicated that in the event the acceptance did not arrive on time, he would assume there was a contract if he did not hear anything from Anderson in five days. The letter arrived on March 2, 1980. Anderson never responded to Heinz's letter. Heinz claims a contract was entered into and is suing thereon.

Required: Answer the following, setting forth reasons for any conclusions stated.

Is there a contract?

No. The offer for the sale of real property is governed by the common law of contracts.

Anderson's letter constituted an offer that stated it would expire at a given time. In addition to stating the time, the letter indicated that acceptance "must be received in her (Anderson's) office" by said time. This language is clear and unambiguous and effectively negated the rule whereby acceptance may take place upon dispatch. Thus, despite use of the same means of communication, acceptance was not effective until receipt by Anderson on March 2, 1980. This was too late. Thus, the purported acceptance was a mere counteroffer by Heinz and had to be accepted in order to create a contract. Silence does not usually constitute acceptance. In fact, the common-law exceptions to this rule are limited in nature and narrowly construed. The law clearly will not permit a party to unilaterally impose silence upon the other as acceptance. The narrow exceptions are the following:

1. The parties intended silence as acceptance.
2. Prior dealing indicates that silence is an acceptable method of acceptance.
3. The custom of the trade or industry recognizes silence as acceptance.

It is clear that our case is not within any of the exceptions; hence, silence does not constitute acceptance, and there is no contract.

III. Contract Formation--Consideration
A. Doctrine of Consideration

12 (November 92)

In determining whether the consideration requirement to form a contract has been satisfied, the consideration exchanged by the parties to the contract must be
   a. Of approximately equal value.
   b. Legally sufficient.
   c. Exchanged simultaneously by the parties.
   d. Fair and reasonable under the circumstances.

11 (May 90)

To satisfy the consideration requirement for a valid contract, the consideration exchanged by the parties must be
   a. Legally sufficient.
   b. Payable in legal tender.
   c. Simultaneously paid and received.
   d. Of the same economic value.

17 (May 85)

Mix offered to sell a parcel of land to Simon for $90,000. The offer was made by Mix in a signed writing and provided that it would not be revoked for five months if Simon promised to pay Mix $250 within 10 days. Simon agreed to do so. Which of the following is correct?
   a. Simon's agreement to pay $250 is insufficient consideration to form an option contract.
   b. Mix may withdraw the offer any time prior to Simon's payment of the $250.
   c. An option contract is formed.
   d. Although an option contract is formed, the duration of such a contract is limited to three months.

26 (November 83)

In general, which of the following requirements must be satisfied in order to have a valid contract?
a. A writing.
b. Consideration.
c. Mutual promises.
d. Signatures of all parties.

3 (November 79)

Which of the following will not be sufficient to satisfy the consideration requirement for a contract?
a. The offeree expends both time and money in studying and analyzing the offer.
b. The offeree makes a promise which is a legal detriment to him.
c. The offeree performs the act requested by the offeror.
d. The offeree makes a promise which benefits the offeror.

22 (November 74)

The common-law contract doctrine of consideration
a. Requires that consideration have a monetary value if it is to be valid.
b. Recognizes that the forebearance from a legal right constitutes consideration.
c. Has been abolished in most jurisdictions if the contract is made under seal.
d. Requires a roughly equal exchange of value by the parties to the contract.

B. Legal Detriment; Preexisting Legal Duties

9 (May 79)

Williams purchased a heating system from Radiant Heating, Inc., for his factory. Williams insisted that a clause be included in the contract calling for service on the heating system to begin not later than the next business day after Williams informed Radiant of a problem.

This service was to be rendered free of charge during the first year of the contract and for a flat fee of $200 per year for the next two years thereafter. During the winter of the second year, the heating system broke down and Williams promptly notified Radiant of the situation. Due to other commitments, Radiant did not send a man over the next day. Williams phoned Radiant and was told that the $200 per year service charge was uneconomical and they could not get a man over there for several days. Williams in desperation promised to pay an additional $100 if Radiant would send a man over that day.

Radiant did so and sent a bill for $100 to Williams. Is Williams legally required to pay this bill and why?
a. No, because the pre-existing legal duty rule applies to this situation.
b. No, because the Statute of Frauds will defeat Radiant's claim.
c. Yes, because Williams made the offer to pay the additional amount.
d. Yes, because the fact that it was uneconomical for Radiant to perform constitutes economic duress which freed Radiant from its obligation to provide the agreed-upon service.

5C (November 78)

Novack, an industrial designer, accepted an offer from Superior Design Corporation to become one of its designers. The contract was for three years and expressly provided that it was irrevocable by either party except for cause during that period of time. The contract was in writing and signed by both parties. After a year, Novack became dissatisfied with the agreed compensation which he was receiving. He had done a brilliant job and several larger corporations were attempting to lure him away.

Novack, therefore, demanded a substantial raise, and Superior agreed in writing to pay him an additional amount as a bonus at the end of the third year. Novack remained with Superior and performed the same duties he had agreed to perform at the time he initially accepted the position. At the end of the three years, Novack sought to collect the additional amount of money promised. Superior denied liability beyond the amount agreed to in the original contract.

Required: Answer the following, setting forth reasons for any conclusions stated.
Can Novack recover the additional compensation from Superior?

> No. The pre-existing legal duty rule applies. Novack has not given any consideration for Superior's promise of additional compensation. The common law rules apply to contracts for services, and modifications of such contracts must be supported by consideration. In essence, Novack was already bound by a valid contract to perform exactly what he did perform under the modified contract. Hence, he did nothing more than he was legally obligated to do. As a result, there is no consideration to support Superior's promise to pay the bonus.
>
> Section 2-209 of the Uniform Commercial Code, which provides that an agreement modifying a contract needs no consideration to be binding, is not applicable to an employment contract because Section 2-209 covers only the sale of goods.

1. Contract Modification--Common Law

21 (November 90)
Which of the following requires consideration to be binding on the parties?
a. Material modification of a contract involving the sale of real estate.
b. Ratification of a contract by a person after reaching the age of majority.
c. A written promise signed by a merchant to keep an offer to sell goods open for 10 days.
d. Material modification of a sale of goods contract under the UCC.

7 (May 75)
Martinson Services, Inc. agreed to rent two floors of office space in Jason's building for five years. An escalation clause in the lease provided for a $200 per month increase in rental in the fifth year of occupancy by Martinson. Near the end of the fourth year, during a serious economic recession, Martinson's business was doing very poorly. Martinson called upon Jason to inform him that Martinson could not honor the lease if the rent was increased in the fifth year. Jason agreed in a signed writing to allow Martinson to remain at the prior rental, and Martinson did so. At the end of the fifth year Martinson moved to another office building. Then, Jason demanded payment of $2,400 from Martinson.
What is the legal standing of the parties involved?
a. A binding accord and satisfaction has resulted between the parties.
b. The agreed upon rent reduction is valid due to the increased burden of performance as a result of events beyond Martinson's control.
c. Martinson's relinquishment of the legal right to breach the contract provides the consideration for the reduction in rent.
d. The writing signed by Jason does not bind him to the agreed reduction in rent.

2. Contract Modification--UCC § 2-209(1)

54 (May 92)
On May 2, Mason orally contracted with Acme Appliances to buy for $480 a washer and dryer for household use. Mason and the Acme salesperson agreed that delivery would be made on July 2. On May 5, Mason telephoned Acme and requested that the delivery date be moved to June 2. The Acme salesperson agreed with this request. On June 2, Acme failed to deliver the washer and dryer to Mason because of an inventory shortage. Acme advised Mason that it would deliver the appliances on July 2 as originally agreed. Mason believes that Acme has breached its agreement with Mason. Acme contends that its agreement to deliver on June 2 was not binding. Acme's contention is
a. Correct, because Mason is not a merchant and was buying the appliances for household use.
b. Correct, because the agreement to change the delivery date was not in writing.
c. Incorrect, because the agreement to change the delivery date was binding.
d. Incorrect, because Acme's agreement to change the delivery date is a firm offer that cannot be withdrawn by Acme.

53 (May 84)

Olsen purchased a used van from Super Sales Co. for $350. A clause in the written contract in boldfaced type provided that the van was being sold "as is." Another clause provided that the contract was intended as the final expression of the parties' agreement. After driving the van for one week, Olsen realized that the engine was burning oil. Olsen telephoned Super and requested a refund. Super refused but orally gave Olsen a warranty on the engine for six months. Three weeks later the engine exploded. Super's oral warranty
- a. Is invalid since the modification of the existing contract required additional consideration.
- b .Is invalid due to the Statute of Frauds.
- c. Is valid and enforceable.
- d. Although valid, proof of its existence will be inadmissible because it contradicts the final written agreement of the parties.

6 (November 82)

In which of the following situations would an oral agreement without any consideration be binding under the Uniform Commercial Code?
- a. Renunciation of a claim or right arising out of an alleged breach.
- b. A firm offer by a merchant to sell or buy goods which gives assurance that it will be held open.
- c. An agreement which is a requirements contract.
- d. An agreement which modifies an existing sales contract.

45 (November 82)

Stand Glue Corp. offered to sell Macal, Inc. all of the glue it would need in the manufacture of its furniture for one year at the rate of $25 per barrel, F.O.B. seller's city. Macal accepted Stand's offer. Four months later, due to inflation, Stand wrote to Macal advising Macal that Stand could no longer supply the glue at $25 per barrel, but offering to fulfill the contract at $28 per barrel instead. Macal, in need of the glue, sent Stand a letter agreeing to pay the price increase. Macal is
- a. Legally obligated to pay only $25 per barrel under the contract with Stand.
- b. Legally obligated to pay $28 per barrel under the contract with Stand.
- c. Not legally obligated to purchase any glue henceforth from Stand since Stand has breached the contract.
- d. Legally obligated to pay $28 per barrel due to the fact inflation represents an unforeseen hardship.

25 (May 74)

Argot wrote Palm offering to sell him specified merchandise with the offer to remain open 30 days. Ten days later, Argot and Palm orally agreed on the terms of the sale, and Argot prepared a letter which he sent to Palm stating, "This incorporates our agreement." The letter specified the goods but failed to include the agreed price. Later, prior to the date specified for delivery Argot agreed in writing to modify the terms of the contract as requested by Palm; there was no consideration for the modification. Based on these facts
- a. Argot's offer was revocable until accepted by Palm.
- b. If Palm seeks to enforce the agreement, Argot may assert the Statute of Frauds as a defense since neither letter specified any price for the goods.
- c. Lack of consideration for the modification of the agreement would not prevent its enforceability.
- d. Neither Argot nor Palm could enforce the agreement since Palm had not signed any writing.

4A (May 82)

Craig Manufacturing Company needed an additional supply of water for its plant. Consequently, Craig advertised for bids. Shaw Drilling Company submitted the lowest bid and was engaged to drill a well. After a contract had been executed and drilling begun, Shaw discovered that the consistency of the soil was much harder than had been previously encountered in the surrounding countryside. In addition, there was an unexpected layer of bedrock. These facts, unknown to both Craig and Shaw when the contract was signed, significantly increased the cost of performing the contract. Therefore, Shaw announced its intention to abandon performance unless it was assured of recovering its cost. Craig agreed in writing to pay the amount of additional cost if Shaw would continue to drill and complete the contract. Shaw, on the strength of this written promise, completed the job. The additional cost amounted to $10,000 which Shaw now seeks to recover. Craig refuses to pay and asserts that the additional burden was a part of the risk assumed and that the only reason it agreed to pay the additional amount was that it needed the additional water supply on time as agreed.

Shaw has commenced legal action to recover the $10,000 in dispute. Craig denies liability.

Required: Answer the following, setting forth reasons for any conclusions stated.
1. What is the legal liability of Craig as a result of the facts described above?
2. Suppose the contract had been for the purchase of computer parts and the manufacturer had encountered a significant increase in labor cost which it wished to pass on to the purchaser. Would the purchaser's subsequent written promise to make an additional payment have been binding?

1. Craig owes nothing beyond the terms of the original contract. The fact situation poses a classic example of a pre-existing legal duty. The common law rule applicable to such situations is to deny recovery for any additional amount promised if the promisee does nothing more than he was obligated to do in any event. This resolution is arrived at by finding that there is no new consideration to support the modification of the original contract. It may be helpful to think in terms of two contracts, the original contract and the modification. The use of the identical consideration present in the first contract is not legal consideration for the second contract. Some jurisdictions have attempted to mitigate the harshness of this result either by statutory provision or by a strained judicial construction of the rule by the courts. The major change has occurred by the adoption of the Uniform Commercial Code throughout the United States, but the Code applies only to contracts relating to personal property.

2. Yes. The drafters of Article 2 (Sales) of the Uniform Commercial Code considered the pre-existing legal duty rule to be unreasonable when applied to commercial transactions involving the purchase or sale of goods. The rule had the effect of defeating the reasonable expectations of businessmen. Code Section 2-209 rejects the pre-existing legal duty rule by providing as follows: "An agreement modifying a contract within this article needs no consideration to be binding." The Code also provides that if the contract as modified is within the provision of the Statute of Frauds, the modification must be in writing. Since the modification needs no consideration and it is contained in a writing signed by the party to be charged, thus satisfying the Statute of Frauds, it is binding.

C. Bargained-For Exchange; Past Consideration

20 (May 95)

Grove is seeking to avoid performing a promise to pay Brook $1,500. Grove is relying on lack of consideration on Brook's part. Grove will prevail if he can establish that
a. Prior to Grove's promise, Brook had already performed the requested act.
b. Brook's only claim of consideration was the relinquishment of a legal right.
c. Brook's asserted consideration is only worth $400.
d. The consideration to be performed by Brook will be performed by a third party.

10 (November 89)

For there to be consideration for a contract, there must be
a. A bargained-for detriment to the promisor(ee) or a benefit to the promisee(or).
b. A manifestation of mutual assent.
c. Genuineness of assent.
d. Substantially equal economic benefits to both parties.

13 (November 85)

In determining whether the consideration requirement has been satisfied to form a contract, the courts will be required to decide whether the consideration
a. Was bargained for.
b. Was fair and adequate.
c. Has sufficient economic value.
d. Conforms to the subjective intent of the parties.

12 (May 82)

Montbanks' son, Charles, was seeking an account executive position with Dobbs, Smith, and Fogarty, Inc., the largest brokerage firm in the United States. Charles was very independent and wished no interference by his father. The firm, after several weeks of deliberation, decided to hire Charles. They made him an offer on April 12, 1979, and Charles readily accepted. Montbanks feared that his son would not be hired. Being unaware of the fact that his son had been hired, Montbanks mailed a letter to Dobbs on April 13 in which he promised to give the brokerage firm $50,000 in commission business if the firm would hire his son. The letter was duly received by Dobbs and they wish to enforce it against Montbanks. Which of the following statements is correct?

  a. Past consideration is no consideration, hence there is no contract.
  b. The pre-existing legal duty rule applies and makes the promise unenforceable.
  c. Dobbs will prevail since the promise is contained in a signed writing.
  d. Dobbs will prevail based upon promissory estoppel.

36 (November 76)

In order to be valid, consideration must

  a. Be stated in the contract.
  b. Be based upon a legal obligation as contrasted with a moral obligation.
  c. Be performed simultaneously by the parties.
  d. Have a monetary value.

7 (May 76)

Consideration to support a contract generally requires

  a. An adequate exchange.
  b. A bargained exchange.
  c. A reasonable price.
  d. An adequate price.

19 (November 74)

Martin Finance Corporation loaned Davis Small $2,500. Small agreed to repay in twelve monthly installments. After Small was late in making a payment, Martin indicated it needed additional protection and requested that Small obtain a surety. Small appealed to his long-time friend, Arthur Black, to help him. As a personal favor to Small, Black agreed and gave Small a written promise to answer for the debt in the event Small should default on the loan. Small defaulted and filed a voluntary petition in bankruptcy. Martin immediately demanded payment by Black. In this situation

  a. Black's undertaking was not supported by consideration; hence, it is unenforceable.
  b. Martin must wait until the bankruptcy proceeding has been concluded and the bankrupt's estate distributed to creditors.
  c. The Statute of Frauds would not apply to Black's undertaking because he was a noncompensated surety.
  d. Small's bankruptcy bars Martin from recovery against Black.

D. Settlement of Claims; Accord and Satisfaction

24 (May 92)

In which of the following situations does the first promise serve as valid consideration for the second promise?

  a. A police officer's promise to catch a thief for a victim's promise to pay a reward.
  b. A builder's promise to complete a contract for a purchaser's promise to extend the time for completion.
  c. A debtor's promise to pay $500 for a creditor's promise to forgive the balance of a $600 liquidated debt.
  d. A debtor's promise to pay $500 for a creditor's promise to forgive the balance of a $600 disputed debt.

1 (November 87)

On June 1, 1986, Nord Corp. engaged Milo & Co., CPAs, to perform certain management advisory services for nine months for a $45,000 fee. The terms of their oral agreement required Milo to commence performance any time before October 1, 1986. On June 30, 1987, after Milo completed the work to Nord's satisfaction, Nord paid

Milo $30,000 by check. Nord conspicuously marked on the check that it constituted payment in full for all services rendered. Nord has refused to pay the remaining $15,000 arguing that, although it believes the $45,000 fee is reasonable, it had received bids of $30,000 and $38,000 from other firms to perform the same services as Milo. Milo indorsed and deposited the check. If Milo commences an action against Nord for the remaining $15,000, Milo will be entitled to recover

    a. $0 because there has been an enforceable accord and satisfaction.
    b. $0 because the Statute of Frauds has <u>not</u> been satisfied.
    c. $8,000 because $38,000 was the highest other bid.
    d. $15,000 because it is the balance due under the agreement.

22 (November 83)

    Smith, CPA, contracted to perform certain services for Jones for $500. Jones claimed that the services were not fully performed and therefore disputed the amount of his obligation. As a result, Jones sent Smith a check for only $425 and marked clearly on the check it was "payment in full." Smith crossed out the words "payment in full" and cashed the check. The majority of courts would hold that the debt is

    a. Liquidated and Smith can collect the remaining $75.
    b. Liquidated, but Jones by adding the words "payment in full" cancelled the balance of the debt owed.
    c. Unliquidated and the cashing of the check by Smith completely discharged the debt.
    d. Unliquidated, but the crossing out of the words "payment in full" by Smith revives the balance of $75 owed.

13 (May 79)

    Keats Publishing Company shipped textbooks and other books for sale at retail to Campus Bookstore. An honest dispute arose over Campus's right to return certain books. Keats maintained that the books in question could <u>not</u> be returned and demanded payment of the full amount. Campus relied upon trade custom which indicated that many publishers accepted the return of such books. Campus returned the books in question and paid for the balance with a check marked "Account Paid in Full to Date." Keats cashed the check. Which of the following is a correct statement?

    a. Keats is entitled to recover damages.
    b. Keats' cashing of the check constituted an accord and satisfaction.
    c. The pre-existing legal duty rule applies and Keats is entitled to full payment for all the books.
    d. The custom of the industry argument would have <u>no</u> merit in a court of law.

E. Mutuality of Consideration

18 (May 88)

    In deciding whether consideration necessary to form a contract exists, a court must determine whether

    a. The consideration given by each party is of roughly equal value.
    b. There is mutuality of consideration.
    c. The consideration has sufficient monetary value.
    d. The consideration conforms to the subjective intent of the parties.

51 (May 82)

    A condition in a contract for the purchase of real property which makes the purchaser's obligation dependent upon his obtaining a given dollar amount of conventional mortgage financing

    a. Can be satisfied by the seller if the seller offers the buyer a demand loan for the amount.
    b. Is a condition subsequent.
    c. Is implied as a matter of law.
    d. Requires the purchaser to use reasonable efforts to obtain the financing.

34 (November 76)

One of a CPA's major concerns regarding contractual questions arising in the examination of a client's financial statement is
a. The proper court to initiate a lawsuit.
b. The question of who has the burden of proof.
c. Whether consideration has been provided by both parties to a contract.
d. The admissibility of evidence in court.

30 (May 74)

A provision in a contract for the sale of goods providing that the seller may accelerate payment at will when he deems himself insecure
a. Is void as against public policy and ignored in determining contract rights.
b. Makes the agreement illusory and prevents a contract.
c. Gives the seller a preferred creditor's status.
d. Is enforceable subject to the good faith belief of the seller.

F. Promissory Estoppel

23 (May 92)

Which of the following will be legally binding despite lack of consideration?
a. An employer's promise to make a cash payment to a deceased employee's family in recognition of the employee's many years of service.
b. A promise to donate money to a charity on which the charity relied in incurring large expenditures.
c. A modification of a signed contract to purchase a parcel of land.
d. A merchant's oral promise to keep an offer open for 60 days.

IV. Capacity and Legality
A. Incapacity--Minority, Mental Illness, and Intoxication

12 (R01)

Green was adjudicated incompetent by a court having proper jurisdiction. Which of the following statements is correct regarding contracts subsequently entered into by Green?
a. All contracts are voidable.
b. All contracts are valid.
c. All contracts are void.
d. All contracts are enforceable.

21 (November 93)

Egan, a minor, contracted with Baker to purchase Baker's used computer for $400. The computer was purchased for Egan's personal use. The agreement provided that Egan would pay $200 down on delivery and $200 thirty days later. Egan took delivery and paid the $200 down payment. Twenty days later, the computer was damaged seriously as a result of Egan's negligence. Five days after the damage occurred and one day after Egan reached the age of majority, Egan attempted to disaffirm the contract with Baker. Egan will
a. Be able to disaffirm despite the fact that Egan was not a minor at the time of disaffirmance.
b. Be able to disaffirm only if Egan does so in writing.
c. Not be able to disaffirm because Egan had failed to pay the balance of the purchase price.
d. Not be able to disaffirm because the computer was damaged as a result of Egan's negligence.

21 (May 93)

All of the following are effective methods of ratifying a contract entered into by a minor <u>except</u>

a. Expressly ratifying the contract after reaching the age of majority.
b. Failing to disaffirm the contract within a reasonable time after reaching the age of majority.
c. Ratifying the contract before reaching the age of majority.
d. Impliedly ratifying the contract after reaching the age of majority.

15 (November 92)

Rail, who was 16 years old, purchased an $800 computer from Elco Electronics. Rail and Elco are located in a state where the age of majority is 18. On several occasions Rail returned the computer to Elco for repairs. Rail was very unhappy with the computer. Two days after reaching the age of 18, Rail was still frustrated with the computer's reliability, and returned it to Elco, demanding an $800 refund. Elco refused, claiming that Rail no longer had a right to disaffirm the contract. Elco's refusal is

a. Correct, because Rail's multiple requests for service acted as a ratification of the contract.
b. Correct, because Rail could have transferred good title to a good faith purchaser for value.
c. Incorrect, because Rail disaffirmed the contract within a reasonable period of time after reaching the age of 18.
d. Incorrect, because Rail could disaffirm the contract at any time.

17 (May 90)

Payne entered into a written agreement to sell a parcel of land to Stevens. At the time the agreement was executed, Payne had consumed alcoholic beverages. Payne's ability to understand the nature and terms of the contract was not impaired. Stevens did not believe that Payne was intoxicated. The contract is

a. Void as a matter of law.
b. Legally binding on both parties.
c. Voidable at Payne's option.
d. Voidable at Steven's option.

11 (November 89)

Kent, a 16-year old, purchased a used car from Mint Motors, Inc. Ten months later, the car was stolen and never recovered. Which of the following statements is correct?

a. The car's theft is a <u>de facto</u> ratification of the purchase because it is impossible to return the car.
b. Kent may disaffirm the purchase because Kent is a minor.
c. Kent effectively ratified the purchase because Kent used the car for an unreasonable period of time.
d. Kent may disaffirm the purchase because Mint, a merchant, is subject to the UCC.

13 (November 86)

Meed entered into a written agreement to sell a parcel of land to Beel for $80,000. At the time the agreement was executed, Meed had consumed a large amount of alcoholic beverages which significantly impaired Meed's ability to understand the nature and terms of the contract. Beel knew Meed was very intoxicated and that the land had been appraised at $125,000. Meed wishes to avoid the contract. The contract is

a. Void.
b. Legally binding on both parties in the absence of fraud or undue influence.
c. Voidable at Meed's option.
d. Voidable at Meed's option only if the intoxication was involuntary.

4 (May 86)

On May 1, 1985, Mint, a 16-year old, purchased a sail boat from Sly Boats. Mint used the boat for six months at which time he advertised it for sale. Which of the following statements is correct?

a. The sale of the boat to Mint was void, thereby requiring Mint to return the boat and Sly to return the money received.
b. The sale of the boat to Mint may be avoided by Sly at its option.
c. Mint's use of the boat for six months after the sale on May 1 constituted a ratification of that contract.
d. Mint may disaffirm the May 1 contract at any time prior to reaching majority.

B. Unenforceability on Public Policy Grounds
1. In General

25 (May 92)

West, an Indiana real estate broker, misrepresented to Zimmer that West was licensed in Kansas under the Kansas statute that regulates real estate brokers and requires all brokers to be licensed. Zimmer signed a contract agreeing to pay West a 5% commission for selling Zimmer's home in Kansas. West did not sign the contract. West sold Zimmer's home. If West sued Zimmer for nonpayment of commission, Zimmer would be

    a.   Liable to West only for the value of services rendered.
    b.   Liable to West for the full commission.
    c.   Not liable to West for any amount because West did not sign the contract.
    d.   Not liable to West for any amount because West violated the Kansas licensing requirements.

22 (November 90)

Which of the following would be unenforceable because the subject matter is illegal?

    a.   A contingent fee charged by an attorney to represent a plaintiff in a negligence action.
    b.   An arbitration clause in a supply contract.
    c.   A restrictive covenant in an employment contract prohibiting a former employee from using the employer's trade secrets.
    d.   An employer's promise not to press embezzlement charges against an employee who agrees to make restitution.

26 (May 89)

Tell, an Ohio real estate broker, misrepresented to Allen that Tell was licensed in Michigan under Michigan's statute regulating real estate brokers. Allen signed a standard form listing contract agreeing to pay Tell a 6% commission for selling Allen's home in Michigan. Tell sold Allen's home. Under the circumstances, Allen is

    a.   Not liable to Tell for any amount because Allen signed a standard form contract.
    b.   Not liable to Tell for any amount because Tell violated the Michigan licensing requirements.
    c.   Liable to Tell only for the value of services rendered under a quasi-contract theory.
    d.   Liable to Tell for the full commission under a promissory estoppel theory.

19 (May 88)

Parr is a CPA licensed to practice in State A. Parr entered into a contract with Jet, Inc., to perform an audit in State B for $50,000 (including expenses). After Parr had satisfactorily performed the audit, Jet discovered that Parr had violated State B's licensing statute by failing to obtain a CPA license in State B. Parr incurred $10,000 in expenses in connection with the audit. Jet refuses to pay any fee to Parr, arguing that it could have engaged a local CPA licensed in State B to perform the same services for $35,000 (including expenses). If Parr sues Jet based on breach of contract, Parr will be entitled to recover a maximum of

    a. $0.
    b. $10,000.
    c. $35,000.
    d. $50,000.

14 (November 86)

Samm, a plumber, entered into a contract for $75,000 with Orr, Inc., to perform certain plumbing services in a building owned by Orr. After Samm had satisfactorily performed the work, Orr discovered that Samm had violated the state licensing statute by failing to obtain a plumbing license. The licensing statute was enacted merely to raise revenue for the state. An independent appraisal of Samm's work indicated that the building's fair market value increased by $70,000 as a result of Samm's work. The cost of the materials which Samm supplied was $35,000. If Samm sues Orr, Samm will be entitled to recover

    a. $0
    b. $35,000
    c. $70,000
    d. $75,000

5 (May 86)

Todd is a licensed real estate broker in Ohio. One of Todd's largest clients, Sun Corp., contracted in writing with Todd to find a purchaser for its plant in New York and agreed to pay him a 6% commission if he were successful. Todd located a buyer who purchased the plant. Unknown to Todd, New York has a real estate broker's licensing statute which is regulatory in nature, intended to protect the public against unqualified persons. Todd violated the licensing statute by failing to obtain a New York license. If Sun refuses to pay Todd any commission and Todd brings an action against Sun, he will be entitled to recover

    a. Nothing.
    b. A fee based on the actual hours spent.
    c. The commission agreed upon.
    d. Out of pocket expenses only.

20 (November 84)

Aqua, Inc., a Florida corporation, entered into a contract for $30,000 with Sing, Inc., to perform plumbing services in a complex owned by Sing in Virginia. After the work was satisfactorily completed, Sing discovered that Aqua violated Virginia's licensing law by failing to obtain a plumbing license. Virginia's licensing statute was regulatory in nature, serving to protect the public against unskilled and dishonest plumbers. Upon Sing's request, independent appraisals of Aqua's work were performed, which indicated that the complex was benefitted to the extent of $25,000. Sing refuses to pay Aqua. If Aqua brings suit it may recover

    a. $30,000.
    b. $25,000.
    c. Nothing.
    d. An amount sufficient to cover its out of pocket costs.

11 (May 84)

Mix entered into a contract with Small which provided that Small would receive $10,000 if he stole trade secrets from Mix's competition. Small performed his part of the contract by delivering the trade secrets to Mix. Mix refuses to pay Small for his services. Under what theory may Small recover?

    a. Quasi contract, in order to prevent the unjust enrichment of Mix.
    b. Promissory estoppel, since Small has changed his position to his detriment.
    c. None, due to the illegal nature of the contract.
    d. Express contract, since both parties bargained for and exchanged promises in forming the contract.

10 (May 83)

Fairbanks, an author, was approached by Nickle Corporation to ghost-write the history of Nickle for $15,000. Larson, the president of Nickle told Fairbanks the job was his if he would agree to cleverly defame its leading competitor, Mogul Corporation, using sly innuendo and clever distortion of the facts. Fairbanks wrote the history. It turned out that the Mogul passages were neither sly nor clever and Mogul obtained a judgment against Nickle. Fairbanks is seeking to collect the final $5,000 installment on the contract. Nickle refused to pay and seeks to recover the $10,000 it has already paid. In the event of a lawsuit

    a. Fairbanks will recover $5,000.
    b. The court will deny relief to either party.
    c. Nickle will recover $10,000.
    d. Fairbanks will recover in quantum meruit for the value of his services.

2. Covenants Not to Compete

13 (November 88)

Parr is the vice-president of research of Lynx, Inc. When hired, Parr signed an employment contract prohibiting Parr from competing with Lynx during and after employment. While employed, Parr acquired knowledge of many of Lynx's trade secrets. If Parr wishes to compete with Lynx and Lynx refuses to give Parr permission, which of the following statements is correct?

    a. Parr has the right to compete with Lynx upon resigning from Lynx.

    b Parr has the right to compete with Lynx only if fired from Lynx.

    c. In determining whether Parr may compete with Lynx, the court should <u>not</u> consider Parr's ability to obtain other employment.

    d. In determining whether Parr may compete with Lynx, the court should consider, among other factors, whether the agreement is necessary to protect Lynx's legitimate business interests.

2 (November 87)

Blue purchased a travel agency business from Drye. The purchase price included payment for Drye's goodwill. The agreement contained a covenant prohibiting Drye from competing with Blue in the travel agency business. Which of the following statements regarding the covenant is <u>not</u> correct?

    a. The restraint must be <u>no</u> more extensive than is reasonably necessary to protect the goodwill purchased by Blue.

    b. The geographic area to which it applies must be reasonable.

    c. The time period for which it is to be effective must be reasonable.

    d. The value to be assigned to it is the excess of the price paid over the seller's cost of all tangible assets.

18 (May 87)

Wert, an employee of Salam Corp., signed an agreement not to compete with Salam during and after being employed with Salam. Wert is the director of research and has knowledge of many of Salam's trade secrets. If Wert's employment with Salam is terminated and Wert wishes to compete with Salam, which of the following statement is <u>not</u> correct?

    a. The agreement is only enforceable if Wert voluntarily terminates his employment with Salam.

    b. The agreement must be necessary to protect Salam's legitimate interests in order to be enforceable.

    c. The geographic area covered by the agreement must be reasonable in order to be enforceable.

    d. The court will consider Wert's ability to obtain other employment against Salam's right to protect its business.

8 (November 82)

Patton is a partner in an accounting firm. His partnership contract contains a clause which states that should Patton leave the firm, he agrees not to compete with the firm for one year, either as an individual or as a member of another accounting firm, anywhere within the city limits of New York City. The accounting firm does most of its business with clients in the states of New York, Pennsylvania and New Jersey. The clause would be held

    a. Legally enforceable in most states.

    b. An illegal restraint of trade under federal antitrust statutes.

    c. Illegal, thereby invalidating the entire contract.

    d. Unconscionable under the Uniform Commercial Code.

12 (May 79)

Philpot purchased the King Pharmacy from Golden. The contract contained a promise by Golden that he would <u>not</u> engage in the practice of pharmacy for one year from the date of the sale within one mile of the location of King Pharmacy. Six months later Golden opened the Queen Pharmacy within less than a mile of King Pharmacy. Which of the following is a correct statement?

a. Golden has <u>not</u> breached the above covenant since he did <u>not</u> use his own name or the name King in connection with the new pharmacy.
b. The covenant is reasonable and enforceable.
c. The contract is an illegal restraint of trade and illegal under federal antitrust laws.
d. The covenant is contrary to public policy and is illegal and void.

35 (May 77)

A contract effecting an unreasonable restraint of trade is invalid or void as against public policy, but a contract containing a covenant <u>not</u> to compete is valid if it is

a. In writing.
b. Filed with the Attorney General.
c. Reasonable as to area and time.
d. For services.

V. Genuine Assent
A. Fraud (Deceit) and Misrepresentation

16 (May 95)

Which of the following facts must be proven for a plaintiff to prevail in a common law negligent misrepresentation action?

a. The defendant made the misrepresentations with a reckless disregard for the truth.
b. The plaintiff justifiably relied on the misrepresentations.
c. The misrepresentations were in writing.
d. The misrepresentations concerned opinion.

23 (November 93)

To prevail in a common law action for fraud in the inducement, a plaintiff must prove that the

a. Defendant was an expert with regard to the misrepresentations.
b. Defendant made the misrepresentations with knowledge of their falsity and with an intention to deceive.
c. Misrepresentations were in writing.
d. Plaintiff was in a fiduciary relationship with the defendant.

28 (May 92)

Which of the following if intentionally misstated by a seller to a buyer, would be considered a fraudulent inducement to make a contract?

a. Nonexpert opinion.
b. Appraised value.
c. Prediction.
d. Immaterial fact.

21 (November 91)

The intent, or scienter, element necessary to establish a cause of action for fraud will be met if the plaintiff can show that the

a. Defendant made a misrepresentation with a reckless disregard for the truth.
b .Defendant made a false representation of fact.
c. Plaintiff actually relied on the defendant's misrepresentation.
d. Plaintiff justifiably relied on the defendant's misrepresentation.

22 (November 91)

Under the UCC Sales Article, a plaintiff who proves fraud in the formation of a contract may
a. Elect to rescind the contract and need <u>not</u> return the consideration received from the other party.
b. Be entitled to rescind the contract and sue for damages resulting from the fraud.
c. Be entitled to punitive damages provided physical injuries resulted from the fraud.
d. Rescind the contract even if there was <u>no</u> reliance on the fraudulent statement.

21 (May 91)

To prevail in a common law action for innocent misrepresentation, the plaintiff must prove
a. The defendant made the false statements with a reckless disregard for the truth.
b .The misrepresentations were in writing.
c. The misrepresentations concerned material facts.
d. Reliance on the misrepresentations was the only factor inducing the plaintiff to enter into the contract.

21 (May 90)

Steele, Inc. wanted to purchase Kalp's distribution business. On March 15, 1990, Kalp provided Steele with copies of audited financial statements for the period ended December 31, 1989. The financial statements reflected inventory in the amount of $1,200,000. On March 29, 1990, Kalp discovered that the December 31 inventory was overstated by at least $400,000. On April 3, 1990, Steele, relying on the financial statements, purchased all of Kalp's business. On April 29, 1990, Steele discovered the inventory overstatement. Steele sued Kalp for fraud. Which of the following statements is correct?
a. Steele will lose because it should <u>not</u> have relied on the inventory valuation in the financial statements.
b. Steele will lose because Kalp was unaware that the inventory valuation was incorrect at the time the financial statements were provided to Steele.
c. Steele will prevail because Kalp had a duty to disclose the fact that the inventory value was overstated.
d. Steele will prevail but will <u>not</u> be able to sue for damages.

14 (November 89)

Bradford sold a parcel of land to Jones who promptly recorded the deed. Bradford then resold the land to Wallace. In a suit against Bradford by Wallace, recovery will be based on the theory of
a. Bilateral mistake.
b. Ignorance of the facts.
c. Unilateral mistake.
d. Fraud.

15 (November 89)

A party to a contract who seeks to rescind the contract because of that party's reliance on the unintentional but materially false statements of the other party will assert
a. Reformation.
b. Actual fraud.
c. Misrepresentation.
d. Constructive fraud.

30 (May 89)

Which of the following remedies is available to a party who has entered into a contract in reliance upon the other contracting party's innocent misrepresentations as to material facts?

	Compensatory damages	Punitive damages	Rescission
a.	No	No	No
b.	Yes	No	Yes
c.	No	No	Yes
d.	Yes	Yes	No

Contracts

25 (May 88)

To establish a cause of action based on fraud in the inducement, one of the elements the plaintiff must generally prove is that

    a.   It is impossible for the plaintiff to perform the terms of the contract.

    b.   The contract is unconscionable.

    c.   The defendant made a false representation of a material fact.

    d.   There has been a mutual mistake of a material fact by the plaintiff and defendant.

5 (November 87)

Park entered into a contract to sell Reed a parcel of land. Park was aware that Reed was purchasing the land with the intention of building a high-rise office building. Park was also aware of the fact that a subsurface soil condition would prevent such construction. The condition was extremely unusual and not readily discoverable in the course of normal inspections or soil evaluations. Park did not disclose the existence of the condition to Reed, nor did Reed make any inquiry of Park as to the suitability of the land for the intended development. Park's silence as to the soil condition

    a.   Renders the contract voidable at Reed's option.

    b.   Entitles Reed only to money damages.

    c.   Renders the contract void.

    d.   Does <u>not</u> affect the validity of the contract.

Items 19 through 21 are based on the following information:

Bob Meyer sold a parcel of land to Sam Stein for $85,000. Meyer agreed to accept as payment Stein's promissory note in the amount of $60,000 and cash of $25,000. During the course of negotiations Stein misrepresented his financial condition. Furthermore, at the closing Stein made improper threats to Meyer when Meyer indicated he did not want to go through with the deal. As a result of the threats, Meyer did execute and deliver a deed to the land. Meyer wishes to rescind the contract and has commenced an action based upon common law fraud, duress, and innocent misrepresentation. Meyer's complaint contains the following allegations:

    I.   Stein materially misrepresented his financial condition.

    II.   Stein had actual or constructive knowledge that the representations made during the negotiations were false.

    III.   Meyer entered into the contract because of Stein's improper threats.

    IV.   Meyer justifiably relied upon Stein's false representations made during the negotiations.

    V.   Meyer suffered physical harm as a result of the improper threats.

19 (November 86)

Which statements contained in Meyer's complaint are necessary to establish the action for common law fraud?

    a.   I and II only.

    b.   I and IV only.

    c.   II and IV only.

    d.   I, II, and IV.

20 (November 86)

Which statement(s) contained in Meyer's complaint would be necessary to establish the action for duress?

    a.   III only.

    b.   III and IV.

    c.   III and V.

    d.   V only.

21 (November 86)

Which statement(s) contained in Meyer's complaint would be necessary to establish the action for innocent misrepresentation?

a. I and II only.
b. I, II, and IV.
c. I and IV only.
d. IV only.

8 (May 86)

Sardy, a famous football player, was asked to autograph a pad of paper held by Maple. Unknown to Sardy, Maple had carefully concealed a contract for the sale of Sardy's home to Maple in the pad which Sardy signed. If Maple seeks to enforce the contract, Sardy's best defense to have the contract declared void would be

a. Fraud in the inducement.
b. Fraud in the execution.
c. Mistake.
d. Duress.

10 (November 85)

One of the elements necessary to establish fraud is that

a. There was a written misrepresentation of fact.
b. The defendant was in a position of trust and confidence with respect to the plaintiff.
c. The defendant made a false statement with actual or constructive knowledge of its falsity.
d. The plaintiff was induced to enter into a contract as the result of an improper threat by the defendant.

19 (May 85)

The primary distinction between an action based on innocent misrepresentation and an action based on common law fraud is that, in the former, a party need not allege and prove

a. That there has been a false representation.
b. The materiality of the misrepresentation.
c. Reasonable reliance on the misrepresentation.
d. That the party making the misrepresentation had actual or constructive knowledge that it was false.

9 (November 82)

In order to establish a common law action for fraud, the aggrieved party must establish that

a. Although the defendant did not in fact know that his statements were false, he made the false statements with a reckless disregard for the truth.
b. The contract entered into is within the Statute of Frauds.
c. There was a written misrepresentation of fact by the defendant.
d. The plaintiff acted as a reasonably prudent businessman in relying upon the misrepresentation.

10 (November 82)

Which of the following is not required in order for the plaintiff to prevail in an action for innocent misrepresentation?

a. That the misrepresentation was intended to induce reliance.
b. That the misrepresentation amounted to gross negligence.
c. That the plaintiff acted promptly and offered to restore what was received.
d. That the plaintiff relied upon the misrepresentation.

Contracts

9 (November 81)

The element which makes fraud or deceit an intentional tort is
a. The materiality of the misrepresentation.
b. Detrimental reliance.
c. Actual reliance by the aggrieved party upon the misrepresentation.
d. Scienter or knowledge of falsity.

2 (November 79)

In the process of negotiating the sale of his manufacturing business to Grand, Sterling made certain untrue statements which Grand relied upon. Grand was induced to purchase the business for $10,000 more than its true value. Grand is not sure whether he should seek relief based upon misrepresentation or fraud. Which of the following is a correct statement?
a. .If Grand merely wishes to rescind the contract and get his money back, misrepresentation is his best recourse.
b. n order to prevail under the fraud theory, Grand must show that Sterling intended for him to rely on the untrue statements; whereas he need not do so if he bases his action on misrepresentation.
c. Both fraud and misrepresentation required Grand to prove that Sterling knew the statements were false.
d. If Grand chooses fraud as his basis for relief, the Statute of Frauds applies.

34 (May 77)

A contract was created by a false representation of a material fact. The fact was known to be false by the person making the representation, and there was an intent to deceive the party who relied on the representation to his detriment. This contract is voidable on the basis of
a. Undue influence.
b. Fraud.
c. Duress.
d. Negligence.

14 (May 76)

Williams induced Jackson to enter into an employment contract by deliberately telling Jackson certain material facts which Williams knew were not true. If there are no other relevant facts, on what legal grounds is the contract voidable?
a. Undue influence.
b. Fraud.
c. Duress.
d. Unilateral mistake of fact.

1 (May 75)

In the event the purchaser seeks to rescind a contract for the purchase of land because of the seller's misrepresentation (as contrasted with seeking damages for the tort of fraud), the plaintiff (purchaser)
a. Need not show knowledge of falsity on the defendant's part (seller) in order to recover.
b. Need not show reliance upon the misrepresentation on his part in order to recover.
c. Can resort to the Statute of Frauds in order to obtain a rescission on the contract.
d. Will prevail only if there was misrepresentation in the execution which renders the contract void.

4B (May 82)

Ogilvie is a wealthy, prominent citizen of Clarion County. Most of his activities and his properties are located in Vista City, the county seat. Among his holdings are large tracts of farmland located in the outlying parts of Clarion. He has not personally examined large portions of his holdings due to the distance factor and the time it would take. One of his agents told him that 95% of the land was fertile and could be used for general farming. Farber, a recent college graduate who inherited a modest amount of money decided to invest in farmland and raise avocados. He had read certain advertising literature extolling the virtues of avocado farming as an investment. He called upon Ogilvie and discussed the purchase of his land. In the process, Ogilvie praised his land as a great investment for the future. He stated that the land was virtually all splendid farmland and that it would be suitable for avocado growing. Farber entered into a contract of purchase and made a deposit of 10% on the purchase price.

On the eve of the closing, Farber learned of the presence of extensive rock formation at or near the surface of the land. These rock formations made avocado growing virtually impossible but still permit limited use for some other types of farming. These rock formations are partially visible and could have been seen if Farber had examined the property. They cover approximately 25% of the land.

Accordingly, Farber refused to perform the original contract and demanded that the unsuitable 25% of the land be severed from the contract and the price diminished accordingly.

Ogilvie asserted that "a contract is a contract" and that the doctrine of caveat emptor is applicable in the sale of land. Specifically, he stated that he committed no fraud because:

1. Nothing he said was a statement of fact. It was opinion or puffing.
2. His statements were not material since most of the land is okay, and the balance can be used for some types of farming.
3. He had not lied since he had no knowledge of the falsity of his statements.
4. Farber could have and should have inspected and by failing to do so he was negligent and cannot recover.

Farber then commenced legal proceedings against Ogilvie based on fraud.

Required: Answer the following, setting forth reasons for any conclusions stated.

In separate paragraphs, discuss the validity of each of Ogilvie's four assertions that he committed no fraud.

Ogilvie's first asserted defense is not valid. Although there was much in Ogilvie's representations that was opinion and/or praise of the land, there were two statements of fact. One, that the land in question was virtually all splendid farmland and two, that it would be suitable for avocado growing. Neither turned out to be true. Thus, part of the first requirement for establishing fraud--a misstatement of fact--is present.

Second, Ogilvie's misstatement of fact was material to the transaction--25 percent of the land is not usable for avocado growing and has only limited utility as farmland. A substantial decrease in utility and value must be categorized as material.

Third, Ogilvie's statement that he had not lied is no defense. Although he had some basis for making a statement about the quality of the land in general, he had no basis for making the statements he made. Even if he was not aware of the facts and cannot be said to have intentionally misstated the facts, he nevertheless manifested a reckless disregard for the truth. The scienter requirement was satisfied when he made positive statements of fact without any knowledge of their truth or falsity.

The final defense is based upon the reliance requirement necessary to establish fraud. Ogilvie argued that Farber's failure to inspect the land when the opportunity was available results in a bar to recovery. However, although Farber's conduct may be categorized as negligent, such conduct does not normally allow the intentional tort-feasor to escape liability. Furthermore, to allow such a defense to prevail in general would have the potential of causing and fostering fraud, particularly on the unsophisticated investor.

3A (May 78)

A CPA firm was engaged to examine the financial statements of Martin Manufacturing Corporation for the year ending December 31, 1977. The facts revealed that Martin was in need of cash to continue its operations and agreed to sell its common stock investment in a subsidiary through a private placement. The buyers insisted that the proceeds be placed in escrow because of the possibility of a major contingent tax liability that might result from a pending government claim. The payment in escrow was completed in late November 1977. The president of Martin told the audit partner that the proceeds from the sale of the subsidiary's common stock, held in escrow, should be shown on the balance sheet as an unrestricted current account receivable. The president was of the opinion that the government's claim was groundless and that Martin needed an "uncluttered" balance sheet and a "clean" auditor's opinion to obtain additional working capital from lenders. The audit partner agreed with the president and issued an unqualified opinion on the Martin financial statements which did not refer to the contingent liability and did not properly describe the escrow arrangement.

The government's claim proved to be valid, and pursuant to the agreement with the buyers, the purchase price of the subsidiary was reduced by $450,000. This adverse development forced Martin into bankruptcy. The CPA firm is being sued for deceit (fraud) by several of Martin's unpaid creditors who extended credit in reliance upon the CPA firm's unqualified opinion on Martin's financial statements.

Required: Answer the following, setting forth reasons for any conclusions stated.

Based on these facts, can Martin's unpaid creditors recover from the CPA firm?

> Yes. The CPA firm is guilty of a common law <u>deceit</u>, commonly referred to as "fraud." The CPA firm was associated with financial statements that were not in conformity with generally accepted accounting principles because of the failure to disclose the restriction on the cash received, as well as the contingent liability. This association constitutes the commission of an actionable tort (deceit) upon the creditors. The fact that there was no privity of contract between the creditors and the accountants is immaterial in relation to an action based on deceit. Where <u>deceit</u> is involved, the defense of lack of privity is not available. Deceit is an intentional tort, and those who engage in it must bear the burden of their wrongdoing, even though they may not have intended harm to those affected.
>
> The common law elements of deceit in general are--
> 1. A false representation of a material fact made by the defendant.
> 2. Knowledge or belief of falsity, technically described as "scienter."
> 3. An intent that the plaintiff rely upon the false representation.
> 4. Justifiable reliance on the false representation.
> 5. Damage as a result of the reliance.
>
> Clearly, the elements of deceit are present. The only element that needs further elaboration is the "scienter" requirement. About the only defense available to the CPA firm would be that it honestly believed that the government's claim was groundless based upon the president's statement. However, even if this were true, the CPA firm did not have a sufficient basis to express an unqualified opinion that the financial statements were fairly presented. The law includes not only representations made with actual knowledge or belief of falsity but also those made with a reckless disregard for the truth. The fact that the CPA firm did not intend to harm anyone is irrelevant. The CPA firm must be considered liable in light of its training, qualifications, and responsibility and its duty to those who would read, and might act upon, financial statements with which the firm is associated.

B. Mistake

17 (May 95)

A building subcontractor submitted a bid for construction of a portion of a high-rise office building. The bid contained material computational errors. The general contractor accepted the bid with knowledge of the errors. Which of the following statements best represents the subcontractor's liability?
   a. Not liable because the contractor knew of the errors.
   b. Not liable because the errors were a result of gross negligence.
   c. Liable because the errors were unilateral.
   d. Liable because the errors were material.

29 (May 92)

If a buyer accepts an offer containing an immaterial unilateral mistake, the resulting contract will be
   a. Void as a matter of law.
   b. Void at the election of the buyer.
   c. Valid as to both parties.
   d. Voidable at the election of the seller.

23 (May 90)

Paco Corp., a building contractor, offered to sell Preston several pieces of used construction equipment. Preston was engaged in the business of buying and selling equipment. Paco's written offer had been prepared by a secretary who typed the total price as $10,900, rather than $109,000, which was the approximate fair market value of the equipment. Preston, on receipt of the offer, immediately accepted it. Paco learned of the error in the offer and refused to deliver the equipment to Preston unless Preston agreed to pay $109,000. Preston has sued Paco for breach of contract. Which of the following statements is correct?

    a.   Paco will <u>not</u> be liable because there has been a mutual mistake of fact.

    b.   Paco will be able to rescind the contract because Preston should have known that the price was erroneous.

    c.   Preston will prevail because Paco is a merchant.

    d.   The contract between Paco and Preston is void because the price set forth in the offer is substantially less than the equipment's fair market value.

16 (November 88)

On April 6, Apple entered into a signed contract with Bean, by which Apple was to sell Bean an antique automobile having a fair market value of $150,000, for $75,000. Apple believed the auto was worth only $75,000. Unknown to either party the auto had been destroyed by fire on April 4. If Bean sues Apple for breach of contract, Apple's best defense is

    a.   Unconscionability.

    b.   Risk of loss had passed to Bean.

    c.   Lack of adequate consideration.

    d.   Mutual mistake.

22 (May 87)

Sting Corp., a general contractor, obtained bids from several plumbers to install piping. Lite, a licensed plumber, submitted a bid for $60,000 which was $20,000 less than the next lowest bid. Lite made an obvious and substantial arithmetic error in his bid. Sting did not have actual knowledge of Lite's mistake. If Sting accepts Lite's bid, Lite

    a.   Must perform the contract for $60,000 since Sting did <u>not</u> have actual knowledge of the error.

    b.   Must perform the contract for $60,000 unless he can show that Sting caused the error.

    c.   Can avoid liability for refusing to install the piping for $60,000 since Sting should have known of Lite's error.

    d.   Can avoid liability for refusing to install the piping for $60,000 only if the error was <u>not</u> due to his negligence.

12 (May 84)

Pam orally agreed to sell Jack her used car for $400. At the time the contract was entered into, the car had been stolen and its whereabouts were unknown. Neither party was aware of these facts at the time the contract was formed. Jack sues Pam for her failure to deliver the car in accordance with their agreement. Pam's best defense would be that the

    a.   Agreement was unenforceable because it was <u>not</u> evidenced by a writing.

    b.   Risk of loss for the car was on Jack.

    c.   Agreement is unconscionable.

    d.   Parties were under a mutual mistake of a material fact at the time the contract was entered into.

14 (May 83)

Silvers entered into a contract which contains a substantial arithmetical error. Silvers asserts mistake as a defense to his performance. Silvers will prevail

    a.   Only if the mistake was a mutual mistake.

    b.   Only if the error was <u>not</u> due to his negligence.

    c.   If the error was unilateral and the other party knew of it.

    d.   If the contract was written by the other party.

3 (November 81)

Madison advertised for the submission of bids on the construction of a parking lot. Kilroy submitted a bid of $112,000. There were nine other bids. Kilroy's bid was $45,000 less than the next lowest bid. The discrepancy was due to the omission of a $46,000 item on the part of Kilroy's staff. Madison accepted the bid and demands either performance or damages from Kilroy. Kilroy is

    a.   Bound by the acceptance at $112,000.
    b.   Not bound by the acceptance but only if Madison knew of the mistake.
    c.   Not bound by the acceptance if the mistake should have been known by Madison.
    d.   Not bound by the bid submitted because there was <u>no</u> subjective meeting of the minds.

C. Duress and Undue Influence

5 (R00)

If a person is induced to enter into a contract by another person because of the close relationship between the parties, the contract may be voidable under which of the following defenses?
    a.   Fraud in the inducement.
    b.   Unconscionability.
    c.   Undue influence.
    d.   Duress.

20 (May 91)

Johns leased an apartment from Olsen. Shortly before the lease expired, Olsen threatened Johns with eviction and physical harm if Johns did not sign a new lease for twice the old rent. Johns, unable the afford the expense to fight eviction, and in fear of physical harm, signed the new lease. Three months later, Johns moved and sued to void the lease claiming duress. The lease will be held
    a.   Void because of the unreasonable increase in rent.
    b.   Voidable because of Olsen's threat to bring eviction proceedings.
    c.   Void because of Johns' financial condition.
    d.   Voidable because of Olsen's threat of physical harm.

23 (November 90)

For a purchaser of land to avoid a contract with the seller based on duress, it must be shown that the seller's improper threats
    a.   Constituted a crime or tort.
    b.   Would have induced a reasonably prudent person to assent to the contract.
    c.   Actually induced the purchaser to assent to the contract.
    d.   Were made with the intent to influence the purchaser.

28 (May 89)

King had several outstanding unsecured loans with National Bank. In addition, King had a separate loan with National that was secured by a mortgage on a farm owned by King. King was delinquent on the mortgage loan but not on the unsecured loans. National asked King to sign renewal notes for the unsecured loans at substantially higher interest rates. When King refused, National informed King that it would foreclose on the farm's mortgage if King did not sign. King signed but later disaffirmed the new unsecured notes and National sued. King's best defense is
    a.   Undue influence.
    b.   Unconscionability.
    c.   Duress.
    d.   Fraud in the inducement.

4 (November 87)

Sisk contracted to sell Bleu a building for $470,000. If Sisk wishes to avoid the contract based on undue influence, one element that Sisk must prove is that Bleu
    a.   Induced Sisk to sell the building by unfair persuasion.
    b.   Was in a fiduciary relationship with Sisk.
    c.   Misrepresented material facts to Sisk.
    d.   Made improper threats to Sisk.

10 (May 86)

Carter owns a parcel of land. Smith, one of Carter's closest friends and an attorney, has persuaded Carter to sell the land to Smith at a price substantially below fair market value. At the time Carter sold the land he was resting in a nursing home recovering from a serious illness. If Carter desires to set aside the sale, which of the following causes of action is most likely to be successful?

    a.   Duress.
    b.   Undue influence.
    c.   Fraud.
    d.   Misrepresentation.

15 (November 85)

John Tuck entered into a contract with Jack Doe. Doe asserts that he entered into the contract under duress. Which of the following best describes a necessary element of duress?

    a.   There must have been a confidential or fiduciary relationship between Tuck and Doe.
    b.   The contract entered into between Tuck and Doe was unconscionable.
    c.   Doe entered into the contract with Tuck because of Tuck's improper threats.
    d.   Tuck must have intended that Doe be influenced by the improper threats.

23 (May 85)

John Dash, an accountant, entered into a written contract with Kay Reese to perform certain tax services for Reese. Shortly thereafter, Reese was assessed additional taxes and she wanted to appeal the assessment. Reese was required to appeal immediately and the workpapers held by Dash were necessary to appeal. Dash refused to furnish Reese with the workpapers unless he was paid a substantially higher fee than was set forth in the contract. Reese reluctantly agreed in order to meet the filing deadline. The contract as revised is

    a.   Voidable at Reese's option based on undue influence.
    b.   Voidable at Reese's option based on duress.
    c.   Void on the ground of undue influence.
    d.   Void on the ground of duress.

15 (May 83)

Smith, an executive of Apex Corporation, became emotionally involved with Jones. At the urging of Jones, and fearing that Jones would sever their relationship, Smith reluctantly signed a contract which was grossly unfair to Apex. Apex's best basis to rescind the contract would be

    a.   Lack of express authority.
    b.   Duress.
    c.   Undue influence.
    d.   Lack of consideration.

14 (May 82)

Paul filed a $20,000 fire loss claim with the Williams Fire Insurance Company. Dickerson, Williams' adjuster, called Paul on the phone and invited him to come to his hotel room to settle the claim. Upon Paul's entry to the room, Dickerson locked the door and placed the key in his pocket. He then accused Paul of having set the building on fire and of having been involved in several previous suspicious fire claims. Dickerson concluded by telling Paul that unless he signed a release in exchange for $500, he would personally see to it that Paul was prosecuted by the company for arson. Visibly shaken by all this, Paul signed the release. Paul has subsequently repudiated the release. The release is <u>not</u> binding because of

    a.   Fraud.
    b.   Lack of consideration.
    c.   Undue influence.
    d.   Duress.

Contracts

VI. Written Agreements
A. Parol Evidence Rule

18 (May 95)

While the parties have entered into a written contract intended as the final expression of their agreement, which of the following agreements will be admitted into evidence because they are <u>not</u> prohibited by the parol evidence rule?

	Subsequent oral <u>agreements</u>	Prior written <u>agreements</u>
a.	Yes	Yes
b.	Yes	No
c.	No	Yes
d.	No	No

24 (November 93)

Which of the following offers of proof are inadmissible under the parol evidence rule when a written contract is intended as the complete agreement of the parties?

    I. Proof of the existence of a subsequent oral modification of the contract.

    II. Proof of the existence of a prior oral agreement that contradicts the written contract.

a. I only.
b. II only.
c. Both I and II.
d. Neither I nor II.

22 (November 92)

In negotiations with Andrews for the lease of Kemp's warehouse, Kemp orally agreed to pay one-half of the cost of the utilities. The written lease, later prepared by Kemp's attorney, provided that Andrews pay all of the utilities. Andrews failed to carefully ready the lease and signed it. When Kemp demanded that Andrews pay all of the utilities, Andrews refused, claiming that the lease did not accurately reflect the oral agreement. Andrews also learned that Kemp intentionally misrepresented the condition of the structure of warehouse during the negotiations between the parties. Andrews sued to rescind the lease and intends to introduce evidence of the parties' oral agreement about sharing the utilities and the fraudulent statements made by Kemp. The parol evidence rule will prevent the admission of evidence concerning the

	Oral agreement regarding who <u>pays the utilities</u>	Fraudulent statements <u>by Kemp</u>
a.	Yes	Yes
b.	No	Yes
c.	Yes	No
d.	No	No

23 (November 92)

Rogers and Lennon entered into a written computer consulting agreement that required Lennon to provide certain weekly reports to Rogers. The agreement also stated that Lennon would provide the computer equipment necessary to perform the services, and that Rogers' computer would not be used. As the parties were executing the agreement, they orally agreed that Lennon could use Rogers' computer. After executing the agreement, Rogers and Lennon orally agreed that Lennon would report on a monthly, rather than weekly, basis. The parties now disagree on Lennon's right to use Rogers' computer and how often Lennon must report to Rogers. In the event of a lawsuit between the parties, the parol evidence rule will

    a. Not apply to any of the parties' agreements because the consulting agreement did <u>not</u> have to be in writing.

    b. Not prevent Lennon from proving the parties' oral agreement that Lennon could use Rogers' computer.

    c. Not prevent the admission into evidence of testimony regarding Lennon's right to report on a monthly basis.

    d. Not apply to the parties' agreement to allow Lennon to use Rogers' computer because it was contemporaneous with the written agreement.

30 (May 92)

Under the parol evidence rule, oral evidence will be excluded if it relates to

    a. A contemporaneous oral agreement relating to a term in the contract.

    b. Failure of a condition precedent.

    c. Lack of contractual capacity.

    d. A modification made several days after the contract was executed.

23 (November 91)

Two individuals signed a contract that was intended to be their entire agreement. The parol evidence rule will prevent the admission of evidence offered to

    a. Explain the meaning of an ambiguity in the written contract.

    b. Establish that fraud had been committed in the formation of the contract.

    c. Prove the existence of a contemporaneous oral agreement modifying the contract.

    d. Prove the existence of a subsequent oral agreement modifying the contract.

16 (November 89)

Ward is attempting to introduce oral evidence in an action relating to a written contract between Ward and Weaver. Weaver has pleaded the parol evidence rule. Ward will be prohibited from introducing parol evidence if it relates to

    a. A modification made several days after the contract was executed.

    b. A change in the meaning of an unambiguous provision in the contract.

    c. Fraud in the inducement

    d. An obvious error in drafting.

12 (May 86)

Price and White entered into an all-inclusive written contract involving the purchase of a building. Their written agreement contained provisions concerning renovation work to the building to be completed by Price. This aspect of the written contract was modified by a contemporaneous oral agreement between the parties. Price relies upon the parol evidence rule to support his position that the written contract is binding on the parties. Which of the following is correct?

    a. Since the Statute of Frauds was satisfied in respect to the contract for the purchase of the building, the parol evidence rule does <u>not</u> apply.

    b. Since the oral agreement related to the same subject matter as the written contract, the parol evidence rule does <u>not</u> apply.

    c. White will be precluded from introducing into evidence proof of the oral agreement because of the parol evidence rule.

    d. The parol evidence rule does <u>not</u> apply to contemporaneous oral agreements.

25 (May 85)

Where the parties have entered into a written contract intended as the final expression of their agreement, the parol evidence rule generally prevents the admission into evidence of any

a. Other written agreement which is referred to in the contract.
b. Contemporaneous oral agreement which explains an ambiguity in the written contract.
c. Prior oral or written agreement and any contemporaneous oral agreement which contradict the terms of the written contract.
d. Subsequent oral modification of the contract.

23 (November 84)

Fred entered into a written contract with Joe to purchase a car. The written contract was intended to be the final and complete agreement of the parties. Fred is unhappy with the performance of the car and has commenced an action for breach of contract based on an oral representation made at the time the written contract was executed. Fred may introduce evidence of the representation if it

a. Completely modifies the written contract.
b. Contradicts the written agreement.
c. Serves to clarify an ambiguous term in the written contract.
d. Falls within the provisions of the Statute of Frauds.

16 (May 83)

Elrod is attempting to introduce oral evidence in court to explain or modify a written a contract he made with Weaver. Weaver has pleaded the parol evidence rule. In which of the following circumstances will Elrod not be able to introduce the oral evidence?

a. The modification asserted was made several days after the written contract had been executed.
b. The contract indicates that it was intended as the "entire contract" between the parties, and the point is covered in detail.
c. There was a mutual mistake of fact by the parties regarding the subject matter of the contract.
d. The contract contains an obvious ambiguity on the point at issue.

41 (May 83)

With respect to written contracts, the parol evidence rule applies

a. Exclusively to the purchase or sale of goods.
b. To subsequent oral modifications.
c. Only to prior or contemporaneous oral modifications.
d. To modifications by prior written or oral agreements.

49 (November 82)

Filmore purchased a Mirale color television set from Allison Appliances, an authorized dealer, for $499. The written contract contained the usual one-year warranty as to parts and labor as long as the set was returned to the manufacturer or one of its authorized dealers. The contract also contained an effective disclaimer of any express warranty protection, other than that which was included in the contract. It further provided that the contract represented the entire agreement and understanding of the parties. Filmore claims that during the bargaining process Surry, Allison's agent, orally promised to service the set at Filmore's residence if anything went wrong within the year. Allison has offered to repair the set if it is brought to the service department, but denies any liability under the alleged oral express agreement. Which of the following would be the best defense for Allison to rely upon in the event Filmore sues?

a. The Statute of Frauds.
b. The parol evidence rule.
c. The fact that all warranty protection was disclaimed other than the express warranty contained in the contract.
d. The fact that Surry, Allison's agent, did not have express authority to make such a promise.

12 (May 81)

Martin agreed to purchase a two-acre home site from Foxworth. The contract was drafted with great care and meticulously set forth the alleged agreement between the parties. It was signed by both parties. Subsequently, Martin claimed that the contract did not embody all of the agreements that the parties had reached in the course of their negotiations. Foxworth has asserted that the parol evidence rule applies. As such, the rule

    a. Applies to both written and oral agreements relating to the contract made prior to the signing of the contract.

    b. Does not apply to oral agreements made at the time of the signing of the contract.

    c. Applies exclusively to written contracts signed by both parties.

    d. Is not applicable if the Statute of Frauds applies.

4 (November 79)

Marsh and Lennon entered into an all inclusive written contract involving the purchase of a tract of land. Lennon claims that there was a contemporaneous oral agreement between the parties which called for the removal by Marsh of several large rocks on the land. Marsh relies upon the parol evidence rule to avoid having to remove the rocks. Which of the following is correct?

    a. The parol evidence rule does not apply to contemporaneous oral agreements.

    b. Since the Statute of Frauds was satisfied in respect to the contract for the purchase of the land, the parol evidence rule does not apply.

    c. Since the oral agreement does not contradict the terms of the written contract, the oral agreement is valid despite the parol evidence rule.

    d. The parol evidence rule applies and Lennon will be precluded from proving the oral promise in the absence of fraud.

33 (May 77)

The parol evidence rule prohibits contradiction of a written contract through the proof of

    a. A previous oral contract.

    b. A subsequent written contract.

    c. The meaning or clarification of the contract's terms.

    d. A subsequent oral contract.

6 (November 76)

Walker and White entered into a written contract involving the purchase of certain used equipment by White. White claims that there were oral understandings between the parties which are included as a part of the contract. Walker pleads the parol evidence rule. This rule applies to

    a. Subsequent oral modifications of the written contract by the parties.

    b. Additional consistent terms even if the contract was not intended as a complete and exclusive listing of all terms of the agreement.

    c. A contemporaneous oral understanding of the parties which contradicts the terms of a written contract intended as the final expression of the agreement between the parties.

    d. Evidence in support of the oral modification based upon the performance by Walker.

24 (November 74)

The parol evidence rule

    a. Requires that certain types of contracts be in writing.

    b. Precludes the use of oral testimony to show that a written contract was fraudulently obtained.

    c. Eliminates the requirement of consideration if the rule is satisfied.

    d. Does not prohibit a subsequent oral modification of a written contract.

B. Statute of Frauds
1. In General

16 (November 92)

Which of the following statements is true with regard to the Statute of Frauds?
a. All contracts involving consideration of more than $500 must be in writing.
b. The written contract must be signed by all parties.
c. The Statute of Frauds applies to contracts that can be fully performed within one year from the date they are made.
d. The contract terms may be stated in more than one document.

26 (May 92)

Carson agreed orally to repair Ives' rare book for $450. Before the work was started, Ives asked Carson to perform additional repairs to the book and agreed to increase the contract price to $650. After Carson completed the work, Ives refused to pay and Carson sued. Ives' defense was based on the Statute of Frauds. What total amount will Carson recover?
a. $0
b. $200
c. $450
d. $650

15 (May 90)

King sent Foster, a real estate developer, a signed offer to sell a specified parcel of land to Foster for $200,000. King, an engineer, had inherited the land. On the same day that King's letter was received, Foster telephoned King and accepted the offer. Which of the following statements is correct under the Statute of Frauds?
a. No contract was formed because Foster did not sign the offer.
b. No contract was formed because King is not a merchant and, therefore, King's letter is not binding on Foster.
c. A contract was formed, although it would be enforceable only against King.
d. A contract was formed and would be enforceable against both King and Foster because Foster is a merchant.

20 (May 90)

With regard to an agreement for the sale of real estate, the Statute of Frauds
a. Does not require that the agreement be signed by all parties.
b. Does not apply if the value of the real estate is less than $500.
c. Requires that the entire agreement be in a single writing.
d. Requires that the purchase price be fair and adequate in relation to the value of the real estate.

16 (November 86)

Stahl Corp. entered into a written contract to purchase a warehouse from Mehl for $85,000. Thereafter, Mehl received an offer from another purchaser to buy the warehouse for $95,000. As a result, Mehl has refused to transfer the warehouse to Stahl. Stahl has commenced an action for specific performance. Mehl has raised the Statute of Frauds as a defense. In order for Stahl to successfully prevail on the Statute of Frauds issue, it must be shown among other requirements that the contract was signed by
a. Mehl.
b. Stahl.
c. Mehl and Stahl at the same time.
d. Mehl and Stahl with proper notarizations affixed to the contracts.

9 (November 85)

The Statute of Frauds

   a. Requires the formalization of a contract in a single writing.

   b. Applies to all contracts having a consideration valued at $500 or more.

   c. Applies to the sale of real estate but <u>not</u> to any leases.

   d. Does <u>not</u> require that the contract be signed by all parties.

12 (May 83)

The Statute of Frauds

   a. Codified common law rules of fraud.

   b. Requires that formal contracts be in writing and signed by the parties to the contract.

   c. Does <u>not</u> apply if the parties waive its application in the contract.

   d. Sometimes results in a contract being enforceable by only one party.

2. Common Law Statute
a. Contracts Involving Real Property

20 (May 88)

On May 1, Dix and Wilk entered into an oral agreement by which Dix agreed to purchase a small parcel of land from Wilk for $450. Dix paid Wilk $100 as a deposit. The following day, Wilk received another offer to purchase the land for $650, the fair market value. Wilk immediately notified Dix that Wilk would not sell the land for $450. If Dix sues Wilk for specific performance, Dix will

   a. Prevail, because the amount of the contract was less than $500.

   b. Prevail, because there was part performance.

   c. Lose, because the fair market value of the land is over $500.

   d. Lose, because the agreement was <u>not</u> in writing and signed by Wilk.

26 (May 78)

Franklin engaged in extensive negotiations with Harlow in connection with the proposed purchase of Harlow's factory building. Which of the following must Franklin satisfy to establish a binding contract for the purchase of the property in question?

   a. Franklin must obtain an agreement signed by <u>both</u> parties.

   b. Franklin must obtain a formal, detailed, all-inclusive document.

   c. Franklin must pay some earnest money at the time of final agreement.

   d. Franklin must have a writing signed by Harlow which states the essential terms of the understanding.

3 (November 91)

In a signed letter dated March 2, 1991, Stake offered to sell Packer a specific vacant parcel of land for $100,000. Stake had inherited the land, along with several apartment buildings in the immediate vicinity. Packer received the offer on March 4. The offer required acceptance by March 10 and required Packer to have the property surveyed by a licensed surveyor so the exact legal description of the property could be determined.

On March 6, Packer sent Stake a counteroffer of $75,000. All other terms and conditions of the offer were unchanged. Stake received Packer's counteroffer on March 8, and, on that day, telephoned Packer and accepted it. On learning that a survey of the vacant parcel would cost about $1,000, Packer telephoned Stake on March 11 requesting that they share the survey cost equally. During this conversation, Stake agreed to Packer's proposal.

During the course of the negotiations leading up to the March communications between Stake and Packer, Stake expressed concern to Packer that a buyer of the land might build apartment units that would compete with those owned by Stake in the immediate vicinity. Packer assured Stake that Packer intended to use the land for a small shopping center. Because of these assurances, Stake was willing to sell the land to Packer. Contrary to what Packer told Stake, Packer had already contracted conditionally with Rolf for Rolf to build a 48-unit apartment development on the vacant land to be purchased from Stake.

During the last week of March, Stake learned that the land to be sold to Packer had a fair market value of $200,000. Also, Stake learned that Packer intended to build apartments on the land. Because of this information, Stake sued Packer to rescind the real estate contract, alleging that:

- Packer committed fraud in the formation of the contract thereby entitling Stake to rescind the contract.
- Stake's innocent mistake as to the fair market value of the land entitles Stake to rescind the contract.
- The contract was not enforceable against Stake because Stake did not sign Packer's March 6 counteroffer.

Required: State whether Stake's allegations are correct and give the reasons for your conclusions.

Stake's first allegation, that Packer committed fraud in the formation of the contract, is correct and Stake may rescind the contract. Packer had assured Stake that the vacant parcel would be used for a shopping center when, in fact, Packer intended to use the land to construct apartment units that would be in direct competition with those owned by Stake. Stake would not have sold the land to Packer had Packer's real intentions been known. Therefore, the elements of fraud are present:

- A false representation;
- Of a fact;
- That is material;
- Made with knowledge of its falsity and intention to deceive;
- That is justifiably relied on.

Stake's second allegation, that the mistake as to the fair market value of the land entitles Stake to rescind the contract, is incorrect. Generally, mistakes as to adequacy of consideration or fairness of a bargain are insufficient grounds to entitle the aggrieved party to rescind a contract.

Stake's third allegation, that the contract was not enforceable against Stake because Stake did not sign the counteroffer, is correct. The contract between Stake and Packer involves real estate and, therefore, the Statute of Frauds requirements must be satisfied. The Statute of Frauds requires that a writing be signed by the party against whom enforcement is sought. The counteroffer is unenforceable against Stake, because Stake did not sign it. As a result, Stake is not obligated to sell the land to Packer under the terms of the counteroffer.

b. Performance Within One Year

27 (May 89)

Able hired Carr to restore Able's antique car for $800. The terms of their oral agreement provided that Carr was to complete the work within 18 months. Actually, the work could be completed within one year. The agreement is
- a. Unenforceable because it covers services with a value in excess of $500.
- b. Unenforceable because it covers a time period in excess of one year.
- c. Enforceable because personal service contracts are exempt from the Statute of Frauds.
- d. Enforceable because the work could be completed within one year.

13 (May 87)

On April 2, 1986, Streb entered into an oral employment contract with Xeon, Inc. for a term of three years at a salary of $2,000 per week. On June 10, 1986, Streb was terminated by Xeon. On July 10, 1986, Streb commenced an action for breach of the employment contract. Xeon has asserted the Statute of Frauds as a defense. On July 30, 1986, Streb died. Under the circumstances, the employment contract is
- a. Unenforceable since the value of the consideration given exceeds $500.
- b. Unenforceable since it was <u>not</u> in writing and signed by Xeon.
- c. Enforceable since it was possible that the contract could have been performed within one year from the making of the contract.
- d. Enforceable since Streb's death occurred within one year from the making of the contract.

6 (May 86)

On April 3, 1985, Fier entered into an oral employment contract with Reich, whereby Reich was hired as a sales manager for a term of one year. Although Fier and Reich did not agree to a definite starting date, Fier indicated that Reich could begin employment that same day or any time prior to April 15, 1985. Reich began working on April 10. On June 15, 1985, Reich was fired without cause. If Reich sues for breach of the employment contract and Fier asserts the Statute of Frauds as a defense, Reich will

  a. Prevail since the contract was capable of being performed within one year.
  b. .Prevail since the UCC Statute of Frauds applies.
  c. Lose since the contract was <u>not</u> in writing and signed by Fier.
  d. Lose since Reich did <u>not</u> begin employment until April 10.

33 (May 81)

Duval Manufacturing Industries, Inc. orally engaged Harris as one of its district sales managers for an 18-month period commencing April 1, 1980. Harris commenced work on that date and performed his duties in a highly competent manner for several months. On October 1, 1980, the company gave Harris a notice of termination as of November 1, 1980, citing a downturn in the market for its products. Harris sues seeking either specific performance or damages for breach of contract. Duval pleads the Statute of Frauds and/or a justified dismissal due to the economic situation. What is the probable outcome of the lawsuit?

  a. Harris will prevail because he has partially performed under the terms of the contract.
  b. Harris will lose because his termination was caused by economic factors beyond Duval's control.
  c. Harris will lose because such a contract must be in writing and signed by a proper agent of Duval.
  d. Harris will prevail because the Statute of Frauds does <u>not</u> apply to contracts such as his.

25 (November 80)

Wallers and Company has decided to expand the scope of its business. In this connection, it contemplates engaging several agents. Which of the following agency relationships is within the Statute of Frauds and thus should be contained in a signed writing?

  a. An irrevocable agency.
  b. A sales agency where the agent normally will sell goods which have a value in excess of $500.
  c. An agency for the forthcoming calendar year which is entered into in mid-December of the prior year.
  d. An agency which is of indefinite duration but which is terminable upon one month's notice.

13 (May 78)

Potter orally engaged Arthur as a salesman on April 5, 1978, for exactly one year commencing on May 1, 1978. Which of the following is correct insofar as the parties are concerned?

  a. If Arthur refuses to perform and takes another job on April 14, 1978, he will <u>not</u> be liable if he pleads the Statute of Frauds.
  b. The contract need <u>not</u> be in writing since its duration is exactly one year.
  c. Potter may obtain the remedy of specific performance if Arthur refuses to perform.
  d. The parol evidence rule applies.

4 (May 93)

West Corp. is involved in the following disputes:

  • On September 16, West's president orally offered to hire Dodd Consultants, Inc. to do computer consulting for West. The offer provided for a three-year contract at $5,000 per month. West agreed that Dodd could have until September 30 to decide whether to accept the offer. If Dodd chose to accept the offer, its acceptance would have to be received by September 30.

    On September 27, Dodd went West a letter accepting the offer. West received the letter on October 2. On September 28, West's president decided that West's accounting staff could handle West's computer problems and notified Dodd by telephone that the offer was withdrawn. Dodd argued that West had no right to revoke its offer, and that Dodd had already accepted the offer by mail.

Dodd claims that it has a binding contract with West because:
- West's offer could not be revoked before September 30.
- Dodd's acceptance was effective on September 27, when the letter accepting the offer was mailed.

West's president claims that if an agreement exists that agreement would not be enforceable against West because of the Statute of Frauds requirement that the contract be in writing.

- On March 1, West signed a lease with Abco Real Estate, Inc. for warehouse space. The lease required that West repair and maintain the warehouse. On April 14, West orally asked Abco to paint the warehouse. Despite the lease provision requiring West to repair and maintain the warehouse, Abco agreed to do so by April 30. On April 29, Abco advised West that Abco had decided not to paint the warehouse. West demanded that Abco paint the warehouse under the April 14 agreement. Abco refused and has taken the following positions:
  - Abco's April 14 agreement to paint the warehouse is not binding on Abco because it was a modification of an existing contract.
  - Because the April 14 agreement was oral and the March 1 lease was in writing, West would not be allowed to introduce evidence in any litigation relating to the April 14 oral agreement.

Required:
- a.   State whether Dodd's claims are correct and give the reasons for your conclusions.
- b.   State whether West's president's claim is correct and give the reasons for your conclusion.
- c.   State whether Abco's positions are correct and give the reasons for your conclusions.

a. Dodd's claim, that West's offer could not be revoked before September 30, is incorrect. Offers can be revoked at any time before acceptance unless the offeror receives consideration to keep the offer open. West did not receive any consideration from Dodd in exchange for its promise to keep the offer open until September 30. Therefore, West effectively revoked its offer during the September 28 telephone conversation.

Dodd's claim, that the September 27 letter accepting West's offer was effective when mailed to West, is incorrect. The general rule is that an acceptance is effective when dispatched if the acceptance is made using a reasonable mode of communication. In this case, the offer required that the acceptance be received by West to be effective. Therefore, Dodd's acceptance could not have been effective until after the offer expired, because it was received after September 30.

b. West's claim, that any agreement that existed between West and Dodd would not be enforceable against West because of the Statute of Frauds, is correct. The term of the agreement was for three years. The Statute of Frauds requires that contracts that cannot be performed within one year from the date made must be in writing. Because this was an oral contract for a period of three years, it would not be enforceable under the Statute of frauds. Dodd's attempted acceptance of the offer would not be such a writing because it was not signed by West and could not be enforceable against West.

c. Abco's first position, that the oral April 14 agreement regarding the painting of the warehouse is not binding, is correct. This agreement was intended to modify the existing lease between the parties. Under common law, agreements modifying existing contracts require consideration to be binding. Abco did not receive any consideration in exchange for its promise to paint the warehouse; therefore, the agreement is not enforceable against Abco.

Abco's second position, that evidence of the April 14 oral agreement could not be admitted into evidence, is incorrect. The parol evidence rule allows the admission of proof of a later oral agreement that modifies an existing written contract.

c.   Suretyship Provision

17 (November 92)
On June 1, 1992, Decker orally guaranteed the payment of a $5,000 note Decker's cousin owed Baker. Decker's agreement with Baker provided that Decker's guaranty would terminate in 18 months. On June 3, 1992, Baker wrote Decker confirming Decker's guaranty. Decker did not object to the confirmation. On August 23,

1992, Decker's cousin defaulted on the note and Baker demanded that Decker honor the guaranty. Decker refused. Which of the following statements is correct?

    a.   Decker is liable under the oral guaranty because Decker did <u>not</u> object to Baker's June 3 letter.

    b.   Decker is <u>not</u> liable under the oral guaranty because it expired more than one year after June 1.

    c.   Decker is liable under the oral guaranty because Baker demanded payment within one year of the date the guaranty was given.

    d.   Decker is <u>not</u> liable under the oral guaranty because Decker's promise was <u>not</u> in writing.

12 (November 89)

    The Statute of Frauds

    a.   Prevents the use of oral evidence to contradict the terms of a written contract.

    b.   Applies to all contracts having consideration valued at $500 or more.

    c.   Requires the independent promise to pay the debt of another to be in writing.

    d.   Applies to all real estate leases.

14 (November 88)

    Payne borrowed $500 from Onest Bank. At the time the loan was made to Payne, Gem orally agreed with Onest that Gem would repay the loan if Payne failed to do so. Gem received no personal benefit as a result of the loan to Payne. Under the circumstances,

    a.   Gem is secondarily liable to repay the loan.

    b.   Both Gem and Payne are primarily liable to repay the loan.

    c.   Gem is free from liability concerning the loan.

    d.   Gem is primarily liable to repay the loan.

d. Effect of Full Performance, Rescission, and Modification

18 (May 90)

    Sand orally promised Frost a $10,000 bonus, in addition to a monthly salary, if Frost would work two years for Sand. If Frost works for the two years, will the Statute of Frauds prevent Frost from collecting the bonus?

    a.   No, because Frost fully performed.

    b.   No, because the contract did <u>not</u> involve an interest in real estate.

    c.   Yes, because the contract could <u>not</u> be performed within one year.

    d.   Yes, because the monthly salary was the consideration for the contract.

21 (November 84)

    An oral contract to sell land will be enforceable if the

    a.   Contract is capable of full performance within one year.

    b.   Total sales price is less than $500.

    c.   Buyer has made a part payment.

    d.   Parties have fully performed the contract.

3. UCC Statute of Frauds
a. § 2-201 Generally--Goods

9 (R00)

    EG Door Co., a manufacturer of custom exterior doors, verbally contracted with Art Contractors to design and build a $2,000 custom door for a house that Art was restoring. After EG had completed substantial work on the door, Art advised EG that the house had been destroyed by fire and Art was canceling the contract. EG finished the door and shipped it to Art. Art refused to accept delivery. Art contends that the contract cannot be enforced because it violated the Statute of Frauds by not being in writing. Under the Sales Article of the UCC, is Art's contention correct?

a. Yes, because the contract was not in writing.

b. Yes, because the contract cannot be fully performed due to the fire.

c. No, because the goods were specially manufactured for Art and cannot be resold in EG's regular course of business.

d. No, because the cancellation of the contract was not made in writing.

46 (May 94)

Webstar Corp. orally agreed to sell Northco, Inc. a computer for $20,000. Northco sent a signed purchase order to Webstar confirming the agreement. Webstar received the purchase order and did not respond. Webstar refused to deliver the computer to Northco, claiming that the purchase order did not satisfy the UCC Statute of Frauds because it was not signed by Webstar. Northco sells computers to the general public and Webstar is a computer wholesaler. Under the UCC Sales Article, Webstar's position is

a. Incorrect because it failed to object to the Northco's purchase order.

b. Incorrect because only the buyer in a sale-of-goods transaction must sign the contract.

c. Correct because it was the party against whom enforcement of the contract is being sought.

d. Correct because the purchase price of the computer exceeded $500.

17 (May 91)

Bond and Spear orally agreed that Bond would buy a car from Spear for $475. Bond paid Spear a $100 deposit. The next day, Spear received an offer of $575, the car's fair market value. Spear immediately notified Bond that Spear would not sell the car to Bond and returned Bond's $100. If Bond sues Spear and Spear defends on the basis of the Statute of Frauds, Bond will probably

a. Lose, because the agreement was for less than the fair market value of the car.

b. Win, because the agreement was for less than $500.

c. Lose, because the agreement was not in writing and signed by Spear.

d. Win, because Bond paid a deposit.

40 (May 90)

To satisfy the UCC Statute of Frauds regarding the sale of goods, which of the following must generally be in writing?

a. Designation of the parties as buyer and seller.

b. Delivery terms.

c. Quantity of the goods.

d. Warranties to be made.

29 (May 89)

To satisfy the UCC Statute of Frauds, a written agreement for the sale of goods must

a. Contain payment terms.

b. Be signed by both buyer and seller.

c. Indicate that a contract for sale has been made.

d. Refer to the time and place of delivery.

47 (November 86)

Greed Co. telephoned Stieb Co. and ordered 30 tables at $100 each. Greed agreed to pay 15% immediately and the balance within thirty days after receipt of the entire shipment. Greed forwarded a check for $450 and Stieb shipped 15 tables the next day, intending to ship the balance by the end of the week. Greed decided that the contract was a bad bargain and repudiated it, asserting the Statute of Frauds. Stieb sued Greed. Which of the following will allow Stieb to enforce the contract in its entirety despite the Statute of Frauds?

a. Stieb shipped 15 tables.

b. Greed paid 15% down.

c. The contract is not within the requirements of the Statute of Frauds.

d. Greed admitted in court that it made the contract in question.

46 (November 85)
Which of the following terms generally must be included in a writing which would otherwise satisfy the UCC Statute of Frauds regarding the sale of goods?
a. The warranties to be granted.
b. The price of the goods.
c. The designation of the parties as buyer and seller.
d. The quantity of the goods.

13 (May 83)
Certain oral contracts fall outside the Statute of Frauds. An example would be a contract between
a. A creditor and a friend of the debtor, providing for the friend's guaranty of the debt in exchange for the creditor's binding extension of time for payment of the debt.
b. A landlord and a tenant for the lease of land for ten years.
c. A school board and a teacher entered into on January 1, for nine months of service to begin on September 1.
d. A retail seller of television sets and a buyer for the sale of a TV set for $399 C.O.D.

8 (November 79)
A salesman for A & C Company called upon the purchasing agent for Major Enterprises, Inc. and offered to sell Major 1,500 screwdriver sets at $1.60 each. Major's purchasing agent accepted and the following day sent A & C a purchase order which bore Major's name and address at the top and also had the purchasing agent's name and title stamped at the bottom with his initials. The purchase order recited the agreement reached orally the prior day. Subsequently, Major decided it did not want the screwdriver sets since it was overstocked in that item. Major thereupon repudiated the contract and asserted the Statute of Frauds as a defense. Under the circumstances, which of the following is correct?
a. The Statute of Frauds does not apply to this transaction since performance is to be completed within one year from the date of the making of the contract.
b. Major will lose but only if its purchasing agent's authority to make the contract was in writing.
c. The fact that an authorized agent of A & C did not sign the purchase order prevent its use by A & C against Major to satisfy the Statute of Frauds.
d. The purchase order is sufficient to satisfy the Statute of Frauds even though the purchasing agent never signed it in full.

11 (November 79)
Which of the following omissions will prevent a writing from satisfying the Statute of Frauds with respect to the sale of goods?
a. It does not indicate that a sale has occurred.
b. It is not signed by both the buyer and seller.
c. The time and place of delivery are not indicated.
d. The payment terms are not contained in the writing.

5 (November 76)
Under what conditions will the Statute of Frauds be a defense under the Uniform Commercial Code where there is a contract for the sale of goods worth more than $500?
a. The seller has completed goods specially manufactured for the buyer which are not salable in the ordinary course of the seller's business.
b. The written memorandum omits several important terms but states the quantity, and it is signed by the party to be charged.
c. The party asserting the Statute of Frauds admits under oath to having made the contract.
d. The goods in question are fungible and actively traded by merchants in the business community.

3 (November 75)
An oral contract for the sale of goods for a price in excess of $500 is enforceable by the seller if
a. The goods are generally suitable for sale to others in the ordinary course of the seller's business.
b. The buyer admits in court that the contract was made.
c. Payment has <u>not</u> yet been made by the buyer.
d. The goods have been received but <u>not</u> accepted by the buyer.

41 (May 75)
Visco Sales, Inc. sent Nails Manufacturing Corporation the following telegram:

We need 2,000 two-pound boxes of your best grade two-inch roofing nails. Ship at once.

Visco Sales, S. Peters,
V.P. of Purchasing

a. The telegram is too indefinite and uncertain to constitute an offer.
b. Acceptance by Nails will <u>not</u> take place until receipt of the shipment by Visco.
c. The telegram is <u>not</u> an offer, but a mere invitation to do business.
d. The telegram constitutes a signed writing which would be enforceable against Visco under the Statute of Frauds, assuming the nails would cost $500 or more.

b. Modifications--§ 2-209(3)

21 (May 88)
Baker and Able signed a contract which required Able to purchase 600 books from Baker at 90¢ per book. Subsequently, Able, in good faith, requested that the price of the books be reduced to 80¢ per book. Baker orally agreed to reduce the price to 80¢. Under the circumstances, the oral agreement is
a. Unenforceable, because Able failed to give consideration, but proof of it will be otherwise admissible into evidence.
b. Unenforceable, due to the Statute of Frauds, and proof of it will be inadmissible into evidence.
c. Enforceable, but proof of it will be inadmissible into evidence.
d. Enforceable, and proof of it will be admissible into evidence.

40 (November 87)
An oral agreement concerning the sale of goods entered into without consideration is binding if the agreement
a. Is a firm offer made by a merchant who promises to hold the offer open for 30 days.
b. Is a waiver of the non-breaching party's rights arising out of a breach of the contract.
c. Contradicts the terms of a subsequent written contract that is intended as the complete and exclusive agreement of the parties.
d. Modifies the price in an existing, enforceable contract from $525 to $475.

55 (November 84)
Where an oral agreement pertaining to goods is entered into without any consideration, the agreement will be binding if it
a. Relates to a requirements contract.
b. Is a firm offer made by a merchant promising to hold the offer open for two months.
c. Modifies the price on an existing sales contract from $600 to $450.
d. Disclaims the implied warranty of fitness for a particular purpose.

50 (November 83)

Which of the following requirements must be met for modification of a sales contract under the Uniform Commercial Code?

    a.   The modification must satisfy the Statute of Frauds if the contract as modified is within its provisions.

    b.   There must be consideration present if the contract is between merchants.

    c.   The parol evidence rule applies and thus a writing is required.

    d.   There must be a writing if the original sales contract is in writing.

27 (May 80)

Ford bought a used typewriter for $625 from Jem Typewriters. The contract provided that the typewriter was sold "with all faults, as is, and at the buyer's risk." The typewriter broke down within a month. Ford took it back to Jem, and after prolonged arguing and negotiating, Jem orally agreed to reduce the price by $50 and refund that amount. Jem has reconsidered his rights and duties and decided <u>not</u> to refund the money. Under the circumstances, which of the following is correct?

    a.   The disclaimer of the implied warranties of merchantability and fitness is invalid.

    b.   The agreement to reduce the price is valid and binding.

    c.   Jem's promise is unenforceable since Ford gave <u>no</u> new consideration.

    d.   Since the contract as modified is subject to the Statute of Frauds, the modification must be in writing.

33 (May 79)

Strattford Theaters made a contract with Avon, Inc. for the purchase of $450 worth of theater supplies. Delivery was to take place in one month. One week after accepting the order, the price of materials and labor increased sharply. In fact, to break even on the contract, Avon would have to charge an additional $600. Avon phoned Strattford and informed them of the situation. Strattford was sympathetic and said they were sorry to hear about the situation but that the best they would be willing to do was split the rise in price with Avon. Avon accepted the modification on Strattford's terms. As a result of the above modification, which of the following is correct?

    a.   Avon's continuing to perform the contract after informing Strattford of the price difficulty constitutes consideration for the modification of the price.

    b.   The oral modification is <u>not</u> effective since there was <u>not</u> consideration.

    c.   The Statute of Frauds applies to the contract as modified.

    d.   The contract contained an implied promise that it was subject to price rises.

38 (May 78)

Haworth Discount Stores mailed its order to Eagle Recordings, Inc. for 100 eight-track cassette recordings of "Swan Songs" by the Paginations at $5.50 per cassette. Eagle promptly wired its acceptance, delivery to take place within two weeks from date of Haworth's order and terms of net 30 days. Before delivery was made by Eagle, the retail price of this recording by the Paginations fell to $4.95. Haworth informed Eagle of this and pleaded with Eagle, "because we have been good customers, give us a break by either reducing the price of $4.95 so we can break even or by allowing us to cancel the order." Eagle's sales manager called Haworth the next day and informed them that the price would be $4.95 per cassette, <u>not</u> the price that appeared on the original invoice. Which of the following is correct insofar as the modification of the initial Haworth-Eagle contract?

    a.   The modification is invalid due to lack of consideration.

    b.   The modification is voidable by Eagle at any time prior to shipment of the 100 cassettes.

    c.   The modification must be written and signed by the parties to be valid if there is <u>no</u> consideration given for the reduced price.

    d.   The modification need <u>not</u> satisfy the Statute of Frauds.

43 (May 77)

On July 14, 1976, Seeley Corp. entered into a written agreement to sell to Boone Corp. 1,200 cartons of certain goods at $.40 per carton, delivery within 30 days. The agreement contained no other terms. On July 15, 1976, Boone and Seeley orally agreed to modify their July 14 agreement so that the new quantity specified was 1,500 cartons, same price and delivery terms. What is the status of this modification?

    a. Enforceable.
    b. Unenforceable under the Statute of Frauds.
    c. Unenforceable for lack of consideration.
    d. Unenforceable because the change is substantial.

2 (November 87)

On May 1, Starr Corp., a manufacturer and supplier of computers, mailed a proposed contract to Magic, Inc., offering to sell 20 items of specified computer equipment for $18,000. Magic was engaged in the business of selling computers to the public. Magic accepted Starr's offer by executing and returning the contract to Starr. Starr failed to sign the contract.

On May 15, Starr advised Magic by telephone that, due to certain market conditions, the price of computer parts had increased. Therefore, in order to avoid a loss on the sale to Magic, Starr requested an increase in the sales price to $20,000, which was orally agreed to by Magic. On May 17, Starr sent to Magic a signed letter acknowledging this agreement. Magic did not respond to the letter.

On September 15, Starr notified Magic that the equipment was ready for delivery. Due to substantial changes in computer technology subsequent to May 15, Magic indicated that it no longer wanted the equipment and that it would not pay for it. Starr was unable to resell the computer equipment for any price despite its reasonable efforts to do so. Therefore, Starr commenced a breach of contract action against Magic. Magic asserted the following defenses:

- The May 1 written contract between Starr and Magic is not enforceable because of the Statute of Frauds.
- Even if the May 1 contract is enforceable, the May 15 oral agreement to change the price of the equipment is not enforceable because the agreement lacked consideration and failed to satisfy the Statute of Frauds.
- In any event, Starr is not entitled to recover the full sales price because the equipment is still in Starr's possession.

Required: Discuss Magic's assertions, indicating whether each is correct or incorrect and setting forth the reasons for any conclusions stated.

Magic's first assertion, that the original contract between Starr and itself is not enforceable because of the Statute of Frauds, is incorrect. The sale of computer equipment is a transaction in goods and thus is governed by the UCC Sales Article. This Article provides that a contract for the sale of goods for the price of $500 or more is not enforceable unless there is some writing sufficient to indicate that a contract for sale has been made between the parties which is signed by the party against whom enforcement is sought. Since the sales price is $18,000, the Statute of Frauds applies. Magic's execution of the written contract will satisfy the Statute of Frauds since Magic is the party against whom enforcement of the contract is being sought.

Magic's second assertion, that the oral agreement to change the price of the equipment is not enforceable because the agreement lacked consideration and failed to satisfy the Statute of Frauds, is incorrect. Under the UCC Sales Article, an agreement to modify a contract for the sale of goods needs no consideration to be binding. However, the modification must meet the test of good faith, which is defined under the UCC as "honesty in fact in the conduct or transaction concerned and the observance of reasonable commercial standards of fair dealing in the trade." Based upon the facts, it appears that a shift in the market that will result in Starr bearing a loss on the sale to Magic will satisfy the requirement of good faith. In addition, the agreement modifying the sales price must meet the requirements of the Statute of Frauds if the contract, as modified, is within its provisions. Under the facts, the contract as modified by Magic and Starr, falls within the provisions of the Statute of Frauds and thus the Statute of Frauds must be satisfied. Magic's oral agreement to the modification is not sufficient to satisfy the Statute of Frauds. However, the Statute of Frauds will be satisfied if: both parties are merchants; a writing in confirmation of the agreement which is sufficient against the sender is received; the recipient receives the writing within a reasonable time; the recipient has reason to know the contents of the writing; and, the recipient fails to give written notice of objection to the contents of the writing within ten days after it is received. As the facts clearly indicate, the mailing of the signed letter by Starr to Magic on May 17 satisfied the aforementioned requirements and thus the modification agreement is enforceable.

Magic's third assertion that Starr is not entitled to recover the full sales price for the equipment is incorrect. The UCC provides that a seller may recover the price of goods identified to a contract and in the possession of the seller if the seller is unable after reasonable effort to resell them at a reasonable price or the circumstances reasonably indicate that such effort will be unavailing. Under the facts of the case at hand, Starr is entitled to recover the full sales price of $20,000 because the equipment could not be resold for any price.

2 (May 85)

Reed, a manufacturer, entered into an oral contract with Rocco, a retailer, to deliver 10 leather jackets to Rocco's place of business within 15 days. The total sales price was $450. Prior to the delivery of the jackets the market price of leather increased drastically. Reed knew Rocco needed the jackets within the 15 days and telephoned Rocco stating that he would be unable to deliver the jackets unless the sales price was increased by $100. Rocco agreed to the new price. The following morning Reed sent Rocco a signed letter indicating the new sales price and that the sale was for 10 leather jackets. Rocco received the letter the next day and has taken no further action.

Reed entered into an oral contract to purchase Smith's vacant building for $50,000, giving $5,000 as a deposit. The parties intended to reduce their agreement to writing at a later date. Pursuant to the oral contract, Reed took possession of the building with Smith's permission and made permanent and substantial improvements. Due to a rise in the price of similar real estate, Smith serves notice on Reed to vacate the premises, contending that the sales contract was unenforceable.

Required: Answer the following, setting forth reasons for any conclusions stated.
    a.   Discuss whether the original sales contract and the subsequent change in price by Reed are enforceable under the UCC Sales Article.
    b.   May Smith require Reed to vacate the building?

    a.   The sale of leather jackets is governed by the Uniform Commercial Code Sales Article which applies to transactions in goods. Under the Uniform Commercial Code, an oral contract for the sale of goods under $500 does not fall within the provisions of the Statute of Frauds. Thus, the contract between Reed and Rocco is enforceable by either party without the necessity of a signed writing since the sales price is $450. The UCC provides that an agreement to modify a contract for the sale of goods needs no consideration to be binding. However, the modification made must meet the test of good faith. The modification must also satisfy the requirements of the Statute of Frauds if the contract, as modified, falls within its provisions. Whether Reed acted in good faith is determined by an examination of the facts. Here, the shift in the market may satisfy the requirement of good faith if Reed can show that he would have suffered a loss had he sold the jackets at $450. However, if Reed refused to sell the jackets at $450 merely to derive a greater profit, with knowledge that Rocco was in immediate need of the goods, the modification may not meet the test of good faith.

Since the sales price increased from $450 to $550, the contract must satisfy the Statute of Frauds in order to be enforceable. The UCC Statute of Frauds may be satisfied by a confirmation if
- Both parties are merchants.
- It is in writing.
- The writing is signed by the sender.
- The writing states the quantity.
- The writing is received by the recipient within a reasonable time.
- The recipient has reason to know the contents of the writing.
- The recipient fails to give written notice of objection to its contents within ten days after receipt.

As the facts clearly indicate, the mailing of the signed letter by Reed to Rocco the day after the contract was orally modified, coupled with Rocco's failure to object within ten days after receipt will satisfy the requirements of the Statute of Frauds.

    b.   No. As a general rule, a contract for the sale of real property must be supported by a written memo signed by the party to be charged. However, an oral contract to sell real property may be removed from the Statute of Frauds where there has been part performance and reasonable reliance on the oral contract. The part payment of the sales price by Reed, in addition to Reed's taking possession of the building with Smith's consent and making permanent and substantial improvements, generally will prevent Smith from setting the contract aside or requiring Reed to vacate the building.

5A (May 76)

Your client, Super Fashion Frocks, Inc., agreed in writing to purchase $520 worth of coat hangers from Display Distributors, Inc., with payment terms of net/30 after delivery. Delivery was to be made within five days from the signing of the contract. Two days prior to the due date for delivery, Display Distributors called and offered a flat $25 discount if payment were made upon delivery instead of the original net/30 terms. Super Fashion Frocks agreed and tendered its check for $495 upon delivery. Display Distributors cashed the check and now seeks to enforce the original contract calling for payment of $520 (i.e., seeks to recover $25 from Super Fashion). It bases its claim upon the following arguments:

1. The Statute of Frauds applies to the contract modification.
2. The Parol Evidence Rule prohibits the introduction of oral evidence modifying the terms of a written agreement.
3. There was no consideration given for Display's promise to take a lesser amount.

Required: Discuss the validity of each argument.

1. The Statute of Frauds is not applicable because the dollar amount is less than $500 after the modification. Since the contract as modified is not included under the Statute of Frauds, the statute has no impact upon the contractual adjustment made by the parties. The Uniform Commercial Code provides that if a modification is agreed upon, it need not be in writing as long as the contract is not within the Statute of Frauds.

2. The Parol Evidence Rule has no application of the facts stated. It prohibits the contradiction of the written terms of a contract by any prior oral agreement or a contemporaneous oral agreement. It is not applicable to a subsequent oral modification of a written contract.

3. Under the Uniform Commercial Code an agreement to modify a contract for the sale of goods requires no consideration. But even if consideration were necessary, Super Fashions provided consideration by paying earlier than required by the terms of the original agreement. Thus, Super Fashion prevails under either rule.

c. Other UCC Statutes of Frauds

42 (May 78)

Hendrickson is a well-known author of popular detective stories, plays, and film scripts for which he obtained copyrights. As a result of some major declines in the values of certain risk ventures to which he was financially committed, he found himself hard-pressed for cash. Consequently, he decided to assign one of his copyrights on an earlier play to Eureka Enterprises. After protracted and often heated negotiations, Hendrickson and Eureka arrived at an oral agreement whereby Hendrickson would transfer to Eureka the copyright for $4,800. Prior to the actual transfer, one of Hendrickson's investments paid off spectacularly and he refused to transfer the copyright to Eureka, alleging the contract to be null and void or at least voidable for several reasons. In light of the circumstances, which of the following is correct?

a. If Hendrickson had received a memorandum of the agreement which would bind Eureka and has <u>not</u> objected to it, he is bound.
b. Unless Eureka gave Hendrickson some earnest money at the time of the oral understanding, the contract is invalid.
c. The contract is voidable by Hendrickson if he pleads the Statute of Frauds.
d. The contract is null and void in that Hendrickson was under extreme mental stress and financial hardship at the time he made the agreement.

(NOTE: This question was omitted by the examiners because it has no correct answer; c would be correct if amount was over $5,000. See UCC § 1-206.)

VII. Third Parties
A. Assignment and Delegation
1. In General

1 (R98)

This question consists of 10 items. Select the **best** answer for each item. **Answer all items.** Your grade will be based on the total number of correct answers.

On January 15, East Corp. orally offered to hire Bean, CPA, to perform management consulting services for East and its subsidiaries. The offer provided for a three-year contract at $10,000 per month. On January 20, East sent Bean a signed memorandum stating the terms of the offer. The memorandum also included a payment clause that hadn't been discussed and the provision that Bean's acceptance of the offer would not be effective unless it was received by East on or before January 25. Bean received the memorandum on January 21, signed it, and mailed it back to East the same day. East received it on January 24. On January 23, East wrote to Bean revoking the offer. Bean received the revocation on January 25.

On March 1, East Corp. orally engaged Snow Consultants to install a corporate local area network system (LAN) for East's financial operations. The engagement was to last until the following February 15 and East would pay Snow $5,000 twice a month. On March 15, East offered Snow $1,000 per month to assist in the design of East's Internet homepage. Snow accepted East's offer. On April 1, citing excess work, Snow advised East that Snow would not assist with the design of the homepage. On April 5, East accepted Snow's withdrawal from the Internet homepage design project. On April 15, Snow notified East that Snow had assigned the fees due Snow on the LAN installation engagement to Band Computer Consultants. On April 30, East notified Snow that the LAN installation agreement was canceled.

Required: Items 1 through 5 are based on the transaction between East Corp. and Bean. An answer may be selected once, more than once, or not at all.

1. What was the effect of the event(s) that took place on January 20?
2. What was the effect of the event(s) that took place on January 21?
3. What was the effect of the event(s) that took place on January 23?
4. What was the effect of the event(s) that took place on January 24?
5. What was the effect of the event(s) that took place on January 25?

List I	
A	Acceptance of a counteroffer.
B	Acceptance of an offer governed by the mailbox rule.
C	Attempted acceptance of an offer.
D	Attempted revocation of an offer.
E	Formation of an enforceable contract.
F	Formation of a contract enforceable only against East.
G	Invalid revocation because of prior acceptance of an offer.
H	Offer revoked by sending a revocation letter.
I	Submission of a counteroffer.
J	Submission of a written offer.

Items 6 through 10 are based on the transaction between East Corp. and Snow Consultants. For each item, select the best answer from List II. An answer may be selected once, more than once, or not at all.

6. What was the effect of the event(s) that took place on March 1?
7. What was the effect of the event(s) that took place on March 15?
8. What was the effect of the event(s) that took place on April 5?
9. What was the effect of the event(s) that took place on April 15?
10. What was the effect of the event(s) that took place on April 30?

	List II
A	Breach of contract.
B	Discharge from performance.
C	Enforceable oral contract modification.
D	Formation of a voidable contract.
E	Formation of an enforceable contract.
F	Formation of a contract unenforceable under the Statute of Frauds.
G	Invalid assignment.
H	Mutual rescission.
I	Novation.
J	Unilateral offer.
K	Valid assignment of rights.
L	Valid assignment of duties.
M	Valid assignment of rights and duties.

21 (May 95)

Generally, which of the following contract rights are assignable?

	Option contract rights	Malpractice insurance policy rights
a.	Yes	Yes
b.	Yes	No
c.	No	Yes
d.	No	No

22 (May 95)

One of the criteria for a valid assignment of a sales contract to a third party is that the assignment must

a. Be supported by adequate consideration from the assignee.
b. Be in writing and signed by the assignor.
c. Not materially increase the other party's risk or duty.
d. Not be revocable by the assignor.

24 (November 92)

Wilcox Co. contracted with Ace Painters, Inc. for Ace to paint Wilcox's warehouse. Ace, without advising Wilcox, assigned the contract to Pure Painting Corp. Pure failed to paint Wilcox's warehouse in accordance with the contract specifications. The contract between Ace and Wilcox was silent with regard to a party's right to assign it. Which of the following statements is correct?

a. Ace remained liable to Wilcox despite the fact that Ace assigned the contract to Pure.
b. Ace would <u>not</u> be liable to Wilcox if Ace had notified Wilcox of the assignment.
c. Ace's duty to paint Wilcox's warehouse was nondelegable.
d. Ace's delegation of the duty to paint Wilcox's warehouse was a breach of the contract.

24 (November 91)

Yost contracted with Egan for Yost to buy certain real property. If the contract is otherwise silent, Yost's rights under the contract are

a. Assignable only with Egan's consent.
b. Nonassignable because they are personal to Yost.
c. Nonassignable as a matter of law.
d. Generally assignable.

22 (May 90)

On August 1, Neptune Fisheries contracted in writing with West Markets to deliver to West 3,000 pounds of lobsters at $4.00 a pound. Delivery of the lobsters was due October 1 with payment due November 1. On August 4, Neptune entered into a contract with Deep Sea Lobster Farms which provided as follows: "Neptune Fisheries assigns all the rights under the contract with West Markets dated August 1 to Deep Sea Lobster Farms." The best interpretation of the August 4 contract would be that it was

    a.   Only an assignment of rights by Neptune.

    b.   Only a delegation of duties by Neptune.

    c.   An assignment of rights and a delegation of duties by Neptune.

    d.   An unenforceable third-party beneficiary contract.

18 (November 89)

Moss entered into a contract to purchase certain real property from Shinn. Which of the following statements is not correct?

    a.   If Shinn fails to perform the contract, Moss can obtain specific performance.

    b.   The contract is nonassignable as a matter of law.

    c.   The Statute of Frauds applies to the contract.

    d.   Any amendment to the contract must be agreed to by both Moss and Shinn.

33 (May 89)

Generally, which one of the following transfers will be valid without the consent of the other party?

    a.   The assignment by the lessee of a lease contract where rent is a percentage of sales.

    b.   The assignment by a purchaser of goods of the right to buy on credit without giving security.

    c.   The assignment by an architect of a contract to design a building.

    d.   The assignment by a patent holder of the right to receive royalties.

21 (May 87)

On May 2, Kurtz Co. assigned its entire interest in a $70,000 account receivable due in 60 days from Long to City Bank for $65,000. On May 4, City notified Long of the assignment. On May 7, Long informed City that Kurtz had committed fraud in the transaction out of which the account receivable arose and that payment would not be made to City. If City commences an action against Long and Long is able to prove Kurtz acted fraudulently,

    a.   Long will be able to successfully assert fraud as a defense.

    b.   City will be entitled to collect $65,000, the amount paid for the assignment.

    c.   City will be entitled to collect $70,000 since fraud in the inducement is a personal defense which was lost on May 2.

    d.   City will be entitled to collect $70,000 since Long's allegation of fraud arose after notice of the assignment.

18 (May 83)

The assignment of a contract right

    a.   Will not be enforceable if it materially varies the obligor's promise.

    b.   Is invalid unless supported by consideration.

    c.   Gives the assignee better rights against the obligor than the assignor had.

    d.   Does not create any rights in the assignee against the assignor until notice is given to the obligor.

11 (November 82)

A common law duty is delegable even though the

    a.   Contract provides that the duty is nondelegable.

    b.   Duty delegated is the payment of money and the delegatee is not of an equal credit worthiness as the delegator.

    c.   Delegation will result in a material variance in performance by the delegatee.

    d.   Duty to be performed involves personal services.

Contracts

5 (November 81)

Fennell and McLeod entered into a binding contract whereby McLeod was to perform routine construction services according to Fennell's blueprints. McLeod assigned the contract to Conerly. After the assignment

    a. Fennell can bring suit under the doctrine of anticipatory breach.

    b. McLeod extinguishes all his rights and duties under the contract.

    c. McLeod extinguishes all his rights but is <u>not</u> relieved of his duties under the contract.

    d. McLeod still has all his rights but is relieved of his duties under the contract.

44 (May 78)

Bonnie Brook Wholesalers ordered 10,000 five-pound bags of standard granulated household sugar from Crane Sugar Plantations, Inc., for delivery within two months. Crane underestimated its existing backlog of orders and overestimated its inventory. As a result Crane found that it would be either unable or extremely hard-pressed to fill the order on time. Consequently, Crane assigned the contract to Devon Sugars, Inc., a smaller local producer and jobber, and paid Devon $200. Midway through the performance Devon defaulted because one of its suppliers' warehouses was destroyed by fire. Bonnie seeks to recover damages for breach of contract from both Crane and Devon. In the event of litigation, which of the following statements is correct?

    a. The unforeseen fire which destroyed the supplier's warehouse negates any liability on Devon's part.

    b. Devon will prevail because Devon has <u>no</u> contractual duty to Bonnie.

    c. Bonnie will <u>not</u> prevail against either Crane or Devon unless Bonnie first exhausts its rights against the supplier whose warehouse was destroyed.

    d. Bonnie will prevail against either Crane or Devon but will be entitled to only one recovery.

3 (November 77)

A CPA was engaged by Jackson & Wilcox, a small retail partnership, to examine its financial statements. The CPA discovered that due to other commitments, the engagement could <u>not</u> be completed on time. The CPA, therefore, unilaterally delegated the duty to Vincent, an equally competent CPA. Under these circumstances, which of the following is true?

    a. The duty to perform the audit engagement is delegable in that it is determined by an objective standard.

    b. If Jackson & Wilcox refused to accept Vincent because of a personal dislike of Vincent by one of the partners, Jackson & Wilcox will be liable for breach of contract.

    c. Jackson & Wilcox must accept the delegation in that Vincent is equally competent.

    d. The duty to perform the audit engagement is nondelegable and Jackson & Wilcox need <u>not</u> accept Vincent as a substitute if they do <u>not</u> wish to do so.

36 (May 75)

On February 1, 1975, Barron Explosives received an order from Super Construction, Inc. for 200 cases of dynamite at $25 per case with terms of 2/10, net/20, for delivery within two months, FOB seller's warehouse. The order was duly accepted in writing by Barron. Super soon discovered that it was already overstocked with dynamite and, therefore, it contacted Chubb Construction Company to see if it would be interested in taking over the contract. Chubb Construction Company indicated it would take over the contract and signed the following agreement on February 10, 1975:

> Super Construction, Inc., hereby assigns its contract for the purchase of 200 cases of dynamite at $25 per case ordered from Barron Explosive on February 1, 1975, to Chubb Construction Company. Chubb Construction hereby accepts.

<u>(Signed) Super, President</u>
Super Construction, Inc.

<u>(Signed) Chubb, President</u>
Chubb Construction Company

Since February 1, 1975, the price of dynamite has increased substantially, and as a result, Super wishes to avoid the assignment and obtain the dynamite for itself. Barron wishes to avoid having to deliver to either party. Which of the following statements best describes the legal status of the parties to the contract?

    a. Barron can avoid its obligation on the contract if it has reasonable grounds for insecurity because Chubb's credit rating is inferior to that of Super's.

    b. The assignment in question transfers to Chubb both the rights and the duties under the contract.

    c. Super can avoid the assignment to Chubb based upon the fact that it is lacking in consideration on Chubb's part.

    d. The contract is not assignable because it would materially vary Barron's duty to perform.

37 (May 75)

Assume that instead of Super Construction assigning the contract Barron Explosives found that it could not perform, and therefore, it assigned the contract to a nearby competitor, Demerest Explosives. Demerest promised Barron it would perform on the Super contract and expressly released Barron from any responsibility. Demerest subsequently defaulted and has refused to deliver.

    a. Barron's delegation of its duty to perform to Demerest Explosives constitutes an anticipatory breach of contract.

    b. Super Construction need not perform since the assignment of the contract materially alters its burden of performing.

    c. Super Construction can immediately proceed against Barron upon default by Demerest.

    d. Super Construction has recourse only against Barron.

23 (November 74)

Charles Lands offered to sell his business to Donald Bright. The assets consisted of real property, merchandise, office equipment, and the rights under certain contracts to purchase goods at an agreed price. In consideration for receipt of the aforementioned assets, Bright was to pay $125,000 and assume all business liabilities owed by Lands. Bright accepted the offer and a written contract was signed by both parties. Under the circumstances, the contract

    a. Represents an assignment of all the business assets and rights Lands owned and a delegation of whatever duties Lands was obligated to perform.

    b. Must be agreed to by all Lands' creditors and the parties who had agreed to deliver goods to Lands.

    c. Frees Lands from all liability to his creditors once the purchase is consummated.

    d. Is too indefinite and uncertain to be enforced.

4 (November 93)

Victor Corp. engaged Bell & Co., CPAs, to audit Victor's financial statements for the year ended December 31, 1992. Victor is in the business of buying, selling, and servicing new and used construction equipment. While reviewing Victor's 1992 records, Bell became aware of the following disputed transactions:

- On September 8, Victor sent Ambel Contractors, Inc. a signed purchase order for several pieces of used construction equipment. Victor's purchase order described twelve different pieces of equipment and indicated the price Victor was willing to pay for each item. As a result of a mathematical error in adding up the total of the various prices, the purchase price offered by Victor was $191,000 rather than the correct amount of $119,000. Ambel, on receipt of the purchase order, was surprised by Victor's high price and immediately sent Victor a written acceptance. Ambel was aware that the fair market value of the equipment was approximately $105,000 to $125,000. Victor discovered the mistake in the purchase order and refused to purchase the equipment from Ambel. Ambel claims that Victor is obligated to purchase the equipment at a price of $191,000, as set forth in the purchase order.

- On October 8, a Victor salesperson orally contracted to service a piece of equipment owned by Clark Masons, Inc. The contract provided that for a period of 36 months, commencing November 1992, Victor would provide routine service for the equipment at a fixed price of $15,000, payable in three annual installments of $5,000 each. On October 29, Clark's president contacted Victor and stated that Clark did not intend to honor the service agreement because there was no written contract between Victor and Clark.

Contracts

- On November 3, Victor received by mail a signed offer from GYX Erectors, Inc. The offer provided that Victor would service certain specified equipment owned by GYX for a two-year period for a total price of $81,000. The offer also provided as follows:

  "We need to know soon whether you can agree to the terms of this proposal. You must accept by November 15, or we will assume you can't meet our terms."

  On November 12, Victor mailed GYX a signed acceptance of GYX's offer. The acceptance was not received by GYX until November 17, and by then GYX had contracted with another party to provide service for its equipment. Victor has taken the position that GYX is obligated to honor its November 3 offer. GYX claims that no contract was formed because Victor's November 12 acceptance was not received timely by GYX.

- On December 19, Victor contracted in writing with Wells Landscaping Corp. The contract required Victor to deliver certain specified new equipment to Wells by December 31. On December 23, Victor determined that it would not be able to deliver the equipment to Wells by December 31 because of an inventory shortage. Therefore, Victor made a written assignment of the contract to Master Equipment, Inc. When Master attempted to deliver the equipment on December 31, Wells refused to accept it, claiming that Victor could not properly delegate its duties under the December 19 contract to another party without the consent of Wells. The contract is silent with regard to this issue.

Required: State whether the claims of Ambel, Clark, GYX, and Wells are correct and give the reasons for your conclusions.

Ambel is incorrect. The general rule is that when a party knows, or reasonably should know, that a mistake has been made in the making of an offer, the mistaken party will be granted relief from the offer. In this case, because Ambel was aware of the approximate fair market value of the equipment, it had reason to be aware of the mathematical error made by Victor and will not be allowed to take advantage of it.

Clark is correct. A contract that cannot by its terms be performed within one year from the date it is made must be evidenced by a writing that satisfies the requirements of the Statute of Frauds. The contract between Victor and Clark is not enforceable by Victor against Clark, because the contract was oral and provided for performance by the parties for longer than one year from the date the contract was entered into.

GYX is incorrect. An acceptance of an offer is effective when dispatched (in this case, when mailed), provided that the appropriate mode of communication is used. The general rule is that an offer shall be interpreted as inviting acceptance in any manner and by any medium reasonable in the circumstances. In this case, GYX made its offer by mail. An acceptance by mail, if properly addressed with adequate postage affixed, would be considered a reasonable manner and method of acceptance. Therefore, Victor's acceptance was effective (and a contract was formed) when the acceptance was mailed on November 12 and not when received by GYX on November 17.

Wells is incorrect. As a general rule, most contracts are assignable and delegable unless: prohibited in the contract, the duties are personal in nature, or the assignment or delegation is prohibited by statute or public policy. Victor was entitled to assign the contract to Master, because none of these exceptions apply to the contract.

2 (November 90)

The following letters were mailed among Jacobs, a real estate developer, Snow, the owner of an undeveloped parcel of land, and Eljay Distributors, Inc., a clothing wholesaler interested in acquiring Snow's parcel to build a warehouse:

a. January 21, 1990--Snow to Jacobs: "My vacant parcel (Lot 2, Birds Addition to Cedar Grove) is available for $125,000 cash; closing within 60 days. You must accept by January 31 if you are interested."
   This was received by Jacobs on January 31.

b. January 29, 1990--Snow to Jacobs: "Ignore my January 21 letter to you; I have decided not to sell my lot at this time."
   This was received by Jacobs on February 3.

c. January 31, 1990--Jacobs to Snow: "Per your January 21 letter, you have got a deal."
   Jacobs inadvertently forgot to sign the January 31 letter, which was received by Snow on February 4.

d. <u>February 2, 1990</u>--Jacobs to Eljay: "In consideration of your promise to pay me $10,000, I hereby assign to you my right to purchase Snow's vacant lot (Lot 2, Birds Addition to Cedar Grove)."

This was received by Eljay on February 5.

All of the letters were signed, except as noted above, and properly stamped and addressed.

Snow has refused to sell the land to Jacobs or Eljay, asserting that no contract exists because:

- Jacobs' acceptance was not received on a timely basis.
- Snow had revoked the January 21 offer.
- Jacobs' acceptance was not signed.
- Jacobs had no right to assign the contract to Eljay.

Required: For each of Snow's assertions, indicate whether the assertion is correct, setting forth reasons for your conclusion.

Snow's assertion that Jacobs' acceptance was not received on a timely basis is incorrect. Jacobs' January 31 acceptance was effective when dispatched (mailed) under the complete-when-posted doctrine because:

- The letter was an authorized means of communication (because Snow's offer was by mail); and
- The letter was properly stamped and addressed.

Therefore, Jacobs' acceptance was effective on January 31, the last possible day under Snow's January 21 offer.

Snow's assertion that the January 21 offer was effectively revoked is incorrect because a revocation is not effective until received. In this case, the revocation was effective on February 3, and Jacobs' acceptance was effective on January 31.

Snow's assertion that Jacobs' failure to sign the January 31 acceptance prevents the formation of a contract is incorrect. The Statute of Frauds, which applies to contracts involving interests in real estate, requires only the signature of the party to be charged with enforcement of the contract. Therefore, because Snow had signed the January 21 offer, which was accepted by Jacobs, the contract is enforceable against Snow.

Snow's assertion that Jacobs had no right to assign the contract is incorrect. Contract rights, including the right to purchase real estate, are generally assignable unless the assignment:

- Would materially increase the risk or burden of the obligor;
- Purports to transfer highly personal contract rights;
- Is validly prohibited by the contract; or
- Is prohibited by law.

None of these limitations applies to the assignment by Jacobs to Eljay.

3C (May 80)

Betty Monash was doing business as Victory Stamp Company. She sold the business as a going concern. The assets of the business consist of an inventory of stamps, various trade fixtures which are an inherent part of the business, a building which houses the retail operation, goodwill, and miscellaneous office equipment. On the liability side, there are numerous trade accounts payable and a first mortgage on the building.

Joe Franklin purchased the business. In addition to a cash payment, he assumed all outstanding debts and promised to hold Monash harmless from any and all liability on the scheduled debts listed in the contract of sale.

Required: Answer the following, setting forth reasons for any conclusions stated.

What is the legal relationship of Monash, Franklin, and the creditors to each other after the consummation of the sale with respect to the outstanding debts of the business?

The sale of the business to Franklin was both an assignment (sale) of all rights and a delegation (assumption) of the duties connected with the business. Consequently, Monash assumes the role of a surety and remains liable to pay the existing debts immediately (for example, the mortgage) upon default by Franklin. The creditor's rights are unaffected. Franklin becomes the principal debtor and in the relationship between Monash and him, he should pay as he promised her. Although his promise was made to Monash only, the creditors are third-party creditor beneficiaries of that promise. Therefore, they have the standing to sue Franklin on that promise despite the lack of privity and even though they have given no consideration for Franklin's promise. They may also proceed on the original promise made by Monash upon which she remains liable.

Contracts

2. Novation

25 (May 90)

Wren purchased a factory from First Federal Realty. Wren paid 20% at the closing and gave a note for the balance secured by a 20-year mortgage. Five years later, Wren found it increasingly difficult to make payments on the note and defaulted. First Federal threatened to accelerate the loan and foreclose if Wren continued in default. First Federal told Wren to make payment or obtain an acceptable third party to assume the obligation. Wren offered the land to Moss, Inc. for $10,000 less than the equity Wren had in the property. This was acceptable to First Federal and at the closing Moss paid the arrearage, assumed the mortgage and note, and had title transferred to its name. First Federal released Wren. The transaction in question is a(an)

 a. Purchase of land subject to a mortgage.
 b. Assignment and delegation.
 c. Third party beneficiary contract.
 d. Novation.

24 (May 88)

Dell owed Stark $9,000. As the result of an unrelated transactions, Stark owed Ball that same amount. The three parties signed an agreement that Dell would pay Ball instead of Stark, and Stark would be discharged from all liability. The agreement among the parties is

 a. A novation.
 b. An executed accord and satisfaction.
 c. Voidable at Ball's option.
 d. Unenforceable for lack of consideration.

13 (May 84)

Mary is seeking to avoid liability on a contract with Jeff. Mary can avoid liability on the contract if

 a. The entire contract has been assigned.
 b. There has been a subsequent unexecuted accord between Jeff and herself.
 c. She has been discharged by a novation.
 d. A third party has agreed to perform her duty and has for a valuable consideration promised to hold Mary harmless on the obligation to Jeff.

8 (May 79)

Arthur sold his house to Michael. Michael agreed to pay the existing mortgage on the house. The Safety Bank, which held the mortgage, released Arthur from liability on the debt. The above declared transaction (relating to the mortgage debt) is

 a. A delegation.
 b. A novation.
 c. Invalid in that bank did <u>not</u> receive any additional consideration from Arthur.
 d. <u>Not</u> a release of Arthur if Michael defaults, and the proceeds from the sale of the mortgaged house are insufficient to justify the debt.

3. Notification

18 (November 88)

Pix borrowed $80,000 from Null Bank. Pix gave Null a promissory note and mortgage. Subsequently, Null assigned the note and mortgage to Reed. Reed failed to record the assignment or notify Pix of the assignment. If Pix pays Null pursuant to the note, Pix will

 a. Be primarily liable to Reed for the payments.
 b. Be secondarily liable to Reed for the payments made to Null.
 c. Not be liable to Reed for the payments made to Null because Reed failed to record the assignment.
 d. Not be liable to Reed for the payments made to Null because Reed failed to give Pix notice of the assignment.

23 (May 88)

Quick Corp. has $270,000 of outstanding accounts receivable. On March 10, 1988, Quick assigned a $30,000 account receivable due from Pine, one of Quick's customers, to Taft Bank for value. On March 30, Pine paid Quick the $30,000. On April 5, Taft notified Pine of the March 10 assignment from Quick to Taft. Taft is entitled to collect $30,000 from

a. Either Quick or Pine.
b. Neither Quick nor Pine.
c. Pine only.
d. Quick only.

Items 20 through 22 are based on the following information:

After substantial oral negotiations, Ida Frost wrote Jim Lane on May 1 offering to pay Lane $160,000 to build a warehouse. The writing contained the terms essential to form a binding contract. It also provided that the offer would remain open until June 1 and that acceptance must be received to be effective. On May 20, Lane mailed a signed acceptance. This was received by Frost on May 22. Lane completed the warehouse on July 15. On July 30, Lane assigned his right to receive payment to Reid Bank which did not notify Frost of the assignment. Two weeks later, Frost paid Lane $155,000 after deducting $5,000 in satisfaction of a dispute between them unrelated to the construction contract.

20 (May 85)

The agreement between Frost and Lane resulted in the formation of a (an)

a. Bilateral contract.
b. Unilateral contract.
c. Quasi contract.
d. Implied in fact contract.

21 (May 85)

Frost's offer

a. Was accepted and a contract duly formed on May 20.
b. Was irrevocable until June 1.
c. Constituted a firm offer under the UCC despite the lack of consideration.
d. Could have been revoked any time prior to the receipt of Lane's acceptance on May 22.

22 (May 85)

If Reid sues Frost on the contract, Reid will be entitled to recover

a. The full $160,000.
b .$160,000, less the $5,000 setoff.
c. Nothing, because notice of the assignment was <u>not</u> given to Frost.
d. Nothing, because it was <u>not</u> the primary beneficiary of the construction contract.

13 (November 82)

Walton owed $10,000 to Grant. Grant assigned his claim against Walton to the Line Finance Company for value on October 15, 1982. On October 25, 1982, Hayes assigned his matured claim for $2,000 against Grant to Walton for value. On October 30, 1982, Line notified Walton of the assignment to them of the $10,000 debt owed by Walton to Grant. Line has demanded payment in full. Insofar as the rights of the various parties are concerned

a. Walton has the right of a $2,000 set-off against the debt which he owed Grant.
b. Walton must pay Line in full, but has the right to obtain a $2,000 reimbursement from Grant.
c. Line is a creditor beneficiary of the debt owed by Walton.
d .The claimed set-off of the Hayes claim for $2,000 is invalid since it is for an amount which is less than the principal debt.

16 (May 78)

Higgins orally contracted to pay $3,500 to Clark for $4,000 of thirty-day accounts receivable that arose in the course of Clark's office equipment business. Higgins subsequently paid the $3,500. What is the legal status of this contract?

a. The contract is unenforceable by Higgins since the Statute of Frauds requirement has not been satisfied.

b. If Higgins failed to notify the debtors whose accounts were purchased, they will, upon payment in good faith to Clark, have no liability to Higgins.

c. The contract in question is illegal because it violates the usury laws.

d. Higgins will be able to collect against the debtors free of the usual defenses which would be assertable against Clark.

B. Third Party Beneficiaries

21 (November 92)

Ferco, Inc. claims to be a creditor beneficiary of a contract between Bell and Allied Industries, Inc. Allied is indebted to Ferco. The contract between Bell and Allied provides that Bell is to purchase certain goods from Allied and pay the purchase price directly to Ferco until Allied's obligation is satisfied. Without justification, Bell failed to pay Ferco and Ferco sued Bell. Ferco will

a. Not prevail, because Ferco lacked privity of contract with either Bell or Allied.

b. Not prevail, because Ferco did not give any consideration to Bell.

c. Prevail, because Ferco was an intended beneficiary of the contract between Allied and Bell.

d. Prevail, provided Ferco was aware of the contract between Bell and Allied at the time the contract was entered into.

Items 33 and 34 are based on the following:

Egan contracted with Barton to buy Barton's business. The contract provided that Egan would pay the business debts Barton owed Ness and that the balance of the purchase price would be paid to Barton over a 10 year period. The contract also required Egan to take out a decreasing term life insurance policy naming Barton and Ness as beneficiaries to ensure that the amounts owned Barton and Ness would be paid if Egan died.

33 (May 92)

Which of the following would describe Ness' status under the contract and insurance policy?

	Contract	Insurance policy
a.	Donee beneficiary	Donee beneficiary
b.	Donee beneficiary	Creditor beneficiary
c.	Creditor beneficiary	Donee beneficiary
d.	Creditor beneficiary	Creditor beneficiary

34 (May 92)

Barton's contract rights were assigned to Vim, and Egan was notified of the assignment. Despite the assignment, Egan continued making payments to Barton. Egan died before completing payment and Vim sued Barton for the insurance proceeds and the other payments on the purchase price received by Barton after the assignment. To which of the following is Vim entitled?

	Payments on purchase price	Insurance proceeds
a.	No	Yes
b.	No	No
c.	Yes	Yes
d.	Yes	No

19 (May 90)

Union Bank lent $200,000 to Wagner. Union required Wagner to obtain a life insurance policy naming Union as beneficiary. While the loan was outstanding, Wagner stopped paying the premiums on the policy. Union paid the premiums, adding the amounts paid to Wagner's loan. Wagner died and the insurance company refused to pay the policy proceeds to Union. Union may

    a.   Recover the policy proceeds because it is a creditor beneficiary.

    b.   Recover the policy proceeds because it is a donee beneficiary.

    c.   Not recover the policy proceeds because it is <u>not</u> in privity of contract with the insurance company.

    d.   Not recover the policy proceeds because it is only an incidental beneficiary.

24 (May 90)

Rice contracted with Locke to build an oil refinery for Locke. The contract provided that Rice was to use United pipe fittings. Rice did not do so. United learned of the contract and, anticipating the order, manufactured additional fittings. United sued Locke and Rice. United is

    a.   Entitled to recover from Rice only, because Rice breached the contract.

    b.   Entitled to recover from either Locke or Rice because it detrimentally relied on the contract.

    c.   Not entitled to recover because it is a donee beneficiary.

    d.   Not entitled to recover because it is an incidental beneficiary.

17 (November 89)

Jones owned an insurance policy on her life, on which she paid all the premiums. Smith was named the beneficiary. Jones died and the insurance company refused to pay the insurance proceeds to Smith. An action by Smith against the insurance company for the insurance proceeds will be

    a.   Successful because Smith is a third party donee beneficiary.

    b.   Successful because Smith is a proper assignee of Jones' rights under the insurance policy.

    c.   Unsuccessful because Smith was <u>not</u> the owner of the policy.

    d.   Unsuccessful because Smith did <u>not</u> pay any of the premiums.

Items 17 and 18 are based on the following information:

Sand sold a warehouse he owned to Quick Corp. The warehouse was encumbered by an outstanding mortgage securing Sand's note to Security Bank. Quick assumed Sand's note and mortgage at the time it purchased the warehouse from Sand. Within three months, Quick defaulted on the note and Security Bank commenced a mortgage foreclosure action. The proceeds of the resulting foreclosure sale were less than the outstanding balance on the note.

17 (November 85)

As to the contract between Sand and Quick, Security is

    a.   A third party creditor beneficiary.

    b.   A third party donee beneficiary.

    c.   A third party incidental beneficiary.

    d.   Not a beneficiary.

18 (November 85)

Which of the following statements is correct regarding the rights and liabilities of the parties?

    a.   Quick's liability is limited to its equity in the warehouse.

    b.   Sand remains liable on the note.

    c.   Security must first proceed against Quick to recover the deficiency before seeking payment from Sand.

    d.   Sand is <u>not</u> liable for the deficiency because Quick assumed the note and mortgage.

26 (May 85)

Fink is the owner of a parcel of land which is encumbered by a mortgage securing Fink's note to State Bank. Fink sold the land to Bloom who assumed the mortgage note. State Bank
   a.   Is a donee beneficiary.
   b.   Is an incidental beneficiary.
   c.   Is a creditor beneficiary.
   d.   Can not collect from Fink if Bloom defaults.

25 (November 84)

Red purchased a life insurance policy from Ace Insurance Co. naming his wife Bertha as the sole beneficiary. In order for Bertha to qualify as a donee beneficiary she must
   a.   Have had knowledge of the insurance contract at the time the contract was entered into.
   b.   Be in privity of contract with Ace.
   c.   Have provided consideration.
   d.   Have been the person intended to be benefitted from the life insurance contract.

17 (May 83)

Nancy is asserting rights as a third party donee beneficiary on a contract made by Johnson and Harding. In order to prevail, Nancy must prove that
   a.   The contract specifically named her as the beneficiary.
   b.   She gave consideration for the donative promise.
   c.   She is related by blood or marriage to the promisee.
   d.   The terms of the contract and surrounding circumstances manifest a clear intent to benefit her.

12 (November 82)

Wilson sold his factory to Glenn. As part of the contract, Glenn assumed the existing mortgage on the property which was held by Security Bank. Regarding the rights and duties of the parties, which of the following is correct?
   a.   The promise by Glenn need not be in writing to be enforceable by Security.
   b.   Security is a creditor beneficiary of Glenn's promise and can recover against him personally in the event of default.
   c.   Security is a mere incidental beneficiary since it was not a party to the assignment.
   d.   Wilson has no further liability to Security.

4 (May 75)

Matson loaned Donalds $1,000 at 8% interest for one year. Two weeks before the due date, Matson called upon Donalds and obtained his agreement in writing to modify the terms of the loan. It was agreed that on the due date Donalds would pay $850 to Cranston, to whom Matson owed that amount, and pay the balance plus interest to his son, Arthur, to whom he wished to make a gift.
   Under the modified terms of the loan, Cranston and/or Arthur have what legal standing?
   a.   Cranston is a creditor beneficiary and Arthur is a donee beneficiary.
   b.   Cranston has the right to prevent Matson's delegation if he gives timely notice.
   c.   If Cranston is to be able to proceed against Donalds, he must have received notice of Donalds' promise to pay him the $850 prior to the due date.
   d.   Arthur is an incidental beneficiary.

VIII. Performance of the Contract
A. Conditions and Excuse of Condition

19 (May 95)

Which of the following types of conditions affecting performance may validly be present in contracts?

	Conditions precedent	Conditions subsequent	Concurrent conditions
a.	Yes	Yes	Yes
b.	Yes	Yes	No
c.	Yes	No	Yes
d.	No	Yes	Yes

25 (November 92)

On June 15, 1990, Alpha, Inc. contracted with Delta Manufacturing, Inc. to buy a vacant parcel of land Delta owned. Alpha intended to build a distribution warehouse on the land because of its location near a major highway. The contract stated that: "Alpha's obligations hereunder are subject to the vacant parcel being rezoned to a commercial zoning classification by July 31, 1991." Which of the following statements is correct?

    a. If the parcel is <u>not</u> rezoned by July 31, and Alpha refuses to purchase it, Alpha would <u>not</u> be in breach of contract.

    b. If the parcel is rezoned by July 31, and Alpha refuses to purchase it, Delta would be able to successfully sue Alpha for specific performance.

    c. The contract is <u>not</u> binding on either party because Alpha's performance is conditional.

    d. If the parcel is rezoned by July 31, and Delta refuses to sell it, Delta's breach would <u>not</u> discharge Alpha's obligation to tender payment.

25 (November 86)

Meek & Co., CPAs was engaged by Reed, the president of Sulk Corp., to issue by June 15, 1986, an opinion on Sulk's financial statements for the fiscal year ended March 31, 1986. Meek's engagement and its fee of $20,000 were approved by Sulk's board of directors. Meek did not issue its opinion until June 30 because of Sulk's failure to supply Meek with the necessary information to complete the audit. Sulk refuses to pay Meek. If Meek sues Sulk, Meek will

    a. Prevail based on the contract.

    b. Prevail based on quasi contract.

    c. Lose, since it breached the contract.

    d. Lose, since the June 15 deadline was a condition precedent to Sulk's performance.

13 (May 81)

Wilcox mailed Norriss an unsigned contract for the purchase of a tract of real property. The contract represented the oral understanding of the parties as to the purchase price, closing date, type of deed, and other details. It called for payment in full in cash or certified check at the closing. Norriss signed the contract, but added above his signature the following:

This contract is subject to my (Norriss) being able to obtain conventional mortgage financing of $100,000 at 13% or less interest for a period of not less than 25 years.

Which of the following is correct?
  a. The parties had already made an enforceable contract prior to Wilcox's mailing of the formalized contract.
  b. Norriss would not be liable on the contract under the circumstances even if he had not added the "conventional mortgage" language since Wilcox had not signed it.
  c. By adding the "conventional mortgage" language above his signature, Norriss created a condition precedent to his contractual obligation and made a counteroffer.
  d. The addition of the "conventional mortgage" language has no legal effect upon the contractual relationship of the parties since it was an implied condition in any event.

32 (November 78)

On July 25, 1978, Archer, the president of Post Corporation, with the approval of the board of directors, engaged Biggs, a CPA, to examine Post's July 31, 1978, financial statements and to issue a report in time for the annual stockholders' meeting to be held on September 5, 1978. Notwithstanding Biggs' reasonable efforts, the report was not ready until September 7 because of delays by Post's staff. Archer, acting on behalf of Post, refused to accept or to pay for the report since it no longer served its intended purpose. In the event Biggs brings a legal action against Post, what is the probable outcome?
  a. The case would be dismissed because it is unethical for a CPA to sue for his fee.
  b. Biggs will be entitled to recover only in quasi contract for the value of the services to the client.
  c. Biggs will not recover since the completion by September 5th was a condition precedent to his recovery.
  d. Biggs will recover because the delay by Post's staff prevents Biggs from performing on time and thereby eliminated the timely performance condition.

21 (May 78)

Ames and Bates have agreed that Bates will sell a parcel of land to Ames for $10,000 if the land is rezoned from residential to industrial use within six months of the agreement. Bates agreed to use his best efforts to obtain the rezoning, and Ames agreed to make a $2,000 good-faith deposit with Bates two weeks after the date of the agreement. What is the status of this agreement?
  a. No contract results because the event is contingent.
  b. The agreement is probably unenforceable because Bates would be required to attempt to influence governmental action.
  c. The parties have entered into a bilateral contract subject to a condition.
  d. Ames is not obligated to make the deposit at the agreed time even though Bates has by then made an effort to procure a rezoning.

10 (May 75)

Barnes agreed to purchase from Damion 1,000 shares of Excelsior Photo, Inc. stock at $100 per share. Barnes was interested in obtaining control of Excelsior, whose stock was very closely held. The stock purchase agreement contained the following clause: "This contract is subject to my (Barnes) obtaining more than 50% of the shares outstanding of Excelsior Photo stock." In this situation
  a. The contract is not binding on Damion because it lacks consideration on Barnes' part, i.e., unless he obtained more than 50%, he is not liable.
  b. The contract is subject to an express condition precedent.
  c. Specific performance would not be available to Barnes if Damion refuses to perform.
  d. While the contract is executory, Damion cannot transfer good title to a third party who takes in good faith.

B. Performance and Breach

13 (R01)

Which of the following actions if taken by one party to a contract generally will discharge the performance required of the other party to the contract?
  a. Material breach of the contract.
  b. Delay in performance.
  c. Tender.
  d. Assignment of rights.

26 (November 93)

Ames Construction Co. contracted to build a warehouse for White Corp. The construction specifications required Ames to use Ace lighting fixtures. Inadvertently, Ames installed Perfection lighting fixtures which are of slightly lesser quality than Ace fixtures, but in all other respects meet White's needs. Which of the following statements is correct?

   a. White's recovery will be limited to monetary damages because Ames' breach of the construction contract was not material.
   b. White will not be able to recover any damages from Ames because the breach was inadvertent.
   c. Ames did not breach the construction contract because the Perfection fixtures were substantially as good as the Ace fixtures.
   d. Ames must install Ace fixtures or White will not be obligated to accept the warehouse.

25 (November 90)

Parc hired Glaze to remodel and furnish an office suite. Glaze submitted plans that Parc approved. After completing all the necessary construction and painting, Glaze purchased minor accessories that Parc rejected because they did not conform to the plans. Parc refused to allow Glaze to complete the project and refused to pay Glaze any part of the contract price. Glaze sued for the value of the work performed. Which of the following statements is correct?

   a. Glaze will lose because Glaze breached the contract by not completing performance.
   b. Glaze will win because Glaze substantially performed and Parc prevented complete performance.
   c. Glaze will lose because Glaze materially breached the contract by buying the accessories.
   d. Glaze will win because Parc committed anticipatory breach.

24 (November 84)

Ketchum Buildings, Inc. contracted with Samson to construct a high-rise office building for $800,000. Ketchum inadvertently used materials which were not in accordance with the contract specifications. Although the breach resulted in minor damages, Samson has refused to pay Ketchum the $100,000 balance due on the contract. Ketchum

   a. Will be denied recovery since any variation of the contract terms constitutes a breach of the entire contract.
   b. Will be denied recovery based on the equitable doctrine of clean hands.
   c. Is entitled to the entire $100,000 since it has substantially performed the contract.
   d. Is entitled to the $100,000 less damages.

19 (May 83)

Kent Construction Company contracted to construct four garages for Magnum, Inc. according to specifications provided by Magnum. Kent deliberately substituted 2 x 4s for the more expensive 2 x 6s called for in the contract in all places where the 2 x 4s would not be readily detected. Magnum's inspection revealed the variance and Magnum is now withholding the final payment on the contract. The contract was for $100,000, and the final payment would be $25,000. Damages were estimated to be $15,000. In a lawsuit for the balance due, Kent will

   a. Prevail on the contract, less damages of $15,000, because it has substantially performed.
   b. Prevail because the damages in question were not substantial in relation to the contract amount.
   c. Lose because the law unqualifiedly requires literal performance of such contracts.
   d. Lose all rights under the contracts because it has intentionally breached it.

35 (May 74)

Ambrose undertook to stage a production of a well-known play. He wired Belle, a famous actress, offering her the lead at $1,000 per week (for six evening performances per week) for six weeks from the specific opening night, plus $1,000 for a week of rehearsal prior to opening. The telegram also said, "Offer ends in three days."

Assuming a contract between Ambrose and Belle and that Belle did not perform after the third week of the six-week run

    a. If Belle were able to perform, a court would probably order specific performance.

    b. If Belle became unable to perform because of illness, Belle could hold Ambrose to his contract if she arranged for the appearance of a substitute star of at least equal fame and ability.

    c. If Belle became ill and it appeared that she would miss a substantial number of performances, Ambrose might terminate the contract but would be liable for payment for performances previously given.

    d. Belle's refusal to perform would <u>not</u> have constituted a breach of contract if Ambrose had been declared a bankrupt.

3A (May 80)

Smithers contracted with the Silverwater Construction Corporation to build a home. The contract contained a detailed set of specifications including the type, quality, and manufacturers' names of the building materials that were to be used. After construction was completed, a rigid inspection was made of the house and the following defects were discovered:

(1) Some of the roofing shingles were improperly laid.

(2) The ceramic tile in the kitchen and three bathrooms was not manufactured by Disco Tile Company as called for in the specifications. The price of the alternate tile was $325 less than the Disco but was of approximately equal quality.

(3) The sewerage pipes that were imbedded in concrete in the basement were also not manufactured by the specified manufacturer. It could not be shown that there was any difference in quality and the price was the same.

(4) Various minor defects such as improperly hung doors.

Silverwater has corrected defects (1) and (4) but has refused to correct defects (2) and (3) because the cost would be substantial. Silverwater claims it is entitled to recover under the contract and demands full payment. Smithers is adamant and is demanding literal performance of the contract or he will not pay.

Required: Answer the following, setting forth reasons for any conclusions stated.

    1. If the dispute goes to court, who will prevail, assuming Silverwater's breach of contract was intentional?

    2. If the dispute goes to court, who will prevail, assuming Silverwater's breach of contract was unintentional?

The general common-low rules require literal performance by a party to a contract. Failure to literally perform constitutes a breach. Since promises are construed to be dependent upon each other, the failure by one party to perform releases the other. However, a strict and literal application of this type of implied condition often results in unfairness and hardship, particularly in cases such as this. Therefore, the courts developed some important exceptions to the literal performance doctrine. The applicable rule is known as the substantial performance doctrine, which applies to construction contracts and is a more specific statement of the material performance rule that applies to contracts other than construction contracts. The general rule holds that if the breach is immaterial, the party who breached may nevertheless recover under the contract, less damages caused by the breach. The substantial performance doctrine requires the builder (party breaching) to prove the following facts.

    <u>a</u>. The defect was not a structural defect.

    <u>b</u>. The breach was relatively minor in relation to the overall performance of the contract. The courts and texts sometimes talk in terms of a 95 percent or better performance.

    <u>c</u>. The breach must be unintentional or, to state it another way, the party breaching must have been acting in good faith.

It would appear that requirements <u>a</u> and <u>b</u> are clearly satisfied on the basis of the facts. Requirement <u>c</u> cannot be determined on the facts given. If Silverwater deliberately (with knowledge) substituted the improper and cheaper tile or sewerage pipes, then it may not be entitled to the benefit of the substantial performance exception. On the other hand, if these breaches were the result of an innocent oversight or mere negligence on its part, recovery should be granted. The recovery must be decreased by the amount of the damages caused by the breach. The substitute of sewer pipe of like quality and value would be considered substantial performance.

C. Effect of Prospective Nonperformance

47 (November 95)

Under the Sales Article of the UCC, which of the following rights is (are) available to the buyer when a seller commits an anticipatory breach of contract?

	Demand assurance of performance	Cancel the contract	Collect punitive damages
a.	Yes	Yes	Yes
b.	Yes	Yes	No
c.	Yes	No	Yes
d.	No	Yes	Yes

55 (November 94)

Under the Sales Article of the UCC, which of the following events will release the buyer from all its obligations under a sales contract?
- a. Destruction of the goods after risk of loss passed to the buyer.
- b. Impracticability of delivery under the terms of the contract.
- c. Anticipatory repudiation by the buyer that is retracted before the seller cancels the contract.
- d. Refusal of the seller to give written assurance of performance when reasonably demanded by the buyer.

19 (November 89)

Nagel and Fields entered into a contract in which Nagel was obligated to deliver certain goods to Fields by September 10. On September 3, Nagel told Fields that Nagel had no intention of delivering the goods required by the contract. Prior to September 10, Fields may successfully sue Nagel under the doctrine of
- a. Promissory estoppel.
- b. Accord and satisfaction.
- c. Anticipatory repudiation.
- d. Substantial performance.

35 (May 89)

Jones, CPA, entered into a signed contract with Foster Corp. to perform accounting and review services. If Jones repudiates the contract prior to the date performance is due to begin, which of the following is not correct?
- a. Foster could successfully maintain an action for breach of contract after the date performance was due to begin.
- b. Foster can obtain a judgment ordering Jones to perform.
- c. Foster could successfully maintain an action for breach of contract prior to the date performance is due to begin.
- d. Foster can obtain a judgment for the monetary damages it incurred as a result of the repudiation.

51 (November 88)

On March 7, 1988, Wax Corp. contracted with Noll Wholesalers to supply Noll with specific electrical parts. Delivery was called for on June 3, 1988. On May 2, 1988, Wax notified Noll that it would not perform and that Noll should look elsewhere. Wax had received a larger and more lucrative contract on April 21, 1988, and its capacity was such that it could not fulfill both orders. The facts
- a. Will prevent Wax from retracting its repudiation of the Noll contract.
- b. Are not sufficient to clearly establish an anticipatory repudiation.
- c. Will permit Noll to sue only after June 3, 1988, the latest performance date.
- d. Will permit Noll to sue immediately after May 2, 1988, even though the performance called for under the contract was not due until June 3, 1988.

27 (May 85)

Bing engaged Dill to perform personal services for $2,200 a month for a period of four months. The contract was entered into orally on July 1, 1984, and performance was to commence September 1, 1984. On August 10, Dill anticipatorily repudiated the contract. As a result, Bing can

    a. Not assign his rights to damages under the contract to a third party.

    b. Obtain specific performance.

    c. Not enforce the contract against Dill since the contract is oral.

    d. Immediately sue for breach of contract.

21 (November 82)

On August 1, 1982, Fields & Boss, CPAs, made a contract with Gil Manufacturing to audit Gil's financial statements for calendar year 1982 and to render an opinion thereon. Gil agreed to an estimated fee of $7,500 for the services. Gil changed its mind and on September 2, 1982, before any services had been performed, notified Fields & Boss that it was repudiating the contract. Which of the following is correct?

    a. The CPA firm may sue for breach of contract immediately and need not wait until after performance is due and refused.

    b. The CPA firm is no longer bound on the contract but can not sue until after January 1, 1983.

    c. The CPA firm remains bound by the contract until January 1, 1983.

    d. There has been a present breach of the contract.

43 (May 75)

On February 1, 1975, Colonial Industries ordered 10,000 of two-inch pipe in 20-foot lengths from the Eire Steel Company. Delivery was to be made on or before March 15, time being of the essence, FOB buyer's loading platform, cash on delivery. Eire Steel accepted the order. On February 15, Eire informed Colonial that its biggest customer had just purchased and taken delivery of its entire stock of two-inch pipe and that it would be impossible for Eire to deliver the pipe until May 15, at the earliest. Colonial demanded that Eire perform as agreed; Eire apologized but reiterated its prior position that it was now impossible for them to perform until the middle of May.

    a. Eire's action of February 15 constituted an anticipatory repudiation of the contract.

    b. Colonial must "cover" (procure the same or similar goods elsewhere) within a reasonable time in order to determine the damages recoverable.

    c. If Colonial waits for performance by Eire and tenders the amount due on March 15, it can recover damages of the difference between the contract price and the market value on March 15.

    d. Because Eire had sold and delivered all its supply of two-inch pipe, it can successfully plead impossibility of performance in order to avoid liability.

22 (May 74)

Bates ordered 1,000 units of merchandise from Watson, a wholesaler, at a unit price of $50 each, with delivery to be made at Bates' warehouse after April 11 but in no event later than April 15 with payment to be made 30 days after delivery. Watson accepted Bates' offer. If Watson notifies Bates on April 10 that he will not be able to deliver the merchandise until May 2

    a. Bates may notify Watson that he is treating the contract as terminated immediately, but if he does so he waives any right to damages for breach of contract.

    b. If Bates elects to do nothing, he will be bound if Watson subsequently tenders the goods on April 15.

    c. Watson's notification is without legal effect until actual breach occurs.

    d. Watson's action gives Bates no right to recovery if Watson can show that a sudden drop in the market occurred and Watson would have suffered a greater loss if the contract had been performed.

4 (November 95)

On July 5, 1995, Korn sent Wilson a written offer to clear Wilson's parking lot whenever it snowed through December 31, 1995. Korn's offer stated that Wilson had until October 1 to accept.

On September 28, 1995, Wilson mailed Korn an acceptance with a request that the agreement continue through March, 1996. Wilson's acceptance was delayed and didn't reach Korn until October 3.

On September 29, 1995, Korn saw weather reports indicating the snowfall for the season would be much heavier than normal. This would substantially increase Korn's costs to perform under the offer.

On September 30, 1995, Korn phoned Wilson to insist that the terms of the agreement be changed. When Wilson refused, Korn orally withdrew the offer and stated that Korn would not perform.

Required:
  a. State and explain the points of law that Korn would argue to show that there was <u>no</u> valid contract.
  b. State and explain the points of law that Wilson would argue to show that there was a valid contract.
  c. Assuming that a valid contract existed:
    1. Determine whether Korn breached the contract and the nature of the breach and
    2. State the common law remedies available to Wilson.

a. Korn would argue two points of law to show there was no valid contract. Korn would argue that the July 5 offer was not accepted by Wilson before it was withdrawn on September 30. An offer can be withdrawn at any time before it is accepted even if it states that it will remain open for a definite period of time.

Korn would also argue that Wilson's response of September 28 was not a valid acceptance because Wilson included additional terms and Wilson's attempt to change the terms of the contract was a rejection and a counteroffer.

b. Wilson would argue two points of law to show there was a valid contract. Wilson would argue that the mailing of the acceptance on September 28 was an effective acceptance under the mailbox rule. There is a valid contract because there was a valid acceptance before the offer was withdrawn.

Wilson would also argue that the attempt to extend the contract was not a condition of acceptance but a requested immaterial modification that did not negate the acceptance.

c. If a valid contract existed, Korn's September 30 telephone call resulted in Korn's anticipatory breach of the contract because Wilson could no longer rely on Korn's performing.

Under common law, Wilson could either cancel the contract or sue to collect compensatory damages for the additional amount it would cost to obtain the services.

D. Breach by Nonperformance; Excuses for Nonperformance

23 (May 95)
Which of the following actions will result in the discharge of a party to a contract?

	Prevention of performance	Accord and satisfaction
a.	Yes	Yes
b.	Yes	No
c.	No	Yes
d.	No	No

24 (May 95)
Under a personal services contract, which of the following circumstances will cause the discharge of a party's duties?
  a. Death of the party who is to receive the services.
  b. Cost of performing the services has doubled.
  c. Bankruptcy of the party who is to receive the services.
  d. Illegality of the services to be performed.

25 (November 91)
On May 25, 1991, Smith contracted with Jackson to repair Smith's cabin cruiser. The work was to begin on May 31, 1991. On May 26, 1991, the boat, while docked at Smith's pier, was destroyed by arson. Which of the following statements is correct with regard to the contract?

    a. Smith would <u>not</u> be liable to Jackson because of mutual mistake.

    b. Smith would be liable to Jackson for the profit Jackson would have made under the contract.

    c. Jackson would <u>not</u> be liable to Smith because performance by the parties would be impossible.

    d. Jackson would be liable to repair another boat owned by Smith.

23 (May 91)

Maco Corp. contracted to sell 1,500 bushels of potatoes to LBC Chips. The contract did not refer to any specific supply source for the potatoes. Maco intended to deliver potatoes grown on its farms. An insect infestation ruined Maco's crop but not the crops of other growers in the area. Maco failed to deliver the potatoes to LBC. LBC sued Maco for breach of contract. Under the circumstances, Maco will

    a. Lose, because it could have purchased potatoes from other growers to deliver to LBC.

    b .Lose, unless it can show that the purchase of substitute potatoes for delivery to LBC would make the contract unprofitable.

    c. Win, because the infestation was an act of nature that could <u>not</u> have been anticipated by Maco.

    d. Win, because both Maco and LBC are assumed to accept the risk of a crop failure.

51 (May 91)

Yost Corp., a computer manufacturer, contracted to sell 15 computers to Ivor Corp., a computer retailer. The contract specified that delivery was to be made by truck to Ivor's warehouse. Instead, Yost shipped the computers by rail. When Ivor claimed that Yost did not comply with the contract, Yost told Ivor that there had been a trucker's strike when the goods were shipped. Ivor refused to pay for the computers. Under these circumstances, Ivor

    a. Is obligated to pay for the computers because Yost made a valid substituted performance.

    b. Is obligated to pay for the computers because title to them passed to Ivor when Ivor received them.

    c. May return the computers and avoid paying for them because of the way Yost delivered them.

    d. May return the computers and avoid paying for them because the contract was void under the theory of commercial impracticability.

34 (May 89)

In September 1988, Cobb Company contracted with Thrifty Oil Company for the del ry of 100,000 gallons of heating oil at the price of 75¢ per gallon at regular specified intervals during the forthcoming winter. Due to an unseasonably warm winter, Cobb took delivery on only 70,000 gallons. In a suit against Cobb for breach of contract, Thrifty will

    a. Lose, because Cobb acted in good faith.

    b. Lose, because both parties are merchants and the UCC recognizes commercial impracticability.

    c. Win, because this is a requirements contract.

    d. Win, because the change of circumstances could have been contemplated by the parties.

37 (November 76)

A contract will be enforceable even if the party seeking to avoid performance alleges and proves

    a. Innocent misrepresentation.

    b. Fraud.

    c. Mutual mistake of material fact.

    d. Extreme hardship.

5 (May 94)

Suburban Properties, Inc. owns and manages several shopping centers.

On May 4, 1993, Suburban received from Bridge Hardware, Inc., one of its tenants, a signed letter proposing that the existing lease between Suburban and Bridge be modified to provide that certain utility costs be equally shared by Bridge and Suburban, effective June 1, 1993. Under the terms of the original lease, Bridge was obligated to pay all utility costs. On May 5, 1993, Suburban sent Bridge a signed letter agreeing to share the utility costs as proposed. Suburban later changed its opinion and refused to share in the utility costs.

On June 4, 1993, Suburban received from Dart Associates, Inc. a signed offer to purchase one of the shopping centers owned by Suburban. The offer provided as follows: a price of $9,250,000; it would not be withdrawn before July 1, 1993; and an acceptance must be received by Dart to be effective. On June 9, 1993, Suburban mailed Dart a signed acceptance. On June 10, before Dart had received Suburban's acceptance, Dart telephoned Suburban and withdrew its offer. Suburban's acceptance was received by Dart on June 12, 1993.

On June 22, 1993, one of Suburban's shopping centers was damaged by a fire, which started when the center was struck by lightning. As a result of the fire, one of the tenants in the shopping center, World Popcorn Corp., was forced to close its business and will be unable to reopen until the damage is repaired. World sued Suburban claiming that Suburban is liable for World's losses resulting from the fire. The lease between Suburban and World is silent in this regard.

Suburban has taken the following positions:

- Suburban's May 5, 1993, agreement to share equally the utility costs with Bridge is not binding on Suburban.
- Dart could not properly revoke its June 4 offer and must purchase the shopping center.
- Suburban is not liable to World for World's losses resulting from the fire.

Required: In separate paragraphs, determine whether Suburban's positions are correct and state the reasons for your conclusions.

Suburban is correct concerning the agreement to share utility costs with Bridge. A modification of a contract requires consideration to be binding on the parties. Suburban is not bound by the lease modification because Suburban did not receive any consideration in exchange for its agreement to share the cost of utilities with Bridge.

Suburban is not correct with regard to the Dart offer. An offer can be revoked at any time prior to acceptance. This is true despite the fact that the offer provides that it will not be withdrawn prior to a stated time. If no consideration is given in exchange for this promise not to withdraw the offer, the promise is not binding on the offeror. The offer provided that Suburban's acceptance would not be effective until received. Dart's June 10 revocation terminated Dart's offer. Thus, Suburban's June 9 acceptance was not effective.

Suburban is correct with regard to World's claim. The general rule is that destruction of, or damage to, the subject matter of a contract without the fault of either party terminates the contract. In this case, Suburban is not liable to World because Suburban is discharged from its contractual duties as a result of the fire, which made performance by it under the lease objectively impossible.

IX. Contract Remedies

1(a) (R97)

On April 1, Thorn and Birch negotiated the sale of Thorn's shopping center to Birch for $2.1 million ($2 million for the buildings and $100,000 for the land). The parties orally agreed on the following terms:

- Birch would make a cash down payment of $600,000.
- Birch would give Thorn a $1.5 million first mortgage on the property to secure the balance of the purchase price.
- The contract would contain an anti-assignment clause prohibiting assignment of the contract of sale or the mortgage.
- The contract would contain a "time of the essence" clause requiring that the closing take place on June 1.

No discussion took place regarding any existing mortgages or liens on the property. On April 14, the parties signed a written contract containing the above provisions.

On April 20, Birch took out a $1.5 million fire insurance policy with Acme Fire Insurance Co. on the buildings. The policy contained a standard 80% coinsurance clause.

On April 25, a title insurance report ordered by Birch revealed that there was an existing $500,000 mortgage on the property that had been recorded the previous February. The title report failed to disclose another mortgage for $50,000 that had been given years earlier by a prior owner of the land and had not been recorded. Thorn was aware of the $500,000 mortgage but not the earlier mortgage. The title report also disclosed that there were unpaid property taxes outstanding.

Contracts

On May 1, Thorn agreed to assign to a third party the prospective mortgage payments Thorn would receive from Birch.

When Birch received the title report and found out about Thorn's assignment of the mortgage payments, Birch accused Thorn of breach of contract for failing to disclose the prior mortgages and for violating the anti-assignment clause in the contract. Birch also insisted on postponing the contract closing date.

Thorn and Birch were able to resolve their differences.

- Birch reduced the mortgage being given to Thorn and assumed the previously recorded mortgage.
- The closing took place on July 1.
- Thorn recorded Birch's mortgage on July 5.
- The previously unrecorded mortgage was recorded on July 10.

On August 1, a fire caused $160,000 damage to the buildings. On that date, the fair market value of the buildings was $2 million. Acme contested payment of the claim, contending that Birch had no insurable interest in the buildings when the policy was taken out. Acme also contended that, even if Birch had an insurable interest, Birch would not be entitled to recover the entire amount of the loss because Birch is a coinsurer.

After the insurance issues were resolved and the buildings repaired, Birch stopped making payments on the mortgages and they were foreclosed. After payment of all foreclosure expenses, there was $1 million available to pay the outstanding mortgages. Thorn's mortgage had a principal and accrued interest balance of $950,000. The mortgage recorded in February had a principal and accrued interest balance of $475,000. The mortgage recorded on July 10 had a principal and accrued interest balance of $60,000.

The above transactions took place in a notice-race jurisdiction.

Required:

a. 1. State whether there was an enforceable contract for the sale of real property and list the requirements necessary to form such a contract.

2. State whether Thorn breached the contract by assigning the mortgage payments and give the reasons supporting your decision.

3. State and explain the remedies available to Birch if a court determined that Thorn, in any way, breached the contract.

---

a. 1. There was an enforceable contract between Thorn and Birch. The requirem. is necessary to form an enforceable contract for the sale of real property are as follows:

> An offer.
> An acceptance.
> Legally sufficient consideration.
> Parties who have the legal capacity to enter into a contract.
> A legal purpose.
> A written contract document.

2. Thorn did not breach the contract by assigning the mortgage payments to a third party. The right to receive a sum of money may be assigned even when a contract contains an anti-assignment clause.

3. If a court determined that Thorn breached the contract, Birch would be entitled to sue for either compensatory damages or specific performance. Compensatory damages would reimburse Birch for all expenses as well as any additional amounts spent in obtaining substitute property as a result of Thorn's actions. Specific performance would require Thorn to complete the sale of the property to Birch because each parcel of real property is unique.

A. Legal Remedies

9 (R99)

Which of the following concepts affect(s) the amount of monetary damages recoverable by the non-breaching party when a contract is breached?

	Forseeability of damages	Mitigation of damages
a.	Yes	Yes
b.	Yes	No
c.	No	Yes
d.	No	No

25 (May 93)

Master Mfg., Inc. contracted with Accur Computer Repair Corp. to maintain Master's computer system. Master's manufacturing process depends on its computer system operating properly at all times. A liquidated damages clause in the contract provided that Accur pay $1,000 to Master for each day that Accur was late responding to a service request. On January 12, Accur was notified that Master's computer system failed. Accur did not respond to Master's service request until January 15. If Master sues Accur under the liquidated damage provision of the contract, Master will

    a.   Win, unless the liquidated damage provision is determined to be a penalty.

    b.   Win, because under all circumstances liquidated damage provisions are enforceable.

    c.   Lose, because Accur's breach was <u>not</u> material.

    d.   Lose, because liquidated damage provisions violate public policy.

24 (May 91)

In general, a clause in a real estate contract entitling the seller to retain the purchaser's downpayment as liquidated damages if the purchaser fails to close the transaction, is enforceable

    a.   In all cases, when the parties have a signed contract.

    b.   If the amount of the downpayment bears a reasonable relationship to the probable loss.

    c.   As a penalty, if the purchaser intentionally defaults.

    d.   Only when the seller cannot compel specific performance.

13 (November 80)

The Balboa Custom Furniture Company sells fine custom furniture. It has been encountering difficulties lately with some customers who have breached their contracts after the furniture they have selected has been customized to their order or the fabric they have selected has been cut or actually installed on the piece of furniture purchased. The company therefore wishes to resort to a liquidated damages clause in its sales contract to encourage performance or provide an acceptable amount of damages. Regarding Balboa's contemplated resort to a liquidated damages clause, which of the following is correct?

    a.   Balboa may not use a liquidated damages clause since it is a merchant and is the preparer of the contract.

    b.   Balboa can simply take a very large deposit which will be forfeited if performance by a customer is not made for any reason.

    c.   The amount of the liquidated damages stipulated in the contract must be reasonable in light of the anticipated or actual harm caused by the breach.

    d.   Even if Balboa uses a liquidated damages clause in its sales contract, it will nevertheless have to establish that the liquidated damages claimed did not exceed actual damages by more than 10%.

22 (May 78)

The Johnson Corporation sent its only pump to the manufacturer to be repaired. It engaged Travis, a local trucking company, both to deliver the equipment to the manufacturer and to redeliver it to Johnson promptly upon completion of the repair. Johnson's entire plant was inoperative without this pump, but the trucking company did not know this. The trucking company delayed several days in its delivery of the repaired pump to Johnson. During the time it expected to be without the Pump, Johnson incurred $5,000 in lost profits. At the end of that time Johnson rented a replacement pump at a cost of $200 per day. As a result of these facts, what is Johnson entitled to recover from Travis?

    a.   The $200 a day cost incurred in renting the pump.

    b.   The $200 a day cost incurred in renting the pump plus the lost profits.

    c.   Actual damages plus punitive damages.

    d.   Nothing because Travis is <u>not</u> liable for damages.

5 (November 77)

Sharp, CPA, was engaged by Peters & Sons, a partnership, to give an opinion on the financial statements which were to be submitted to several prospective partners as part of a planned expansion of the firm. Sharp's fee was fixed on a per diem basis. After a period of intensive work, Sharp completed about half of the necessary field work. Then due to unanticipated demands upon his time by other clients, Sharp was forced to abandon the work. The planned expansion of the firm failed to materialize because the prospective partners lost interest when the audit report was <u>not</u> promptly available. Sharp offers to complete the task at a later date. This offer was refused. Peters & Sons suffered damages of $4,000 as a result. Under the circumstances, what is the probable outcome of a lawsuit between Sharp and Peters & Sons?

    a.   Sharp will be compensated for the reasonable value of the services actually performed.

    b.   Peters & Sons will recover damages for breach of contract.

    c.   Peters & Sons will recover both punitive damages and damages for breach of contract.

    d.   Neither Sharp nor Peters & Sons will recover against the other.

B. Equitable Remedies

32 (May 92)

To cancel a contract and to restore the parties to their original positions before the contract, the parties should execute a

    a.   Novation

    b.   Release

    c.   Rescission

    d.   Revocation

35 (May 92)

Kaye contracted to sell Hodges a building for $310,000. The contract required Hodges to pay the entire amount at closing. Kaye refused to close the sale of the building. Hodges sued Kaye. To what relief is Hodges entitled?

    a.   Punitive damages and compensatory damages.

    b.   Specific performance and compensatory damages.

    c.   Consequential damages or punitive damages.

    d.   Compensatory damages or specific performance.

48 (May 90)

Eagle Corporation solicited bids for various parts it uses in the manufacture of jet engines. Eagle received six offers and selected the offer of Sky Corporation. The written contract specified a price for 100,000 units, delivery on June 1 at Sky's plant, with payment on July 1. On June 1, Sky had completed a 200,000 unit run of parts similar to those under contract for Eagle and various other customers. Sky had not identified the parts to specific contracts. When Eagle's truck arrived to pick up the parts on June 1, Sky refused to deliver claiming the contract price was too low. Eagle was unable to cover in a reasonable time. Its production lines were in danger of shutdown because the parts were not delivered. Eagle would probably

    a.   Have as its only remedy the right of replevin.

    b.   Have the right of replevin only if Eagle tendered the purchase price on June 1.

    c.   Have as its only remedy the right to recover dollar damages.

    d.   Have the right to obtain specific performance.

25 (May 87)

Lark, CPA, entered into a signed contract with Bale Corp. to perform management advisory services for Bale. If Lark repudiates the contract prior to the date performance is due to begin, which of the following is not correct?

    a.   Bale could successfully maintain an action for breach of contract prior to the date performance is due to begin.

    b.   Bale can obtain a judgment for the monetary damages it incurred as a result of the repudiation.

    c.   Bale could successfully maintain an action for breach of contract after the date performance was due to begin.

    d.   Bale can obtain a judgment ordering Lark to perform.

18 (November 86)

Price signed a contract to sell Wyatt a parcel of land for $90,000. The entire sales price was payable at the closing. Price has decided to keep the land. If Wyatt commences an action against Price, what relief is Wyatt most likely to receive?

    a.   Specific performance.

    b.   Compensatory damages and specific performance.

    c.   Punitive damages.

    d.   Compensatory damages and punitive damages.

20 (May 83)

Myers entered into a contract to purchase a valuable rare coin from Eisen. Myers tendered payment which was refused by Eisen. Upon Eisen's breach, Myers brought suit to obtain the coin. The court will grant Myers

    a.   Compensatory damages.

    b.   Specific performance.

    c.   Reformation.

    d.   Restitution.

13 (May 82)

Foster offered to sell Lebow his garage for $27,000. The offer was in writing and signed by Foster. Foster gave Lebow five days to decide. On the fourth day Foster accepted a better offer from Dilby, who was unaware of the offer to Lebow. Foster subsequently conveyed the property to Dilby. Unaware of the sale to Dilby, Lebow telephoned Foster on the fifth day and unconditionally accepted the offer. Under the circumstances, Lebow

    a.   Is entitled to specific performance by Foster.

    b.   Has no rights against Foster.

    c.   Is entitled to damages.

    d.   Can obtain specific performance by Dilby upon depositing in court the $27,000 he agreed to pay.

2 (May 76)

The remedy of specific performance is available where the subject matter of the contract involves

    a.   Services.

    b.   Goods with a price of $500 or more.

    c.   Fraud.

    d.   Land.

C. Statutes of Limitation

11 (R97)

Which of the following statements is correct regarding the effect of the expiration of the period of the statute of limitations on a contract?

    a.   Once the period of the statute of limitations has expired, the contract is void.

    b.   The expiration of the period of the statute of limitations extinguishes the contract's underlying obligation.

    c.   A cause of action barred by the statute of limitations may not be revived.

    d.   The running of the statute of limitations bars access to judicial remedies.

25 (May 95)

Ordinarily, in an action for breach of a construction contract, the statute of limitations time period would be computed from the date the
    a.   Contract is negotiated.
    b.   Contract is breached.
    c.   Construction is begun.
    d.   Contract is signed.

22 (November 93)

Teller brought a lawsuit against Kerr ten years after an oral contract was made and eight years after it was breached. Kerr raised the statute of limitations as a defense. Which of the following allegations would be most important to Kerr's defense?
    a.   The contract was oral.
    b.   The contract could not be performed within one year from the date made.
    c.   The action was not timely brought because the contract was entered into ten years prior to the commencement of the lawsuit.
    d.   The action was not timely brought because the contract was allegedly breached eight years prior to the commencement of the lawsuit.

22 (May 93)

Which of the following statements correctly applies to a typical statute of limitations?
    a.   The statute requires that a legal action for breach of contract be commenced within a certain period of time after the breach occurs.
    b.   The statute provides that only the party against whom enforcement of a contract is sought must have signed the contract.
    c.   The statute limits the right of a party to recover damages for misrepresentation unless the false statements were intentionally made.
    d.   The statute prohibits the admission into evidence of proof of oral statements about the meaning of a written contract.

19 (November 92)

The statute of limitations for an alleged breach of contract
    a.   Does not apply if the contract was oral.
    b.   Requires that a lawsuit be commenced and a judgment rendered within a prescribed period of time.
    c.   Is determined on a case by case basis.
    d.   Generally commences on the date of the breach.

15 (May 91)

In 1959, Dart bought an office building from Graco under a written contract signed only by Dart. In 1991, Dart discovered that Graco made certain false representations during their negotiations concerning the building's foundation. Dart could have reasonably discovered the foundation problems by 1965. Dart sued Graco claiming fraud in the formation of the contract. Which of the following statements is correct?
    a.   The parol evidence rule will prevent the admission into evidence of proof concerning Dart's allegations.
    b.   Dart will be able to rescind the contract because both parties did not sign it.
    c.   Dart must prove that the alleged misrepresentations were part of the written contract because the contract involved real estate.
    d.   The statute of limitations would likely prevent Dart from prevailing because of the length of time that has passed.

22 (May 88)

On May 1, 1972, Mix, CPA, entered into an oral contract with Dell to provide certain accounting services to Dell. The contract was fully performed by both parties in 1974. On April 25, 1988, Dell commenced a breach of contract action against Mix claiming that Mix had improperly performed the accounting services. Mix's best defense to the action would likely be the

   a. Parol evidence rule.
   b. Statute of limitations.
   c. Statute of Frauds.
   d. Lack of consideration.

7 (May 86)

Simon has been sued by Major for breach of a real estate contract. Simon has raised the statute of limitations as a defense to Major's lawsuit. Under the circumstances, the statute of limitations

   a. Runs continuously under all circumstances commencing at the time the contract is breached.
   b. Does not apply to the contract between Simon and Major because it involves real estate.
   c. Will prevent recovery where the time set forth in the statute has expired.
   d. Is four years in all states.

2 (November 81)

When a lengthy delay has occurred between the breach of a contract and the commencement of the lawsuit, the statute of limitations defense may be raised. The statute

   a. Is three years irrespective of the type of legal action the plaintiff is bringing.
   b. Does not apply to an action brought in a court of equity.
   c. Is a defense to recovery if the requisite period of time has elapsed.
   d. Fixes a period of time in which the plaintiff must commence the action or be barred from recovery, regardless of the defendant's conduct during the period.

PART IV -- SURETYSHIP

TABLE OF CONTENTS

PART IV

SURETYSHIP

I. Introduction to Suretyship
A. Relationship in General; Creation of Suretyship

22 (November 82)

Which of the following transactions does not establish Samp as a surety?
a.   Samp says: "Ship goods to my son and I will pay for them."
b.   Samp signs commercial paper as an accommodation indorser for one of his suppliers.
c.   Samp guarantees a debt of a corporation he controls.
d.   Samp sells an office building to Park, and, as a part of the consideration, Park assumes Samp's mortgage on the property.

17 (November 77)

Which of the following transactions does not create a surety relationship?
a.   The assumption of a mortgage by the purchaser of a parcel of real estate.
b.   The blank indorsement of a check.
c.   Signing a non-negotiable promissory note as an accommodation maker.
d.   Obtaining professional malpractice insurance by a CPA.

11 (May 76)

The Martin Corporation was a small family-owned corporation whose owners were also the directors and officers. The corporation's bankers insisted that if any further credit were to be extended to the corporation the owners must guarantee payment by the corporation. This guaranty was agreed to by the owners in writing, and an additional $50,000 loan was granted to Martin Corporation. Which of the following best describes the legal significance of these events?
a.   The guaranty by the owners need not have been in writing since it was primarily for their own benefit.
b.   Once the owners agreed to the undertaking they automatically assumed responsibility for all of the corporation's prior debts.
c.   In the absence of specific provisions to the contrary, the owners are immediately liable on the debt in the event of the corporation's default.
d.   Since the owners each participated equally in the guaranty, each can be held liable by the bank, but only to the extent of his proportionate share in relation to the others.

12 (November 75)

Sims became an agent for Paul with the power to sell goods furnished by Paul but with the requirement that Sims would guarantee payment to Paul for all credit sales made by Sims. Under the circumstances
a.   Sims is an agent coupled with an interest.
b.   The Statute of Frauds applies to the above arrangement regardless of the amount of sales Sims makes.
c.   Sims is a surety vis-à-vis any credit sales he makes on Paul's behalf.
d.   The relationship between Sims and Paul is subject to the Federal Fair Labor Standards Act.

27 (November 74)

Lester Dunbar sold to Walter Masters real property on which Charles Endicott held a first mortgage which had been created at the time Dunbar purchased the property. Under the terms of the written purchase agreement, Masters expressly assumed the mortgage debt. Subsequent to the purchase, Masters defaulted in his payment of the mortgage debt. Endicott thereupon sought to enforce payment of the mortgage debt against Masters personally. Masters contends that Endicott should have proceeded against Dunbar, the original mortgagor, because he is primarily liable for the mortgage debt. Based upon the above facts

    a. Masters is correct in his assertion.

    b. Endicott lost all rights against Dunbar upon learning of the sale to Masters and having made no objection thereto.

    c. Dunbar is, in fact, a surety and must satisfy the mortgage if Masters does not.

    d. Upon default, Endicott must elect to proceed against one of the parties involved and by so doing has made a binding election, thereby releasing the other.

11 (May 74)

Andrews borrowed $20,000 from State Bank giving a mortgage on his building to State in that amount. Subsequently when the balance of the mortgage debt was $19,000, Andrews entered into a contract to sell the building to Baum for $25,000 with Baum to assume the mortgage at the closing date and pay Andrews $6,000. Baum obtained a loan of $6,000 from Thomas secured by a second mortgage, and Inch guaranteed payment of Baum's debt to Thomas. Under the circumstances described above

    a. If State Bank is notified of the transaction and makes no protest, Andrews is discharged.

    b. Absent any action by State Bank, Andrews is a surety on the first mortgage debt which Baum assumed.

    c. If Baum defaults on the first mortgage, payment by Andrews would not give Andrews a right of reimbursement from Baum.

    d. Inch and Andrews would be cosureties on the two mortgages.

B. Sureties and Guarantors

24 (May 94)

A party contracts to guaranty the collection of the debts of another. As a result of the guaranty, which of the following statements is correct?

    a. The creditor may proceed against the guarantor without attempting to collect from the debtor.

    b. The guaranty must be in writing.

    c. The guarantor may use any defenses available to the debtor.

    d. The creditor must be notified of the debtor's default by the guarantor.

26 (November 90)

Sorus and Ace have agreed, in writing, to act as guarantors of collection on a debt owed by Pepper to Towns, Inc. The debt is evidenced by a promissory note. If Pepper defaults, Towns will be entitled to recover from Sorus and Ace unless

    a. Sorus and Ace are in the process of exercising their rights against Pepper.

    b. Sorus and Ace prove that Pepper was insolvent at the time the note was signed.

    c. Pepper dies before the note is due.

    d. Towns had not attempted to enforce the promissory note against Pepper.

25 (November 81)

When the debtor has defaulted on its obligation, the creditor is entitled to recover from the surety, unless which of the following is present?

    a. The surety is in the process of exercising its right of exoneration against the debtor.

    b. The debtor has died or become insolvent.

    c. The creditor could collect the entire debt from the debtor's collateral in his possession.

    d. The surety is a guarantor of collection and the creditor failed to exercise due diligence in enforcing his remedies against the debtor.

27 (November 81)

Marbury Surety, Inc. agreed to act as a guarantor of collection of Madison's trade accounts for one year beginning on April 30, 1980, and was compensated for same. Madison's trade debtors are in default in payment of $3,853 as of May 1, 1981. As a result

a. Marbury is liable to Madison without any action on Madison's part to collect the amounts due.
b. Madison can enforce the guarantee even if it is <u>not</u> in writing since Marbury is a <u>del</u> <u>credere</u> agent.
c. The relationship between the parties must be filed in the appropriate county office since it is a continuing security transaction.
d. Marbury is liable for those debts for which a judgment is obtained and returned unsatisfied.

39 (May 80)

Nolan Surety Company has agreed to serve as a guarantor of collection (a form of conditional guaranty) of the accounts receivable of the Dunbar Sales Corporation. The duration of the guarantee is one year and the maximum liability assumed is $3,000. Nolan charged the appropriate fee for acting in this capacity. Which of the following statements <u>best</u> describes the difference between a guarantor of collection and the typical surety relationship?
a. A guaranty need <u>not</u> be in writing providing the duration is less than a year.
b. The guarantor is <u>not</u> immediately liable upon default; the creditor must first proceed against the debtor.
c. A guaranty is only available from a surety who is a compensated surety.
d. A guaranty is only used in connection with the sale of goods which have been guaranteed by the seller.

27 (November 76)

Barnes has agreed to become the conditional guarantor of collection on credit extended by Ace Supply Company on a contract for the sale of goods by Ace to Wilcox not exceeding $5,000.
a. If Wilcox defaults, Barnes is immediately liable for the amount of the debt outstanding.
b. A discharge in bankruptcy obtained by Wilcox will discharge Barnes.
c. Upon default, Barnes must proceed against Wilcox on Ace's behalf if Ace so requests.
d. Ace must first proceed against Wilcox before it is entitled to recover from Barnes.

20 (November 74)

Winslow Enterprises, Inc. sought an increased line of credit from New National Bank. New National insisted that Winslow obtain an acceptable surety. Winslow's president persuaded Peter Josephs, a Winslow board member and major stockholder, to agree to become its surety. Josephs stipulated, however, that he would become the surety only if he could do so as a conditional guarantor. New National was unhappy about the arrangement, but it agreed to accept Josephs' conditions because he was an excellent customer and a multimillionaire. Under these circumstances
a. The surety agreement need <u>not</u> be in writing because it was directly beneficial to Josephs.
b. New National must first give timely notice of default to Josephs and then proceed to judgment against Winslow before it can collect from Josephs.
c. There is a conflict of interest between Josephs and Winslow which necessitates his resignation as a Winslow board member.
d. The rights, duties, and obligations of Josephs as a conditional guarantor are the same as those of a usual surety.

II. The Suretyship Contract

25 (November 78)

Which of the following contractual prerequisites is <u>not</u> generally necessary to establish a legally enforceable surety relationship?
a. A signed writing.
b. The solvency of the principal debtor.
c. Separate consideration for the surety's promise.
d. The legal capacity of the surety.

18 (November 77)

Which of the following <u>best</u> describes what is required of a noncompensated surety?
a. The noncompensated surety must have the legal capacity to make contracts generally.
b. The noncompensated surety <u>cannot</u> be a corporation.

    c.   The noncompensated surety benefits by a rule which requires a creditor to first proceed against the principal debtor before the surety can be held liable.

    d.   The noncompensated surety must <u>not</u> directly or indirectly benefit from the undertaking.

26 (November 76)

Anthony is a surety on a debt owed by Victor to Day.

    a.   Day must satisfy the Uniform Commercial Code's filing requirements in order to perfect his security interest.

    b.   The surety undertaking need <u>not</u> be in writing if the surety is obtained by Victor at Day's request.

    c.   The extension of credit by Day to Victor, contingent upon Anthony's agreeing to act as surety, provides the consideration for Anthony's promise.

    d.   Upon default, Anthony would be allowed to deduct a personal claim that he has against Victor from his required payment to Day.

19 (November 74)

Martin Finance Corporation loaned David Small $2,500. Small agreed to repay in twelve monthly installments. After Small was late in making a payment, Martin indicated it needed additional protection and requested that Small obtain a surety. Small appealed to his longtime friend, Arthur Black, to help him. As a personal favor to Small, Black agreed and gave Small a written promise to answer for the debt in the event Small should default on the loan. Small defaulted and filed a voluntary petition in bankruptcy. Martin immediately demanded payment by Black. In this situation

    a.   Black's undertaking was <u>not</u> supported by consideration; hence, it is unenforceable.

    b.   Martin must wait until the bankruptcy proceeding has been concluded and the bankrupt's estate distributed to creditors.

    c.   The Statute of Frauds would <u>not</u> apply to Black's undertaking because he was a noncompensated surety.

    d.   Small's bankruptcy bars Martin from recovery against Black.

III. Relationship Between Surety and Principal--Reimbursement, Exoneration, and Subrogation

30 (November 95)

When a principal debtor defaults and a surety pays the creditor the entire obligation, which of the following remedies gives the surety the best method of collecting from the debtor?

    a.   Exoneration.

    b.   Contribution.

    c.   Subrogation.

    d.   Attachment.

20 (November 89)

Burns borrowed $240,000 from Dollar Bank as additional working capital for his business. Dollar required that the loan be collateralized to the extent of 20%, and that an acceptable surety for the entire amount be obtained. Surety Co. agreed to act as surety on the loan and Burns pledged $48,000 of negotiable bearer bonds. Burns defaulted. Which of the following statements is correct?

    a.   Dollar must first liquidate the collateral before it can proceed against Surety.

    b.   Surety is liable in full immediately upon default by Burns, but will be entitled to the collateral upon satisfaction of the debt.

    c.   Dollar must first proceed against Burns and obtain a judgment before it can proceed against the collateral.

    d.   Surety may proceed against Burns for the full amount of the loan even if Surety settles with Dollar for a lower amount.

21 (November 89)

If a debtor defaults and the debtor's surety satisfies the obligation, the surety acquires the right of

    a.   Subrogation.

    b.   Primary lien.

    c.   Indemnification.

    d.   Satisfaction.

28 (November 86)

Queen paid Pax & Co. to become the surety on a loan which Queen obtained from Squire. The loan is due and Pax wishes to compel Queen to pay Squire. Pax has not made any payments to Squire in its capacity as Queen's surety. Pax will be most successful if it exercises its right to

    a. Reimbursement (Indemnification).
    b. Contribution.
    c. Exoneration.
    d. Subrogation.

27 (May 83)

The right of subrogation

    a. May permit the surety to assert rights he otherwise could not assert.
    b. Is denied in bankruptcy.
    c. Arises only to the extent that it is provided in the surety agreement.
    d. Can not be asserted by a cosurety unless he includes all other cosureties.

26 (November 81)

Dependable Surety Company, Inc. issued a surety bond for value received which guaranteed: (1) completion of a construction contract Mason had made with Lund and (2) payment by Mason of his workmen. Mason defaulted and did not complete the contract. The workers were not paid for their last week's work. Mason had in fact become insolvent, and a petition in bankruptcy was filed two months after the issuance of the bond. What is the effect upon Dependable as a result of the above events?

    a. If Dependable pays damages to Lund as a result of the default on the contract, Dependable is entitled to recover in the bankruptcy proceedings the entire amount it paid prior to the payment of the general creditors of Mason.
    b. If Dependable pays the workers in full, it is entitled to the same priority in the bankruptcy proceedings that the workers would have had.
    c. If Dependable has another separate claim against Lund, Dependable may not set it off against any rights Lund may have under this contract.
    d. As a compensated surety, Dependable would be discharged from its surety obligation by Mason's bankruptcy.

35 (May 81)

Doral is the surety on a loan made by Nelson to Gordon. Which statement describes Doral's legal relationship or status among the respective parties?

    a. As between Gordon and Doral, Doral has the ultimate liability.
    b. Upon default by Gordon and payment by Doral, Doral is entitled to subrogation to the rights of Nelson or to obtain reimbursement from Gordon.
    c. Doral is a fiduciary insofar as Nelson is concerned.
    d. Doral is not liable immediately upon default by Gordon, unless the agreement so provides.

38 (May 81)

Reginald, who is insolvent, defaulted on a loan upon which Jayne was the surety. Edward, the creditor, demanded payment from Jayne of the amount owed by Reginald. The loan was also secured by a mortgage which Edward has the right to foreclose. Which of the following is Jayne's best legal course of action?

    a. Seek specific performance by Reginald.
    b. Refuse to pay until Reginald has been petitioned into bankruptcy and the matter has been decided by the trustee in bankruptcy.
    c. Pay Edward and resort to the subrogation rights to the collateral.
    d. Refuse to pay because Edward must first resort to the collateral.

Suretyship

36 (May 80)

Dilworth provided collateral to Maxim to secure Dilworth's performance of an obligation owed to Maxim. Maxim also obtained the Protection Surety Company as a surety for Dilworth's performance. Dilworth has defaulted and Protection has discharged the obligation in full. Which of the following is the correct legal basis for Protection's assertion of rights to the collateral?

    a.   Promissory estoppel.
    b.   Exoneration.
    c.   Indemnification.
    d.   Subrogation.

42 (May 80)

Moncrief is a surety on a $100,000 obligation owed by Vicars to Sampson. The debt is also secured by a $50,000 mortgage to Sampson on Vicars' factory. Vicars is in bankruptcy. Moncrief has satisfied the debt. Which of the following is a correct statement?

    a.   Moncrief is a secured creditor to the extent of the $50,000 mortgage and a general creditor for the balance.
    b.   Moncrief would not be entitled to a priority in bankruptcy, even though Sampson could validly claim it.
    c.   Moncrief is only entitled to the standing of a general creditor in bankruptcy.
    d.   Moncrief is entitled to nothing in bankruptcy since this was a risk he assumed.

5 (May 79)

Dunlop loaned Barkum $20,000 which was secured by a security agreement covering Barkum's machinery and equipment. A financing statement was properly filed covering the machinery and equipment. In addition, Delson was a surety on the Barkum loan. Barkum is now insolvent and a petition in bankruptcy has been filed against him. Delson paid the amount owed ($17,000) to Dunlop. The property was sold for $12,000. Which of the following is correct?

    a.   Delson has the right of a secured creditor to the $12,000 via subrogation to Dunlop's rights and the standing of general creditor for the balance.
    b.   To the extent Delson is not fully satisfied for the $17,000 he paid Dunlop, his claim against Barkum will not be discharged in bankruptcy.
    c.   Delson's best strategy would have been to proceed against Barkum in his own right for reimbursement.
    d.   Delson should have asserted his right of exoneration.

32 (November 76)

The surety's right of subrogation

    a.   Is not available in a bankruptcy proceeding.
    b.   Must be explicitly stated and defined in the surety undertaking.
    c.   Does not apply to situations where the creditor holds security insufficient to satisfy the debt.
    d.   Allows the surety, upon satisfying the obligation, to succeed to the creditor's rights.

12 (May 76)

Parker owed Charles $100,000 secured by a first mortgage on Parker's plant and land. Simons was the surety on the obligation but his liability was limited to $50,000. Parker defaulted on the debt and Charles demanded and received payment of $50,000 from Simons. Charles subsequently foreclosed the mortgage and upon sale of the mortgaged property netted $75,000, Simons claims a right of subrogation for his loss. Under the right of subrogation Simons should receive

    a.   Nothing.
    b. $25,000.
    c. $37,500.
    d. $50,000.

26 (November 74)

Alfred Matz negotiated with Basic Construction Company, Inc. to construct an apartment house. Desiring additional assurance of completion or payment of damages in the event of default, Matz insisted that a performance bond be posted. Basic obtained First Fidelity Surety Bonding Company as the surety on the undertaking. In addition to the normal terms of such contracts, First Fidelity insisted upon the right to complete the building in the event of default by Basic. The contract was drafted and signed by all the parties involved. Under the circumstances

a. Basic Construction is the third-party beneficiary of the contract.
b. If Basic Construction refuses to perform, Matz can obtain a court order obligating First Fidelity to complete construction.
c. First Fidelity has assumed the primary obligation to perform.
d. First Fidelity would be entitled to any and all rights that Matz would have against Basic in the event Basic defaults and First Fidelity pays.

4B (November 79)

Barclay Surety, Inc. is the surety on a construction contract that the Gilmore Construction Company made with Shadow Realty, Inc. By the terms of the surety obligation, Barclay is not only bound to Shadow, but also is bound to satisfy materialmen and laborers in connection with the contract. Gilmore defaulted, and Barclay elected to complete the project and pay all claims and obligations in connection with the contract, including all unpaid materialmen and laborers' claims against Gilmore. The total cost to complete exceeded the construction contract payments Barclay received from Shadow. Some of the materialmen who were satisfied had either liens or security interests against Gilmore. Gilmore has filed a voluntary bankruptcy petition.

Required: Answer the following, setting forth reasons for any conclusions stated.
What rights does Barclay have as a result of the above facts?

Barclay is, of course, entitled to reimbursement from Gilmore. However, since Gilmore is bankrupt, Barclay will receive the same percentage on the dollar as will all other general creditors of Gilmore's estate. However, Barclay is subrogated to the rights of the materialmen and laborers it has satisfied. Specifically, it would have the right to assert the liens and security interests of the materialmen. Furthermore, wage earners are entitled to a limited priority in a bankruptcy proceeding, which Barclay could assert.

IV. Relationship Between Surety and Creditor--In General
A. Application of Collateral

30 (November 94)

Which of the following rights does a surety have?

	Right to compel the creditor to collect from the principal debtor	Right to compel the creditor to proceed against the principal debtor's collateral
a.	Yes	Yes
b.	Yes	No
c.	No	Yes
d.	No	No

19 (November 77)

Franks is a surety on a $5,000 debt owed by Smith to Jones. Jones also holds as collateral property worth $4,000 belonging to Smith. Under these circumstances, which of the following statements is true?

a. Franks has the right to the property immediately upon default.
b. Jones need <u>not</u> first proceed against the collateral in order to hold Franks liable.
c. Jones may return the collateral to Smith at any time prior to default without impairing his rights against Franks.
d. Jones must file a financing statement in order to perfect his rights in the collateral he holds.

B. Payments by Debtor

13 (May 74)

Park owed Collins $1,000 and $2,000, respectively, on two separate unsecured obligations. Smythe had become a surety on the $2,000 debt at the request of Park when Park became indebted to Collins. Both debts matured on June 1. Park was able to pay only $600 at that time, and he forwarded that amount to Collins without instructions. Under these circumstances

a. Collins must apply the funds pro rata in proportion to the two debts.

b. Collins must apply the $600 to the $2,000 debt if there is no surety on the $1,000 debt.

c. Smythe will be discharged to the extent of $400 if Collins on request of Smythe fails to apply $400 to the $2,000 debt.

d. Collins is free to apply the $600 to the debts as he sees fit.

V. Relationship Between Surety and Creditor--Surety's Defenses
A. In General

26 (May 95)

Green was unable to repay a loan from State Bank when due. State refused to renew the loan unless Green provided an acceptable surety. Green asked Royal, a friend, to act as surety on the loan. To induce Royal to agree to become a surety, Green fraudulently represented Green's financial condition and promised Royal discounts on merchandise sold at Green's store. Royal agreed to act as surety and the loan was renewed. Later, Green's obligation to State was discharged in Green's bankruptcy. State wants to hold Royal liable. Royal may avoid liability

a. If Royal can show that State was aware of the fraudulent representations.

b. If Royal was an uncompensated surety.

c. Because the discharge in bankruptcy will prevent Royal from having a right of reimbursement.

d. Because the arrangement was void at the inception.

15 (November 82)

Markum contacted the Variable Loan Company for a business loan. Variable refused to make the loan unless adequate security or an acceptable surety could be provided. Markum asked Duffy, one of his trade customers, to act as surety on the loan. In order to induce Duffy to sign, Markum made certain fraudulent representations and submitted a materially false financial statement. He also promised Duffy favorable treatment if Duffy would agree to act as surety for him. Markum is now insolvent and Variable seeks to hold Duffy liable. Duffy may avoid liability

a. Since the surety undertaking was void at the inception.

b. Based upon fraud if Duffy can show Variable was aware of the fraud.

c. Because Variable had a duty to warn Duffy about Markum's financial condition and did not do so.

d. Because the law of suretyship favors the surety where neither the surety nor the creditor is at fault.

23 (May 82)

Which of the following defenses by a surety will be effective to avoid liability?

a. Lack of consideration to support the surety undertaking.

b. Insolvency in the bankruptcy sense by the debtor.

c. Incompetency of the debtor to make the contract in question.

d. Fraudulent statements by the principal-debtor which induced the surety to assume the obligation and which were unknown to the creditor.

36 (May 81)

Don loaned $10,000 to Jon, and Robert agreed to act as surety. Robert's agreement to act as surety was induced by (1) fraudulent misrepresentations made by Don concerning Jon's financial status and (2) a bogus unaudited financial statement of which Don had no knowledge, and which was independently submitted by Jon to Robert. Which of the following is correct?

a. Don's fraudulent misrepresentations will <u>not</u> provide Robert with a valid defense unless they were contained in a signed writing.
b. Robert will be liable on his surety undertaking despite the facts since the defenses are personal defenses.
c. Robert's reliance upon Jon's financial statements makes Robert's surety undertaking voidable.
d. Don's fraudulent misrepresentations provide Robert with a defense which will prevent Don from enforcing the surety undertaking.

31 (May 77)

A surety will <u>not</u> be liable on an undertaking if
a. The principal is a minor.
b. The underlying obligation was illegal.
c. The principal was insolvent at the time of the surety's agreement to act as surety.
d. The surety was mistaken as to the legal implications of the surety agreement.

16 (May 76)

Young, a minor, purchased a car from Ace Auto Sales by making a down payment and signing a note for the balance. The note was guaranteed by Rich. Subsequently, Young sought to return the car and <u>not</u> pay off the note because Ace made false representations concerning the car's mileage at the time of sale. Which of the following <u>best</u> describes the legal implications in these circumstances?
a. <u>Neither</u> Young <u>nor</u> Rich is liable on the note solely because Young is a minor.
b. Young's attempt to return the car, in and of itself, released Rich of any liability.
c. The fraud perpetrated upon Young is a valid defense to Rich's guaranty.
d. There are <u>no</u> valid defenses for Rich and Young and the only recourse is to seek to reduce the amount owed based upon a counterclaim for fraud.

10 (May 74)

Bob purchased a car from Jones. At Bob's request, Paul guaranteed payment at the time of sale. Which of the following defenses can Paul successfully assert against Jones when sued following nonpayment of the debt by Bob at maturity?
a. Death of Bob.
b. Infancy of Bob.
c. Nondisclosure of facts known to Jones at the time of sale which were unknown to Paul and materially increased the risk.
d. Lack of consideration by Jones to Paul for guaranteeing payment.

B. Tender of Performance

29 (November 95)

Which of the following acts always will result in the total release of a compensated surety?
a. The creditor changes the manner of the principal debtor's payment.
b. The creditor extends the principal debtor's time to pay.
c. The principal debtor's obligation is partially released.
d. The principal debtor's performance is tendered.

24 (May 84)

Which of the following defenses will release a surety from liability?
a. Insanity of the principal debtor at the time the contract was entered into.
b. Failure by the creditor to promptly notify the surety of the principal debtor's default.
c. Refusal by the creditor, with knowledge of the surety relationship, to accept the principal debtor's unconditional tender of payment in full.
d. Release by the creditor of the principal debtor's obligation without the surety's consent but with the creditor's reservation of his rights against the surety.

44 (May 80)

Cornwith agreed to serve as a surety on a loan by Super Credit Corporation to Fairfax, one of Cornwith's major customers. The relationship between Fairfax and Super deteriorated to a point of hatred as a result of several late payments on the loan. On the due date of the final payment, Fairfax appeared 15 minutes before closing and tendered payment of the entire amount owing to Super. The office manager of Super told Fairfax that he was too late and would have to pay the next day with additional interest and penalties. Fairfax again tendered the payment, which was again refused. It is now several months later and Super is seeking to collect from either Cornwith or Fairfax or both. What are Super's rights under the circumstances?

    a. It cannot collect anything from either party.
    b. The tender of performance released Cornwith from his obligation.
    c. The tender of performance was too late and rightfully refused.
    d. Cornwith is released only to the extent that the refusal to accept the tender harmed him.

30 (May 77)

Ludwig was approached by Cranston to borrow $10,000. Ludwig demanded that a surety be obtained. Marcross agreed to act as the surety on the loan. Upon default by Cranston, which of the following defenses would defeat Ludwig's claim against Marcross?

    a. Fraud by Cranston in obtaining Marcross's surety undertaking.
    b. Tender of performance by Cranston to Ludwig, which was refused.
    c. The fact that Cranston was in unsound financial condition at the time the loan was made.
    d. Lack of consideration given by Ludwig to Marcross in obtaining the surety undertaking.

28 (November 74)

William Joyce, a creditor, has instituted suit seeking recovery from Howard Frank as a surety. Frank's <u>best</u> defense would be to assert

    a. The debtor's infancy.
    b. Fraud by the debtor which induced him to act as surety.
    c. Tender of performance by the debtor.
    d. Failure of the creditor to first proceed against the debtor.

C. Modification of Principal's Duty; Impairment of Security

25 (May 94)

Which of the following events will release a noncompensated surety from liability?

    a. Release of the principal debtor's obligation by the creditor but with the reservation of the creditor's rights against the surety.
    b. Modification by the principal debtor and creditor of their contract that materially increases the surety's risk of loss.
    c. Filing of an involuntary petition in bankruptcy against the principal debtor.
    d. Insanity of the principal debtor at the time the contract was entered into with the creditor.

Items 26 and 27 are based on the following information:

State Bank loaned Barr $80,000 and received securities valued at $20,000 from Barr as collateral. At the request of State, Barr entered into an agreement with Rice and Noll to act as cosureties on the loan. The agreement provided that Rice and Noll's maximum liability would be $80,000 each.

26 (May 87)

Which of the following defenses asserted by Rice will completely release Rice from liability to State?

    a. State and Barr entered into a binding agreement to extend the time for payment that increased the sureties' risk and was agreed to without the sureties' consent.
    b. Fraud by Barr which induced Rice to enter into the surety contract and which was unknown to State.
    c. Release of Barr's obligation by State without Rice's or Noll's consent but with State's reservation of its rights against Rice.
    d. Return of the collateral to Barr by State without Rice's or Noll's consent.

27 (May 87)

If State releases Noll without Rice's consent and Barr subsequently defaults at a time when the collateral held by State is worthless and the loan balance is $80,000, Rice's maximum potential liability will be

    a. $0.

    b. $40,000.

    c. $60,000.

    d. $80,000.

24 (November 82)

Knott obtained a loan of $10,000 from Charles on January 1, 1982, payable on April 15, 1982. At the time of the loan, Beck became a noncompensated surety thereon by written agreement. On April 15, 1982, Knott was unable to pay and wrote to Charles requesting an extension of time. Charles made no reply, but did not take any immediate action to recover. On May 30, 1982, Charles demanded payment from Knott and, failing to collect from him, proceeded against Beck. Based upon the facts stated

    a.   Charles was obligated to obtain a judgment against Knott returned unsatisfied before he could collect from Beck.

    b.   Beck is released from his surety obligation because Charles granted Knott an extension of time.

    c.   Charles may recover against Beck despite the fact Beck was a noncompensated surety.

    d.   Beck is released because Charles delayed in proceeding against Knott.

25 (November 82)

Which of the following will release a surety from liability?

    a.   Release of the principal debtor from liability with the consent of the surety.

    b.   Delegation of the debtor's obligation to another party with the acquiescence of the creditor.

    c.   Lack of capacity because the debtor is a minor.

    d.   Discharge of the debtor in bankruptcy.

24 (November 81)

Dustin is a very cautious lender. When approached by Lanier regarding a $2,000 loan, he not only demanded an acceptable surety but also collateral equal to 50% of the loan. Lanier obtained King Surety Company as his surety and pledged rare coins worth $1,000 with Dustin. Dustin was assured by Lanier one week before the due date of the loan that he would have no difficulty in making payment. He persuaded Dustin to return the coins since they had increased in value and he had a prospective buyer. What is the legal effect of the release of the collateral upon King Surety?

    a.   It totally releases King Surety.

    b.   It does not release King Surety if the collateral was obtained after its promise.

    c.   It releases King Surety to the extent of the value of the security.

    d.   It does not release King Surety unless the collateral was given to Dustin with the express understanding that it was for the benefit of King Surety as well as Dustin.

29 (November 81)

Allen was the surety for the payment of rent by Lear under a lease from Rosenthal Rentals. The lease was for two years. A clause in the lease stated that at the expiration of the lease, the lessee had the privilege to renew upon thirty days' prior written notice or, if the lessee remained in possession after its expiration, it was agreed that the lease was to continue for two years more. There was a default in the payment of rent during the extended term of the lease and Rosenthal is suing Allen for the rent due based upon the guarantee. Allen contends that he is liable only for the initial term of the lease and not for the extended term. Allen is

    a.   Not liable since it does not appear that a judgment against Lear has been returned unsatisfied.

    b.   Not liable because there has been a material alteration of the surety undertaking.

    c.   Not liable because there was a binding extension of time.

    d.   Liable on the surety undertaking which would include the additional two years.

Suretyship

1 (May 79)

Martinson borrowed $50,000 from Wisdom Finance Company. The loan was evidenced by a non-negotiable promissory note secured by a first mortgage on Martinson's ranch. One of the terms of the note required acceleration of repayment in the event that Wisdom "deemed itself insecure." When the value of the property declined, Wisdom notified Martinson that pursuant to the terms of the note, it "deemed itself insecure" and demanded that either additional collateral or an acceptable surety be provided. Martinson arranged for Clark, a personal friend, to act as surety on the loan. Clark signed the note as an indorser and Wisdom agreed in writing not to accelerate repayment of the loan during the life of the debt. Martinson has defaulted. Which of the following is a correct statement?

    a.   Clark's promise is not supported by consideration, hence is unenforceable.

    b.   Clark is a guarantor of collection and his obligation is conditioned upon Wisdom's first proceeding against Martinson.

    c.   Release of the mortgage by Wisdom would release Clark to the extent of the value of the property.

    d.   Wisdom must first foreclose the mortgage before it can proceed against Clark.

20 (November 78)

Maxwell was the head cashier of the Amalgamated Merchants Bank. The Excelsior Surety Company bonded Maxwell for $200,000. An internal audit revealed a $1,000 embezzlement by Maxwell. Maxwell persuaded the bank not to report him, and he promised to pay the money back within ten days. The bank acquiesced and neither the police nor Excelsior was informed of the theft. Maxwell shortly thereafter embezzled $75,000 and fled. Excelsior refuses to pay. Is Excelsior liable? Why?

    a.   Excelsior is liable since the combined total of the embezzlements is less than the face amount of the surety bond.

    b.   Excelsior is liable for $75,000, but not the $1,000 since a separate arrangement was agreed to by Amalgamated with Maxwell.

    c.   Excelsior is liable since it is a compensated surety and as such assumed the risk.

    d.   Excelsior is not liable since the failure to give notice of the first embezzlement is a valid defense.

24 (November 76)

A surety can avoid liability on his surety undertaking if he can show

    a.   Death of the creditor.

    b.   Bankruptcy of the creditor.

    c.   A material alteration by the debtor and creditor of the contract which the surety guaranteed.

    d.   Lack of capacity of the debtor.

15 (May 76)

Which of the following defenses asserted by a surety should be effective in a suit by a creditor?

    a.   Insolvency of the creditor and the principal debtor.

    b.   Death of the principal debtor.

    c.   Failure of the creditor to foreclose a mortgage on property which he holds to secure the principal debtor's performance.

    d.   A material variance of the surety's undertaking as a result of a modification in the principal debtor's obligation.

VI. Cosureties

(R03)

Teller, Kerr, and Ace are co-sureties on a $120,000 loan with maximum liabilities of $20,000, $40,000, and $60,000, respectively. The debtor defaulted on the loan when the loan balance was $60,000. Ace paid the lender $48,000 in full settlement of all claims against Teller, Kerr, and Ace. What amount may Ace collect from Kerr?

    a. $0

    b. $16,000

    c. $20,000

    d. $28,000

28 (November 95)

Which of the following rights does one cosurety generally have against another cosurety?

a. Exoneration.
b. Subrogation.
c. Reimbursement.
d. Contribution.

31 (November 94)

Ingot Corp. lent Flange $50,000. At Ingot's request, Flange entered into an agreement with Quill and West for them to act as compensated cosureties on the loan in the amount of $100,000 each. Ingot released West without Quill's or Flange's consent, and Flange later defaulted on the loan. Which of the following statements is correct?

a. Quill will be liable for 50% of the loan balance.
b. Quill will be liable for the entire loan balance.
c. Ingot's release of West will have <u>no</u> effect on Flange's and Quill's liability to Ingot.
d. Flange will be released for 50% of the loan balance.

25 (November 93)

Nash, Owen, and Polk are cosureties with maximum liabilities of $40,000, $60,000 and $80,000, respectively. The amount of the loan on which they have agreed to act as cosureties is $180,000. The debtor defaulted at a time when the loan balance was $180,000. Nash paid the lender $36,000 in full settlement of all claims against Nash, Owen, and Polk. The total amount that Nash may recover from Owen and Polk is

a. $0
b. $24,000
c. $28,000
d. $140,000

26 (November 92)

Ivor borrowed $420,000 from Lear Bank. At Lear's request, Ivor entered into an agreement with Ash, Kane, and Queen for them to act as cosureties on the loan. The agreement between Ivor and the cosureties provided that the maximum liability for each cosurety was: Ash, $84,000; Kane, $126,000; and Queen, $210,000. After making several payments, Ivor defaulted on the loan. The balance was $280,000. If Queen pays $210,000 and Ivor subsequently pays $70,000, what amounts may Queen recover from Ash and Kane?

a. $0 from Ash and $0 from Kane.
b. $42,000 from Ash and $63,000 from Kane.
c. $70,000 from Ash and $70,000 from Kane.
d. $56,000 from Ash and $84,000 from Kane.

28 (November 92)

A distinction between a surety and a cosurety is that only a cosurety is entitled to

a. Reimbursement (Indemnification).
b. Subrogation.
c. Contribution.
d. Exoneration.

26 (November 91)

Mane Bank lent Eller $120,000 and received securities valued at $30,000 as collateral. At Mane's request, Salem and Rey agreed to act as uncompensated cosureties on the loan. The agreement provided that Salem's and Rey's maximum liability would be $120,000 each.

Mane released Rey without Salem's consent. Eller later defaulted when the collateral held by Mane was worthless and the loan balance was $90,000. Salem's maximum liability is

a. $30,000
b. $45,000
c. $60,000
d. $90,000

27 (May 91)

Lane promised to lend Turner $240,000 if Turner obtained sureties to secure the loan. Turner agreed with Rivers, Clark, and Zane for them to act as cosureties on the loan from Lane. The agreement between Turner and the cosureties provided that compensation be paid to each of the cosureties. It further indicated that the maximum liability of each cosurety would be as follows: Rivers $240,000, Clark $80,000, and Zane $160,000. Lane accepted the commitments of the sureties and made the loan to Turner. After paying ten installments totaling $100,000, Turner defaulted. Clark's debts, including the surety obligation to Lane on the Turner loan, were discharged in bankruptcy. Later, Rivers properly paid the entire outstanding debt of $140,000. What amount may Rivers recover from Zane?

a. $0
b. $56,000
c. $70,000
d. $84,000

21 (November 88)

Ott and Bane agreed to act as cosureties on an $80,000 loan that Cread Bank made to Dash. Ott and Bane are each liable for the entire $80,000 loan. Subsequently, Cread released Ott from liability without Bane's consent and without reserving its rights against Bane. If Dash subsequently defaults, Cread will be entitled to collect a maximum of

a. $0 from Bane.
b. $0 from Dash.
c. $40,000 from Bane.
d. $40,000 from Dash.

29 (May 87)

A distinction between a surety and a cosurety is that only a cosurety is entitled to

a. Contribution.
b. Exoneration.
c. Subrogation.
d. Reimbursement (Indemnification).

32 (November 85)

West promised to make Noll a loan of $180,000 if Noll obtained sureties to secure the loan. Noll entered into an agreement with Carr, Gray, and Pine to act as cosureties on his loan from West. The agreement between Noll and the cosureties provided for compensation to be paid to each of the cosureties. It further indicated that the maximum liability of each cosurety would be as follows: Carr $180,000, Gray $60,000, and Pine $120,000. West accepted the commitment of the sureties and made the loan to Noll. After paying nine installments totaling $90,000, Noll defaulted. Gray's debts (including his surety obligation to West on the Noll loan) were discharged in bankruptcy. Subsequently, Carr properly paid the entire debt outstanding of $90,000. What amounts may Carr recover from the cosureties?

	Gray	Pine
a.	$0	$30,000
b.	$0	$36,000
c.	$15,000	$30,000
d.	$30,000	$30,000

Items 22 and 23 are based on the following information:

Jane wishes to obtain a loan of $90,000 from Silver Corp. At the request of Silver, Jane has entered into an agreement with Bing, Piper, and Long to act as cosureties on the loan. The agreement between Jane and the cosureties stated that the maximum liability of each cosurety is: Bing $60,000, Piper $30,000, and Long $90,000. Based upon the surety relationship, Silver agreed to make the loan. After paying three installments totalling $30,000, Jane defaulted.

22 (May 84)

Prior to making payment, the cosureties may seek the remedy of

a. Contribution.

b. Indemnification.

c. Subrogation.

d. Exoneration.

23 (May 84)

If Long properly paid the entire debt outstanding of $60,000, what amount may Long recover from the cosureties?

a. $30,000 from Bing and $30,000 from Piper.

b. $20,000 from Bing and $20,000 from Piper.

c. $20,000 from Bing and $10,000 from Piper.

d. $15,000 from Bing and $15,000 from Piper.

26 (May 83)

A release of a cosurety by the creditor

a. Will have <u>no</u> effect on the obligation of the other cosurety.

b. Will release the other cosurety entirely.

c. Will release the other cosurety to the extent that his right to contribution has been adversely affected.

d. Need <u>not</u> be a binding release in order to affect the rights of the parties.

20 (November 82)

Gray and Far are cosureties on a loan of $100,000 made by the Durham Bank to Wilson Fabric, Inc. Gray guaranteed the loan in full and Far guaranteed $50,000 of the loan. Each was aware of the cosurety relationship. Gray received $50,000 of collateral from Wilson as a condition precedent to his serving as cosurety. Wilson has defaulted on the loan. With respect to their ultimate liabilities

a. Gray is liable for $50,000 but has the exclusive benefit of resort to the collateral to repay his loss.

b. Gray and Far will each be liable for $50,000.

c. Since Gray received collateral and Far did not, the relationship is actually one of sub-suretyship with Gray being liable for the entire amount.

d. In the final settlement between the sureties, Far will be liable for a net amount of $16,667.

25 (May 82)

In relation to the principal debtor, the creditor and a fellow cosurety, the cosurety is <u>not</u> entitled to

a. Exoneration against the debtor under any circumstances.

b. A pro-rata contribution by his fellow surety or sureties if he pays the full amount.

c. Be subrogated to the rights of the creditor upon satisfaction of the debt.

d. Avoid performance because his cosurety refuses to perform.

41 (May 80)

Simpson and Thomas made separate contracts of suretyship with Allan to guarantee repayment of a $12,000 loan Allan made to Parker. Simpson's guarantee was for $12,000 and Thomas' for $8,000. In the event Simpson pays the full amount ($12,000), what may he recover from Thomas?

a. Nothing since their contracts were separate.

b. $4,800.

c. $6,000.

d. $8,000.

Suretyship

7 (May 79)

Crawford and Blackwell separately agreed to act as sureties on a loan of $25,000 by Lux to Factor. Each promised to pay the full $25,000 upon default of Factor. Lux subsequently released Blackwell from his surety undertaking. Which of the following is a correct statement?

    a.   The release has <u>no</u> effect upon Crawford's right to contribution if he is obligated to pay.

    b.   The release of Blackwell had <u>no</u> effect upon Crawford's liability.

    c.   The release of Blackwell also totally released Crawford.

    d.   The release of Blackwell also released Crawford to the extent of $12,500.

21 (November 78)

Adams, Baker, and Carter are cosureties on a $250,000 loan by the Wilson National Bank to Marathon Motors, Inc. Adams is a surety for the full amount of the debt; Baker's obligation is limited to $100,000; and Carter has agreed to pay $50,000 upon default. In the event of default by Marathon on the entire $250,000 loan, what is the liability of Adams, Baker, and Carter?

    a.   Baker is liable for the first $100,000; Carter, the next $50,000; and Adams, the balance.

    b.   Baker and Adams are each liable for $100,000 and Carter for $50,000.

    c.   If both Baker and Carter know of Adam's obligation for the full amount, then they are <u>not</u> liable unless Adams can <u>not</u> satisfy the debt.

    d.   Adams is liable for $156,250; Baker, $62,500; and Carter, $31,250.

24 (November 78)

Ace Corporation loaned $10,000 to King Enterprises, Inc., one of its best customers. The loan was for three years and was evidenced by a note duly executed by King's president on behalf of the corporation. In addition, Walsh and Paxton, King's principal shareholders, had orally guaranteed the repayment of the loan. With respect to Walsh and Paxton, which of the following is a correct statement?

    a.   Unless otherwise indicated, each guaranteed $5,000 of the loan.

    b.   They will be denied the usual surety defenses.

    c.   They are cosureties and, as such, their surety undertaking must be in a signed writing.

    d.   Some additional consideration, independent of the making of the loan by Ace, must pass directly to Walsh and Paxton.

32 (May 77)

What rights or defenses does a cosurety have?

    a.   The same legal rights against fellow sureties as a surety would have against a sub-surety.

    b.   The same rights as a single surety would have, but in addition, has the right of contribution from cosureties.

    c.   A defense against liability for more than a proportionate share of the undertaking.

    d.   A defense against liability unless all cosureties are sued jointly.

31 (November 76)

In order to establish a cosurety relationship the two or more sureties must

    a.   Be aware of each others existence at the time of their contract.

    b.   Sign the same contract creating the debt and the cosurety relationship.

    c.   Be bound to answer for the same debt or duty of the debtor.

    d.   Be bound for the same amount and share equally in the obligation to satisfy the creditor.

25 (November 74)

In order to have a cosurety relationship

    a.   Each surety must sign the original loan and surety agreement at the time credit is extended.

    b.   Each surety must be bound to answer for the same duty and share in the loss upon default.

    c.   The creditor must agree to proceed against them jointly in the event of default.

    d.   Any collateral provided by the debtor must be held jointly or divided equally among the sureties.

3B (November 83)

Mars Finance Company was approached by Grant, the president of Hoover Corp., for a loan of $25,000 for Hoover. After careful evaluation of Hoover's financial condition, Mars decided it would not make the loan unless the loan was collateralized or guaranteed by one or more sureties for a total of $30,000. Hoover agreed to provide collateral in the form of a security interest in Hoover's equipment. The initial valuation of the equipment was $20,000 and Hoover obtained Victory Surety Company as a surety for the additional $10,000. Prior to the granting of the loan, the final valuation on the equipment was set at $15,000 and Mars insisted on additional surety protection of $5,000. Grant personally assumed this additional surety obligation. Hoover has defaulted and Mars first proceeded against the collateral, which was sold for $17,000. It then proceeded against Victory for the balance. Victory paid the $8,000 and now seeks a $4,000 contribution from Grant.

Grant asserts the following defenses and arguments in order to avoid or limit his liability:
- That he is not liable since Mars elected to proceed against the collateral.
- That Mars by suing Victory for the deficiency, released him.
- That he is not a cosurety because Victory did not know of his existence until after default and his surety obligation was not assumed at the time nor was it equal in amount, hence, there is no right of contribution.
- That in no event is he liable for the full $4,000 sought by Victory.

Required: Answer the following, setting forth reasons for any conclusions stated.

Discuss in separate paragraphs each of the above defenses asserted by Grant and indicate the amount of Grant's liability.

> Grant is incorrect in his first three assertions and correct in connection with his fourth assertion for the following reasons:
> - The law is clear regarding the right to collateral and its effect between the creditor and the surety. The creditor has the right to resort to any available collateral. Resort to the collateral by the creditor in no way affects the creditor's right to proceed against a surety or sureties for the balance.
> - A creditor may choose to sue one or more of the sureties without impairing his rights against those not sued. Similarly, he has the right to sue one surety if he wishes, and such a choice does not release the surety who was not sued insofar as the rights of his fellow surety to seek contribution. Suing one but not all of the sureties does not constitute a release by the creditor.
> - All of the defenses asserted in the fact situation are invalid. Grant is a cosurety since he is answering for the same debt as Victory, and there is a right of contribution which Victory may assert against Grant.
> - Since Grant's surety undertaking was one-third of the combined surety undertakings, he is liable for $2,666.67 only and not the full $4,000.

3A (November 80)

Hardaway Lending, Inc. had a 4 year $800,000 callable loan to Superior Metals, Inc. outstanding. The loan was callable at the end of each year upon Hardaway's giving 60 days written notice. Two and one-half years remained of the four years. Hardaway reviewed the loan and decided that Superior Metals was no longer a prime lending risk and it therefore decided to call the loan. The required written notice was sent to and received by Superior 60 days prior to the expiration of the second year. Merriweather, Superior's chief executive officer and principal shareholder, requested Hardaway to continue the loan at least for another year. Hardaway agreed, provided that an acceptable commercial surety would guarantee $400,000 of the loan and Merriweather would personally guarantee repayment in full. These conditions were satisfied and the loan was permitted to continue. The following year the loan was called and Superior defaulted. Hardaway released the commercial surety but retained its rights against Merriweather and demanded that Merriweather pay the full amount of the loan. Merriweather refused, asserting the following:
-There was no consideration for his promise. The loan was already outstanding and he personally received nothing.
-Hardaway must first proceed against Superior before it can collect from Merriweather.
-Hardaway had released the commercial surety, thereby releasing Merriweather.

Required: Answer the following, setting forth reasons for any conclusions stated.

Discuss the validity of each of Merriweather's assertions.

The first two defenses asserted by Merriweather are invalid. The third defense is partially valid.

Consideration on Hardaway's part consisted of foregoing the right to call the Superior Metals loan. The fact that the loan was already outstanding is irrelevant. By permitting the loan to remain outstanding for an additional year instead of calling it, Hardaway relinquished a legal right, which is adequate consideration for Merriweather's surety promise. Consideration need not pass to the surety; in fact, it usually primarily benefits the principal debtor.

There is no requirement that the creditor first proceed against the debtor before it can proceed against the surety, unless the surety undertaking expressly provides such a condition. Basic to the usual surety undertaking is the right of the creditor to proceed immediately against the surety. Essentially, that is the reason for the surety.

Hardaway's release of the commercial surety from its $400,000 surety undertaking partially released Merriweather. The release had the legal effect of impairing Merriweather's right of contribution against its cosurety (the commercial surety). Thus, Merriweather is released to the extent of 1/3 ($400,000 (commercial surety's guarantee)/$1,200,000 (the aggregate of the cosureties's guarantees)) of the principal amount ($800,000), or $266,667.

4C (November 75)

Fox Construction Corporation obtained a $20 million contract from the United States government to construct a federal office building. The contract required Fox to obtain a surety (or sureties) guaranteeing performance of the contract. After contacting several surety companies, Fox learned that no one company would write a bond for that amount. However, Fox was able to obtain a $10 million bond from Ace Surety Company and a $5 million bond each from Empire Surety and the Excelsior Surety Company. Fox breached the contract and, as a result, the United States government suffered a $2 million loss.

Required:
1. What are the rights of the United States against the three surety companies? Explain.
2. When finally settled, for what amount will each surety company be liable? Explain.

1. The United States could proceed against one or more of the cosureties to collect the $2 million damages resulting from Fox's having breached the construction contract. The three surety companies are cosureties on the Fox Construction Corporation obligation. As such, they are jointly and severally liable. Assuming Ace pays the entire amount ($2 million), it will have a right of contribution from the other sureties as discussed below.

2. Ace will be liable for $1 million, Empire for $500,000 and Excelsior for $500,000. In the event that a cosurety pays more than its proportionate share of the surety obligation, it has a right of contribution from its fellow sureties in proportion to the several undertaking. Thus, if Ace were to pay the $2 million liability, it would have the right to receive $500,000 each from Empire and Excelsior.

PART V – BANKRUPTCY*

TABLE OF CONTENTS

*Answers consistent with Bankruptcy Reform Act of 1978 (Bankruptcy Code) as amended through 2004.

PART V

BANKRUPTCY

I. Introduction to Debtor-Creditor Relations

13 (R96)

Which of the following will enable a creditor to collect money from a debtor's wages?
a. An order of receivership.
b. An order of garnishment.
c. A writ of execution.
d. A writ of attachment.

26 (November 95)

Which of the following statements is (are) correct regarding debtors' rights?
    I. State exemption statutes prevent all of a debtor's personal property from being sold to pay a federal tax lien.
    II. Federal social security benefits received by a debtor are exempt from garnishment by creditors.
a. I only.
b. II only.
c. Both I and II.
d. Neither I nor II.

27 (November 95)

Which of the following liens generally require(s) the lienholder to give notice of legal action before selling the debtor's property to satisfy the debt?

	Mechanic's lien	Artisan's lien
a.	Yes	Yes
b.	Yes	No
c.	No	Yes
d.	No	No

26 (November 94)

Under the Federal Fair Debt Collection Practices Act, which of the following would a collection service using improper debt collection practices be subject to?
a. Abolishment of the debt.
b. Reduction of the debt.
c. Civil lawsuit for damages for violating the Act.
d. Criminal prosecution for violating the Act.

193

Bankruptcy

28 (November 94)

Which of the following prejudgment remedies would be available to a creditor when a debtor owns <u>no</u> real property?

	Writ of attachment	Garnishment
a.	Yes	Yes
b.	Yes	No
c.	No	Yes
d.	No	No

21 (May 94)

A debtor may attempt to conceal or transfer property to prevent a creditor from satisfying a judgment. Which of the following actions will be considered an indication of fraudulent conveyance?

	Debtor remaining in possession after conveyance	Secret conveyance	Debtor retains an equitable benefit in the property conveyed
a.	Yes	Yes	Yes
b.	No	Yes	Yes
c.	Yes	Yes	No
d.	Yes	No	Yes

22 (May 94)

A homestead exemption ordinarily could exempt a debtor's equity in certain property from post-judgment collection by a creditor. To which of the following creditors will this exemption apply?

	Valid home mortgage lien	Valid IRS tax lien
a.	Yes	Yes
b.	Yes	No
c.	No	Yes
d.	No	No

23 (May 94)

Which of the following methods will allow a creditor to collect money from a debtor's wages?

a. Arrest.
b. Mechanic's lien.
c. Order of receivership.
d. Writ of garnishment.

II. Straight Bankruptcy--Chapter 7
A. Commencing a Chapter 7 Case

(R03)

Hall, CPA, is an unsecured creditor of Tree Co. for $15,000. Tree has a total of 10 creditors, all of whom are unsecured. Tree has not paid any of the creditors for three months. Under Chapter 11 of the federal Bankruptcy Code, which of the following statements is correct?

a. Hall and two other unsecured creditors must join in the involuntary petition in bankruptcy.
b. Hall may file an involuntary petition in bankruptcy against Tree.
c. Tree may <u>not</u> be petitioned involuntarily into bankruptcy under the provisions of Chapter 11.
d. Tree may <u>not</u> be petitioned involuntarily into bankruptcy because there are less than 12 unsecured creditors.

27 (November 93)

The filing of an involuntary bankruptcy petition under the Federal Bankruptcy Code
a. Terminates liens on exempt property.
b. Terminates all security interests in property in the bankruptcy estate.
c. Stops the debtor from incurring new debts.
d. Stops the enforcement of judgment liens against property in the bankruptcy estate.

28 (November 93)

Which of the following requirements must be met for creditors to file an involuntary bankruptcy petition under Chapter 7 of the Federal Bankruptcy Code?
a. The debtor must owe one creditor more than $5,000.
b. The debtor has <u>not</u> been paying its *bona fide* debts as they become due.
c. There must <u>not</u> be more than 12 creditors.
d. At least one fully secured creditor must join in the petition.

29 (November 93)

Which of the following conditions, if any, must a debtor meet to file a voluntary bankruptcy petition under Chapter 7 of the Federal Bankruptcy Code?

	Insolvency	Three or more creditors
a.	Yes	Yes
b.	Yes	No
c.	No	Yes
d.	No	No

30 (November 92)

A party involuntarily petitioned into bankruptcy under Chapter 7 of the Federal Bankruptcy Code who succeeds in having the petition dismissed could recover

	Court costs and attorney's fees	Compensatory damages	Punitive damages
a.	Yes	Yes	Yes
b.	Yes	Yes	No
c.	No	Yes	Yes
d.	Yes	No	No

30 (May 91)

A voluntary petition filed under the liquidation provisions of Chapter 7 of the Federal Bankruptcy Code
a. Is <u>not</u> available to a corporation unless it has previously filed a petition under the reorganization provisions of Chapter 11 of the Federal Bankruptcy Code.
b. Automatically stays collection actions against the debtor <u>except</u> by secured creditors.
c. Will be dismissed unless the debtor has 12 or more unsecured creditors whose claims total at least $5,000.
d. Does <u>not</u> require the debtor to show that the debtor's liabilities exceed the fair market value of assets.

29 (November 90)

A contested involuntary petition in bankruptcy will be dismissed if the debtor
a. Owes unsecured obligations exceeding $5,000 to less than three creditors.
b. Had all its property taken to enforce a lien within 120 days of filing.
c. Is failing to pay undisputed debts as they become due.
d. Is an individual engaged in the business of farming.

Bankruptcy

25 (November 89)

Filing a valid petition in bankruptcy acts as an automatic stay of actions to

	Garnish the debtor's wages	Collect alimony from the debtor
a.	Yes	Yes
b.	Yes	No
c.	No	Yes
d.	No	No

32 (May 88)

Which of the following statements is correct with respect to a voluntary bankruptcy proceeding under the liquidation provisions of the Bankruptcy Code?

a. The debtor must be insolvent.

b. The liabilities of the debtor must total $5,000 or more.

c. It may be properly commenced and maintained by any person who is insolvent.

d. The filing of the bankruptcy petition constitutes an order for relief.

22 (May 83)

An involuntary petition in bankruptcy

a. Will be denied if a majority of creditors in amount and in number have agreed to a common law composition agreement.

b. Can be filed by creditors only once in a seven-year period.

c. May be successfully opposed by the debtor by proof that the debtor is solvent in the bankruptcy sense.

d. If not contested will result in the entry of an order for relief by the bankruptcy judge.

16 (November 82)

An otherwise valid petition for involuntary bankruptcy has been filed against Mohawk Corporation. This will be sufficient to obtain an order for relief against Mohawk provided

a. Mohawk is generally not paying debts as they become due.

b. A custodian has been appointed to take charge of substantially all of Mohawk's debts within four months of filing.

c. The creditor or creditors can establish that Mohawk is bankrupt in the bankruptcy sense.

d. The majority of creditors join the filing if there are more than two creditors involved.

18 (May 82)

Mac, doing business as Mac's Restaurant, has an involuntary petition in bankruptcy filed against him. Which of the following is a correct legal statement regarding such a filing?

a. Mac has the right to controvert the validity of the petition and if Mac is successful, the petition will be dismissed and Mac may recover his costs including a reasonable attorney's fee.

b. The filing of the petition by a majority of the creditors creates a binding presumption that Mac is insolvent.

c. A single creditor may file the petition regardless of the number of creditors if its provable claim exceeds $7,500.

d. A trustee is appointed upon the filing of the petition and is vested by operation of law with the bankrupt's title as of the date of the filing.

B. Property of the Estate

6 (R00)

Under the liquidation provisions of Chapter 7 of the federal Bankruptcy Code, certain property acquired by the debtor after the filing of the petition becomes part of the bankruptcy estate. An example of such property is

a. Inheritances received by the debtor within 180 days after the filing of the petition.

b. Child support payments received by the debtor within one year after the filing of the petition.

c. Social Security payments received by the debtor within 180 days after the filing of the petition.

d. Wages earned by the debtor within one year after the filing of the petition.

34 (November 94)

Under the liquidation provisions of Chapter 7 of the Federal Bankruptcy Code, which of the following statements applies to a person who has voluntarily filed for and received a discharge in bankruptcy?

    a.   The person will be discharged from all debts.

    b.   The person can obtain another voluntary discharge in bankruptcy under Chapter 7 after three years have elapsed from the date of the prior filing.

    c.   The person must surrender for distribution to the creditors amounts received as an inheritance, if the receipt occurs within 180 days after filing the bankruptcy petition.

    d.   The person is precluded from owning or operating a similar business for two years.

27 (November 89)

Which of the following assets would be included in a debtor's bankruptcy estate in a liquidation proceeding?

    a.   Proceeds from a life insurance policy received 90 days after the petition was filed.

    b.   An inheritance received 270 days after the petition was filed.

    c.   Property from a divorce settlement received 365 days after the petition was filed.

    d.   Wages earned by the debtor after the petition was filed.

28 (November 88)

The Bankruptcy Code provides that a debtor is entitled to claim as exempt property the right to receive

	Social security benefits	Disability benefits
a.	No	No
b.	Yes	No
c.	Yes	Yes
d.	No	Yes

C. Collecting Estate Property--General Trustee Powers

27 (November 90)

On June 5, 1989, Gold rented equipment under a four-year lease. On March 8, 1990, Gold was petitioned involuntarily into bankruptcy under the Federal Bankruptcy Code's liquidation provisions. A trustee was appointed. The fair market value of the equipment exceeds the balance of the lease payments due. The trustee

    a.   May <u>not</u> reject the equipment lease because the fair market value of the equipment exceeds the balance of the lease payments due.

    b.   May elect <u>not</u> to assume the equipment lease.

    c.   Must assume the equipment lease because its term exceeds one year.

    d.   Must assume and subsequently assign the equipment lease.

28 (November 84)

The trustee in bankruptcy of a landlord-debtor under a Chapter 7 liquidation

    a.   Must be elected by the creditors immediately after a bankruptcy petition is filed.

    b.   May <u>not</u> be appointed by the court after the order for relief has been entered.

    c.   Must reject the executory contracts of the debtor.

    d.   May assign the leases of the debtor.

41 (May 81)

In a bankruptcy proceeding, the trustee

    a.   Must be an attorney admitted to practice in the federal district in which the bankrupt is located.

    b.   Will receive a fee based upon the time and fair value of the services rendered, regardless of the size of the estate.

    c.   May <u>not</u> have had any dealings with the bankrupt within the past year.

    d.   Is the representative of the bankrupt's estate and as such has the capacity to sue and be sued on its behalf.

D. Collecting Estate Property--Trustees Avoidance Powers

30 (November 93)

Which of the following transfers by a debtor, within ninety days of filing for bankruptcy, could be set aside as a preferential payment?

   a.   Making a gift to charity.
   b.   Paying a business utility bill.
   c.   Borrowing money from a bank secured by giving a mortgage on business property.
   d.   Prepaying an installment loan on inventory.

Items 37 through 39 are based on the following:

On August 1, 1992, Hall filed a voluntary petition under Chapter 7 of the Federal Bankruptcy Code.

Hall's assets are sufficient to pay general creditors 40% of their claims.

The following transactions occurred before the filing:

   ▪   On May 15, 1992, Hall gave a mortgage on Hall's home to National Bank to secure payment of a loan National had given Hall two years earlier. When the loan was made, Hall's twin was a National employee.
   ▪   On June 1, 1992, Hall purchased a boat from Olsen for $10,000 cash.
   ▪   On July 1, 1992, Hall paid off an outstanding credit card balance of $500. The original debt had been $2,500.

37 (November 92)

The National mortgage was

   a.   Preferential, because National would be considered an insider.
   b.   Preferential, because the mortgage was given to secure an antecedent debt.
   c.   Not preferential, because Hall is presumed insolvent when the mortgage was given.
   d.   Not preferential, because the mortgage was a security interest.

38 (November 92)

The payment to Olsen was

   a.   Preferential, because the payment was made within 90 days of the filing of the petition.
   b.   Preferential, because the payment enabled Olsen to receive more than the other general creditors.
   c.   Not preferential, because Hall is presumed insolvent when the payment was made.
   d.   Not preferential, because the payment was a contemporaneous exchange for new value.

39 (November 92)

The credit card payment was

   a.   Preferential, because the payment was made within 90 days of the filing of the petition.
   b.   Preferential, because the payment was on account of an antecedent debt.
   c.   Not preferential, because the payment was for a consumer debt of less than $600.
   d.   Not preferential, because the payment was less than 40% of the original debt.

Items 33 and 34 are based on the following:

On May 1, 1991, two months after becoming insolvent, Quick Corp., an appliance wholesaler, filed a voluntary petition for bankruptcy under the provisions of Chapter 7 of the Federal Bankruptcy Code. On October 15, 1990, Quick's board of directors had authorized and paid Erly $50,000 to repay Erly's April 1, 1990, loan to the corporation. Erly is a sibling of Quick's president. On March 15, 1991, Quick paid Kray $100,000 for inventory delivered that day.

33 (May 91)

Which of the following is <u>not</u> relevant in determining whether the repayment of Erly's loan is a voidable preferential transfer?

   a.   Erly is an insider.
   b.   Quick's payment to Erly was made on account of an antecedent debt.
   c.   Quick's solvency when the loan was made by Erly.
   d.   Quick's payment to Erly was made within one year of the filing of the bankruptcy petition.

34 (May 91)

Quick's payment to Kray would
a. Not be voidable, because it was a contemporaneous exchange.
b. Not be voidable, unless Kray knew about Quick's insolvency.
c. Be voidable, because it was made within 90 days of the bankruptcy filing.
d. Be voidable, because it enabled Kray to receive more than it otherwise would receive from the bankruptcy estate.

34 (May 87)

One of the elements necessary to establish that a preferential transfer has been made under the Bankruptcy Code by the debtor to a creditor is that the
a. Debtor was insolvent at the time of the transfer.
b. Creditor was an insider and the transfer occurred within 90 days of the filing of the bankruptcy petition.
c. Transfer was in fact a contemporaneous exchange for new value given to the debtor.
d. Transfer was made by the debtor with actual intent to hinder, delay, or defraud other creditors.

18 (May 84)

Under the Bankruptcy Code, one of the elements that must be established in order for the trustee in bankruptcy to void a preferential transfer to a creditor who is not an insider is that
a. The transferee-creditor received more than he would have received in a liquidation proceeding under the Bankruptcy Code.
b. Permission was received from the bankruptcy judge prior to the trustee's signing an order avoiding the transfer.
c. The transfer was in fact a contemporaneous exchange for new value given to the debtor.
d. The transferee-creditor knew or had reason to know that the debtor was insolvent.

44 (May 81)

In order to establish a preference under the federal bankruptcy act, which of the following is the trustee required to show where the preferred party is <u>not</u> an insider?
a. That the preferred party had reasonable cause to believe that the debtor was insolvent.
b. That the debtor committed an act of bankruptcy.
c. That the transfer was for an antecedent debt.
d. That the transfer was made within 60 days of the filing of the petition.

3 (May 80)

The federal bankruptcy act contains several important terms. One such term is "insider." The term is used in connection with preferences and preferential transfers. Which among the following is <u>not</u> an "insider"?
a. A secured creditor having a security interest in at least 25% or more of the debtor's property.
b. A partnership in which the debtor is a general partner.
c. A corporation of which the debtor is a director.
d. A close blood relative of the debtor.

2 (May 94)

Items 70 through 72 are based on the following:

On May 1, 1994, Able Corp. was petitioned involuntarily into bankruptcy under the provisions of Chapter 7 of the Federal Bankruptcy Code. The following transactions occurred before the bankruptcy petition was filed:
- On January 15, 1994, Able paid Vista Bank the $1,000 balance due on an unsecured business loan.
- On February 28, 1994, Able paid $1,000 to Owen, an officer of Able, who had lent Able money.
- On March 1, 1994, Able bought a computer for use in its business from Core Computer Co. for $2,000 cash.

Assuming the bankruptcy petition was validly filed, for each item determine whether the statement is True or False.

70. The payment to Vista Bank would be set aside as a preferential transfer.
71. The payment to Owen would be set aside as a preferential transfer.
72. The purchase from Core Computer Co. would be set aside as a preferential transfer.

Bankruptcy

5 (May 85)

On July 1, Sam Baker, a sole proprietor operating a drugstore, was involuntarily petitioned into bankruptcy by his creditors. At that time, and for at least 60 days prior thereto, Baker was unable to pay his current obligations and also had a negative net worth. Prior to the filing of the petition Baker made the following transfers

-May 17--Paid Nix, an unsecured creditor, the full $7,500 outstanding on a loan obtained from Nix on April 10. . . .

At the time the petition was filed, Baker owned a rental warehouse and was involved in a divorce proceeding. The trustee in bankruptcy has informed Baker that the debtor's (Baker's) estate will include the following non-exempt property:

-Rents received from July 1 through November 1 on the warehouse.

-Property received on October 10 as a result of the Bakers' final divorce decree.

Required: Answer the following, setting forth reasons for any conclusions stated.

In separate paragraphs, discuss whether the trustee in bankruptcy can properly avoid or set aside the transfer made by Baker? Was the trustee correct by including in the debtor's estate rents on the warehouse and the property received as a result of the final divorce decree?

The trustee in bankruptcy may properly avoid or set aside the payment made by Baker to Nix on May 17 since it meets all the requirements necessary to establish a preferential transfer. In order to establish a preference, the trustee must show that the transfer

-Was to or for the benefit of a creditor.

-Was made for or on account of an antecedent debt owed by the debtor before such transfer was made.

-Was made while the debtor was insolvent.

-Was made within 90 days prior to the filing of the petition (when the creditor is not an insider).

-Enables the creditor to receive more than such creditor would receive in a liquidation proceeding.

There is a rebuttable presumption that the debtor is insolvent during the ninety days preceding the filing of the petition.

The trustee was correct by including in the estate rents and property received as a result of the final divorce decree. Generally, property acquired after the filing of a bankruptcy petition is not part of the debtor's estate in bankruptcy but belongs to the debtor individually. However, there are certain exceptions to this rule. One such exception is rents earned on property of the debtor's estate. Thus, the rents received from July 1 through November 1 will be included in Baker's estate. Another such exception is property received by the debtor as a result of a final divorce decree within 180 days of the filing of the bankruptcy petition. Thus, the receipt of property by Baker on October 10 as a result of a final divorce decree falls within the 180 days after the filing of the bankruptcy petition on July 1 and is therefore included in the debtor's estate.

3B (November 80)

In connection with the audit of One-Up, Inc., a question has arisen regarding the validity of a $10,000 purchase money security interest in certain machinery sold to Essex Company on March 2nd. Essex was petitioned into bankruptcy on May 1st by its creditors. The trustee is seeking to avoid One-Up's security interest on the grounds that it is a preferential transfer, hence voidable. The machinery in question was sold to Essex on the following terms: $1,000 down and the balance plus interest at nine percent (9%) to be paid over a three year period. One-Up obtained a signed security agreement which created a security interest in the property on March 2nd, the date of the sale. A financing statement was filed on March 10th.

Required: Answer the following, setting forth reasons for any conclusions stated.

1. Would One-Up's security interest in the machinery by a voidable preference?

2. In general, what are the requirements necessary to permit the trustee to successfully assert a preferential transfer and thereby set aside a creditor's security interest?

1. No. The Bankruptcy Reform Act of 1978 has not only modified the requirements for establishing a voidable preference, it has also specified transactions that do not constitute preferences. One such transaction is the creditor's taking a security interest in property acquired by the debtor as a contemporaneous exchange for new value given to the debtor to enable him to acquire such property (a purchase money security interest). The security interest must be perfected (filed) within 20 days after attachment. The Act is in harmony with the secured transactions provisions of the Uniform Commercial Code. Thus, One-Up has a valid security interest in the machinery it sold to Essex.

2. The Bankruptcy Reform Act of 1978 does not require that the creditor have knowledge or reasonable cause to believe the debtor is insolvent in the bankruptcy sense. Instead, under the Act, where such insolvency exists on or within ninety days before the filing of the petition, knowledge of insolvency by the transferee need not be established. The Act also assumes that the debtor's insolvency is presumed if the transfer alleged to be preferential is made within 90 days. Finally, the time period in which transfers may be set aside is 90 days unless the transferee is an "insider." If the transfer is to an insider, the trustee may avoid transfers made within one year prior to the filing of the petition. Thus, the trustee may avoid as preferential any transfer of property of the debtor that is

- To or for the benefit of a creditor.
- For or on account of an antecedent debt owed by the debtor before such transfer was made.
- Made while the debtor was insolvent in the bankruptcy sense (however, if the transfer is made within 90 days, the debtor's insolvency is presumed).
- Made on or within 90 days of the filing of the petition (or if made after the 90 days but within one year prior to the date of the filing of the petition and the transfer was to an "insider," it may be set aside). . . .
- Such that it enables the creditor to receive more than he would if it were a straight liquidation proceeding.

The bankruptcy act contains a lengthy definition of the term "insider" that includes common relationships that the transferee has to the debtor, which, in case of an individual debtor, could be certain relatives, a partnership in which he is a general partner, his fellow general partners, or a corporation controlled by him.

E. Claims and Exemptions

28 (November 90)

Flax, a sole proprietor, has been petitioned involuntarily into bankruptcy under the Federal Bankruptcy Code's liquidation provisions. Simon & Co., CPAs, has been appointed trustee of the bankruptcy estate. If Simon also wishes to act as the tax return preparer for the estate, which of the following statements is correct?

a. Simon is prohibited from serving as both trustee and preparer under any circumstances because serving in that dual capacity would be a conflict of interest.

b. Although Simon may serve as both trustee and preparer, it is entitled to receive a fee only for the services rendered as a preparer.

c. Simon may employ itself to prepare tax returns if authorized by the court and may receive a separate fee for services rendered in each capacity.

d. Although Simon may serve as both trustee and preparer, its fee for services rendered in each capacity will be determined solely by the size of the estate.

42 (May 81)

Haplow engaged Turnbow as his attorney when threatened by several creditors with a bankruptcy proceeding. Haplow's assets consisted of $85,000 and his debts were $125,000. A petition was subsequently filed and was uncontested. Several of the creditors are concerned that the suspected large legal fees charged by Turnbow will diminish the size of the distributable estate. What are the rules or limitations which apply to such fees?

a. None, since it is within the attorney-client privileged relationship.

b. The fee is presumptively valid as long as arrived at in an arm's-length negotiation.

c. Turnbow must file with the court a statement of compensation paid or agreed to for review as to its reasonableness.

d. The trustee must approve the fee.

F. Priorities

2 (R98)

Question Number 2 consists of 5 items. Select the **best** answer for each item. **Answer all items**. Your grade will be based on the total number of correct answers.

On June 1, 1998, Hart Corp. was involuntarily petitioned into bankruptcy under the liquidation provisions of Chapter 7 of the federal Bankruptcy Code. When the petition was filed, Hart's creditors included:

Bankruptcy

Secured creditors	Amount owed
Thorn Bank - 1st mortgage on factory building owned by Hart	$250,000
Owen Corp. - perfected purchase money security interest in Hart's inventory	100,000

Unsecured creditors	
Core Realty - office rent for March, April, and May 1998	$14,000
Vista Office Services - Cleaning services for February and March 1998	2,000
Local Telephone Co. - Telephone charges for March, April, and May 1998	9,000
Gene Wren (employee) - May 1998 wages	4,000

All of Hart's assets were sold. The factory building was sold for $300,000 and the inventory was sold for $70,000. After paying the administration expenses of the bankruptcy, secured creditors up to the amount realized from the collateral, and general creditors having priority, there was enough cash left to pay each general creditor 50 cents on the dollar.

Required:

For **Items 1 and 2**, select the best answer from List I. An answer may be selected once, more than once, or not at all.

List I	
A	Core.
B	Local.
C	Owen.
D	Thorn.
E	Vista.
F	Wren.

1. Which creditor alone can petition Hart into involuntary bankruptcy?
2. Which unsecured creditor will be paid in full?

For **Items 3 through 5**, select the best answer from List II. An answer may be selected once, more than once, or not at all.

List II	
A	$0
B	$7,000
C	$9,000
D	$12,000
E	$70,000
F	$85,000
G	$100,000
H	$250,000
I	$275,000
J	$300,000

3. What would be the total amount paid to Thorn from the bankruptcy estate?
4. What would be the total amount paid to Owen from the bankruptcy estate?
5. What would be the total amount paid to Core from the bankruptcy estate?

Items 28 through 30 are based on the following:

Dart Inc., a closely held corporation, was petitioned involuntarily into bankruptcy under the liquidation provisions of Chapter 7 of the Federal Bankruptcy Code. Dart contested the petition.

Dart has not been paying its business debts as they became due, has defaulted on its mortgage loan payments, and owes back taxes to the IRS. The total cash value of Dart's bankruptcy estate after the sale of all assets and payment of administration expenses is $100,000.

Dart has the following creditors:

- Fracon Bank is owed $75,000 principal and accrued interest on a mortgage loan secured by Dart's real property. The property was valued at and sold, in bankruptcy, for $70,000.
- The IRS has a $12,000 recorded judgment for unpaid corporate income tax.
- JOG Office Supplies has an unsecured claim of $3,000 that was timely filed.
- Nanstar Electric Co. has an unsecured claim of $1,200 that was not timely filed.
- Decoy Publications has a claim of $14,000, of which $2,000 is secured by Dart's inventory that was valued and sold, in bankruptcy, for $2,000. The claim was timely filed.

28 (May 95)

Which of the following creditors must join in the filing of the involuntary petition?
   I. JOG Office Supplies
   II. Nanstar Electric Co.
   III. Decoy Publications
a. I, II, & III.
b. II & III.
c. I & II.
d. III only.

29 (May 95)

Which of the following statements would correctly describe the result of Dart's opposing the petition?
a. Dart will win because the petition should have been filed under Chapter 11.
b. Dart will win because there are not more than 12 creditors.
c. Dart will lose because it is not paying its debts as they become due.
d. Dart will lose because of its debt to the IRS.

30 (May 95)

Which of the following events will follow the filing of the Chapter 7 involuntary petition?

	A trustee will be appointed	A stay against creditor collection proceedings will go into effect
a.	Yes	Yes
b.	Yes	No
c.	No	Yes
d.	No	No

39 (November 93)

Which of the following types of claims would be paid first in the distribution of a bankruptcy estate under the liquidation provisions of Chapter 7 of the Federal Bankruptcy Code if the petition was filed July 15, 1993?
a. A secured debt properly perfected on March 20, 1993.
b. Inventory purchased and delivered August 1, 1993.
c. Employee wages due April 30, 1993.
d. Federal tax lien filed June 30, 1993.

Bankruptcy

30 (November 91)

Which of the following claims would have the highest priority in the distribution of a bankruptcy estate under the liquidation provisions of Chapter 7 of the Federal Bankruptcy Code if the petition was filed June 1, 1991?

a. Federal tax lien filed May 15, 1991.
b. A secured debt properly perfected on February 10, 1991.
c. Trustee's administration costs filed September 30, 1991.
d. Employee wages due March 30, 1991.

Items 42 through 45 are based on the following:

On February 28, 1991, Master, Inc. had total assets with a fair market value of $1,200,000 and total liabilities of $990,000. On January 15, 1991, Master made a monthly installment note payment to Acme Distributors Corp., a creditor holding a properly perfected security interest in equipment having a fair market value greater than the balance due on the note. On March 15, 1991, Master voluntarily filed a petition in bankruptcy under the liquidation provisions of Chapter 7 of the Federal Bankruptcy Code. One year later, the equipment was sold for less than the balance due on the note to Acme.

42 (November 91)

If a creditor challenged Master's right to file, the petition would be dismissed

a. If Master had less than 12 creditors at the time of filing.
b. Unless Master can show that a reorganization under Chapter 11 of the Federal Bankruptcy Code would have been unsuccessful.
c. Unless Master can show that it is unable to pay its debts in the ordinary course of business or as they come due.
d. If Master is an insurance company.

43 (November 91)

If Master's voluntary petition is filed properly,

a. Master will be entitled to conduct its business as a debtor-in-possession unless the court appoints a trustee.
b. A trustee must be appointed by the creditors.
c. Lawsuits by Master's creditors will be stayed by the Federal Bankruptcy Code.
d. The unsecured creditors must elect a creditors' committee of three to eleven members to consult with the trustee.

44 (November 91)

Master's payment to Acme could

a. Be set aside as a preferential transfer because the fair market value of the collateral was greater than the installment note balance.
b. Be set aside as a preferential transfer unless Acme showed that Master was solvent on January 15, 1991.
c. Not be set aside as a preferential transfer because Acme was oversecured.
d. Not be set aside as a preferential transfer if Acme showed that Master was solvent on March 15, 1991.

45 (November 91)

Which of the following statements correctly describes Acme's distribution from Master's bankruptcy estate?

a. Acme will receive the total amount it is owed, even if the proceeds from the sale of the collateral were less than the balance owed by Master.
b. Acme will have the same priority as unsecured general creditors to the extent that the proceeds from the sale of its collateral are insufficient to satisfy the amount owed by Master.
c. The total proceeds from the sale of the collateral will be paid to Acme even if they are less than the balance owed by Master, provided there is sufficient cash to pay all administrative costs associated with the bankruptcy.
d. Acme will receive only the proceeds from the sale of the collateral in full satisfaction of the debt owed by Master.

34 (November 90)

On May 24, Knurl, an appliance dealer, filed for bankruptcy under the provisions of Chapter 7 of the Federal Bankruptcy Code. A trustee was appointed and an order for relief was entered. Knurl's non-exempt property was converted to cash, which is available to satisfy the following claims and expenses:

Claim by Card Corp. (one of Knurl's suppliers) for toasters ordered on May 11, and delivered on credit to Knurl on May 15.	$50,000
Fee earned by the bankruptcy trustee.	$12,000
Claim by Hill Co. for the delivery of televisions to Knurl on credit. The televisions were delivered on April 9, and a financing statement was properly filed on April 10. These televisions were sold by the trustee with Hill's consent for $7,000, their fair market value.	$ 7,000
Fees earned by the attorneys for the bankruptcy estate.	$ 8,000

The cash available for distribution includes the proceeds from the sale of the televisions. What amount will be distributed to Card if the cash available for distribution is $50,000?
   a. $23,000
   b. $30,000
   c. $31,000
   d. $43,000

28 (November 89)
   Which of the following unsecured debts of $500 each would have the highest relative priority in the distribution of a bankruptcy estate in a liquidation proceeding?
   a. Tax claims of state and municipal governmental units.
   b. Liabilities to employee benefit plans arising from services rendered during the month preceding the filing of the petition.
   c. Claims owed to customers who gave deposits for the purchase of undelivered consumer goods.
   d. Wages earned by employees during the month preceding the filing of the petition.

23 (November 88)
   On July 15, 1988, White, a sole proprietor, was involuntarily petitioned into bankruptcy under the liquidation provisions of the Bankruptcy Code. White's non-exempt property has been converted to $13,000 cash, which is available to satisfy the following claims:

Unsecured claim for 1986 state income tax	$10,000
Fee owed to Best & Co., CPA, for services rendered from April 1, 1988, through June 30, 1988	$ 6,000
Unsecured claim by Stieb for wages earned as an employee of White during March, 1988	$ 3,000

There are no other claims.
   What is the maximum amount that will be distributed for the payment of the 1986 state income tax?
   a. $ 4,000
   b. $ 5,000
   c. $ 7,000
   d. $10,000

Bankruptcy

20 (May 82)

The Bankruptcy Reform Act of 1978 provides that certain allowed expenses and claims are entitled to a priority. Which of the following is <u>not</u> entitled to such a priority?

a. Claims of governmental units for taxes.
b. Wage claims, but to a limited extent.
c. Rents payable within the four months preceding bankruptcy, but to a limited extent.
d. Unsecured claims for contributions to employee benefit plans, but to a limited extent.

22 (May 82)

Clark is a surety on a $100,000 obligation owed by Thompson to Owens. The debt is also secured by a $50,000 mortgage to Owens on Thompson's factory. Thompson is in bankruptcy. Clark has satisfied the debt. Clark is

a. Only entitled to the standing of a general creditor in bankruptcy.
b. A secured creditor to the extent of the $50,000 mortgage and a general creditor for the balance.
c. Entitled to nothing in bankruptcy since this was a risk he assumed.
d. Not entitled to priority in bankruptcy, even though Owens could validly claim it.

43 (May 81)

If a secured party's claim exceeds the value of the collateral of a bankrupt, he will be paid the total amount realized from the sale of the security and will

a. Not have any claim for the balance.
b. Become a general creditor for the balance.
c. Retain a secured creditor status for the balance.
d. Be paid the balance only after all general creditors are paid.

3 (November 95)

Items 71 through 75 are based on the following:

On June 1, 1995, Rusk Corp. was petitioned involuntarily into bankruptcy. At the time of the filing, Rusk had the following creditors:

- Safe Bank, for the balance due on the secured note and mortgage on Rusk's warehouse.
- Employee salary claims.
- 1994 federal income taxes due.
- Accountant's fees outstanding.
- Utility bills outstanding.

Prior to the bankruptcy filing, but while insolvent, Rusk engaged in the following transactions:

- On February 1, 1995, Rusk repaid all corporate directors' loans made to the corporation.
- On May 1, 1995, Rusk purchased raw materials for use in its manufacturing business and paid cash to the supplier.

Required: **Items 71 through 75** relate to Rusk's creditors and the February 1 and May 1 transactions. For each item, select from List I whether only statement I is correct, whether only statement II is correct, whether both statements I and II are correct, or whether neither statement I nor II is correct.

List I
A   I only.
B   II only.
C   Both I and II.
D   Neither I nor II.

71. I. Safe Bank's claim will be the first paid of the listed claims because Safe is a secured creditor.
II. Safe Bank will receive the entire amount of the balance of the mortgage due as a secured creditor regardless of the amount received from the sale of the warehouse.

206

72. I. The employee salary claims will be paid in full after the payment of any secured party.
    II. The employee salary claims up to $4,925 per claimant will be paid before payment of any general creditors' claims.

73. I. The claim for 1994 federal income taxes due will be paid as a secured creditor claim.
    II. The claim for 1994 federal income taxes due will be paid prior to the general creditor claims.

74. I. The February 1 repayments of the directors' loans were preferential transfers even though the payments were made more than 90 days before the filing of the petition.
    II. The February 1 repayments of the directors' loans were preferential transfers because the payments were made to insiders.

75. I. The May 1 purchase and payment was <u>not</u> a preferential transfer because it was a transaction in the ordinary course of business.
    II. The May 1 purchase and payment was a preferential transfer because it occurred within 90 days of the filing of the petition.

2 (May 93)

On April 15, 1992, Wren Corp., an appliance wholesaler, was petitioned involuntarily into bankruptcy under the liquidation provisions of Chapter 7 of the Federal Bankruptcy Code.

When the petition was filed, Wren's creditors included:

Secured creditors	Amount owed
Fifth Bank - 1st mortgage on warehouse owned by Wren	$50,000
Hart Manufacturing Corp. - perfected purchase money security interest in inventory	30,000
TVN Computers, Inc. - perfected security interest in office computers	15,000

Unsecured creditors	Amount owed
IRS - 1990 federal income taxes	$20,000
Acme Office Cleaners - services for January, February, and March 1992	750
Ted Smith (employee) - February and March 1992 wages	2,400
Joan Sims (employee) - March 1992 commissions	1,500
Power Electric Co. - electricity charges for January, February, and March 1992	600
Soft Office Supplies - supplies purchased in 1991	2,000

The following transactions occurred before the bankruptcy petition was filed:
- On December 31, 1991, Wren paid off a $5,000 loan from Mary Lake, the sister of one of Wren's directors.
- On January 30, 1992, Wren donated $2,000 to Universal Charities.
- On February 1, 1992, Wren gave Young Finance Co. a security agreement covering Wren's office fixtures to secure a loan previously made by Young.
- On March 1, 1992, Wren made the final $1,000 monthly payment to Integral Appliance Corp. on a two-year note.
- On April 1, 1992, Wren purchased from Safety Co., a new burglar alarm system for its factory, for $5,000 cash.

All of Wren's assets were liquidated. The warehouse was sold for $75,000, the computers were sold for $12,000, and the inventory was sold for $25,000. After paying, the bankruptcy administration expenses of $8,000, secured creditors, and priority general creditors, there was enough cash to pay each non-priority general creditor 50 cents on the dollar.

Bankruptcy

Required:

a. Items 61 through 65 represent the transactions that occurred before the filing of the bankruptcy petition. For each transaction, determine if the transaction would be set aside as a preferential transfer by the bankruptcy court. Answer Y if the transaction would be set aside or N if the transfer would <u>not</u> be set aside.

61. Payment to Mary Lake
62. Donation to Universal Charities
63. Security agreement to Young Finance Co.
64. Payment to Integral Appliance Corp.
65. Purchase from Safety Co.

b. Items 66 through 70 represent creditor claims against the bankruptcy estate. Select from List I each creditor's order of payment in relation to the other creditors named in items 66 through 70.

		List I
66.	Bankruptcy administration expense	A. First
67.	Acme Office Cleaners	B. Second
68.	Fifth Bank	C. Third
69.	IRS	D. Fourth
70.	Joan Sims	E. Fifth

4 (May 92)

Techno, Inc. is a computer equipment dealer. On February 3, 1992, Techno was four months behind in its payments to Allied Building Maintenance, Cleen Janitorial Services, Inc., and Jones and Associates, CPAs, all of whom provide monthly services to Techno. In an attempt to settle with these three creditors, Techno offered each of them a reduced lump-sum payment for the past due obligations and full payment for future services. These creditors rejected Techno's offer and on April 9, 1992, Allied, Cleen and Jones filed an involuntary petition in bankruptcy against Techno under the provisions of Chapter 7 of the Federal Bankruptcy Code. At the time of the filing, Techno's liability to the three creditors was $9,100, all of which was unsecured.

Techno, at the time of the filing, had liabilities of $229,000 (owed to 23 creditors) and assets with a fair market value of $191,000. During the entire year before the bankruptcy filing, Techno's liabilities exceeded the fair market value of its assets.

Included in Techno's liabilities was an installment loan payable to Dollar Finance Co., properly secured by cash registers and other equipment.

The bankruptcy court approved the involuntary petition.

On April 21, 1992, Dollar filed a motion for relief from automatic stay in bankruptcy court claiming it was entitled to take possession of the cash registers and other equipment securing its loan. Dollar plans to sell these assets immediately and apply the proceeds to the loan balance. The fair market value of the collateral is less than the loan balance and Dollar claims to lack adequate protection. Also, Dollar claims it is entitled to receive a priority distribution, before distribution to unsecured creditors, for the amount Techno owes Dollar less the proceeds from the sale of the collateral.

During the course of the bankruptcy proceeding, the following transactions were disclosed:

- On October 6, 1991, Techno paid its president $9,900 as repayment of an unsecured loan made to the corporation on September 18, 1989.
- On February 19, 1992, Techno paid $1,150 to Alexis Computers, Inc. for eight color computer monitors. These monitors were delivered to Techno on February 9, 1992, and placed in inventory.
- On January 12, 1992, Techno bought a new delivery truck from Maple Motors for $7,900 cash. On the date of the bankruptcy filing, the truck was worth $7,000.

208

Required:

Answer the following questions and give the reasons for your conclusions.

a. What circumstances had to exist to allow Allied, Cleen, and Jones to file an involuntary bankruptcy petition against Techno?

b. 1. Will Dollar's motion for relief be granted?

2. Will Dollar's claim for priority be approved by the bankruptcy court?

c. Are the payments to Techno's president, Alexis, and Maple preferential transfers?

---

a. An involuntary bankruptcy petition may be filed against a debtor having 12 or more creditors by at least three creditors having unsecured claims of at least $12,300, provided the debtor is not paying its undisputed debts as they become due.

b. 1. Dollar's motion for relief will be granted. Dollar's claim that it is entitled to take possession of the collateral securing its loan is correct. Generally, a secured creditor is allowed to take possession of its collateral if there is no equity in it (that is, the debt balance exceeds the collateral's fair market value). Dollar would then be entitled to sell the collateral and apply the proceeds to the loan balance.

2. Dollar's claim that it is entitled to a priority distribution to the extent that the proceeds from the sale of its collateral are less than the loan balance will not be approved by the bankruptcy court. Dollar is entitled to the value of its collateral. As to any deficiency, Dollar will be treated as an unsecured creditor.

c. The payment to Techno's president would be regarded as a preferential transfer. Because the president is an "insider," any payments made on the unsecured loan during the year preceding the bankruptcy filing would be considered a preferential transfer.

The payment to Alexis was not a preferential transfer because it was made in the ordinary course of business and under ordinary business terms.

The $7,900 payment to Maple for the truck was not a preferential transfer because it was not made on account of an antecedent debt, but as a contemporaneous exchange for new value.

---

3 (November 87)

On July 1, 1986, Mix was petitioned by Able into bankruptcy under the liquidation provisions of the Bankruptcy Code. Able and Baker are unsecured creditors of Mix, owed $20,000 and $40,000 respectively. Mix also owes Carr $80,000, secured by a valid perfected security interest in bankruptcy on Mix's machinery, valued at $20,000. Mix has no other debts, except for 1986 federal income taxes.

Shortly after the filing of the petition Lang was appointed trustee in Mix's bankruptcy. In Lang's capacity as trustee, Lang:

- Engaged Ring & Co., CPAs, as the accountants for the bankruptcy estate.
- Included as part of the bankruptcy estate, an inheritance that Mix became entitled to receive on December 15, 1986 and that Mix actually received on January 15, 1987.

Lang has sold the property in the estate (including the sale of Mix's machinery for $20,000, which Carr consented to) and now the sole asset of the estate is $60,000 cash. Lang wishes to distribute the $60,000 so as to satisfy the following claims and expenses of the estate:

- Unsecured claim for 1986 federal income taxes	$ 6,000
- Carr's claim	80,000
- Able's and Baker's claims	60,000
- Expenses necessary to maintain and sell the	
- unsecured property of the estate	1,000
- Ring's fee for services rendered	3,000

There are no other claims.

Required: Answer the following, setting forth reasons for any conclusions stated.

a. Under the facts, were the requirements necessary for the filing of a valid petition in bankruptcy met? Discuss.

b. Discuss whether Lang's actions in engaging Ring and including the inheritance in the bankruptcy estate were proper.

c. Indicate the order in which the $60,000 should be distributed to satisfy the claims and expenses of the bankruptcy estate, assuming all necessary court approvals have been obtained.

a. Yes. The requirements necessary for the filing of a valid petition in bankruptcy have been met. An involuntary case may be commenced against a person by the filing of a petition where the aggregate amount of unsecured claims is at least $12,300 and a sufficient number of creditors join in the filing of the petition. Where there are fewer than 12 creditors only one creditor need file the petition. Under the facts, the petition was validly filed against Mix because Able's unsecured claim was more than $12,300 and because there were fewer than 12 creditors.

b. Lang's action as trustee to appoint Ring as the accountant for the bankruptcy estate was proper if such action was with the bankruptcy court's approval. The trustee, with the court's approval, may engage professional persons such as accountants on any reasonable terms and conditions.

Lang's inclusion of the inheritance in the property of the estate was also correct because property of the estate includes property that the debtor acquires or becomes entitled to acquire by inheritance within 180 days after the filing of the petition. By acquiring the right to inherit the property on December 15, 1986, which was less than 180 days after the filing of the petition on July 1, 1986, Mix's inheritance was properly included in the bankruptcy estate. Thus, Mix's receipt of the inheritance more than 180 days after the filing of the petition does not prevent the inclusion of the inheritance in the property of the estate.

c. The $60,000 will be distributed to satisfy the claims and expenses of the bankruptcy estate in the following order of priority:

1.	Carr's claim to the extent of the sale proceeds of the machinery in which Carr had a valid perfected security interest in bankruptcy.	$20,000
2.	Administrative expenses including the expenses to maintain and sell the unsecured property of the estate ($1,000) and Ring's fee for services rendered ($3,000).	4,000
3.	Unsecured claim for federal income taxes.	6,000
4.	The unsecured claims of Able and Baker and the balance of Carr's claim, which have equal priority, will be paid proportionately as follows:	

Able $- -$ $\dfrac{\$20,000}{\$120,000} \times \$30,000$ 5,000

Baker $- -$ $\dfrac{\$40,000}{\$120,000} \times \$30,000$ 10,000

Carr $- -$ $\dfrac{\$60,000}{\$120,000} \times \$30,000$ <u>15,000</u>

Total distributions   <u>$60,000</u>

G. Debts and Debtors Not Discharged

12 (R97)

Under the liquidation provisions of Chapter 7 of the federal Bankruptcy Code, a debtor will be denied a discharge in bankruptcy if the debtor

a. Fails to list a creditor.
b. Owes alimony and support payments.
c. Cannot pay administration expenses.
d. Refuses to satisfactorily explain a loss of assets.

33 (November 94)

Which of the following claims will <u>not</u> be discharged in bankruptcy?

a. A claim that arises from alimony or maintenance.
b. A claim that arises out of the debtor's breach of a contract.
c. A claim brought by a secured creditor that remains unsatisfied after the sale of the collateral.
d. A claim brought by a judgment creditor whose judgment resulted from the debtor's negligent operation of a motor vehicle.

31 (November 93)

Which of the following acts by a debtor could result in a bankruptcy court revoking the debtor's discharge?

    I. Failure to list one creditor.
    II. Failure to answer correctly material questions on the bankruptcy petition.

a. I only.
b. II only.
c. Both I and II.
d. Neither I nor II.

31 (May 91)

In general, which of the following debts will be discharged under the voluntary liquidation provisions of Chapter 7 of the Federal Bankruptcy Code?

a. A debt due to the negligence of the debtor arising before filing the bankruptcy petition.
b. Alimony payments owed the debtor's spouse under a separation agreement entered into two years before the filing of the bankruptcy petition.
c. A debt incurred more than 90 days before the filing of the bankruptcy petition and <u>not</u> disclosed in the petition.
d. Income taxes due within two years before the filing of the bankruptcy petition.

30 (November 90)

Larson, an unemployed carpenter, filed for voluntary bankruptcy on August 14, 1990. Larson's liabilities are listed below.

Credit card charges due May 2, 1989	$3,000
Bank loan incurred June 1990	5,000
Medical expenses incurred June 1983	7,000
Alimony due during 1988	1,000

Under the provisions of Chapter 7 of the Federal Bankruptcy Code, Larson's discharge will <u>not</u> apply to the unpaid

a. Credit card charges.
b. Bank loan.
c. Medical expenses.
d. Alimony.

32 (November 90)

Chapter 7 of the Federal Bankruptcy Code will deny a debtor a discharge when the debtor

a. Made a preferential transfer to a creditor.
b. Accidentally destroyed information relevant to the bankruptcy proceeding.
c. Obtained a Chapter 7 discharge 10 years previously.
d. Is a corporation or a partnership.

33 (November 90)

A claim will <u>not</u> be discharged in a bankruptcy proceeding if it

a. Is brought by a secured creditor and remains unsatisfied after receipt of the proceeds from the disposition of the collateral.
b. Is for unintentional torts that resulted in bodily injury to the claimant.
c. Arises from an extension of credit based upon false representations.
d. Arises out of the breach of a contract by the debtor.

Bankruptcy

22 (November 89)

Rolf, an individual, filed a voluntary petition in bankruptcy. A general discharge in bankruptcy will be denied if Rolf

a. Negligently made preferential transfers to certain creditors within 90 days of filing the petition.
b. Unjustifiably failed to preserve Rolf's books and records.
c. Filed a fraudulent federal income tax return two years prior to filing the petition.
d. Obtained a loan by using financial statements that Rolf knew were false.

Items 25 through 27 are based on the following:

On May 5, 1988, Bold obtained a $90,000 judgment in a malpractice action against Aker, a physician. On June 2, 1988, Aker obtained a $75,000 loan from Tint Finance Co. by knowingly making certain false representations to Tint. On July 7, 1988, Aker filed a voluntary petition in bankruptcy under the liquidation provisions of the Bankruptcy Code. Both Bold and Tint filed claims in Aker's bankruptcy proceeding. Assets in Aker's bankruptcy estate are exempt.

25 (November 88)

Bold's claim

a. Will be excepted from Aker's discharge in bankruptcy.
b. Will cause Aker to be denied a discharge in bankruptcy.
c. Will be set aside as a preference.
d. Will be discharged in Aker's bankruptcy proceeding.

26 (November 88)

Tint's claim

a. Will be excepted from Aker's discharge in bankruptcy.
b. Will cause Aker to be denied a discharge in bankruptcy.
c. Will be set aside as a preference.
d. Will be discharged in Aker's bankruptcy proceeding.

27 (November 88)

For this item only, assume that on June 9, 1988, Aker transferred property he owned to his son. The property was collateral for Aker's obligation to Simon. Aker transferred the property with the intent to defraud Simon. Which of the following statements is correct?

a. Only Simon's debt will be excepted from Aker's discharge in bankruptcy.
b. Aker will be denied a discharge in bankruptcy.
c. The transfer will be set aside because it constitutes a preference.
d. Aker will receive a discharge in bankruptcy of all debts.

33 (May 87)

Dark Corp. is a general creditor of Blue. Blue filed a petition in bankruptcy under the liquidation provisions of the Bankruptcy Code. Dark wishes to have the bankruptcy court either deny Blue a general discharge or not have its debt discharged. The discharge will be granted and it will include Dark's debt even if

a. Dark's debt is unscheduled.
b. Dark was a secured creditor which was **not** fully satisfied from the proceeds obtained upon disposition of the collateral.
c. Blue has unjustifiably failed to preserve the records from which Blue's financial condition might be ascertained.
d. Blue had filed for and received a previous discharge in bankruptcy under the liquidation provisions within six years of the filing of the present petition.

16 (May 84)

A debtor will be denied a discharge in bankruptcy if the debtor

a. Failed to timely list a portion of his debts.

b. Unjustifiably failed to preserve his books and records which could have been used to ascertain the debtor's financial condition.

c. Has negligently made preferential transfers to favored creditors within 90 days of the filing of the bankruptcy petition.

d. Has committed several willful and malicious acts which resulted in bodily injury to others.

17 (November 82)

The Bankruptcy Reform Act of 1978 distinguishes between an exception to discharge of a debt or debts and a denial of discharge. Which of the following types of conduct will result in a denial of discharge?

a. Obtaining of money or credit by resort to actual fraud.

b. Fraud or defalcation while acting in a fiduciary capacity.

c. Transfer by the debtor, with an intent to hinder a creditor, of property within one year before the date of filing of the petition.

d. Willful and malicious injury by the debtor to another entity or its property.

35 (May 80)

Hapless is a bankrupt. In connection with a debt owed to the Suburban Finance Company, he used a false financial statement to induce it to loan him $500. Hapless is seeking a discharge in bankruptcy. Which of the following is a correct statement?

a. Hapless will be denied a discharge of any of his debts.

b. Even if it can be proved that Suburban did <u>not</u> rely upon the financial statement, Hapless will be denied a discharge either in whole or in part.

c. Hapless will be denied a discharge of the Suburban debt.

d. Hapless will be totally discharged despite the false financial statement.

1 (R96)

In 1995, Fender was petitioned involuntarily into bankruptcy under the liquidation provisions of Chapter 7 of the Federal Bankruptcy Code.

At the time of the filing, Fender listed the following unsecured claims:

Judgment creditor	$6,000
Alimony and maintenance due under divorce decree	1,200
IRS assessment for 1993 taxes	500
1994 state income tax due	750
Unsecured personal loan from Ranch Bank	7,000
Rent on residence	2,000
Electricity charges on residence	200
Ace Finance Co.	1,000

The Ace Finance Company claim is listed because, in 1993, Fender agreed to guarantee payment of a $1,000 loan by Ace Finance Co. to Fender's cousin. The cousin defaulted on the loan and Ace is attempting to collect from Fender.

Fender had not been paying bills and obligations as they became due.

Required:

a. State and name the fewest number of creditors which would have had to join in filing the petition against Fender and give the reasons for your decision.

b. State which two creditor claims would be satisfied first from the bankruptcy estate and give the reasons for your decision.

c. State which claim(s) would not be discharged if unpaid and give the reasons for your decision.

d. State whether Fender's guarantee of payment would be discharged and give the reasons for your decision.

a. Ranch Bank and the judgment creditor would have had to join in the involuntary bankruptcy petition. Fender had fewer than 12 unsecured creditors. Under the liquidation provisions of Chapter 7 of the Federal Bankruptcy Code, when there are fewer than 12 creditors one or more creditors having unsecured claims in the aggregate of $12,300 must join in the petition.

b. The IRS assessment for 1993 taxes and the 1994 state tax income taxes due would be paid first.

Taxes due and owing within three years of the bankruptcy, unless evidenced by liens or otherwise secured, are considered to be general creditor claims but are accorded a higher priority than the other general creditor claims.

c. The alimony and maintenance claim and the tax claims would not be discharged if unpaid because these are two of the types of debts specifically excepted from discharge under the Federal Bankruptcy Code.

d. Fender's discharge in bankruptcy would discharge the guarantee of payment given to Ace. Bankruptcy of the guarantor is an absolute defense to payment, and any claim by Ace would be included in the bankruptcy proceeding and be discharged.

2 (May 90)

On February 1, 1990, Drake, a sole proprietor operating a retail clothing store, filed a bankruptcy petition under the liquidation provisions of the Bankruptcy Code. For at least six months prior to the filing of the petition, Drake had been unable to pay current business and personal obligations as they came due. Total liabilities substantially exceeded the total assets. A trustee was appointed who has converted all of Drake's non-exempt property to cash in the amount of $96,000. Drake's bankruptcy petition reflects a total of $310,000 of debts, including the following:

- A judgment against Drake in the amount of $19,500 as a result of an automobile accident caused by Drake's negligence.
- Unpaid federal income taxes in the amount of $4,300 for the year 1983. (Drake filed an accurate tax return for 1983.)
- A $3,200 obligation payable on June 1, 1990, described as being owed to Martin Office Equipment, when, in fact, the debt is owed to Bartin Computer Supplies (Bartin has no knowledge of Drake's bankruptcy and the time for filing claims has expired).
- Unpaid child support in the amount of $780 arising from a support order incorporated in Drake's 1982 divorce judgment.

Prior to the filing of the petition, Drake entered into the following transactions:

- January 13, 1990--paid Safe Bank $7,500, the full amount due on an unsecured loan given by Safe on November 13, 1989 (Drake had used the loan proceeds to purchase a family automobile).
- October 21, 1989--conveyed to his brother, in repayment of a $2,000 debt, a painting that cost Drake $125 and which had a fair market value of $2,000.
- November 15, 1989--borrowed $23,000 from Home Savings and Loan Association, giving Home a first mortgage on Drake's residence, which has a fair market value of $100,000.
- November 9, 1989--paid $4,300 to Max Clothing Distributors for clothing delivered to Drake 60 days earlier (Drake had for several years purchased inventory from Max and his other suppliers on 60-day credit terms).

Required: Answer the following questions, setting forth reasons for any conclusions stated.

a. Will the four debts described above be discharged in Drake's bankruptcy?

b. What factors must the bankruptcy trustee show to set aside a transaction as a preferential transfer?

c. State whether each transaction entered into by Drake is a preferential or non-preferential transfer.

a. The judgment against Drake arising from his negligence is dischargeable in his bankruptcy.

The unpaid federal income taxes are also dischargeable because they became due and owing more than three years prior to the filing of the bankruptcy petition.

The obligation to Bartin will not be discharged because the debt was not included in Drake's bankruptcy petition schedules and the creditor did not have notice or actual knowledge of the bankruptcy in time to file a proof of claim.

The unpaid child support is not dischargeable in Drake's bankruptcy.

b. To establish a preferential transfer that can be set aside, the bankruptcy trustee must show

- A voluntary or involuntary transfer of non-exempt property to a creditor.
- The transfer was made during the ninety days immediately preceding the bankruptcy filing (or within one

year in the case of an "insider").
- The transfer was on account of an antecedent debt.
- The transfer was made while the debtor was insolvent.
- The transfer allows the creditor to receive a greater percentage than would otherwise be received in the bankruptcy proceeding.

c. The payment to Safe will be regarded as a preference and may be set aside by the trustee.

The transfer by Drake to his brother can be set aside as a preference since his brother would be considered an insider and payment was made within one year of filing.

Giving the mortgage to Home is not a preference because it was not on account of an antecedent debt.

The payment to Max is not a preference because it was made in the ordinary course of the business of Max and Drake under ordinary business terms.

2 (May 89)

On March 23, 1989, Tine, a sole proprietor, was involuntarily petitioned into bankruptcy under the liquidation provisions of the Bankruptcy Code. For the six-month period before the filing of the bankruptcy petition, Tine had been unable to pay current obligations as they became due. At the time the petition was filed, Tine had a negative net worth.

Before March 23, 1989, Tine entered into the following transactions:
- On December 29, 1988, Tine borrowed $250,000 from Safe Finance. On January 31, 1989, after learning of Tine's financial problems, Safe requested that Tine execute a mortgage on Tine's residence naming Safe as mortgagee. On January 31, 1989, Tine executed the mortgage and delivered it to Safe and it was recorded that same day. The residence had a fair market value of $300,000 at all times.
- On May 5, 1988, Rich Bank loaned Tine $50,000 based on Tine's personal financial statements. Tine knew the financial statements submitted to Rich substantially overstated Tine's net worth because of misrepresentations that were difficult to detect.

Required: Answer the following, setting forth reasons for any conclusions stated. Assuming that the requirements necessary for the commencement of an involuntary bankruptcy were met, discuss the following:

1. What action may the court take regarding the transactions between Tine and Safe?

2. What action may the court take regarding the transaction between Tine and Rich if Rich challenges the discharge of its debt?

1. The court may declare the January 31, 1989, mortgage delivered to Safe by Tine to be void as a preference. A preference occurs if there is a transfer of the interest in property:
- To or for the benefit of a creditor;
- For or on account of an antecedent debt owed by the debtor before such transfer was made;
- Made while the debtor was insolvent;
- Made within 90 days before the date of the filing of the bankruptcy petition (when the creditor is not an insider);
- That enables the creditor to receive more than the creditor would receive in a liquidation proceeding.

Under the facts of this case, the mortgage delivered by Tine to Safe was for Safe's benefit, on account of the $250,000 owed to Safe, given while Tine was unable to pay his current obligations (was insolvent), given on January 31, 1989 (which was within 90 days before the filing of the bankruptcy petition on March 23, 1989), and enabled Safe to receive more than it would have received in a liquidation proceeding ($250,000 as a secured creditor vs. a lesser amount as an unsecured creditor in liquidation).

2. The court can except Tine's debt to Rich Bank from Tine's discharge in bankruptcy. In general, the bankruptcy court will except a debt from discharge if the debtor obtains money by use of a statement in writing respecting the debtor's financial condition that is materially false; the creditor to whom the debtor is liable for money reasonably relied on the statement, and the debtor caused the statement to be made or published with intent to deceive.

Based on the facts of this case, Tine obtained a $50,000 loan after furnishing Rich with personal financial statements, that he knew substantially overstated his net worth. Because it was difficult to detect the overstatement, Rich's reliance on the financial statements was reasonable. Therefore, the requirements necessary to except Rich's debt from Tine's discharge have been met.

5 (May 86)

Ed Walsh, a sole proprietor, filed a petition in bankruptcy under the liquidation provisions of Chapter 7 of the Bankruptcy Code. Salam Corp., one of Walsh's largest creditors, wishes to prevent Walsh from receiving a discharge in bankruptcy or in the alternative to have its debt excepted from a discharge. Salam asserts to the trustee in bankruptcy that:
- Walsh neither listed nor scheduled Salam's debt at anytime during the bankruptcy proceeding.
- Walsh failed to preserve his financial records which are necessary to ascertain his financial condition.
- Walsh obtained money from Salam by using false financial statements.

Required: Answer the following, setting forth reasons for any conclusions stated.
    a. Discuss the assertions of Salam, indicating the consequences if such assertions are proven correct.
    b. If Walsh obtains a discharge in bankruptcy and certain creditors of Walsh wish to have the discharge revoked, discuss the various bases upon which such revocation may be granted, indicating who may request the revocation and the time within which an action requesting such revocation must be made.

    a. The failure by Walsh to list or schedule a debt at anytime during the bankruptcy proceeding, if proven, would result in that debt being excepted from a discharge in bankruptcy. Such is the rule where the creditor is unable to file a proof of claim in time and lacks notice or actual knowledge of the case.

Proof of Walsh's failure to preserve financial records necessary to ascertain his financial condition, if unjustified, would result in Walsh being denied a discharge in bankruptcy. The purpose of this rule is to deny the debtor a discharge for his wrongdoing in connection with the bankruptcy proceeding.

The effect of Walsh obtaining money by use of false financial statements, if proven, would result in Salam's debt being excepted from a discharge in bankruptcy. In order to obtain such an exception from discharge Salam must establish that the money was obtained by the use of a statement in writing in respect to Walsh's financial condition that is materially false, on which Salam reasonably relied, and which Walsh made or published with intent to deceive.

    b. On request of the trustee in bankruptcy or a creditor, and after notice and a hearing, the court will revoke a previously granted discharge in bankruptcy if:
- Such discharge was obtained through the fraud of the debtor and the party requesting that the discharge be revoked did not know of such fraud until after the discharge was granted: or
- The debtor acquired property that is property of the estate, or became entitled to acquire property that would be property of the estate, and knowingly and fraudulently failed to report the acquisition of, or entitlement to, such property, or to deliver or surrender such property to the trustee; or
- The debtor has refused (1) to obey any lawful order of the court, (2) has refused to testify on the ground of privilege against self-incrimination despite being granted immunity, or (3) has refused to testify after improperly invoking the constitutional privilege against self-incrimination.

The trustee in bankruptcy or a creditor may request a revocation of a discharge in bankruptcy under the first ground set forth above if such action is commenced within one year after the discharge was granted. If the requested revocation is based on the second or third grounds set forth above, then revocation must be sought within one year after the granting of such discharge or the date the case was closed, whichever is later.

III. Rehabilitation--Chapters 11, 12, and 13

Items 34 and 35 are based on the following:

Strong Corp. filed a voluntary petition in bankruptcy under the reorganization provisions of Chapter 11 of the Federal Bankruptcy Code. A reorganization plan was filed and agreed to by all necessary parties. The court confirmed the plan and a final decree was entered.

34 (May 95)

Which of the following parties ordinarily must confirm the plan?

	1/2 of the secured creditors	2/3 of the shareholders
a.	Yes	Yes
b.	Yes	No
c.	No	Yes
d.	No	No

35 (May 95)

Which of the following statements best describes the effect of the entry of the court's final decree?
a. Strong Corp. will be discharged from all its debts and liabilities.
b. Strong Corp. will be discharged only from the debts owed creditors who agreed to the reorganization plan.
c. Strong Corp. will be discharged from all its debts and liabilities that arose before the date of confirmation of the plan.
d. Strong Corp. will be discharged from all its debts and liabilities that arose before the confirmation of the plan, except as otherwise provided in the plan, the order of confirmation, or the Bankruptcy Code.

37 (November 94)

Under the reorganization provisions of Chapter 11 of the Federal Bankruptcy Code, after a reorganization plan is confirmed, and a final decree closing the proceedings entered, which of the following events usually occurs?
a. A reorganized corporate debtor will be liquidated.
b. A reorganized corporate debtor will be discharged from all debts except as otherwise provided in the plan and applicable law.
c. A trustee will continue to operate the debtor's business.
d. A reorganized individual debtor will not be allowed to continue in the same business.

32 (November 93)

Robin Corp. incurred substantial operating losses for the past three years. Unable to meet its current obligations, Robin filed a petition for reorganization under Chapter 11 of the Federal Bankruptcy Code. Which of the following statements is correct?
a. The creditors' committee must select a trustee to manage Robin's affairs.
b. The reorganization plan may only be filed by Robin.
c. A creditors' committee, if appointed, will consist of unsecured creditors.
d. Robin may continue in business only with the approval of a trustee.

33 (November 93)

A reorganization under Chapter 11 of the Federal Bankruptcy Code requires all of the following except the
a. Liquidation of the debtor.
b. The filing of a reorganization plan.
c. Confirmation of the reorganization plan by the court.
d. Opportunity for each class of claims to accept the reorganization plan.

34 (November 93)

Which of the following statements is correct with respect to the reorganization provisions of Chapter 11 of the Federal Bankruptcy Code?
a. A trustee must always be appointed.
b. The debtor must be insolvent if the bankruptcy petition was filed voluntarily.
c. A reorganization plan may be filed by a creditor anytime after the petition date.
d. The commencement of a bankruptcy case may be voluntary or involuntary.

Bankruptcy

31 (November 92)

Under Chapter 11 of the Federal Bankruptcy Code, which of the following actions is necessary before the court may confirm a reorganization plan?
   a. Provision for full payment of administration expenses.
   b. Acceptance of the plan by all classes of claimants.
   c. Preparation of a contingent plan of liquidation.
   d. Appointment of a trustee.

32 (November 92)

Under Chapter 11 of the Federal Bankruptcy Code, which of the following would not be eligible for reorganization?
   a. Retail sole proprietorship.
   b. Advertising partnership.
   c. CPA professional corporation.
   d. Savings and loan corporation.

29 (November 89)

As an alternative to bankruptcy liquidation, a business may reorganize under Chapter 11 of the Bankruptcy Code. Such a reorganization
   a. Requires the appointment of a trustee to administer the debtor organization.
   b. May be commenced by filing either a voluntary or involuntary petition.
   c. Never requires the appointment of a creditors' committee.
   d. May not be confirmed unless all creditors accept the plan.

26 (November 85)

Lux Corp. has been suffering large losses for the past two years. Because of its inability to meet current obligations, Lux has filed a petition for reorganization under Chapter 11 of the Bankruptcy Code. The reorganization provisions under the Bankruptcy Code
   a. Require that the court appoint a trustee in all cases.
   b. Permit Lux to remain in possession of its assets.
   c. Apply only to involuntary bankruptcy.
   d. Will apply to Lux only if Lux is required to register pursuant to the federal securities laws.

24 (May 83)

Hard Times, Inc. is insolvent. Its liabilities exceed its assets by $13 million. Hard Times is owned by its president, Waters, and members of his family. Waters, whose assets are estimated at less than a million dollars, guaranteed the loans of the corporation. A consortium of banks is the principal creditor of Hard Times having loaned it $8 million, the bulk of which is unsecured. The banks decided to seek reorganization of Hard Times and Waters has agreed to cooperate. Regarding the proposed reorganization
   a. Waters' cooperation is necessary since he must sign the petition for a reorganization.
   b. If a petition in bankruptcy is filed against Hard Times, Waters will also have his personal bankruptcy status resolved and relief granted.
   c. Only a duly constituted creditors committee may file a plan of reorganization of Hard Times.
   d. Hard Times will remain in possession unless a request is made to the court for the appointment of a trustee.

19 (November 82)

Chapter 11 of the Bankruptcy Reform Act of 1978 deals with reorganizations. This Chapter
   a. Is exclusively available to corporations.
   b. Permits the debtor-in-possession to continue to operate the business in the same manner as a Chapter 11 trustee.
   c. Provides for filing of voluntary petitions but prohibits the filing of involuntary petitions.
   d. Provides separate procedures for corporations with publicly-held securities.

IV. Collective Creditors' Remedies Outside Bankruptcy

27 (November 94)

Which of the following actions between a debtor and its creditors will generally cause the debtor's release from its debts?

	Composition of creditors	Assignment for the benefit of creditors
a.	Yes	Yes
b.	Yes	No
c.	No	Yes
d.	No	No

40 (May 81)

A client has joined other creditors of the Martin Construction Company in a composition agreement seeking to avoid the necessity of a bankruptcy proceeding against Martin. Which statement describes the composition agreement?

a. It provides a temporary delay, not to exceed six months, insofar as the debtor's obligation to repay the debts included in the composition.

b. It does not discharge any of the debts included until performance by the debtor has taken place.

c. It provides for the appointment of a receiver to take over and operate the debtor's business.

d. It must be approved by all creditors.

PART VI -- SECURITIES REGULATION; OTHER GOVERNMENT REGULATION

TABLE OF CONTENTS

PART VI

SECURITIES REGULATION; OTHER
GOVERNMENT REGULATION

I. Securities Act of 1933
A. Definition of "Security"

6 (R96)

Under the registration requirements of the Securities Act of 1933, which of the following items is (are) considered securities?

	Investment contracts	Collateral-trust certificates
a.	Yes	Yes
b.	Yes	No
c.	No	Yes
d.	No	No

30 (May 93)

Which of the following is <u>least</u> likely to be considered a security under the Securities Act of 1933?
a. Stock options.
b. Warrants.
c. General partnership interests.
d. Limited partnership interests.

34 (November 86)

One of the clients of Sherman & Pryor, CPAs, plans to form a limited partnership and offer to the public in interstate commerce 2,000 limited partnership units at $5,000 per unit. Which of the following is correct?
a. The dollar amount in question is sufficiently small so as to provide an absolute exemption from the Securities Act of 1933.
b. The Securities Act of 1933 requires a registration despite the fact that the client is <u>not</u> selling stock and the purchasers have limited liability.
c. Under the Securities Act of 1933, Sherman & Pryor has <u>no</u> responsibility for financial statements since the limited partnership is a new entity.
d. Sherman & Pryor may disclaim any liability under the federal securities acts by an unambiguous, bold-faced disclaimer of liability on its audit report.

28 (November 79)

Which of the following is exempt from registration under the Securities Act of 1933?
a. First mortgage bonds.
b. The usual annuity contract issued by an insurer.
c. Convertible preferred stock.
d. Limited partnership interests.

B. Registration Requirements

41 (November 94)

Under the Securities Act of 1933, which of the following statements most accurately reflects how securities registration affects an investor?

a. The investor is provided with information on the stockholders of the offering corporation.

b. The investor is provided with information on the principal purposes for which the offering's proceeds will be used.

c. The investor is guaranteed by the SEC that the facts contained in the registration statement are accurate.

d. The investor is assured by the SEC against loss resulting from purchasing the security.

43 (November 94)

Which of the following requirements must be met by an issuer of securities who wants to make an offering by using shelf registration?

	Original registration statement must be kept updated	The offeror must be a first-time issuer of securities
a.	Yes	Yes
b.	Yes	No
c.	No	Yes
d.	No	No

31 (May 94)

Which of the following statements concerning the prospectus required by the Securities Act of 1933 is correct?

a. The prospectus is part of the registration statement.

b. The prospectus should enable the SEC to pass on the merits of the securities.

c. The prospectus must be filed after an offer to sell.

d. The prospectus is prohibited from being distributed to the public until the SEC approves the accuracy of the facts embodied therein.

32 (May 94)

A preliminary prospectus, permitted under SEC Regulations, is known as the

a. Unaudited prospectus.

b. Qualified prospectus.

c. "Blue-sky" prospectus.

d. "Red-herring" prospectus.

33 (May 94)

A tombstone advertisement

a. May be substituted for the prospectus under certain circumstances.

b. May contain an offer to sell securities.

c. Notifies prospective investors that a previously-offered security has been withdrawn from the market and is therefore effectively "dead."

d. Makes known the availability of a prospectus.

29 (May 93)

Which of the following disclosures must be contained in a securities registration statement filed under the Securities Act of 1933?

a. A list of all existing stockholders.

b. The principal purposes for which the offering proceeds will be used.

c. A copy of the corporation's latest proxy solicitation statement.

d. The names of all prospective accredited investors.

Items 39 and 40 are based on the following:

World Corp. wanted to make a public offering of its common stock. On May 10, World prepared and filed a registration statement with the SEC. On May 20, World placed a "tombstone ad" announcing that it was making a public offering. On May 25, World issued a preliminary prospectus and the registration statement became effective on May 30.

39 (May 92)

On what date may World first make oral offers to sell the shares?

a. May 10.
b. May 20.
c. May 25.
d. May 30.

40 (May 92)

On what date may World first sell the shares?

a. May 10.
b. May 20.
c. May 25.
d. May 30.

36 (November 91)

When a common stock offering requires registration under the Securities Act of 1933,

a. The registration statement is automatically effective when filed with the SEC.
b. The issuer would act unlawfully if it were to sell the common stock without providing the investor with a prospectus.
c. The SEC will determine the investment value of the common stock before approving the offering.
d. The issuer may make sales 10 days after filing the registration statement.

37 (November 91)

Under the Securities Act of 1933, an initial offering of securities must be registered with the SEC, unless

a. The offering is made through a broker-dealer licensed in the states in which the securities are to be sold.
b. The offering prospectus makes a fair and full disclosure of all risks associated with purchasing the securities.
c. The issuer's financial condition meets certain standards established by the SEC.
d. The type of security or the offering involved is exempt from registration.

40 (May 91)

Universal Corp. intends to sell its common stock to the public in an interstate offering that will be registered under the Securities Act of 1933. Under the Act,

a. Universal can make offers to sell its stock before filing a registration statement, provided that it does not actually issue stock certificates until after the registration is effective.
b. Universal's registration statement becomes effective at the time it is filed, assuming the SEC does not object within 20 days thereafter.
c. A prospectus must be delivered to each purchaser of Universal's common stock unless the purchaser qualifies as an accredited investor.
d. Universal's filing of a registration statement with the SEC does not automatically result in compliance with the "blue-sky" laws of the states in which the offering will be made.

41 (May 91)

The registration of a security under the Securities Act of 1933 provides an investor with

a. A guarantee by the SEC that the facts contained in the registration statement are accurate.
b. An assurance against loss resulting from purchasing the security.
c. Information on the principal purposes for which the offering's proceeds will be used.
d. Information on the issuing corporation's trade secrets.

Securities Regulation

39 (November 90)

The registration requirements of the Securities Act of 1933 are intended to provide information to the SEC to enable it to
a. Evaluate the financial merits of the securities being offered.
b. Ensure that investors are provided with adequate information on which to base investment decisions.
c. Prevent public offerings of securities when management fraud or unethical conduct is suspected.
d. Assure investors of the accuracy of the facts presented in the financial statements.

29 (May 90)

Under the Securities Act of 1933, the registration of an interstate securities offering is
a. Required only in transactions involving more than $500,000.
b. Mandatory, unless the cost to the issuer is prohibitive.
c. Required, unless there is an applicable exemption.
d. Intended to prevent the marketing of securities which pose serious financial risks.

40 (May 89)

Acme Corp. intends to make a public offering in several states of 250,000 shares of its common stock. Under the Securities Act of 1933,
a. Acme must sell the common stock through licensed securities dealers.
b. Acme must, in all events, file a registration statement with the SEC because the offering will be made in several states.
c. Acme's use of any prospectus delivered to an unsophisticated investor must be accompanied by a simplified explanation of the offering.
d. Acme may make an oral offer to sell the common stock to a prospective investor after a registration statement has been filed but before it becomes effective.

41 (May 89)

Pace Corp. previously issued 300,000 shares of its common stock. The shares are now actively traded on a national securities exchange. The original offering was exempt from registration under the Securities Act of 1933. Pace has $2,500,000 in assets and 425 shareholders. With regard to the Securities Exchange Act of 1934, Pace is
a. Required to file a registration statement because its assets exceed $2,000,000 in value.
b. Required to file a registration statement even though it has fewer than 500 shareholders.
c. Not required to file a registration statement because the original offering of its stock was exempt from registration.
d. Not required to file a registration statement unless insiders own at least 5% of its outstanding shares of stock.

37 (May 88)

Unless an exemption applies to an offering of securities, the Securities Act of 1933 requires preparation and filing of a

	Registration statement	Prospectus
a.	Yes	Yes
b.	Yes	No
c.	No	Yes
d.	No	No

8 (November 87)

After the filing of the registration statement with the SEC but prior to the effective date, the underwriter is allowed to do which of the following?
  I. Make oral offers to sell the security.
  II. Issue a preliminary prospectus ("red herring").
a. I only.
b. II only.
c. I and II.
d. Neither I nor II.

41 (May 87)

The registration requirements of the Securities Act of 1933 apply to

a. The issuance of a stock dividend without commissions or other consideration paid.
b. The issuance of stock warrants.
c. Securities issued by a federally chartered savings and loan association.
d. Securities issued by a common carrier regulated by the Interstate Commerce Commission.

32 (November 86)

Donn & Co. is considering the sale of $11 million of its common stock to the public in interstate commerce. In this connection, Donn has been correctly advised that registration of the securities with the SEC is

a. Not required if the states in which the securities are to be sold have securities acts modeled after the federal act and Donn files in those states.
b. Required in that it is necessary for the SEC to approve the merits of the securities offered.
c. Not required if the securities are to be sold through a registered brokerage firm.
d. Required and must include audited financial statements as an integral part of its registration.

43 (May 79)

Tweed Manufacturing, Inc. plans to issue $5 million of common stock to the public in interstate commerce after its registration statement with the SEC becomes effective. What, if anything, must Tweed do in respect to those states in which the securities are to be sold?

a. Nothing; since approval by the SEC automatically constitutes satisfaction of any state requirements.
b. Make a filing in those states which have laws governing such offerings and obtain their approval.
c. Simultaneously apply to the SEC for permission to market the securities in the various states without further clearance.
d. File in the appropriate state office of the state in which it maintains its principal office of business, obtain clearance, and forward a certified copy of that state's clearance to all other states.

3 (May 77)

Under the Securities Act of 1933, subject to some exceptions and limitations, it is unlawful to use the mails or instruments of interstate commerce to sell or offer to sell a security to the public underline

a. A surety bond sufficient to cover potential liability to investors is obtained and filed with the Securities and Exchange Commission.
b. The offer is made through underwriters qualified to offer the securities on a nationwide basis.
c. A registration statement has been properly filed with the Securities and Exchange Commission, has been found to be acceptable, and is in effect.
d. The Securities and Exchange Commission approves of the financial merit of the offering.

2 (May 82)

Various Enterprises Corporation is a medium-sized conglomerate listed on the American Stock Exchange. It is constantly in the process of acquiring smaller corporations and is invariably in need of additional money. Among its diversified holdings is a citrus grove which it purchased eight years ago as an investment. The grove's current fair market value is in excess of $2 million. Various also owns 800,000 shares of Resistance Corporation which it acquired in the open market over a period of years. These shares represent a 17% minority interest in Resistance and are worth approximately $2.5 million. Various does its short-term financing with a consortium of banking institutions. Several of these loans are maturing; in addition to renewing these loans, it wishes to increase its short-term debt from $3 to $4 million.

In light of the above, Various is considering resorting to one or all of the following alternatives in order to raise additional working capital.

- An offering of 500 citrus grove units at $5,000 per unit. Each unit would give the purchaser a 0.2% ownership interest in the citrus grove development. Various would furnish management and operation services for a fee under a management contract and net proceeds would be paid to the unit purchasers. The offering would be confined almost exclusively to the state in which the groves are located or in the adjacent state in which Various is incorporated.

Securities Regulation

- An increase in the short-term borrowing by $1 million from the banking institution which currently provides short-term funds. The existing debt would be consolidated, extended and increased to $4 million and would mature over a nine-month period. This would be evidenced by a short-term note.

- Sale of the 17% minority interest in Resistance Corporation in the open market through its brokers over a period of time and in such a way so as to minimize decreasing the value of the stock. The stock is to be sold in an orderly manner in the ordinary course of the broker's business.

Required: Answer the following, setting forth reasons for any conclusions stated.

In separate paragraphs discuss the impact of the registration requirements of the Securities Act of 1933 on each of the above proposed alternatives.

The impact of the registration requirements of the Securities Act of 1933 on each of the proposals is as follows:

- The offering of the participation units in the citrus groves, although ostensibly the sale of an interest in land, constitutes an offer to sell, or the sale of, securities within the meaning of § 2 of the Securities Act of 1933. Although land itself is not a security, the offering of the land in conjunction with a management contract has been held to constitute the offering of a security. Since interstate commerce and communications are to be used and since there is no apparent transactional exemption available, a registration under the 1933 Act is required. Whatever hope there was of an intrastate offering exclusion is dashed by the fact that the units will be offered and sold in two states.

- The short-term borrowings evidenced by the promissory notes of Various Enterprises are exempt from registration. This exemption from categorization as a security for purposes of registration under the Act applies to commercial paper such as notes, drafts, checks, and similar paper arising out of a current transaction that have a maturity not exceeding nine months. In addition, the private placement exemption is applicable.

- If Various is deemed to be a controlling person insofar as Resistance is concerned, it must register the securities in question before it can legally sell them. The Securities Act of 1933 provides in connection with its definition of the term "underwriter," that, "the term 'issuer' shall include, in addition to an issuer, any person directly or indirectly controlling or controlled by the issuer, or any person under direct or indirect common control with the issuer."

Securities Act rule 405(f) further defines the term "control." It states that "the term 'control' . . . means the possession, direct or indirect, of the power to direct or cause the direction of the policies of a person, whether through the ownership of voting securities, by contract, or otherwise." It is obvious that "control" as defined is a question of fact. In general, a controlling person has the power to influence the management and policies of the issuer. If an individual is an officer, director, or member of the executive committee, a low percentage of stock would suffice. Actual or practical control is sufficient and the power to exercise control will also be sufficient even if it is not exercised. Stock ownership is looked to and majority ownership naturally constitutes control. Although ownership of 17 percent of the stock is certainly not conclusive, it is a substantial block of stock and, if any of the above factors is also present, it would be most likely that Various would be a controlling person. Thus, although not the issuer of the stock, it would need to register the securities. This resembles a secondary offering of a large block by the owners of the corporation. This sale through the brokers will in no way insulate the transaction from registration.

5A (November 75)

Boswell Realty Corporation, whose sole business is land development, purchased a large tract of land on which it intended to construct a high-rise apartment-house complex. In order to finance the construction, Boswell offered to sell $3,000,000 worth of shares in Boswell Realty to about 1,000 prospective investors located throughout the United States.

Required:

1. Discuss the implications of the Securities Act of 1933 to Boswell's offering to sell shares in the corporation.

2. The Securities Act of 1933 is considered a disclosure statute. Briefly describe the means provided and the principal types of information required to accomplish this objective of disclosure.

1. The offering is subject to registration under the Securities Act of 1933. Despite the fact that the underlying property is real property, the shares represent the ownership in the corporation which in turn owns the real property. When these shares are offered for sale in interstate commerce (or by the use of instrumentalities of interstate commerce), the registration requirements of the Securities Act of 1933 must be met. These include filing a registration statement with the Securities and Exchange Commission (SEC) and giving a copy of the prospectus to each prospective purchaser of the registered securities.

228

2. The means of disclosure are the registration statement and the prospectus. The registration statement is filed with the SEC. The prospectus, which contains much of the information included in the registration statement, must be furnished to prospective investors of the registered securities. Both documents must contain full and accurate disclosure of all relevant information relating to such things as the company's business, its officers and directors, its securities, its financial position and earnings, and details about the underwriting. With rare exception, all information in a registration statement is part of the public record and open to public inspection. Photocopies of part or all of the registration statement may be obtained from the SEC at nominal costs.

C. Exemption from 1933 Act Registration
1. Exempt Securities

42 (November 94)

Which of the following securities would be regulated by the provisions of the Securities Act of 1933?
a.   Securities issued by not-for-profit, charitable organizations.
b.   Securities guaranteed by domestic governmental organizations.
c.   Securities issued by savings and loan associations.
d.   Securities issued by insurance companies.

33 (May 93)

The Securities Act of 1933 provides an exemption from registration for

	Bonds issued by a municipality for governmental purposes	Securities issued by a not-for-profit charitable organization
a.	Yes	Yes
b.	Yes	No
c.	No	Yes
d.	No	No

34 (May 93)

Which of the following securities is exempt from registration under the Securities Act of 1933?
a.   Shares of nonvoting common stock, provided their par value is less than $1.00.
b.   A class of stock given in exchange for another class by the issuer to its existing stockholders without the issuer paying a commission.
c.   Limited partnership interests sold for the purpose of acquiring funds to invest in bonds issued by the United States.
d.   Corporate debentures that were previously subject to an effective registration statement, provided they are convertible into shares of common stock.

43 (May 92)

Under the Securities Act of 1933, which of the following securities must be registered?
a.   Bonds of a railroad corporation.
b.   Common stock of an insurance corporation.
c.   Preferred stock of a domestic bank corporation.
d.   Long-term notes of a charitable corporation.

35 (November 91)

Exemption from registration under the Securities Act of 1933 would be available for
a.   Promissory notes maturing in 12 months.
b.   Securities of a bank.
c.   Limited partnership interests.
d.   Corporate bonds.

45 (May 91)

Which of the following securities is exempt from the registration requirements of the Securities Act of 1933?

a. Common stock with <u>no</u> par value.
b. Warrants to purchase preferred stock.
c. Bonds issued by a charitable foundation.
d. Convertible debentures issued by a corporation.

39 (November 89)

Which of the following types of securities are generally exempt from registration under the Securities Act of 1933?

	Securities of nonprofit charitable organizations	Securities of savings and loan associations
a.	Yes	Yes
b.	Yes	No
c.	No	Yes
d.	No	No

42 (May 88)

In general, the Securities Act of 1933 provides for an exemption from registration for

	A stock dividend issued to existing shareholders	Bonds issued by a municipality for governmental purposes
a.	Yes	No
b.	Yes	Yes
c.	No	Yes
d.	No	No

42 (November 84)

Which of the following is subject to the registration requirements of the Securities Act of 1933?

a. Public sale of its bonds by a municipality.
b. Public sale by a corporation of its negotiable five-year notes.
c. Public sale of stock issued by a common carrier regulated by the Interstate Commerce Commission.
d. Issuance of stock by a corporation to its existing stockholders pursuant to a stock split.

2. Small or Limited Offering Exemptions

(R03)

Miner Corp. wants to make a $5 million public stock offering under the exempt transaction limited offering provisions of the Securities Act of 1933. What must Miner do to comply with the Act?

a. File a registration statement.
b. Advertise the offering.
c. Issue a "red herring" prospectus.
d. Limit sales of the offering to <u>no</u> more than 35 unaccredited investors.

44 (November 94)

Under the Securities Act of 1933, which of the following statements concerning an offering of securities sold under a transaction exemption is correct?

a. The offering is exempt from the anti-fraud provisions of the 1933 Act.
b. The offering is subject to the registration requirements of the 1933 Act.
c. Resales of the offering are exempt from the provisions of the 1933 Act.
d. Resales of the offering must be made under a registration or a different exemption provision of the 1933 Act.

37 (May 94)

Which of the following transactions will be exempt from the full registration requirements of the Securities Act of 1933?

    a.   All intrastate offerings.

    b.   All offerings made under Regulation A.

    c.   Any resale of a security purchased under a Regulation D offering.

    d.   Any stockbroker transaction.

40 (May 94)

Under Regulation D of the Securities Act of 1933, which of the following conditions apply to private placement offerings? The securities

    a.   Cannot be sold for longer than a six month period.

    b.   Cannot be the subject of an immediate unregistered reoffering to the public.

    c.   Must be sold to accredited institutional investors.

    d.   Must be sold to fewer than 20 nonaccredited investors.

40 (November 93)

An offering made under the provisions of Regulation A of the Securities Act of 1933 requires that the issuer

    a.   File an offering circular with the SEC.

    b.   Sell only to accredited investors.

    c.   Provide investors with the prior four years' audited financial statements.

    d.   Provide investors with a proxy registration statement.

Items 43 and 44 are based on the following:

Pix, Corp. is making a $6,000,000 stock offering. Pix wants the offering exempt from registration under the Securities Act of 1933.

43 (November 93)

Which of the following provisions of the Act would Pix have to comply with for the offering to be exempt?

    a.   Regulation A.

    b.   Regulation D, Rule 504.

    c.   Regulation D, Rule 505.

    d.   Regulation D, Rule 506.

44 (November 93)

Which of the following requirements would Pix have to comply with when selling the securities?

    a.   No more than 35 investors.

    b.   No more than 35 nonaccredited investors.

    c.   Accredited investors only.

    d.   Nonaccredited investors only.

45 (November 93)

Frey, Inc. intends to make a $2,000,000 common stock offering under Rule 505 of Regulation D of the Securities Act of 1933. Frey

    a.   May sell the stock to an unlimited number of investors.

    b.   May make the offering through a general advertising.

    c.   Must notify the SEC within 15 days after the first sale of the offering.

    d.   Must provide all investors with a prospectus.

Securities Regulation

35 (May 93)

Regulation D of the Securities Act of 1933

a. Restricts the number of purchasers of an offering to 35.

b. Permits an exempt offering to be sold to both accredited and nonaccredited investors.

c. Is limited to offers and sales of common stock that do not exceed $1.5 million.

d. Is exclusively available to small business corporations as defined by Regulation D.

40 (November 91)

Kamp is offering $10 million of its securities. Under Rule 506 of Regulation D of the Securities Act of 1933,

a. The securities may be debentures.

b. Kamp must be a corporation.

c. There must be more than 35 purchasers.

d. Kamp may make a general solicitation in connection with the offering.

43 (November 90)

Imperial Corp. is offering $450,000 of its securities under Rule 504 of Regulation D of the Securities Act of 1933. Under Rule 504, Imperial is required to

a. Provide full financial information to all non-accredited purchasers.

b. Make the offering through general solicitation.

c. Register the offering under the provisions of the Securities Exchange Act of 1934.

d. Notify the SEC within 15 days after the first sale of the securities.

44 (November 90)

Hamilton Corp. is making a $4,500,000 securities offering under Rule 505 of Regulation D of the Securities Act of 1933. Under this regulation, Hamilton is

a. Required to provide full financial information to accredited investors only.

b. Allowed to make the offering through a general solicitation.

c. Limited to selling to no more than 35 non-accredited investors.

d. Allowed to sell to an unlimited number of investors both accredited and non-accredited.

45 (November 90)

A $10,000,000 offering of corporate stock intended to be made pursuant to the provisions of Rule 506 of Regulation D of the Securities Act of 1933 would not be exempt under Rule 506 if

a. The offering was made through a general solicitation or advertising.

b. Some of the investors are non-accredited.

c. There are more than 35 accredited investors.

d. The SEC was notified 14 days after the first sale of the securities.

33 (May 90)

Pate Corp. is offering $3 million of its securities solely to accredited investors. Under Regulation D of the Securities Act of 1933, Pate is

a. Not required to provide any specified information to the accredited investors.

b. Permitted to make a general solicitation.

c. Not allowed to sell to investors using purchaser representatives.

d. Required to provide accredited investors with audited financial statements for the three most recent fiscal years.

37 (May 90)

Zack Limited Partnership intends to sell $6,000,000 of its limited partnership interests. Zack conducts all of its business activities in the state in which it was organized. Zack intends to use the offering proceeds to acquire municipal bonds. Which of the following statements is correct concerning the offering and the registration exemptions that might be available to Zack under the Securities Act of 1933?

a. The offering is exempt from registration because of the intended use of the offering proceeds.

b. Under Rule 147 (regarding intrastate offerings), Zack may make up to five offers to non-residents without jeopardizing the Rule 147 exemption.

c. If Zack complies with the requirements of Regulation D, any subsequent resale of a limited partnership interest by a purchaser is automatically exempt from registration.

d. If Zack complies with the requirements of Regulation D, Zack may make an unlimited number of offers to sell the limited partnership interests.

35 (November 89)

An issuer making an offering under the provisions of Regulation A of the Securities Act of 1933 must file a(an)

a. Prospectus.

b. Offering statement.

c. Shelf registration.

d. Proxy.

37 (November 89)

Rule 504 of Regulation D of the Securities Act of 1933 provides issuers with an exemption from registration for certain small issues. Which of the following statements is correct?

a. The rule allows sales to an unlimited number of investors.

b. The rule requires certain financial information to be furnished to the investors.

c. The issuer must offer the securities through general public advertising.

d. The issuer is not required to file anything with the SEC.

Items 44 and 45 are based on the following:

Maco Limited Partnership intends to sell $6,000,000 of its limited partnership interests. The state in which Maco was organized is also the state in which it carries on all of its business activities.

44 (May 89)

If Maco intends to offer the limited partnership interests in reliance on Rule 147, the intrastate registration exception under the Securities Act of 1933, which one of the following statements is correct?

a. Maco may make up to five offers to nonresidents without the offering being ineligible for the Rule 147 exemption.

b. The offering is not exempt under Rule 147 because it exceeds $5,000,000.

c. Under Rule 147, certain restrictions apply to resales of the limited partnership interests by purchasers.

d. Rule 147 limits to 100 the number of purchasers of the limited partnership interests.

45 (May 89)

If Maco intends to offer the limited partnership interests in reliance on Rule 506 of Regulation D under the Securities Act of 1933 to prospective investors residing in several states, which of the following statements is correct?

a. The offering will be exempt from the anti-fraud provisions of the Securities Exchange Act of 1934.

b. Any subsequent resale of a limited partnership interest by a purchaser will be exempt from registration.

c. Maco may make an unlimited number of offers to sell the limited partnership interests.

d. No more than 35 purchasers may acquire the limited partnership interests.

39 (May 88)

In order to raise $375,000, Penn Corp. is offering its securities under Rule 504 of Regulation D of the Securities Act of 1933. Under Rule 504, the offering

a. Must be sold to accredited investors.

b. Can not be sold to more than 35 non-accredited investors.

c. Can be sold to an unlimited number of accredited and non-accredited investors.

d. Will not subject the issuer to the antifraud provisions of the Securities Act of 1933.

Securities Regulation

45 (May 87)

Regulation D of the Securities Act of 1933 is available to issuers without regard to the dollar amount of an offering only when the

    a.   Purchasers are all accredited investors.

    b.   Number of purchasers who are non-accredited is 35 or less.

    c.   Issuer is <u>not</u> a reporting company under the Securities Exchange Act of 1934.

    d.   Issuer is <u>not</u> an investment company.

22 (May 86)

Regulation D under the Securities Act of 1933

    a.   Eliminates all small offerings made pursuant to Regulation A of the Securities Act of 1933.

    b.   Permits an exempt offering by a corporation even though it is a "reporting" corporation under the Securities Exchange Act of 1934.

    c.   Is limited to offers and sales of common stock which do <u>not</u> exceed $5 million.

    d.   Is exclusively available to "small business corporations" as defined by Regulation D.

40 (November 80)

Theobold Construction Company, Inc. is considering a public stock offering for the first time. It wishes to raise $1.2 million by a common stock offering and do this in the least expansive manner. In this connection, it is considering making an offering pursuant to Regulation A. Which of the following statements is correct regarding such an offering?

    a.   Such an offering can <u>not</u> be made to more than 250 people.

    b.   The maximum amount of securities permitted to be offered under Regulation A is $1 million.

    c.   Only those corporations which have had an initial registration under the Securities Act of 1933 are eligible.

    d.   Even if Regulation A applies, Theobold is required to distribute an offering circular.

3 (November 95)

Items 76 through 80 are based on the following:

Coffee Corp., a publicly-held corporation, wants to make an $8,000,000 exempt offering of its shares as a private placement offering under Regulation D, Rule 506, of the Securities Act of 1933. Coffee has more than 500 shareholders and assets in excess of $1 billion, and has its shares listed on a national securities exchange.

Required: Items 76 through 80 relate to the application of the provisions of the Securities Act of 1933 and the Securities Exchange Act of 1934 to Coffee Corp. and the offering. For each item, select from List II whether only statement I is correct, whether only statement II is correct, whether both statements I and II are correct, or whether neither statement I nor II is correct.

List II	
A	I only.
B	II only.
C	Both I and II.
D	Neither I nor II.

76.   I.   Coffee Corp. may make the Regulation D, Rule 506, exempt offering.

          II.   Coffee Corp., because it is required to report under the Securities Exchange Act of 1934, may <u>not</u> make an exempt offering.

77.   I.   Shares sold under a Regulation D, Rule 506, exempt offering may only be purchased by accredited investors.

          II.   Shares sold under a Regulation D, Rule 506, exempt offering may be purchased by any number of investors provided there are <u>no</u> more than 35 non-accredited investors.

78.   I.   An exempt offering under Regulation D, Rule 506, must <u>not</u> be for more than $10,000,000.

          II.   An exempt offering under Regulation D, Rule 506, has <u>no</u> dollar limit.

79.   I.   Regulation D, Rule 506, requires that all investors in the exempt offering be notified that for nine months after the last sale <u>no</u> resale may be made to a nonresident.

        II.   Regulation D, Rule 506, requires that the issuer exercise reasonable care to assure that purchasers of the exempt offering are buying for investment and are <u>not</u> underwriters.

80.   I.   The SEC must be notified by Coffee Corp. within 5 days of the first sale of the exempt offering securities.

        II.   Coffee Corp. must include an SEC notification of the first sale of the exempt offering securities in Coffee's next filed Quarterly Report (Form 10-Q).

2 (November 92)

Question Number 2 is based on the following information. Question Number 2 consists of Items 61 through 75.

Butler Manufacturing Corp. planned to raise capital for a plant expansion by borrowing from banks and making several stock offerings. Butler engaged Weaver, CPA, to audit its December 31, 1989, financial statements. Butler told Weaver that the financial statements would be given to certain named banks and included in the prospectuses for the stock offerings.

In performing the audit, Weaver did not confirm accounts receivable and, as a result, failed to discover a material overstatement of accounts receivable. Also, Weaver was aware of a pending class action product liability lawsuit that was not disclosed in Butler's financial statements. Despite being advised by Butler's legal counsel that Butler's potential liability under the lawsuit would result in material losses, Weaver issued an unqualified opinion on Butler's financial statements.

In May 1990, Union Bank, one of the named banks, relied on the financial statements and Weaver's opinion in giving Butler a $500,000 loan.

Butler raised an additional $16,450,000 through the following stock offerings, which were sold completely:

- June 1990--Butler made a $450,000 unregistered offering of Class B nonvoting common stock under Rule 504 of Regulation D of the Securities Act of 1933. This offering was sold over two years to 30 nonaccredited investors and 20 accredited investors by general solicitation. The SEC was notified eight days after the first sale of this offering.

- September 1990--Butler made a $10,000,000 unregistered offering of Class A voting common stock under Rule 506 of Regulation D of the Securities Act of 1933. This offering was sold over two years to 200 accredited investors and 30 nonaccredited investors through a private placement. The SEC was notified 14 days after the first sale of this offering.

- November 1990--Butler made a $6,000,000 unregistered offering of preferred stock under Rule 505 of Regulation D of the Securities Act of 1933. This offering was sold during a one-year period to 40 nonaccredited investors by private placement. The SEC was notified 18 days after the first sale of this offering.

Shortly after obtaining the Union loan, Butler began experiencing financial problems but was able to stay in business because of the money raised by the offerings. Butler was found liable in the product liability suit. This resulted in a judgment Butler could not pay. Butler also defaulted on the Union loan and was involuntarily petitioned into bankruptcy. This caused Union to sustain a loss and Butler's stockholders to lose their investments.

As a result:

- The SEC claimed that all three of Butler's offerings were made improperly and were not exempt from registration.
- Union sued Weaver for
    - Negligence
    - Common Law Fraud
- The stockholders who purchased Butler's stock through the offerings sued Weaver, alleging fraud under Section 10(b) and Rule 10b-5 of the Securities Exchange Act of 1934.

These transactions took place in a jurisdiction providing for accountant's liability for negligence to known and intended users of financial statements.

Securities Regulation

2 (November 92)

a.   Items 61 through 65 are questions related to the June 1990 offering made under Rule 504 of Regulation D of the Securities Act of 1933. For each item answer either yes (Y) or no (N).

61.   Did the offering comply with the dollar limitation of Rule 504?
62.   Did the offering comply with the method of sale restrictions?
63.   Was the offering sold during the applicable time limit?
64.   Was the SEC notified timely of the first sale of the securities?
65.   Was the SEC correct in claiming that this offering was not exempt from registration?

b.   Items 66 through 70 are questions related to the September 1990 offering made under Rule 506 of Regulation D of the Securities Act of 1933. For each item answer either yes (Y) or no (N).

66.   Did the offering comply with the dollar limitation of Rule 506?
67.   Did the offering comply with the method of sale restrictions?
68.   Was the offering sold to the correct number of investors?
69.   Was the SEC notified timely of the first sale of the securities?
70.   Was the SEC correct in claiming that this offering was not exempt from registration?

c.   Items 71 through 75 are questions related to the November 1990 offering made under Rule 505 of Regulation D of the Securities Act of 1933. For each item answer either yes (Y) or no (N).

71.   Did the offering comply with the dollar limitation of Rule 505?
72.   Was the offering sold during the applicable time limit?
73.   Was the offering sold to the correct number of investors?
74.   Was the SEC notified timely of the first sale of the securities?
75.   Was the SEC correct in claiming that this offering was not exempt from registration?

4A (November 78)

Glover Corporation is a small rapidly-expanding manufacturing company. In 1977, Glover made a public offering of its shares for $400,000 in accordance with Regulation A, issued by the Securities and Exchange Commission pursuant to the Securities Act of 1933. The shares are not listed on any exchange, but are sometimes bought and sold in interstate commerce. At the end of 1977, Glover had total assets of $900,000, 429 shareholders, and sales of $650,000 for the year.

Required: Answer the following, setting forth reasons for any conclusions stated.
1.   What is a Regulation A offering and what are the general requirements which must be met in order to qualify for making such an offering?
2.   What difference is there in the potential liability of the parties making an offering under Regulation A as contrasted with a full registration?

1. The Securities Act of 1933 gives the Securities and Exchange Commission authority to exempt certain small public offerings from full registration. The dollar amount of the offering may not exceed $5.0 million. In order to obtain an exemption, the issuer must meet the filing requirements contained in Regulation A. These requirements are not as onerous as a full registration, although considerable documentation is required. The financial statements generally need not be audited, and supplemental disclosures are not as extensive. Sales must be made only by an offering circular, which is similar to a prospectus, and it must be supplied to each purchaser.
2. None. The same liability for a false statement or a material omission that applies to a full registration applies to a Regulation A offering.

3. Intrastate Offering Exemption

52 (November 94)

Which of the following statements concerning an initial intrastate securities offering made by an issuer residing in and doing business in that state is correct?
   a. The offering would be exempt from the registration requirements of the Securities Act of 1933.
   b. The offering would be subject to the registration requirements of the Securities Exchange Act of 1934.
   c. The offering would be regulated by the SEC.
   d. The shares of the offering could <u>not</u> be resold to investors outside the state for at least one year.

32 (May 90)

Which of the following are exempt from the registration requirements of the Securities Act of 1933?
   a. Bankers' acceptances with maturities at the time of issue ranging from one to two years.
   b. Participation interests in money market funds that consist wholly of short-term commercial paper.
   c. Corporate stock offered and sold only to residents of the state in which the issuer was incorporated and is doing all of its business.
   d. All industrial development bonds issued by municipalities.

4 (May 77)

Under which of the following circumstances is a public offering of securities exempt from the registration requirements of the Securities Act of 1933?
   a. There was a prior registration within one year.
   b. The corporation is a public utility subject to regulation by the Federal Power Commission.
   c. The corporation was closely held prior to the offering.
   d. The issuing corporation and all prospective security owners are located within one state, and the entire offering, sale, and distribution is made within that state.

4B (May 81)

Marigold Corporation is incorporated in one of the states of the United States and does substantially all of its business within that state. It is considering reliance upon the intrastate exemption to the Securities Act of 1933 in order to offer and sell its securities without registering them under the 1933 Act. Its proposed offering will consist of $800,000 of common stock and $1 million of debentures. Most of the people it has talked to about the feasibility of such an offering are very wary of such a course of action and warn of significant limitations and dangers inherent in such action.

Required: Answer the following, setting forth reasons for any conclusions stated.
   1. What are the requirements, limitations, and problems that are typically encountered in an intrastate offering?
   2. Even if the Securities Act's requirements for the exemption can be satisfied, what must be done from the standpoint of state law?

> 1. The Securities Act of 1933 exempts from registration "any security which is part of an issue offered and sold only to persons resident within a single state ... where the issuer of such security is a corporation incorporated by and doing business within such state." If an offering otherwise qualifies for this exemption, the use of the facilities of interstate commerce is permitted. According to the facts, Marigold could qualify for the intrastate exemption.
>
> However, very strict requirements apply to the offerees and purchasers: They must all be "residents" of the single state in question. Consequently, an offer to one nonresident can nullify the entire exemption. Meticulous care must be taken to ensure that no offers or sales are made to nonresidents, which, from a practical standpoint, may be extremely difficult to ascertain. A further limitation applies to issuers. Since the underlying rationale of the exemption as articulated by the SEC is "to provide for local financing for local industries carried out through local investment," the judicial and administrative interpretations of "doing business" have been strict. Essentially, the SEC has ruled that an issuer is doing business within the state if it derives 80 percent of its revenues from the state, has 80 percent of its assets within the state, intends to use 80 percent of the proceeds from the offering within the state, and has its principal office within the state.
>
> Were the above requirements and limitations not enough, an added requirement regarding resale of the distributed securities must be satisfied. In effect, there must not be a resale of the securities to nonresidents for a period of nine months.

2. Even if an exemption of federal registration is available, state law must be complied with. State securities laws popularly known as "blue sky" laws are not entirely uniform; however, at least a minimum filing generally will be required as well as a clearance to offer and sell the securities within the state.

4. Secondary Trading Exemptions

48 (November 94)

Which of the following facts will result in an offering of securities being exempt from registration under the Securities Act of 1933?
a. The securities are nonvoting preferred stock.
b. The issuing corporation was closely held prior to the offering.
c. The sale or offer to sell the securities is made by a person other than an issuer, underwriter, or dealer.
d. The securities are AAA-rated debentures that are collateralized by first mortgages on property that has a market value of 200% of the offering price.

24 (May 86)

Dee is the owner of 12% of the shares of common stock of D & M Corporation which she acquired in 1975. She is the treasurer and a director of D & M. The corporation registered its securities in 1984 and made a public offering pursuant to the Securities Act of 1933. If Dee decides to sell part of her holdings in D & M, the shares
a. Would be exempt from registration since the corporation previously registered them within three years.
b. Must be registered regardless of the amount sold or manner in which they are sold.
c. Would be exempt from registration because she is not an issuer.
d. Must be registered if Dee sells 50% of her shares through her broker to the public.

31 (November 82)

Which of the following securities or security transactions is automatically exempt under the Securities Act of 1933 from the Act's registration requirements?
a. An offering of $3,000,000 or less of stock to 25 or fewer persons.
b. A $10 million offering of first mortgage bonds to the public.
c. An exchange by a corporation of its own securities with existing shareholders without payment of brokerage commissions.
d. Sale by a director of her shares of stock providing that she owns less than 10% of the corporation's stock and that the sale is on a registered stock exchange.

48 (May 79)

Harvey Wilson is a senior vice president, 15% shareholder, and a member of the Board of Directors of Winslow, Inc. Wilson has decided to sell 10% of his stock in the company. Which of the following methods of disposition would subject him to SEC registration requirements?
a. A redemption of the stock by the corporation.
b. The sale by several brokerage houses of the stock in the ordinary course of business.
c. The sale of the stock to an insurance company which will hold the stock for long-term investment purposes.
d. The sale to a corporate officer who currently owns 5% of the stock of Winslow and who will hold the purchased stock for long-term investment.

6 (May 78)

Mr. Jackson owns approximately 40% of the shares of common stock of Triad Corporation. The rest of the shares are widely distributed among over 2,000 shareholders. Jackson has had a number of personal problems related to other business ventures and would like to raise about $2,000,000 through the sale of some of his shares. He accordingly approached Underwood & Sons, an investment banking house in which he knew one of the principals, to purchase his Triad shares to distribute the shares to the public at a reasonable price through its offices in the United States. Any profit on the sales could be retained by Underwood pursuant to an agreement reached between Jackson and Underwood. In this situation

a. The securities to be sold probably do <u>not</u> need to be registered with the Securities and Exchange Commission.
b. Underwood & Son probably is <u>not</u> an underwriter as defined in the federal securities law.
c. Jackson probably is considered the issuer under federal securities law.
d. Under federal securities law, <u>no</u> prospectus is required to be filed in connection with this contemplated transaction.

30 (May 76)

The Securities Act of 1933 specifically exempts from registration, securities offered by any person
a. Other than an issuer, underwriter, or dealer.
b. Who is an issuer of a public offering.
c. If the securities in question have previously been registered.
d. In a small company.

D. Liability Under the 1933 Act

(R03)

Under the Securities Act of 1933, which of the following acts by an accountant may subject the accountant to criminal penalties?
a. Negligently making a false entry in financial statements included in a registration statement.
b. Giving an unqualified opinion on negligently prepared financial statements in an audit report included in a registration statement.
c. Willfully including materially misstated financial statements in a registration statement.
d. Failing to use due diligence in the preparation of financial statements included in a registration statement.

39 (May 94)

If securities are exempt from the registration provisions of the Securities Act of 1933, any fraud committed in the course of selling such securities can be challenged by

	SEC	Person defrauded
a.	Yes	Yes
b.	Yes	No
c.	No	Yes
d.	No	No

37 (November 93)

One of the elements necessary to recover damages if there has been a material misstatement in a registration statement filed under the Securities Act of 1933 is that the
a. Issuer and plaintiff were in privity of contract with each other.
b. Issuer failed to exercise due care in connection with the sale of the securities.
c. Plaintiff gave value for the security.
d. Plaintiff suffered a loss.

5 (May 93)

To be successful in a civil action under Section 11 of the Securities Act of 1933 concerning liability for a misleading registration statement, the plaintiff must prove the

	Defendant's intent to deceive	Plaintiff's reliance on the registration statement
a.	No	Yes
b.	No	No
c.	Yes	No
d.	Yes	Yes

32 (November 88)

A plaintiff wishes to recover damages from the issuer for losses resulting from material misstatements in a securities registration statement. In order to be successful, one of the elements the plaintiff must prove is that the

    a. Plaintiff was in privity of contract with the issuer or that the issuer knew of the plaintiff.

    b. Plaintiff acquired the securities.

    c. Issuer acted negligently.

    d. Issuers acted fraudulently.

20 (May 86)

A requirement of a private action to recover damages for violation of the registration requirements of the Securities Act of 1933 is that

    a. The securities be purchased from an underwriter.

    b. A registration statement has been filed.

    c. The issuer or other defendants commit either negligence or fraud in the sale of the securities.

    d. The plaintiff has acquired the securities in question.

2B (May 83)

Able Corporation decided to make a public offering of bonds to raise needed capital. On June 30, 1982, it publicly sold $2,500,000 of 12% debentures in accordance with the registration requirements of the Securities Act of 1933.

The financial statements filed with the registration statement contained the unqualified opinion of Baker & Co., CPAs. The statements overstated Able's net income and net worth. Through negligence Baker did not detect the overstatements. As a result, the bonds, which originally sold for $1,000 per bond, have dropped in value to $700.

Ira is an investor who purchased $10,000 of the bonds. He promptly brought an action against Baker under the Securities Act of 1933.

Required: Answer the following, setting forth reasons for any conclusions stated.

Will Ira prevail on his claim under the Securities Act of 1933?

Yes. Ira will prevail and recover damages from Baker. He will base his action on § 11 of the Securities Act of 1933. Section 11 imposes liability on experts, including accountants, whose opinions appear in a registration statement. The experts are liable to all those who in reliance on their opinions purchase securities in a public offering under the 1933 Act. Ira does not have to prove Baker was negligent in auditing Able. All he need allege and prove is that there is a material false statement or omission of a material fact in the registration statement. The only defense that Baker may assert is that it exercised the degree of care that would be exercised by certified public accountants in similar circumstances. This is commonly referred to as the "due diligence" defense. Negligence by Baker is therefore a violation of § 11, and makes Baker liable to Ira for his damages.

2B (May 80)

The directors of Clarion Corporation, their accountants, and their attorneys met to discuss the desirability of this highly successful corporation going public. In this connection, the discussion turned to the potential liability of the corporation and the parties involved in the preparation and signing of the registration statement under the Securities Act of 1933. Craft, Watkins, and Glenn are the largest shareholders. Craft is the Chairman of the Board; Watkins is the Vice Chairman; and Glenn is the Chief Executive Officer. It has been decided that they will sign the registration statement. There are two other directors who are also executives and shareholders of the corporation. All of the board members are going to have a percentage of their shares included in the offering. The firm of Witherspoon & Friendly, CPAs, will issue an opinion as to the financial statements of the corporation which will accompany the filing of the registration statement, and Blackstone & Abernathy, Attorneys-at-Law, will render legal services and provide any necessary opinion letters.

Required: Answer the following, setting forth reasons for any conclusions stated.

Discuss the types of potential liability and defenses pursuant to the Securities Act of 1933 that each of the above parties or classes of parties may be subject to as a result of going public.

The Securities Act of 1933 permits an aggrieved party to sue various parties connected with the registration statement for an untrue statement of a material fact in the registration statement or the omission of a material fact required to be stated therein or necessary to make the statements therein not misleading. Those having potential liability include issuers of the security, those who signed the registration statement, every director, underwriter, and expert.

Any acquirer of the security may sue unless it is proved that at the time of such acquisition he knew of such untruth or omission.

Since all the directors and signers are also issuers along with the corporation, they may be sued in that capacity, since with the one exception mentioned above, issuers may not avoid liability for untrue statements or omissions. They are insurers of the truth contained in the registration statement; that is, they are liable without fault.

Contrast their liability with that of the accountants and lawyers who are both experts. As such, they are not liable for parts of the registration statement on which they did not render an expert opinion. Moreover, as experts, they have the benefit of the "due diligence" defense. That is, liability can be avoided if it can be shown by the expert that he had, after reasonable investigation, reasonable ground to believe and did believe at the time such part of the registration statement became effective that the parts for which he gave expert opinion were true and that there was no omission to state a material fact required to be stated.

The Act also provides certain defenses based on the amount of damages and their relationship to the misstatements or omissions.

II.   Securities Exchange Act of 1934

15 (R01)

Dean, Inc., a publicly traded corporation, paid a $10,000 bribe to a local zoning official. The bribe was recorded in Dean's financial statements as a consulting fee. Dean's unaudited financial statements were submitted to the SEC as part of a quarterly filing. Which of the following federal statutes did Dean violate?

   a.   Federal Trade Commission Act.
   b.   Securities Act of 1933.
   c.   Securities Exchange Act of 1934.
   d.   North American Free Trade Act.

Items 45 through 47 are based on the following:

Link Corp. is subject to the reporting provisions of the Securities Exchange Act of 1934.

45 (November 94)

Which of the following situations would require Link to be subject to the reporting provisions of the 1934 Act?

	Shares listed on a national securities exchange	More than one class of stock
a.	Yes	Yes
b.	Yes	No
c.	No	Yes
d.	No	No

46 (November 94)

Which of the following documents must Link file with the SEC?

	Quarterly reports (Form 10-Q)	Proxy statements
a.	Yes	Yes
b.	Yes	No
c.	No	Yes
d.	No	No

47 (November 94)

Which of the following reports must also be submitted to the SEC?

	Report by any party making a tender offer to purchase Link's stock	Report of proxy solicitations by Link stockholders
a.	Yes	Yes
b.	Yes	No
c.	No	Yes
d.	No	No

34 (May 94)

Which of the following factors, by itself, requires a corporation to comply with the reporting requirements of the Securities Exchange Act of 1934?
a. Six hundred employees.
b. Shares listed on a national securities exchange.
c. Total assets of $2 million.
d. Four hundred holders of equity securities.

35 (May 94)

Which of the following events must be reported to the SEC under the reporting provisions of the Securities Exchange Act of 1934?

	Tender offers	Insider trading	Soliciting proxies
a.	Yes	Yes	Yes
b.	Yes	Yes	No
c.	Yes	No	Yes
d.	No	Yes	Yes

41 (November 93)

Adler, Inc. is a reporting company under the Securities Exchange Act of 1934. The only security it has issued is voting common stock. Which of the following statements is correct?
a. Because Adler is a reporting company, it is <u>not</u> required to file a registration statement under the Securities Act of 1933 for any future offerings of its common stock.
b. Adler need <u>not</u> file its proxy statements with the SEC because it has only one class of stock outstanding.
c. Any person who owns more than 10% of Adler's common stock must file a report with the SEC.
d. It is unnecessary for the required annual report (Form 10K) to include audited financial statements.

31 (May 93)

Corporations that are exempt from registration under the Securities Exchange Act of 1934 are subject to the Act's
a. Antifraud provisions.
b. Proxy solicitation provisions.
c. Provisions dealing with the filing of annual reports.
d. Provisions imposing periodic audits.

32 (May 93)

Under the Securities Exchange Act of 1934, a corporation with common stock listed on a national stock exchange
a. Is prohibited from making private placement offerings.
b. Is subject to having the registration of its securities suspended or revoked.
c. Must submit Form 10-K to the SEC except in those years in which the corporation has made a public offering.
d. Must distribute copies of Form 10-K to its stockholders.

Items 41 and 42 are based on the following:

Integral Corp. has assets in excess of $4 million, has 350 stockholders, and has issued common and preferred stock. Integral is subject to the reporting provisions of the Securities Exchange Act of 1934. For its 1991 fiscal year, Integral filed the following with the SEC: quarterly reports, an annual report, and a periodic report listing newly appointed officers of the corporation. Integral did not notify the SEC of stockholder "short swing" profits; did not report that a competitor made a tender offer to Integral's stockholders; and did not report changes in the price of its stock as sold on the New York Stock Exchange.

41 (May 92)

Under the SEC reporting requirements, which of the following was Integral required to do?
a. Report the tender offer to the SEC.
b. Notify the SEC of stockholder "short swing" profits.
c. File the periodic report listing newly appointed officers.
d. Report the changes in the market price of its stock.

42 (May 92)

Under the Securities Exchange Act of 1934, Integral must be registered with the SEC because
a. It issues both common and preferred stock.
b. Its shares are listed on a national stock exchange.
c. It has more than 300 stockholders.
d. Its shares are traded in interstate commerce.

39 (November 91)

The reporting and registration provisions of the Securities Exchange Act of 1934
a. Do <u>not</u> require registration by a corporation if its stock was originally issued under an offering exempt from registration under the Securities Act of 1933.
b. Do <u>not</u> require registration by a corporation unless its stock is listed on a national securities exchange.
c. Require a corporation reporting under the Act to register any offering of its securities under the Securities Act of 1933.
d. Require a corporation reporting under the Act to file its proxy statements with the SEC even if it has only one class of stock outstanding.

42 (May 91)

Which of the following statements is correct regarding the proxy solicitation requirements of Section 14(a) of the Securities Exchange Act of 1934?
a. A corporation does <u>not</u> have to file proxy revocation solicitations with the SEC if it is a reporting company under the Securities Exchange Act of 1934.
b. Current unaudited financial statements must be sent to each stockholder with every proxy solicitation.

    c.   A corporation must file its proxy statements with the SEC if it is a reporting company under the Securities Exchange Act of 1934.

    d.   In a proxy solicitation by management relating to election of officers, all stockholder proposals must be included in the proxy statement.

40 (November 90)

The registration provisions of the Securities Exchange Act of 1934 require disclosure of all of the following information except the

    a.   Names of owners of at least five (5) percent of any class of nonexempt equity security.

    b.   Bonus and profit-sharing arrangements.

    c.   Financial structure and nature of the business.

    d.   Names of officers and directors.

30 (May 90)

Dice, Inc. is a reporting company under the Securities Exchange Act of 1934. The only security Dice issued is voting common stock. With regard to Dice's proxy solicitation requirements, which of the following statements is correct?

    a.   Dice must file its proxy statements with the SEC even though it has only one class of stock outstanding.

    b.   Dice's current unaudited financial statements must be sent to each shareholder with every proxy solicitation.

    c.   Shareholder proposals need not be included in the proxy statements unless consented to by a majority of Dice's board of directors.

    d.   Dice need not provide any particular information to its shareholders unless Dice is soliciting proxies from them.

31 (May 90)

Under the Securities Exchange Act of 1934, which of the following individuals would not be subject to the insider reporting provisions?

    a.   An owner of ten percent of a corporation's stock.

    b.   An owner of five percent of a corporation's voting stock.

    c.   The vice-president of marketing.

    d.   A member of the board of directors.

33 (November 88)

Which of the following statements is correct concerning corporations subject to the reporting requirements of the Securities Exchange Act of 1934?

    a.   The annual report (Form 10-K) need not include audited financial statements.

    b.   The annual report (Form 10-K) must be filed with the SEC within 20 days of the end of the corporation's fiscal year.

    c.   A quarterly report (Form 10-Q) need only be filed with the SEC by those corporations that are also subject to the registration requirements of the Securities Act of 1933.

    d.   A monthly report (Form 8-K) must be filed with the SEC after the end of any month in which a materially important event occurs.

38 (May 88)

Which of the following statements is correct with respect to the Securities Exchange Act of 1934?

    a.   Issuers whose securities are registered under the Act are required to comply with its reporting requirements.

    b.   The Act applies only to issuers whose securities are traded on a national securities exchange.

    c.   The Act subjects all issuers of securities to its registration requirements if the issuer has more than $2.5 million of assets or more than 250 shareholders.

    d.   The antifraud provisions of the Act do not apply to issuers of securities that are exempt from the Act's registration requirements.

40 (May 88)

If securities are registered under the Securities Exchange Act of 1934, which of the following disclosure provisions apply?

	Notice of sales of the registered securities by the corporation's officers must be filed with the SEC	Proxy material for the registered securities must be filed with the SEC
a.	No	Yes
b.	Yes	No
c.	Yes	Yes
d.	No	No

12 (November 87)

The reporting requirements of the Securities Exchange Act of 1934 and its rules
a. Apply only to issuers, underwriters, and dealers.
b. Apply to a corporation that registered under the Securities Act of 1933 but that did <u>not</u> register under the Securities Exchange Act of 1934.
c. Require all corporations engaged in interstate commerce to file an annual report.
d. Require all corporations engaged in interstate commerce to file quarterly audited financial statements.

39 (May 87)

Which of the following statements is correct with respect to the registration requirements of the Securities Exchange Act of 1934?
a. They require issuers of non-exempt securities traded on a national securities exchange to register with the SEC.
b. They permit issuers who comply with the Securities Act of 1933 to avoid the registration requirements of the Securities Exchange Act of 1934.
c. They permit issuers who comply with those requirements to avoid state registration requirements.
d. They permit issuers who comply with those requirements to avoid the registration requirements of the Securities Act of 1933.

40 (May 87)

On May 1, Apel purchased 7% of Stork Corp.'s preferred stock which was traded on a national securities exchange. After the purchase Apel owned 9% of the outstanding preferred stock. Stork is registered under the Securities Exchange Act of 1934. With respect to the purchase, Apel
a. Is <u>not</u> required to file any report or information with the SEC since Apel owns less than 10% of the preferred stock.
b. Is <u>not</u> required to file any report or information with the SEC since the security purchased was preferred stock.
c. Must file with the SEC, the issuer, and the national securities exchange information concerning the purpose of the acquisition.
d. Must file only with the SEC information concerning the source of the funds used to purchase the preferred stock.

33 (November 86)

Tulip Corp. is a registered and reporting corporation under the Securities Exchange Act of 1934. As such it
a. Can offer and sell its securities to the public without the necessity of registering its securities pursuant to the Securities Act of 1933.
b. Can <u>not</u> make a tender offer for the equity securities of another registered and reporting corporation without the consent of the SEC.
c. Must file annual reports (Form 10-K) with the SEC.
d. Must distribute a copy of the annual report (Form 10-K) to each of its shareholders.

35 (November 86)

The Securities Exchange Act of 1934

a. Applies exclusively to issuers whose securities are listed on an organized stock exchange.

b. Has <u>no</u> application to issuers who are <u>not</u> required to register.

c. Imposes additional requirements on those issuers who must register and report.

d. Requires registration and reporting by all issuers with $2 million or more of assets or which have 1,000 or more shareholders.

41 (November 80)

Shariff is a citizen of a foreign country. He has just purchased six percent (6%) of the outstanding common shares of Stratosphere Metals, Inc., a company listed on a national stock exchange. He has instructed the brokerage firm that quietly and efficiently handled the execution of the purchase order that he wants the securities to be held in street name. What are the legal implications of the above transactions? Shariff must

a. Immediately have the securities registered in his own name and take delivery of them.

b. Sell the securities because he has violated the antifraud provisions of the Securities Exchange Act of 1934.

c. Notify Stratosphere Metals, Inc. of his acquisition and file certain information as to his identity and background with the SEC.

d. Notify the SEC and Stratosphere Metals, Inc. only if he acquires ten percent (10%) or more of Stratosphere's common shares.

5 (May 95)

Perry, a staff accountant with Orlean Associates, CPAs, reviewed the following transactions engaged in by Orlean's two clients: World Corp. and Unity Corp.

WORLD CORP.

During 1994, World Corp. made a $4,000,000 offering of its stock. The offering was sold to 50 nonaccredited investors and 150 accredited investors. There was a general advertising of the offering. All purchasers were provided with material information concerning World Corp. The offering was completely sold by the end of 1994. The SEC was notified 30 days after the first sale of the offering.

World did not register the offering and contends that the offering and any subsequent resale of the securities are completely exempt from registration under Regulation D, Rule 505, of the Securities Act of 1933.

UNITY CORP.

Unity Corp. has 750 equity stockholders and assets in excess of $100,000,000. Unity's stock is traded on a national stock exchange. Unity contends that it is not a covered corporation and is not required to comply with the reporting provisions of the Securities Exchange Act of 1934.

Required:

a. 1. State whether World is correct in its contention that the offering is exempt from registration under Regulation D, Rule 505, of the Securities Act of 1933. Give the reason(s) for your conclusion.

2. State whether World is correct in its contention that on subsequent resale the securities are completely exempt from registration. Give the reason(s) for your conclusion.

b. 1. State whether Unity is correct in its contention that it is not a covered corporation and is not required to comply with the reporting requirements of the Securities Exchange Act of 1934 and give the reason(s) for your conclusion.

2. Identify and describe two principal reports a covered corporation must file with the SEC.

a. 1. World is incorrect in its first contention that the offering is exempt from registration under Regulation D, Rule 505, of the Securities Act of 1933. World did not comply with the requirements of Rule 505 for the following reasons: the offering was sold to more than 35 nonaccredited investors; there was a general advertising of the offering; and the SEC was notified more than 15 days after the first sale of the offering.

2. World is also incorrect in its second contention that the securities of the offering would be completely exempt from registration if the offering were exempt. Securities originally purchased under a Regulation D limited offering exemption are restricted securities. They must be registered prior to resale unless sold subject to another exemption.

b. 1.   Unity is incorrect in its contention that it is not required to comply with the reporting requirements of the Securities Exchange Act of 1934. Unity must comply because it has more than 500 stockholders and total assets in excess of $5,000,000. Alternately, Unity must comply because its shares are traded on a national securities exchange.

2.   A covered corporation must file the following reports with the SEC: Quarterly Reports (10-Q's); Annual Reports (10-K's); and Current Reports (8-K's). These reports are intended to provide a complete, current statement of all business operations and matters affecting the value of the corporation's securities.

III. Antitrust Law
A. Introduction—Scope and Remedies

21 (November 79)

Wanton Corporation, its president, and several other officers of the corporation are found guilty of conspiring with its major competitor to fix prices. Which of the following sanctions would not be applicable under federal antitrust laws?
  a.   Suspension of corporate right to engage in interstate commerce for not more than one year.
  b.   Treble damages.
  c.   Seizure of Wanton's property illegally shipped in interstate commerce.
  d.   Fines against Wanton and fines and imprisonment of its president and officers.
  e.   All of the above sanctions may be imposed.

12 (November 78)

The Ripper Corporation has been found guilty of widespread price fixing along with several of its competitors in the sale of a certain product. As a result of these facts, Ripper and its officers may be subject to various sanctions, penalties, or liabilities. Which of the following would not be applicable?
  a.   Fines and imprisonment imposed against the principal officers responsible.
  b.   Fines imposed against the corporation.
  c.   Treble damages awarded to third parties who purchased the product from the corporation and suffered damages.
  d.   A prohibition against the corporation from engaging in the sale of the product in question in interstate commerce for a period of not more than six months.

B. Sherman Act
1. Section 1—Contracts and Combinations in Restraint of Trade
a. Scope

43 (November 75)

Inns Corporation operated a major hotel in a metropolitan city. An annual festival week brought many tourists to the city resulting in peak demand for accommodations. The local Tourism Bureau, of which Inns was an active member, embarked on a campaign to increase tourist trade in the area and asked all suppliers of goods to hotels and restaurants to contribute 1% of sales revenue to the bureau. Bureau members also were of the opinion that higher prices could be charged during the festival week without hurting the tourist trade. Which of the following actions would most likely violate the antitrust laws?
  a.   Rental of Inns' main ballroom on the key day of the festival at a price below that offered by other hotels.
  b.   The raising of rates on hotel rooms during festival week when other hotels also raise their rates.
  c.   Inns' notification to its purchasing officer to confine its purchases to suppliers contributing to the Tourism Bureau as agreed with other bureau members.
  d.   Inns' policy of purchasing soap products from only one manufacturer even though there were offers of lower prices for similar goods from other manufacturers.

45 (November 74)

The Waller Corporation competes with the Graves Corporation in interstate commerce. Without communicating with Graves or anyone else, Waller decided <u>not</u> to sell to Redondo Company who had ordered certain products from Waller. Redondo then sued Waller for damages pursuant to the antitrust laws. Redondo claims damages of $50,000 for loss of profits and capital. In this situation, Waller is

a. Liable to Redondo for $150,000.
b. Liable to Redondo for $50,000.
c. Liable to Redondo only for loss of capital.
d. <u>Not</u> liable to Redondo.

48 (November 74)

The Sherman Act is <u>not</u> directed at trade restraints involving

a. Monopolization.
b. Attempts to monopolize.
c. Contracts and combinations.
d. Price discrimination.

b. Horizontal Price Fixing

8 (May 78)

The four largest manufacturers in their industry have had a combined share of the market in excess of 80% each year for several years. As members of a trade association, certain officers of these corporations meet periodically to discuss various topics of mutual interest. Matters discussed include engineering design, production methods, product costs, market shares, merchandising policy, and inventory levels. Open discussion of pricing is scrupulously avoided. However, the representatives usually see each other after the association meetings and pricing is frequently discussed. These representatives have maintained prices in accordance with an informal oral agreement terminable at will by any company wishing to withdraw. They have never reduced their agreement to a written document or memorandum. The four corporations compete with each other in interstate commerce. Which of the following applies?

a. The members of the trade association may validly appoint the trade association as their representative to set minimum prices.
b. If the trade association suggested it, the distributors of the four corporations may legally enter an agreement among themselves to follow the industry leader's pricing policy.
c. The trade association could legally allocate marketing areas among its members.
d. The four corporations have illegally entered into a price maintenance agreement among themselves.

17 (November 76)

What pricing agreements among competitors are legal?

a. An agreement which is aimed at lowering prices.
b. An agreement which is aimed at eliminating cut-throat competition by stabilizing prices.
c. An agreement which seeks to fix prices reasonably and fairly for the consumers' benefit.
d. None, because competitors are forbidden to enter into agreements which determine the price of the product they sell.

42 (November 75)

Boswell Woolen Yarns, Inc. is one of your audit clients. It has been a member of the Woolen Yarns Manufacturers Association of America which has represented 75% of the woolen yarn manufacturers of America for the past ten years. Until recently, the association has served primarily as a public relations and lobbying agent for its members. Now, as a result of severe inflation and competition from manufacturers of other types of fabrics, e.g., super nylon, orlon, etc., it has been proposed by the association and the overwhelming majority of its members that the association provide its members with suggested minimum and maximum prices to be charged and maximum production levels for each member. If the plan is implemented

a. The association and its members, including your client, have engaged in an illegal contract, combination, or conspiracy in restraint of trade.

b. There are <u>no</u> antitrust implications regarding such an arrangement as long as the parties are <u>not</u> compelled to join in the plan.

c. And the association is appointed by its members as their agent to engage in such activities, the arrangement will <u>not</u> be considered a violation of the antitrust laws even if its members could <u>not</u> have done so themselves.

d. Meeting competition from other non-wool manufacturers is a complete defense against any alleged antitrust violations.

45 (November 75)

One of your CPA firm's clients, Destination Garages, Inc., has entered into an agreement with its principal competitor, Parking Unlimited, Inc., to eliminate cut-throat competition. They have agreed to charge a uniform hourly rate in the different areas in which they compete. The garages are mainly located in Metropolis, but some are located in another state which is just across the state line from Metropolis. It is agreed that the rates to be charged are (1) always to be reasonable and (2) to be based upon the rate structure charged by the leading parking lot operator in Central City, the capital of the state in which Metropolis is located. What is the status of the agreement between Destination Garages and Parking Unlimited in regard to federal antitrust law?

a. Because the garages are real property, antitrust law does <u>not</u> apply.

b. Because the "product" sold is a service, antitrust law does <u>not</u> apply.

c. Regardless of the fact that the prices agreed upon are aimed at avoiding cut-throat competition, are always to be reasonable to the public, and are based upon another company's rates, the prices agreed upon are, nevertheless, in violation of the antitrust law.

d. If Destination Garages can show that it was in fact merely meeting competition from other parking lots, it would have a complete defense against any alleged antitrust violation.

47 (November 75)

Paperbox Company is one of four equal-sized paper-carton container companies whose sales constitute 90% of paper container sales in the relevant market. Competition has been intense. In order to control costs within reasonable limits the chief executive officers of the four companies have agreed that they will set a maximum price, agreed upon by them, to be paid for the pulp they purchase. From an antitrust standpoint

a. <u>No</u> antitrust violation occurs if the price set is reasonable.

b. The agreement is a *per se* violation of the antitrust laws.

c. <u>No</u> antitrust violation occurs if the suppliers of raw pulp agree that the price is reasonable and works in the best interest of all parties.

d. The agreement will <u>not</u> violate the antitrust laws if it can be shown that it is necessary to prevent insolvency of one of the parties to the agreement who controls 30% of the market.

c. Resale Price Maintenance—Vertical Price Fixing

1 (May 80)

Jay Manufacturing Company sells high quality, high-priced lawn mowers to retailers throughout the United States. Jay unilaterally announced suggested retail prices in its advertisements. Jay also informed retailers that its products would not be sold to them if the retailers used them as "loss leaders" or "come-ons." There was no requirement that any retailer agree to sell at the suggested prices or refrain from selling at whatever price they wished. Monroe Sales, Inc., a large home supply discounter, persistently engaged in a loss-leader selling of the Jay mower. Jay has terminated sales to Monroe and declined to do any further business with it. Monroe claims that Jay has violated the antitrust laws. Under the circumstances, which is a correct statement?

a. The arrangement in question is an illegal joint boycott.

b. The arrangement in question amounts to price-fixing and is illegal *per se*.

c. The mere unilateral refusal to deal with Monroe is <u>not</u> illegal under antitrust laws.

d. Even if it were found that in fact the overwhelming preponderance of retailers had willingly agreed to follow the suggested prices, Jay would <u>not</u> have violated antitrust laws.

35 (November 79)

 The Donner Corporation has obtained a patent on a revolutionary coin-operated washing machine. It is far superior to the existing machines currently in use. Which of the following actions taken by Donner will <u>not</u> result in a violation of federal antitrust law?

 a. Entering into resale price maintenance contracts with distributors for machines it sells.

 b. Obtaining a near total monopolization of the market as a result of the patent.

 c. Requiring the purchasers of the machines to buy from Donner all their other commonplace supplies connected with the use of the machine.

 d. Joining in a boycott with other appliance manufacturers to eliminate a troublesome discount distributor.

12 (May 78)

 The Diablo Oven Company entered into agreements with retail merchants whereby they agreed not to sell beneath Diablo's minimum "suggested" retail price of $85 in exchange for Diablo's agreeing not to sell its ovens at retail in their respective territories. The agreement does not preclude the retail merchants from selling competing ovens. What is the legal status of the agreement?

 a. It is legal if the product is a trade name or trademarked item.

 b. It is legal if the power to fix maximum prices is <u>not</u> relinquished.

 c. It is illegal unless it can be shown that the parties to the agreement were preventing cut-throat competition.

 d. It is illegal even though the price fixed is reasonable.

45 (November 77)

 Marks Corporation manufactures expensive pens and pencils. It does business throughout the United States. Its top brand is the Silvertip pen. Fellows Outlets, Inc., ordered 100 of the most expensive pens in the Silvertip line. The contract for the sale provided that the retail price to be charged by Fellows was not to be less than $35 per pen. In the event that Fellows did not wish to comply with the above stipulation, it was further provided that the pens must be promptly returned and the purchase price less costs to Marks would be refunded. Fellows agreed to the above terms in writing. Which of the following is true under the circumstances?

 a. The contract is illegal.

 b. Since the price stipulated is merely a minimum resale price-fixing arrangement, the contract is legal.

 c. The right to promptly returns the pens and receive a refund validates the contract.

 d. Vertical price-fixing arrangements are exempt from illegality if state law so permits.

d. Allocation of Markets

32 (November 81)

 Which of the following is a *per se* violation of the federal antitrust laws?

 a. Exclusive territorial rights to sell and corresponding limitations on selling outside the allocated territory by a manufacturer and its distributors.

 b. Unilateral refusal to deal with a troublesome wholesaler.

 c. Tacit agreement with several leading competitors to respect established customer relationships of each other.

 d. Sale of a patented product at an unreasonably high price.

44 (November 74)

 Territorial allocation of competitors' markets is

 a. Subject to the rule of reason.

 b. A *per se* violation of the Sherman Act.

 c. Never a *per se* violation of the Sherman Act.

 d. Legal if the allocation involves territories rather than customers.

e. Limitation of Supply; Bid Rigging

34 (November 83)

Certain members of the Tri-State Railway Construction Association decided that something must be done about the disastrous competition, which, when coupled with the depressed status of the industry and economy, was causing financial chaos for many of its members. They met privately after one of the association meetings and decided to allocate construction projects among themselves based upon an historical share of the market. Under the arrangement, a certain designated company would submit the low bid, thereby ensuring that the company would obtain the job. Such an arrangement is

    a. Illegal *per se*, and a criminal violation of the antitrust law.

    b. Illegal under the rule of reason, but <u>not</u> a criminal violation of the antitrust law.

    c. Legally justifiable due to the economic conditions in the marketplace.

    d. Legal under antitrust law since it does <u>not</u> fix prices.

f. Non-Price Vertical Restraints

31 (November 81)

Sunrise Company has a distribution system comprised of distributors and retailers. Each distributor has a defined geographic area in which it has the exclusive right to sell to retailers and to which sales are restricted. Franchised retailers are authorized to sell Sunrise's products only within specified locations. Both distributors and retailers are forbidden to sell to nonfranchised retailers. Under present law this marketing arrangement will be

    a. Judged under the rule of reason, whether or not title passes.

    b. Illegal *per se* if title passes to the distributor or retailer, but judged under the rule of reason if title does <u>not</u> pass (as under an agency or consignment).

    c. Illegal *per se*, whether or not title passes.

    d. Illegal *per se* if title does <u>not</u> pass, but judged under the rule of reason if title passes.

18 (November 80)

Divoc Corporation manufactured and sold a high quality line of distinctive calculators. In order to fully realize the potential of the products, it decided to engage in a franchising arrangement with selected outlets throughout the country. Its basic arrangement was to grant to each dealer the exclusive right to sell in a designated area and each dealer agreed not to sell outside its allotted geographic area. Which of the following <u>best</u> describes the status of the law?

    a. Such arrangements are *per se* illegal.

    b. Divoc <u>must</u> sell on consignment, thereby retaining title, in order to avoid illegality.

    c. Such franchising arrangements will be tested under the rule of reason and as long as they are found to be reasonable they are legal.

    d. Such arrangements are specifically declared to be illegal under existing antitrust statutes.

2. Section 2—Monopolization; Attempts and Conspiracies to Monopolize

27 (May 82)

The United States Department of Justice has alleged that Variable Resources, Inc., the largest manufacturer and seller of variable speed drive motors, is a monopolist. It is seeking an injunction ordering divestiture by Variable of a significant portion of its manufacturing facilities. Variable denies it has monopolized the variable speed drive motor market. Which of the following statements is correct insofar as the government's action against Variable is concerned?

    a. The government must prove that Variable is the sole source of a significant portion of the market.

    b. In order to establish monopolization, the government must prove that Variable has at least 75% of the market.

    c. If Variable has the power to control prices or exclude competition, it has monopoly power.

    d. As long as Variable has not been a party to a contract, combination, or conspiracy in restraint of trade, it cannot be found to be guilty of monopolization.

5 (May 80)

The Duplex Corporation has been charged by the United States Justice Department with an "attempt to monopolize" the duplex industry. In defending itself against such a charge, Duplex will prevail if it can establish

    a. It had <u>no</u> intent to monopolize the duplex industry.

    b. Its percentage share of the relevant market was less than 90%.

    c. Its activities do <u>not</u> constitute an unreasonable restraint of trade.

    d. It does <u>not</u> have monopoly power.

37 (November 79)

The Justice Department is contemplating commencing an action against Lion Corporation for monopolizing the off-shore oil drilling business in violation of Section 2 of the Sherman Act. Which of the following would be Lion's <u>best</u> defense against such an action?

    a. Since the drilling is off-shore, interstate commerce is not involved.

    b. The monopoly was originally the result of a long since expired patent.

    c. Lion had <u>no</u> specific wrongful intent to monopolize.

    d. Lion's market share is such that it does <u>not</u> have the power to fix prices or to exclude competitors.

C. Clayton Act
1. Section 2—Robinson-Patman Act

32 (May 83)

Pratt Company manufactures and sells distinctive clocks. Its best selling item is a reproduction of a rare antique grandfather clock. Taylor Co. purchased 100 of the clocks from Pratt at $99 each. Much to Taylor's chagrin it discovered that Stewart, one of its competitors, had purchased the same clock from Pratt at $94 per clock. Taylor has complained and threatened legal action. In the event the issue is litigated

    a. Taylor has a presumption in its favor that it has been harmed by price discrimination.

    b. Pratt will prevail if it can show it did <u>not</u> intend to harm Taylor.

    c. Pratt will prevail if it can show that it sold the clocks at the lower price to all customers such as Stewart who had been doing business with it continuously for ten years or more.

    d. Pratt will prevail if it can establish that there were several other clock companies with which Taylor could deal if Taylor were dissatisfied.

34 (November 81)

Robinson's pricing policies have come under attack by several of its retailers. In fact, one of those retailers, Patman, has instigated legal action against Robinson alleging that Robinson charges other favored retailers prices for its products which are lower than those charged to it. Patman's legal action against Robinson

    a. Will fail unless Patman can show that there has been an injury to competition.

    b. Will be sufficient if the complaint alleges that Robinson charged different prices to different customers and there is a reasonable possibility that competition may be adversely affected.

    c. Is groundless since one has the legal right to sell at whatever price one wishes as long as the price is determined unilaterally.

    d. Is to be tested under the rule of reason and if the different prices charged are found to be reasonable, the complaint will be dismissed.

41 (November 77)

Devold Enterprises, Inc., sells frozen baked goods to chain stores, wholesalers, restaurant suppliers, and retailers in interstate commerce. It naturally seeks to avoid violation of the Robinson-Patman Act, which proscribes price discrimination. Which of the following will permit Devold to <u>avoid</u> potential violations of the Act?

    a. Its volume of sales is less than $300,000 per year.

    b. It pays for local advertising of selected large volume retailers.

    c. It provides free marketing advice and provides displays to its customers strictly based on their relative volume of purchases and the relative amount of sales of its products.

    d. It pays brokerage commissions to favored customers.

46 (November 74)

FunTime Corporation sells radios in interstate commerce for $2.75 per radio to Birchall, Devlin, Cates, and Rosenthal, each sole proprietors. The radios cost $2.00 each to make. Mahoney Corporation, a competitor of FunTime, has legally offered to sell the same product to Birchall at $2.50 each. FunTime then in good faith sold the radios to Birchall at $2.50 each. Birchall, Devlin, Cates, and Rosenthal compete with one another. Under these circumstances FunTime is

    a.   Liable to Devlin, Cates, and Rosenthal for price discrimination.

    b.   Liable to Mahoney Corporation for price discrimination.

    c.   Liable to Mahoney Corporation for unlawful predatory price cutting.

    d.   <u>Not</u> liable for price discrimination.

2. Section 3—Tying Contracts and Exclusive Dealings

46 (November 77)

You were the auditor examining the financial statements of Mason Corporation and noted an extraordinary increase in the sales of certain items. Further inquiry revealed that Mason sold various interrelated products which it manufactured. One of the items was manufactured almost exclusively by them. This unique product was in great demand and was sold throughout the United States. Mason realized the importance of the product to its purchasers and decided to capitalize on the situation by requiring all purchasers to take at least two of its other products if they wished to obtain the item over which it had almost complete market control. At the spring sales meeting the president of Mason informed the entire sales force that they were to henceforth sell only to those customers who agreed to take the additional products. He indicated that this was a great opportunity to substantially increase sales of other items. Under the circumstances, which of the following <u>best</u> describes the situation?

    a.   The plan is both ingenious and legal and should have been resorted to long ago.

    b.   The arrangement is an illegal tying agreement.

    c.   Since Mason did <u>not</u> have complete market control over the unique product in question, the arrangement is legal.

    d.   As long as the other products which must be taken are sold at a fair price to the buyers, the arrangement is legal.

42 (November 74)

Nashville Baseball Corporation has a contract that provides it with exclusive rights to supply baseballs to the National and American Baseball Leagues as long as it meets the price and quality of baseballs offered by competitors. Excelsior Corporation offered a superior baseball at a reduced price. Nashville met the quality and price proposal submitted by Excelsior and retained its exclusive suppliership. Under these circumstances

    a.   If Nashville meets the price and quality offer of Excelsior, it has <u>not</u> violated the federal antitrust laws.

    b.   Nashville has obtained an exclusive dealing arrangement which will be tested under the provisions of the Clayton Act.

    c.   Nashville is <u>not</u> engaged in interstate commerce because it sells all its baseballs to the league buyers in Tennessee.

    d.   Nashville has <u>not</u> violated the antitrust laws because it must meet competition from other suppliers.

43 (November 74)

George Corporation entered into contracts to supply all of the requirements of 1,000 dealers in New England. In these contracts the dealers agreed <u>not</u> to sell products competitive with those of George. These dealers constituted 20% of the total number of dealers in the area. George Corporation may

    a.   Be enjoined from enforcing the contracts if they might substantially lessen competition.

    b.   Be enjoined only to the extent that is own outlets operated by its agents are involved.

    c.   <u>Not</u> be enjoined because only 20% of the New England dealers are involved.

    d.   Be enjoined for violating the Robinson-Patman Act.

3. Section 7—Mergers

35 (November 83)

In a pure conglomerate merger
   a. The government must establish an actual restraint on competition in the marketplace in order to prevent the merger.
   b. The acquiring corporation <u>neither</u> competes with <u>nor</u> sells to or buys from the acquired corporation.
   c. The merger is prima facie valid unless the government can prove the acquiring corporation had an intent to monopolize.
   d. Some form of additional anticompetitive behavior must be established (e.g., price fixing) in order to provide the basis for the government's obtaining injunctive relief.

47 (November 74)

White Corporation acquired 100% of the stock of King Corporation, a competitor of White. Both companies are of substantial size with respect to their involvement in interstate commerce. This acquisition would
   a. Be legal under the Clayton Act unless the acquisition were certain to create a monopoly in any line of commerce in any section of the country.
   b. Constitute a *per se* violation under the Clayton Act.
   c. Be illegal under the Clayton Act if its effect might be to substantially lessen competition.
   d. Be illegal under the Clayton Act only if its effect were certain to lessen competition substantially.

D. Federal Trade Commission Act

37 (November 83)

If a defendant is charged with an unfair method of competition under the Federal Trade Commission Act
   a. The FTC may prevail despite the fact that the conduct alleged to be illegal did <u>not</u> violate either the Sherman or Clayton Act.
   b. Criminal sanctions can generally be imposed against a defendant even though the defendant has <u>not</u> violated an FTC order to cease and desist.
   c. There can be <u>no</u> violation of the Act unless one or more of the specifically enumerated unfair methods of competition are established.
   d. The complaint must be based upon the purchase or sale of goods, wares, or commodities in interstate commerce.

28 (May 82)

The Federal Trade Commission Act sets forth a legislative yardstick or standard to be applied with respect to anti-competitive practices. Which of the following is an <u>incorrect</u> statement with respect to the Act's scope and application?
   a. The Act's legislative yardstick provides the basis under which the Federal Trade Commission proceeds against violators of the other antitrust laws.
   b. The Act applies not only to goods in interstate commerce, but to services as well.
   c. The Act provides the basis for an action for treble damages by a private party who is adversely affected by a violation of the Act.
   d. The Act permits the Federal Trade Commission to reach violations which are in their incipiency, but which have not yet reached the threshold level of illegality under the Sherman or Clayton Acts.

IV. Employment Law
A. Federal Insurance Contributions Act

31 (November 95)

Under the Federal Insurance Contributions Act (FICA), which of the following acts will cause an employer to be liable for penalties?

	Failure to supply taxpayer identification numbers	Failure to make timely FICA deposits
a.	Yes	Yes
b.	Yes	No
c.	No	Yes
d.	No	No

26 (May 94)

Syl Corp. does <u>not</u> withhold FICA taxes from its employees' compensation. Syl voluntarily pays the entire FICA tax for its share and the amounts that it could have withheld from the employees. The employees' share of FICA taxes paid by Syl to the IRS is
- a. Deductible by Syl as additional compensation that is includable in the employees' taxable income.
- b. Not deductible by Syl because it does <u>not</u> meet the deductibility requirement as an ordinary and necessary business expense.
- c. A nontaxable gift to each employee, provided that the amount is less than $1,000 annually to each employee.
- d. Subject to prescribed penalties imposed on Syl for its failure to withhold required payroll taxes.

26 (May 93)

Which of the following forms of income, if in excess of the annual exempt amount, will cause a reduction in a retired person's social security benefits?
- a. Annual proceeds from an annuity.
- b. Director's fees.
- c. Pension payments.
- d. Closely held corporation stock dividends.

36 (May 92)

An employer who fails to withhold Federal Insurance Contributions Act (FICA) taxes from covered employees' wages, but who pays both the employer and employee shares would
- a. Be entitled to a refund from the IRS for the employees' share.
- b. Be allowed <u>no</u> federal tax deduction for any payments.
- c. Have a right to be reimbursed by the employees for the employees' share.
- d. Owe penalties and interest for failure to collect the tax.

32 (November 91)

Which of the following types of income is subject to taxation under the provisions of the Federal Insurance Contributions Act (FICA)?
- a. Interest earned on municipal bonds.
- b. Capital gains of $3,000.
- c. Car received as a productivity award.
- d. Dividends of $2,500.

36 (May 91)

Social security benefits may include all of the following <u>except</u>
- a. Payments to divorced spouses.
- b. Payments to disabled children.
- c. Medicare payments.
- d. Medicaid payments.

Other Government Regulation

36 (November 90)

Under the Federal Insurance Contributions Act (FICA), all of the following are considered wages <u>except</u>

a. Contingent fees.
b. Reimbursed travel expenses.
c. Bonuses.
d. Commissions.

26 (May 90)

Tower drives a truck for Musgrove Produce, Inc. The truck is owned by Musgrove. Tower is paid on the basis of a formula that takes into consideration the length of the trip, cargo, and fuel consumed. Tower is responsible for repairing or replacing all flat tires. Musgrove is responsible for all other truck maintenance. Tower drives only for Musgrove. If Tower is a common law employee and <u>not</u> an independent contractor, which of the following statements is correct?

a. All social security retirement benefits are fully includable in the determination of Tower's federal taxable income if certain gross income limitations are exceeded.
b. Musgrove remains primarily liable for Tower's share of FICA taxes if it fails to withhold and pay the taxes on Tower's wages.
c. Musgrove would <u>not</u> have to withhold FICA taxes if Tower elected to make FICA contributions as a self-employed person.
d. Bonuses or vacation pay that are paid to Tower by Musgrove are <u>not</u> subject to FICA taxes because they are <u>not</u> regarded as regular compensation.

37 (May 89)

Under the Federal Insurance Contributions Act (FICA) and the Social Security Act (SSA),

a. Persons who are self-employed are <u>not</u> required to make FICA contributions.
b. Employees who participate in private retirement plans are <u>not</u> required to make FICA contributions.
c. Death benefits are payable to an employee's survivors only if the employee dies before reaching the age of retirement.
d. The receipt of earned income by a person who is also receiving social security retirement benefits may result in a reduction of such benefits.

43 (May 88)

Which of the following statements is correct with respect to social security taxes and benefits?

a. An individual whose gross income exceeds certain maximum limitations is required to include the entire amount received as disability benefits in the computation of taxable income.
b. Benefits are available to a qualifying individual or that individual's family only upon retirement or disability.
c. An employer that erroneously underwithholds and underpays an employee's share of social security taxes will be liable for the unpaid balance of the employee's share.
d. An individual whose private pension benefits exceed certain maximum limitations will have social security retirement benefits reduced.

37 (May 87)

The Social Security tax base is calculated on

a. A self-employed person's net profit from self-employment.
b. A self-employed person's gross income from self-employment.
c. An employee's gross wages less the deduction permitted for contributions to an individual retirement account.
d. An employee's taxable income.

39 (November 86)

Social Security benefits may be obtained by

a. Qualifying individuals who are also receiving benefits from a private pension plan.
b. Qualifying individuals or their families only upon such individual's disability or retirement.
c. Children of a deceased worker who was entitled to benefits until such children reach age 25 or complete their education, whichever occurs first.
d. Only those individuals who have made payment while employed.

18 (May 86)

Which of the following statements is correct regarding Social Security benefits?

a. Retirement benefits paid in excess of recipient's contributions will be included in the determination of the recipient's federal taxable income regardless of his gross income.

b. Upon the death of the recipient, immediate family members within certain age limits are entitled to a death benefit equal to the unpaid portion of the deceased recipient's contributions.

c. Retirement benefits are fully includable in the determination of the recipient's federal taxable income if his gross income exceeds certain maximum limitations.

d. Individuals who have made <u>no</u> contributions may be eligible for some benefits.

22 (November 85)

Jay White, an engineer, entered into a contract with Sky, Inc., agreeing to provide Sky with certain specified consulting services. After performing the services, White was paid pursuant to the contract but Social Security taxes were not withheld from his check since Sky considered White an independent contractor. The IRS has asserted that White was an employee and claims that a deficiency exists due to Sky's failure to withhold and pay Social Security taxes. Which of the following factors is most likely to support the IRS's position that White is an employee?

a. White was paid in one lump sum after all the services were performed.

b. White provided his own office and supplies.

c. Sky supervised and controlled the manner in which White performed the services.

d. Sky reserved the right to inspect White's work.

B. Federal Unemployment Tax Act

32 (November 95)

Taxes payable under the Federal Unemployment Tax Act (FUTA) are

a. Calculated as a fixed percentage of all compensation paid to an employee.

b. Deductible by the employer as a business expense for federal income tax purposes.

c. Payable by employers for all employees.

d. Withheld from the wages of all covered employees.

36 (May 95)

Which of the following payments are deducted from an employee's salary?

	Unemployment compensation insurance	Worker's compensation insurance
a.	Yes	Yes
b.	Yes	No
c.	No	Yes
d.	No	No

35 (November 94)

For the entire year 1993, Ral Supermarket, Inc. conducted its business operations without any permanent or full-time employees. Ral employed temporary and part-time workers during each of the 52 weeks in the year. Under the provisions of the Federal Unemployment Tax Act (FUTA), which of the following statements is correct regarding Ral's obligation to file a federal unemployment tax return for 1993?

a. Ral must file a 1993 FUTA return only if aggregate wages exceeded $100,000 during 1993.

b. Ral must file a 1993 FUTA return because it had at least one employee during at least 20 weeks of 1993.

c. Ral is obligated to file a 1993 FUTA return only if at least one worker earned $50 or more in any calendar quarter of 1993.

d. Ral does <u>not</u> have to file a 1993 FUTA return because it had <u>no</u> permanent or full-time employees in 1993.

37 (May 92)

Unemployment tax payable under the Federal Unemployment Tax Act (FUTA), is
a. Payable by all employers.
b. Deducted from employee wages.
c. Paid to the Social Security Administration.
d. A tax deductible employer's expense.

33 (November 91)

An unemployed CPA generally would receive unemployment compensation benefits if the CPA
a. Was fired as a result of the employer's business reversals.
b. Refused to accept a job as an accountant while receiving extended benefits.
c. Was fired for embezzling from a client.
d. Left work voluntarily without good cause.

37 (November 90)

The Federal Unemployment Tax Act (FUTA)
a. Requires both the employer and employee to pay FUTA taxes, although the amounts to be paid by each are different.
b. Does not apply to businesses with fewer than 35 employees.
c. Does not apply to employers that conduct business only in one state and employ only residents of that state.
d. Allows the employer to take a credit against the FUTA tax if contributions are made to a state unemployment fund.

31 (November 89)

Which of the following statement is not correct concerning federal unemployment insurance?
a. Federal law provides general guidelines, standards, and requirements for the program.
b. The states administer the benefit payments under the program.
c. The program is funded by taxes imposed on employers and employees.
d. The federal unemployment tax is calculated as a fixed percentage of each covered employee's salary up to a stated maximum.

36 (May 89)

The Federal Unemployment Tax Act
a. Imposes a tax on all employers doing business in the U.S.
b. Requires contributions to be made by the employer and employee equally.
c. Allows an employer to take a credit against the federal unemployment tax if contributions are made to a state unemployment fund.
d. Permits an employee to receive unemployment benefits that are limited to the contributions made to that employee's account.

45 (May 88)

In general, which of the following statements is correct with respect to unemployment compensation?
a. An employee who is unable to work because of a disability is entitled to unemployment compensation.
b. An individual who has been discharged from employment because of work-connected misconduct is ineligible for unemployment compensation.
c. The maximum period during which unemployment compensation may be collected is uniform throughout the United States.
d. The maximum amount of weekly unemployment compensation payments made by a state is determined by federal law.

16 (May 86)

With respect to federal unemployment taxes and unemployment compensation, which of the following statements is correct?

    a.   The Federal Unemployment Tax Act requires both the employer and employee to make payments to an approved state unemployment fund.

    b.   Federal unemployment taxes are offset by a credit equal to the amount the employer contributes to an approved state unemployment fund.

    c.   Unemployment compensation received in excess of the employer's contributions is, in all cases, fully includable in the recipient's gross income for federal income tax purposes.

    d.   Payments made by a corporate employer for federal unemployment taxes are deductible as a business expense for federal income tax purposes.

C. Employee Protection and Equal Employment Opportunity Laws

4 (R97)

Which of the following statements is (are) correct regarding the authority of the Occupational Safety and Health Administration (OSHA)?

    I.   OSHA is authorized to establish standards that protect employees from exposure to substances that may be harmful to their health.

    II.   OSHA is authorized to develop safety equipment and require employers to instruct employees in its use.

    a.   I only.

    b.   II only.

    c.   Both I and II.

    d.   Neither I nor II.

35 (November 95)

Under the Age Discrimination in Employment Act, which of the following remedies is (are) available to a covered employee?

	Early retirement	Back pay
a.	Yes	Yes
b.	Yes	No
c.	No	Yes
d.	No	No

36 (November 95)

Which of the following Acts prohibit(s) an employer from discriminating among employees based on sex?

	Equal Pay Act	Title VII of the Civil Rights Act
a.	Yes	Yes
b.	Yes	No
c.	No	Yes
d.	No	No

37 (November 95)

Under the Fair Labor Standards Act, which of the following pay bases may be used to pay covered, nonexempt employees who earn, on average, the minimum hourly wage?

	Hourly	Weekly	Monthly
a.	Yes	Yes	Yes
b.	Yes	Yes	No
c.	Yes	No	Yes
d.	No	Yes	Yes

39 (November 95)

Under the Employee Retirement Income Security Act of 1974 (ERISA), which of the following areas of private employer pension plans is (are) regulated?

	Employee vesting	Plan funding
a.	Yes	Yes
b.	Yes	No
c.	No	Yes
d.	No	No

40 (November 95)

Which of the following employee benefits is (are) exempt from the provisions of the National Labor Relations Act?

	Sick pay	Vacation pay
a.	Yes	Yes
b.	Yes	No
c.	No	Yes
d.	No	No

37 (May 95)

Under which of the following conditions is an on-site inspection of a workplace by an investigator from the Occupational Safety and Health Administration (OSHA) permissible?
   a.   Only if OSHA obtains a search warrant after showing probable cause.
   b.   Only if the inspection is conducted after working hours.
   c.   At the request of employees.
   d.   After OSHA provides the employer with at least 24 hours notice of the prospective inspection.

38 (May 95)

Under the provisions of the Americans With Disabilities Act of 1990, in which of the following areas is a disabled person protected from discrimination?

	Public transportation	Privately operated public accommodations
a.	Yes	Yes
b.	Yes	No
c.	No	Yes
d.	No	No

39 (May 95)

When verifying a client's compliance with statutes governing employees' wages and hours, an auditor should check the client's personnel records against relevant provisions of which of the following statutes?
a. National Labor Relations Act.
b. Fair Labor Standards Act.
c. Taft-Hartley Act.
d. Americans With Disabilities Act.

40 (May 95)

Under the provisions of the Employee Retirement Income Security Act of 1974 (ERISA), which of the following statements is correct?
a. Employees are entitled to have an employer established pension plan.
b. Employers are prevented from unduly delaying an employee's participation in a pension plan.
c. Employers are prevented from managing retirement plans.
d. Employees are entitled to make investment decisions.

38 (November 94)

Under the Federal Age Discrimination in Employment Act, which of the following practices would be prohibited?

	Compulsory retirement of employees below the age of 65	Termination of employees between the ages of 65 and 70 for cause
a.	Yes	Yes
b.	Yes	No
c.	No	Yes
d.	No	No

27 (May 94)

Which of the following statements is correct regarding the scope and provisions of the Occupational Safety and Health Act (OSHA)?
a. OSHA requires employers to provide employees a workplace free from risk.
b. OSHA prohibits an employer from discharging an employee for revealing OSHA violations.
c. OSHA may inspect a workplace at any time regardless of employer objection.
d. OSHA preempts state regulation of workplace safety.

28 (May 94)

Under Title VII of the 1964 Civil Rights Act, which of the following forms of discrimination is not prohibited?
a. Sex.
b. Age.
c. Race.
d. Religion.

29 (May 94)

Which of the following statements is correct under the Federal Fair Labor Standards Act?
a. Some workers may be included within the minimum wage provisions but exempt from the overtime provisions.
b. Some workers may be included within the overtime provisions but exempt from the minimum wage provisions.
c. All workers are required to be included within both the minimum wage provisions and the overtime provisions.
d. Possible exemptions from the minimum wage provisions and the overtime provisions must be determined by the union contract in effect at the time.

40 (November 94)

Which of the following statements correctly describes the funding of noncontributory pension plans?

a. All of the funds are provided by the employees.

b. All of the funds are provided by the employer.

c. The employer and employee each provide 50% of the funds.

d. The employer provides 90% of the funds, and each employee contributes 10%.

PART VII -- NEGOTIABLE INSTRUMENTS,* DOCUMENTS OF TITLE, AND LETTERS OF CREDIT

TABLE OF CONTENTS

PART VII -- NEGOTIABLE INSTRUMENTS;* DOCUMENTS OF TITLE, AND LETTERS OF CREDIT

TABLE OF CONTENTS (continued)

*Answers consistent with Revised UCC Articles 3 and 4 (1990).

PART VII

NEGOTIBLE INSTRUMENTS, DOCUMENTS OF TITLE, AND LETTERS OF CREDIT

I. Introduction to Negotiable Instruments

(R03)

Third Corp. agreed to purchase goods from Silk Corp. Third could not pay for the goods immediately. A draft was then drawn by Silk ordering Third to pay Silk the price of the goods at a specified future date. Third signed the draft and returned it to Silk. Under the Negotiable Instruments Article of the UCC, what type of draft was created?

    a.   A trade acceptance.

    b.   A letter of credit.

    c.   A bank draft.

    d.   A check.

14 (R99)

Which of the following instruments is subject to the provisions of the Negotiable Instruments Article of the UCC?

    a.   A bill of lading.

    b.   A warehouse receipt.

    c.   A certificate of deposit.

    d.   An investment security.

41 (May 95)

Under the Commercial Paper Article of the UCC, which of the following documents would be considered an order to pay?

        I.   Draft

       II.   Certificate of deposit

    a.   I only.

    b.   II only.

    c.   Both I and II.

    d.   Neither I nor II.

42 (May 95)

```
To: Middlesex National Bank
    Nassau, N.Y.

                                          September 15, 1994

Pay to the order of _____ Robert Silver _____      $4,000.00

_____ Four Thousand and xx/100 _____  Dollars

_____ on October 1, 1994 _____

                                          __/s/ Lynn Dexter__
                                              Lynn Dexter
```

The above instrument is a

a. Draft.
b. Postdated check.
c. Trade acceptance.
d. Promissory note.

33 (November 92)

Which of the following negotiable instruments is subject to the UCC Commercial Paper Article?

a. Corporate bearer bond with a maturity date of January 1, 2001.
b. Installment note payable on the first day of each month.
c. Warehouse receipt.
d. Bill of lading payable to order.

40 (November 89)

A trade acceptance is an instrument drawn by a

a. Seller obligating the seller or designee to make payment.
b. Buyer obligating the buyer or designee to make payment.
c. Seller ordering the buyer or designee to make payment.
d. Buyer ordering the seller or designee to make payment.

46 (May 89)

On April 2, 1989, Harris agreed to sell a computer to Cross for $390. At the time of delivery, Cross gave Harris $90 and a written instrument, signed by Cross, in which Cross promised to pay Harris the balance on April 20, 1989. The instrument also made a reference to the sale of the computer. Under the UCC Commercial Paper Article, the instrument is a

a. Promissory note.
b. Non-negotiable draft.
c. Trade acceptance.
d. Negotiable time draft.

59 (May 89)

A trade acceptance usually

a. Is an order to deliver goods to a named person.
b. Provides that the drawer is also the payee.
c. Is not regarded as commercial paper under the UCC.
d. Must be made payable "to the order of" a named person.

36 (November 88)

A bank issues a negotiable instrument that acknowledges receipt of $50,000. The instrument also provides that the bank will repay the $50,000 plus 8% interest per annum to the bearer 90 days from the date of the instrument. The instrument is a

a. Certificate of deposit.
b. Time draft.
c. Trade or banker's acceptance.
d. Cashier's check.

47 (May 88)

Assuming each of the following is negotiable, which qualifies as a draft under the UCC Commercial Paper Article?

a. A warehouse receipt.
b. A demand promissory note.
c. A document of title.
d. A trade acceptance.

26 (May 86)

An instrument reads as follows:

```
                                                    April 1, 1986
   Pay
   to the
   Order of  Donald Kent, Fifteen days after date    ,      $100.00


    One hundred and no/100                               Dollars


   Union Corp.
   Ridgefield, Connecticut                         /s/ Dale Cox
                                                     Dale Cox


   re:  down payment on auto purchase
```

The instrument
- a. Is non-negotiable since it incorporates the auto purchase transaction by reference.
- b. Is a negotiable time draft.
- c. Is a negotiable sight draft.
- d. Is a non-negotiable trade acceptance.

36 (November 85)

An instrument complies with the requirements for negotiability contained in the UCC Article on Commercial Paper. The instrument contains language expressly acknowledging the receipt of $40,000 by Mint Bank and an agreement to repay principal with interest at 11% six months from date. The instrument is
- a. A banker's acceptance.
- b. A banker's draft.
- c. A negotiable certificate of deposit.
- d. Non-negotiable because of the additional language.

33 (May 85)

The following instrument was received by Kerr:

```
   Madison, Wisconsin                           April 5, 1985

   Sixty days after date pay to the order of Donald Kerr, one hundred and
   fifty dollars ($150).  Value received and charge the trade account of
   Olympia Sales Corp., N.Y.

                                              Olympia Sales Corp.

                                         by:    /s/ Carl Starr
                                                   President

   To:  New City Bank
   U.N. Plaza, New York, N.Y.
```

The instrument is a
- a. Negotiable time draft.
- b. Check.
- c. Promissory note.
- d. Trade acceptance.

46 (November 84)

    Which of the following is covered under the UCC Article on commercial paper?

    a.   An investment security.

    b.   A negotiable document of title.

    c.   A promissory note payable 10 days after presentment.

    d.   A negotiable warehouse receipt.

47 (November 84)

    Sinka Corp. has the following instrument in its possession:

	No. 121
Oct. 3, 1984	<u>51-109</u>
	332
Pay to the order of <u> Sinka Corp. </u>	$2,500.00
<u> Two Thousand Five Hundred and 00/100</u>	Dollars
<u> Fifteen days after presentment</u>	
Bocca Trust Company	
Portland, Oregon	
Memo: For purchase of stock	
	<u> /s/ Ludwig Bond</u>
	Ludwig Bond

The above instrument is

    a.   A draft.

    b.   Non-negotiable.

    c.   A check.

    d.   A trade acceptance.

36 (May 84)

    Assuming each of the following instruments is negotiable, which qualifies as commercial paper?

    a.   Bearer documents of title.

    b.   Investment securities indorsed in blank.

    c.   Foreign currency.

    d.   A foreign draft.

37 (May 84)

    Assuming each of the following is negotiable, which qualifies as a draft?

    a.   A bearer bond.

    b.   A trade acceptance.

    c.   A certificate of deposit.

    d.   A demand promissory note.

35 (November 82)

Alex & Co. has in its possession, the following instrument:

September 2, 1982

I, Henry Hardy, do hereby acknowledge my debt to Walker Corporation arising out of my purchase of soybeans and promise to pay to Walker or to its bearer, SIX HUNDRED DOLLARS, thirty days after presentment of this instrument to me at my principal place of business.

　　　　　　　　　　　　　　　　　/s/ Henry Hardy
　　　　　　　　　　　　　　　　Henry Hardy

Re: $600.00 - Soybean purchase

The above instrument is
   a.   Non-negotiable.
   b.   A negotiable promissory note.
   c.   A trade acceptance.
   d.   A negotiable bill of lading.

37 (November 82)

Alex & Co. has the following instrument in its possession:

October 5, 1982

To: Henry Futterman Suppliers
281 Cascade Boulevard
Spokane, Washington 99208

　　　　　　　　　　　　　　　　　　$950.00

Pay to the order of Alex & Co.
Nine hundred fifty and 00/100 dollars
one month after acceptance.

　　　　　　　　　　　　　　　Alex & Co.

　　　　　　　　　　　By　　/s/ Charles Alex
　　　　　　　　　　　　　Managing Partner

Alex & Co.
264 Liberty Avenue
Philadelphia, PA 19117

Accepted by:　/s/ Laura Futterman, Treasurer
　　　　　　　Henry Futterman, Suppliers

Date:　October 15, 1982

The above instrument is
   a.   Non-negotiable since the payee is also the drawer.
   b.   A time promissory note.
   c.   A trade acceptance which imposes primary liability upon Henry Futterman Suppliers after acceptance.
   d.   A negotiable investment security under the Uniform Commercial Code.

37 (May 82)

Although the scope of the Uniform Commercial Code is broad insofar as inclusion of instruments within the definition of commercial paper, it excludes certain instruments from its coverage. Which of the following is <u>not</u> commercial paper?

   a. A promissory note payable 30 days after presentment for payment.
   b. A draft which is an order to pay.
   c. A negotiable certificate of deposit issued by a bank.
   d. An investment security which is payable to bearer.

II. Negotiability
A. Formal Requisites of Negotiability
1. Writing Signed by the Maker or Drawer
2. Unconditional Promise or Order

38 (November 88)

A secured promissory note would be non-negotiable if it provided that

   a. Additional collateral must be tendered if there is a decline in market value of the original collateral.
   b. Upon default, the maker waives a trial by jury.
   c. The maker is entitled to a 5% discount if the note is prepaid.
   d. It is subject to the terms of the mortgage given by the maker to the payee.

36 (May 85)

Your client, MDS Discount Services, Inc., purchased the following instrument from John Cross on February 15, 1985. Cross had received it in connection with the sale to Dann Corp. of real property he owned located in Utah. Cross indorsed it in blank and received $24,000 from MDS.

$26,000.00   Boston Massachusetts
                                           February 2, 1985

     Sixty days after date, I promise to pay to the order of John Cross Twenty Six Thousand & 00/100 Dollars at the Second National Bank of Provo, Utah.

     Value received with interest at the rate of 14% per annum. This instrument arises out of the sale of real estate located in the state of Utah. It is further agreed that this instrument is:

   1. Subject to all implied and constructive conditions.
   2. Secured by a first mortgage given as per the sale of the real estate mentioned above.
   3. To be paid out of funds deposited in the City Bank of Wabash, Illinois.

                                            Dann Corp.

                            by   <u>/s/ Joan Dann</u>
                                President

The instrument is

   a. Non-negotiable due to the language contained in clause number 1.
   b. Non-negotiable since it incorporates by reference the terms of the mortgage indicated in clause number 2.
   c. Negotiable since it contains the words "value received" and specifies the required recitation of the transaction out of which it arose.
   d. Negotiable despite the language contained in clauses numbered 1, 2, and 3.

43 (May 82)

Which of the following provisions contained in an otherwise negotiable instrument will cause it to be non-negotiable?

a. It is payable in Mexican pesos.
b. It contains an unrestricted acceleration clause.
c. It grants to the holder an option to purchase land.
d. It is limited to payment out of the entire assets of a partnership.

46 (November 80)

Anderson agreed to purchase Parker's real property. Anderson's purchase was dependent upon his being able to sell certain real property that he owned. Anderson gave Parker an instrument for the purchase price. Assuming the instrument is otherwise negotiable, which one of the statements below, written on the face of the instrument, will render it non-negotiable?

a. A statement that Parker's cashing or indorsing the instrument acknowledges full satisfaction of Anderson's obligation.
b. A statement that payment of the instrument is contingent upon Anderson's sale of his real property.
c. A statement that the instrument is secured by a first mortgage on Parker's property and that upon default in payment the entire amount of the instrument is due.
d. A statement that the instrument is subject to the usual implied and constructive conditions applicable to such transactions.

42 (May 76)

A promise or order is conditional if the instrument states

a. That it is secured by a mortgage or other security device.
b. The purpose for which it was given.
c. That it is subject to the provisions of another agreement.
d. The account which is to be charged.

2 (May 74)

An instrument is non-negotiable if it

a. Is payable in a foreign currency.
b. States it is secured by a mortgage.
c. States that it is subject to any other agreement.
d. Is issued by a partnership and limited to payment from partnership assets.

3. Fixed Amount of Money

8 (R00)

Under the Negotiable Instruments Article of the UCC, which of the following statements is(are) correct regarding the requirements for an instrument to be negotiable?

    I. The instrument must be in writing, be signed by both the drawer and the drawee, and contain an unconditional promise or order to pay.
    II. The instrument must state a fixed amount of money, be payable on demand or at a definite time, and be payable to order or to bearer.

a. I only.
b. II only.
c. Both I and II.
d. Neither I nor II.

44 (May 95)

Under the Commercial Paper Article of the UCC, which of the following circumstances would prevent a promissory note from being negotiable?
 a. An extension clause that allows the maker to elect to extend the time for payment to a date specified in the note.
 b. An acceleration clause that allows the holder to move up the maturity date of the note in the event of default.
 c. A person having a power of attorney signs the note on behalf of the maker.
 d. A clause that allows the maker to satisfy the note by the performance of services or the payment of money.

46 (November 90)

Holt, MT	$4,000	April 15, 1990

Fifty days after date, or sooner, the undersigned promises to pay to the order of

Union Co.

Four Thousand

Salem Bank, Holt, MT

at   Dollars

Ten percent interest per annum.

This instrument is secured by the maker's business inventory.

EASY, INC.

BY: /s/ Thomas Foy

Thomas Foy, President

Assuming all other requirements of negotiability are satisfied, this instrument is
 a. Not negotiable because of a lack of a definite time for payment.
 b. Not negotiable because the amount due is unspecified.
 c. Negotiable because it is secured by the maker's inventory.
 d. Negotiable because it is payable in a sum certain in money.

49 (May 89)

Which one of the following aspects of an otherwise negotiable promissory note will render it non-negotiable?
 a. The maker is obligated to pay a sum certain to the payee but may instead deliver to the payee goods of equal value.
 b. The maker has the right to prepay the note, subject to a prepayment penalty of 10% of the amount prepaid.
 c. The maker is obligated to pay the payee's costs of collection upon default by the maker.
 d. The maker intentionally using a rubber stamp to sign the note.

37 (November 88)

Which of the following would cause a promissory note to be non-negotiable?
 a. An acceleration clause that allows the holder to move up the maturity date of the note in the event of default.
 b. An extension clause that allows the maker to elect to extend the time for payment to a date specified in the note.
 c. A clause that allows the maker to satisfy the note by the performance of services or the payment of money.
 d. A due date is <u>not</u> specified in the note.

41 (November 82)

Ash Company has in its possession the following note:

> October 15, 1982
>
> I, Joseph Gorman, promise to pay or deliver to Harold Smalley or to his order ONE THOUSAND DOLLARS ($1,000) or at his option to deliver an amount of stock in the Sunrise Corporation which, on the due date of this instrument, is worth not less than ONE THOUSAND DOLLARS ($1,000). This note is due and payable on the 1st of November, 1982.
>
> /s/ Joseph Gorman
> Joseph Gorman

This note is

a. Not commercial paper, but instead a negotiable investment security.
b. A negotiable promissory note since it is payable to Smalley's order and contains an unconditional promise to pay $1,000 if the holder so elects.
c. Non-negotiable since it gives Smalley the option to take stock instead of cash.
d. Nontransferable.

4. Payable on Demand or at a Definite Time

40 (May 93)

An instrument reads as follows:

> $10,000   Ludlow, Vermont   February 1, 1993
>
> I promise to pay to the order of Custer Corp. $10,000 within 10 days after the sale of my two-carat diamond ring. I pledge the sale proceeds to secure my obligation hereunder.
>
> /s/ R. Harris
> R. Harris

Which of the following statements correctly describes the above instrument?

a. The instrument is nonnegotiable because it is <u>not</u> payable at a definite time.
b. The instrument is nonnegotiable because it is secured by the proceeds of the sale of the ring.
c. The instrument is a negotiable promissory note.
d. The instrument is a negotiable sight draft payable on demand.

34 (November 92)

Which of the following conditions, if present on an otherwise negotiable instrument, would affect the instrument's negotiability?

a. The instrument is payable after six months after the death of the maker.
b. The instrument is payable at a definite time subject to an acceleration clause in the event of a default.
c. The instrument is postdated.
d. The instrument contains a promise to provide additional collateral if there is a decrease in value of the existing collateral.

Negotiable Instruments

Items 46 and 47 relate to the following instrument:

May 19, 1991

I promise to pay to the order of A. B. Shark $1,000 (One thousand and one hundred dollars) with interest thereon at the rate of 12% per annum.

/s/ T. T. Tile
T. T. Tile

Guraranty

I personally guaranty payment by T. T. Tile.

/s/ N. A. Abner
N. A. Abner

---

46 (November 91)

The instrument is a
a. Promissory demand note.
b. Sight draft.
c. Check.
d. Trade acceptance.

47 (November 91)

The instrument is
a. Nonnegotiable even though it is payable on demand.
b. Nonnegotiable because the numeric amount differs from the written amount.
c. Negotiable even though a payment date is not specified.
d. Negotiable because of Abner's guaranty.

46 (May 88)

Ard is holding the following instrument:

I, Rosemary Larkin, hereby promise to pay to the bearer twenty thousand dollars ($20,000). This document is given by me as a payment of the balance due on my purchase of a 1984 Winnebago mobile home from Ed Dill and is payable when I am able to obtain a bank loan.

/s/ Rosemary Larkin
Rosemary Larkin

This instrument is not negotiable because it
a. Refers to the contract out of which it arose.
b. Is payable to bearer rather than to a named payee.
c. Is not dated on the face of the instrument.
d. Is not payable at a definite time.

43 (November 86)

Which of the following prevents an instrument from being negotiable?
a. An indorsement on the back of the instrument which reads: "Pay Smith only."
b. An instrument which is payable after completion of a contractual obligation which is certain to happen but uncertain as to the time of occurrence.
c. The fact that it is unclear whether the instrument is intended to be a note or a draft.
d. The capacity in which the party signed was unclear.

34 (May 85)

Jason contracted to sell his business to Farr. Upon execution of the contract by Farr, he delivered a note in lieu of earnest money which recited the nature of the transaction and indicated that it was payable on the date of the closing which was to be determined by the mutual consent of the parties. The note is
a. Non-negotiable because <u>no</u> consideration is given.
b. Non-negotiable because of the recitation of the transaction which gave rise to it.
c. Non-negotiable since it is <u>not</u> payable at a definite time.
d. Negotiable.

40 (November 81)

A client has in its possession the instrument below.

> I, Margaret Dunlop, hereby promise to pay to the order of Caldwell
> Motors five thousand dollars ($5,000) upon the receipt of the final
> distribution from the estate of my deceased uncle, Carlton Dunlop. This
> negotiable instrument is given by me as the down payment on my
> purchase of a 1981 Lincoln Continental to be delivered in two weeks.
>
>   /s/ Margaret Dunlop
>   Margaret Dunlop

The instrument is
a. Negotiable.
b. Not negotiable as it is undated.
c. Not negotiable in that it is subject to the two week delivery term regarding the purchase of the Lincoln Continental.
d. Not negotiable because it is <u>not</u> payable at a definite time.

3 (November 80)

Your client, Globe, Inc., has in its possession an undated instrument which is payable 30 days after date. It is believed that the instrument was issued on or about August 10, 1980, by Dixie Manufacturing, Inc., to Harding Enterprises in payment of goods purchased. On August 13, 1980, it was negotiated to Desert Products, Inc., and thereafter to Globe on the 15th. Globe took for value, in good faith and without notice of any defense. It has been learned that the goods shipped by Harding to Dixie are defective. Which of the following is correct?
a. Since the time of payment is indefinite, the instrument is non-negotiable and Globe can <u>not</u> qualify as a holder in due course.
b. By issuing an undated instrument payable 30 days after date, Dixie was reserving the right to avoid liability on it until it filled in or authorized the filling in of the date.
c. Since the defense involves a rightful rejection of the goods delivered, it is valid against Globe.
d. Globe can validly fill in the date and will qualify as a holder in due course.

5. Payable to "Order" or to "Bearer"

43 (May 95)

Under the Commercial Paper Article of the UCC, for an instrument to be negotiable it must
a. Be payable to order or to bearer.
b. Be signed by the payee.
c. Contain references to all agreements between the parties.
d. Contains necessary conditions of payment.

48 (May 89)

The following instrument is in the possession of Bill North:

> On May 30, 1989, I promise to pay Bill North, the bearer of this
> document, $1,800.
>
>

    /s/ Joseph Peppers

    Joseph Peppers

>
> Re: Auto Purchase Contract

This instrument is

a. Non-negotiable because it is undated.
b. Non-negotiable because it is <u>not</u> payable to order or bearer.
c. Negotiable even though it makes reference to the contract out of which it arose.
d. Negotiable because it is payable at a definite time.

48 (November 87)

A company has in its possession the following instrument:

> $500.00   Dayton, Ohio   October 2, 1987
>
> Sixty days after date I promise to pay to the order of
>
>

    Cash

    Five Hundred   Dollars

>
> at   Miami, Florida
>
> Value received with interest at the rate of nine percent per annum.
>
> This instrument is secured by a conditional sales contract.
>
> no. 11   <u>Due December 1, 1987</u>   <u>/s/ Craig Burke</u>
>
>   Craig Burke

This instrument is

a. Not negotiable until December 1, 1987.
b. A negotiable bearer note.
c. A negotiable time draft.
d. A non-negotiable note since it states that it is secured by a conditional sales contract.

7 (November 80)

Rapid Delivery, Inc., has in its possession the following instrument which it purchased for value.

> March 1, 1980
>
> Thirty days from date, I, Harold Kales, do hereby promise to pay Ronald
> Green four hundred dollars and no cents ($400.00). This note is given
> for value received.
>
>

    /s/ Harold Kales

    Harold Kales

Which of the following is correct?
a. The instrument is negotiable.
b. The instrument is non-negotiable, and therefore Rapid has obtained no rights on the instrument.
c. Rapid is an assignee of the instrument and has the same rights as the assignor had on it.
d. The instrument is nontransferable on its face.

19 (May 77)

Arthur Fox purchased a large order of business supplies from Spencer & Company by paying 10% in cash and giving Spencer & Company the following instrument to cover the balance due:

> Los Angeles, Calif.
> February 2, 1977
>
> For value received, I, Arthur Fox, hereby promise to pay my debt of One thousand thirty and 26/100's ($1,030.26) to Spencer & Company or to their order. The instrument is due not later than March 2, 1978, but the maker may at his option pay within one month of the date of this instrument and receive a 1% discount.
>
> /s/ Arthur Fox

Which of the following is true with respect to this instrument?
a. The instrument is a trade draft.
b. Since Fox can pay earlier than the due date, the instrument is thereby rendered non-negotiable.
c. The language "For value received" is necessary in order to satisfy the requirements of negotiability.
d. The instrument is negotiable.

39 (May 76)

Your client, Robert Rose, has the following instrument in his possession.

> March 1, 1976
>
> One month from date, I, Charles Wallace, do hereby promise to pay Edward Carlson seven hundred and fifty dollars ($750.00).
>
> /s/ Charles Wallace

Edward Carlson wrote "pay to the order of Robert Rose" on the back and delivered it to Rose.
a. Robert Rose is a holder in due course.
b. The instrument is a negotiable promissory note.
c. Edward Carlson is a holder in due course.
d. All defenses, real and personal, are assertable by Wallace against Rose.

5 (May 90)

On February 12, 1990, Mayfair & Associates, CPAs, was engaged to audit the financial statements of University Book Distributors, Inc. University operates as a retail and wholesale distributor of books, newspapers, magazines, and other periodicals. In conjunction with the audit of University's cash, notes, and accounts receivable, University's controller gave Mayfair's staff accountant certain instruments that University had received from its customers during 1989 in the ordinary course of its business. The instruments are:

- A signed promissory note dated June 30, 1989, in the amount of $3,100 payable "to Harris on December 31, 1989." The maker of the note was Peters and it was indorsed in blank by Harris, who delivered it to University as payment for a shipment of magazines. University demanded that Peters pay the note but Peters refused, claiming that he gave the note as a result of misrepresentations by Harris related to a real estate transaction between the two of them. University advised Harris immediately of Peters' refusal to pay.

Negotiable Instruments

- A signed promissory note dated July 31, 1989, in the amount of $1,800 payable "to the order of Able on January 15, 1990." The maker of the note was Cole and it further provided that it was given "pursuant to that certain construction contract dated June 1, 1989." The note had been given to University as payment for books by one of its customers, Baker, who did not indorse it. The note bears Able's blank indorsement. University demanded payment from Cole. Cole refused to honor the note claiming that:
- The note's reference to the construction contract renders it non-negotiable; and
- University has no rights to the note because it was not indorsed by Baker.

University immediately advised Baker of Cole's refusal to pay.

University is uncertain of its rights under the two notes.

Required: Answer the following questions, setting forth reasons for your conclusions.
  a. With regard to the note executed by Peters, is University a holder in due course?
  b. Can Peters raise Harris' alleged misrepresentations as a defense to University's demand for payment?
  c. Are Cole's claims valid?

  a. University is not a holder in due course (HDC) with regard to Peters' note. To be an HDC, University must:
   - Be a holder of a negotiable instrument.
   - Take it for value.
   - Take it in good faith.
   - Take it without notice that it is overdue or has been dishonored.
   - Take it without notice of any defense or claim to it.

All of the above requirements are met except the first. Peters' note is not negotiable because it is not made payable to bearer or to the order of a named payee.

  b. University is an assignee of Harris' rights under Peters' note. Therefore, University "stands in the shoes" of Harris, and Peters can raise Harris' alleged misrepresentations as a defense against University.

  c. 1. Cole's first claim is incorrect. The promissory note Cole executed is negotiable despite the reference to the construction contract, because it does not make the note subject to the other contract; rather, the reference is only a recital of that contract's existence.

  2. Cole's second claim is incorrect. University acquired rights to the promissory note without Baker's indorsement because the note had been converted to a bearer instrument as a result of Able's blank indorsement. Bearer paper can be negotiated by delivery alone.

6B (November 75)

On September 30, 1975, Dayton Blasting Company purchased 25 cases of blasting caps from Whitten Blasting Cap Company. In this connection, it gave Whitten the following instrument:

September 30, 1975

Dayton Blasting Company hereby promises to pay Whitten Blasting Cap Company Six Hundred Fifty Dollars ($650.00) on December 1, 1975, plus interest at 6% per annum from date.

Dayton Blasting Company

By ___/s/ Malcolm Smalley___
MALCOLM SMALLEY, President

Whitten promptly transferred the above instrument to Vincent Luck for $600. James Whitten, president of Whitten, indorsed the instrument on the back as follows: "Pay to the order of Vincent Luck" signed Whitten Blasting Cap Company per James Whitten, President.

Approximately half of the blasting caps were defective and Dayton refused to pay on the instrument. Dayton returned the defective cases and used the balance.

Required: What are Vincent Luck's rights on the instrument in question? Explain.

Vincent Luck is an assignee of the contract rights evidenced by the instrument. He is not a holder in due course because the instrument does not contain the words of negotiability, i.e., pay to order, or bearer. The indorsement, "Pay to the order of Vincent Luck" and signed by Whitten, does not cure the defect. Thus, Luck takes the instrument subject to all defenses assertable by Dayton Blasting.

However, Luck does take all of Whitten's rights as an assignee. Because Dayton used approximately 50% of the cases of caps, Luck should be able to recover for them.

6A (November 74)

Magnum Enterprises, Inc., received a note from one of its major customers, Bilbo Sales, Inc., in connection with the purchase of $100,000 of merchandise. The note provided as follows:

August 1, 1974

Bilbo Sales, Inc., hereby promises to pay Magnum Enterprises, Inc., One Hundred Thousand Dollars ($100,000) within thirty days from August 1, 1974, for the purchase of goods delivered on July 26, 1974, receipt of which is hereby acknowledged. Bilbo Sales hereby confesses judgment on said note and agrees to pay any and all costs of collection in the event of wrongful default.

Walter Bilbo,
President

Magnum had promptly discounted the note with the Third National Bank.

Upon examination of the merchandise, Bilbo promptly informed Magnum that the goods were not as warranted. Magnum responded by informing Bilbo that the note had been sold to Third National Bank and that whatever problems it had must first be resolved with the bank because it was the holder in due course.

Required: In the event that Bilbo was properly dissatisfied with the merchandise, can it assert the defense of breach of warranty against Third National? Explain.

Yes. The note in question is non-negotiable because it is not payable to Magnum's order or to bearer. As such, all defenses, including personal defenses, are assertable against the transferee, Third National. Third National is a mere assignee of Magnum's rights on the note and contract and, therefore, is subject to all the defenses which Bilbo could assert against Magnum, including breach of warranty.

B. Rules of Construction and Incomplete Instruments

44 (November 86)

Your client has in its possession the following instrument:

```
                                              No. 1625

FAIR FOOD WHOLESALERS, INC.
22 Woodrow Wilson Hayes Lane
Columbus, Ohio                        Jan. 10, 1986


On demand the undersigned promises to pay to


Bearer                                        $1,200.00

Twelve hundred & ten/100's                        Dollars


                           Fair Food Wholesalers, Inc.

                           By    /s/ James Duff
                                James Duff, President

For: _____
```

The instrument is
   a. A non-negotiable promissory note.
   b. Non-negotiable because the instrument is incomplete.
   c. A negotiable time draft.
   d. Negotiable despite the inconsistency between the amount in words and the amount in numbers.

III. Negotiation
A. Introduction to Negotiation

2(a) (R96)

This question consists of two parts. Each part consists of 5 items. Select the **best** answer for each item. **Answer all items.** Your grade will be based on the total number of correct answers.

a. Under the Negotiable Instruments Article of the UCC, a note must conform to certain requirements to be negotiable. Similarly, a note's negotiability may be restricted or prevented.

Required: Items 1 through 5 are examples of terms, conditions, and indorsements that may appear on a note. For each item, select the effect each term, condition, or indorsement would have on the note's negotiability from List I. An answer may be selected once, more than once, or not at all.
   1. The note is postdated.
   2. No place of payment is indicated on the note.
   3. The note is payable to the order of a named individual.
   4. The note is indorsed "For Collection."
   5. The note is payable in either money or goods.

	List I
A	Has no effect on negotiability.
B	Restricts negotiability.
C	Must be negotiated by delivery.
D	Must be indorsed to be negotiated.
E	Results in nonnegotiability.

45 (May 95)

Under the Commercial Paper Article of the UCC, which of the following requirements must be met for a transferee of order paper to become a holder?

      I. Possession

     II. Indorsement of transferor

a. I only.

b. II only.

c. Both I and II.

d. Neither I nor II.

41 (May 93)

The following indorsements appear on the back of a negotiable promissory note payable to Lake Corp.

> Pay to John Smith only
> /s/ Frank Parker, President of
> Lake Corp.
>
> /s/ John Smith
>
> Pay to the order of Sharp, Inc., without
> recourse, but only if Sharp delivers
> computers purchased by Mary Harris
> by March 15, 1993
> /s/ Mary Harris
>
> /s/ Sarah Sharp, President of
> Sharp, Inc.

Which of the following statements is correct?

a. The note became nonnegotiable as a result of Parker's indorsement.

b. Harris' indorsement was a conditional promise to pay and caused the note to be nonnegotiable.

c. Smith's indorsement effectively prevented further negotiation of the note.

d. Harris' signature was <u>not</u> required to effectively negotiable the note to Sharp.

36 (November 92)

One of the requirements to qualify as a holder of a negotiable bearer check is that the transferee must

a. Receive the check that was originally made payable to bearer.

b. Take the check in good faith.

c. Give value for the check.

d. Have possession of the check.

47 (November 87)

In order to negotiate bearer paper, one must
   a. Indorse the paper.
   b. Indorse and deliver the paper with consideration.
   c. Deliver the paper.
   d. Deliver and indorse the paper.

60 (November 82)

Drummond broke into the Apex Drug Store and took all of the cash and checks which were in the cash register. The checks reflect payments made to Apex for goods sold. Drummond disposed of the checks and has disappeared. Apex is worried about its ability to recover the checks from those now in possession of them. Which of the following is correct?
   a. Apex will prevail as long as its signature was necessary to negotiate the checks in question.
   b. Since there was no valid transfer by Apex to Drummond, subsequent parties have no better rights than the thief had.
   c. Apex will prevail only if the checks were payable to cash.
   d. Apex will not prevail on any of the checks since it was the only party that could have prevented the theft.

35 (November 81)

Howard Corporation has the following instrument which it purchased in good faith and for value from Luft Manufacturing, Inc.

```
                                               July 2, 1981

   McHugh Wholesalers, Inc.
   Pullman, Washington


   Pay to the order of Luft Manufacturing, Inc., one thousand seven hundred
   dollars ($1,700) three months after acceptance.


                         /s/ Peter Crandall, President
                          Peter Crandall, President
                          Luft Manufacturing, Inc.



   Accepted  July 12, 1981

   McHugh Wholesalers, Inc.

   By  /s/ Charles Towne, President
```

Crandall indorsed the instrument on the back in his capacity as president of Luft when it was transferred to Howard on July 15, 1981.
   The instrument
   a. Would be treated as a promissory note since the drawee is <u>not</u> a bank.
   b. Is a negotiable draft and Howard is a holder in due course.
   c. Is <u>not</u> negotiable under Article 3 (commercial paper) of the Uniform Commercial Code, although it may be negotiable under another Article.
   d. Is <u>not</u> negotiable since the drawer and the payee are the same person.

21 (May 80)

An instrument is order paper when it is
a. Payable to the order of cash on its face.
b. Indorsed to John Smith by Marvin Frank, the payee.
c. Payable to the order of Marvin Frank and indorsed in blank.
d. Payable to a specified person or bearer.

46 (November 78)

Maxwell is a holder in due course of a check which was originally payable to the order of Clark and has the following indorsements on its back:

```
/s/ Clark

Pay to the order of White

/s/ Smithers

Without Recourse

/s/ White

/s/ Dobbins
```

Which of the following statements about this check is correct?
a. If the bank refuses to pay, Maxwell's only recourse is to sue Dobbins.
b. The instrument was bearer paper in Dobbins' hands.
c. Clark's signature was not necessary to negotiate the instrument.
d. White has no warranty liability to Maxwell on the instrument.

50 (November 78)

An instrument reads as follows:

```
$5,000.00              Boise, Idaho          October 1, 1978

Thirty days after date I promise to pay to the

Order of _____ Cash _____

at 120 BROADWAY, _____ New York City _____

Value received with interest at the rate of eight percent per annum.
This instrument arises out of a separate agreement.

No. 20    Due October 31, 1978              /s/ A. G. Loeb
```

Which of the following statements about this instrument is correct?
a. The instrument is negotiable.
b. The instrument is order paper.
c. The instrument is a time draft.
d. Failure to make a timely presentment will excuse Loeb from liability.

25 (May 77)

Price has in his possession an otherwise negotiable instrument which reads:

"I, Waldo, hereby promise to pay to the order of Mark or bearer...."

Which of the following is true with respect to the above instrument?
a. Mark's signature is required to negotiate the instrument.
b. The instrument is non-negotiable.
c. If Mark indorses the instrument, Mark assumes potentially greater liability to subsequent transferees than if Mark transfers it by mere delivery.
d. Since the instrument is payable to Mark's order, it is a draft.

7 (May 74)

Teff entered Archer's office and stole from Archer some radios and Archer's wallet containing identification. Subsequently, representing himself as Archer, Teff induced Bane to purchase one of the stolen radios for a fair price. Bane gave Teff his check made out to Archer. Teff indorsed the check "Pay to the order of Crown, Archer" and transferred it to Crown for cash in the amount of the check. Crown indorsed the check "Pay to the order of Fox, Crown" and transferred the check to Fox to be applied to his account.
Bane's check was
a. Void ab initio.
b. Bearer paper when Crown took it.
c. Order paper initially and negotiated by Teff to Crown.
d. Non-negotiable absent a valid indorsement by the real Archer.

16 (May 74)

Fitz received from Gayle a negotiable instrument payable to the order of Gayle. Fitz received the instrument for value, but Gayle inadvertently did not indorse the instrument.
a. Fitz will be treated as the holder of a bearer negotiable instrument.
b. If Fitz later obtains Gayle's unqualified indorsement, Fitz's rights as a holder in due course are determined as of the time of indorsement.
c. Fitz has a right to require Gayle to indorse, but Gayle may satisfy the right by a qualified indorsement.
d. Fitz has no right after accepting the transferred instrument to require Gayle to indorse where he made no such request at the time of the transfer.

B. Indorsements
1. Blank v. Special Indorsement

46 (May 92)

The following indorsements appear on the back of a negotiable promissory note made payable "to bearer." Clark has possession of the note.

Pay to Sam North
/s/ Alice Fox

/s/ Sam North
(without recourse)

Which of the following statements is correct?
a. Clark's unqualified indorsement is required to further negotiate the note.
b. To negotiate the note, Clark must have given value for it.
c. Clark is not a holder because North's qualified indorsement makes the note nonnegotiable.
d. Clark can negotiate the note by delivery alone.

49 (November 90)

The following note was executed by Elizabeth Quinton on April 17, 1990 and delivered to Ian Wolf:

(Face)

April 17, 1990
On demand, the undersigned promises to pay to the order of Ian Wolf
Seven Thousand and 00/100---------------------------------DOLLARS
/s/ Elizabeth Quinton Elizabeth Quinton

(Back)

/s/ Ian Wolf Ian Wolf
Pay: George Vernon
/s/ Samuel Thorn Samuel Thorn
Pay: Alan Yule
/s/ George Vernon George Vernon
/s/ Alan Yule Alan Yule

In sequence, beginning with Wolf's receipt of the note, this note is properly characterized as what type of commercial paper?

a. Bearer, bearer, order, order, order.
b. Order, bearer, order, order, bearer.
c. Order, order, bearer, order, bearer.
d. Bearer, order, order, order, bearer.

41 (May 90)

Fred Anchor is the holder of the following check:

Peter Mason	
Champaign, Illinois	4/30 19 90
Pay to the order of _____Mary Nix or bearer_____	$93.00
Ninety-Three---	Dollars
Second Bank 0453-0978	
	/s/ Peter Mason

285

The check is indorsed on the back as follows:

> /s/ Mary Nix
> Pay to John Jacobs
> /s/ Mark Harris
> /s/ John Jacobs
> (without recourse)

Jacobs gave the check to his son as a gift, who transferred it to Anchor for $78.00. Which of the following statements is correct?

    a.   The unqualified indorsement of Jacobs was necessary in order to negotiate the check to his son.

    b.   Nix's indorsement was required to negotiate the check to any subsequent holder.

    c.   Anchor does <u>not</u> qualify as a holder because less than full consideration was given for the check.

    d.   The check is bearer paper in Jacobs' son's hands.

41 (November 86)

Hand executed and delivered to Rex a $1,000 negotiable note payable to Rex or bearer. Rex then negotiated it to Ford and indorsed it on the back by merely signing his name. Which of the following is a correct statement?

    a.   Rex's indorsement was a special indorsement.

    b.   Rex's indorsement was necessary to Ford's qualification as a holder.

    c.   The instrument initially being bearer paper can <u>not</u> be converted to order paper.

    d.   The instrument is bearer paper and Ford can convert it to order paper by writing "pay to the order of Ford" above Rex's signature.

37 (November 85)

Jane Lane, a sole proprietor, has in her possession several checks which she received from her customers. Lane is concerned about the safety of the checks since she believes that many of them are bearer paper which may be cashed without indorsement. The checks in Lane's possession will be considered order paper rather than bearer paper if they were made payable (in the drawer's handwriting) to the order of

    a.   Cash.

    b.   Ted Tint, and indorsed by Ted Tint in blank.

    c.   Bearer, and indorsed by Ken Kent making them payable to Jane Lane.

    d.   Bearer, and indorsed by Sam Sole in blank.

2. Qualified v. Unqualified Indorsement

48 (May 95)

Under the Commercial Paper Article of the UCC, which of the following statements best describes the effect of a person indorsing a check "without recourse"?

    a.   The person has <u>no</u> liability to prior indorsers.

    b.   The person makes <u>no</u> promise or guarantee of payment on dishonor.

    c.   The person gives <u>no</u> warranty protection to later transferees.

    d.   The person converts the check into order paper.

41 (May 84)

Ed Moss has a negotiable draft in his possession. The draft was originally payable to the order of John Davis. The instrument was indorsed as follows:

> (1) Carl Bass
> (2) John Davis
> (3) Pay to the order of Nix & Co.
> (4) Pay to Ed Moss, without recourse,
>   Nix & Co. per Jane Kirk,
>   President
> (5) For deposit, Ed Moss

Which of the following is correct regarding the above indorsements?
- a. Number 1 prevents further negotiation since Bass is not the payee.
- b. Number 2 does not change the instrument to bearer paper since it was originally payable to the order of Davis.
- c. Number 4 eliminates all the contractual liability of the indorser.
- d. Number 5 prevents any further negotiation.

42 (May 82)

Balquist sold a negotiable instrument payable to her order to Farley. In transferring the instrument to Farley, she forgot to indorse it. Accordingly,
- a. Farley qualifies as a holder in due course.
- b. Farley has a specifically enforceable right to obtain Balquist's unqualified indorsement.
- c. Farley obtains a better right to payment of the instrument than Balquist had.
- d. Once the signature of Balquist is obtained, Farley's rights as a holder in due course relate back to the time of transfer.

3 (May 94)

Items 73 through 78 are based on the following documents:

Document I (face)	Document I (back)
April 1, 1994 On demand, the undersigned promises to pay to the order of MARK EDEN Three Thousand Two Hundred and no/100 ($3,300.00).....dollars _/s/Alice Long_ Alice Long	/s/ Mark Eden Pay Joyce Noon /s/ Harold Storm

Document II (face)

	April 15, 1994
On May 1, 1994, or sooner, pay to the order of	
EDWARD THARP	
Two Thousand and NO/100 ($2,000.00)................ ....dollars	
To: Henry Gage	/s/ Patricia Rite
100 East Way	Patricia Rite
Capital City, ND	

Document II (back)

/s/ Edward Tharp

/s/ Nancy Ferry
without recourse

/s/ Ann Archer

Required: Items 73 through 78 relate to the nature and negotiability of the above documents and the nature of several of the indorsements. For each item select from List A the response that best completes that statement. A response may be selected more than once.

List A

73. Document I is a (type of instrument)
74. Document II is a (type of instrument)
75. Document I is (negotiability)
76. Document II is (negotiability)
77. The indorsement by Mark Eden is (type of indorsement)
78. The indorsement by Nancy Ferry is (type of indorsement)

A. Blank
B. Check
C. Draft
D. Negotiable
E. Nonnegotiable
F. Promissory Note
G. Qualified
H. Special

3. Restrictive v. Nonrestrictive Indorsement

17 (R01)

Under the Negotiable Instruments Article of the UCC, an indorsement of an instrument "for deposit only" is an example of what type of indorsement?
a. Blank.
b. Qualified.
c. Restrictive.
d. Special.

39 (November 85)

John Daly received a check which was originally made payable to the order of one of his customers, Al Pine. The following indorsement was written on the back of the check:

> Al Pine, without recourse, for
> collection only

The indorsement on this check would be classified as
a. Blank, unqualified, and nonrestrictive.
b. Blank, qualified, and restrictive.
c. Special, unqualified, and restrictive.
d. Special, qualified, and nonrestrictive.

28 (May 79)

Johnson lost a check that he had received for professional services rendered. The instrument on its face was payable to Johnson's order. He had indorsed it on the back by signing his name and printing "for deposit only" above his name. Assuming the check is found by Alcatraz, a dishonest person who attempts to cash it, which of the following is correct?

    a. Any transferee of the instrument must pay or apply any value given by him for the instrument consistent with the indorsement.

    b. The indorsement is a blank indorsement and a holder in due course who cashed it for Alcatraz would prevail.

    c. The indorsement prevents further transfer or negotiation by anyone.

    d. If Alcatraz simply signs his name beneath Johnson's indorsement, he can convert it into bearer paper and a holder in due course would take free of the restriction.

18 (May 77)

Kenneth Nelson has a negotiable check in his possession. It was originally payable to the order of Donna Baker. The back of the instrument contained the following indorsements:

    /s/ Donna Baker

    /s/ Harold Sharp, without recourse

    Pay Kenneth Nelson
    /s/ Judy Lally

    For deposit only
    /s/ Kenneth Nelson

Which of the following statements is true with respect to these indorsements?

    a. Kenneth Nelson's restrictive indorsement "for deposit only" does not prevent further negotiation.

    b. Kenneth Nelson cannot be a holder in due course because of Sharp's indorsement.

    c. Harold Sharp eliminates all potential liability to himself via the "without recourse" indorsement.

    d. Once Donna Baker signed the instrument in blank, it became a bearer instrument and remained so despite the subsequent indorsements.

IV. Holders in Due Course
A. General Requirements
1. Taking for Value
a. Executory Promises

48 (May 88)

The value requirement in determining whether a person is a holder in due course with respect to a check will not be satisfied by the taking of the check

    a. As security for an obligation to the extent of the obligation.

    b. As payment for an antecedent debt.

    c. In exchange for another negotiable instrument.

    d. In exchange for a promise to perform services in the future.

42 (November 85)

Frey paid Holt $2,500 by check pursuant to an agreement between them whereby Holt promised to perform in Frey's theater within the next year. Holt indorsed the check, making it payable to Len Able. Holt's status with regard to the check was one of a(n)

    a. Assignee since a payee may not also be a holder in due course.

    b. Holder since Holt's promise failed to satisfy the value requirement necessary to become a holder in due course.

    c. Holder in due course under the shelter rule since Able's right as a holder in due course revert to Holt.

    d. Holder in due course since all the requirements have been satisfied.

b. Antecedent Debt as Value

40 (May 76)

Carter fraudulently misrepresented the quality and capabilities of certain machinery he sold to Dobbins. Carter obtained a check for $2,000, the amount agreed upon, at the time he made delivery. The machinery proved to be virtually worthless. Dobbins promptly stopped payment on the check. Carter negotiated the check to Marvel in satisfaction of a prior loan of $600 and received $1,400 in cash. Marvel, who had accepted the check in good faith, presented the check for payment which was refused by Dobbins' bank.

    a.   Even if Marvel is a holder in due course, Dobbins has a real defense.

    b.   Marvel can only collect for $1,400 cash in that he did <u>not</u> give new value beyond that amount.

    c.   Marvel will be able to collect the full amount from Dobbins.

    d.   Dobbins' timely stop order eliminates his liability on the check.

c. Value Must be Given Without Notice

36 (May 82)

Industrial Factors, Inc. discounted a $4,000 promissory note, payable in two years, for $3,000. It paid $1,000 initially and promised to pay the balance ($2,000) within 30 days. Industrial paid the balance within the 30 days, but before doing so learned that the note had been obtained originally by fraudulent misrepresentation in connection with the sale of land which induced the maker to issue the note. For what amount will Industrial qualify as a holder in due course?

    a.   None because the 25% discount is presumptive or prima facie evidence that Industrial is <u>not</u> a holder in due course.

    b. $1,000.

    c. $3,000.

    d. $4,000.

36 (November 77)

Baker sold goods to Abrams for $300, taking Abrams' negotiable note in payment, with the agreement that Baker would deliver the goods immediately. Baker sold and indorsed the note to Cantrell, an innocent party, for $250 of which $50 was paid in cash and $200 was to be paid in 10 days. Baker did <u>not</u> deliver the goods for which the note had been given before the 10 days expired, and Abrams so informed Cantrell. Cantrell paid the remaining $200 to Baker on the 10th day as agreed. Cantrell sued Abrams for the $300. Which of the following statements is a correct legal solution or proposition?

    a.   The total failure to deliver any of the goods constitutes a defense which will prevail even against a holder in due course.

    b.   Cantrell can only recover $50.

    c.   Cantrell can only recover $250.

    d.   Cantrell can recover the full $300.

2. Taking in Good Faith
3. Taking Without Notice

47 (May 95)

Under the Commercial Paper Article of the UCC, which of the following circumstances would prevent a person from becoming a holder in due course of an instrument?

    a.   The person was notified that payment was refused.

    b.   The person was notified that one of the prior indorsers was discharged.

    c.   The note was collateral for a loan.

    d.   The note was purchased at a discount.

40 (November 88)

A purchaser of a negotiable instrument would least likely be a holder in due course if, at the time of purchase, the instrument is

a. Purchased at a discount.
b. Collateral for a loan.
c. Payable to bearer on demand.
d. Overdue by three weeks.

4. Payee as Holder in Due Course

1 (November 80)

Who among the following can personally qualify as a holder in due course?

a. A payee.
b. A reacquirer who was not initially a holder in due course.
c. A holder to whom the instrument was negotiated as a gift.
d. A holder who had notice of a defect but who took from a prior holder in due course.

5. Shelter Provision

46 (May 95)

Under the Commercial Paper Article of the UCC, which of the following requirements must be met for a person to be a holder in due course of a promissory note?

a. The note must be payable to bearer.
b. The note must be negotiable.
c. All prior holders must have been holders in due course.
d. The holder must be the payee of the note.

38 (May 90)

Bond fraudulently induced Teal to make a note payable to Wilk, to whom Bond was indebted. Bond delivered the note to Wilk. Wilk negotiated the instrument to Monk, who purchased it with knowledge of the fraud and after it was overdue. If Wilk qualifies as a holder in due course, which of the following statements is correct?

a. Monk has the standing of a holder in due course through Wilk.
b. Teal can successfully assert the defense of fraud in the inducement against Monk.
c. Monk personally qualifies as a holder in due course.
d. Teal can successfully assert the defense of fraud in the inducement against Wilk.

41 (November 85)

Hunt has in his possession a negotiable instrument which was originally payable to the order of Carr. It was transferred to Hunt by a mere delivery by Drake, who took it from Carr in good faith in satisfaction of an antecedent debt. The back of the instrument read as follows, "Pay to the order of Drake in satisfaction of my prior purchase of a new video calculator, signed Carr." Which of the following is correct?

a. Hunt has the right to assert Drake's rights, including his standing as a holder in due course and also has the right to obtain Drake's signature.
b. Drake's taking the instrument for an antecedent debt prevents him from qualifying as a holder in due course.
c. Carr's indorsement was a special indorsement; thus Drake's signature was <u>not</u> required in order to negotiate it.
d. Hunt is a holder in due course.

Negotiable Instruments

42 (November 78)

Marlin ordered merchandise from Plant to be delivered the following day and gave Plant a check payable to its order drawn on Marlin's account in First Bank. It was agreed that the check would <u>not</u> be transferred unless delivery was received and accepted. The goods were <u>not</u> delivered and Marlin notified Plant that he exercised his right to rescind. Plant, nevertheless, negotiated the check for full value to Rose who took it in good faith and without notice of any defense. Rose then negotiated it for full value to Quirk who knew of Plant's breach of the agreement. Marlin promptly stopped payment on the check and refuses to pay it. Under these circumstances, which of the following statements is correct?

    a.   Marlin would have a valid defense in a suit by Rose for the amount of the check.

    b.   Marlin would have a valid defense in a suit by Quirk for the amount of the check.

    c.   Despite the fact that Quirk can <u>not</u> personally qualify as a holder in due course, he can assert Rose's standing as such.

    d.   A stop payment order will <u>not</u> prevent a holder in due course from collecting from the bank.

3 (May 91)

River Oaks is a wholesale distributor of automobile parts. River Oaks received the promissory note shown below from First Auto, Inc., as security for payment of a $4,400 auto parts shipment. When River Oaks accepted the note as collateral for the First Auto obligation, River Oaks was aware that the maker of the note, Hillcraft, Inc. was claiming that the note was unenforceable because Alexco Co. had breached the license agreement under which Hillcraft had given the note. First Auto had acquired the note from Smith in exchange for repairing several cars owned by Smith. At the time First Auto received the note, First Auto was unaware of the dispute between Hillcraft and Alexco. Also, Smith, who paid Alexco $3,500 for the note, was unaware of Hillcraft's allegations that Alexco had breached the license agreement.

PROMISSORY NOTE

                                                          Date: <u>1/14/90</u>

     <u>Hillcraft, Inc.</u>   promises to pay to

     <u>Alexco Co. or bearer</u>   the sum of <u>$4,400</u>

       <u>Four Thousand and 00/100</u>   Dollars

on or before   <u>May 15, 1991 (maker may elect to extend</u>

   <u>due date by 30 days)</u>   with interest thereon

at the rate of   <u>9½%</u>   per annum.

                                   Hillcraft, Inc.
                                   By: <u>/s/ P. J. Hill</u>
                                   P. J. Hill, President

Reference: <u>Alexco Licensing Agreement</u>

The reverse side of the note was indorsed as follows:

> Pay to the order of First Auto without recourse
>
> /s/ E. Smith
> E. Smith
>
> Pay to the order of River Oaks Co.
>
> First Auto
> By: /s/ G. First
> G. First, President

First Auto is now insolvent and unable to satisfy its obligation to River Oaks. Therefore, River Oaks has demanded that Hillcraft pay $4,400, but Hillcraft has refused, asserting:

- The note is nonnegotiable because it references the license agreement and is not payable at a definite time or on demand.
- River Oaks is not a holder in due course of the note because it received the note as security for amounts owed by First Auto.
- River Oaks is not a holder in due course because it was aware of the dispute between Hillcraft and Alexco.
- Hillcraft can raise the alleged breach by Alexco as a defense to payment.
- River Oaks has no right to the note because it was not indorsed by Alexco.
- The maximum amount that Hillcraft would owe under the note is $4,000, plus accrued interest.

Required:

State whether each of Hillcraft's assertions are correct and give the reasons for your conclusions.

Hillcraft's first assertion, that the note is nonnegotiable because it references the license agreement and is not payable at a definite time or on demand, is incorrect. The note is negotiable despite the reference to the license agreement because it does not make the note subject to the terms of the agreement; rather, the reference is regarded only as a recital of its existence.

Also, Hillcraft's right to extend the time for payment does not make the note nonnegotiable because the extension period is for a definite period of time.

Hillcraft's second assertion, that River Oaks is not a holder in due course (HDC) because it received the note as security for an existing debt and, therefore, did not give value for it, is incorrect. Under the UCC Commercial Paper Article, a holder does give value for an instrument when it is taken in payment of, or as security for, an antecedent claim.

Hillcraft's third assertion, that River Oaks is not an HDC because River Oaks was aware of Alexco's alleged breach of the license agreement, is correct. If a holder of a note is aware of a dispute when it acquires the note, that holder cannot be an HDC because it took with notice.

Hillcraft's fourth assertion, that it can raise the alleged breach by Alexco as a defense to payment of the note, is incorrect. Even though River Oaks is not an HDC under the UCC "shelter provision," it is entitled to the protection of an HDC because it took the instrument from First Auto, which was an HDC. Therefore, River Oaks did not take the note subject to Hillcraft's defense based on the alleged breach by Alexco. Hillcraft's defense is considered a personal defense and can only be used by Hillcraft against Alexco.

Hillcraft's fifth assertion, that River Oaks has no right to the note because it was not indorsed by Alexco, is incorrect. River Oaks acquired rights to the Hillcraft note without Alexco's indorsement because the note was a bearer instrument as a result of it being payable to "Alexco Company or bearer." A bearer instrument can be negotiated by delivery alone.

Hillcraft's final assertion, that the maximum amount Hillcraft would owe under the note is $4,000, plus accrued interest, is correct. If there is a conflict between a number written in numerals and also described by words, the words take precedence. Therefore, Hillcraft's maximum potential principal liability is $4,000 under the note.

5A (May 83)

Dunhill fraudulently obtained a negotiable promissory note from Beeler by misrepresentation of a material fact. Dunhill subsequently negotiated the note to Gordon, a holder in due course. Pine, a business associate of Dunhill, was aware of the fraud perpetrated by Dunhill. Pine purchased the note for value from Gordon. Upon presentment, Beeler has defaulted on the note.

Required: Answer the following, setting forth reasons for any conclusions stated.
1. What are the rights of Pine against Beeler?
2. What are the rights of Pine against Dunhill?

1. Pine is not a holder in due course because he has knowledge of a defense against the note. However, Pine has the rights of a holder in due course because he acquired the note through Gordon, who was a holder in due course. The rule where a transferee not a holder in due course acquires the rights of one by taking from a holder in due course is known as the "shelter rule." Through these rights, Pine is entitled to recover the proceeds of the note from Beeler. The defense of fraud in the inducement is a personal defense and not valid against a holder in due course or one with the rights of a holder in due course.

2. As one with the rights of a holder in due course, Pine is entitled to proceed against any person whose signature appears on the note, provided he gives notice of dishonor. When Dunhill negotiated the note to Gordon, Dunhill's signature on the note made him secondarily liable. As a result, if Pine brings suit against Dunhill, Pine would prevail because of Dunhill's secondary liability.

B. Rights of a Holder in Due Course
1. Taking Free of Claims

49 (November 83)

Filmore had a negotiable instrument in its possession which it had received in payment of certain equipment it had sold to Marker Merchandising. The instrument was originally payable to the order of Charles Danforth or bearer. It was indorsed specially by Danforth to Marker which in turn negotiated it to Filmore via a blank indorsement. The instrument in question, along with some cash and other negotiable instruments, was stolen from Filmore on October 1, 1981. Which of the following is correct?
a. A holder in due course will prevail against Filmore's claim to the instrument.
b. Filmore's signature was necessary in order to further negotiate the instrument.
c. The theft constitutes a common law conversion which prevents anyone from obtaining a better title to the instrument than the owner.
d. Once an instrument is bearer paper it is always bearer paper.

2. Personal Defenses
a. In General

Items 36 through 39 are based on the following:

On February 15, 1993, P. D. Stone obtained the following instrument from Astor Co. for $1,000. Stone was aware that Helco, Inc. disputed liability under the instrument because of an alleged breach by Astor of the referenced computer purchase agreement. On March 1, 1993, Willard Bank obtained the instrument from Stone for $3,900. Willard had no knowledge that Helco disputed liability under the instrument.

February 12, 1993

Helco, Inc. promises to pay to Astor Co. or bearer the sum of $4,900 (four thousand four hundred and 00/100 dollars) on March 12, 1993 (maker may elect to extend due date to March 31, 1993) with interest thereon at the rate of 12% per annum.

HELCO, INC.

By: ___/s/ A. J. Help___
A. J. Help, President

Reference: Computer purchase agreement dated February 12, 1993

The reverse side of the instrument is indorsed as follows:

Pay to the order of Willard Bank,
without recourse.

/s/ P. D. Stone
P. D. Stone

---

36 (May 93)

The instrument is a
a. Promissory note.
b. Sight draft.
c. Check.
d. Trade acceptance.

37 (May 93)

The instrument is
a. Nonnegotiable, because of the reference to the computer purchase agreement.
b. Nonnegotiable, because the numerical amount differs from the written amount.
c. Negotiable, even though the maker has the right to extend the time for payment.
d. Negotiable, when held by Astor, but nonnegotiable when held by Willard Bank.

38 (May 93)

Which of the following statements is correct?
a. Willard Bank <u>cannot</u> be a holder in due course because Stone's indorsement was without recourse.
b. Willard Bank must indorse the instrument to negotiate it.
c. Neither Willard Bank <u>nor</u> Stone are holders in due course.
d. Stone's indorsement was required for Willard Bank to be a holder in due course.

39 (May 93)

If Willard Bank demands payment from Helco and Helco refuses to pay the instrument because of Astor's breach of the computer purchase agreement, which of the following statements would be correct?
a. Willard Bank is <u>not</u> a holder in due course because Stone was <u>not</u> a holder in due course.
b. Helco will <u>not</u> be liable to Willard Bank because of Astor's breach.
c. Stone will be the only party liable to Willard Bank because he was aware of the dispute between Helco and Astor.
d. Helco will be liable to Willard Bank because Willard Bank is a holder in due course.

48 (November 90)

A maker of a note will have a valid defense against a holder in due course as a result of any of the following conditions except

    a.   Lack of consideration.

    b.   Infancy.

    c.   Forgery.

    d.   Fraud in the execution.

51 (May 89)

To the extent that a holder of a negotiable promissory note is a holder in due course, the holder takes the note free from which of the following defenses?

    a.   Non-performance of a condition precedent.

    b.   Discharge of the maker in bankruptcy.

    c.   Minority of the maker where it is a defense to enforcement of a contract.

    d.   Forgery of the maker's signature.

29 (May 79)

Archer has in his possession a bearer negotiable instrument. He took it by negotiation from Perth who had stolen it from Cox's office along with cash and other property. The robbery of Cox's office had received appropriate coverage in the local papers in the area in which both Archer and Cox reside. Archer did <u>not</u> know that Perth had stolen the instrument when he purchased it at a 20% discount. Cox refuses to pay and Archer had commenced legal action asserting that he is a holder in due course. Which of the following statements is correct?

    a.   Even if all other requisites are satisfied, Archer's title is defective in that there was <u>no</u> delivery by Cox of the instrument.

    b.   Archer is a holder in due course and will prevail.

    c.   Archer is prevented from qualifying as a holder in due course because there had been general notice published in the community about the robbery.

    d.   The discount in and of itself prevents Archer from qualifying as a holder in due course or at least prevents him from so qualifying as to the 20%.

35 (November 77)

Gardner Owen purchased some bearer bonds from P & L Securities, Inc. and gave them a promissory note. P & L Securities negotiated the instrument, for value, to Barbara Stapp by a blank indorsement. Stapp had no knowledge of the securities transaction. Stapp presented the instrument to Owen for payment on the due date. Owen refused to pay the note alleging a failure of consideration and that the securities were absolutely worthless. Stapp sued Owen on the note. What is the probable outcome of the lawsuit?

    a.   Stapp will prevail because Owen's defenses is a personal defense which is <u>not</u> assertable against Stapp.

    b.   Owen will prevail because his defense is a real defense which is assertable against Stapp.

    c.   Stapp will be required to institute suit against P & L Securities.

    d.   Owen will be required to give the bearer bonds to Stapp.

2B (November 83)

Hardy & Company was encountering financial difficulties. Melba, a persistent creditor whose account was overdue, demanded a check for the amount owed to him. Hardy's president said that this was impossible since the checking account was already overdrawn. However, he indicated he would be willing to draw on funds owed by one of the company's customers. He drafted and presented to Melba the following instrument.

October 1, 1983

TO:
Stitch Fabrications, Inc.
2272 University Avenue
Pueblo, Colorado 81001

Pay Hardy & Company, ONE THOUSAND and no/100 dollars
($1,000.00) 30 days after acceptance, for value received in connection
with our shipment of August 11, 1983.

Hardy & Company

by /s/ Charles Hardy_____, President

242 Oak Lake Drive
Hinsdale, Illinois 60521

Accepted by: _____

Hardy indorsed the instrument on the back as follows:

Pay to the order of Walter Melba

Hardy & Company

_/s/ Charles Hardy___, President

Melba asserts that he is a holder in due course.

Required: Answer the following, setting forth reasons for any conclusions stated.
1. What type of instrument is the above? How and in what circumstances is it used?
2. Is it negotiable?
3. Assume that the instrument is negotiable and accepted by Stitch, but prior to payment, Stitch discovers the goods are defective. May Stitch successfully assert this defense against Melba to avoid payment of the instrument?

1. The instrument in question is a draft and is commonly known as a trade acceptance. Such an instrument arises out of a sales transaction, whereby the seller is authorized to draw upon the purchaser for payment of the goods. Normally, as is the case here, the seller is both the drawer and the payee. The instrument is then presented for the buyer's acceptance.

2. No. The instrument lacks the "magic" words of negotiability on its face. That is, it is not payable to order or bearer but instead payable solely to Hardy & Company. The indorsement on the back of the instrument neither cures the defect nor provides the requisite words of negotiability. Hence, the instrument is not negotiable. The "for value received . . . " does not in any way affect negotiability.

3. No. Melba would be a holder in due course. He took in good faith and gave value even though the value in question is an antecedent indebtedness. The Uniform Commercial Code specifically provides that an antecedent indebtedness is value. Therefore, Melba as a holder in due course takes free of the so-called personal defenses. Breach of warranty and contractual defenses are personal defenses and a holder in due course such as Melba is not subject to them.

Negotiable Instruments

2A (May 78)

Your CPA firm was engaged to audit the Meglo Corporation. During the audit you examined the following instrument:

April 2, 1977

Charles Noreen
21 West 21st Street
St. Louis, Missouri

I, Charles Noreen, do hereby promise to pay to Roger Smith, Two Thousand Dollars ($2,000) one year from date, with 8% interest upon due presentment.

FOR: Payment for used IBM typewriters.

/s/ Charles Noreen

Meglo purchased the instrument from Smith on April 10, 1977, for $1,700. Meglo received the instrument with Smith's signature and the words "Pay to the order of Meglo Corporation" on the back. Upon maturity, Meglo presented the instrument to Noreen, who refused to pay. Noreen alleged that the typewriters were defective and did not satisfy certain warranties given in connection with the purchase of the used IBM typewriters which were guaranteed for one year. Noreen had promptly notified Smith of this fact and had told him he would not pay the full amount due.

Required: Answer the following, setting forth reasons for any conclusions stated.
1. Is the instrument in question negotiable commercial paper?
2. Assuming that the instrument is negotiable, does Meglo qualify as a holder in due course entitled to collect the full $2,000?
3. Assuming that the instrument is negotiable, is Noreen's defense valid against a holder in due course?
4. Assuming that the instrument is non-negotiable, what is the legal effect of the transfer by Smith to Meglo?

1. No. Although it meets all of the other requisites of negotiability pursuant to the Uniform Commercial Code, it lacks the specific terminology of negotiability. That is, it is neither payable to Smith's "order" nor payable to "bearer." Consequently, it is a non-negotiable promissory note. This defect is not cured by Smith's indorsement despite the fact he used the words "pay to the order of." The indication of the nature of the transaction is legally insignificant.

2. Yes. The note is not overdue, and Meglo took it for value and without notice or knowledge of any defect in it. The only possible assertion that could be made by Noreen to defeat Meglo's status as a holder in due course is that the size of the discount was so large as to indicate a lack of good faith. In the absence of any further information, a $300 discount on a one-year note such as this is not of such amount as to suggest a lack of good faith. Under these circumstances Meglo would collect the full $2,000.

3. No. It is a mere personal defense and as such would not prevail against a subsequent holder in due course.

4. Since the instrument is not negotiable it cannot be "negotiated" to another person so as to enable him to qualify as a holder in due course. However, the transferor does assign all his rights to collect on the promise. Therefore, even if the typewriters were defective, Meglo would be entitled to sue on the promise and collect the amount due, decreased by damages for breach of warranty.

6A (November 75)

Harry Fisk operates a local tuna cannery. On May 31, 1975, your client, Fair Food Wholesalers, Inc., purchased 100 cases of tuna for $12 per case, FOB Fisk's warehouse. The contract expressly stipulated that the tuna was to be first quality and all white meat in "solid chunks." It was further agreed that Fair Food had until June 10, 1975 to inspect the tuna before the transaction became final. Consequently, on May 31, 1975, Fair Food gave Fisk the following instrument:

```
                                                    No. 1625
        FAIR FOOD WHOLESALERS, INC.
                                                     1-12
                                                     210
        June 10, 1975


        Pay to the
        order of _____ Bearer _____ $1,200.00


        Twelve hundred & no/100's _____  Dollars


                               Fair Food Wholesalers, Inc.


                               By ___/s/ James Duff___
                                  James Duff, President


        CENTURY BANK
        2 Broadlane
        Providence, R.I.


        For tuna purchase from
        Harry Fisk per contract dated May 31, 1975
```

Fisk had orally agreed not to transfer the above instrument until June 10 or at the time final acceptance was manifested by Fair Food if this was earlier.

Fisk disregarded this agreement and promptly transferred the instrument to one of his creditors, Ross, who was threatening to force Fisk into bankruptcy. Ross took the instrument in good faith and without notice of any claim or defense in satisfaction of indebtedness arising from previous sales to Fisk which were overdue. The instrument was not indorsed by Fisk.

On June 10, 1975, Fair Food sample tested the tuna and found that it was not first quality and that it was not all white meat in solid chunks. Fair Food promptly notified Century Bank to stop payment on the instrument. Century did so and Ross is seeking recovery against Fair Food. In addition, Fair Food notified Fisk that it rejected the shipment and that it was holding the tuna on Fisk's behalf awaiting instructions from Fisk for disposition.

Required:

What are Ross's rights, if any, against Fair Food and Century Bank on the instrument? Explain.

Ross qualifies as a holder in due course and, as such, takes the instrument free of any and all personal defenses, i.e., in this case, breach of warranty. First, the instrument is negotiable despite the postdating of the check and the fact that it recites the transaction out of which it arose. Furthermore, because it is payable to bearer, no indorsement by Fisk is necessary to negotiate it to Ross. Nor can Fair Food rely upon the fact that no new value was given in exchange for the instrument at the time of negotiation. The Uniform Commercial Code recognizes an antecedent debt as value for satisfying the value requirement to qualify as a holder in due course. As indicated in the facts, Ross took the instrument in good faith and without notice of any claim or defense. Thus, Ross takes the instrument free of any personal defenses assertable by Fair Food against Fisk.

6B (November 74)

Herman Watts sold a used printing press to Marshall Offset, Inc. for two thousand dollars ($2,000). Watts requested that Marshall make the check payable to the order of the Foremost Finance Company because Watts was in arrears on a loan it owed to Foremost. That same day Watts delivered the check to Foremost which, in turn, presented the check and received payment from Marshall's bank.

Marshall subsequently discovered serious defects in the printing press purchased from Watts. The defects unquestionably represented a breach of the express warranties given by Watts in the contract of sale. Immediately upon discovery of the defect, Marshall notified his bank to stop payment but this was several days after the bank had processed the check.

Watts is hopelessly insolvent. Marshall seeks to rescind the transaction and recover the payment on the check from Foremost or its own bank.

Required:

What legal remedies are available to Marshall in the situation described? Explain.

Marshall has no rights against Foremost or its own bank. Both qualify as holders in due course and will prevail against the personal defense of breach of warranty. The fact that the check was initially made payable to the order of Foremost does not prevent Foremost from qualifying as a holder in due course if it gave value and took the check in good faith. An antecedent debt constitutes value, and there is no indication of any facts which would establish a lack of good faith on Foremost's part. The bank also qualifies as a holder in due course. The stop order is ineffective because it was initiated too late. Thus, Marshall's only recourse is to proceed against Watts.

b. Unauthorized Completion

49 (November 91)

Cobb gave Garson a signed check with the amount payable left blank. Garson was to fill in, as the amount, the price of fuel oil Garson was to deliver to Cobb at a later date. Garson estimated the amount at $700, but told Cobb it would be no more than $900. Garson did not deliver the fuel oil, but filled in the amount of $1,000 on the check. Garson then negotiated the check to Josephs in satisfaction of a $500 debt with the $500 balance paid to Garson in cash. Cobb stopped payment and Josephs is seeking to collect $1,000 from Cobb. Cobb's maximum liability to Josephs will be

    a. $0
    b. $ 500
    c. $ 900
    d. $1,000

39 (May 90)

A holder in due course will take free of which of the following defenses?

    a. Infancy, to the extent that it is a defense to a simple contract.
    b. Discharge of the maker in bankruptcy.
    c. A wrongful filling-in of the amount payable that was omitted from the instrument.
    d. Duress of a nature that renders the obligation of the party a nullity.

44 (November 89)

Silver Corp. sold 20 tons of steel to River Corp. with payment to be by River's check. The price of steel was fluctuating daily. Silver requested that the amount of River's check be left blank and Silver would fill in the current market price. River complied with Silver's request. Within two days, Silver received River's check. Although the market price of 20 tons of steel at the time Silver received River's check was $80,000, Silver filled in the check for $100,000 and negotiated it to Hatch Corp. Hatch took the check in good faith, without notice of Silver's act or any other defense, and in payment of an antecedent debt. River will

    a. Not be liable to Hatch, because the check was materially altered by Silver.
    b. Not be liable to Hatch, because Hatch failed to give value when it acquired the check from Silver.
    c. Be liable to Hatch for $100,000.
    d. Be liable to Hatch, but only for $80,000.

38 (November 81)

Clarkson received a check from Shipley which was incomplete as to the amount. The check was given as payment in advance on the purchase of 100 CB radios. The amount was left blank because Clarkson had the right to substitute other CB models if available for those ordered, which would change the price. It was agreed that in no event would the purchase price exceed $1,800. Desperate for cash, Clarkson wrongfully substituted much more expensive CB radios thereby increasing the purchase price to $2,200. Clarkson then negotiated the check to Marshall, one of his suppliers. Clarkson filled in the $2,200 in Marshall's presence showing him the shipping order and invoice applicable to the sale to Shipley. Marshall accepted the check in payment of $1,400 overdue debts and $800 in cash. Under the circumstances, Marshall is

    a.   A holder in due course but only to the extent of the $800 in cash.
    b.   A holder in due course and entitled to recover the full amount.
    c.   Not a holder in due course because the amount filled in was greater than authorized.
    d.   Not a holder in due course because the instrument was completed in his presence.

42 (November 81)

Dilworth, an employee of Excelsior Super Markets, Inc., stole his payroll check from the cashier before it was completed. The check was properly made out to his order but the amount payable had not been filled in because Dilworth's final time sheet had not yet been received. Dilworth filled in the amount which was $300 in excess of his proper pay and cashed it at the Good Luck Tavern. Good Luck took the check in good faith and without suspecting that the instrument had been improperly completed. Excelsior's bank paid the instrument in due course. Excelsior is demanding that the bank credit its account for the $300 or that it be paid by Good Luck. Which of the following is correct?

    a.   Good Luck has <u>no</u> liability for the return of the $300.
    b.   Excelsior's bank must credit Excelsior's account for the $300.
    c.   A theft defense would be good against all parties including Good Luck.
    d.   Only in the event that negligence on Excelsior's part can be shown will Excelsior bear the loss.

25 (May 79)

Martindale Retail Fish Stores, Inc. purchased a large quantity of fish from the Seashore Fish Wholesalers. The exact amount was <u>not</u> ascertainable at the moment, and Martindale, rather than waiting for the exact amount, gave Seashore a check which was blank as to the amount. Seashore promised <u>not</u> to fill in any amount until it had talked to Martindale's purchasing agent and had the amount approved. Seashore disregarded this agreement and filled in an amount that was $300 in excess of the correct price. The instrument was promptly negotiated to Clambake & Company, one of Seashore's persistent creditors, in payment of an account due. Martindale promptly stopped payment. For what amount will Martindale be liable to Clambake? Why?

    a.   Nothing because Martindale can assert the real defense of material alteration.
    b.   Nothing because Clambake did not give value and the stop order is effective against it.
    c.   Only the correct amount because the wrongful filling in of the check for the $300 excess amount was illegal.
    d.   The full amount because the check is in the hands of a holder in due course.

35 (May 76)

During the course of your audit you discover a dispute concerning one of your client's checks. The check had been sent to a supplier but without indicating the sum on the face of the instrument. The supplier fraudulently filled in the check for $500 more than amount indicated in the letter which accompanied the check. A subsequent holder in due course is asserting the right to recover the full amount stated in the completed instrument.

    a.   Alteration is a complete defense against all parties.
    b.   The holder in due course can only collect an amount equal to the authorized amount.
    c.   The holder in due course may enforce the instrument as completed.
    d.   The holder in due course must first proceed against the fraudulent supplier.

3. Real Defenses

49 (May 95)

Under the Commercial Paper Article of the UCC, in a nonconsumer transaction, which of the following are real defenses available against a holder in due course?

	Material alteration	Discharge in bankruptcy	Breach of contract
a.	No	Yes	Yes
b.	Yes	Yes	No
c.	No	No	Yes
d.	Yes	No	No

40 (November 92)

A maker of a note will have a real defense against a holder in due course as a result of any of the following conditions except

    a. Discharge in bankruptcy.

    b. Forgery.

    c. Fraud in the execution.

    d. Lack of consideration.

47 (May 92)

To the extent that a holder of a negotiable promissory note is a holder in due course, the holder takes the note free of which of the following defenses?

    a. Minority of the maker where it is a defense to enforcement of a contract.

    b. Forgery of the maker's signature.

    c. Discharge of the maker in bankruptcy.

    d. Nonperformance of a condition precedent.

50 (November 87)

A holder in due course of a negotiable promissory note will take the note subject to which of the following defenses?

    a. Fraud in the inducement.

    b. Failure of consideration.

    c. Unauthorized signature.

    d. Breach of contract.

52 (November 84)

Which of the following is a valid defense against a holder in due course of a negotiable instrument?

    a. Execution of the instrument by one without authority to sign the instrument.

    b. Fraudulent statements made to the drawer as to the value of the consideration given for the instrument.

    c. Duress on the drawer which renders the instrument voidable at the drawer's option.

    d. Delivery of the instrument subject to a condition precedent which has yet to be performed.

44 (May 84)

Which of the following defenses may be successfully asserted by the maker against a holder in due course?

    a. Wrongful filling in of an incomplete instrument by a prior holder.

    b. Total failure to perform the contractual undertaking for which the instrument was given.

    c. Fraudulent misrepresentations as to the consideration given by a prior holder in exchange for the negotiable instrument.

    d. Discharge of the maker of the instrument in bankruptcy proceedings.

43 (November 82)

Dodger fraudulently induced Tell to issue a check to his order for $900 in payment for some nearly worthless securities. Dodger took the check and artfully raised the amount from $900 to $1,900. He promptly negotiated the check to Bay who took in good faith and for value. Tell, upon learning of the fraud, issued a stop order to its bank. Which of the following is correct?

    a.   Dodger has a real defense which will prevent any of the parties from collecting anything.

    b.   The stop order was ineffective against Bay since it was issued after the negotiation to Bay.

    c.   Bay as a holder in due course will prevail against Tell but only to the extent of $900.

    d.   Had there been no raising of the amount by Dodger, the bank would be obligated to pay Bay despite the stop order.

38 (May 82)

Cindy Lake is a holder in due course of a negotiable promissory note for $1,000. Which of the following defenses of the maker may be validly asserted against her?

    a.   A total failure of consideration on the part of the party to whom it was issued.

    b.   A wrongful filling in of the amount on the instrument by the party to whom it was issued.

    c.   Non-performance of a condition precedent to its transfer by the party to whom it was issued.

    d.   Infancy of the maker to the extent that it is a defense to a simple contract.

43 (November 81)

Wilbur executed and delivered a check for $80 payable to the order of Muldowney. Muldowney raised the amount to $800, and negotiated it to Lester, who took the check in good faith and for value without notice of the alteration. When Lester presented it for payment to the bank, the bank refused to honor it due to insufficient funds in Wilbur's account. Lester is seeking to collect the $800 from Wilbur. Which of the following is correct?

    a.   Lester is a holder in due course, but is only entitled to collect $80 from Wilbur unless Wilbur's negligence facilitated the alteration.

    b.   The bank's dishonor of the instrument was wrongful.

    c.   Wilbur is liable for $800 since Lester is a holder in due course and the defense is a personal defense.

    d.   The material alteration of the check by Muldowney released Wilbur from all liability to subsequent parties.

32 (May 79)

Franco & Sons, Inc. was engaged in the furniture manufacturing business. One of its bi-weekly paychecks was payable to Stein, who negotiated it to White in payment of a gambling debt. White proceeded to raise the amount of the check from $300 to $800 and negotiated it to Carson, a holder in due course, for cash. Upon presentment by Carson at the drawee bank, the teller detected the raising of the amount and contacted Franco who stopped payment on the check. Franco refuses to pay Carson. Carson is seeking to recover the $800. Under the circumstances, which of the following is a correct statement?

    a.   Franco is liable, but only for $300.

    b.   Franco is liable for the $800.

    c.   Stein is liable for the $800.

    d.   Franco has <u>no</u> liability to Carson.

1 (May 74)

John executed and delivered his check for $2,000 on May 1 payable to the order of Ken who indorsed the check to the order of Lyons for value. Despite John's care in executing the check, Lyons was able to raise the amount to $20,000 and on May 3 transferred it by blank indorsement to Marks who took the check for value and in good faith without notice of the alteration. If the drawee bank refuses to honor the check because of insufficient funds

    a.   Marks would have an action against the bank for failure to pay available funds in John's account.

    b.   Marks would bear the entire loss since the check was nullified by the alteration, though he would have an action against Lyons.

    c.   Marks, as a holder in due course, could recover $20,000 from John.

    d.   Marks, as a holder in due course, could recover $2,000 from John.

3B (November 79)

Grover had an $80 check payable to the order of Parker that Parker had indorsed in blank. The check was drawn by Madison on State Bank. Grover deftly raised the amount to $800 and cashed it at Friendly Check Cashing Company. Friendly promptly presented it at State Bank where it was dishonored as an overdraft. Grover has been apprehended by the police and is awaiting trial. He has no known assets. Friendly is seeking collection on the instrument against any or all of the other parties involved.

Required: Answer the following, setting forth reasons for any conclusions stated.
Will Friendly recover against Madison, State Bank, or Parker?

Grover materially altered the instrument within the meaning of Uniform Commercial Code § 3-407, which provides that a holder in due course, such as Friendly, in all cases may enforce the instrument according to its original tenor. Thus, Friendly would be entitled to recover $80, the original tenor of the instrument, from Madison.

Friendly is entitled to nothing from State Bank. The bank rightfully dishonored the instrument, but even had it done so wrongfully, Friendly has no relationship to the bank and hence no right to recover from it.

Parker, as a transferor of the instrument by indorsement, gave certain implied warranties, including that the instrument had not been materially altered. This warranty is at the time of transfer and is not a warranty that the instrument will not be subsequently altered, as it was in this case. Although there would appear to be no recourse against Parker under the alteration warranty, in the event of dishonor by the maker, Parker is liable on the instrument according to its tenor ($80) at the time of indorsement.

There is one possibility for full recovery against Madison; Friendly must assert and prove that Madison was negligent in the way he drafted the instrument and thereby contributed to the alteration.

V. Liability of Parties--Contract Liability
A. Primary v. Secondary Liability

50 (May 95)

```
Pay to Ann Tyler
/s/ Paul Tyler

/s/ Ann Tyler


/s/ Mary Thomas

/s/ Betty Ash

Pay George Green Only
/s/ Susan Town
```

Susan Town, on receiving the above instrument, struck Betty Ash's indorsement. Under the Commercial Paper Article of the UCC, which of the indorsers of the above instrument will be completely discharged from secondary liability to later indorsers of the instrument?

a. Ann Tyler
b. Mary Thomas
c. Betty Ash
d. Susan Town

42 (May 93)

Robb, a minor, executed a promissory note payable to bearer and delivered it to Dodsen in payment for a stereo system. Dodsen negotiated the note for value to Mellon by delivery alone and without indorsement. Mellon indorsed the note in blank and negotiated it to Bloom for value. Bloom's demand for payment was refused by Robb because the note was executed when Robb was a minor. Bloom gave prompt notice of Robb's default to Dodsen and Mellon. None of the holders of the note were aware of Robb's minority. Which of the following parties will be liable to Bloom?

	Dodsen	Mellon
a.	Yes	Yes
b.	Yes	No
c.	No	No
d.	No	Yes

28 (May 86)

Frank Supply Co. held the following instrument:

Clark Novelties, Inc.   April 12, 1986
29 State Street
Spokane, Washington

Pay to the order of Frank Supply Co. on April 30, 1986 ten thousand and 00/100 dollars ($10,000.00).

                                             Smith Industries, Inc.

                                             ___/s/ J. C. Kahn___
                                             J. C. Kahn, President

ACCEPTED: Clark Novelties, Inc.
BY:
/s/ Mitchell Clark
Mitchell Clark, President

Date: April 20, 1986

As a result of an audit examination of this instrument which was properly indorsed by Frank to your client, it may be correctly concluded that

a. Smith was primarily liable on the instrument prior to acceptance.

b. The instrument is non-negotiable and thus no one has rights under the instrument.

c. No one was primarily liable on the instrument at the time of issue, April 12, 1986.

d. Upon acceptance, Clark Novelties, Inc. became primarily liable and Smith was released from all liability.

41 (May 82)

Your client, Ensign Factors Corporation, has purchased the trade acceptance shown below from Mason Art Productions, Inc. It has been properly indorsed in blank on the back by Mason.

```
                                                October 15, 1981
Adams Wholesalers, Inc.
49 Buena Vista Avenue
Santa Monica, California

Pay to the order of Mason Art Productions, Inc., ten thousand and
00/00 dollars ($10,000.00).


                                    ____/s/ Gilda Loucksi____
                                    Gilda Loucksi, President
                                    Mason Art Productions, Inc.


Accepted  October 24, 1981


Adams Wholesalers, Inc.
By /s/ Charles Lurch, President
```

As to the rights of Ensign, which of the following is correct?
  a. The instrument is non-negotiable, hence Ensign is an assignee.
  b. Until acceptance, Mason had primary liability on the instrument.
  c. After acceptance by Adams Wholesalers, Adams is primarily liable and Mason is secondarily liable.
  d. After acceptance by Adams, Mason is primarily liable, and Adams is secondarily liable.

38 (November 82)

Kirk made a check payable to Haskin's order for a debt she owed on open account. Haskin negotiated the check by a blank indorsement to Carlson who deposited it in his checking account. The bank returned the check with the notation that payment was refused due to insufficient funds. Kirk is insolvent. Under the circumstances
  a. Kirk has a real defense assertable against all parties including Carlson, a holder in due course.
  b. If Kirk files for bankruptcy, Haskin or Carlson could successfully assert that there had been an assignment of whatever funds were in Kirk's checking account.
  c. If there is a proper presentment, and notice is properly given by Carlson to Haskin, Carlson may recover the amount of the check from Haskin.
  d. Haskin or Carlson can correctly assert the standing of a secured creditor.

34 (November 77)

Wilson drew a sight draft on Foxx, a customer who owed Wilson money on an open account, payable to the order of Burton, one of Wilson's creditors. Burton presented it to Foxx. After examining the draft as to its authenticity and after checking the amount against outstanding debts to Wilson, Foxx wrote on its face "Accepted--payable in 10 days" and signed it. When Burton returned at the end of the ten days, Foxx told him he could not pay and was hard pressed for cash. Burton did not notify Wilson of these facts. Two days later when Burton again presented the instrument for payment, Burton was told that Foxx's creditors had filed a petition in bankruptcy that morning. Which of the following statements is correct?
  a. The instrument in question is a type of demand promissory note.
  b. Wilson had primary liability on the draft at its inception.
  c. Foxx was secondarily liable on the instrument prior to acceptance.
  d. Foxx assumed primary liability at the time of acceptance.

306

36 (May 76)

Fenster has a negotiable trade acceptance in his possession. It is signed by Edwards and orders Wilberforce, a trade debtor of Edwards, to pay Fenster ten days after acceptance. Wilberforce has <u>not</u> yet accepted the instrument.

    a.   The instrument is not negotiable until acceptance.

    b.   Wilberforce <u>cannot</u> refuse to accept the instrument without incurring liability to Fenster.

    c.   <u>No</u> one presently has primary liability on the instrument.

    d.   A mere refusal to accept as contrasted with a refusal to pay will not constitute a dishonor.

9 (May 74)

Teff entered Archer's office and stole from Archer some radios and Archer's wallet containing identification. Subsequently, representing himself as Archer, Teff induced Bane to purchase one of the stolen radios for a fair price. Bane gave Teff his check made out to Archer. Teff indorsed the check "Pay to the order of Crown, Archer" and transferred it to Crown for cash in the amount of the check. Crown indorsed the check "Pay to the order of Fox, Crown" and transferred the check to Fox to be applied to his account.

If the drawee bank refuses to honor the check on timely presentment by Fox, he

    a.   Has a cause of action against the bank.

    b.   Can only succeed in an action against Teff because of his fraudulent acts.

    c.   Must proceed against Bane before resorting to any right against any of the indorsers.

    d.   Can, after timely notice of dishonor, require Crown to pay the amount of the check.

3 (November 94)

During an audit of Trent Realty Corp.'s financial statements, Clark, CPA, reviewed the following instruments:

A. Instrument 1.

$300,000   Belle, MD September 15, 1993 For value received, ten years after date, I promise to pay to the order of Dart Finance Co. Three Hundred Thousand and 00/100 dollars with interest at 9% per annum compounded annually until fully paid. This instrument arises out of the sale of land located in MD. It is further agreed that: 1. Maker will pay all costs of collection including reasonable attorney fees. 2. Maker may prepay the amount outstanding on any anniversary date of this instrument.   <u>/s/ G. Evans</u>   G. Evans

The following transactions relate to Instrument 1.

    ▪   On March 15, 1994, Dart indorsed the instrument in blank and sold it to Morton for $275,000.

    ▪   On July 10, 1994, Evans informed Morton that Dart had fraudulently induced Evans into signing the instrument.

    ▪   On August 15, 1994, Trent, which knew of Evans' claim against Dart, purchased the instrument from Morton for $50,000.

Required: Items 76 through 80 relate to Instrument 1. For each item, select from List I the correct answer. An answer may be selected once, more than once, or not at all.

List I

76. Instrument 1 is a (type of instrument)

77. Instrument 1 is (negotiability)

78. Morton is considered a (type of ownership)

79. Trent is considered a (type of ownership)

80. Trent could recover on the instrument from (liable party(s))

A. Draft
B. Promissory note
C. Security Agreement
D. Holder
E. Holder in due course
F. Holder with rights of a holder in due course under the Shelter Provision
G. Negotiable
H. Nonnegotiable
I. Evans, Morton, and Dart
J. Morton and Dart
K. Only Dart

B. Instrument 2.

Front

```
To: Pure Bank
Upton, VT
                                          April 5, 1994

Pay to the order of M. West $1,500.00 One Thousand Five Hundred and
00/100 Dollars on May 1, 1994

                                    /s/ W. Fields
                                    W. Fields
```

Back

```
/s/ M. West

Pay to C. Larr
/s/ T. Keetin

/s/ C. Larr
without recourse
```

Required: Items 81 through 88 relate to Instrument 2. For each item, select from List II the correct answer. An answer may be selected once, more than once, or not at all.

List II

81. Instrument 2 is a (type of instrument)

82. Instrument 2 is (negotiability)

83. West's indorsement makes the instrument (type of instrument)

84. Keetin's indorsement makes the instrument (type of instrument)

85. Larr's indorsement makes the instrument (type of instrument)

86. West's indorsement would be considered (type of indorsement)

87. Keetin's indorsement would be considered (type of indorsement)

88. Larr's indorsement would be considered (type of indorsement)

A. Bearer paper
B. Blank
C. Check
D. Draft
E. Negotiable
F. Nonnegotiable
G. Note
H. Order paper
I. Qualified
J. Special

B. Certified Checks

41 (November 92)

A check has the following indorsements on the back:

```
/s/ Paul Folk
without recourse

/s/ George Hopkins
payment guaranteed

/s/ Ann Quarry
collection guaranteed

/s/ Rachel Ott
```

Which of the following conditions occurring subsequent to the indorsements would **discharge all of the indorsers**?
a. Lack of notice of dishonor.
b. Late presentment.
c. Insolvency of the maker.
d. Certification of the check.

41 (November 89)

For which of the following negotiable instruments is a bank <u>not</u> an acceptor?
a. Cashier's check.
b. Certified check.
c. Certificate of deposit.
d. Bank acceptance.

C. Accommodation Parties

43 (May 93)

Vex Corp. executed a negotiable promissory note payable to Tamp, Inc. The note was collateralized by some of Vex's business assets. Tamp negotiated the note to Miller for value. Miller indorsed the note in blank and negotiated it to Bilco for value. Before the note became due, Bilco agreed to release Vex's collateral. Vex refused to pay Bilco when the note became due. Bilco promptly notified Miller and Tamp of Vex's default. Which of the following statements is correct?
a. Bilco will be unable to collect from Miller because Miller's indorsement was in blank.
b. Bilco will be able to collect from either Tamp or Miller because Bilco was a holder in due course.
c. Bilco will be unable to collect from either Tamp or Miller because Bilco's release of the collateral.
d. Bilco will be able to collect from Tamp because Tamp was the original payee.

6 (November 80)

Marshall Franks purchased $1,050 worth of inventory for his business from Micro Enterprises. Micro insisted on the signature of Franks' former partner, Hobart, before credit would be extended. Hobart reluctantly signed. Franks delivered the following instrument to Micro:

January 15, 1980

We, the undersigned, do hereby promise to pay to the order of Micro Enterprises, Inc., One Thousand and Fifty Dollars ($1,050.00) on the 15th of April, 1980.

/s/ Marshall Franks
Marshall Franks

/s/ Norman Hobart
Norman Hobart

Memo:
N. Hobart signed as an
accommodation for Franks

Franks defaulted on the due date. Which of the following is correct?
a. The instrument is non-negotiable.
b. Hobart is liable on the instrument but only for $525.
c. Since it was known to Micro that Hobart signed as an accommodation party, Micro must first proceed against Franks.
d. Hobart is liable on the instrument for the full amount and is obligated to satisfy it immediately upon default.

27 (November 77)
The typical conditional guarantor of collection is
a. Liable only upon the creditor's establishing that the debtor has fled the jurisdiction.
b. Liable upon the creditor establishing that he has had a judgment returned unsatisfied.
c. Not entitled to the usual defenses asserted by other typical types of sureties.
d. Not entitled to the right of subrogation.

39 (November 77)
Wixstad asked Montrose, his father-in-law, to sign a note as an accommodation co-maker. Montrose did this for Wixstad as a personal favor to his daughter. Both indorsed the note for value to Carlton who had knowledge that Montrose had signed the note for Wixstad's accommodation only. With respect to Montrose's rights and liabilities, which of the following is correct?
a. Carlton has the right to treat either or both parties as primarily liable on the note.
b. Carlton's best basis for recovery is to sue Montrose as an indorser.
c. Montrose has no liability beyond one-half of the face value of the note plus interest.
d. In the event Wixstad defaults on the note, notice must be promptly given to Montrose in order to hold him liable.

34 (May 76)
One who signs as an accommodation party to a negotiable instrument
a. Has the same liability on the instrument whether he signs as an accommodation maker or as an accommodation indorser.
b. Has a right of recourse against the party he accommodated.
c. Cannot be held liable against a subsequent holder in due course if the party he accommodated has a contract (personal) defense against the party to whom the instrument was originally issued.
d. Has no liability to any subsequent taker who knew of the accommodation.

VI. Liability of Parties--Forgery and Alteration
A. Basic Concepts of Forgery and Alteration--Unauthorized Signatures, Warranties on Presentment and Transfer, and Alteration

9 (November 80)

An otherwise valid negotiable bearer note is signed with the forged signature of Darby. Archer, who believed he knew Darby's signature, bought the note in good faith from Harding, the forger. Archer transferred the note without indorsement to Barker, in partial payment of a debt. Barker then sold the note to Chase for 80% of its face amount and delivered it without indorsement. When Chase presented the note for payment at maturity, Darby refused to honor it, pleading forgery. Chase gave proper notice of dishonor to Barker and to Archer. Which of the following statements best describes the situation from Chase's standpoint?

    a. Chase can not qualify as a holder in due course for the reason that he did not pay face value for the note.

    b. Chase can hold Barker liable on the ground that Barker warranted to Chase that neither Darby nor Archer had any defense valid against Barker.

    c. Chase can hold Archer liable on the ground that Archer warranted to Chase that Darby's signature was genuine.

    d. Chase can not hold Harding, the forger, liable on the note because his signature does not appear on it and thus, he made no warranties to Chase.

3 (May 74)

The transferor of a bearer negotiable instrument who transfers without indorsing but for full consideration

    a. Is liable to all subsequent holders if there exists a personal defense to the instrument maintainable by the primary party and the transferor was aware of the defense.

    b. Warranties to his immediate transferee that he has good title.

    c. Makes no warranty that prior signatures are genuine or authorized.

    d. Engages that he will pay the instrument if his immediate transferor is unable to obtain payment upon due presentment and dishonor because of insufficient funds and due notice is given the transferor.

5B (November 76)

Davidson was one of Fenner Corporation's chief stock clerks. His net weekly salary was $125. Unfortunately, he lost a substantial sum of money betting on sports events, and he owed $2,000 to the loan sharks. Under these circumstances, he decided to raise the amount of his paychecks to $725 per week. His strategem was to wait until the assistant treasurer, in whose office the paymaster check imprinting machine was located, was away from his desk. He would then go into the office and artfully strike the number 7 over the number 1 and raise the paycheck amount from $125 to $725. The checks were promptly negotiated to Smith, a holder in due course, who cashed them at his own bank, and the checks were subsequently paid by Fenner's bank, Beacon National. The fraudulent scheme was discovered within a week after Beacon returned Fenner's canceled checks for the month. By that time five weekly paychecks had been raised by Davidson and cashed by Smith. Fenner promptly notified Beacon of the fraud.

Required: Answer the following, setting forth reasons for any conclusions stated.

    1. To whom is Davidson liable?

    2. What are the rights and liabilities of Fenner?

    3. What are the rights and liabilities of Beacon?

    4. What are the rights and liabilities of Smith?

1. The embezzler, Davidson, is liable to whichever party bears the ultimate loss.

2. Fenner Corporation would normally be able to recover $600 per check from Beacon National because it has a real defense (material alteration), which is valid even against a holder in due course. However, Beacon National has a possible defense of contributory negligence by Fenner on the basis that Fenner did not exercise proper safeguards to prevent improper use of the check-imprinting machine. The Uniform Commercial Code provides that any person who by his negligence substantially contributes to a material alteration of the instrument is precluded from asserting the alteration against a holder in due course or against a drawee or other payor who pays the instrument in good faith and in accordance with the reasonable commercial standards of the drawee's or payor's business. In any event, Fenner is still liable to the extent of the original amount of $125 per check.

3. Normally, Beacon National must credit Fenner's account for the overpayments. It in turn has an action against the parties indorsing the instruments based upon a breach of their warranty that there were not material alterations. However, as discussed above, the possible defense of contributory negligence would be equally applicable here.

4. Smith as a holder in due course, has the same rights and liabilities as Beacon National as they are given above.

B. Forgery and Alteration--Specific Problems
1. Payment on Forged Drawer's or Maker's Signature; Payment on Forged Indorsement

15 (May 80)

Mask stole one of Bloom's checks. The check was already signed by Bloom and made payable to Duval. The check was drawn on United Trust Company. Mask forged Duval's signature on the back of the check and cashed the check at the Corner Check Cashing Company which in turn deposited it with its bank, Town National Bank of Toka. Town National proceeded to collect on the check from United. None of the parties mentioned was negligent. Who will bear the loss assuming the amount <u>cannot</u> be recovered from Mask?

    a. Bloom.
    b. Duval.
    c. United Trust Company.
    d. Corner Check Cashing Company.

30 (May 80)

Robb stole one of Markum's blank checks, made it payable to himself, and forged Markum's signature to it. The check was drawn on the Unity Trust Company. Robb cashed the check at the Friendly Check Cashing Company which in turn deposited it with its bank, the Farmer's National. Farmer's National proceeded to collect on the check from Unity Trust. The theft and forgery were quickly discovered by Markum who promptly notified Unity. None of the parties mentioned was negligent. Who will bear the loss, assuming the amount <u>cannot</u> be recovered from Robb.

    a. Markum.
    b. Unity Trust Company.
    c. Friendly Check Cashing Company.
    d. Farmer's National.

30 (May 79)

Path stole a check made out to the order of Marks. Path forged the name of Marks on the back and made the instrument payable to himself. He then negotiated the check to Harrison for cash by signing his own name on the back of the instrument in Harrison's presence. Harrison was unaware of any of the facts surrounding the theft or forged indorsement and presented the check for payment. Central County Bank, the drawee bank, paid it. Disregarding Path, which of the following will bear the loss?

    a. The drawer of the check payable to Marks.
    b. Central County Bank.
    c. Marks.
    d. Harrison.

2. Impostors and Fictitious Payees

19 (May 80)

Gomer developed a fraudulent system whereby he could obtain checks payable to the order of certain repairmen who serviced various large corporations. Gomer observed the delivery trucks of repairmen who did business with the corporations, and then he submitted bills on the bogus letterhead of the repairmen to the selected large corporations. The return envelope for payment indicated a local post office box. When the checks arrived, Gomer would forge the payees' signatures and cash the checks. The parties cashing the checks are holders in due course. Who will bear the loss assuming the amount cannot be recovered from Gomer?

    a.   The defrauded corporations.

    b.   The drawee banks.

    c.   Intermediate parties who indorsed the instruments for collection.

    d.   The ultimate recipients of the proceeds of the checks even though they are holders in due course.

47 (November 78)

Davidson bore a remarkable physical resemblance to Ford, one of the town's most prominent citizens. He presented himself one day at the Friendly Finance Company, represented himself as Ford, and requested a loan of $500. The manager mistakenly, but honestly, believed that Davidson was Ford. Accordingly, being anxious to please so prominent a citizen, the manager required no collateral and promptly delivered to Davidson a $500 check payable to the order of Ford. Davidson took the check and signed Ford's name to it on the back and negotiated it to Robbins, who took in the ordinary course of business (in good faith and for value). Upon learning the real facts, Friendly stopped payment on the check. Robbins now seeks recovery against Friendly. Under these circumstances, which of the following statements is correct?

    a.   Friendly could not validly stop payment on the check.

    b.   Davidson's signature of Ford's name on the check constitutes a forgery and is a real defense which is valid against Robbins.

    c.   Since both Friendly and Robbins were mistaken as to Davidson's real identity, they will share the loss equally.

    d.   Davidson's signature of Ford's name on the check is effective and Robbins will prevail against Friendly.

43 (November 77)

Hawkins, the assistant to the controller of a general partnership, told the controller that the firm owed Samuel $500. The alleged Samuel represented by Hawkins to be a creditor was a fictitious person. Relying upon Hawkins' statement, the controller signed the firm's name to a check. Hawkins indorsed the check on its back, signing the name "Henry Samuel," and cashed it at a liquor store. People's Bank charged the firm's account for the $500 and returned it with the rest of the checks for the month. Subsequently, the auditors detected the fraudulent conduct on Hawkins' part. Which of the following statements is true regarding the liability of the various parties involved?

    a.   The partnership has a real defense which will allow it to avoid liability.

    b.   The liquor store cannot qualify as a holder in due course since Samuel was a fictitious person.

    c.   The partnership is liable on the check despite the fact that Samuel is a fictitious person and the signature is considered a forgery.

    d.   People's Bank will not prevail as against the partnership since the payee was a fictitious person.

VII. Bank Deposits and Collections; Relationship Between Payor Bank and Its Customer

39 (November 88)

In general, which of the following statements is correct concerning the priority among checks drawn on a particular account and presented to the drawee bank on a particular day?

    a.   The checks may be charged to the account in any order convenient to the bank.

    b.   The checks may be charged to the account in any order provided no charge creates an overdraft.

    c.   The checks must be charged to the account in the order in which the checks were dated.

    d.   The checks must be charged to the account in the order of lowest amount to highest amount to minimize the number of dishonored checks.

8 (November 80)

Harrison obtained from Bristow his $11,500 check drawn on the Union National Bank in payment for bogus uranium stock. He immediately negotiated it by a blank indorsement to Dunlop in return for $1,000 in cash and her check for $10,400. Dunlop qualified as a holder in due course. She deposited the check in her checking account in the Oceanside Bank. Upon discovering that the stock was bogus, Bristow notified Union National to stop payment on his check, which it did. The check was returned to Oceanside Bank, which in turn debited Dunlop's account and returned the check to her. Which of the following statements is correct?

    a. Dunlop can collect from Union National Bank since Bristow's stop payment order was invalid in that the defense was only a personal defense.

    b. Oceanside's debiting of Dunlop's account was improper since she qualified as a holder in due course.

    c. Dunlop can recover $11,500 from Bristow despite the stop order, since she qualified as a holder in due course.

    d. Dunlop will be entitled to collect only $1,000.

5A (November 76)

Barton Fashion, Inc. was in poor financial condition and desperate for cash. Wilcox, its major owner and president, contacted Marvel Department Store, Inc. and offered to sell them 2,000 genuine alligator handbags at a bargain price. Wilcox presented several of the bags to Marvel's chief purchasing officer. These were duly examined and found to be of first quality in every respect. Marvel's chief purchasing officer placed an order with Barton for the 2,000 handbags. Payment was to be made upon delivery and inspection by Marvel. In fact, Barton had about 100 real alligator bags, the rest were clever imitations. Wilcox had the cartons packed in such a way that the genuine alligator bags were on the top of each carton. The shipment was made, and Marvel's initial inspection revealed that everything was apparently in order. Marvel delivered a check to Barton's agent who turned it over to Wilcox. Wilcox as president of Barton promptly negotiated the check to Walker, one of Barton's creditors who was threatening to file bankruptcy proceedings against Barton. Barton received $3,000 in cash and full credit against its debt to Walker for the balance of the check. Upon discovery of the fraud, Marvel promptly notified its bank, First Commerce, to stop payment on the check. When the check was presented for payment the next day, payment was refused.

Required: Answer the following, setting forth reasons for any conclusions stated.

    1. What are the rights of Walker against First Commerce?

    2. What are the rights of Walker against Marvel?

    3. What are the rights of Marvel against Walker?

    4. What are the rights of Marvel against Barton?

    1. Walker has no rights against First Commerce. First Commerce validly obeyed its customer's stop order. Hence, under the circumstances it had no potential liability to Walker.

    2. Walker, as a holder in due course, has a valid claim against Marvel. The defense in question is a mere personal defense and as such is not available against a holder in due course. Furthermore, Walker may collect in full; both the cash and antecedent indebtedness constitute "value" under the Uniform Commercial Code.

    3. Marvel has the right to recover any damages for loss from Wilcox because Wilcox acted in a fraudulent manner by misrepresentation followed by concealment of goods that did not conform to the contract. The fact that Wilcox was acting in an agency capacity will not relieve him from liability to Marvel.

    4. Barton is liable to Marvel for the actions taken by its agent, Wilcox, who acted in a fraudulent manner. The basic rule establishing the principal's liability for his agent's tort is applicable. Furthermore, Barton received the benefit of the $3,000 cash paid on the check and credit for the balance on its indebtedness owing to Walker.

VIII. Documents of Title and Letters of Credit

20 (R01)

Under the Documents of Title Article of the UCC, which of the following statements is(are) correct regarding a common carrier's duty to deliver goods subject to a negotiable, bearer bill of lading?

    I. The carrier may deliver the goods to any party designated by the holder of the bill of lading.

    II. A carrier who, without court order, delivers goods to a party claiming the goods under a missing negotiable bill of lading is liable to any person injured by the misdelivery.

   a. I only.

   b. II only.

   c. Both I and II.

   d. Neither I nor II.

16 (R99)

Under the Documents of Title Article of the UCC, which of the following acts may excuse or limit a common carrier's liability for damage to goods in transit?

   a. Vandalism.

   b. Power outage.

   c. Willful acts of third parties.

   d. Providing for a contractual dollar liability limitation.

5 (R97)

Under the Documents of Title Article of the UCC, which of the following terms must be contained in a warehouse receipt?

    I. A statement indicating whether the goods received will be delivered to the bearer, to a specified person, or to a specified person or his/her order.

    II. The location of the warehouse where the goods are stored.

a. I only.

b. II only.

c. Both I and II.

d. Neither I nor II.

15 (R97)

Under the Documents of Title Article of the UCC, a negotiable document of title is "duly negotiated" when it is negotiated to

   a. Any holder by indorsement.

   b. Any holder by delivery.

   c. A holder who takes the document in payment of a money obligation.

   d. A holder who takes the document for value, in good faith, and without notice of any defense or claim to it.

15 (R96)

Under the Documents of Title Article of the UCC, which of the following statements is (are) correct regarding a common carrier's duty to deliver goods subject to a negotiable, bearer bill of lading?

    I. The carrier may deliver the goods to any party designated by the holder of the bill of lading.

    II. A carrier who, without court order, delivers goods to a party claiming the goods under a missing negotiable bill of lading is liable to any person injured by the misdelivery.

   a. I only.

   b. II only.

   c. Both I and II.

   d. Neither I nor II.

59 (November 95)

A common carrier bailee generally would avoid liability for loss of goods entrusted to its care if the goods are

a. Stolen by an unknown person.
b. Negligently destroyed by an employee.
c. Destroyed by the derailment of the train carrying them due to railroad employee negligence.
d. Improperly packed by the party shipping them.

58 (May 95)

Which of the following standards of liability best characterizes the obligation of a common carrier in a bailment relationship?

a. Reasonable care.
b. Gross negligence.
c. Shared liability.
d. Strict liability.

46 (November 93)

Field Corp. issued a negotiable warehouse receipt to Hall for goods stored in Field's warehouse. Hall's goods were lost due to Field's failure to exercise such care as a reasonably carefully person would under like circumstances. The state in which this transaction occurred follows the UCC rule with respect to a warehouseman's liability for lost goods. The warehouse receipt is silent on this point. Under the circumstances, Field is

a. Liable because it is strictly liable for any loss.
b. Liable because it was negligent.
c. Not liable because the warehouse receipt was negotiable.
d. Not liable unless Hall can establish that Field was grossly negligent.

47 (November 93)

Which of the following statements is correct concerning a bill of lading in the possession of Major Corp. that was issued by a common carrier and provides that the goods are to be delivered "to bearer"?

a. The carrier's lien for any unpaid shipping charges does <u>not</u> entitle it to sell the goods to enforce the lien.
b. The carrier will <u>not</u> be liable for delivering the goods to a person other than Major.
c. The carrier may require Major to indorse the bill of lading prior to delivering the goods.
d. The bill of lading can be negotiated by Major by delivery alone and without indorsement.

44 (May 93)

Under the UCC, a bill of lading

a. Will <u>never</u> be enforceable if altered.
b. Is issued by a consignee of goods.
c. Will <u>never</u> be negotiable unless it is indorsed.
d. Is negotiable if the goods are to be delivered to bearer.

42 (November 92)

Burke stole several negotiable warehouse receipts from Grove Co. The receipts were deliverable to Grove's order. Burke indorsed Grove's name and sold the warehouse receipts to Federated Wholesalers, a bona fide purchaser. In an action by Federated against Grove,

a. Grove will prevail, because Burke <u>cannot</u> validly negotiable the warehouse receipts.
b. Grove will prevail, because the warehouser must be notified before any valid negotiation of a warehouse receipt is effective.
c. Federated will prevail, because the warehouse receipts were converted to bearer instruments by Burke's indorsement.
d. Federated will prevail, because it took the negotiable warehouse receipts as a bona fide purchaser for value.

43 (November 92)

Under a nonnegotiable bill of lading, a carrier who accepts goods for shipment, must deliver the goods to
  a. Any holder of the bill of lading.
  b. Any party subsequently named by the seller.
  c. The seller who was issued the bill of lading.
  d. The consignee of the bill of lading.

49 (May 92)

Under the UCC, a warehouse receipt
  a. Is negotiable if, by its terms, the goods are to be delivered to bearer or to the order of a named person.
  b. Will not be negotiable if it contains a contractual limitation on the warehouser's liability.
  c. May qualify as both a negotiable warehouse receipt and negotiable commercial paper if the instrument is payable either in cash or by the delivery of goods.
  d. May be issued only by a bonded and licensed warehouser.

47 (May 91)

Which of the following statements is correct concerning a common carrier that issues a bill of lading stating that the goods are to be delivered "to the order of Ajax"?
  a. The carrier's lien on the goods covered by the bill of lading for storage or transportation expenses is ineffective against the bill of lading's purchaser.
  b. The carrier may not, as a matter of public policy, limits its liability for the goods by the terms of the bill.
  c. The carrier must deliver the goods only to Ajax or to a person who presents the bill of lading properly indorsed by Ajax.
  d. The carrier would have liability only to Ajax because the bill of lading is nonnegotiable.

42 (November 88)

Which of the following is not a warranty made by the seller of a negotiable warehouse receipt to the purchaser of the document?
  a. The document transfer is fully effective with respect to the goods it represents.
  b. The warehouseman will honor the document.
  c. The seller has no knowledge of any facts that would impair the document's validity.
  d. The document is genuine.

49 (May 88)

The procedure necessary to negotiate a document of title depends principally on whether the document is
  a. An order document or a bearer document.
  b. Issued by a bailee or a consignee.
  c. A receipt for goods stored or goods already shipped.
  d. A bill of lading or a warehouse receipt.

40 (May 85)

Unless otherwise agreed, which of the following warranties will not be conferred by a person negotiating a negotiable warehouse receipt for value to his immediate purchaser?
  a. The document is genuine.
  b. The transferor is without knowledge of any fact which would impair its validity or worth.
  c. The goods represented by the warehouse receipt are of merchantable quality.
  d. Negotiation by the transferor is rightful and fully effective with respect to the title to the document.

46 (May 84)

Woody Pyle, a public warehouseman, issued Merlin a negotiable warehouse receipt for fungible goods stored. Pyle

    a.   May <u>not</u> limit the amount of his liability for his own negligence.

    b.   Will be absolutely liable for any damages in the absence of a statute or a provision on the warehouse receipt to the contrary.

    c.   May commingle Merlin's goods with similar fungible goods of other bailors.

    d.   Is obligated to deliver the goods to Merlin despite Merlin's improper refusal to pay the storage charges due.

47 (November 83)

Thieves broke into the warehouse of Monogram Airways and stole a shipment of computer parts belonging to Valley Instruments. Valley had in its possession a negotiable bill of lading covering the shipment. The thieves transported the stolen parts to another state and placed the parts in a bonded warehouse. The thieves received a negotiable warehouse receipt which they used to secure a loan of $20,000 from Reliable Finance. These facts were revealed upon apprehension of the thieves. Regarding the rights of the parties

    a.   Reliable is entitled to a $20,000 payment before relinquishment of the parts.

    b.   Monogram will be the ultimate loser of the $20,000.

    c.   Valley is entitled to recover the parts free of Reliable's $20,000 claim.

    d.   Valley is <u>not</u> entitled to the parts but may obtain damages from Monogram.

44 (May 83)

Under the Uniform Commercial Code's rule, a warehouseman

    a.   Is liable as an insurer.

    b.   Will <u>not</u> be liable for the nonreceipt or misdescription of the goods stored even to a good faith purchaser for value of a warehouse receipt.

    c.   Can <u>not</u> limit its liability in respect to loss or damage to goods while in its possession.

    d.   Is liable for damages which could have been avoided through the exercise of due care.

45 (May 83)

A negotiable bill of lading

    a.   Is one type of commercial paper as defined by the Uniform Commercial Code.

    b.   Can give certain good faith purchasers greater rights to the bill of lading or the goods than the transferor had.

    c.   Can <u>not</u> result in a loss to the owner if lost or stolen, provided prompt notice is given to the carrier in possession of the goods.

    d.   Does <u>not</u> give the rightful possessor the ownership of the goods.

47 (November 81)

Boyd Corporation owned 100 cases of canned fish and stored them in a public warehouse. It asked for and received from the bailee a negotiable warehouse receipt payable to bearer. It sold the document in the ordinary course of business for cash to the Payton Corporation. Boyd delivered the document and indorsed it "Deliver to order of Payton Corporation, signed Boyd Corporation." A thief then stole the document and forged the signature of the Payton Corporation. The thief sold and delivered the document to Slate Corporation who bought it for cash in good faith and in the ordinary course of business. Which of the following is correct?

    a.   Slate has legal title to the document.

    b.   Payton has legal title to the document.

    c.   Boyd has legal title to the document.

    d.   Payton can recover the document from Slate but must reimburse Slate for the resultant damages.

25 (November 77)

Safekeeping, Inc., a public warehouse operator, issued negotiable warehouse receipts to the owner of whiskey stored in the warehouse. As required by law each receipt set forth the storage and other charges for which Safekeeping claimed liens on the whiskey. Safekeeping then became bankrupt and the warehouse was sold to another warehouse operator at a judicial foreclosure sale. The foreclosure sale was for the benefit of all creditors who held claims against Safekeeping. Which of the following is a correct legal conclusion?

    a. The judicial foreclosure sale extinguished the legal and equitable interest of the holder of the warehouse receipts in the whiskey held for storage by Safekeeping.

    b. The trustee in bankruptcy appointed for Safekeeping was immediately vested with legal title to the whiskey upon the filing of the bankruptcy petition.

    c. The negotiable warehouse receipts represent legal ownership of the whiskey, and the owner of the receipts is entitled to the property.

    d. The successor warehouse operator is <u>not</u> entitled to the whiskey and can <u>not</u> collect the storage and other charges against the owner.

PART VIII -- SALES

TABLE OF CONTENTS

PART VIII

SALES

I. The Sales Contract--General Obligations
A. Introduction; Seller's Duty of Delivery; Buyer's Duty of Payment

48 (November 95)

Under the Sales Article of the UCC, and unless otherwise agreed to, the seller's obligation to the buyer is to
   a. Deliver the goods to the buyer's place of business.
   b. Hold conforming goods and give the buyer whatever notification is reasonably necessary to enable the buyer to take delivery.
   c. Deliver all goods called for in the contract to a common carrier.
   d. Set aside conforming goods for inspection by the buyer before delivery.

56 (November 93)

Smith contracted in writing to sell Peters a used personal computer for $600. The contract did not specifically address the time for payment, place of delivery, or Peters' right to inspect the computer. Which of the following statements is correct?
   a. Smith is obligated to deliver the computer to Peters' home.
   b. Peters is entitled to inspect the computer before paying for it.
   c. Peters may not pay for the computer using a personal check unless Smith agrees.
   d. Smith is not entitled to payment until 30 days after Peters receives the computer.

54 (May 87)

If a contract for the sale of goods includes a C. & F. shipping term and the seller has fulfilled all of its obligations, the
   a. Title to the goods will pass to the buyer when the goods are received by the buyer at the place of destination.
   b. Risk of loss will pass to the buyer upon delivery of the goods to the carrier.
   c. Buyer retains the right to inspect the goods prior to making payment.
   d. Seller must obtain an insurance policy at its own expense for the buyer's benefit.

43 (May 78)

Wilson Corporation entered into a contract to sell goods to Marvin who has a place of business in the same town as Wilson. The contract was clear with respect to price and quantity, but failed to designate the place of delivery. Which of the following statements is correct?
   a. The contract is unenforceable because of indefiniteness.
   b. The place for delivery must be designated by the parties within five days or the contract is voidable.
   c. The seller's place of business is the proper place for delivery.
   d. The buyer's place of business is the proper place for delivery.

46 (May 77)

In connection with risk and expense associated with the delivery of goods to a carrier for shipment under a sales contract, the term "F.O.B. the place of shipment" means that
   a. The seller bears the risk but not the expense.
   b. The buyer bears the risk but not the expense.
   c. The seller bears the risk and expense.
   d. The buyer bears the risk and expense.

47 (May 77)

In connection with risk and expense associated with the delivery of goods to a destination under a sales contract, the term "F.O.B. place of destination" means that
    a. The seller bears the risk and expense.
    b. The buyer bears the risk and expense.
    c. The seller bears the risk but not the expense.
    d. The buyer bears the risk but not the expense.

48 (May 77)

In connection with a contract for the sale of goods, the term "C.I.F." means that the price includes
    a. The cost of the goods exclusive of insurance and freight.
    b. The cost of the goods plus freight but exclusive of insurance.
    c. The cost of the goods plus insurance but exclusive of freight.
    d. The cost of the goods, freight, and insurance.

6 (November 75)

Suggs Company agreed to sell certain goods to Barr Corporation pursuant to a written contract. No shipment or delivery date was specified in the contract. Based on these facts
    a. The time for shipment is within a reasonable time.
    b. The time for shipment must be agreed upon.
    c. The time for shipment is within 3 months.
    d. The contract fails for indefiniteness.

B. Open Price and Quantity Terms
1. Open Price Term--§ 2-305

12 (November 76)

Martin, a wholesale distributor, made a contract for the purchase of 10,000 gallons of gasoline from the Wilberforce Oil Company. The price was to be determined in accordance with the refinery price as of the close of business on the delivery date. Credit terms were net/30 after delivery. Under these circumstances which of the following statements is true?
    a. If Martin pays upon delivery, he is entitled to a 2% discount.
    b. The contract being silent on the place of delivery, Martin has the right to expect delivery at his place of business.
    c. Although the price has some degree of uncertainty, the contract is enforceable.
    d. Because the goods involved are tangible, specific performance is a remedy available to Martin.

2. Open Quantity Term: Requirements and Output Contracts--§ 2-306

19 (R01)

A sheep rancher agreed, in writing, to sell all the wool shorn during the shearing season to a weaver. The contract failed to establish the price and a minimum quantity of wool. After the shearing season, the rancher refused to deliver the wool. The weaver sued the rancher for breach of contract. Under the Sales Article of the UCC, will the weaver win?
    a. Yes, because this was an output contract.
    b. Yes, because both price and quantity terms were omitted.
    c. No, because quantity cannot be omitted for a contract to be enforceable.
    d. No, because the omission of price and quantity terms prevents the formation of a contract.

51 (November 89)

Mayker, Inc. and Oylco contracted to have Oylco be the exclusive provider of Mayker's fuel oil for three months. The stated price was subject to increases of up to a total of 10% if the market price increased. The market price rose 25% and Mayker tripled its normal order. Oylco seeks to avoid performance. Oylco's best argument in support of its position is that
    a.   There was <u>no</u> meeting of the minds.
    b.   The contract was unconscionable.
    c.   The quantity was <u>not</u> definite and certain enough.
    d.   Mayker ordered amounts of oil unreasonably greater than its normal requirements.

11 (November 80)

Bass Electric Co. has entered an agreement to buy its actual requirements of copper wiring for six months from the Seymour Metal Wire Company and Seymour Metal has agreed to sell all the copper wiring Bass will require for six months. The agreement between the two companies is
    a.   Unenforceable because it is too indefinite.
    b.   Unenforceable because it lacks mutuality of obligation.
    c.   Unenforceable because of lack of consideration.
    d.   Valid and enforceable.

34 (May 79)

Mara Oil, Inc. had a contract with Gotham Apartments to supply it with its fuel oil needs for the year, approximately 10,000 gallons. The price was fixed at ten cents above the price per gallon that Mara paid for its oil. Due to an exceptionally cold winter, Mara found that its capacity to fulfill this contract was doubtful. Therefore, it contracted Sands Oil Company and offered to assign the contract to it for $100. Sands agreed. Which of the following is correct as a result of the above assignment?
    a.   The contract with Gotham was neither assignable nor delegable.
    b.   Mara is now released from any further obligation to perform the Gotham contract.
    c.   Mara has effectively assigned to Sands its rights and delegated its duties under the terms of the contract with Gotham.
    d.   In the event Sands breaches the contract with Gotham, Mara has <u>no</u> liability.

44 (May 79)

Major Steel Manufacturing, Inc. signed a contract on October 2, 1978, with the Hard Coal & Coke Company for its annual supply of coal for three years commencing on June 1, 1979, at a price to be determined by taking the average monthly retail price per ton, less a ten cent per ton quantity discount. On March 15, 1979, Major discovered that it could readily fulfill its requirements elsewhere at a much greater discount. Major is seeking to avoid its obligation. Which of the following is correct?
    a.   The pricing term is too indefinite and uncertain hence there is <u>no</u> contract.
    b.   Since the amount of coal required is unknown at the time of the making of the contract, the contract is too indefinite and uncertain to be valid.
    c.   Major is obligated to take its normal annual coal requirements from Hard or respond in damages.
    d.   There is <u>no</u> contract since Major could conceivably require <u>no</u> coal during the years in question.

5B (May 76)

Mark Candy Wholesalers, Inc. entered into a contract with Brown & Sons, a family partnership, which owned three small candy stores. Mark agreed to supply Brown & Sons with "its entire requirements of candy for its stores for one year" at fixed prices. Brown agreed to purchase its requirements exclusively from Mark. The price of sugar increased drastically shortly after the first month of performance. Mark breached the contract because the prices at which it was required to deliver imposed a severe financial hardship which would be ruinous. Mark asserts the following legal justifications for its actions:
    1.   The contract is unenforceable for want of consideration in that Brown & Sons did not agree to take any candy at all. That is, Brown & Sons was not specifically required to purchase candy if it did not require any.

2. The contract is too indefinite and uncertain as to the quantity which might be ordered and hence is unenforceable.

3. Performance is excused on the ground of legal impossibility because of the severe financial hardship imposed upon Mark as a result of the drastic rise in the price of sugar. This unforeseen event falls within the rule of implied conditions and makes the contract voidable.

Required: Discuss the validity of each of the legal justifications asserted by Mark.

1. This asserted legal justification is invalid. First, Brown & Sons did give consideration in that they promised to purchase their candy needs exclusively from Mark. Second, the courts have sustained the validity of such requirement contracts based upon a logical interpretation of the agreement on the buyer's part to act in good faith and to take his usual or normal amount of the product involved.

2. This asserted legal justification is also invalid. Although some limited indefiniteness and uncertainty is present, this will not invalidate the agreement. The Uniform Commercial Code provides that a contract of sale does not fail for indefiniteness even though one or more terms are left open if the parties have intended to make a contract and there is a reasonably certain basis for giving an appropriate remedy. Furthermore, the Code provides that when a contract measures the quantity in terms of output of the seller or requirements of the buyer, it means such actual output or requirements as may occur in good faith. Mark's good faith is presumed, and prior requirements may be used to ascertain the quantities.

3. The asserted legal justification based upon a drastic change in price is invalid. The courts will not recognize a subsequent implied condition of this nature to permit a party to avoid his obligation under a contract. Moreover, while the modern trend of the courts may be somewhat more lenient in finding the existence of impossibility, they will not excuse performance unless the performance is rendered physically and objectively impossible.

The development of an additional financial burden or hardship upon a party to a contract is not sufficient to provide a legal excuse for his non-performance. To excuse performance in these circumstances would seriously hamper the conduct of business transactions and impair the validity of many contracts.

C. Auction Sales--§ 2-328

50 (May 84)
Which of the following statements is correct with regard to an auction of goods?
   a. The auctioneer may withdraw the goods at any time prior to completion of the sale unless the goods are put up without reserve.
   b. A bidder may retract his bid before the completion of the sale only if the auction is without reserve.
   c. A bidder's retraction of his bid will revive the prior bid if the sale is with reserve.
   d. In a sale with reserve, a bid made while the hammer is falling automatically reopens the bidding.

II. The Sales Contract--Title and Risk of Loss
A. Passage of Title

19 (May 87)
Baker fraudulently induced Able to sell Baker a painting for $200. Subsequently, Baker sold the painting for $10,000 to Gold, a good faith purchaser. Able is entitled to
   a. Rescind the contract with Baker.
   b. Recover the painting from Gold.
   c. Recover damages from Baker.
   d. Rescind Baker's contract with Gold.

47 (May 82)

A claim has been made by Donnegal to certain goods in your client's possession. Donnegal will be entitled to the goods if it can be shown that Variance, the party from whom your client purchased the goods, obtained them by

    a.   Deceiving Donnegal as to his identity at the time of the purchase.

    b.   Giving Donnegal his check which was later dishonored.

    c.   Obtaining the goods from Donnegal by fraud, punishable as larceny under criminal law.

    d.   Purchasing goods which had been previously stolen from Donnegal.

B. Identification

14 (R97)

Under the Sales Article of the UCC, unless a contract provides otherwise, before title to goods can pass from a seller to a buyer, the goods must be

    a.   Tendered to the buyer.

    b.   Identified to the contract.

    c.   Accepted by the buyer.

    d.   Paid for.

45 (May 90)

Pulse Corp. maintained a warehouse where it stored its manufactured goods. Pulse received an order from Star. Shortly after Pulse identified the goods to be shipped to Star, but before moving them to the loading dock, a fire destroyed the warehouse and its contents. With respect to the goods, which of the following statements is correct?

    a.   Pulse has title but <u>no</u> insurable interest.

    b.   Star has title and an insurable interest.

    c.   Pulse has title and an insurable interest.

    d.   Star has title but <u>no</u> insurable interest.

58 (November 81)

Mammoth Furniture, Inc. is in the retail furniture business and has stores located in principal cities in the United States. Its designers created a unique coffee table. After obtaining prices and schedules, Mammoth ordered 2,000 tables to be made to its design and specifications for sale as a part of its annual spring sales promotion campaign. Which of the following represents the earliest time Mammoth will have an insurable interest in the tables?

    a.   Upon shipment of conforming goods by the seller.

    b.   When the goods are marked or otherwise designated by the seller as the goods to which the contract refers.

    c.   At the time the contract is made.

    d.   At the time the goods are in Mammoth's possession.

C. Risk of Loss

15 (R99)

Under the Sales Article of the UCC, when a contract for the sale of goods stipulates that the seller ship the goods by common carrier "F.O.B. purchaser's loading dock," which of the parties bears the risk of loss during shipment?

    a.   The purchaser, because risk of loss passes when the goods are delivered to the carrier.

    b.   The purchaser, because title to the goods passes at the time of shipment.

    c.   The seller, because risk of loss passes only when the goods reach the purchaser's loading dock.

    d.   The seller, because risk of loss remains with the seller until the goods are accepted by the purchaser.

12 (R98)

Under the Sales Article of the UCC and the United Nations Convention for the International Sale of Goods (CISG), absent specific terms in an international sales shipment contract, when will risk of loss pass to the buyer?

a. When the goods are delivered to the first carrier for transmission to the buyer.
b. When the goods are tendered to the buyer.
c. At the conclusion of the execution of the contract.
d. At the time the goods are identified to the contract.

45 (November 95)

Under the Sales Article of the UCC, which of the following factors is most important in determining who bears the risk of loss in a sale of goods contract?

a. The method of shipping the goods.
b. The contract's shipping terms.
c. Title to the goods.
d. How the goods were lost.

46 (November 95)

Under the Sales Article of the UCC, in an F.O.B. place of shipment contract, the risk of loss passes to the buyer when the goods

a. Are identified to the contract.
b. Are placed on the seller's loading dock.
c. Are delivered to the carrier.
d. Reach the buyer's loading dock.

54 (November 94)

Under the Sales Article of the UCC, which of the following events will result in the risk of loss passing from a merchant seller to a buyer?

	Tender of the goods at the seller's place of business	Use of the seller's truck to deliver the goods
a.	Yes	Yes
b.	Yes	No
c.	No	Yes
d.	No	No

45 (May 94)

Quick Corp. agreed to purchase 200 typewriters from Union Suppliers, Inc. Union is a wholesaler of appliances and Quick is an appliance retailer. The contract required Union to ship the typewriters to Quick by common carrier, "F.O.B. Union Suppliers, Inc. Loading Dock." Which of the parties bears the risk of loss during shipment?

a. Union, because the risk of loss passes only when Quick receives the typewriters.
b. Union, because both parties are merchants.
c. Quick, because title to the typewriters passed to Quick at the time of shipment.
d. Quick, because the risk of loss passes when the typewriters are delivered to the carrier.

49 (November 93)

Which of the following statements applies to a sale on approval under the UCC Sales Article?

a. Both the buyer and seller must be merchants.
b. The buyer must be purchasing the goods for resale.
c. Risk of loss for the goods passes to the buyer when the goods are accepted after the trial period.
d. Title to the goods passes to the buyer on delivery of the goods to the buyer.

55 (November 93)

Bond purchased a painting from Wool, who is not in the business of selling art. Wool tendered delivery of the painting after receiving payment in full from Bond. Bond informed Wool that Bond would be unable to take possession of the painting until later that day. Thieves stole the painting before Bond returned. The risk of loss

    a.   Passed to Bond at Wool's tender of delivery.

    b.   Passed to Bond at the time the contract was formed and payment was made.

    c.   Remained with Wool, because the parties agreed on a later time of delivery.

    d.   Remained with Wool, because Bond had <u>not</u> yet received the painting.

Items 51 through 53 are based on the following:

On May 2, Lace Corp., an appliance wholesaler, offered to sell appliances worth $3,000 to Parco, Inc., a household appliances retailer. The offer was signed by Lace's president, and provided that it would not be withdrawn before June 1. It also included the shipping terms: "FOB--Parco's warehouse." On May 29, Parco mailed an acceptance of Lace's offer. Lace received the acceptance June 2.

51 (May 92)

Which of the following statements is correct if Lace sent Parco a telegram revoking its offer, and Parco received the telegram on May 25?

    a.   A contract was formed on May 2.

    b.   Lace's revocation effectively terminated its offer on May 25.

    c.   Lace's revocation was ineffective because the offer could <u>not</u> be revoked before June 1.

    d.   No contract was formed because Lace received Parco's acceptance after June 1.

52 (May 92)

Risk of loss for the appliances will pass to Parco when they are

    a.   Identified to the contract.

    b.   Shipped by Lace.

    c.   Tendered at Parco's warehouse.

    d.   Accepted by Parco.

53 (May 92)

If Lace inadvertently ships the wrong appliances to Parco and Parco rejects them two days after receipt, title to the goods will

    a.   Pass to Parco when they are identified to the contract.

    b.   Pass to Parco when they are shipped.

    c.   Remain with Parco until the goods are returned to Lace.

    d.   Revert to Lace when they are rejected by Parco.

44 (May 90)

Cey Corp. entered into a contract to sell parts to Deck, Ltd. The contract provided that the goods would be shipped "F.O.B. Cey's warehouse." Cey shipped parts different from those specified in the contract. Deck rejected the parts. A few hours after Deck informed Cey that the parts were rejected, they were destroyed by fire in Deck's warehouse. Cey believed that the parts were conforming to the contract. Which of the following statements is correct?

    a.   Regardless of whether the parts were conforming, Deck will bear the loss because the contract was a shipment contract.

    b.   If the parts were nonconforming, Deck had the right to reject them, but the risk of loss remains with Deck until Cey takes possession of the parts.

    c.   If the parts were conforming, risk of loss does <u>not</u> pass to Deck until a reasonable period of time after they are delivered to Deck.

    d.   If the parts were nonconforming, Cey will bear the risk of loss, even though the contract was a shipment contract.

48 (November 89)

Which of the following factors is most important in deciding who bears the risk of loss between merchants when goods are destroyed during shipment?
  a. The agreement of the parties.
  b. Whether the goods are perishable.
  c. Who has title at the time of the loss.
  d. The terms of applicable insurance policies.

49 (November 89)

On Monday, Wolfe paid Aston Co., a furniture retailer, $500 for a table. On Thursday, Aston notified Wolfe that the table was ready to be picked up. On Saturday, while Aston was still in possession of the table, it was destroyed in a fire. Who bears the loss of the table?
  a. Wolfe, because Wolfe had title to the table at the time of loss.
  b. Aston, unless Wolfe is a merchant.
  c. Wolfe, unless Aston breached the contract.
  d. Aston, because Wolfe had not yet taken possession of the table.

46 (November 88)

If goods have been delivered to a buyer pursuant to a sale or return contract, the
  a. Buyer may use the goods but not sell them.
  b. Seller is liable for the expenses incurred by the buyer in returning the goods to the seller.
  c. Title to the goods remains with the seller.
  d. Risk of loss for the goods passed to the buyer.

39 (November 87)

Sand Corp. sold and delivered a photocopier to Barr for use in Barr's business. According to their agreement, Barr may return the copier within 30 days. During the 30-day period, if Barr has not returned the copier or indicated acceptance of it, which of the following statements is correct with respect to risk of loss and title?
  a. Risk of loss and title passed to Barr.
  b. Risk of loss and title remain with Sand.
  c. Risk of loss passed to Barr but title remains with Sand.
  d. Risk of loss remains with Sand but title passed to Barr.

55 (May 87)

Which of the following is most important in determining who bears the risk of loss in a sale of goods contract?
  a. The shipping terms.
  b. The agreement of the parties.
  c. Who has title to the goods.
  d. Who has possession of the goods.

45 (November 85)

Bell Co. owned 20 engines which it deposited in a public warehouse on May 5, receiving a negotiable warehouse receipt in its name. Bell sold the engines to Spark Corp. On which of the following dates did the risk of loss transfer from Bell to Spark?
  a. June 11--Spark signed a contract to buy the engines from Bell for $19,000. Delivery was to be at the warehouse.
  b. June 12--Spark paid for the engines.
  c. June 13--Bell negotiated the warehouse receipt to Spark.
  d. June 14--Spark received delivery of the engines at the warehouse.

49 (May 84)

Bell by telegram to Major Corp. ordered 10,000 yards of fabric, first quality, 50% wool and 50% cotton. The shipping terms were F.O.B. Bell's factory in Akron, Ohio. Major accepted the order and packed the fabric for shipment. In the process it discovered that one-half of the fabric packed had been commingled with fabric which was 30% wool and 70% cotton. Since Major did not have any additional 50% wool fabric, it decided to send the shipment to Bell as an accommodation. The goods were shipped and later the same day Major wired Bell its apology informing Bell of the facts and indicating that the 5,000 yards of 30% wool would be priced at $2 a yard less. The carrier delivering the goods was destroyed on the way to Akron. Under the circumstances, who bears the risk of loss?

    a.   Bell, since Bell has title to the goods.
    b.   Major, because the order was <u>not</u> a signed writing.
    c.   Bell, since the shipping terms were F.O.B. Bell's place of business.
    d.   Major, since they shipped goods which failed to conform to the contract.

17 (May 81)

A dispute has arisen between two merchants over the question of who has the risk of loss in a given sales transaction. The contract does not specifically cover the point. The goods were shipped to the buyer who rightfully rejected them. Which of the following factors will be the most important factor in resolving their dispute?

    a.   Who has title to the goods.
    b.   The shipping terms.
    c.   The credit terms.
    d.   The fact that a breach has occurred.

33 (May 80)

Buyer ordered goods from Seller. The contract required Seller to deliver them f.o.b. Buyer's place of business. Buyer inspected the goods, discovered they failed to conform to the contract, and rightfully rejected them. In the event of loss of the goods, which of the following is a correct statement?

    a.   Seller initially had the risk of loss and it remains with him after delivery.
    b.   Risk of loss passes to Buyer upon tender of the goods f.o.b. Buyer's place of business.
    c.   Buyer initially had the risk of loss, but it is shifted to Seller upon rightful rejection.
    d.   If Seller used a public carrier to transport the goods to Buyer, risk of loss is on Buyer during transit.

39 (May 79)

Duval Liquor Wholesalers, Inc. stored its inventory of goods in the Reliable Warehouse Company. Duval's shipments would arrive by truck and be deposited with Reliable who would in turn issue negotiable warehouse receipts to Duval. Duval would resell the liquor by transferring the negotiable warehouse receipts to the buyer who was responsible for transporting it to his place of business. In one of the sales of liquor to a retailer, the liquor was badly damaged and a question has arisen as to who has the risk of loss, Duval or the retailer. If the contract is silent on this point, when did the risk of loss pass to the retailer?

    a.   When the goods have been placed on the warehouseman's delivery dock awaiting pick up by the retailer.
    b.   When the goods have been identified to the contract.
    c.   On his receipt of the negotiable warehouse receipts covering the goods.
    d.   When the goods have been properly loaded upon the retailer's carrier.

2 (May 88)

Mirk & Co., CPAs, has been engaged to audit Spear Corp.'s 1987 financial statements. Spear is engaged in the business of buying and selling computers. Spear has adopted a calendar year for accounting purposes. While conducting the audit, Mirk reviewed the following transactions occurring in December 1987.

    ■   On December 20, Spear sold five computers to Pica Corp. The contract required Spear to ship the computers by common carrier. The shipping terms of the contract were "F.O.B.--Spear's loading dock." The computers were shipped on December 30, and on January 1, 1988, while the computers were in transit, the common carrier was involved in an accident causing a fire that totally destroyed the computers. Pica discovered, upon a review of a copy of the common carrier's bill of lading, that the destroyed computers were not the models it had ordered.

- On December 21, Spear purchased and took delivery of 15 computers from Larson for $20,000. Larson had purchased the computers from Xeon Co., paying Xeon with a check that Larson's bank refused to honor because of insufficient funds. Spear was unaware that Larson's check was dishonored.
- On December 22, Spear entered into a sale on approval contract with Rusk Corp. for two computers. Rusk is engaged exclusively in the business of selling furniture. The contract required Rusk to notify Spear within 15 days after delivery if it did not want to keep the computers. Rusk took delivery of the computers on December 21, and, as of December 31, had not yet decided whether to keep the computers.

With regard to the transactions described above, Mirk wishes to resolve the following issues that were not addressed in the specific contracts:

As of December 31, 1987, which of the parties bear the risk of loss for the computers with regard to the:

- December 20 transaction with Pica?
- December 22 transaction with Rusk?

As of December 31, 1987, which of the parties has title to the computers with regard to the:

- December 21 transaction with Larson?
- December 22 transaction with Rusk?

What rights do the general creditors of Rusk have to the computers delivered to Rusk pursuant to the December 22 transaction with Spear?

Required: Discuss the issues raised by Mirk, setting forth your conclusions and reasons therefor.

As of December 31, 1987, Spear bears the risk of loss for the computers on the December 20 contract with Pica. The shipping term "F.O.B.--Spear's loading dock" designates a shipment contract. In general, risk of loss passes to the buyer (Pica) in a shipment contract when the goods are duly delivered to the carrier. However, where a tender or delivery of goods so fails to conform to the contract as to give a right of rejection, the risk of their loss remains on the seller until cure or acceptance. Thus, the failure of the shipment to conform to the contract constitutes a breach that permits Pica to reject the computers, thereby resulting in Spear bearing the risk of loss for the computers while they are in transit.

With respect to the December 22 contract, the risk of loss as of December 31, 1987 remains with Spear. Unless otherwise agreed, the risk of loss in a sale on approval contract does not pass to the buyer until the buyer accepts the goods. Under the facts of this case, Rusk had not yet accepted the computers as of December 31, 1987. Therefore, the risk of loss on the computers as of December 31, 1987, remains with Spear.

As of December 31, 1987, Spear has title to the 15 computers purchased from Larson under the December 21 contract because a person with voidable title has the power to transfer good title to a good faith purchaser for value. Larson has voidable title because he paid for the computers with an insufficient funds check. Spear is a good faith purchaser for value because it paid Larson $20,000 and was unaware that Larson's check to Xeon was dishonored. The UCC Sales Article provides that when goods have been delivered under a transaction of purchase, the purchaser has the power to transfer good title even though the delivery was in exchange for a check that is later dishonored. Thus, Spear has good title to the computers as of December 31, 1987, despite Larson's check being dishonored, because it purchased and received the computers on December 21, 1987.

With respect to the December 22 sale on approval contract, title to the two computers remains with the seller until the buyer accepts the computers, because the contract is silent as to when title passes. Therefore, as of December 31, 1987, Spear retains title to the two computers because Rusk had not yet notified Spear whether it would accept the computers, and the time for such notification had not yet passed.

Because the December 22 contract between Spear and Rusk is a sale on approval contract, the computers are not subject to the claims of the creditors of the buyer (Rusk) until acceptance.

5B (May 83)

Dennison Corporation, a Los Angeles-based manufacturer, recently ordered some hardware from Elba Corporation, a Boston-based seller of fine tools. Unfortunately, all of the hardware was destroyed while in transit by the carrier. Further examination revealed that while one set of tools was shipped under terms F.O.B. Los Angeles, the other set was shipped under terms F.O.B. Boston.

Required: Answer the following, setting forth reasons for any conclusions stated.

1. Which party will bear the risk of loss for each set of tools destroyed in transit assuming conforming goods were shipped?

2. Assume that Dennison also purchased some tools from San Francisco-based Drew Corporation which were shipped under terms F.O.B. San Francisco. The property is found defective upon arrival in Los Angeles. Which party will bear the risk of loss if the property is destroyed immediately after receipt?

1. Although the parties involved are permitted to allocate risk of loss in any manner they deem appropriate, assuming that there was no provision in the agreement regarding risk of loss, the Uniform Commercial Code sets forth very specific rules which depart sharply from the common law concept dependent upon whether title had been transferred. Sales contracts that require the seller to ship the goods F.O.B. seller's location are known as "shipment" contracts while contracts requiring the seller to deliver to a particular destination are known as "destination" contracts.

The first set of tools was sold under "destination" terms which means that risk of loss passed to Dennison only when the goods arrived at that destination and were duly tendered to enable Dennison to take delivery. Thus, Elba would bear the risk of loss.

Regarding the second set which entailed "shipment" terms, risk of loss passed when the goods were properly delivered to the carrier. Thus, although the property was destroyed prior to delivery, risk of loss had already passed to Dennison.

2. Drew. The UCC sets forth specific provisions regarding the effect of breach (both by the seller and buyer) on risk of loss. Assuming a seller's breach, as is the case here, the Code provides that where a tender or delivery of goods so fails to conform to the contract as to give a right of rejection, the risk of loss remains on the seller until cure or acceptance.

5B (November 78)

On May 30, 1978, Hargrove ordered 1,000 spools of nylon yarn from Flowers, Inc. of Norfolk, Virginia. The shipping terms were "F.O.B., Norfolk & Western RR at Norfolk." The transaction was to be a cash sale for the negotiable bill of lading covering the goods. Title to the goods was expressly reserved in Flowers. The yarn ordered by Hargrove was delivered to the railroad and loaded in a boxcar on June 1, 1978. Flowers obtained a negotiable bill of lading made out to its own order. The boxcar was destroyed the next day while the goods were in transit. Hargrove refused to pay for the yarn and Flowers sued Hargrove for the purchase price.

Required: Answer the following, setting forth reasons for any conclusions stated.

Who will prevail?

Flowers will prevail because Hargrove has the risk of loss. The shipping terms determine who had the risk of loss. Section 2-509(1) of the Uniform Commercial Code provides that "Where the contract requires or authorizes the seller to ship the goods by carrier, (a) if it does not require him to deliver at a particular destination, the risk of loss passes to the buyer when the goods are duly delivered to the carrier, even though the shipment is under reservation. . . ."

The facts that title was reserved by Flowers and that Flowers retained the negotiable bill of lading do not affect the determination of who is to bear the risk of loss. The Code makes it clear that title is irrelevant in determining the risk of loss.

III.   The Sales Contract--Remedies

1 (R98)

On June 1, Classic Corp., a manufacturer of desk chairs, orally agreed to sell 100 leather desk chairs to Rand Stores, a chain of retail furniture stores, for $50,000. The parties agreed that delivery would be completed by September 1, and the shipping terms were "F.O.B. seller's loading dock." On June 5, Classic sent Rand a signed memorandum of agreement containing the terms orally agreed to. Rand received the memorandum on June 7 and made no response.

On July 31, Classic identified the chairs to be shipped to Rand and placed them on its loading dock to be picked up by the common carrier the next day. That night, a fire on the loading dock destroyed 50 of the chairs. On August 1, the remaining 50 chairs were delivered to the common carrier together with 50 vinyl chairs. The truck carrying the chairs was involved in an accident, resulting in extensive damage to 10 of the leather chairs and 25 of the vinyl chairs.

On August 10, the chairs were delivered to Rand. On August 12, Rand notified Classic that Rand was accepting 40 of the leather chairs and 10 of the vinyl chairs, but the rest of the shipment was being rejected. Rand also informed Classic that due to Classic's failure to perform under the terms of the contract, Rand would seek all remedies available under the Sales Article of the UCC.

Classic contended that it has no liability to Rand and that the shipment was strictly an accommodation to Rand because Rand failed to sign the memorandum of agreement, thus preventing a contract from being formed.

The above parties and transactions are governed by the provisions of the Sales Article of the UCC.

Required:

    a.   Determine whether Classic's contention is correct and give the reasons for your conclusion.

    b.   Assuming that a valid contract exists between Classic and Rand, answer the following questions and give the reasons for your conclusions. Do not consider any possible liability owed by the common carrier.

        1.   Who bears the risk of loss for the 50 destroyed leather chairs?

        2.   Who bears the risk of loss for the 25 damaged vinyl chairs?

        3.   What is the earliest date that title to any of the chairs would pass to Rand?

    c.   With what UCC requirements must Rand comply to be entitled to recover damages from Classic?

    d.   Assuming that a valid contract exists between Classic and Rand, state the applicable remedies to which Rand would be entitled. Do not consider any possible liability owed by the common carrier.

    a. Classic's contention is incorrect.   Under the provisions of the Sales Article of the UCC, a written memorandum stating an agreement between merchants does not have to be signed by both parties. The contract is enforceable against Classic because Classic signed the memorandum and against Rand because Rand did not object to the memorandum within 10 days of receiving it.

    b. 1.   Classic bears the risk of loss for the 50 leather chairs destroyed in the fire. Even though the goods were identified to the contract and placed on the loading dock, the risk of loss remains with Classic. The shipping terms "F.O.B. seller's loading dock" provide that risk of loss remains with the seller until the goods are delivered to the common carrier. The 50 leather chairs destroyed in the fire had not yet been delivered to the carrier.

        2.   Classic bears the risk of loss for the damaged vinyl chairs. Even though these goods were delivered to the common carrier, the risk of loss did not pass to Rand because the vinyl chairs were nonconforming goods.

        3.   August 1 was the earliest date that title to any of the chairs passed to Rand. Title passed when goods identified to the contract were delivered to the carrier.

    c. Under the Sales Article of the UCC, for Rand to be entitled to damages from Classic, Rand must comply with the following requirements:

      ▪   Rand has to notify Classic of the rejection of the goods within a reasonable time.

      ▪   Rand must act in good faith with respect to the rejected goods by following any reasonable instructions from Classic.

      ▪   Rand must give Classic the opportunity to cure until the contract time of performance expires.

    d. Rand would be entitled to the following remedies:

      ▪   The right to cancel the contract.

      ▪   The right of cover.

      ▪   The right to recover monetary damages for nondelivery.

A. Buyers' Obligations--Rejection; Cure; Acceptance and Revocation of Acceptance

56 (November 94)

Rowe Corp. purchased goods from Stair Co. that were shipped C.O.D. Under the Sales Article of the UCC, which of the following rights does Rowe have?

a. The right to inspect the goods before paying.
b. The right to possession of the goods before paying.
c. The right to reject nonconforming goods.
d. The right to delay payment for a reasonable period of time.

48 (November 85)

Kirk Corp. sold Nix an Ajax freezer, Model 24, for $490. The contract required delivery to be made by June 23. On June 12, Kirk delivered an Ajax freezer, Model 52, to Nix. Nix immediately notified Kirk that the wrong freezer had been delivered and indicated that the delivery of a correct freezer would not be acceptable. Kirk wishes to deliver an Ajax freezer, Model 24 on June 23. Which of the following statements is correct?

a. Kirk may deliver the freezer on June 23 without further notice to Nix.
b. Kirk may deliver the freezer on June 23 if it first seasonably notifies Nix of its intent to do so.
c. Nix must accept the nonconforming freezer but may recover damages.
d. Nix always may reject the nonconforming freezer and refuse delivery of a conforming freezer on June 23.

56 (November 84)

Mix Clothing shipped 300 custom suits to Tara Retailers. The suits arrived on Thursday, earlier than Tara had anticipated and on an exceptionally busy day for its receiving department. They were perfunctorily examined and sent to a nearby warehouse for storage until needed. On the following day, upon closer examination, it was discovered that the quality of the linings of the suits was inferior to that specified in the sales contract. Which of the following is correct insofar as Tara's rights are concerned?

a. Tara must retain the suits since it accepted them and had an opportunity to inspect them upon delivery.
b. Tara had <u>no</u> rights if the linings were of merchantable quality.
c. Tara can reject the suits upon subsequent discovery of the defects.
d. Tara's only course of action is rescission.

9 (November 76)

Kent, a wholesale distributor of cameras, entered into a contract with Williams. Williams agreed to purchase 100 cameras with certain optional attachments. The contract was made on October 1, 1976, for delivery by October 15, 1976; terms: 2/10, net 30. Kent shipped the cameras on October 6 and they were delivered on October 10. The shipment did <u>not</u> conform to the contract, in that one of the attachments was <u>not</u> included. Williams immediately notified Kent that he was rejecting the goods. For maximum legal advantage Kent's most appropriate action is to

a. Bring an action for the price less an allowance for the missing attachment.
b. Notify Williams promptly of his intention to cure the defect and make a conforming delivery by October 15.
c. Terminate his contract with Williams and recover for breach of contract.
d. Sue Williams for specific performance.

23 (May 74)

Bates ordered 1,000 units of merchandise from Watson, a wholesaler, at a unit price of $50 each, with delivery to be made at Bates' warehouse after April 11 but in <u>no</u> event later than April 15 with payment to be made 30 days after delivery. Watson accepted Bates' offer. If Watson ships the goods to Bates and the shipment arrives on April 12

    a.   Bates must inspect all items at the time delivery is tendered or waive any defects.

    b.   Bates may inspect the goods prior to accepting delivery but may <u>not</u> accept conforming goods while rejecting the nonconforming goods if he wishes to preserve his remedies for any breach of contract as to the latter.

    c.   If Watson delivers 1,000 units of a newer model of the merchandise ordered reasonably believing it to be acceptable and Bates rejects the merchandise as nonconforming, Watson may hold Bates to the contract terms by reasonably notifying Bates of his intent to cure and delivering conforming units by April 15.

    d.   If the goods are damaged but salable as damaged merchandise, Bates must immediately seek to sell them and then he may recover any loss as damages from Watson.

4 (November 91)

On October 10, Vesta Electronics contracted with Zap Audio to sell Zap 200 18" stereo speakers. The contract provided that the speakers would be shipped F.O.B. seller's loading dock. The contract was silent as to when risk of loss for the speakers would pass to Zap. Delivery was to be completed by November 10.

On October 18, Vesta identified the speakers to be shipped to Zap and moved them to the loading dock. Before the carrier picked up the goods, a fire on Vesta's loading dock destroyed 50 of the speakers. On October 20, Vesta shipped, by common carrier, the remaining 150 18" speakers and 50 16" speakers. The truck carrying the speakers was involved in an accident resulting in damage to 25 of the 16" speakers. Zap received the 200 speakers on October 25, and on October 27 notified Vesta that 100 of the 18" speakers were being accepted but the rest of the shipment was being rejected. Zap also informed Vesta that, due to Vesta's failure to comply with the terms of the contract, Zap would contest paying the contract price and would sue for damages.

The above parties and transactions are subject to the Uniform Commercial Code (UCC).

Required: Answer the following questions, and give the reasons for your conclusions.
    a.   1.   Who bears the risk of loss for the 50 destroyed 18" speakers?
           2.   Who bears the risk of loss for the 25 damaged 16" speakers?
    b.   1.   Was Zap's rejection of the 16" speakers valid?
           2.   Was Zap's acceptance of some of the 18" speakers valid?
    c.   Under the UCC, what duties are required of Zap after rejecting all or part of the shipment?

    a.   1.   Vesta Electronics would bear the risk of loss for the 18" speakers destroyed by the fire on its loading dock. Even though Vesta identified and segregated the goods on its loading dock, the risk of loss remained with the seller because the contract's shipping terms "F.O.B. seller's loading dock" made it a shipping contract. Thus, risk of loss does not pass to Zap until the goods are delivered to the carrier.

           2.   The risk of loss for the 16" speakers also remained with Vesta. Even though the goods were delivered to the common carrier, risk of loss did not pass because Vesta shipped nonconforming goods.

    b.   1.   Zap may validly reject the 16" speakers because any buyer may reject nonconforming goods. To avoid potential liability, the rejection must be made within a reasonable time of receipt and must be communicated to the seller.

           2.   Zap may also validly accept some of the 18" speakers. A buyer may accept none, all, or any commercial unit of a shipment when nonconforming goods are shipped.

    c.   To be entitled to damages, Zap must comply with the UCC by notifying Vesta of the rejection of the goods within a reasonable time; acting in good faith with respect to the rejected goods by following any reasonable instructions of the seller; and giving Vesta the opportunity to cure until the contract time of performance expires.

B. Buyers' Remedies
1. Recovery of Damages (Including Cover Under § 2-712)

36 (May 86)

On May 1, Frost entered into a signed contract for the sale of 5,000 pounds of sugar to Kemp Co. at 30¢ per pound. Delivery was to be made on June 10. Due to a sudden rise in sugar prices, Frost sent Kemp a letter stating that it would not sell the sugar to Kemp. Kemp received the letter on May 15 at which time the market price of sugar was 40¢ per pound. Although Kemp could have reasonably purchased sugar elsewhere in the market, it chose not to do so. On June 10, the market price of sugar was 50¢ per pound. In addition to incidental damages, Kemp is entitled to damages of

    a. $500.
    b. $500 plus consequential damages.
    c. $1,000.
    d. $1,000 plus consequential damages.

13 (November 79)

On March 11, Vizar Sales Corporation telegraphed Watson Company:

> Will sell 1,000 cases of coffee for $28 a case for delivery at our place of business on April 15. You may pick them up at our loading platform."

Watson telegraphed its acceptance on March 12. On March 20, coffee prices rose to $30 a case. Vizar telegraphed Watson on March 21 that it repudiated the sale and would not make delivery. The telegram was received by Watson on March 22 when the price was $32; Watson could have covered at that price but chose not to do so. On April 15 the coffee was selling at $35 a case. Watson tendered $28,000 to Vizar and indicated it was ready to take delivery. Vizar refused to deliver. What relief, if any, is Watson entitled to?

    a. Specific performance, because it made a valid tender of performance.
    b. Nothing, because it failed to cover.
    c. Damages of $4,000 (the difference between the contract price and the fair market value at the time Watson learned of the breach).
    d. Damages of $7,000 (the difference between the contract price and the fair market value at the time delivery should have been made).

38 (May 79)

If a seller repudiates his contract with a buyer for the sale of 100 radios, what recourse does the buyer have?

    a. He can "cover," i.e., procure the goods elsewhere and recover the difference.
    b. He must await the seller's performance for a commercially reasonable time after repudiation.
    c. He can obtain specific performance by the seller.
    d. He can recover punitive damages.

29 (May 74)

When a contract for the sale of merchandise has been breached by the seller's failure to deliver goods conforming to the contract, the buyer's remedy of "cover"

    a. Is exclusive if substitute goods are readily available.
    b. Is normally limited to nondelivery of fungible goods.
    c. Limits primary damages (as distinguished from incidental and consequential damages) to the difference between the contract price and the market price of comparable goods at the time the buyer learns of the breach.
    d. Requires a reduction in damages claimed for expenses saved in consequence of the seller's breach.

5B (May 82)

Nielson Wholesalers, Inc. ordered 1,000 scissors at $2.50 a pair from Wilmot, Inc. on February 1, 1982. Delivery was to be made not later than March 10. Wilmot accepted the order in writing on February 4. The terms were 2/10, net/30, F.O.B. seller's loading platform in Baltimore. Due to unexpected additional orders and a miscalculation of the backlog of orders, Wilmot subsequently determined that it could not perform by March 10. On February 15, Wilmot notified Nielson that it would not be able to perform, and cancelled the contract. Wilmot pleaded a reasonable mistake and impossibility of performance as its justification for cancelling. At the time the notice of cancellation was received, identical scissors were available from other manufacturers at $2.70. Nielson chose not to purchase the 1,000 scissors elsewhere, but instead notified Wilmot that it rejected the purported cancellation and would await delivery as agreed. Wilmot did not deliver on March 10, by which time the price of the scissors had risen to $3.00 a pair. Nielson is seeking to recover damages from Wilmot for breach of contract.

Required: Answer the following, setting forth reasons for any conclusions stated.
1. Will Nielson prevail and, if so, how much will it recover?
2. Would Nielson be entitled to specific performance under the circumstances?
3. Assuming that Wilmot discovers that Nielson was insolvent, will this excuse performance?

1. Yes. Wilmot's asserted legal defenses are without merit. Recovery by Nielson will be limited to 20 cents per pair, which is the difference between the contract price and the additional amount that it would have cost to purchase the goods elsewhere at the time the buyer learned of the breach. When the notice of cancellation was received, the contract price was $2.50 and the market price was $2.70.

2. No. Specific performance would not be available under the circumstances. Money damages are adequate in that it would be compensated for the amount it would have to pay to buy the goods elsewhere. Hence, it would be in as good a position as it would have been otherwise.

3. No. The Uniform Commercial Code covers these points specifically. If a seller discovers after the making of the contract, but prior to the delivery of the goods, that his customer is insolvent, he still cannot terminate the contract. However, Wilmot has the right to refuse delivery except for cash payment.

2. Recovery of Identified Goods

47 (May 94)

Under the UCC Sales Article, which of the following legal remedies would a buyer <u>not</u> have when a seller fails to transfer and deliver goods identified to the contract?
a. Suit for specific performance.
b. Suit for punitive damages.
c. Purchase substitute goods (cover).
d. Recover the identified goods (capture).

47 (May 90)

On September 10, Bell Corp. entered into a contract to purchase 50 lamps from Glow Manufacturing. Bell prepaid 40% of the purchase price. Glow became insolvent on September 19 before segregating, in its inventory, the lamps to be delivered to Bell. Bell will <u>not</u> be able to recover the lamps because
a. Bell is regarded as a merchant.
b. The lamps were <u>not</u> identified to the contract.
c. Glow became insolvent fewer than 10 days after receipt of Bell's prepayment.
d. Bell did <u>not</u> pay the full price at the time of purchase.

47 (May 84)

Darrow purchased 100 sets of bookends from Benson Manufacturing, Inc. Darrow made substantial prepayments of the purchase price. Benson is insolvent and the goods have not been delivered as promised. Darrow wants the bookends. Under the circumstances, which of the following will prevent Darrow from obtaining the bookends?

a. The fact that he did <u>not</u> pay the full price at the time of the purchase even though he has made a tender of the balance and holds it available to Benson upon delivery.

b. The fact that he can obtain a judgment for damages.

c. The fact that he was <u>not</u> aware of Benson's insolvency at the time he purchased the bookends.

d. The fact that the goods have <u>not</u> been identified to his contract.

C. Sellers' Remedies
1. Recovery of Damages (Including Purchase Price Under § 2-709)

11 (R98)

Under the Sales Article of the UCC, the remedies available to a seller when a buyer breaches a contract for the sale of goods may include

	The right to resell goods identified to the contract	The right to stop a carrier from delivering the goods
a.	Yes	Yes
b.	Yes	No
c.	No	Yes
d.	No	No

50 (November 95)

Under the Sales Article of the UCC, which of the following rights is available to a seller when a buyer materially breaches a sales contract?

	Right to cancel the contract	Right to recover damages
a.	Yes	Yes
b.	Yes	No
c.	No	Yes
d.	No	No

57 (November 93)

Cara Fabricating Co. and Taso Corp. agreed orally that Taso would custom manufacture a compressor for Cara at a price of $120,000. After Taso completed the work at a cost of $90,000, Cara notified Taso that the compressor was no longer needed. Taso is holding the compressor and has requested payment from Cara. Taso has been unable to resell the compressor for any price. Taso incurred storage fees of $2,000. If Cara refuses to pay Taso and Taso sues Cara, the most Taso will be entitled to recover is

a. $92,000
b. $105,000
c. $120,000
d. $122,000

56 (May 92)

On February 15, Mazur Corp. contracted to sell 1,000 bushels of wheat to Good Bread, Inc. at $6.00 per bushel with delivery to be made on June 23. On June 1, Good advised Mazur that it would not accept or pay for the wheat. On June 2, Mazur sold the wheat to another customer at the market price of $5.00 per bushel. Mazur had advised Good that it intended to resell the wheat. Which of the following statements is correct?

a. Mazur can successfully sue Good for the difference between the resale price and the contract price.
b. Mazur can resell the wheat only after June 23.
c. Good can retract its anticipatory breach at any time before June 23.
d. Good can successfully sue Mazur for specific performance.

59 (May 92)

Under the UCC Sales Article, a seller will be entitled to recover the full contract price from the buyer when the
a. Goods are destroyed after title passed to the buyer.
b. Goods are destroyed while risk of loss is with the buyer.
c. Buyer revokes its acceptance of the goods.
d. Buyer rejects some of the goods.

52 (November 89)

Under the UCC Sales Article, if a buyer wrongfully rejects goods, the aggrieved seller may

	Resell the goods and sue for damages	Cancel the agreement
a.	Yes	Yes
b.	Yes	No
c.	No	Yes
d.	No	No

43 (May 85)

Flax telephoned Sky Corp. and ordered a specially manufactured air conditioner for $1,900. Subsequently, Flax realized that he miscalculated the area which was to be cooled and concluded that the air conditioner would not be acceptable. Sky had already completed work on the air conditioner, demanded payment, and was unable to resell the unit at a reasonable price. If Flax refuses to pay and Sky brings an action seeking as damages the price plus reasonable storage charges of $50, Sky will recover
a. Nothing, because of the Statute of Frauds.
b. Only its lost profit.
c. The full $1,950.
d. Only $1,900.

58 (November 83)

Marvin contracted to purchase goods from Ling. Subsequently, Marvin breached the contract and Ling is seeking to recover the contract price. Ling can recover the price if
a. Ling does not seek to recover any damages in addition to the price.
b. The goods have been destroyed and Ling's insurance coverage is inadequate, regardless of risk of loss.
c. Ling has identified the goods to the contract and the circumstances indicate that a reasonable effort to resell the goods at a reasonable price would be to no avail.
d. Marvin anticipatorily repudiated the contract and specific performance is not available.

34 (May 80)

Milgore, the vice president of Deluxe Restaurants, telephoned Specialty Restaurant Supplies and ordered a made-to-order dishwashing unit for one of its restaurants. Due to the specifications, the machine was not adaptable for use by other restauranteurs. The agreed price was $2,500. The machine was constructed as agreed but Deluxe has refused to pay for it. Which of the following is correct?
a. Milgore obviously lacked the authority to make such a contract.
b. The Statute of Frauds applies and will bar recovery by Specialty.
c. Specialty can successfully maintain an action for the price.
d. Specialty must resell the machine and recover damages based upon the resale price.

39 (May 78)

Badger Corporation sold goods to Watson. Watson has arbitrarily refused to pay the purchase price. Under what circumstances will Badger not be able to recover the price if it seeks this remedy instead of other possible remedies?

    a.   If Watson refused to accept delivery and the goods were resold in the ordinary course of business.

    b.   If Watson accepted the goods but seeks to return them.

    c.   If the goods sold were destroyed shortly after the risk of loss passed to the buyer.

    d.   If the goods were identified to the contract and Badger made a reasonable effort to resell them at a reasonable price but was unable to do so.

2. On Discovery of Buyer's Insolvency--§§ 2-702, 2-705

Items 52 and 53 are based on the following information:

On April 5, 1987, Anker, Inc. furnished Bold Corp. with Anker's financial statements dated March 31, 1987. The financial statements contained misrepresentations which indicated that Anker was solvent when in fact it was insolvent. Based on Anker's financial statements, Bold agreed to sell Anker 90 computers, "F.O.B. - Bold's loading dock." On April 14, Anker received 60 of the computers. The remaining 30 computers are in the possession of the common carrier and in transit to Anker.

52 (May 87)

If on April 28, Bold discovered that Anker was insolvent, then with respect to the computers delivered to Anker on April 14, Bold may

    a.   Reclaim the computers upon making a demand.

    b.   Reclaim the computers irrespective of the rights of any subsequent third party.

    c.   Not reclaim the computers since ten days have elapsed from its delivery.

    d.   Not reclaim the computers since it is entitled to recover the price of the computers.

53 (May 87)

With respect to the remaining 30 computers in transit, which of the following statements is correct if Anker refuses to pay Bold in cash and Anker is <u>not</u> in possession of a negotiable document of title covering the computers?

    a.   Bold may stop delivery of the computers to Anker since their contract is void due to Anker's furnishing of the false financial statements.

    b.   Bold may stop delivery of the computers to Anker despite the fact that title had passed to Anker.

    c.   Bold must deliver the computers to Anker on credit since Anker has <u>not</u> breached the contract.

    d.   Bold must deliver the computers to Anker since the risk of loss had passed to Anker.

51 (May 84)

Sanders Hardware Company received an order for $900 of assorted hardware from Richards & Company. The shipping terms were F.O.B. Lester Freight Line, seller's place of business, 2/10, net/30. Sanders packed and crated the hardware for shipment and it was loaded upon Lester's truck. While the goods were in transit to Richards, Sanders learned that Richards was insolvent in the equity sense (unable to pay its debts in the ordinary course of business). Sanders promptly wired Lester's office in Denver, Colorado, and instructed them to stop shipment of the goods to Richards and to store them until further instructions. Lester complied with these instructions. Regarding the rights, duties, and liabilities of the parties, which of the following is correct?

    a.   Sanders' stoppage in transit was improper if Richards' assets exceeded his liabilities.

    b.   Richards is entitled to the hardware if it pays cash.

    c.   Once Sanders correctly learned of Richards' insolvency, it had no further duty or obligation to Richards.

    d.   The fact that Richards became insolvent in no way affects the rights, duties, and obligations of the parties.

38 (May 80)

Martha Supermarkets ordered 1,000 cases of giant pitted olives from Grove Packers and Wholesalers. The olives were to be packed, labeled and shipped in 30 days. The payment terms were 2/10, net/30 upon delivery. After the order was nearly ready for shipment, Grove learned that Martha was <u>not</u> paying its debts as they became due. Martha insisted on delivery according to the terms of the contract. Which of the following is correct?

Sales

a. Upon discovery of Martha's financial condition, Grove was relieved from any duty under the contract.
b. Martha has the right of performance since it was <u>not</u> insolvent in the bankruptcy sense.
c. Grove must perform but it is entitled to demand cash.
d. The terms of the contract provided credit to Martha and Grove is bound by it.

D. Statute of Limitations--§ 2-725

13 (November 89)

Unless the parties have otherwise agreed, an action for the breach of a contract within the UCC Sales Article must be commenced within
a. Four years after the cause of action has accrued.
b. Six years after the cause of action has accrued.
c. Four years after the effective date of the contract.
d. Six years after the effective date of the contract.

17 (November 86)

Sklar, CPA, purchased from Wiz Corp. two computers. Sklar discovered material defects in the computers 10 months after taking delivery. Three years after discovering the defects, Sklar commenced an action for breach of warranty against Wiz. Wiz has raised the statute of limitations as a defense. The original contract between Wiz and Sklar contained a conspicuous clause providing that the statute of limitations for breach of warranty actions would be limited to 18 months. Under the circumstances, Sklar will
a. Win because the action was commenced within the four-year period as measured from the date of delivery.
b. Win because the action was commenced within the four-year period as measured from the time he discovered the breach or should have discovered the breach.
c. Lose because the clause providing that the statute of limitations would be limited to 18 months is enforceable.
d. Lose because the statute of limitations is three years from the date of delivery with respect to written contracts.

54 (May 84)

Park purchased from Derek Truck Sales a truck which had serious mechanical problems. Park learned of the defects six months after the date of sale. Five years after the date of sale Park commenced an action for breach of warranty against Derek. Derek asserts the statute of limitations as a defense. Which of the following statements made by Derek is correct?
a. A clause in the original contract reducing the statute of limitations to nine months is enforceable.
b. Park was required to bring the action within the statute of limitation as measured from Derek's tender of delivery.
c. Park was required to bring the action within the statute of limitation as measured from the time the breach was discovered or should have been discovered.
d. Park is precluded from asserting under any circumstances that the statute of limitations stopped running.

59 (November 83)

Dodd Company sold Barney & Company 10,000 ball point pens. The shipment, upon inspection, was found to be nonconforming and Barney rejected the pens. Barney purchased the pens elsewhere at a price which was $525 more than the contract price. The Dodd sales contract contained a clause which purported to reduce the statute of limitations provision of the Uniform Commercial Code to one year. Barney has done nothing about the breach except to return the pens and demand payment of the $525 damages. Dodd has totally ignored Barney's claim. The statute of limitations
a. Is four years according to the Uniform Commercial Code and can <u>not</u> be reduced by the original agreement.
b. Will totally bar recovery unless suit is commenced within the time specified in the contract.
c. May be extended by the parties but <u>not</u> beyond five years.
d. Can <u>not</u> be reduced by the parties to a period less than two years.

V. The Sales Contract--Warranties
A. Express Warranties--§ 2-313

13 (R97)

Under the Sales Article of the UCC, most goods sold by merchants are covered by certain warranties. An example of an express warranty would be a warranty of

a. Usage of trade.
b. Fitness for a particular purpose.
c. Merchantability.
d. Conformity of goods to sample.

60 (May 92)

Which of the following factors result(s) in an express warranty with respect to a sale of goods?

    I.   The seller's description of the goods is part of the basis of the bargain.

    II.   The seller selects goods knowing the buyer's intended use.

a. I only.
b. II only.
c. Both I and II.
d. Neither I nor II.

43 (May 90)

An important factor in determining if an express warranty has been created is whether the

a. Statements made by the seller became part of the basis of the bargain.
b. Sale was made by a merchant in the regular course of business.
c. Statements made by the seller were in writing.
d. Seller intended to create a warranty.

45 (November 88)

Which of the following factors will be most important in determining whether an express warranty has been created concerning goods sold?

a. The seller gave a description of the goods that is part of the basis of the bargain.
b. The buyer or seller is a merchant with respect to the goods being sold.
c. Whether the seller intended to create the express warranty.
d. Whether the buyer relied on the seller's statements.

32 (May 80)

Target Company, Inc. ordered a generator from Maximum Voltage Corporation. A dispute has arisen over the effect of a provision in the specifications that the generator have a 5,000 kilowatt capacity. The specifications were attached to the contract and were incorporated by reference in the main body of the contract. The generator did not have this capacity but instead had a maximum capacity of 4,800 kilowatts. The contract had a disclaimer clause which effectively negated both of the implied warranties of quality. Target is seeking to avoid the contract based upon breach of warranty and Maximum is relying on its disclaimer. Which of the following is a correct statement?

a. The 5,000 kilowatt term contained in the specifications does not constitute a warranty.
b. The disclaimer effectively negated any and all warranty protection claimed by Target.
c. The description language (5,000 kilowatt) contained in the specifications is an express warranty and has not been effectively disclaimed.
d. The parol evidence rule will prevent Target from asserting the 5,000 kilowatt term as a warranty.

Sales

37 (May 79)

Marco Auto, Inc. made many untrue statements in the course of inducing Rockford to purchase a used auto for $3,500. The car in question turned out to have some serious faults. Which of the following untrue statements made by Marco should Rockford use in seeking recovery from Marco for breach of warranty?

    a. "I refused a $3,800 offer for this very same auto from another buyer last week."
    b. "This auto is one of the best autos we have for sale."
    c. "At this price the auto is a real steal."
    d. "I can guarantee that you will never regret this purchase."

2 (November 75)

In a contract for the sale of goods, express warranties by the seller are created by any

    a. Reasonable implication based upon the seller's acts.
    b. Description of the goods which is made part of the basis of the contract.
    c. Expression of the value of the goods.
    d. Statement of seller's opinion.

7A (November 77)

Max Motors, Inc. sold a 1973 used station wagon to Sarah Constance for $3,350. Constance has corresponded with Max Motors on several occasions and has alleged that Fogarty, an experienced salesman for Max Motors, made several express oral warranties in connection with her purchase of the car. Constance alleges that there has been breach of warranty and as a result she has suffered damages to the extent of $1,025 for expenses incurred to repair the car. Constance also indicated that in the event she does not receive a refund of $1,025, she will take appropriate legal action to obtain satisfaction.

In various letters, Constance stated that she went to Max Motors and contacted Fogarty. Before she finally made a deal for the car, she asked many questions about the car. Fogarty assured her that the car was in good condition and that he had driven the car several times. In addition, Fogarty stated that "This is a car I can recommend and it is in A-1 shape."

Constance informed Fogarty that her husband had been transferred to another state, that her child was only two years old, and that she needed the car so she could join her husband. She stated that Fogarty assured her that he knew the car and knew the person who traded it in and it was "mechanically perfect." He also told her that, "it would get any place she wanted to go and not to worry." Constance indicated she knew nothing about cars but would like to drive it. Fogarty replied this was not possible because he was the only man on duty at the lot that day and he could not leave to accompany her as required by company policy.

Constance stated she purchased the car in reliance on the statements made by Fogarty. Unfortunately, these statements proved to be incorrect. The car began knocking and finally broke down after being driven about 300 miles. The car was repaired by Master Mechanics and a copy of a receipted bill for $1,025 accompanied one of her letters to Max Motors.

Fogarty indicated that he believed what he stated was true, as far as he knew the car wasn't in bad condition, and he knew of no important defects in the car. He also indicated he told Constance that he could not warrant the car because it was over two years old and had in excess of 50,000 miles.

Required: Answer the following, setting forth reasons for any conclusions stated.

    1. Is it likely that Constance will prevail in a legal action against Max Motors? Discuss all relevant issues.
    2. Identify, but do not discuss, other warranties that Constance might rely upon in addition to the oral express warranties.

1. Yes. The main issue is whether Fogarty's statements constitute an affirmation of fact as contrasted with mere opinion.

This issue has been resolved in many cases in favor of purchasers, such as Constance. It often is difficult to draw the line between an affirmation of fact, which when relied upon constitutes a warranty, and mere sales talk, which is a statement of the seller's opinion. However the combination of the various statements made by Fogarty and perhaps the language "mechanically perfect" constituted a warranty under the circumstances.

Furthermore, the relative expertise of the parties is validly taken into account under such circumstances. Fogarty was a used car salesman with long experience and was familiar with the mechanical aspects of automobiles. It would be only natural for Constance to take his statements as being something more than idle chatter. Her total lack of knowledge of automobiles and their engines would lead her to rely on Fogarty's representations.

In addition, all the other elements necessary to establish an oral express warranty are present. Fogarty's good faith or honest belief in the truth of his statements is irrelevant. Knowledge of falsity has nothing to do with warranty. The Uniform Commercial Code reads as follows: "Any affirmation of fact or promise made by the seller to the buyer which relates to the goods and becomes part of the basis of the bargain creates an express warranty that the goods shall conform to the affirmation or promise." Additionally, the Code states, "It is not necessary to the creation of an express warranty that the seller use familiar words, such as warrants or guarantees or that . . . a specific intention to make a warranty be present."

The facts clearly indicate that the affirmation or promise was a basis of the bargain; that is, that the language was intended to be relied upon by the buyer and it was. Finally, the buyer relied upon it to her detriment and suffered damages as a result. Although the Uniform Commercial Code includes cautionary language that an affirmation merely of the value of the goods or a statement purporting to be merely the seller's opinion or commendation of the goods does not create a warranty, it appears that the facts clearly establish an oral express warranty.

Another issue is the legal effect of Fogarty's statement that he could not give a warranty on the auto sold. Does this validly disclaim the oral express warranty protection? There is a general hostility manifested by the Uniform Commercial Code and the courts to allowing broad uninformative disclaimers to legally negate warranty protection. Warranties are not to be disclaimed without due notice and fairness shown to the purchaser under the circumstances. Where there are words tending to negate an oral express warranty, the purported disclaimer shall be constructed whenever reasonable as consistent with the warranty. Hence, a purported negation or limitation is inoperative to the extent that such a construction is unreasonable. Thus, it appears that the warranty has not been disclaimed.

2. Constance might rely upon the implied warranties of merchantability and fitness for a particular purpose.

B. Implied Warranties--Merchantability and Fitness--§§ 2-314, 2-315

51 (November 94)

Under the Sales Article of the UCC, which of the following statements is correct regarding the warranty of merchantability arising when there has been a sale of goods by a merchant seller?

a. The warranty must be in writing.
b. The warranty arises when the buyer relies on the seller's skill in selecting the goods purchased.
c. The warranty cannot be disclaimed.
d. The warranty arises as a matter of law when the seller ordinarily sells the goods purchased.

55 (May 92)

Which of the following conditions must be met for an implied warranty of fitness for a particular purpose to arise in connection with a sale of goods?

    I. The warranty must be in writing.
    II. The seller must know that the buyer was relying on the seller in selecting the goods.

a. I only.
b. II only.
c. Both I and II.
d. Neither I nor II.

47 (November 88)

Which of the following is necessary in order for the warranty of merchantability to arise where there has been a sale of goods?

        I.   The seller must be a merchant with respect to goods of that kind.

        II.   The warranty must be in writing.

        III.   The buyer must have relied on the seller's skill or judgment in selecting the goods.

  a. I and III only.

  b. I, II, and III.

  c. II and III only.

  d. I only.

50 (May 88)

Under the UCC Sales Article, which of the following warranties requires the seller to be a merchant with respect to the goods being sold in order for the warranty to apply?

	Implied warranty of fitness for a particular purpose	Implied warranty of merchantability
a.	Yes	Yes
b.	No	No
c.	Yes	No
d.	No	Yes

54 (November 84)

Wally, a CPA and a neighbor of Rita's, offered to sell Rita his power chain saw for $400. Rita stated that she knew nothing about chain saws but would buy the saw if it were capable of cutting down the trees in her backyard, which had an average diameter of five feet. Wally assured Rita that the saw "would do the job." Relying on Wally's assurance, Rita purchased the saw. Wally has created a warranty that

  a. The saw is of an average fair quality.

  b. The saw is fit for the ordinary purposes for which it is used.

  c. The saw is capable of cutting the trees in Rita's backyard.

  d. Is unenforceable because it is <u>not</u> in writing.

54 (November 83)

The Uniform Commercial Code implies a warranty of merchantability to protect buyers of goods. To be subject to this warranty the goods need <u>not</u> be

  a. Fit for all of the purposes for which the buyer intends to use the goods.

  b. Adequately packaged and labeled.

  c. Sold by a merchant.

  d. In conformity with any promises or affirmations of fact made on the container or label.

C. Warranty of Title and Against Infringement--§ 2-312

43 (November 95)

Under the Sales Article of the UCC, the warranty of title

  a. Provides that the seller cannot disclaim the warranty if the sale is made to a bona fide purchaser for value.

  b. Provides that the seller deliver the goods free from any lien of which the buyer lacked knowledge when the contract was made.

  c. Applies only if it is in writing and signed by the seller.

  d. Applies only if the seller is a merchant.

Items 51 and 52 are based on the following:

On May 2, Handy Hardware sent Ram Industries a signed purchase order that stated, in part, as follows:

"Ship for May 8 delivery 300 Model A-X socket sets at current dealer price. Terms 2/10/net 30."

Ram received Handy's purchase order on May 4. On May 5, Ram discovered that it had only 200 Model A-X socket sets and 100 Model W-Z socket sets in stock. Ram shipped the Model A-X and Model W-Z sets to Handy without any explanation concerning the shipment. The socket sets were received by Handy on May 8.

51 (November 93)

Which of the following statements concerning the shipment is correct?
a. Ram's shipment is an acceptance of Handy's offer.
b. Ram's shipment is a counteroffer.
c. Handy's order must be accepted by Ram in writing before Ram ships the socket sets.
d. Handy's order can only be accepted by Ram shipping conforming goods.

52 (November 93)

Assuming a contract exists between Handy and Ram, which of the following implied warranties would result?
      I. Implied warranty of merchantability.
     II. Implied warranty of fitness for a particular purpose.
     III. Implied warranty of title.
a. I only.
b. III only.
c. I and III only.
d. I, II and III.

48 (May 91)

With respect to the sale of goods, the warranty of title
a. Applies only if the seller is a merchant.
b. Applies only if it is in writing and signed by the seller.
c. Provides that the seller deliver the goods free from any lien of which the buyer lacked knowledge when the contract was made.
d. Provides that the seller cannot disclaim the warranty if the sale is made to a bona fide purchaser for value.

14 (May 81)

The Uniform Commercial Code provides for a warranty against infringement. Its primary purpose is to protect the buyer of goods from infringement of the rights of third parties. This warranty
a. Only applies if the sale is between merchants.
b. Must be expressly stated in the contract or the Statute of Frauds will prevent its enforceability.
c. Protects the seller if the buyer furnishes specifications which result in an infringement.
d. Can not be disclaimed.

16 (May 81)

Ace Auto Sales, Inc. sold Williams a secondhand car for $9,000. One day Williams parked the car in a shopping center parking lot. When Williams returned to the car, Montrose and several policemen were waiting. It turned out that the car had been stolen from Montrose who was rightfully claiming ownership. Subsequently, the car was returned by Williams to Montrose. Williams seeks recourse against Ace Auto Sales who had sold him the car with the usual disclaimer of warranty. Which of the following is correct?

a. Since Ace Auto Sales' contract of sale disclaimed "any and all warranties" arising in connection with its sale to Williams, Williams must bear the loss.

b. Since Ace Auto and Williams were both innocent of any wrongdoing in connection with the theft of the auto, the loss will rest upon the party ultimately in possession.

c. Had Williams litigated the question of Montrose's ownership to the auto, he would have won since possession is nine-tenths of the law.

d. Ace Auto will bear the loss since a warranty of title in Williams' favor arose upon the sale of the auto.

35 (November 78)

Gordon purchased 100 automatic sprinklers from Thompson, a jobber. Conrad was the rightful owner of the sprinklers which had been stolen from his warehouse. He had the sheriff repossess them and has asserted his ownership of them. Gordon's bill of sale specifically indicated that it made no implied warranties. The bill of sale did not contain any warranties of title. Which of the following is correct based on the above facts?

a. The title warranties have been effectively negated.

b. It is not possible to disclaim the title warranties.

c. Gordon's best course of action is to assert his superior title to the sprinklers since he is a good faith purchaser for value.

d. Thompson is liable in that he warranted that the title conveyed was good and his transfer rightful.

36 (November 78)

Parks furnished specifications and ordered 1,000 specially-constructed folding tables from Metal Manufacturing Company, Inc. The tables were unique in design and had not appeared in the local market. Metal completed the job and delivered the order to Parks. Parks sold about 600 of the tables when Unusual Tables, Inc. sued both Parks and Metal for patent infringement. If Unusual wins, what is the status of Parks and Metal?

a. Metal is liable to Parks for breach of the warranty against infringement.

b. Parks is liable to Metal for breach of the warranty against infringement.

c. The warranty against infringement is not available to either Parks or Metal.

d. Parks and Metal are jointly and severally liable and, as such, must pay the judgment in equal amounts.

7 (November 75)

Unless specifically excluded, a contract for the sale of goods includes a warranty of

a. Good title.

b. Fairness.

c. Usefulness.

d. Adequate consideration.

4 (November 90)

Pharo Aviation, Inc. sells and services used airplanes. Sanders, Pharo's service department manager, negotiated with Secure Equipment Co. for the purchase of a used tug for moving airplanes in and out of Pharo's hangar. Secure sells and services tugs and related equipment. Sanders was unfamiliar with the various models, specifications, and capacities of the tugs sold by Secure; however, Sanders knew that the tug purchased needed to have the capacity to move airplanes weighing up to 10,000 pounds. Sanders and the sales representative discussed this specific need because Sanders was uncertain as to which tug would meet Pharo's requirements. The sales representative then recommended a particular make and model of tug. Sanders agreed to rely on the sales representative's advice and signed a purchase contract with Secure.

About a week after Sanders took delivery, the following occurred:

- Sanders determined that the tug did not have the capacity to move airplanes weighing over 5,000 pounds.

- Sanders was advised correctly by Maco Equipment Distributors, Inc. that Maco was the rightful owner of the tug, which it had left with Secure for repairs.

Pharo has commenced a lawsuit against Secure claiming that implied warranties were created by the contract with Secure and that these have been breached. Maco has claimed that it is entitled to the tug and has demanded its return from Pharo.

Required: Answer each of the following questions, and set forth the reasons for your conclusions.

a. Were any implied warranties created by the contract between Pharo and Secure and, if so, were any of those warranties breached?

b. Is Maco entitled to the return of the tug?

a. Under the UCC Sales Article, the contract between Pharo and Secure creates the following implied warranties:

- Implied warranty of merchantability;
- Implied warranty of fitness for a particular purpose;
- Implied warranty of title.

The implied warranty of merchantability requires the tug to be merchantable; that is, fit for the ordinary purpose intended. It is probable that the tug was fit for such ordinary purposes and, therefore, the implied warranty of merchantability was not breached.

The implied warranty of fitness for a particular purpose requires that the tug be fit for the particular purpose for which it was purchased. To show that the implied warranty of fitness for a particular purpose is present as a result of the contract Pharo must show that:

- Secure knew of the particular needs of Pharo;
- Pharo relied on Secure to select a suitable tug;
- Secure knew that Pharo was relying on Secure to select a tug suitable for Pharo's needs.

The implied warranty of fitness for a particular purpose has been breached because the tug was not suitable for Pharo's particular needs (i.e., to move airplanes weighing up to 10,000 pounds).

The implied warranty of title requires that:

- Secure have good title;
- The transfer to Pharo would be rightful
- The tug would be delivered free from any security interest or other lien.

The implied warranty of title has been breached because Maco was the rightful owner.

b. Maco will not be entitled to recover the tug from Pharo because:

- Maco had entrusted the tug to Secure, which deals in similar goods;
- That, as a result of such entrustment, Secure had the power to transfer Maco's rights to the tug to a buyer in the ordinary course of business;
- Pharo was a buyer in the ordinary course of business because Pharo purchased the tug in good faith and without knowledge of Maco's ownership interest.

D. Warranty Disclaimers
1. Title--§ 2-312(2)

43 (May 94)

Vick bought a used boat from Ocean marina that disclaimed "any and all warranties" in connection with the sale. Ocean was unaware the boat had been stolen from Kidd. Vick surrendered it to Kidd when confronted with proof of the theft. Vick sued Ocean. Who is likely to prevail and why?

a. Vick, because the implied warranty of title has been breached.
b. Vick, because a merchant cannot disclaim implied warranties.
c. Ocean, because of the disclaimer of warranties.
d. Ocean, because Vick surrendered the boat to Kidd.

42 (May 90)

Under the UCC Sales Article, the warranty of title may be excluded by

a. Merchants or non-merchants provided the exclusion is in writing.
b. Non-merchant sellers only.
c. The seller's statement that it is selling only such right or title that it has.
d. Use of an "as is" disclaimer.

52 (November 83)

Gold sold Sable ten fur coats. The contract contained no specific provision regarding title warranties. It did, however, contain a provision which indicated that the coats were sold "with all faults and defects." Two of the coats sold to Sable had been stolen and were reclaimed by the rightful owner. Which of the following is a correct statement?

a. The implied warranty of title is eliminated by the parol evidence rule.
b. The contract automatically contained a warranty that the title conveyed is good and can only be excluded by specific language.
c. Since there was no express title warranty, Sable assumed the risk.
d. The disclaimer "with all faults and defects" effectively negates any and all warranties.

7B (November 77)

A claim has been asserted against Ajax Motors for $7,000 arising out of the sale of a used 1975 automobile. Knox purchased the automobile in February 1977 and subsequently learned that it was a stolen car. The serial numbers had been changed, but it has been conclusively determined that the car belongs to Watts who has duly repossessed it. The contract contained a disclaimer which read as follows: "Ajax Motors hereby disclaims any and all warranties, express or implied, which are not contained in the contract." Knox has brought a legal action against Ajax Motors alleging breach of contract.

Required: Answer the following, setting forth reasons for any conclusions stated.

What is the probable outcome of such a legal action? Discuss fully the legal basis upon which Watts is relying and any defense that Ajax Motors may assert.

> The case should be decided in favor of Knox. The basis for recovery would be the title warranties provided under the Uniform Commercial Code which states that the title conveyed should be good and its transfer rightful, but here Watts was the rightful owner and entitled to repossess the car. The Code does not indicate whether such a warranty is to be construed as an express or implied warranty. However, it can only be excluded by specific language or circumstances that give the buyer reason to know that the person selling does not claim title in himself. From this it would appear that a seller would have to clearly indicate that he does not purport to own the item in question and that the buyer is assuming the risk that the title is defective. Such was not the case. However, Ajax Motors will undoubtedly claim that the disclaimer is legally operative.

2. Other Warranties--§ 2-316

50 (May 91)

Under the UCC Sales Article, the implied warranty of merchantability
a. May be disclaimed by a seller's oral statement that mentions merchantability.
b. Arises only in contracts involving a merchant seller and a merchant buyer.
c. Is breached if the goods are not fit for all purposes for which the buyer intends to use the goods.
d. Must be part of the basis of the bargain to be binding on the seller.

Items 55 through 58 are based on the following:

Lazur Corp. entered into a contract with Baker Suppliers, Inc. to purchase a used word processor from Baker. Lazur is engaged in the business of selling new and used word processors to the general public. The contract required Baker to ship the goods to Lazur by common carrier pursuant to the following provision in the contract: "F.O.B.--Baker Suppliers, Inc. loading dock." Baker also represented in the contract that the word processor had been used for only 10 hours by its previous owner. The contract included the provision that the word processor had been used for only 10 hours by its previous owner. The contract included the provision that the word processor was being sold "as is" and this provision was in a larger and different type style than the remainder of the contract.

55 (May 89)

With regard to the contract between Lazur and Baker,

    a.   An implied warranty of merchantability does <u>not</u> arise unless both Lazur and Baker are merchants.

    b.   The "as is" provision effectively disclaims the implied warranty of title.

    c.   No express warranties are created by the contract.

    d.   The "as is" provision would <u>not</u> prevent Baker from being liable for a breach of any express warranties created by the contract.

56 (May 89)

<u>For this item only</u>, assume that during shipment to Lazur the word processor was serious damaged when the carrier's truck was involved in an accident. When the carrier attempted to deliver the word processor, Lazur rejected it and has refused to pay Baker the purchase price. Under the UCC Sales Article:

    a.   Lazur rightfully rejected the damaged computer.

    b.   The risk of loss for the computer was on Lazur during shipment.

    c.   At the time of the accident, risk of loss for the computer was on Baker because title to the computer had <u>not</u> yet passed to Lazur.

    d.   Lazur will <u>not</u> be liable to Baker for the purchase price of the computer because of the F.O.B. provision in the contract.

57 (May 89)

<u>For this item only</u>, assume that the contract between Lazur and Baker is otherwise silent. Under the UCC Sales Article,

    a.   Lazur must pay Baker the purchase price before Baker is required to ship the word processor to Lazur.

    b.   Baker does <u>not</u> warrant that it owns the word processor.

    c.   Lazur will be entitled to inspect the word processor before it accepts or pays for it.

    d.   Title to the word processor passes to Lazur when it takes physical possession.

58 (May 89)

<u>For this item only</u>, assume that Lazur refused to accept the word processor even though it was in all respects conforming to the contract and that the contract is otherwise silent. Under the UCC Sales Article,

    a.   Baker can successfully sue for specific performance and make Lazur accept and pay for the word processor.

    b.   Baker may resell the word processor to another buyer.

    c.   Baker must sue for the difference between the market value of the word processor and the contract price plus its incidental damages.

    d.   Baker cannot successfully sue for consequential damages unless it attempts to resell the word processor.

39 (May 83)

In general, disclaimers of implied warranty protection are

    a.   Permitted if they are explicit and understandable and the buyer is aware of their existence.

    b.   Not binding on remote purchasers with notice thereof.

    c.   Void because they are against public policy.

    d.   Invalid unless in writing and signed by the buyer.

47 (November 82)

Webster purchased a drill press for $475 from Martinson Hardware, Inc. The press has proved to be defective and Webster wishes to rescind the purchase based upon a breach of implied warranty. Which of the following will preclude Webster's recovery from Martinson?

    a.   The press sold to Webster was a demonstration model and sold at a substantial discount; hence, Webster received no implied warranties.

    b.   Webster examined the press carefully, but as regards the defects, they were hidden defects which a reasonable examination would <u>not</u> have detected.

    c.   Martinson informed Webster that they were closing out the model at a loss due to certain deficiencies and that it was sold "with all faults."

    d.   The fact that it was the negligence of the manufacturer which caused the trouble and that the defect could <u>not</u> have been discovered by Martinson without actually taking the press apart.

40 (May 78)

Viscount Appliances sold Conway a refrigerator. Viscount wishes to disclaim the implied warranty of fitness for a particular purpose. Which of the following will effectively disclaim this warranty?

    a.   The fact that the refrigerator is widely advertised and was sold under its brand name.

    b.   A conspicuous written statement which states that "any and all warranty protection is hereby disclaimed."

    c.   A conspicuous written statement indicating that "there are <u>no</u> warranties which extend beyond the description contained in the contract of sale."

    d.   An inconspicuous written statement which specifically negates the warranty.

45 (May 77)

In connection with a contract for the sale of goods, in which of the following ways can the implied warranty of merchantability be excluded by the seller?

    a.   By an oral statement which mentions merchantability.

    b.   By a written statement without mentioning merchantability.

    c.   By an oral statement which does <u>not</u> mention merchantability.

    d.   By an inconspicuous written statement which mentions merchantability.

34 (May 75)

Carter purchased goods from Dunn for $450. Dunn orally made an express warranty of fitness of the goods for the particular purpose described by Carter. In addition, Dunn orally disclaimed "all warranty protection." The express warranty of fitness

    a.   Is irrelevant in any event, but it is superseded by the Uniform Commercial Code section which creates an implied warranty of fitness.

    b.   Is valid even though <u>not</u> in writing.

    c.   Is effectively negated by the general disclaimer clause assuming both the warranty and disclaimer are in writing.

    d.   Coupled with the disclaimer, effectively negates all Carter's implied warranty protection.

V.   Products Liability

44 (November 95)

To establish a cause of action based on strict liability in tort for personal injuries that result from the use of a defective product, one of the elements the injured party must prove is that the seller

    a.   Was aware of the defect in the product.

    b.   Sold the product to the injured party.

    c.   Failed to exercise due care.

    d.   Sold the product in a defective condition.

53 (November 94)

High sues the manufacturer, wholesaler, and retailer for bodily injuries caused by a power saw High purchased. Which of the following statements is correct under strict liability theory?

    a.   Contributory negligence on High's part will always be a bar to recovery.

    b.   The manufacturer will avoid liability if it can show it followed the custom of the industry.

    c.   Privity will be a bar to recovery insofar as the wholesaler is concerned if the wholesaler did <u>not</u> have a reasonable opportunity to inspect.

    d.   High may recover even if he <u>cannot</u> show any negligence was involved.

44 (May 94)

Larch Corp. manufactured and sold Oak a stove. The sale documents included a disclaimer of warranty for personal injury. The stove was defective. It exploded causing serious injuries to Oak's spouse. Larch was notified one week after the explosion. Under the UCC Sales Article, which of the following statements concerning Larch's liability for personal injury to Oak's spouse would be correct?

a. Larch <u>cannot</u> be liable because of a lack of privity with Oak's spouse.
b. Larch will <u>not</u> be liable because of a failure to give proper notice.
c. Larch will be liable because the disclaimer was <u>not</u> a disclaimer of all liability.
d. Larch will be liable because liability for personal injury <u>cannot</u> be disclaimed.

54 (November 93)

To establish a cause of action based on strict liability in tort for personal injuries resulting from using a defective product, one of the elements of the plaintiff must prove is that the seller (defendant)

a. Failed to exercise due care.
b. Was in privity of contract with the plaintiff.
c. Defectively designed the product.
d. Was engaged in the business of selling the product.

57 (May 92)

Under the UCC Sales Article, an action for breach of the implied warranty of merchantability by a party who sustains personal injuries may be successful against the seller of the product only when

a. The seller is a merchant of the product involved.
b. An action based on negligence can also be successfully maintained.
c. The injured party is in privity of contract with the seller.
d. An action based on strict liability in tort can also be successfully maintained.

45 (November 89)

Which of the following factors is least important in determining whether a manufacturer is strictly liable in tort for a defective product?

a. The negligence of the manufacturer.
b. The contributory negligence of the plaintiff.
c. Modifications to the product by the wholesaler.
d. Whether the product caused injuries.

46 (November 86)

Kent suffered an injury due to a malfunction of a chain saw he had purchased from Grey Hardware. The saw was manufactured by Dill Tool Corp. Kent has commenced an action against Grey and Dill based upon strict liability. Which of the following is a correct statement.

a. Dill will <u>not</u> be liable if it manufactured the saw in a non-negligent manner.
b. Privity will <u>not</u> be a valid defense against Kent's suit.
c. The lawsuit will be dismissed since strict liability has <u>not</u> been applied in product liability cases in the majority of jurisdictions.
d. Kent's suit against Grey will be dismissed since Grey was <u>not</u> at fault.

42 (May 85)

The Uniform Commercial Code's position on privity of warranty as to personal injuries

a. Allows the buyer's family the right to sue only the party from whom the buyer purchased the product.
b. Resulted in a single uniform rule being adopted throughout most of the United States.
c. Prohibits the exclusion on privity grounds of third parties from the warranty protection it has granted.
d. Applies exclusively to manufacturers.

37 (May 80)

Pure Food Company packed and sold quality food products to wholesalers and fancy food retailers. One of its most popular items was "southern style" baked beans. Charleston purchased a large can of the beans from the Superior Quality Grocery. Charleston's mother bit into a heaping spoonful of the beans at a family outing and fractured her jaw. The evidence revealed that the beans contained a brown stone, the size of a marble. In a subsequent lawsuit by Mrs. Charleston, which of the following is correct?

    a.   Mrs. Charleston can collect against Superior Quality for negligence.

    b.   Privity will <u>not</u> be a bar in a lawsuit against either Pure Food or Superior Quality.

    c.   The various sellers involved could have effectively excluded or limited the rights of third parties to sue them.

    d.   Privity is a bar to recovery by Mrs. Charleston, although her son may sue Superior Quality.

40 (May 75)

Marvin purchased a new 1975 automobile from Excellent Auto Sales. The car was fully warranted by the manufacturer, Specific Motors, for one year or 20,000 miles whichever occurred sooner. There was <u>no</u> warranty disclaimer by either the manufacturer or the retailer. The car contained a hidden defect insofar as the retailer was concerned, i.e., one that could <u>not</u> be discovered with reasonable care except during manufacture. The defect caused Marvin to have a serious accident which damaged the car and injured him. Which of the following statements is true regarding the status of Marvin's contract?

    a.   Marvin is <u>not</u> in privity of contract with Specific Motors.

    b.   Excellent Auto has <u>no</u> liability to Marvin in that it could <u>not</u> have discovered the defect.

    c.   The Uniform Commercial Code abolished the privity requirement in cases such as this.

    d.   Marvin may recover only for the damage to the car and the replacement of the defective parts.

4 (November 85)

John Barr purchased a new fork-lift for use in his business from Fiber Corp. Fiber designs, manufactures, and assembles fork-lifts, shipping them directly to customers throughout the U.S. The contract between Barr and Fiber contained a clause in fine print disclaiming "all warranties express or implied other than the limited warranty provided for on the face of this contract." The limited warranty included in the contract provided that "the buyer's sole and exclusive remedy shall be repair or replacement of defective parts and the seller shall not be liable for damages or personal injuries." The contract was a standard form used by Fiber, and as a matter of policy Fiber did not negotiate the terms and conditions of the contract with its customers.

Within one week of the purchase date, Barr was seriously injured when the steering wheel locked causing him to lose control of the fork-lift. Barr brings an action against Fiber for the personal injuries that he sustained based on the following causes of action:

- Negligence
- Breach of warranty
- Strict liability in tort

Fiber has asserted that the action brought by Barr should be dismissed due to the disclaimer.

Required: Answer the following, setting forth reasons for any conclusions stated.

    a.   Discuss in separate paragraphs the prerequisites necessary to sustain each of the three causes of action asserted by Barr.

    b.   Discuss the validity of the disclaimer with regard to the breach of warranty cause of action.

a. <u>Negligence</u>. In order to establish a cause of action based on negligence Barr must establish the following elements:

- That the defendant owed a legal duty to the plaintiff.
- That the defendant breached that duty.
- That the plaintiff sustained an actual loss or damages.
- That the breach of duty was the proximate cause of the plaintiff's actual loss or damages.

In determining if negligence is present the court will consider whether the defendant acted as a reasonably prudent person under the circumstances. Included in the reasonably prudent person test is whether the risk of harm was foreseeable.

<u>Breach of Warranty</u>. Since the sale of goods (the fork-lift) is involved in the contract, the UCC Sales Article applies. Because the seller would be regarded as a merchant, an implied warranty of merchantability is created. In order to establish a breach of this warranty, the plaintiff (Barr) must show:

- That the fork-lift was not fit for the ordinary purposes intended and
- That as a result of the breach of warranty, the plaintiff sustained a loss.

<u>Strict Liability in Tort</u>. Generally, the elements necessary to establish a cause of action based on strict liability in tort are as follows:

- That the product was in defective condition when it left the possession or control of the seller.
- That the product was unreasonably dangerous to the consumer or user.
- That the cause of the consumer's or user's injury was the defect.
- That the seller engaged in the business of selling such a product.
- That the product was one which the seller expected to and did reach the consumer or user without substantial changes in the condition in which it was sold.

Proof of fault is not a requirement to establish a cause of action in strict liability.

b. A proper disclaimer will permit the seller to exclude the implied warranty of merchantability. Under the facts, the disclaimer would appear to be invalid since a written disclaimer of the implied warranty of merchantability must be conspicuous and, arguably, the language in the contract is not acceptable under the UCC. In this case the disclaimer was in fine print and therefore not conspicuous. In addition, the disclaimer may be considered unconscionable since the contract was standardized and no bargaining of the terms of the contract was permitted. It should be pointed out that although consequential damages may be limited or excluded, in the case of consumer goods limitation of consequential damages for personal injuries is prima facie unconscionable. However, since the facts do not relate to consumer goods, such limitation of damages is not prima facie unconscionable but may be proved to be unconscionable.

PART IX -- SECURED TRANSACTIONS*

TABLE OF CONTENTS

*Answers consistent with Revised UCC Article 9 (2000).

PART IX

SECURED TRANSACTIONS

I. Introduction to Secured Transactions
A. Introduction to Article 9
1. Basic Definitions; Types of Security Interests and Collateral

45 (May 75)

Case Corporation manufactures electric drills and sells them to retail hardware stores. Under the Uniform Commercial Code, it is likely that
  a. The drills are inventory in Case's hands.
  b. The drills are equipment in Case's hands.
  c. The raw materials on hand to be used in the manufacturing of the drills are not inventory in Case's hands.
  d. The drills are considered equipment in the hands of the hardware stores who purchased them.

2. Scope of Article 9

38 (November 80)

Which of the following is included within the scope of the Secured Transactions Article of the Code?
  a. The outright sale of accounts receivable.
  b. A landlord's lien.
  c. The assignment of a claim for wages.
  d. The sale of chattel paper as a part of the sale of a business out of which it arose.

18 (May 79)

Migrane Financial does a wide variety of lending. It provides funds to manufacturers, middlemen, retailers, consumers and home owners. In all instances it intends to create a security interest in the loan transactions it enters into. To which of the following will Article 9 (Secured Transactions) of the Uniform Commercial Code not apply?
  a. A second mortgage on the borrower's home.
  b. An equipment lease.
  c. The sale of accounts.
  d. Field warehousing.

35 (November 75)

The scope of secured transactions in the Uniform Commercial Code does not include
  a. Pledges.
  b. Transactions where title has not passed.
  c. After-acquired collateral.
  d. Sale of corporate debentures.

37 (November 75)

Article 9 (Secured Transactions) of the Uniform Commercial Code
  a. Does not apply if the secured transaction involves personal property which has a value of less than $500.
  b. Has been adopted by the Congress of the United States and thus is the law of all the states.
  c. Only codified most of the majority rules existing at common law are contained in widely adopted state statutes applicable to secured transactions.
  d. Does not apply to purchase-money real estate mortgages.

359

B. Attachment of a Security Interest

57 (November 94)

Under the Secured Transactions Article of the UCC, which of the following requirements is necessary to have a security interest attach?

	Debtor has rights in the collateral	Proper filing of a security agreement	Value given by the creditor
a.	Yes	Yes	Yes
b.	Yes	Yes	No
c.	Yes	No	Yes
d.	No	Yes	Yes

48 (May 94)

Under the UCC Secured Transactions Article, which of the following events will always prevent a security interest from attaching?
   a.   Failure to have a written security agreement.
   b.   Failure of the creditor to have possession of the collateral.
   c.   Failure of the debtor to have rights in the collateral.
   d.   Failure of the creditor to give present consideration for the security interest.

58 (November 93)

Winslow Co., which is in the business of selling furniture, borrowed $60,000 from Pine Bank. Winslow executed a promissory note for that amount and used all of its accounts receivable as collateral for the loan. Winslow executed a security agreement that described the collateral. Winslow did not file a financing statement. Which of the following statements best describes this transaction?
   a.   Perfection of the security interest occurred even though Winslow did <u>not</u> file a financing statement.
   b.   Perfection of the security interest occurred by Pine having an interest in accounts receivable.
   c.   Attachment of the security interest did <u>not</u> occur because Winslow failed to file a financing statement.
   d.   Attachment of the security interest occurred when the loan was made and Winslow executed the security agreement.

46 (May 93)

On March 1, Green went to Easy Car Sales to buy a car. Green spoke to a salesperson and agreed to buy a car that Easy had in its showroom. On March 5, Green made a $500 downpayment and signed a security agreement to secure the payment of the balance of the purchase price. On March 10, Green picked up the car. On March 15, Easy filed the security agreement. On what date did Easy's security interest attach?
   a.   March 1.
   b.   March 5.
   c.   March 10.
   d.   March 15.

45 (November 92)

Under the UCC Secured Transactions Article, which of the following conditions must be satisfied for a security interest to attach?
   a.   The debtor must have title to the collateral.
   b.   The debtor must agree to the creation of the security interest.
   c.   The creditor must be in possession of part of the collateral.
   d.   The creditor must properly file a financing statement.

46 (November 92)

Under the UCC Secured Transactions Article, when collateral is in a secured party's possession, which of the following conditions must also be satisfied to have attachment?
a. There must be a written security agreement.
b. The public must be notified.
c. The secured party must receive consideration.
d. The debtor must have rights to the collateral.

57 (May 91)

Pix Co., which is engaged in the business of selling appliances, borrowed $18,000 from the Lux Bank. Pix executed a promissory note for that amount and pledged all of its customer installment receivables as collateral for the loan. Pix executed a security agreement that described the collateral, but Lux did not file a financing statement. With respect to this transaction
a. Attachment of the security interest did <u>not</u> occur because Pix failed to file a financing statement.
b. Perfection of the security interest occurred despite Lux's failure to file a financing statement.
c. Attachment of the security interest took place when the loan was made and Pix executed the security agreement.
d. Perfection of the security interest did <u>not</u> occur because accounts receivable are intangibles.

50 (November 89)

Under the UCC Secured Transactions Article, for a security interest to attach, the
a. Debtor must agree to the creation of the security interest.
b. Creditor must properly file a financing statement.
c. Debtor must be denied all rights in the collateral.
d. Creditor must take and hold the collateral.

53 (November 88)

Dart Co., which is engaged in the business of selling appliances, borrowed $8,000 from Arco Bank. Dart executed a promissory note for that amount and pledged all of its customer installment receivables as collateral for the loan. Dart executed a security agreement which described the collateral, but Arco did not file a financing statement. With respect to this transaction
a. Attachment of the security interest took place when Dart executed the security agreement.
b. Attachment of the security interest did <u>not</u> occur because Arco failed to file a financing statement.
c. Perfection of the security interest occurred despite Arco's failure to file a financing statement.
d. The UCC Secured Transactions Article does <u>not</u> apply because Arco failed to file a financing statement.

42 (November 87)

In order for a security interest in goods to attach, one of the requirements is that the debtor must
a. Sign a financing statement that adequately describes the goods.
b. Sign a security agreement that adequately describes the goods.
c. Receive the goods from the creditor.
d. Have rights in the goods.

58 (May 87)

Which of the following requirements is <u>not</u> necessary in order to have a security interest attach?
a. There must be a proper filing.
b. Value must be given by the creditor.
c. Either the creditor must take possession or the debtor must sign a security agreement that describes the collateral.
d. The debtor must have rights in the collateral.

Secured Transactions

Items 44 and 45 are based on the following information:

On June 3, Muni Finance loaned Page Corp. $20,000 to purchase four computers for use in Page's trucking business. Page contemporaneously executed a promissory note and security agreement. On June 7, Page purchased the computers with the $20,000, obtaining possession that same day. On June 10, Mort, a judgment creditor of Page, levied on the computers.

44 (May 85)

Which of the following statements is correct?

a. Muni failed to qualify as a purchase money secured lender.
b. Muni's security interest attached on June 3.
c. Muni's security interest attached on June 7.
d. Muni's security interest did <u>not</u> attach.

45 (May 85)

If Muni files a financing statement on June 11, which of the parties will have a priority security interest in the computers?

a. Mort, since he lacked notice of Muni's security interest.
b. Mort, since Muni failed to file before Mort levied on the computers.
c. Muni, since its security interest was perfected within the permissible time limits.
d. Muni, since its security interest was automatically perfected upon attachment.

50 (May 83)

Attachment under Article 9 of the Uniform Commercial Code applies primarily to the rights of

a. Third party creditors.
b. Parties to secured transactions.
c. Holders in due course.
d. Warehousemen.

52 (November 82)

Lombard, Inc. manufactures exclusive designer apparel. It sells through franchised clothing stores on consignment, retaining a security interest in the goods. Gifford is one of Lombard's franchisees pursuant to a detailed contract signed by both Lombard and Gifford. In order for the security interest to be valid against Gifford with respect to the designer apparel in Gifford's possession, Lombard

a. Must retain title to the goods.
b. Does not have to do anything further.
c. Must file a financing statement.
d. Must perfect its security interest against Gifford's creditors.

54 (November 82)

Two Uniform Commercial Code concepts relating to secured transactions are "attachment" and "perfection." Which of the following is correct in connection with the similarities and differences between these two concepts?

a. They are mutually exclusive and wholly independent of each other.
b. Attachment relates primarily to the rights against the debtor and perfection relates primarily to the rights against third parties.
c. Satisfaction of one automatically satisfies the other.
d. It is <u>not</u> possible to have a simultaneous attachment and perfection.

47 (May 75)

On May 1, Dixie Corporation borrowed $100,000 from Clark Bank. The bank filed a financing statement on that date. On May 5, Dixie signed a security agreement granting the bank a security interest in its inventory, its accounts receivable, and the proceeds from the sale of its inventory and collection of its accounts receivable. The bank's security interest

a. Was perfected on May 1.
b. Was <u>not</u> perfected until a copy of the security agreement was filed.
c. Was perfected on May 5.
d. Attached on May 1.

4B (May 76)

On January 14, 1976, Thelma Corporation sold and delivered to Dey Corporation inventory goods priced at $5,000 on terms which required payment within 30 days after delivery. Because of business reverses, Dey found that it was unable to pay the amount due Thelma. On February 9, 1976, Thelma's credit manager validly filed a properly signed financing statement. On February 18, 1976, he met with Dey's officers to effect a plan of repayment. At this meeting Thelma obtained a $5,000 promissory note and security agreement signed by Dey and secured by Dey's presently existing and thereafter acquired inventory.

Required: Does Thelma have a perfected security interest? Explain.

Yes, Thelma has a perfected security interest in the inventory as of February 18, 1976.

According to the Uniform Commercial Code, a security interest is not enforceable (or does not attach) against a debtor with respect to the collateral unless (1) the debtor has signed a security agreement that contains a description of the collateral (or the collateral is in the possession of the secured party pursuant to agreement), (2) value has been given by the creditor, and (3) the debtor has rights in the collateral. Attachment or enforceability generally occurs as soon as all of these events occur. Here, Thelma Corporation has given value by delivering the $5,000 in goods to Dey Corporation. Dey, having taken title to the goods, has rights in them. Dey signed a security agreement providing that any obligation covered by the security agreement is to be secured by after-acquired collateral. Thus, Thelma has a security interest that has attached to Dey's present inventory and that will continue to be a floating charge on Dey's subsequently acquired or changing stock of inventory.

Generally, a financing statement must be filed to perfect all security interests except where the collateral is in the possession of the secured party. The Code provides that a security interest is perfected as soon as filing plus all the events required for attachment have occurred. If the filing is effected before the security interest attaches, it is perfected at the time when it attaches. Thus, a financing statement may be filed before a security agreement is made or a security interest otherwise attaches. Here, the filing on February 9, 1976, of the financing statement prior to reaching an agreement on the secured transaction on February 18, 1976, was proper. Thelma is a secured party with a perfected security interest generally enforceable against Dey and against third parties.

C. Perfection of a Security Interest

2(b) (R96)

Under the Secured Transactions Article of the UCC, any transaction intended to establish a security interest in personal property is governed by requirements for the creation and satisfaction of that interest.

Required: Items 6 through 10 relate to situations involved in the creation and/or satisfaction of a security interest. For each item, select the effect that will result from each situation from List II. An answer may be selected once, more than once, or not at all.

6. The security interest obtained by a creditor who lends money to a debtor to purchase goods used in the debtor's business will be
7. A seller of consumer goods who obtains an oral security agreement from a purchaser in the ordinary course of business will have
8. A creditor who is transferred collateral to hold as security by a debtor, pursuant to agreement, will have
9. A creditor who files a financing statement would, at the most, have
10. A creditor who files a financing statement on October 15 will have priority over another creditor who has a signed but unfiled security agreement dated October 1 because of

	List II - Effect
A	An attached security interest.
B	A priority due to attachment.
C	A priority due to perfection.
D	A priority due to chronological order.
E	A purchase money security interest.
F	A security interest in receivables.
G	A security interest perfected by filing.
H	A security interest perfected without filing.
I	No security interest.

53 (November 89)

Perfection of a security interest permits the secured party to protect its interest by

    a.   Avoiding the need to file a financing statement.

    b.   Preventing another creditor from obtaining a security interest in the same collateral.

    c.   Establishing priority over the claims of most subsequent secured creditors.

    d.   Denying the debtor the right to possess the collateral.

58 (November 84)

Milo Manufacturing Corp. sells baseball equipment to distributors, who in turn sell the equipment to various retailers throughout the U.S. The retailers then sell the equipment to consumers who use the equipment for their own personal use. In all cases, the equipment is sold on credit with a security interest taken in the equipment by each of the respective sellers. Which of the following is correct?

    a.   The security interests of all of the sellers remain valid and will take priority even against good faith purchasers for value, despite the fact that resales were contemplated.

    b.   The baseball equipment is inventory in the hands of all parties concerned.

    c.   Milo's security interest is automatically perfected since Milo qualifies as a purchase money secured party.

    d.   Milo and the distributors must file a financing statement or take possession of the baseball equipment in order to perfect their security interests.

37 (November 80)

The Secured Transaction Article of the Code recognizes various methods of perfecting a security interest in collateral. Which of the following is <u>not</u> recognized by the Code?

    a.   Filing.

    b.   Possession.

    c.   Consent.

    d.   Attachment.

26 (November 77)

As a secured creditor under the Uniform Commercial Code, Dawson has invariably perfected a security interest in goods which provide the underlying security for various loans. Under the circumstances, which of the following is correct?

    a.   Dawson is assured that the debts will be repaid.

    b.   Dawson's security interest can <u>not</u> be perfected by possession.

    c.   Dawson is entitled to "resort to" or obtain the property even as against a trustee in bankruptcy.

    d.   Dawson has a priority in bankruptcy and therefore is entitled to defeat the claims of all creditors which are asserted against the goods.

1. By Possession

50 (May 94)

Under the UCC Secured Transactions Article, which of the following actions will best perfect a security interest in a negotiable instrument against any other party?

a. Filing a security agreement.
b. Taking possession of the instrument.
c. Perfecting by attachment.
d. Obtaining a duly executed financing statement.

48 (May 93)

Which of the following transactions would illustrate a secured party perfecting its security interest by taking possession of the collateral?

a. A bank receiving a mortgage on real property.
b. A wholesaler borrowing to purchase inventory.
c. A consumer borrowing to buy a car.
d. A pawnbroker lending money.

47 (May 83)

Attachment and perfection will occur simultaneously when

a. The security agreement so provides.
b. There is a purchase money security interest taken in inventory.
c. Attachment is by possession.
d. The goods are sold on consignment.

49 (May 78)

Gladstone Warehousing, Inc. is an independent bonded warehouse company. It issued a warehouse receipt for 10,000 bales of cotton belonging to Travis. The word "NEGOTIABLE" was conspicuously printed on the warehouse receipt it issued to Travis. The warehouse receipt also contained a statement in large, clear print that the cotton would only be surrendered upon return of the receipt and payment of all storage fees. Travis was a prominent plantation owner engaged in the cotton growing business. Travis pledged the warehouse receipt with Southern National Bank in exchange for a $50,000 personal loan. A financing statement was not filed. Under the circumstances, which of the following is correct?

a. Travis' business creditors cannot obtain the warehouse receipt from Southern National unless they repay Travis' outstanding loan.
b. The bank does not have a perfected security interest in the cotton since it did not file a financing statement.
c. Travis' personal creditors have first claim, superior to all other parties, to the cotton in question because the loan was a personal loan and constituted a fraud upon the personal creditors.
d. The fact that the word "NEGOTIABLE" and the statement regarding the return of the receipt were conspicuously printed upon the receipt is not binding upon anyone except Travis.

28 (November 77)

Weatherall seeks to create a valid perfected security interest in goods under the provisions of the Uniform Commercial Code. Which of the following acts or actions will establish this?

a. Weatherall obtains a written agreement under which Weatherall takes possession of the security.
b. Weatherall obtains an unsigned written security agreement.
c. Weatherall obtains a security agreement signed only by the debtor.
d. Weatherall files a financing statement which is not in itself a security agreement.

2. By Filing

47 (November 92)

Under the UCC Secured Transactions Article, what is the effect of perfecting a security interest by filing a financing statement?

    a.   The secured party can enforce its security interest against the debtor.

    b.   The secured party has permanent priority in the collateral even if the collateral is removed to another state.

    c.   The debtor is protected against all other parties who acquire an interest in the collateral after the filing.

    d.   The secured party has priority in the collateral over most creditors who acquire a security interest in the same collateral after the filing.

48 (November 92)

A secured creditor wants to file a financing statement to perfect its security interest. Under the UCC Secured Transactions Article, which of the following must be included in the financing statement.

    a.   A listing or description of the collateral.

    b.   An after-acquired property provision.

    c.   The creditor's signature.

    d.   The collateral's location.

60 (May 89)

Burn Manufacturing borrowed $500,000 from Howard Finance Co., secured by Burn's present and future inventory, accounts receivable, and the proceeds thereof. The parties signed a financing statement that described the collateral and it was filed in the appropriate state office. Burn subsequently defaulted in the repayment of the loan and Howard attempted to enforce its security interest. Burn contended that Howard's security interest was unenforceable. In addition, Green, who subsequently gave credit to Burn without knowledge of Howard's security interest, is also attempting to defeat Howard's alleged security interest. The security interest in question is valid with respect to

    a.   Both Burn and Green.

    b.   Neither Burn nor Green.

    c.   Burn but <u>not</u> Green.

    d.   Green but <u>not</u> Burn.

59 (May 87)

If a manufacturer assigns 90% of its accounts receivable to a factor, perfection will occur by

	Filing a financing statement	Possession	Attachment
a.	Yes	Yes	No
b.	Yes	No	No
c.	No	No	Yes
d.	No	Yes	No

56 (November 82)

On October 1, 1982, Winslow Corporation obtained a loan commitment of $250,000 from Liberty National Bank. Liberty filed a financing statement on October 2, 1982. On October 5, 1982, the $250,000 loan was consummated and Winslow signed a security agreement granting the bank a security interest in inventory, accounts receivable, and proceeds from the sale of the inventory and collection of the accounts receivable. Liberty's security interest was perfected

    a.   On October 1.

    b.   On October 2.

    c.   On October 5.

    d.   By attachment.

33 (November 80)

The Gordon Manufacturing Company manufactures various types of lathes. It sold on credit 25 general-use lathes to Hardware City, a large retail outlet. Hardware City sold one of the lathes to Johnson for use in his home repair business, reserving a security interest for the unpaid balance. However, Hardware City did <u>not</u> file a financing statement. Johnson's creditors are asserting rights against the lathe. Which of the following statements is correct?

    a.   The lathe is a consumer good in Johnson's hands.

    b.   No filing was necessary to perfect a security interest in the lathe against Johnson's creditors.

    c.   Gordon Manufacturing could assert rights against the lathe sold to Johnson in the event Hardware City defaults in its payments.

    d.   The lathe was inventory in both Gordon and Hardware's hands and is equipment in Johnson's, and both Gordon and Hardware City must file to perfect their interests.

36 (November 75)

On June 10, Central Corporation sold goods to Bowie Corporation for $5,000. Bowie signed a financing statement containing the names and addresses of the parties and describing the collateral. Central filed the financing statement on June 21, noting the same in its accounting books.

    a.   Central need <u>not</u> sign the financing statement to perfect its security interest in the collateral.

    b.   Central must file the financing statement prior to the sale if a security interest is to be perfected.

    c.   Central must sign the financing statement in order to perfect its security interest.

    d.   Central had a perfected security interest in the collateral even before the financing statement was filed.

3. Automatic Perfection--Purchase Money Security Interests in Consumer Goods

58 (November 94)

Under the Secured Transactions Article of the UCC, which of the following purchasers will own consumer goods free of a perfected security interest in the goods?

    a.   A merchant who purchases the goods for resale.

    b.   A merchant who purchases the goods for use in its business.

    c.   A consumer who purchases the goods from a consumer purchaser who gave the security interest.

    d.   A consumer who purchases the goods in the ordinary course of business.

59 (November 93)

Grey Corp. sells computers to the public. Grey sold and delivered a computer to West on credit. West executed and delivered to Grey a promissory note for the purchase price and a security agreement covering the computer. West purchased the computer for personal use. Grey did not file a financing statement. Is Grey's security interest perfected?

    a.   Yes, because Grey retained ownership of the computer.

    b.   Yes, because it was perfected at the time of attachment.

    c.   No, because the computer was a consumer good.

    d.   No, because Grey failed to file a financing statement.

47 (May 93)

Mars, Inc. manufactures and sells VCRs on credit directly to wholesalers, retailers, and consumers. Mars can perfect its security interest in the VCRs it sells without having to file a financing statement or take possession of the VCRs if the sale is made to

    a.   Retailers.

    b.   Wholesalers that sell to distributors for resale.

    c.   Consumers.

    d.   Wholesalers that sell to buyers in the ordinary course of business.

60 (May 91)

Wine purchased a computer using the proceeds of a loan from MJC Finance Company. Wine gave MJC a security interest in the computer. Wine executed a security agreement and financing statement, which was filed by MJC. Wine used the computer to monitor Wine's personal investments. Later, Wine sold the computer to Jacobs, for Jacobs' family use. Jacobs was unaware of MJC's security interest. Wine now is in default under the MJC loan. May MJC repossess the computer from Jacobs?

    a. No, because Jacobs was unaware of the MJC security interest.
    b. No, because Jacobs intended to use the computer for family or household purposes.
    c. Yes, because MJC's security interest was perfected before Jacobs' purchase.
    d. Yes, because Jacobs' purchase of the computer made Jacobs personally liable to MJC.

48 (May 85)

Foxx purchased a stereo for personal use from Dix Audio, a retail seller of appliances. Foxx paid 30% of the $600 sales price and agreed to pay the balance in 12 equal principal payments plus interest. Foxx executed a security agreement giving Dix a security interest in the stereo. Dix properly filed a financing statement immediately. After making six payments Foxx defaulted.

If after making the third installment payment, Foxx sold the stereo to Lutz for personal use, who would have a superior interest in the stereo assuming Lutz lacked knowledge of Dix's security interest?

    a. Dix, since it filed a financing statement.
    b. Dix, since more than 30% of the purchase price had been paid.
    c. Lutz, since title passed from Foxx to Lutz.
    d. Lutz, since he purchased without knowledge of Dix's security interest and for personal use.

50 (May 85)

Minor Corp. manufactures exercise equipment for sale to health clubs and to retailers. Minor also sells directly to consumers in its wholly-owned retail outlets. Minor has created a subsidiary, Minor Finance Corp., for the purpose of financing the purchase of its products by the various customers. In which of the following situations does Minor Finance <u>not</u> have to file a financing statement to perfect its security interest against competing creditors in the equipment sold by Minor?

    a. Sales made to retailers who in turn sell to buyers in the ordinary course of business.
    b. Sales made to any buyer when the equipment becomes a fixture.
    c. Sales made to health clubs.
    d. Sales made to consumers who purchase for their own personal use.

57 (May 84)

Rich Electronics sells various brand name television and stereo sets at discount prices. Rich maintains a large inventory which it obtains from various manufacturers on credit. These manufacturer-creditors have all filed and taken security interests in the goods and proceeds therefrom which they have sold to Rich on credit. Rich in turn sells to hundreds of ultimate consumers; some pay cash but most buy on credit. Rich takes a security interest but does not file a financing statement for credit sales. Which of the following is correct?

    a. Since Rich takes a purchase money security interest in the consumer goods sold, its security interest is perfected upon attachment.
    b. The appliance manufacturers can enforce their security interests against the goods in the hands of the purchasers who paid cash for them.
    c. A subsequent sale by one of Rich's customers to a bona fide purchaser will be subject to Rich's security interest.
    d. The goods in Rich's hands are consumer goods.

51 (May 83)

Fogel purchased a TV set for $900 from Hamilton Appliance Store. Hamilton took a promissory note signed by Fogel and a security interest for the $800 balance due on the set. It was Hamilton's policy not to file a financing statement until the purchaser defaulted. Fogel obtained a loan of $500 from Reliable Finance which took and recorded a security interest in the set. A month later, Fogel defaulted on several loans outstanding and one of his creditors, Harp, obtained a judgment against Fogel which was properly recorded. After making several payments, Fogel defaulted on a payment due to Hamilton, who then recorded a financing statement subsequent to Reliable's filing and the entry of the Harp judgment. Subsequently, at a garage sale, Fogel sold the set for $300 to Mobray. Which of the parties has the priority claim to the set?

    a.   Reliable.

    b.   Hamilton.

    c.   Harp.

    d.   Mobray.

58 (November 82)

Clearview Manufacturing, Inc. sells golf equipment to wholesale distributors, who sell to retailers, who in turn sell to golfers. In most instances, the golf equipment is sold on credit with a security interest in the goods taken by each of the respective sellers. With respect to the above described transactions

    a.   The only parties who qualify as purchase money secured parties are the retailers.

    b.   The security interests of all of the parties remain valid even against good faith purchasers despite the fact that resale was contemplated.

    c.   Except for the retailers, all of the sellers must file or have possession of the goods in order to perfect their security interests.

    d.   The golf equipment is inventory in the hands of all the parties involved.

48 (May 82)

Johnstone Hardware Company sold a $450 drill press to Markum for use in his home workshop. Markum paid 20% initially and promised to pay the balance in monthly installments over a period of one year. Johnstone took a purchase money security interest in the drill press to secure payment. Markum promised not to sell or otherwise transfer the drill press without Johnstone's consent. Johnstone did not file a financing statement in connection with the transaction. Markum subsequently found himself hard pressed to make the payments and defaulted. He then sold the drill press to his neighbor Harper for $250 without disclosing Johnstone's interest and without Johnstone's consent. Under the circumstances

    a.   The security agreement need not be in writing and signed in order to be valid since the purchase price of the drill press is less than $500.

    b.   No one can obtain superior rights to the drill press in that transfer of the press was prohibited without Johnstone's consent.

    c.   Johnstone's security interest is perfected against the other creditors of Markum, but not against Harper.

    d.   Harper would take the drill press free of Johnstone's security interest even if Johnstone had filed.

46 (November 81)

A purchase money security interest

    a.   May be taken or retained only by the seller of collateral.

    b.   Is exempt from the Uniform Commercial Code's filing requirements.

    c.   Entitles the person who is the original purchase money lender to certain additional rights and advantages, which are nontransferable.

    d.   Entitles the purchase money lender to a priority through a twenty-day grace period for filing.

25 (November 79)

In respect to obtaining a purchase money security interest, which of the following requirements must be met?

    a.   The property sold may only be consumer goods.

    b.   Only a seller may obtain a purchase money security interest.

    c.   Such a security interest must be filed in all cases to be perfected.

    d.   Credit advanced to the buyer must be used to obtain the property which serves as the collateral.

34 (November 75)

In the case of consumer goods, a buyer from the original purchaser takes the goods free of a perfected security interest if

    a. He buys without knowledge of the security interest, for value, for his own personal purposes, and the secured party has <u>not</u> filed a financing statement covering such goods.

    b. He buys without knowledge of the security interest, for value, for his own personal purposes, and prior to the purchase the secured party has filed a financing statement covering such goods.

    c. He buys with knowledge of the security interest, and after the purchase the secured party files a financing statement covering such goods.

    d. He buys with knowledge of the security interest, and the secured party has <u>not</u> filed a financing statement covering such goods prior to delivery of the goods.

39 (November 75)

Your client, Ace Auto Sales, sold a 1974 Skylark Magnificent to Marcus on the installment basis. Marcus signed an installment agreement for the balance due ($2,000) on the purchase price. Ace's policy was <u>not</u> to file a financing statement in the appropriate recordation office. Marcus subsequently sold the car to Franks without disclosing the debt owed to Ace. Franks purchased the car in good faith, knowing nothing about the debt owed by Marcus to Ace. Marcus is bankrupt. Wallace, a general creditor of Marcus has asserted rights to the car in question. Under the circumstances

    a. Marcus takes title free and clear of any claims because Ace did <u>not</u> file.

    b. Ace can defeat the claim of Franks in that Franks is a mere third party beneficiary.

    c. Ace's rights against Marcus under the contract of sale are unimpaired despite the lack of filing.

    d. In the final analysis Wallace will prevail.

4 (November 84)

Tom Sauer purchased a computer and a stereo from Zen Sounds, Inc. for personal use. With regard to the computer, Sauer signed an installment purchase note and a security agreement. Under the terms of the note Sauer was to pay $100 down and $50 a month for 20 months. The security agreement included a description of the computer. However, Zen did not file a financing statement. Sauer paid $800 cash for the stereo.

Two months later, Sauer sold the computer to Ralph for $600 cash. Ralph purchased the computer for personal use without knowledge of Zen's security interest.

Three months later, Sauer brought the stereo back to Zen for repair. Inadvertently, one of Zen's sales persons sold the stereo to Ned, a buyer in the ordinary course of business.

Required: Answer the following, setting forth reasons for any conclusions stated.

    a. Did Zen fulfill the requirements necessary for the attachment and perfection of its security interest in the computer?

    b. Will Ralph take the computer free of Zen's security interest?

    c. As between Sauer and Ned, who has title to the stereo?

    a. Yes. In order for a security interest in collateral to attach, the following three requirements must be met:

(1) The collateral is in the possession of the secured party pursuant to agreement, or the debtor has signed a security agreement that contains a description of the collateral; (2) value has been given by the secured party; and (3) the debtor has rights in the collateral.

Zen, under the stated facts has fulfilled all three requirements, thereby creating an enforceable security interest that has attached to the computer. Since the transaction involves a purchase money security interest in consumer goods--that is, goods used or bought primarily for personal, family, or household purposes--it is not necessary for the secured party to file a financing statement or take possession of the collateral in order to perfect its interest. The security interest is perfected when the three requirements set forth have been fulfilled.

    b. Yes. Generally, a secured party with a perfected security interest has priority over all subsequent claims to the same collateral. However, in the case of consumer goods, where perfection is achieved solely by attachment, a subsequent buyer will take free of such prior perfected security interests if he buys without knowledge of the security interest, for value, for his own personal, family, or household use and before a financing statement is filed by the secured party. Since Ralph has complied with those qualifications, he will take the computer free of Zen's perfected security interest.

c. Ned. The UCC sales provisions state that any entrusting of possession of goods to a merchant who deals in goods of that kind gives such merchant the power to transfer all rights of the entruster to a buyer in the ordinary course of business. Furthermore, the entruster, in delivering and acquiescing in the merchant's retention of possession of the goods, must be the rightful owner in order for the merchant to acquire the power to transfer complete ownership and title. Since Sauer's delivery of the stereo to Zen constituted an entrusting, Zen acquired the power to transfer title and ownership to Ned. Thus, upon Ned's purchase of the stereo in good faith and without knowledge of Sauer's true ownership interests, Ned acquired title to the stereo.

2A (November 78)

National Finance Company engages in a wide variety of secured transactions which may be broken down into three categories.

I. Consumer loans in connection with the purchase of automobiles, appliances, and furniture. National makes these loans in two ways. First, it makes direct loans to the consumer-borrower who then makes the purchase with the proceeds. Second, it is contacted by the seller and provides the financing for the purchase by the customer. In either case National takes a security interest in the property purchased.

II. Collateralized loans to borrowers who deliver possession of property, such as diamonds, to National to secure repayment of their loans.

III. Loans to merchants to finance their inventory purchases. National takes a security interest in the inventory and proceeds.

Except for category III, National does not file a financing statement.

Required: Answer the following, setting forth reasons for any conclusions stated.

1. When does National's security interest in the various types of property attach?
2. As a secured creditor, against what parties must National protect itself?
3. Does National have a perfected security interest in any of the above property? If so, against whom?
4. If the facts indicate that National does not have a perfected security interest against all parties, what should it do?
5. Can National fully protect itself against all subsequent parties who might claim superior rights to the property involved?

1. The Uniform Commercial Code provides that a security interest attaches in property when three events occur. First, collateral is in possession of the secured party pursuant to agreement, or the debtor has signed a security agreement that contains a description of the collateral. Second, value has been given by the creditor. Third, the debtor has rights in the collateral.

Insofar as National is concerned, a security interest in all three categories of secured transactions has attached. In categories I and III, there must be a security agreement signed by the debtor. Regarding the collateralized property in category II, possession pursuant to agreement without a signed writing is sufficient. In all instances, value has been given and the debtor has rights in the collateral.

2. There are four potential parties against whom National must protect itself. These are the debtor, the debtor's creditors, the trustee in bankruptcy, and subsequent purchasers for value from the debtor.

3. National's rights against the debtor are contained in the security agreement and the Uniform Commercial Code provisions relating to the agreement and the relationship between the parties. It is not necessary to file a financing statement in order to obtain these rights against the debtor; the agreement itself is sufficient.

To perfect a security interest against other parties, the creditor must either take possession (as in category II) or file a financing statement except where the creditor has taken "a purchase-money security interest in consumer goods." In the latter case, perfection occurs at the time the security interest attaches, but it is only valid against the debtor's creditors and a trustee in bankruptcy and not against a bona fide purchaser unless a financing statement has been filed. Whether National uses either method described in category I to finance the purchase of the consumer goods, it will have a purchase-money security interest if it gave value to enable the debtor to acquire rights in or the use of collateral if such value is in fact so used.

Where a creditor provides financing for a debtor to enable him to obtain and resell inventory items, the security interest is perfected by filing. However, since resale is clearly contemplated, purchasers for value take free of the perfected security interest.

4. The only practical suggestion would be to file a financing statement in respect to the loans described in category I, which would then provide protection against subsequent purchasers from the debtor. National already is protected against the other parties in category I upon attachment of the security interest.

5. No. As indicated above, where the goods are inventory in the hands of the debtor, a purchaser for value in the ordinary course of business takes free of the creditor's perfected security interest. In such cases, it is not possible for the lender to completely protect itself against all parties without obtaining possession.

7B (May 77)

You have been assigned by the CPA firm of Stanford, Cox & Walsh to audit the accounts of Super Appliances, Inc., a retail discount chain. Super sells almost exclusively to retail customers in the ordinary course of business. It typically requires 25% as a down payment and takes a promissory note and a signed security agreement for the balance. However, if the purchase price of the appliance or appliances purchased by the customer exceeds $500, it arranges with a local financing company, Friendly Finance, to have credit extended to the customer. In such cases, Friendly supplies the 75% financing and takes a promissory note and a signed security agreement. A financing statement is neither obtained nor recorded by Super or Friendly.

Required: Answer the following, setting forth reasons for any conclusions stated.

1. Does Super or Friendly have a "purchase-money security interest" in respect to the appliances sold to Super's customers?

2. What is the legal importance of the distinction between a "purchase-money security interest" and the usual nonpossessory security interest?

1. Yes. Both Super, the seller, and Friendly, who financed many of the purchases by Super's customers, qualify as "purchase money security" lenders. The Uniform Commercial Code provides that a security interest is a "purchase money security interest" to the extent that it is--

(a) taken or retained by the seller of the collateral to secure all or part of its price; or

(b) taken by a person who, by making advances or incurring an obligation, gives value to enable the debtor to acquire rights in or the use of collateral if such value is in fact so used.

Those items financed by Super meet the requirements of (a) and those items financed by Friendly meet the requirements of (b).

2. A nonpossessory security interest is one in which the lender or seller does not have possession of the property subject to the security interest. In such situations, the lender or seller perfects the security interest against third parties by filing a financing statement. An exception is made for the purchase-money security interest relating to consumer goods (for example, installment sales to the consumer) wherein the lender or seller is protected against other creditors of the debtor (but not bona fide consumer purchasers for value from the debtor) without the necessity of filing a financing statement. Hence, bothersome and costly paperwork is eliminated unless the secured party wishes to protect itself from a fraudulent sale by the consumer to a bona fide purchaser for value. The risk is relatively unimportant in relation to the cost of filing, consequently many sellers and commercial lenders assume this risk themselves.

D. Default

60 (November 94)
Under the Secured Transactions Article of the UCC, which of the following remedies is available to a secured creditor when a debtor fails to make a payment when due?

	Proceed against the collateral	Obtain a general judgment against the debtor
a.	Yes	Yes
b.	Yes	No
c.	No	Yes
d.	No	No

Items 54 and 55 are based on the following:
Drew bought a computer for personal use from Hale Corp. for $3,000. Drew paid $2,000 in cash and signed a security agreement for the balance. Hale properly filed the security agreement. Drew defaulted in paying the balance of the purchase price. Hale asked Drew to pay the balance. When Drew refused, Hale peacefully repossessed the computer.

54 (May 94)
Under the UCC Secured Transactions Article, which of the following remedies will Hale have?
a. Obtain a deficiency judgment against Drew for the amount owed.
b. Sell the computer and retain any surplus over the amount owed.
c. Retain the computer over Drew's objection.
d. Sell the computer without notifying Drew.

55 (May 94)
Under the UCC Secured Transactions Article, which of the following rights will Drew have?
a. Redeem the computer after Hale sells it.
b. Recover the sale price from Hale after Hale sells the computer.
c. Force Hale to sell the computer.
d. Prevent Hale from selling the computer.

53 (November 93)
In what order are the following obligations paid after a secured creditor rightfully sells the debtor's collateral after repossession?
       I. Debt owed to any junior security holder.
      II. Secured party's reasonable sale expenses.
     III. Debt owed to the secured party.
a. I, II, III.
b. II, I, III.
c. II, III, I.
d. III, II, I.

50 (May 93)

Under the UCC Secured Transactions Article, which of the following statements is correct concerning the disposition of collateral by a secured creditor after a debtor's default?

    a. A good faith purchaser for value and without knowledge of any defects in the sale takes free of any subordinate liens or security interests.

    b. The debtor may <u>not</u> redeem the collateral after the default.

    c. Secured creditors with subordinate claims retain the right to redeem the collateral after the collateral is sold to a third party.

    d. The collateral may only be disposed of at a public sale.

50 (November 92)

Under the UCC Secured Transactions Article, if a debtor is in default under a payment obligation secured by goods, the secured party has the right to

	Peacefully repossess the goods without judicial process	Reduce the claim to a judgment	Sell the goods and apply the proceeds toward the debt
a.	Yes	Yes	Yes
b.	No	Yes	Yes
c.	Yes	Yes	No
d.	Yes	No	Yes

44 (November 87)

Bean defaulted on a promissory note payable to Gray Co. The note was secured by a piece of equipment owned by Bean. Gray perfected its security interest on May 29, 1987. Bean had also pledged the same equipment as collateral for another loan from Smith Co. after he had given the security interest to Gary. Smith's security interest was perfected on June 30, 1987. Bean is current in his payments to Smith. Subsequently, Gray took possession of the equipment and sold it at a private sale to Walsh, a good faith purchaser for value. Walsh will take the equipment

    a. Free of Smith's security interest because Bean is current in his payments to Smith.

    b. Free of Smith's security interest because Walsh acted in good faith and gave value.

    c. Subject to Smith's security interest because the equipment was sold at a private sale.

    d. Subject to Smith's security interest because Smith is a purchase money secured creditor.

57 (May 87)

Under the UCC, collateral sold at a public sale by a secured party to a good faith purchaser for value after the debtor's default

    a. Transfers to the purchaser marketable and insurable title to the collateral.

    b. May be redeemed by the debtor within 30 days after the sale.

    c. Remains subject to security interests which are senior to that being discharged at the sale.

    d. May be redeemed by judicial lien creditors whose claims are subordinate to that being discharged at the sale.

50 (November 85)

Under the UCC, collateral which has been sold in a private sale by a secured party to a good faith purchaser for value after the debtor's default

    a. May be redeemed by the debtor within 10 days after the disposition.

    b. May be redeemed by creditors with subordinate claims.

    c. Remains subject to the security interests of subordinate lien creditors in all cases where the collateral is disposed of at a private sale.

    d. Discharges the security interest pursuant to which such sale was made and any security interest or lien subordinate thereto.

47 (May 85)

Foxx purchased a stereo for personal use from Dix Audio, a retail seller of appliances. Foxx paid 30% of the $600 sales price and agreed to pay the balance in 12 equal principal payments plus interest. Foxx executed a security agreement giving Dix a security interest in the stereo. Dix properly filed a financing statement immediately. After making six payments Foxx defaulted. If Dix takes possession of the stereo, it

    a. Must dispose of the stereo at a public sale.

    b. Must dispose of the stereo within 90 days after taking possession or be liable to the debtor.

    c. May retain possession of the stereo, thereby discharging Foxx of any deficiency.

    d. May retain possession of the stereo and collect any deficiency plus costs from Foxx.

57 (November 84)

Pine has a security interest in certain goods purchased by Byron on an installment contract. Byron has defaulted on the payments resulting in Pine's taking possession of the collateral. Which of the following is correct?

    a. Byron may waive his right of redemption at the time he executes the security agreement.

    b. Pine must sell the collateral if Byron has paid more than 60% of the cash price on a purchase money security interest in business equipment.

    c. The collateral may be sold by Pine at a private sale and, if the collateral is consumer goods, without notice to other secured parties.

    d. Unless otherwise agreed, Pine must pay Byron for any increase in value of the collateral while the collateral is in Pine's possession.

52 (May 83)

Gilbert borrowed $10,000 from Merchant National Bank and signed a negotiable promissory note which contained an acceleration clause. In addition, securities valued at $11,000 at the time of the loan were pledged as collateral. Gilbert has defaulted on the loan repayments. At the time of default, $9,250, plus interest of $450, was due, and the securities had a value of $8,000. Merchant

    a. Must first proceed against the collateral before proceeding against Gilbert personally on the note.

    b. Can not invoke the acceleration clause in the note until ten days after the notice of default is given to Gilbert.

    c. Must give Gilbert 30 days after default in which to refinance the loan.

    d. Is entitled to proceed against Gilbert on either the note or the collateral or both.

50 (May 78)

Vega Manufacturing, Inc. manufactures and sells hi-fi systems and components to the trade and at retail. Repossession is frequently made from customers who are in default. Which of the following statements is correct concerning the rights of the defaulting debtors who have had property repossessed by Vega?

    a. Vega has the right to retain all the goods repossessed as long as it gives notice and cancels the debt.

    b. It is unimportant whether the goods repossessed are defined as consumer goods, inventory, or something else in respect to the debtor's rights upon repossession.

    c. If the defaulting debtor voluntarily signs a statement renouncing his rights in the collateral, the creditor must nevertheless resell them for the debtor's benefit.

    d. If a debtor has paid sixty percent or more of the purchase price of consumer goods in satisfaction of a purchase money security interest, the debtor has the right to have the creditor dispose of the goods.

II. Secured Transactions--Priorities
A. General Rules of Priority
1. Lien Creditors

52 (May 94)

Under the UCC Secured Transactions Article, what is the order of priority for the following security interests in store equipment?

      I. Security interest perfected by filing on April 15, 1994.

      II. Security interest attached on April 1, 1994.

      III. Purchase money security interest attached April 11, 1994 and perfected by filing on April 20, 1994.

  a. I, III, II.

  b. II, I, III.

  c. III, I, II.

  d. III, II, I.

60 (November 93)

Noninventory goods were purchased and delivered on June 15, 1993. Several security interests exist in these goods. Which of the following security interests has priority over the others?

  a. Security interest in future goods attached June 10, 1993.

  b. Security interest attached June 15, 1993.

  c. Security interest perfected June 20, 1993.

  d. Purchase money security interest perfected June 24, 1993.

32 (May 91)

Peters Co. repairs computers. On February 9, 1991, Stark Electronics Corp. sold Peters a circuit tester on credit. Peters executed an installment note for the purchase price, a security agreement covering the tester, and a financing statement that Stark filed on February 11, 1991. On April 13, 1991, creditors other than Stark filed an involuntary petition in bankruptcy against Peters. What is Stark's status in Peters' bankruptcy?

  a. Stark will be treated as an unsecured creditor because Stark did <u>not</u> join in the filing against Peters.

  b. Stark's security interest constitutes a voidable preference because the financing statement was <u>not</u> filed until February 11.

  c. Stark's security interest constitutes a voidable preference because the financing statement was filed within 90 days before the bankruptcy proceeding was filed.

  d. Stark is a secured creditor and can assert a claim to the circuit tester that will be superior to the claims of Peters' other creditors.

59 (May 91)

On June 15, Harper purchased equipment for $100,000 from Imperial Corp. for use in its manufacturing process. Harper paid for the equipment with funds borrowed from Eastern Bank. Harper gave Eastern a security agreement and financing statement covering Harper's existing and after-acquired equipment. On June 21, Harper was petitioned involuntarily into bankruptcy under Chapter 7 of the Federal Bankruptcy Code. A bankruptcy trustee was appointed. On June 23, Eastern filed the financing statement. Which of the parties will have a superior security interest in the equipment?

  a. The trustee in bankruptcy, because the filing of the financing statement after the commencement of the bankruptcy case would be deemed a preferential transfer.

  b. The trustee in bankruptcy, because the trustee become a lien creditor before Eastern perfected its security interest.

  c. Eastern, because it had a perfected purchase money security interest without having to file a financing statement.

  d. Eastern, because it perfected its security interest within the permissible time limits.

43 (November 87)

On May 8, Westar Corp. sold 20 typewriters to Saper for use in Saper's business. Saper paid for the typewriters by executing a promissory note that was secured by the typewriters. Saper also executed a security agreement. On May 9, Saper filed a petition in bankruptcy and a trustee was appointed. On May 16, Westar filed a financing statement covering the typewriters. Westar claims that it has a superior interest in the typewriters. The trustee in bankruptcy disagrees. Which of the parties is correct?

   a. The trustee, because the filing of a petition in bankruptcy cuts off Westar's rights as of the date of filing.
   b. The trustee, because the petition was filed prior to Westar's filing of the financing statement.
   c. Westar, because it perfected its security interest within ten days after Saper took possession of the typewriters.
   d. Westar, because its security interest was automatically perfected upon attachment.

39 (May 86)

Cross has an unperfected security interest in the inventory of Safe, Inc. The unperfected security interest

   a. Is superior to the interest of subsequent lenders who obtain a perfected security interest in the property.
   b. Is subordinate to lien creditors of Safe who become such prior to any subsequent perfection by Cross.
   c. Causes Cross to lose important rights against Safe as an entity.
   d. May only be perfected by Cross filing a financing statement.

23 (May 78)

Robert Cunningham owns a shop in which he repairs electrical appliances. Three months ago Electrical Supply Company sold Cunningham on credit, a machine for testing electrical appliances and obtained a perfected security interest at that time to secure payment of the balance due. Cunningham's creditors have now filed an involuntary petition in bankruptcy against him. What is the status of Electrical Supply?

   a. Electrical Supply is a secured creditor that has the right, if not paid, to assert its rights against the machine sold to Cunningham to enforce its claim.
   b. Electrical Supply must surrender its perfected security interest to the trustee in bankruptcy and share as a general creditor of the bankrupt's estate.
   c. Electrical Supply's perfected security interest constitutes a preference and is voidable.
   d. Electrical Supply must elect to resort exclusively to its secured interest or to relinquish it and obtain the same share as a general creditor.

2. Buyers of Collateral--(Particularly Buyers in the Ordinary Course of Business)

51 (May 94)

Under the UCC Secured Transactions Article, perfection of a security interest by a creditor provides added protection against other parties in the event the debtor does not pay its debts. Which of the following parties is not affected by perfection of a security interest?

   a. Other prospective creditors of the debtor.
   b. The trustee in a bankruptcy case.
   c. A buyer in the ordinary course of business.
   d. A subsequent personal injury judgment creditor.

49 (November 92)

On July 8, Ace, a refrigerator wholesaler, purchased 50 refrigerators. This comprised Ace's entire inventory and was financed under an agreement with Rome Bank that gave Rome a security interest in all refrigerators on Ace's premises, all future acquired refrigerators, and the proceeds of sales. On July 12, Rome filed a financing statement that adequately identified the collateral. On August 15, Ace sold one refrigerator to Cray for personal use and four refrigerators to Zone Co. for its business. Which of the following statements is correct?

    a.   The refrigerators sold to Zone will be subject to Rome's security interest.

    b.   The refrigerator sold to Cray will <u>not</u> be subject to Rome's security interest.

    c.   The security interest does <u>not</u> include the proceeds from the sale of the refrigerators to Zone.

    d.   The security interest may <u>not</u> cover after-acquired property even if the parties agree.

47 (May 89)

Acorn Marina, Inc. sells and services boat motors. On April 1, 1989, Acorn financed the purchase of its entire inventory with GAC Finance Company. GAC required Acorn to execute a security agreement and financing statement covering the inventory and proceeds of sale. On April 14, 1989, GAC properly filed the financing statement pursuant to the UCC Secured Transactions Article. On April 27, 1989, Acorn sold one of the motors to Wilks for use in his charter business. Wilks, who had once worked for Acorn, knew that Acorn regularly financed its inventory with GAC. Acorn has defaulted on its obligations to GAC. The motor purchased by Wilks is

    a.   Subject to the GAC security interest because Wilks should have known that GAC financed the inventory purchase by Acorn.

    b.   Subject to the GAC security interest because Wilks purchased the motor for a commercial use.

    c.   Not subject to the GAC security interest because Wilks is regarded as a buyer in the ordinary course of Acorn's business.

    d.   Not subject to the GAC security interest because GAC failed to file the financing statement until more than 10 days after April 1, 1989.

54 (November 88)

With regard to a prior perfected security interest in goods for which a financing statement has been filed, which of the following parties is most likely to have a superior interest in the same collateral?

    a.   A buyer in the ordinary course of business who purchased the goods from a merchant.

    b.   A subsequent buyer of consumer goods who purchased the goods from another consumer.

    c.   The trustee in bankruptcy of the debtor.

    d.   Lien creditors of the debtor.

38 (May 86)

The UCC establishes the rights of a secured creditor of a merchant in relation to various types of third parties. Regarding these third parties, which of the following is most likely to have an interest superior to that of a secured party who has a prior perfected security interest?

    a.   Purchasers from the merchant in the ordinary course of business.

    b.   General creditors of the merchant.

    c.   Lien creditors of the merchant.

    d.   Trustee in bankruptcy.

59 (November 84)

Sax purchased from Bosch Tools a new saw for his home workshop for cash. One week later, Sax was called by Cary Finance. Cary explained to Sax that it had been financing Bosch's purchases from the manufacturers and that to protect its interest it had obtained a perfected security interest in Bosch's entire inventory of hardware and power tools, including the saw which Sax bought. Cary further explained that Bosch had defaulted on a payment due to Cary, and Cary intended to assert its security interest in the saw and repossess it unless Sax was willing to make payment of $100 for a release of Cary's security interest. If Sax refuses to make the payment, which of the following statements is correct?

    a.   Even if Sax had both actual notice and constructive notice via recordation of Cary's interest, he will prevail if Cary seeks to repossess the saw.

    b.   Cary's security interest in the saw in question is invalid against all parties unless its filing specifically described and designated the particular saw Sax purchased.

    c.   Sax must pay the $100 or the saw can be validly repossessed and sold to satisfy the amount Bosch owes Cary and any excess paid to Sax.

    d.   Sax will <u>not</u> take free of Cary's security interest if he was aware of said interest at the time he purchased the saw.

57 (November 82)

Thrush, a wholesaler of television sets, contracted to sell 100 sets to Kelly, a retailer. Kelly signed a security agreement with the 100 sets as collateral. The security agreement provided that Thrush's security interest extended to the inventory, to any proceeds therefrom, and to the after-acquired inventory of Kelly. Thrush filed his security interest centrally. Later, Kelly sold one of the sets to Haynes who purchased with knowledge of Thrush's perfected security interest. Haynes gave a note for the purchase price and signed a security agreement using the set as collateral. Kelly is now in default. Thrush can

    a.   Not repossess the set from Haynes, but is entitled to any payments Haynes makes to Kelly on his note.

    b.   Repossess the set from Haynes as he has a purchase money security interest.

    c.   Repossess the set as his perfection is first, and first in time is first in right.

    d.   Repossess the set in Haynes' possession because Haynes knew of Thrush's perfected security interest at the time of purchase.

32 (November 80)

The Jolly Finance Company provides the financing for Triple J Appliance Company's inventory. As a part of its sales promotion and public relations campaign Jolly Finance placed posters in Triple J's stores indicating that Triple J is another satisfied customer of Jolly and that the goods purchased at Triple J are available through the financing by Jolly. Jolly also files a financing statement which covers the financed inventory. Victor Restaurants purchased four hi-fi sets for use in its restaurants and had read one of the Jolly posters. Triple J has defaulted on its loan and Jolly Finance is seeking to repossess the hi-fi sets. Which of the following is correct?

    a.   Jolly has a perfected security interest in the hi-fi sets which is good against Victor.

    b.   Victor's knowledge of the financing arrangement between Jolly and Triple J does <u>not</u> affect its rights to the hi-fi sets.

    c.   Jolly's filing was unnecessary to perfect its security interest in Triple J's inventory since it was perfected upon attachment.

    d.   The hi-fi sets are consumer goods in Victor's hands.

5 (November 90)

Wizard Computer Co. sells computers to the general public. On April 30, Wizard financed the purchase of its computer inventory with National Bank. Wizard executed and delivered a promissory note and a security agreement covering the inventory. National filed a financing statement on the same day.

On May 1, Wizard sold a computer out of its inventory to Kast, who intended to use it to do some household budgeting. Kast made a 10% downpayment toward the purchase price. Kast executed and delivered to Wizard a promissory note for the balance and a security agreement covering the computer. Kast was aware that Wizard financed its inventory with National. Wizard did not file a financing statement.

On May 6, Kast, who was dissatisfied with the computer, sold it on credit to Marc, who intended to use it to assist in family budgeting. Marc, who was unaware that Kast had purchased the computer on credit, paid 25% of the purchase price and executed and delivered to Kast a promissory note for the balance and a security agreement covering the computer. Kast did not file a financing statement.

On May 12, Marc borrowed $6,000 from Alcor Finance. Marc gave Alcor a promissory note for the loan amount and a security agreement covering the computer and other household appliances owned by Marc. Alcor did not file a financing statement.

Marc failed to pay Alcor or Kast. In turn, Kast has been unable to pay Wizard. On June 2, Wizard defaulted on its obligation to National.

Kast and Marc take the following positions:

    ▪   Kast asserts that the computer was purchased from Wizard free of National's security interest.

    ▪   Marc asserts that the computer was purchased from Kast free of Wizard's security interest.

    ▪   Marc asserts that Alcor's security interest is unenforceable against Marc because Alcor failed to file a financing statement.

Required: For each assertion, indicate whether it is correct, and set forth the reasons for your conclusions.

Kast's assertion that the computer was purchased from Wizard free of National's security interest is correct. Kast, as a buyer in the ordinary course, purchased the computer free of any security interest given by Wizard. The fact that Kast was aware of the existence of National's security interest does not affect this conclusion.

Marc's assertion that the computer was purchased from Kast free of Wizard's security interest is correct. Marc purchased the computer from Kast free of Wizard's security interest because:

- Marc had no knowledge of the security interest;
- Marc was buying the computer for household use;
- Wizard's security interest had not been perfected by filing prior to Marc's purchase.

Marc's assertion that Alcor's security interest is unenforceable against Marc because Alcor failed to file a financing statement is incorrect. On attachment of Alcor's security interest, it became enforceable against Marc. Attachment has occurred because:

- The security party (Alcor) gave value;
- The debtor (Marc) has rights in the collateral;
- The debtor (Marc) has executed and delivered a security agreement covering the collateral to the creditor (Alcor).

Alcor's failure to perfect its security interest has no effect on the enforceability of the security interest against Marc.

4C (May 76)

Sill Corporation operates a retail appliance store. About a year ago, Sill borrowed $3,000 from Castle to supplement its working capital. At that time it granted to Castle a security interest in its present and future inventory pursuant to a written security agreement signed by both parties. Castle duly filed a properly executed financing statement a few days later. In the ordinary course of business, a customer purchased a $500 television set from Sill. The customer knew of the existence of Castle's security interest.

Required: What rights does Castle have against Sill's customer? Explain.

None. The Uniform Commercial Code provides that a retail customer in the ordinary course of business takes free of a security interest created by his seller even though the security interest is perfected and even though the buyer knows of its existence. A buyer in the ordinary course of business is, generally, a person who, in good faith and without knowledge that the sale to him is in violation of the ownership rights or security interest of a third party in the goods, buys goods from someone in the business of selling them.

By duly filing a financing statement, Castle perfected its security interest in then-existing as well as after-acquired inventory. Even though Castle held a perfected security interest in Sill's inventory, the customer who purchased the television set from Sill in the ordinary course of business took the property free of Castle's security interest.

3. Conflicting Security Interests in Same Collateral

54 (November 89)

Roth and Dixon both claim a security interest in the same collateral. Roth's security interest attached on January 1, 1989, and was perfected by filing on March 1, 1989. Dixon's security interest attached on February 1, 1989, and was perfected on April 1, 1989, by taking possession of the collateral. Which of the following statements is correct?

a. Roth's security interest has priority because Roth perfected before Dixon perfected.
b. Dixon's security interest has priority because Dixon's interest attached before Roth's interest was perfected.
c. Roth's security interest has priority because Roth's security interest attached before Dixon's security interest attached.
d. Dixon's security interest has priority because Dixon is in possession of the collateral.

51 (November 86)

On May 2, Safe Bank agreed to loan Tyler Corp. $50,000. Tyler signed a security agreement and financing statement covering its existing equipment. On May 4, Safe filed the financing statement. On May 7, State Bank loaned Tyler $60,000. State had notified Safe on May 5 of its intention to make the loan. Tyler signed a security agreement and financing statement covering the same existing equipment. On May 8, State filed the financing statement. On May 10, Safe loaned Tyler $50,000. If Tyler defaults on both loans, who will have a priority security interest in the equipment?

    a.   State, since it was the first to perfect its security interest.

    b.   State, since it properly notified Safe prior to making the loan.

    c.   Safe, since it was the first to file.

    d.   Safe, since it has a purchase money security interest in the equipment which was perfected within the permissible time limits.

4. Liens Arising by Operation of Law

49 (November 85)

A typewriter, which was subject to a prior UCC security interest, was delivered to Ed Fogel for repair. Fogel is engaged in the business of repairing typewriters. Fogel repaired the typewriter. However, the owner of the typewriter now refuses to pay for the services performed by Fogel. The state in which Fogel operates his business has a statute which gives Fogel a mechanics lien on the typewriter. Fogel's mechanics lien

    a.   Takes priority over a prior perfected security interest under all circumstances.

    b.   Is subject to a prior perfected purchase money security interest under all circumstances.

    c.   Is subject to a prior unperfected security interest where the statute is silent as to priority.

    d.   Takes priority over a prior perfected security interest unless the statute expressly provides otherwise.

B. Floating Lien Priority Rules
1. After-Acquired Property Clauses

49 (May 94)

Under the UCC Secured Transactions Article, which of the following after-acquired property may be attached to a security agreement given to a secured lender?

	Inventory	Equipment
a.	Yes	Yes
b.	Yes	No
c.	No	Yes
d.	No	No

33 (November 75)

Maxim Corporation, a wholesaler, was indebted to the Wilson Manufacturing Corporation in the amount of $50,000 arising out of the sale of goods delivered to Maxim on credit. Wilson and Maxim signed a security agreement creating a security interest in certain collateral of Maxim. The collateral was described in the security agreement as "the inventory of Maxim Corporation, presently existing and thereafter acquired." In general, this description of the collateral

    a.   Applies only to inventory sold by Wilson to Maxim.

    b.   Is sufficient to cover all inventory.

    c.   Is insufficient because it attempts to cover after-acquired inventory.

    d.   Must be more specific for the security interest to be perfected against subsequent creditors.

2. Proceeds Priority Rules

26 (November 79)

Vista Motor Sales, a corporation engaged in selling motor vehicles at retail, borrowed money from Sunshine Finance Company and gave Sunshine a properly executed security agreement in its present and future inventory and in the proceeds therefrom to secure the loan. Sunshine's security interest was duly perfected under the laws of the state where Vista does business and maintains its entire inventory. Thereafter, Vista sold a new pickup truck from its inventory to Archer and received Archer's certified check in payment of the full price. Under the circumstances, which of the following is correct?

    a.   Sunshine must file an amendment to the financing statement every time Vista receives a substantial number of additional vehicles from the manufacturer if Sunshine is to obtain a valid security interest in subsequently delivered inventory.

    b.   Sunshine's security interest in the certified check Vista received is perfected against Vista's other creditors.

    c.   Unless Sunshine specifically included proceeds in the financing statement it filed, it has no rights to them.

    d.   The term "proceeds" does not include used cars received by Vista since they will be resold.

7A (May 74)

Monolith Industries, Inc., manufactures appliances and has been the major supplier of appliances to Wilber Force Corporation, a chain of retail appliance stores. The financing arrangement between Monolith and Wilber Force calls for the sale by Monolith to Wilber Force of appliances to be resold to the public through Wilber Force's chain of appliance stores. Title to the merchandise has been retained by Monolith until receipt of payment. Monthly accountings and payments have been rendered by Wilber Force to Monolith.

Monolith filed a financing statement with the appropriate jurisdictions involved pursuant to the Uniform Commercial Code. The financing statement clearly revealed the debtor-creditor relationship between the parties, described the goods in general terms, and set forth Monolith's security interest in the various appliances sold to Wilber Force. It also contained a provision asserting Monolith's rights against any and all proceeds arising from the sale of said appliances by Wilber Force.

Wilber Force is in financial difficulty. Monolith is asserting rights to certain chattel paper (i.e., installment-sales contracts and non-negotiable notes) received by Wilber Force arising from the sale of Monolith appliances to its retail customers. Double Discount Corporation purchased the chattel paper in question from Wilber Force in the ordinary course of its business and took possession of all the paper at the time it was purchased. Double Discount was aware of Monolith's security interest in the inventory. Both Monolith and Double Discount claim ownership of the paper.

Required:

    1.   Does Monolith have a perfected security interest? Explain.

    2.   Assuming Monolith has a perfected security interest, does it include proceeds? Explain.

    3.   Does Monolith have any rights against Double Discount regarding the chattel paper? Explain.

    1. Yes. The Uniform Commercial Code clearly recognizes the validity of a security interest in inventory supplied by a manufacturer, such as Monolith. This type of arrangement was previously known as "trust receipts financing." The Code has simplified the requirements for perfection of a security interest in inventory against the other creditors of the purchaser-debtor (Wilber Force). Title is irrelevant and the description is sufficient if it "reasonably identifies what is described." Thus, having filed in the appropriate jurisdictions, Monolith has a perfected security interest in the ever-changing inventory it supplies to Wilber Force.

    2. Yes. The Code also recognizes the validity of a perfected security interest in the proceeds from the sale of inventory covered by a filed financing statement. This is true whether the financing statement does or does not specifically include proceeds. Therefore, Monolith's security interest includes proceeds such as chattel paper.

    3. No. Where a purchaser (Double Discount) of chattel paper and non-negotiable notes gives new value (i.e., pays for the paper) and takes possession of the paper in the ordinary course of its business, as was the case here, it has a claim which is superior to that of the inventory financier (Monolith). This result attains here even though Monolith's financing statement includes proceeds. The Code provides that the purchaser of the paper retains his priority over the inventory financier unless the paper indicates that it has been assigned to a person other than the

purchaser. Hence, Monolith has no rights against Double Discount. (Answer revised to conform to Revised Article 9 (1999).)

3. Conflicting Security Interests in Same Collateral (Including Consignments)

20 (May 79)

Bigelow manufactures mopeds and sells them through franchised dealers who are authorized to resell them to the ultimate consumer or return them. Bigelow delivers the mopeds on consignment to these retailers. The consignment agreement clearly states that the agreement is intended to create a security interest for Bigelow in the mopeds delivered on consignment. Bigelow wishes to protect itself against the other creditors of and purchasers from the retailers who might assert rights against the mopeds. Under the circumstances, Bigelow

    a. Must file a financing statement and give notice to certain creditors in order to perfect his security interest.

    b. Will have rights against purchasers in the ordinary course of business who were aware of the fact that Bigelow had filed.

    c. Need take no further action to protect itself, since the consignment is a sale or return and title is reserved in Bigelow.

    d. Will have a perfected security interest in the mopeds upon attachment.

3 (May 95)

On January 2, 1994, Gray Interiors Corp., a retailer of sofas, contracted with Shore Furniture Co. to purchase 150 sofas for its inventory. The purchase price was $250,000. Gray paid $50,000 cash and gave Shore a note and security agreement for the balance. On March 1, 1994, the sofas were delivered. On March 10, 1994, Shore filed a financing statement.

On February 1, 1994, Gray negotiated a $1,000,000 line of credit with Float Bank, pledged its present and future inventory as security, and gave Float a security agreement. On February 20, 1994, Gray borrowed $100,000 from the line of credit. On March 5, 1994, Float filed a financing statement.

On April 1, 1994, Dove, a consumer purchaser in the ordinary course of business, purchased a sofa from Gray. Dove was aware of both security interests.

Required: Items 79 through 84 refer to the above fact pattern. For each item, determine whether A, B, or C is correct.

79.   Shore's security interest in the sofas attached on
        A. January 2, 1994.
        B. March 1, 1994.
        C. March 10, 1994.

80.   Shore's security interest in the sofas was perfected on
        A. January 2, 1994.
        B. March 1, 1994.
        C. March 10, 1994.

81.   Float's security interest in Gray's inventory attached on
        A. February 1, 1994.
        B. March 1, 1994.
        C. March 5, 1994.

82.   Float's security interest in Gray's inventory was perfected on
        A. February 1, 1994.
        B. February 20, 1994.
        C. March 5, 1994.

83. A. Shore's security interest has priority because it was a purchase money security interest.
    B. Float's security interest has priority because Float's financing statement was filed before Shore's.
    C. Float's security interest has priority because Float's interest attached before Shore's.

84. A. Dove purchased the sofa subject to Shore's security interest.
    B. Dove purchased the sofa subject to both the Shore and Float security interests.
    C. Dove purchased the sofa free of either the Shore or Float security interests.

4 (May 88)

Dunn & Co., CPAs, is auditing the 1987 financial statements of its client, Safe Finance. While performing the audit, Dunn learned of certain transactions that occurred during 1987 that may have an adverse impact on Safe's financial statements. The following transactions are of most concern to Dunn:

- On May 5, Safe sold certain equipment to Lux, who contemporaneously executed and delivered to Safe a promissory note and security agreement covering the equipment. Lux purchased the equipment for use in its business. On May 8, City Bank loaned Lux $50,000, taking a promissory note and security agreement from Lux that covered all of Lux's existing and after-acquired equipment. On May 11, Lux was involuntarily petitioned into bankruptcy under the liquidation provisions of the Bankruptcy Code and a trustee was appointed. On May 12, City filed a financing statement covering all of Lux's equipment. On May 14, Safe filed a financing statement covering the equipment it had sold to Lux on May 5.

- On July 10, Safe loaned $600,000 to Cam Corp., which used the funds to refinance existing debts. Cam duly executed and delivered to Safe a promissory note and a security agreement covering Cam's existing and after-acquired inventory of machine parts. On July 12, Safe filed a financing statement covering Cam's inventory of machine parts. On July 15, Best Bank loaned Cam $200,000. Contemporaneous with the loan, Cam executed and delivered to Best a promissory note and security agreement covering all of Cam's inventory of machine parts and any after-acquired inventory. Best had already filed a financing statement covering Cam's inventory on June 20, after Best agreed to make the loan to Cam. On July 14, Dix, in good faith, purchased certain machine parts from Cam's inventory and received delivery that same day.

Required: Define a purchase money security interest. In separate paragraphs, discuss whether Safe has a priority security interest over:

- The trustee in Lux's bankruptcy with regard to the equipment sold by Safe on May 5.
- City with regard to the equipment sold by Safe on May 5.
- Best with regard to Cam's existing and after-acquired inventory of machine parts.
- Dix with regard to the machine parts purchased on July 14 by Dix.

A purchase money security interest is an interest in personal property or fixtures that secures payment or performance of an obligation and that is (1) taken or retained by the seller of the collateral to secure all or part of its price, or (2) taken by a person who by making advances of incurring an obligation gives value to enable the debtor to acquire rights in or the use of collateral if such value is in fact so used.

Safe's security interest has priority over the rights of the trustee in bankruptcy. The UCC Article on Secured Transactions states that a lien creditor includes a trustee in bankruptcy from the date of the filing of the petition. Under the general rule, an unperfected security interest is subordinate to the rights of a person who becomes a lien creditor before the security interest is perfected. However, if the secured party files with respect to a purchase money security interest before or within 20 days after the debtor receives possession of the collateral, he takes priority over the rights of a lien creditor that arise between the time the security interest attaches and the time of filing. Under the facts of our case, Safe has a purchase money security interest in the equipment because the security interest was taken by Safe to secure the price. Therefore, because Safe filed a financing statement on May 14 (within 20 days after Lux received possession of the equipment) it has a priority security interest over the trustee in bankruptcy (lien creditor) whose claim arose between the time the security interest attached (May 5) and the time of filing (May 14).

Safe has a priority security interest in the equipment over City. A purchase money security interest in collateral other than inventory has priority over a conflicting security interest in the same collateral if the purchase money security interest is perfected at the time the debtor receives possession of the collateral or within 20 days thereafter. Because Safe has a purchase money security interest in the equipment that was perfected by filing a financing statement on May 14 (within 20 days after Lux received possession of the equipment on May 5), Safe has a priority security interest over City despite City's perfection of its security interest on May 12.

Best's security interest in the inventory has priority over Safe's security interest. In general, conflicting perfected security interests rank according to priority in time of filing or perfection. Priority dates from the time a filing is first made covering the collateral or the time the security interest is first perfected, whichever is earlier, provided that there is no period thereafter when there is neither a filing nor perfection. In this case, because both Best's and Safe's security interests were perfected by filing, the first to file (Best) will have a priority security interest. The fact that Best filed a financing statement prior to making the loan will not affect Best's priority.

Safe will not have a priority security interest over Dix because Dix is a buyer in the ordinary course of business and will take free of Safe's perfected security interest. Dix is a buyer in the ordinary course of business because Dix acted in good faith when purchasing the machine parts in the regular course of Cam's business. The UCC Article on Secured Transactions states that a buyer in the ordinary course of business takes free of a security interest created by his seller even though the security interest is perfected and even though the buyer knows of its existence. Therefore, Dix will take the machine parts purchased from Cam's inventory on July 14, free from Safe's security interest which was perfected on July 12. (Answer revised to conform to Revised Article 9 (1999).)

3A (May 81)

Walpole Electric Products, Inc. manufactures a wide variety of electrical appliances. Walpole uses the consignment as an integral part of its marketing plan. The consignments are "true" consignments rather than consignments intended as security interests. Unsold goods may be returned to the owner-consignor. Walpole contracted with Petty Distributors, Inc., an electrical appliance wholesaler, to market its products under this consignment arrangement. Subsequently, Petty became insolvent and made a general assignment for the benefit of creditors. Klinger, the assignee, took possession of all of Petty's inventory, including all the Walpole electrical products. Walpole has demanded return of its appliances asserting that the relationship created by the consignment between itself and Petty was one of agency and that Petty never owned the appliances. Furthermore, Walpole argues that under the consignment arrangement there is no obligation owing by Petty at any time, thus there is nothing to secure under the secured transactions provisions of the Uniform Commercial Code. Klinger has denied the validity of these assertions claiming that the consignment is subject to the Code's filing provisions unless the Code has otherwise been satisfied. Walpole sues to repossess the goods.

Required: Answer the following, setting forth reasons for any conclusions stated.
1. What are the requirements, if any, to perfect a true consignment such as discussed above?
2. Will Walpole prevail?

In order to prevail against the creditors of a party to whom goods have been consigned, the consignor must comply with the requirements of Article 9 of the Uniform Commercial Code; that is, Article 9 treats virtually all consignments, whether intended for security or not, as secured transactions governed by Article 9. For example, § 9-109(a)(4) provides that Article 9 applies to consignments, and § 1-201(37) defines "security interest" to include "any interest of a consignor" in the goods. Further, § 9-103(d) provides that the "security interest of a consignor in goods that are the subject of a consignment is a purchase money security interest in inventory." Walpole has failed to take the steps necessary to perfect a security interest in inventory (for example, filing a financing statement). Thus, Walpole will lose because it has an unperfected security interest, which loses to a lien creditor such as Klinger. (Answer revised to conform to Revised Article 9 (1999).)

C. Priorities in Fixtures

29 (May 78)

Donaldson, Inc. loaned Watson Enterprises $50,000 secured by a real estate mortgage which included the land, buildings, and "all other property which is added to the real property or which is considered as real property as a matter of law." Star Company also loaned Watson $25,000 and obtained a security interest in all of Watson's "inventory, accounts receivable, fixtures, and other tangible personal property." There is insufficient property to satisfy the two creditors. Consequently, Donaldson is attempting to include all property possible under the terms and scope of its real property mortgage. If Donaldson is successful in this regard, then Star will receive a lesser amount in satisfaction of its claim. What is the probable outcome of Donaldson's action?
   a.   Donaldson will <u>not</u> prevail if the property in question is detachable trade fixtures.
   b.   Donaldson will prevail if Star failed to file a financing statement.
   c.   Donaldson will prevail if it was the first lender and duly filed its real property mortgage.
   d.   The problem will be decided by taking all of Watson's property (real and personal) subject to the two secured creditors' claims and dividing it in proportion to the respective debts.

D. Field Warehousing

55 (November 82)

Tawney Manufacturing approached Worldwide Lenders for a loan of $50,000 to purchase vital components it used in its manufacturing process. Worldwide decided to grant the loan but only if Tawney would agree to a field warehousing arrangement. Pursuant to their understanding, Worldwide paid for the purchase of the components, took a negotiable bill of lading for them, and surrendered the bill of lading in exchange for negotiable warehouse receipts issued by the bonded warehouse company that had established a field warehouse in Tawney's storage facility. Worldwide did not file a financing statement. Under the circumstances, Worldwide
   a.   Has a security interest in the goods which has attached and is perfected.
   b.   Does <u>not</u> have a security interest which has attached since Tawney has not signed a security agreement.
   c.   Must file an executed financing statement in order to perfect its security interest.
   d.   Must <u>not</u> relinquish control over any of the components to Tawney for whatever purpose, unless it is paid in cash for those released.

24 (November 77)

Field warehousing is a well-established means of securing a loan. As such, it resembles a pledge in many legal respects. Which of the following is correct?
   a.   The field warehouseman must maintain physical control of and dominion over the property.
   b.   A filing is required in order to perfect such a financing arrangement.
   c.   Temporary relinquishment of control for any purpose will suspend the validity of the arrangement insofar as other creditors are concerned.
   d.   The property in question must be physically moved to a new location although it may be a part of the borrower's facilities.

4B (May 80)

Norwood Furniture, Inc. found that its credit rating was such that it was unable to obtain a line of unsecured credit. National Bank indicated that it would be willing to supply funds based upon a "pledge" of Norwood's furniture inventory which was located in two warehouses. The bank would receive notes and bearer negotiable warehouse receipts covering the merchandise securing the loans. An independent warehouseman was to have complete control over the areas in the warehouse set aside as field warehousing facilities. The Hastings Field Warehousing Corporation was selected to serve as the independent warehouseman. It was to retain keys to the posted area in which the inventory was contained. Negotiable bearer warehouse receipts were issued to Norwood when it delivered the merchandise to Hastings. The receipts were then delivered by Norwood to National to secure the loans which were made at 80% of the market value of the furniture indicated on the receipts. Upon occasion, Norwood would take temporary possession of the furniture for the purposes of packaging it, surrendering the warehouse receipt for this limited purpose. As orders were filled out of the field warehouse inventory, the requisite receipt would be relinquished by National, the merchandise obtained by Norwood, and other items substituted with a new receipt issued.

Required: Answer the following, setting forth reasons for any conclusions stated.
1. Based upon the facts given, is the field warehousing arrangement valid?
2. When does a security interest in the negotiable warehouse receipts attach?
3. What, if anything, is necessary to perfect a security interest in goods covered by negotiable warehouse receipts?
4. What are the dangers, if any, that National faces by relinquishing the warehouse receipts to Norwood?

1. Yes. Independent dominion and control by the field warehouseman is the essential test that must be met in order to create a valid security interest in the field warehoused goods. If the debtor (Norwood) were allowed to retain dominion and control of the goods placed in the field warehouse on its premises, the validity of the field warehousing arrangement would be questionable. But where the warehouseman is an independent warehousing company and where the formalities are adhered to (that is, posting, and the keys are in the warehouseman's exclusive control), the arrangement will withstand an attack upon its validity.

2. The Uniform Commercial Code provides that a security interest attaches when

a. The collateral is in possession of the secured party pursuant to agreement or the debtor has signed a security agreement that contains a description of the collateral.

b. Value has been given.

c. The debtor has rights to the collateral.

Typically the security interests in such situations arise upon delivery of the warehouse receipts to the creditor.

3. Nothing. A security interest in goods covered by negotiable documents may be perfected by taking possession of the documents. When possession is obtained, no filing is necessary.

4. The danger inherent in relinquishing the negotiable document of title to Norwood is that he may "duly negotiate" it to a holder. The Code provides that "such holders take priority over an earlier security interest even though perfected. Filing . . . does not constitute notice of the security interest to such holders. . . ."

Negotiation of a negotiable bearer document of title is by delivery alone. The instrument is "duly negotiated" when negotiated "to a holder who purchasers it in good faith without notice of any defense against or claim to it on the part of any person and for value, unless it is established that the negotiation is not in the regular course of business or financing or involved receiving the document in settlement or payment of a money obligation."

6A (November 76)

Pierce Auto Parts, Inc. needed additional working capital for a six-month period. It has a large inventory in its possession consisting of finished products, work in process, and raw materials. Merrill Financing Corporation was contacted regarding a $25,000 loan. Merrill was willing to make a loan, but only if it was secured by collateral. Merrill obviously did not wish to take physical possession of the inventory, and Pierce needed access to the work-in-process inventory in order to finish the auto parts which required minor additional work, packaging, and labeling. Hence, the parties agreed to enter into a field warehousing arrangement covering the finished inventory and the nearly completed work-in-process inventory. The raw materials were not included because they were already subject to the secured interest of another creditor who had duly filed a financing statement.

Required: Answer the following, setting forth reasons for any conclusions stated.
1. Discuss the procedures used in, and the business and legal aspects of, field warehousing.
2. How may Merrill perfect its security interest?
3. Suppose the raw materials are subsequently field warehoused by Merrill for an additional $5,000 loan. What rights will Merrill have?

1. Field warehousing is a very practical and useful device used essentially as a financing arrangement rather than a storage operation. The term connotes the use of the debtor's own facilities or premises (his "field") as the place of the warehouse. Thus, the expense in moving and storing the property in an independent warehouse is avoided. An area is normally set aside and fenced in, and signs are posted indicating the creation of such relationship. Locks are typically changed, and a bonded warehouseman is put in charge of the operation to control the segregated field warehouse. The warehouseman may be an employee of the debtor or an employee of an independent warehouse. Typically, negotiable warehouse receipts are issued covering the property warehoused, and these are retained by the creditor as collateral for a loan or other form of credit. So long as a bona fide field warehousing arrangement is entered into and maintained, its validity is well recognized. The chief elements necessary to validate such an arrangement are the independence of the field warehouseman and his control over the property subject to the arrangement. In fact, this is a type of pledge, and through the warehouseman, the lender must have physical dominion over the property. Temporary relinquishment of the property to the debtor for limited purposes such as labelling or packaging is permitted.

2. The usual method of perfecting the security interest of the lender in such an arrangement is the physical dominion and control over the property, as in a pledge. However, the Uniform Commercial Code also permits filing a financing statement as an additional method of perfecting the security interest of the lender.

3. Merrill's rights are clearly subordinate to the claims of the prior interest of the other creditor who has duly perfected his security interest by filing. Merrill's rights will have value only to the extent that the raw materials are worth more than the prior creditor's claim.

PART X -- PROPERTY

TABLE OF CONTENTS

*Answers consistent with Revised Uniform Principal and Income Act (1997).

PART X

PROPERTY

I. Fixtures

56 (November 95)

Which of the following factors help determine whether an item of personal property is a fixture?
  I. Degree of the item's attachment to the property.
  II. Intent of the person who had the item installed.
  a. I only.
  b. II only.
  c. Both I and II.
  d. Neither I nor II.

55 (May 95)

Which of the following factors help determine whether an item of personal property has become a fixture?

	Manner of affixation	Value of the item	Intent of the annexor
a.	Yes	Yes	Yes
b.	Yes	Yes	No
c.	Yes	No	Yes
d.	No	Yes	Yes

51 (November 91)

A tenant's personal property will become a fixture and belong to the landlord if its removal would
  a. Increase the value of the personal property.
  b. Cause a material change to the personal property.
  c. Result in substantial harm to the landlord's property.
  d. Change the use of the landlord's property back to its prior use.

53 (November 87)

Which of the following factors is least significant in determining whether an item of personal property has become a fixture?
  a. The extent of injury that would be caused to the real property by the removal of the item.
  b. The value of the item.
  c. The manner of attachment.
  d. The adaptability of the item to the real estate.

51 (November 85)

Mini, Inc. entered into a five-year lease with Rein Realtors. The lease was signed by both parties and immediately recorded. The leased building was to be used by Mini in connection with its business operations. To make it suitable for that purpose, Mini attached a piece of equipment to the wall of the building. Which of the following is most important in determining whether the equipment became a fixture?
  a. Whether the equipment can be removed without material damage to the building.
  b. Whether the attachment is customary for the type of building.
  c. The fair market value of the equipment at the time the lease expires.
  d. The fact that the equipment was subject to depreciation.

Property

53 (May 83)

Wilmont owned a tract of waterfront property on Big Lake. During Wilmont's ownership of the land, several frame bungalows were placed on the land by tenants who rented the land from Wilmont. In addition to paying rent, the tenants paid for the maintenance and insurance of the bungalows, repaired, altered and sold them, without permission or hindrance from Wilmont. The bungalows rested on surface cinderblock and were not bolted to the ground. The buildings could be removed without injury to either the buildings or the land. Wilmont sold the land to Marsh. The deed to Marsh recited that Wilmont sold the land, with buildings thereon, "subject to the rights of tenants, if any, . . ." When the tenants attempted to remove the bungalows, Marsh claimed ownership of them. In deciding who owns the bungalows, which of the following is least significant?

    a. The leasehold agreement itself, to the extent it manifested the intent of the parties.
    b. The mode and degree of annexation of the buildings to the land.
    c. The degree to which removal would cause injury to the buildings or the land.
    d. The fact that the deed included a general clause relating to the buildings.

38 (May 77)

Under certain circumstances personal property may be converted into and become a part of real property. Which of the following is least relevant in ascertaining whether this has occurred?

    a. The mode and degree of annexation.
    b. The use and purpose the property serves in relation to the real property.
    c. The legal formalities which the parties satisfied in relation to the property in question, such as a signed, sealed, and witnessed document.
    d. The actual intent of the parties.

4 (May 87)

On June 1, 1972, Fein, Inc. leased a warehouse to Ted Major for use in his trucking business. Among the essential terms of the lease are the following:

- The lease term is 15 years.
- The monthly rent is $1,500.
- Major was required to replace the outside wood surface of the warehouse with aluminum siding by December 31, 1972 and, in consideration of this, Fein reduced the monthly rent from its market rate of $1,700 to $1,500.

On June 10, 1972, Major had the aluminum siding installed on the warehouse at a cost of $17,000. On June 15, 1982, Major installed a mainframe computer and several computer terminals in the warehouse at a cost of $250,000.

The lease on the warehouse is silent with respect to Major's right to remove the aluminum siding or computer and terminals upon the expiration of the lease.

On June 2, 1985, Fein obtained a fire insurance policy insuring the warehouse in the amount of $140,000. The policy contains an 80% coinsurance clause. On April 2, 1987, a fire caused $40,000 worth of damage to the roof of the warehouse. Fein had purchased the warehouse for $90,000 in 1960. On April 2, 1987, the cost less depreciation of the warehouse was $25,000 and its fair market value was $200,000.

Fein has asserted the following with respect to the above facts:

- That it is entitled to retain ownership of the aluminum siding at the expiration of the lease.
- That it is entitled to retain ownership of the computer and terminals at the expiration of the lease.
- That it has an insurable interest in the warehouse and therefore is entitled to recover $40,000 as a result of the fire damage to the warehouse.

Required: Discuss Fein's assertions indicating whether such assertions are correct.

Fein's first assertion that it is entitled to retain ownership of the aluminum siding at the expiration of the lease is correct. The ownership of the aluminum siding will remain with Fein since it was converted from personal property to real property by virtue of it becoming a fixture. Since the lease between Fein and Major is silent as to Major's right to remove the aluminum siding, the facts and circumstances surrounding the installation of the aluminum siding must be evaluated. One significant factor which indicates that the parties may have impliedly agreed that the aluminum siding is to remain with Fein after the lease expires is the reduction in the monthly rent by $200 over 15 years in exchange for the installation of the aluminum siding by Major. In the absence of an agreement, the most important factor is the annexor's (Major's) objective intent in having added the aluminum siding to the real property. Major's intent may be inferred from such things as the following: manner by which the item is attached to the realty, the extent of damage to the realty caused by the removal of the item, the nature or purpose of the item, and the interest of the annexor in the realty at the time of the annexation of the item. Under the foregoing tests it is likely that the aluminum siding has become a fixture which is so permanently affixed to the warehouse that it probably could not be removed without doing substantial damage to the warehouse. Thus, the aluminum siding has become a part of the realty (warehouse).

Fein's second assertion that it is entitled to retain ownership of the computer and computer terminals at the expiration of the lease is incorrect. Although the computers may also have become a fixture under the tests mentioned above, they were installed in order for the lessee (Major) to pursue its trade or business and were likely not intended to be permanent. Thus, the computers would be classified as trade fixtures which may be removed by Major at the expiration of the lease if it can be accomplished without doing material damage to the warehouse.

Fein's assertion that it has an insurable interest in the warehouse is correct. Fein has an insurable interest in the warehouse since it was the owner (lessor) of the warehouse at the time of the fire and suffered a financial loss. However, Fein's belief that it is entitled to recover $40,000 as a result of the fire damage to the warehouse is incorrect as to the amount. The amount which Fein may recover is determined by the following formula where a coinsurance clause is present:

$$\frac{\text{Insurance Carried (Policy Amount)}}{\text{Insurance Required (Coinsurance \%} \times \text{Fair Market Value of the Property at the Time of the Loss)}} \times \text{The Amount of Loss}$$

$$\frac{140,000}{.80 \times 200,000} \times 40,000 - \$35,000$$

The result generally will be the amount which the insured (Fein) is entitled to recover. In applying the formula to the facts in this case the amount of insurance which Fein carried was less than the insurance required. Therefore, Fein is entitled to receive only $35,000.

5B (November 82)

Darby Corporation, a manufacturer of power tools, leased a building for 20 years from Grayson Corporation commencing January 1, 1981. During January 1981, Darby affixed to the building a central air conditioning system and certain heavy manufacturing machinery, each with an estimated useful life of 30 years.

While auditing Darby's financial statements for the year ended December 31, 1981, the auditor noted that Darby was depreciating the air conditioning system and machinery, for financial accounting purposes, over their estimated useful lives of 30 years. In reading the lease, the auditor further noted that there was no provision with respect to the removal by the lessee of the central air conditioning system or machinery upon expiration of the lease. To verify that the appropriate estimated useful lives are being utilized for recording depreciation, the auditor is interested in establishing the rightful ownership of these assets upon the expiration of the lease. The auditor knows that in order to determine ownership of the assets at the expiration of the lease, one must first determine whether the assets would be considered personalty or realty.

Property

Required: Answer the following, setting forth reasons for any conclusions stated.

What major factors would likely be considered by a court in determining whether the air conditioning system and the machinery are to be regarded as personalty or realty, and what would be the likely determination with respect to each?

Based upon the facts of the problem and the legal criteria discussed below, it appears that the manufacturing machinery retains its character as personalty and therefore can be removed by Darby at the expiration of the building lease and is properly being depreciated over its estimated useful life of 30 years. The central air conditioning system, however, appears to be realty and therefore cannot be removed by Darby at the expiration of the building lease. It should therefore be depreciated by Darby over the term of the lease, that is, 20 years.

In order to determine the rightful ownership of the central air conditioning system and the manufacturing machinery upon expiration of the building lease, one needs to determine if either or both should be regarded as realty by virtue of being fixtures. Whether a particular item of personalty becomes a fixture depends on whether there has been an annexation to the realty and an intention that the item become a fixture. The intention is inferred from such matters as (1) the nature of the item, (2) the manner of its attachment to the realty, and (3) the possible injury to the realty that might be caused by its removal.

In Darby's case, both the central air conditioning system and the machinery would likely be fixtures under this analysis. However, when personal property is attached to realty for the particular purpose of increasing the business profits of a tenant during a lease term, such personal property is ordinarily classified as a trade fixture. The manufacturing machinery clearly fits into this category, since it is directly used to increase Darby's business profits. A trade fixture may be removed by the lessee unless it is so built into the realty that it becomes an integral part thereof. Accordingly, if it can be removed at the building's lease term with no material damage to the building, it may be removed.

It is unlikely that the central air conditioning system would be considered to be a trade fixture. Thus, it is subject to the general rules applicable to fixtures discussed above. As a result, it has become realty and cannot be removed at the end of the lease.

5B (May 79)

The Merchants and Mechanics County Bank expanded its services and facilities as a result of the economic growth of the community it serves. In this connection, it provided safe deposit facilities for the first time. A large vault was constructed as a part of the renovation and expansion of the bank building. Merchants purchased a bank vault door from Foolproof Vault Doors, Inc. for $65,000 and installed it at the vault entrance. The state in which Merchants was located had a real property tax but did not have a personal property tax. When the tax assessor appraised the bank building after completion of the renovation and expansion, he included the bank vault door as a part of the real property. Merchants has filed an objection claiming the vault door was initially personal property and remains so after installation in the bank.

There are no specific statutes or regulations determinative of the issue. Therefore, the question will be decided according to common law principles of property law.

Required: Answer the following, setting forth reasons for any conclusions stated.

1. What is the likely outcome as to the classification of the bank vault door?

2. The above situation involves a dispute between a tax authority and the owner of property. In what other circumstances might a dispute arise with respect to the classification of property as either real or personal property?

1. Based upon the facts of the problem and the legal criteria discussed below, the vault door will probably be classified as real property. The criteria applicable are these:

- Annexation--the mode and degree to which the chattel is physically attached to the real property.
- Adaptation--the extent to which the chattel is used in promoting the purpose for which the real property is used.
- Intention--whether the chattel was intended as a permanent improvement of the real property.

Applying these criteria to the facts demonstrates that the degree of annexation of a vault door is by necessity very high. Furthermore, the adaptation of the personal property (the vault door) the use of the real property by the bank also argues for a finding in favor of real property classification. Finally, the last criterion, the intent of the bank to make a permanent improvement of the real property, appears to have been satisfied. Taking these criteria together, it would appear that the bank door has become real property.

2. In addition to tax collectors, disputes involving the categorization of property as real or personal have arisen in respect of--

- Real property mortgagees versus creditors of the same debtor who have a security interest in personal property (chattel mortgagees).
- Landlord versus tenant upon expiration of the lease and the question of what property may be removed.
- Takers under a will versus the executor in cases where different takers will receive the property, based upon its classification.
- The seller versus the purchaser of real property, where a dispute arises concerning the removal of certain property by the seller.
- The mortgagor versus mortgagee, when the question arises regarding what property is included under the scope of the mortgage.

II. Real Property Ownership
A. Freehold Estates in Property

14 (R98)

What interest in real property generally gives the holder of that interest the right to sell the property?

a. Easement.
b. Leasehold.
c. License.
d. Fee simple.

40 (May 77)

Abrams owned a fee simple absolute interest in certain real property. Abrams conveyed it to Fox for Fox's lifetime with the remainder interest upon Fox's death to Charles. What are the rights of Fox and Charles in the real property?

a. Charles may <u>not</u> sell his interest in the property until the death of Fox.
b. Fox has a possessory interest in the land and Charles has a future interest.
c. Charles must outlive Fox in order to obtain any interest in the real property.
d. Any conveyance by either Fox or Charles must be joined in by the other party in order to be valid.

8 (May 75)

Franklin's will left his ranch "to his wife, Joan, for her life, and upon her death to his sons, George and Harry, as joint tenants." Because of the provisions in Franklin's will

a. Joan <u>cannot</u> convey her interest in the ranch except to George and Harry.
b. The ranch must be included in Joan's estate for federal estate tax purposes upon her death.
c. If George predeceases Harry, Harry will obtain all right, title, and interest in the ranch.
d. Joan holds the ranch in trust for the benefit of George and Harry.

B. Co-ownership of Property

51 (November 95)

Long, Fall, and Pear own a building as joint tenants with the right of survivorship. Long gave Long's interest in the building to Green by executing and delivering a deed to Green. Neither Fall nor Pear consented to this transfer. Fall and Pear subsequently died. After their deaths, Green's interest in the building would consist of

a. A 1/3 interest as a joint tenant.
b. A 1/3 interest as a tenant in common.
c. No interest because Fall and Pear did <u>not</u> consent to the transfer.
d. Total ownership due to the deaths of Fall and Pear.

Property

51 (May 95)

On August 15, 1994, Tower, Nolan, and Oak were deeded a piece of land as tenants in common. The deed provided that Tower owned 1/2 the property and Nolan and Oak owned 1/4 each. If Oak dies, the property will be owned as follows:

    a.   Tower 1/2, Nolan 1/4, Oak's heirs 1/4.
    b.   Tower 1/3, Nolan 1/3, Oak's heirs 1/3.
    c.   Tower 5/8, Nolan 3/8.
    d.   Tower 1/2, Nolan 1/2.

56 (May 94)

Court, Fell, and Miles own a parcel of land as joint tenants with right of survivorship. Court's interest was sold to Plank. As a result of the sale from Court to Plank,

    a.   Fell, Miles, and Plank each own one-third of the land as joint tenants.
    b.   Fell and Miles each own one-third of the land as tenants in common.
    c.   Plank owns one-third of the land as a tenant in common.
    d.   Plank owns one-third of the land as a joint tenant.

52 (May 93)

Which of the following unities (elements) are required to establish a joint tenancy?

	Time	Title	Interest	Possession
a.	Yes	Yes	Yes	Yes
b.	Yes	Yes	No	No
c.	No	No	Yes	Yes
d.	Yes	No	Yes	No

56 (November 88)

Green and Nunn own a 40-acre parcel of land as joint tenants with the right of survivorship. Nunn wishes to sell the land to Ink. If Nunn alone executes and delivers a deed to Ink, what will be the result?

    a.   Green will retain a 1/2 undivided interest in the 40-acre parcel, and will be unable to set aside Nunn's conveyance to Ink.
    b.   Ink will obtain an interest in 1/2 of the parcel, or 20 acres.
    c.   Ink will share ownership of the 40 acres with Green as a joint tenant with a right of survivorship.
    d.   The conveyance will be invalid because Green did not sign the deed.

Items 53 and 54 are based on the following information:

Boch and Kent are equal owners of a warehouse. Boch died leaving a will that gave his wife all of his right, title, and interest in his real estate.

53 (May 88)

If Boch and Kent owned the warehouse at all times as joint tenants with the right of survivorship, Boch's interest

    a.   Will pass to his wife after the will is probated.
    b.   Will not be included in his gross estate for federal estate tax purposes.
    c.   Could not be transferred before Boch's death without Kent's consent.
    d.   Passed to Kent upon Boch's death.

54 (May 88)

If Boch and Kent owned the warehouse at all times as tenants in common, which of the following statements is correct?

    a.   Boch's interest will pass to his wife after the will is probated.
    b.   Upon Boch's death, all tenancies in common terminated.
    c.   Boch's interest will not be included in his gross estate for federal estate tax purposes.
    d.   Upon Boch's death, his interest passed to Kent.

Items 54 and 55 are based on the following information:

Hill, Knox, and Lark own a building as joint tenants with the right of survivorship. Hill donated her interest in the building to Care Charity by executing and delivering a deed to Care. Both Knox and Lark refused to consent to Hill's transfer to Care. Subsequently, Hill and Knox died.

54 (November 87)

As a result of Hill's transfer to Care, Care acquired

a. A 1/3 interest in the building as a joint tenant.
b. A 1/3 interest in the building as a tenant in common.
c. No interest in the building because Knox and Lark refused to consent to the transfer.
d. No interest in the building because it failed to qualify as a bona fide purchaser for value.

55 (November 87)

As a result of Hill's and Knox's death,

a. Lark owns the entire interest in the building.
b. Lark owns a 2/3 interest in the building as a tenant in common.
c. Care and Lark each own a 1/2 interest in the building as joint tenants.
d. Knox's heirs and Lark each own a 1/3 interest in the building as tenants in common.

Items 56 and 57 are based on the following information:

On July 1, 1986, A, B, C, and D purchased a parcel of land as tenants in common each owning an equal share. On July 10, A died leaving a will. Subsequently, B died intestate.

56 (November 86)

After A and B's death,

a. C and D will each own a 1/2 interest in the land.
b. C and D will each own a 1/4 interest in the land.
c. C and D will each own a 1/3 interest in the land.
d. The tenancy in common will terminate.

57 (November 86)

If C sells her interest in the land to X,

a. The tenancy in common will terminate.
b. D and X will each own a 1/2 interest in the land.
c. D and X will each own a 1/3 interest in the land.
d. D and X will each own a 1/4 interest in the land.

Items 43 and 44 are based on the following information:

Abel, Boyd, and Cox are relatives who own a parcel of undeveloped land as joint tenants with right of survivorship. Abel sold his interest in the land to Zahn.

43 (May 86)

As a result of the sale from Abel to Zahn,

a. Zahn will acquire a 1/3 interest in the land as a joint tenant.
b. Zahn will acquire a 1/3 interest in the land as a tenant in common.
c. Boyd and Cox will each own a 1/3 interest in the land as tenants in common.
d. Boyd and Cox must consent before Zahn will acquire any interest in the land.

Property

44 (May 86)

If both Boyd and Zahn die, which of the following is correct with respect to the ownership of the land?

   a.   Cox and Zahn's heirs are tenants in common with ownership interests as follows: Cox 2/3 and Zahn's heirs 1/3.
   b.   Cox and Zahn's heirs are joint tenants with ownership interests as follows: Cox 2/3 and Zahn's heirs 1/3.
   c.   Cox, Boyd's heirs, and Zahn's heirs each own a 1/3 interest as tenants in common.
   d.   Cox owns the entire interest.

53 (November 85)

Jane and her brother each own a 1/2 interest in certain real property as tenants in common. Jane's interest

   a.   Is considered personal property.
   b.   Will pass to her brother by operation of law upon Jane's death.
   c.   Will pass upon her death to the person Jane designates in her will.
   d.   May not be transferred during Jane's lifetime without her brother's consent.

50 (May 81)

The last will and testament of Jean Bond left various specific property and sums of money to relatives and friends. She left the residue of her estate equally to her favorite niece and nephew. Which of the various properties described below will become a part of Bond's estate and be distributed in accordance with her last will and testament?

   a.   A joint savings account which listed her sister, who is still living, as the joint tenant.
   b.   The entire family homestead which she had owned in joint tenancy with her old brother who predeceased her and which was still recorded as jointly owned.
   c.   Several substantial gifts that she made in contemplation of death to various charities.
   d.   A life beneficiary policy which designated a former partner as the beneficiary.

50 (November 80)

Paul Good's will left all of his commercial real property to his wife Dorothy for life and the remainder to his two daughters, Joan and Doris, as tenants in common. All beneficiaries are alive and over 21 years of age. Regarding the rights of the parties, which of the following is a correct statement?

   a.   Dorothy may not elect to take against the will and receive a statutory share instead.
   b.   The daughters must survive Dorothy in order to receive any interest in the property.
   c.   Either of the daughters may sell her interest in the property without the consent of their mother or the other daughter.
   d.   If only one daughter is alive upon the death of Dorothy, she is entitled to the entire property.

26 (May 80)

Dombres is considering purchasing Blackacre. The title search revealed that the property was willed by Adams jointly to his children, Donald and Martha. The language contained in the will is unclear as to whether a joint tenancy or a tenancy in common was intended. Donald is dead and Martha has agreed to convey her entire interest by quit-claim deed to Dombres. The purchase price is equal to the full fair market price of the property. Dombres is not interested in anything less than the entire title to the tract. Under the circumstances, which of the following is correct?

   a.   There is a statutory preference which favors the finding of a joint tenancy.
   b.   Whether the will created a joint tenancy or a tenancy in common is irrelevant since Martha is the only survivor.
   c.   Dombres will not obtain title to the entire tract of land by Martha's conveyance.
   d.   There is no way or means whereby Dombres may obtain a clear title under the circumstances.

10 (November 79)

Marcross and two business associates own real property as tenants in common that they have invested in as a speculation. The speculation proved to be highly successful, and the land is now worth substantially more than their investment. Which of the following is a correct legal incident of ownership of the property?

a. Upon the death of any of the other tenants, the deceased's interest passes to the survivor(s) unless there is a will.
b. Each of the co-tenants owns an undivided interest in the whole.
c. A co-tenant can <u>not</u> sell his interest in the property without the consent of the other tenants.
d. Upon the death of a co-tenant, his estate is entitled to the amount of the original investment, but <u>not</u> the appreciation.

41 (November 78)

Winslow conveyed a 20-acre tract of land to his two children, George and Martha, "equally as tenants in common." What is the legal effect of this form of conveyance?
a. George and Martha are joint owners with a right to survivorship.
b. Each must first offer the other the right to purchase the property before he or she can sell to a third party.
c. Neither may convey his or her interest in the property unless both join in the conveyance.
d. Each owns an undivided interest in the whole, which he or she may dispose of by deed or by will.

27 (May 78)

Olson conveyed real property to his sons, Sampson and David, but the deed was ambiguous as to the type of estate created and the interest each son had in relation to the other. David died intestate shortly after Olson. David's widow and children are contending that they have rights in the property. Which of the following would be the widow's and children's **best** argument to claim valid rights in the real property?
a. The conveyance by Olson created a life estate in Sampson with a contingent remainder interest in David.
b. The conveyance by Olson created a joint tenancy with a right to survivorship.
c. The conveyance by Olson created a tenancy in common.
d. The widow is entitled to her statutory share.

39 (May 77)

A joint tenant's interest in real property
a. Can only be created by deed.
b. Need <u>not</u> be created at the same time <u>nor</u> pursuant to the same instrument.
c. Will <u>not</u> pass under the laws of intestate succession.
d. <u>Cannot</u> be sold or severed during the life of the joint tenancy.

26 (May 76)

A joint tenancy
a. <u>Cannot</u> be created by deed.
b. Will be found to exist by judicial preference if it is unclear as to whether a joint tenancy or tenancy in common was intended by the grantor.
c. <u>Cannot</u> be created in respect to personal property.
d. Provides a right of survivorship in the surviving joint tenant.

C. Landlord and Tenant

13 (R98)

Which of the following rights is (are) generally given to a lessee of residential property?
      I. A covenant of quiet enjoyment.
      II. An implied warranty of habitability
a. I only.
b. II only.
c. Both I and II.
d. Neither I nor II.

Property

53 (November 95)

Which of the following provisions must be included to have an enforceable written residential lease?

	A description of the leased premises	A due date for the payment of rent
a.	Yes	Yes
b.	Yes	No
c.	No	Yes
d.	No	No

52 (May 95)

Which of the following provisions must be included in a residential lease agreement?

a. A description of the leased premises.
b. The due date for payment of rent.
c. A requirement that the tenant have public liability insurance.
d. A requirement that the landlord will perform all structural repairs to the property.

53 (November 92)

Which of the following forms of tenancy will be created if a tenant stays in possession of the leased premises without the landlord's consent, after the tenant's one-year written lease expires?

a. Tenancy at will.
b. Tenancy for years.
c. Tenancy from period to period.
d. Tenancy at sufferance.

53 (November 91)

To be enforceable, a residential real estate lease must

a. Require the tenant to obtain liability insurance.
b. Entitle the tenant to exclusive possession of the leased property.
c. Specify a due date for rent.
d. Be in writing.

52 (November 90)

Bronson is a residential tenant with a 10-year written lease. In the absence of specific provisions in the lease to the contrary, which of the following statements is correct?

a. The premises may not be sublet for less than the full remaining lease term.
b. Bronson may not assign the lease.
c. The landlord's death will automatically terminate the lease.
d. Bronson's purchase of the property will terminate the lease.

53 (May 90)

A tenant renting an apartment under a three-year written lease that does not contain any specific restrictions may be evicted for

a. Counterfeiting money in the apartment.
b. Keeping a dog in the apartment.
c. Failing to maintain a liability insurance policy on the apartment.
d. Making structural repairs to the apartment.

54 (May 90)

Delta Corp. leased 60,000 square feet in an office building from Tanner under a written 25-year lease. Which of the following statements is correct?

    a.   Tanner's death will terminate the lease and Delta will be able to recover any resulting damages from Tanner's estate.

    b.   Tanner's sale of the office building will terminate the lease unless both Delta and the buyer consented to the assumption of the lease by the buyer.

    c.   In the absence of a provision in the lease to the contrary, Delta does <u>not</u> need Tanner's consent to assign the lease to another party.

    d.   In the absence of a provision in the lease to the contrary, Delta would need Tanner's consent to enter into a sublease with another party.

55 (May 88)

Sisk is a tenant of Met Co. and has two years remaining on a six-year lease executed by Sisk and Met. The lease prohibits subletting but is silent as to Sisk's right to assign the lease. Sisk assigned the lease to Kern Corp. which assumed all of Sisk's obligations under the lease. Met objects to the assignment. Which of the following statements is correct?

    a.   The assignment to Kern is voidable at Met's option.

    b.   Sisk would have been relieved from liability on the lease with Met if Sisk obtained Met's consent to the assignment.

    c.   Sisk will remain liable to Met for the rent provided for in the lease.

    d.   With respect to the rent provided for in the lease, Kern is liable to Sisk but <u>not</u> to Met.

56 (November 87)

Drake Corp. entered into a five-year lease with Samon that provided for Drake's occupancy of three floors of a high-rise office building at a monthly rent of $16,000. The lease provided that "lessee may sublet the premises but only with the landlord's (Samon's) prior written consent." The lease was silent as to whether Drake could assign the lease. Which of the following statements is correct?

    a.   Subletting of the premises with Samon's consent will relieve Drake from its obligation to pay rent.

    b.   Assignment of the lease with Samon's consent will relieve Drake from its obligation to pay rent.

    c.   Samon may refuse to consent to a subsequent sublet even if she has consented to a prior sublet.

    d.   Subletting of the premises without Samon's consent is void.

41 (May 86)

Mack & Watts, CPAs, wishes to relocate its office. Its existing lease is for four years, with one year remaining. Its landlord is not agreeable to canceling the lease. The lease also prohibits a sublease without the landlord's consent but is silent as to an assignment. Mack & Watts has found a financially responsible and respectable prospective subtenant but is convinced that the landlord will not consent to the sublease. Which of the following statements is correct?

    a.   A sublease without the landlord's consent would not be a breach of the lease.

    b.   An assignment by Mack & Watts would be a breach of the lease.

    c.   An assignment by Mack & Watts would <u>not</u> relieve it of liability under the lease.

    d.   A sublease with the landlord's consent would relieve Mack & Watts of liability under the lease.

52 (November 85)

Mini, Inc. entered into a five-year lease with Rein Realtors. The lease was signed by both parties and immediately recorded. The leased building was to be used by Mini in connection with its business operations. To make it suitable for that purpose, Mini attached a piece of equipment to the wall of the building. Which of the following statements is correct regarding Mini's rights and liabilities?

    a.   Mini is prohibited from assigning the lease if it is silent in this regard.

    b.   Mini has a possessory interest in the building.

    c.   Mini is strictly liable for all injuries sustained by any person in the building during the term of the lease.

    d.   Mini's rights under the lease are automatically terminated by Rein's sale of the building to a third party.

48 (November 80)

Charles is a commercial tenant of Luxor Buildings, Inc. The term of the lease is five years and two years have elapsed. The lease prohibits subletting, but does not contain any provision relating to assignment. Charles approached Luxor and asked whether Luxor could release him from the balance of the term of the lease for $500. Luxor refused unless Charles would agree to pay $2,000. Charles located Whitney who was interested in renting in Luxor's building and transferred the entire balance of the lease to Whitney in consideration of his promise to pay Luxor the monthly rental and otherwise perform Charles' obligations under the lease. Luxor objects. Which of the following statements is correct?

    a.   The assignment is invalid without Luxor's consent.

    b.   The assignment does not extinguish Charles' obligation to pay the rent if Whitney defaults.

    c.   The assignment need not be in writing.

    d.   A prohibition of the right to sublet contained in the lease completely prohibits an assignment.

41 (November 76)

Vance obtained a 25-year leasehold interest in an office building from the owner Stanfield.

    a.   Vance's interest is nonassignable.

    b.   The conveyance of the ownership of the building by Stanfield to Wax will terminate Vance's leasehold interest.

    c.   Stanfield's death will not terminate Vance's leasehold interest.

    d.   Vance's death will terminate the leasehold interest.

11 (May 75)

Unlimited Fashions, Inc. leased a store in the Suburban Styles Shopping Center for five years at $1,500 a month. The lease contained a provision which prohibited assignment of the lease. After occupying the premises for two years, Unlimited sublet the premises to Fantastic Frocks for the balance of its term, less one day, at $2,000 per month. Unlimited moved out on a Sunday and removed all its personal property and trade fixtures such as portable clothing racks, cash registers, detachable counters, etc. Which of the following best describes the legal status of the parties involved?

    a.   Unlimited has not breached its contract with Suburban.

    b.   Suburban is entitled to the additional $500 rental paid each month by Fantastic to Unlimited.

    c.   Removal of the trade fixtures in question by Unlimited was improper and it can be held liable to Suburban for their fair value.

    d.   Fantastic is a tenant of Suburban.

5A (May 79)

Hammar Hardware Company, Inc. purchased all the assets and assumed all the liabilities of JoMar Hardware for $60,000. Among the assets and liabilities included in the sale was a lease of the building in which the business was located. The lessor-owner was Marathon Realty, Inc., and the remaining unexpired term of the lease was nine years. The lease did not contain a provision dealing with the assignment of the leasehold. Incidental to the purchase, Hammar expressly promised JoMar that it would pay the rental due Marathon over the life of the lease and would hold JoMar harmless from any future liability thereon.

When Marathon learned of the proposed transaction, it strenuously objected to the assignment of the lease and to the occupancy by Hammar. Later, after this dispute was resolved and prior to expiration of the lease, Hammar abandoned the building and ceased doing business in the area. Marathon has demanded payment by JoMar of the rent as it matures over the balance of the term of the lease.

Required: Answer the following, setting forth reasons for any conclusions stated.

    1.   Was the consent of Marathon necessary in order to assign the lease?

    2.   Is JoMar liable on the lease?

    3.   If Marathon were to proceed against Hammar, would Hammar be liable under the lease?

1. No. In the absence of a restriction on the right to assign specifically stated in the lease, a lessee may assign his leasehold interest to another. Only in unusual circumstances, where the lease involves special elements of personal trust and confidence as contrasted with mere payment for occupancy, will the courts limit the right to assign.

2. Yes. Although JoMar may effectively assign the lease, which in effect is an assignment of the right to occupy the leasehold premises and a delegation of its duty to pay Marathon, it cannot shed its liability to Marathon for the rental payments. In the absence of a release, JoMar remains liable. The transaction described in the fact situation is in the nature of a surety relationship.

3. Yes. Marathon is a third-party creditor beneficiary of Hammar's promise to JoMar. As such, Marathon can assert rights on the promise even though it was not a party to the contract. Marathon is not barred by lack of privity or the fact that it gave no consideration to Hammar for the promise.

4B (May 74)

Reynolds leased a manufacturing building from Philip under a written lease for a period of five years at a specified rental and with a provision that the lessor would keep the structure in repair.

Reynolds subleased a portion of the lower floor to Signor giving him access through a hallway from the main entrance. Philip subsequently mortgaged the building, and Central Savings, the mortgagee, ultimately foreclosed and acquired good title to the property. Reynolds was unable to get Central Savings to make certain minor repairs and had withheld rent in an amount equal to the repairs he was forced to make. Central Savings meanwhile notified both Reynolds and Signor that the lease was terminated and that both were to pay rent directly to it for one month and then vacate.

Required:
1. Discuss Reynolds' right to withhold rent in the amount of repairs.
2. Absent a breach by the tenants, discuss Central Savings' right to:
   a. Evict the tenants.
   b. Require Signor to pay the rent directly to it.

1. Reynolds had no right to withhold rent in the amount of repairs. Covenants by lessor and lessee are deemed independent unless it is clear that the parties intended the contrary. However, if the breach were sufficiently serious, it might furnish the basis for a claim of constructive eviction. This does not seem to be the case on the facts.

2a. Central Savings has no right to evict the tenants. When the lease preceded the mortgage, the tenant's term is not affected by the later mortgage absent an agreement by the tenant to the contrary.

2b. Signor is a sublessee and, as such, a tenant of Reynolds. Absent a provision in the lease prohibiting the sublease, Reynolds committed no breach by the subletting, and the sublessee, as a tenant of the sublessor, has no direct obligations to the lessor.

III. Real Property Transfer
A. Voluntary Transfer of Real Property by Sale--Conveyancing

52 (November 95)

A method of transferring ownership of real property that most likely would be considered an arm's-length transaction is transfer by
   a. Inheritance.
   b. Eminent domain.
   c. Adverse possession.
   d. Sale

Property

54 (November 95)

Which of the following elements must be contained in a valid deed?

	Purchase price	Description of the land
a.	Yes	Yes
b.	Yes	No
c.	No	Yes
d.	No	No

53 (May 95)

For a deed to be effective between a purchaser and seller of real estate, one of the conditions is that the deed must
a. Be recorded within the permissible statutory time limits.
b. Be delivered by the seller with an intent to transfer title.
c. Contain the actual sales price.
d. Contains the signatures of the seller and purchaser.

57 (May 94)

Which of the following is a defect in marketable title to real property?
a. Recorded zoning restrictions.
b. Recorded easements referred to in the contract of sale.
c. Unrecorded lawsuit for negligence against the seller.
d. Unrecorded easement.

53 (May 93)

Which of the following warranties is (are) contained in a general warranty deed?
    I. The grantor has the right to convey the property.
    II. The grantee will <u>not</u> be disturbed in possession of the property by the grantor or some third party's lawful claim of ownership.
a. I only.
b. II only.
c. I and II.
d. Neither I nor II.

54 (May 93)

A standard title insurance policy will generally insure that
a. There are <u>no</u> other deeds to the property.
b. The purchaser has good record title as of the policy's date.
c. All taxes and assessments are paid.
d. The insurance protection will be transferable to a subsequent purchaser.

51 (November 92)

Which of the following would change if an asset is treated as personal property rather than as real property?

	Requirements for transfer	Creditor's rights
a.	Yes	No
b.	No	Yes
c.	Yes	Yes
d.	No	No

54 (November 91)

A purchaser who obtains real estate title insurance will

a. Have coverage for the title exceptions listed in the policy.
b. Be insured against all defects of record other than those excepted in the policy.
c. Have coverage for title defects that result from events that happen after the effective date of the policy.
d. Be entitled to transfer the policy to subsequent owners.

53 (November 90)

Unless an exception to title is noted in the title insurance policy, a title insurance company will be liable to a land purchaser for

a. Closing costs.
b. Recorded easements.
c. Unrecorded easements.
d. Zoning violations.

56 (November 90)

Which of the following deeds will give a real property purchaser the greatest protection?

a. Quitclaim.
b. Bargain and sale.
c. Special warranty.
d. General warranty.

55 (May 90)

On February 2, Mazo deeded a warehouse to Parko for $450,000. Parko did not record the deed. On February 12, Mazo deeded the same warehouse to Nexis for $430,000. Nexis was aware of the prior conveyance to Parko. Nexis recorded its deed before Parko recorded. Who would prevail under the following recording statutes?

	Notice statute	Race statute	Race-Notice statute
a.	Nexis	Parko	Parko
b.	Parko	Nexis	Parko
c.	Parko	Nexis	Nexis
d.	Parko	Parko	Nexis

56 (November 89)

A buyer of real estate who receives a title insurance policy will

a. Take title free of all defects.
b. Be able to transfer the policy to a subsequent buyer of the real estate.
c. Not have coverage for title exceptions listed in the insurance policy.
d. Not have coverage greater than the amount of any first mortgage.

58 (November 88)

Which of the following deeds gives the grantee the least amount of protection?

a. Bargain and sale deed.
b. Grant deed.
c. Quitclaim deed.
d. Warranty deed.

Property

58 (November 86)

Which of the following warranty (warranties) is (are) given by a general warranty deed?
   I.   The grantor owns the property being conveyed.
   II. The grantee will <u>not</u> be disturbed in her possession of the property by the grantor or some third party's lawful claim of ownership.
   III. The grantor has the right to convey the property.
   a. I only.
   b. I, II, and III.
   c. I and III only.
   d. II and III only.

46 (May 86)

Dash has agreed to sell a warehouse for $300,000 to Bosch. The contract provided that Dash will convey to Bosch whatever interest Dash may have in the warehouse. Under the terms of the contract, Bosch is entitled to receive a(an)
   a. Insurable deed.
   b. Quitclaim deed.
   c. General warranty deed.
   d. Special warranty deed.

54 (November 85)

Real estate title insurance
   a. May be transferred to a subsequent bona fide purchaser for value.
   b. Assures that the purchaser will take title free and clear of all defects.
   c. Assures that the purchaser will take title free and clear of all record defects since all exceptions to title must be cleared prior to the purchaser taking possession of the realty.
   d. Is generally <u>not</u> required where the contract is silent on this point.

Items 52 and 53 are based on the following information:

On July 1, Bean deeded her home to Park. The deed was never recorded. On July 5, Bean deeded the same home to Noll. On July 9, Noll executed a deed, conveying his title to the same home to Baxter. On July 10, Noll and Baxter duly recorded their respective deeds.

52 (May 85)

In order for Noll's deed from Bean to be effective it must
   a. Contain the actual purchase price paid by Noll.
   b. Be signed by Noll.
   c. Include a satisfactory description of the property.
   d. Be recorded with Bean's seal affixed to the deed.

53 (May 85)

If Noll and Baxter are bona fide purchasers for value, which of the following statements is correct?
   a. Baxter's interest is superior to Park's.
   b. Bean's deed to Park was void as between Bean and Park because it was <u>not</u> recorded.
   c. Bean's deed to Noll was void because she had <u>no</u> interest to convey.
   d. Baxter can recover the purchase price from Noll.

55 (May 85)

Lake purchased a home from Walsh for $95,000. Lake obtained a $60,000 loan from Safe Bank to finance the purchase, executing a promissory note and mortgage. The recording of the mortgage by Safe

a. Gives the world actual notice of Safe's interest.
b. Protects Safe's interest against the claims of subsequent bona fide purchasers for value.
c. Is necessary in order that Safe have rights against Lake under the promissory note.
d. Is necessary in order to protect Safe's interest against the claim of a subsequent transferee who does not give value.

55 (May 83)

Smith purchased a tract of land. To protect himself, he ordered title insurance from Valor Title Insurance Company. The policy was the usual one issued by title companies. Accordingly

a. Valor will not be permitted to take exceptions to its coverage if it agreed to insure and prepared the title abstract.
b. The title policy is assignable in the event Smith subsequently sells the property.
c. The title policy provides protection against defects in record title only.
d. Valor will be liable for any title defect which arises, even though the defect could not have been discovered through the exercise of reasonable care.

56 (May 83)

Purdy purchased real property from Hart and received a warranty deed with full covenants. Recordation of this deed is

a. Not necessary if the deed provides that recordation is not required.
b. Necessary to vest the purchaser's legal title to the property conveyed.
c. Required primarily for the purpose of providing the local taxing authorities with the information necessary to assess taxes.
d. Irrelevant if the subsequent party claiming superior title had actual notice of the unrecorded deed.

52 (May 82)

Park purchased Marshall's department store. At the closing, Park delivered a certified check for the balance due and Marshall gave Park a warranty deed with full covenants to the property. The deed

a. Must be recorded to be valid between the parties.
b. Must recite the actual consideration given by Park.
c. Must be in writing and contain the signature of both parties duly witnessed.
d. Usually represents an exclusive integration of the duties of the seller.

53 (May 82)

Fulcrum Enterprises, Inc. contracted to purchase a four acre tract of land from Devlin as a site for its proposed factory. The contract of sale is silent on the type of deed to be received by Fulcrum and does not contain any title exceptions. The title search revealed that there are 51 zoning laws which affect Fulcrum's use of the land and that back taxes are due. A survey revealed a stone wall encroaching upon a portion of the land Devlin is purporting to convey. A survey made 23 years ago also had revealed the wall. Regarding the rights and duties of Fulcrum, which of the following is correct?

a. Fulcrum is entitled to a warranty deed with full covenants from Devlin at the closing.
b. The existence of the zoning laws above will permit Fulcrum to avoid the contract.
c. Fulcrum must take the land subject to the back taxes.
d. The wall results in a potential breach of the implied warranty of marketability.

47 (November 80)

Gilgo has entered into a contract for the purchase of land from the Wicklow Land Company. A title search reveals certain defects in the title to the land to be conveyed by Wicklow. Wicklow has demanded that Gilgo accept the deed and pay the balance of the purchase price. Furthermore, Wicklow has informed Gilgo that unless Gilgo proceeds with the closing, Wicklow will hold Gilgo liable for breach of contract. Wicklow has pointed out to

Gilgo that the contract says nothing about defects and that he must take the property "as is." Which of the following is correct?

    a. Gilgo can rely on the implied warranty of merchantability.

    b. Wicklow is right in that if there is <u>no</u> express warranty against title defects, none exists.

    c. Gilgo will prevail because he is entitled to a perfect title from Wicklow.

    d. Gilgo will win if the title is <u>not</u> marketable.

31 (May 78)

In connection with the audit of Fiske & Company, you found it necessary to examine a deed to certain property owned by the client. In this connection, which of the following statements is correct?

    a. A deed purporting to convey real property, but which omits the day of the month, is invalid.

    b. A deed which lacks the signature of the grantor is valid.

    c. A quitclaim deed which purports to transfer to the grantee "whatever title the grantor has" is invalid.

    d. A deed which purports to convey real property and recites a consideration of $1 and other valuable consideration is valid.

44 (May 77)

Fitz decided to purchase a two-acre tract in an industrial park from Expansion, Inc., the developer. The usual contract of sale was drafted and signed by the parties. However, it is silent in respect to marketable title and the type of deed to be delivered at the closing. What effect does the omission of these items from the contract have?

    a. The contract is subject to an implied covenant that Fitz will receive marketable title at the closing.

    b. Expansion must deliver a warranty deed with full covenants.

    c. In the event Expansion decides to withdraw the property from the market because of rising land prices, Fitz could obtain damages but <u>not</u> specific performance.

    d. Fitz should have a title search within 30 days after the closing in order to make sure the title is clear.

43 (November 76)

The failure to record a deed will

    a. <u>Not</u> affect the rights between the parties to the deed.

    b. Constitute a fraud upon the creditors of the seller.

    c. Defeat the rights of the buyer if the seller subsequently conveys the property to a third party who has actual knowledge of the prior conveyance.

    d. Be disregarded in respect to the rights of subsequent third parties if the deed is a mere quitclaim.

23 (May 76)

Maxwell purchased real property from Plumb and received a warranty deed at the closing. Maxwell neglected to record the deed. In this situation:

    a. A subsequent purchaser from Plumb will obtain a better title to the real property than Maxwell even if the subsequent purchaser is aware of Maxwell's prior purchase.

    b. Maxwell must record his deed in order to perfect his rights against Plumb.

    c. Recordation would provide constructive notice of Maxwell's rights to subsequent purchasers of the real property even though they do <u>not</u> have actual notice.

    d. Maxwell lacks an insurable interest in the property and any fire insurance policy he obtains is void.

27 (May 76)

Arthur entered into a contract for the sale of real property to Vance for $50,000. Arthur owned the property free and clear of all mortgages. Arthur received $2,500 upon the signing of the contract and agreed to take $22,500 in cash or certified check at the closing and a first mortgage for the balance. In this situation:

    a. The mortgage in question need not be recorded by Arthur to perfect his interest against third parties in that it is a purchase-money security interest.

    b. Arthur's contract gave Vance an implied covenant that his title would be marketable at the time of the closing.

    c. If the contract is silent on the point, Arthur must deliver a full warranty deed with covenants at the closing.

    d. If Arthur breaches the contract, Vance's only recourse is to sue for damages based upon breach of contract.

2 (May 75)

A contract for the purchase and sale of real property:

a. Must be signed by both parties in order to be binding on either.

b. Must be contained in a formalized, signed, and notarized document if the contrast is to be enforceable.

c. Is <u>not</u> assignable unless specifically authorized in the contract.

d. Contains an implied promise that the title to the property to be conveyed is marketable.

17 (May 75)

Harrison purchased Bigacre from Whitmore. The deed described the real property conveyed and the granting clause read: "Seller hereby releases, surrenders, and relinquishes to buyer any right, title, or interest that he may have in Bigacre." The deed contained no covenants. What is Harrison's legal status concerning title to Bigacre?

a. Harrison has obtained a quitclaim deed.

b. If an adverse claimant ousts Harrison from Bigacre, Harrison will have recourse against Whitmore.

c. The only warranty contained in the deed is an implied warranty of marketability of title.

d. Harrison's deed is neither insurable nor recordable.

B. Financing Real Property--Mortgages

55 (November 95)

Rich purchased property from Sklar for $200,000. Rich obtained a $150,000 loan from Marsh Bank to finance the purchase, executing a promissory note and a mortgage. By recording the mortgage, Marsh protects its

a. Rights against Rich under the promissory note.

b. Rights against the claims of subsequent bona fide purchasers for value.

c. Priority against a previously filed real estate tax lien on the property.

d. Priority against all parties having earlier claims to the property.

54 (May 95)

Generally, which of the following federal acts regulate mortgage lenders?

	Real Estate Settlement Procedures Act (RESPA)	Federal Trade Commission Act
a.	Yes	Yes
b.	Yes	No
c.	No	Yes
d.	No	No

58 (May 94)

Which of the following conditions must be met to have an enforceable mortgage?

a. An accurate description of the property must be included in the mortgage.

b. A negotiable promissory note must accompany the mortgage.

c. Present consideration must be given in exchange for the mortgage.

d. The amount of the debt and the interest rate must be stated in the mortgage.

55 (May 93)

In general, which of the following statements is correct with respect to a real estate mortgage?

a. The mortgage may <u>not</u> be given to secure an antecedent debt.

b. The mortgage must contain the actual amount of the underlying debt.

c. The mortgage must be signed by both the mortgagor (borrower) and mortgagee (lender).

d. The mortgagee may assign the mortgage to a third party without the mortgagor's consent.

Property

57 (May 93)

On May 1, 1991, Chance bought a piece of property by taking subject to an existing unrecorded mortgage held by Hay Bank. On April 1, 1992, Chance borrowed money from Link Finance and gave Link a mortgage on the property. Link did not know about the Hay mortgage and did not record its mortgage until July 1, 1992. On June 1, 1992, Chance borrowed money from Zone Bank and gave Zone a mortgage on the same property. Zone knew about the Link mortgage but did not know about the Hay mortgage. Zone recorded its mortgage on June 15, 1992. Which mortgage would have priority if these transactions took place in a notice-race jurisdiction?

   a.   The Hay mortgage because it was first in time.

   b.   The Link mortgage because Zone had notice of the Link mortgage.

   c.   The Zone mortgage because it was the first recorded mortgage.

   d.   The Zone and Link mortgages share priority because neither had notice of the Hay mortgage.

55 (November 92)

Generally, in addition to being in writing, a real estate mortgage must

   a.   Be signed by both the mortgagor and mortgagee.

   b.   Be recorded to validate the mortgagee's rights against the mortgagor.

   c.   Contain a description of the real estate covered by the mortgage.

   d.   Contain the actual amount of the underlying debt and the interest rate.

Items 58 through 60 are based on the following:

On February 1, Frost bought a building from Elgin, Inc. for $250,000. To complete the purchase, Frost borrowed $200,000 from Independent Bank and gave Independent a mortgage for that amount; gave Elgin a second mortgage for $25,000; and paid $25,000 in cash. Independent recorded its mortgage on February 2 and Elgin recorded its mortgage on March 12.

The following transactions also took place

   ▪   On March 1, Frost gave Scott a $20,000 mortgage on the building to secure a personal loan Scott had previously made to Frost.

   ▪   On March 10, Scott recorded this mortgage.

   ▪   On March 15, Scott learned about both prior mortgages.

   ▪   On June 1, Frost stopped making payments on all the mortgages.

   ▪   On August 1, the mortgages were foreclosed. Frost, on that date, owed Independent, $195,000; Elgin, $24,000; and Scott, $19,000

A judicial sale of the building resulted in proceeds of $220,000 after expenses were deducted. The above transactions took place in a notice-race jurisdiction.

58 (November 92)

What amount of the proceeds will Scott receive?

   a. $0

   b. $1,000

   c. $12,500

   d. $19,000

59 (November 92)

Why would Scott receive this amount?

   a.   Scott knew of the Elgin mortgage.

   b.   Scott's mortgage was recorded before Elgin's and before Scott knew of Elgin's mortgage.

   c.   Elgin's mortgage was first in time.

   d.   After Independent is fully paid, Elgin and Scott share the remaining proceeds equally.

60 (November 92)
   Frost may redeem the property before the judicial sale only if
   a. There is a statutory right of redemption.
   b. It is probable that the sale price will result in a deficiency.
   c. All mortgages are paid in full.
   d. All mortgagees are paid a penalty fee.

55 (November 91)
   A mortgage on real property must
   a. Be acknowledged by the mortgagee.
   b. State the exact amount of the debt.
   c. State the consideration given for the mortgage.
   d. Be delivered to the mortgagee.

56 (November 91)
   If a mortgagee fails to records it mortgage in a jurisdiction with a notice-race recording statute,
   a. A subsequent recording mortgagee who has <u>no</u> knowledge of the prior mortgage will have a superior security interest.
   b. A subsequent recording mortgagee who has knowledge of the prior mortgage will have a superior security interest.
   c. A subsequent purchaser for value who has <u>no</u> knowledge of the mortgage will take the property subject to the mortgage.
   d. A subsequent purchaser for value who has knowledge of the mortgage will take the property free of the prior security interest.

57 (November 91)
   Which of the following is correct regarding foreclosure of a purchase money mortgage by judicial sale of the property?
   a. The mortgagor has the right to any remaining sale proceeds after the mortgagee is paid.
   b. The purchaser at the sale is liable for any deficiency owed the mortgagee.
   c. The court must confirm any price received at the sale.
   d. The mortgagor can never be liable for a deficiency owed the mortgagee.

58 (November 91)
   Wyn bought real estate from Duke and gave Duke a purchase money mortgage. Duke forgot to record the mortgage. Two months later, Wyn gave a mortgage on the same property to Goode to secure a property improvement loan. Goode recorded this mortgage nine days later. Goode knew about the Duke mortgage. If these events took place in a notice-race statute jurisdiction, which mortgage would have priority?
   a. Duke's, because it was the first mortgage given.
   b. Duke's, because Goode knew of the Duke mortgage.
   c. Goode's, because it was the first mortgage recorded.
   d. Goode's, because it was recorded within ten days.

19 (May 91)
   Wilk bought an apartment building from Dix Corp. There was a mortgage on the building securing Dix's promissory note to Xeon Finance Co. Wilk took title subject to Xeon's mortgage. Wilk did not make the payments on the note due Xeon and the building was sold at foreclosure sale. If the proceeds of the foreclosure sale are less than the balance due on the note, which of the following statements is correct regarding the deficiency?
   a. Xeon must attempt to collect the deficiency from Wilk before suing Dix.
   b. Dix will <u>not</u> be liable for any of the deficiency because Wilk assumed the note and mortgage.
   c. Xeon may collect the deficiency from either Dix or Wilk.
   d. Dix will be liable for the entire deficiency.

24 (November 90)

Omega Corp. owned a factory that was encumbered by a mortgage securing Omega's note to Eagle Bank. Omega sold the factory to Spear, Inc., which assumed the mortgage note. Later, Spear defaulted on the note, which had an outstanding balance of $15,000. To recover the outstanding balance, Eagle

- a. May sue Spear only after suing Omega.
- b. May sue either Spear or Omega.
- c. Must sue both Spear and Omega.
- d. Must sue Spear first and then proceed against Omega for any deficiency.

54 (November 90)

Sklar Corp. owns a factory that has a fair market value of $90,000. Dall Bank holds an $80,000 first mortgage and Rice Finance holds a $20,000 second mortgage on the factory. Sklar has discontinued payments to Dall and Rice, who have foreclosed on their mortgages. If the factory is properly sold to Bond at a judicial sale for $90,000, after expenses,

- a. Rice will receive $10,000 out of the proceeds.
- b. Dall will receive $77,500 out of the proceeds.
- c. Bond will take the factory subject to the unsatisfied portion of any mortgage.
- d. Rice has a right of redemption after the judicial sale.

55 (November 90)

To be enforceable against the mortgagor, a mortgage must meet all the following requirements except

- a. Be delivered to the mortgagee.
- b. Be in writing and signed by the mortgagor.
- c. Be recorded by the mortgagee.
- d. Include a description of the debt and land involved.

58 (November 90)

Ritz owned a building on which there was a duly recorded first mortgage held by Lyn and a recorded second mortgage held by Jay. Ritz sold the building to Nunn. Nunn assumed the Jay mortgage and had no actual knowledge of the Lyn mortgage. Nunn defaulted on the payments to Jay. If both Lyn and Jay foreclosed, and the proceeds of the sale were insufficient to pay both Lyn and Jay,

- a. Jay would be paid after Lyn was fully paid.
- b. Jay and Lyn would be paid proportionately.
- c. Nunn would be personally liable to Lyn but not to Jay.
- d. Nunn would be personally liable to Lyn and Jay.

59 (November 90)

Gilmore borrowed $60,000 from Dix Bank. The loan was used to remodel a building owned by Gilmore as investment property and was secured by a second mortgage that Dix did not record. FCA Loan Company has a recorded first mortgage on the building. If Gilmore defaults on both mortgages, Dix

- a. Will not be entitled to any mortgage foreclosure sale proceeds, even if such proceeds are in excess of the amount owed to FCA.
- b. Will be unable to successfully claim any security interest in the building.
- c. Will be entitled to share in any foreclosure sale proceeds pro rata with FCA.
- d. Will be able to successfully claim a security interest that is subordinate to FCA's security interest.

56 (May 90)

On April 6, Ford purchased a warehouse from Atwood for $150,000. Atwood had executed two mortgages on the property: a purchase money mortgage given to Lang on March 2, which was not recorded; and a mortgage given to Young on March 9, which was recorded the same day. Ford was unaware of the mortgage to Lang. Under the circumstances,

a. Ford will take title to the warehouse subject only to Lang's mortgage.
b. Ford will take title to the warehouse free of Lang's mortgage.
c. Lang's mortgage is superior to Young's mortgage because Lang's mortgage is a purchase money mortgage.
d. Lang's mortgage is superior to Young's mortgage because Lang's mortgage was given first in time.

57 (May 90)

Sussex, Inc. had given a first mortgage when it purchased its plant and warehouse. Sussex needed additional working capital. It decided to obtain financing by giving a second mortgage on the plant and warehouse. Which of the following statements is true with respect to the mortgages?
a. Default on payment of the second mortgage will constitute default on the first mortgage.
b. The second mortgage may not be prepaid without the consent of the first mortgagee.
c. The second mortgagee may not pay off the first mortgage to protect its security.
d. If both mortgages are foreclosed, the first mortgage must be fully paid before paying the second mortgage.

58 (May 90)

If a mortgagor defaults in the payment of a purchase money mortgage, and the mortgagee forecloses, the mortgagor may do any of the following except
a. Obtain any excess monies resulting from a judicial sale after payment of the mortgagee.
b. Remain in possession of the property after a foreclosure sale if the equity in the property exceeds the balance due on the mortgage.
c. Refinance the mortgage with another lender and repay the original mortgage.
d. Assert the equitable right of redemption by paying the mortgagee.

57 (November 89)

If a borrower is in default under a purchase money mortgage loan, the
a. Lender can file suit to have the borrower declared insolvent.
b. Person who sold the real estate to the borrower can be forced to assume the mortgage debt.
c. Lender may file suit for foreclosure.
d. Lender may unilaterally obtain title without a foreclosure suit.

17 (November 88)

Bond purchased from Spear Corp. an apartment building that was encumbered by a mortgage securing Spear's promissory note to Fale Finance Co. Bond assumed Spear's note and mortgage. Subsequently, Bond defaulted on the note payable to Fale and, as a result, the building was sold at a foreclosure sale. If the proceeds of the foreclosure sale are less than the balance due on the note, which of the following statements is correct?
a. Fale must sue both Spear and Bond to collect the deficiency because they are jointly and severally liable.
b. Spear will be liable for the deficiency.
c. Fale must attempt to collect the deficiency from Bond before suing Spear.
d. Spear will not be liable for the deficiency because Bond assumed the note and mortgage.

59 (November 88)

In general, a mortgage on real estate
a. Must be recorded to validate the mortgagee's (lender's) rights against the mortgagor (borrower).
b. Must be signed by the mortgagee and mortgagor to create an enforceable instrument.
c. Encumbers the mortgagor's legal title to the real estate.
d. Gives the mortgagee the right to possess the real estate.

60 (November 88)

In 1982, Smith gave a mortgage to State Bank to secure a $100,000 loan. The mortgage was silent as to whether it would secure any other loans made by State to Smith. In 1984 Smith gave a second mortgage to Penn Bank to secure an $80,000 loan. Both mortgages described the same land and were properly recorded shortly after being executed by Smith. By 1988 Smith had repaid State Bank $40,000 of the $100,000 debt. State Bank then loaned Smith an additional $20,000 without taking any new security. Within a few days, Smith defaulted on the loans from

both banks and the first and second mortgages were foreclosed. The balance on the Penn loan was $20,000. The net proceeds of the foreclosure sale were $70,000. State is entitled to receive from the proceeds a maximum of
a. $52,500.
b. $56,000.
c. $60,000.
d. $70,000.

52 (May 88)

In general, which of the following statements is correct with respect to a real estate mortgage?
a. The mortgage must be in writing and signed by both the mortgagor (borrower) and mortgagee (lender).
b. The mortgagee may assign the mortgage to a third party without the mortgagor's consent.
c. The mortgage need <u>not</u> contain a description of the real estate covered by the mortgage.
d. The mortgage must contain the actual amount of the underlying debt and the rate of interest.

56 (May 88)

Bell obtained a $30,000 loan from Arco Bank, executing a promissory note and mortgage. The loan was secured by a building that Bell purchased from Marx for $50,000. Arco's recording of the mortgage
a. Generally does <u>not</u> affect the rights of Bell and Arco against each other under the promissory note.
b. Generally creates a possessory security interest in Arco.
c. Cuts off the rights of all prior and subsequent lessees of the building.
d. Transfers legal title to the building to Arco.

51 (November 87)

Fine Bank loaned Aker $80,000 to purchase a condominium. Aker executed a promissory note and a mortgage that encumbered the condominium. Fine failed to record the mortgage. With respect to the above transaction, Fine
a. Will hold legal title to the condominium until the note is paid.
b. Must file a financing statement to perfect its security interest in the condominium, because the condominium is personal property.
c. Must sign the note and mortgage in order for them to be effective.
d. Is entitled to collect the $80,000 from Aker despite its failure to record the mortgage.

52 (November 87)

Lusk borrowed $20,000 from Marco Finance. The loan was secured by a mortgage on a four-unit apartment building owned by Lusk. The proceeds of the loan were used by Lusk to purchase a business. The mortgage was duly recorded 60 days after Marco loaned the money to Lusk. Six months after borrowing the money from Marco, Lusk leased one of the apartments to Rudd for $800 per month. Neither Rudd nor Lusk notified Marco of the lease. Subsequently, Lusk defaulted on the note to Marco and Marco has commenced foreclosure proceedings. Under the circumstances,
a. Marco's mortgage is junior to Rudd's lease because the mortgage was <u>not</u> a purchase money mortgage.
b. Marco's mortgage is junior to Rudd's lease because Marco failed to record the mortgage for 60 days after the closing.
c. Rudd's lease is subject to Marco's mortgage because Marco recorded its mortgage prior to the time Rudd's leasehold interest arose.
d. Rudd's lease is subject to Marco's mortgage because of the failure to notify Marco of the lease.

23 (May 87)

Krieg was the owner of an office building encumbered by a mortgage securing Krieg's promissory note to Muni Bank. Park purchased the building subject to Muni's mortgage. As a result of the sale to Park,
a. Muni is <u>not</u> a third party creditor beneficiary.
b. Krieg is a third party creditor beneficiary.
c. Park is liable for any deficiency resulting from a default on the note.
d. Krieg was automatically released from any liability on the note.

414

53 (November 86)

Which of the following statements is correct with respect to a real estate mortgage?
a. It must be signed only by the mortgagor (borrower).
b. It must be recorded in order to be effective between the mortgagor and mortgagee.
c. It does not have to be recorded to be effective against third parties without notice if it is a purchase money mortgage.
d. It is effective even if not delivered to the mortgagee.

54 (November 86)

Watts gave a mortgage on a vacant lot to Fast to secure payment of a note. Fast assigned the note and mortgage to Beal who paid 85% of the face value for it. Neither Fast nor Beal recorded the mortgage. Subsequently, Fast assigned the same note and mortgage to Rusk who paid 75% of the face value for it and who had no notice of the prior assignment to Beal. Rusk promptly recorded the mortgage and the assignment. Watts has made no payments on the note. The jurisdiction has a notice-type of recordation statute. Under the circumstances
a. The assignments to Beal and Rusk are ineffective because Fast failed to record the mortgage.
b. Equity will require that Beal and Rusk share in the proceeds of the note equally as their interests may appear.
c. Rusk is entitled to recover only 75% of the face value of the note.
d. Rusk is entitled to the full face amount of the Watts note.

55 (November 86)

In a notice-type recordation jurisdiction, failure by the mortgagee to record its mortgage
a. Releases the mortgagor (borrower) from the underlying obligation to pay.
b. Permits a subsequent mortgagee without knowledge of the prior mortgage to have a superior security interest.
c. Permits a subsequent purchaser for value with knowledge of the mortgage to take the property free of the prior security interest.
d. Permits a subsequent mortgagee with knowledge of the prior mortgage to have a superior security interest provided he promptly records his mortgage.

47 (May 86)

Which of the following statements pertaining to a mortgage on a building is incorrect?
a. The mortgagor customarily retains legal title to the building despite the mortgage.
b. The recording of the mortgage is necessary to validate the rights and liabilities of the mortgagor and mortgagee against each other.
c. The mortgage must be in writing and signed by the mortgagor.
d. The mortgage must contain a description of the property subject to the mortgage.

48 (May 86)

Which of the following statements regarding the recording of a real estate mortgage in a state having a notice-race statute is correct?
a. By recording, the mortgagee will acquire additional rights against the mortgagor.
b. The mortgagee must file a financing statement with the appropriate state agency.
c. The recording of a mortgage is necessary to defeat the claims of a purchaser for value who had knowledge of the mortgage.
d. The recording of the mortgage will be important in determining priority among parties who claim an interest in the real estate.

49 (May 86)

Glenn borrowed $80,000 from City Bank. He executed a promissory note and secured the loan with a mortgage on business real estate he owned as a sole proprietor. Glenn neglected to advise City that he had previously mortgaged the property to Ball, who had failed to record his mortgage. City promptly recorded its mortgage.

Property

Subsequently, Glenn conveyed his business assets including the property to a newly-created corporation in exchange for all of its stock. Which of the following is correct?

a. Ball's mortgage is prior in time and would take priority over City's mortgage.

b. Glenn's corporation will take the property subject to both mortgages.

c. The corporation will be deemed to have assumed both mortgages.

d. On foreclosure, Glenn could not be called upon to pay City any deficiency.

Items 55 and 56 are based on the following information:

On June 1, 1985, Byrd Corp. purchased a high-rise building from Slade Corp. for $375,000. The building was encumbered by a mortgage and note dated May 1, 1980 executed by Slade. The mortgage had been duly recorded by the mortgagee, Fale Bank. The outstanding balance on the mortgage at the time of Byrd's purchase was $300,000. Byrd acquired the property subject to the mortgage held by Fale and, in addition, gave a mortgage on the building to Foxx Finance to secure a non-purchase money promissory note in the sum of $50,000. Prior to any payments being made on either loan, Byrd defaulted. As a result, the building was properly sold at a foreclosure sale for $280,000.

55 (November 85)

Which of the following statements is correct regarding Byrd's and Slade's liability to Fale?

a. Byrd is liable to Fale for any deficiency.

b. Byrd is secondarily liable to Fale as a surety.

c. Slade was automatically released from all liability to Fale upon Byrd's acquisition of the building subject to the mortgage.

d. Slade is liable to Fale for any resulting deficiency.

56 (November 85)

As a result of the foreclosure sale

a. Fale is entitled to receive the full $280,000 out of the proceeds.

b. Fale is entitled to receive $240,000 out of the proceeds.

c. Foxx is entitled to receive its full $50,000 from either Byrd or Slade.

d. Foxx is entitled to receive $50,000 out of the proceeds.

57 (November 85)

Farr obtained a $45,000 loan from State Bank, executing a promissory note and mortgage. The loan was secured by a factory which Farr purchased from Datz for $79,000. State's recording of the mortgage

a. Cuts off the rights of all prior and subsequent lessees of the factory.

b. Transfers legal title to the factory to State.

c. Generally creates a possessory security interest in State.

d. Generally does not affect the rights of Farr and State against each other under the promissory note.

56 (May 85)

Gray owned a warehouse free and clear of any encumbrances. Gray borrowed $30,000 from Harp Finance and executed a promissory note secured by a mortgage on the warehouse. The state within which the warehouse was located had a notice-race recording statute applicable to real property. Harp did not record its mortgage. Thereafter, Gray applied for a loan with King Bank, supplying King with certified financial statements which disclosed Harp's mortgage. After review of the financial statements, King approved Gray's loan for $25,000, taking an executed promissory note secured by a mortgage on the warehouse. King promptly recorded its mortgage. Which party's mortgage will be superior?

a. Harp's, since King had notice of Harp's interest.

b. Harp's, since it obtained a purchase money security interest.

c. King's, since it was the first to file.

d. King's, since a title search would fail to reveal Harp's interest.

57 (May 85)
A mortgagor who defaults on his mortgage payments will <u>not</u> be successful if he attempts to
a. Assert the equitable right to redeem.
b. Redeem the property after a judicial foreclosure sale has taken place.
c. Obtain any excess resulting from a judicial foreclosure sale.
d. Contest the validity of the price received at a judicial foreclosure sale by asserting that a higher price could have been received at a later date.

57 (May 83)
Which of the following is an <u>incorrect</u> statement regarding a real property mortgage?
a. It transfers title to the real property to the mortgagee.
b. It is invariably accompanied by a negotiable promissory note which refers to the mortgage.
c. It creates an interest in real property and is therefore subject to the Statute of Frauds.
d. It creates a nonpossessory security interest in the mortgagee.

58 (May 83)
Recordation of a real property mortgage
a. Is required to validate the rights of the parties to the mortgage.
b. Will <u>not</u> be effective if improperly filed even if the party claiming superior title had actual notice of its existence.
c. Perfects the interest of the mortgagee against subsequent bona fide purchasers for value.
d. Must be filed in the recordation office where the mortgagee's principal place of business is located.

59 (May 83)
Moch sold her farm to Watkins and took back a purchase money mortgage on the farm. Moch failed to record the mortgage. Moch's mortgage will be valid against all of the following parties <u>except</u>
a. The heirs or estate of Watkins.
b. A subsequent mortgagee who took a second mortgage since he had heard there was a prior mortgage.
c. A subsequent bona fide purchaser from Watkins.
d. A friend of Watkins to whom the farm was given as a gift and who took without knowledge of the mortgage.

60 (May 83)
Peters defaulted on a purchase money mortgage held by Fairmont Realty. Fairmont's attempts to obtain payment have been futile and the mortgage payments are several months in arrears. Consequently, Fairmont decided to resort to its rights against the property. Fairmont foreclosed on the mortgage. Peters has all of the following rights <u>except</u>
a. To remain in possession as long as his equity in the property exceeds the amount of debt.
b. An equity of redemption.
c. To refinance the mortgage with another lender and repay the original mortgage.
d. A statutory right of redemption.

54 (May 82)
Linderman purchased a tract of land from Noteworthy for $250,000. Noteworthy revealed the fact that there was an existing first mortgage of $100,000 on the property which would be satisfied out of the proceeds of the sale. Effective Title Company's title search and policy revealed only the first mortgage. Noteworthy did not reveal that there was a $50,000 unrecorded second mortgage on the property held by his father, Vincent. The first mortgage was satisfied at the closing and Linderman presumed he had clear title to the property. A month after the closing, Vincent appeared and claimed that Linderman was obligated to pay the principal and interest on the mortgage he held. Noteworthy has fled the jurisdiction. As among Linderman, Vincent, and Effective, which of the following is correct?

Property

a. Vincent will prevail since he had a valid second mortgage.
b. Effective must pay on its title policy since it is an insurer.
c. Linderman's failure to obtain an affidavit from Noteworthy representing that there was no other mortgage outstanding will result in his taking subject to the Vincent mortgage.
d. Linderman will take free of the Vincent mortgage.

53 (May 81)

Lutz sold his moving and warehouse business, including all the personal and real property used therein, to Allen Van Lines, Inc. The real property was encumbered by a $300,000 first mortgage upon which Lutz was personally liable. Allen acquired the property subject to the mortgage. Two years later, when the mortgage outstanding was $260,000, Allen decided to abandon the business location because it had become unprofitable and the value of the real property was less than the outstanding mortgage. Allen moved to another location and refused to pay the installments due on the mortgage. What is the legal status of the parties in regard to the mortgage?

a. Allen took the real property free of the mortgage.
b. Allen breached its contract with Lutz when it abandoned the location and defaulted on the mortgage.
c. Lutz must satisfy the mortgage debt in the event that foreclosure yields an amount less than the unpaid balance.
d. If Lutz pays off the mortgage, he will be able to successfully sue Allen because Lutz is subrogated to the mortgagee's rights against Allen.

54 (May 81)

Tremont Enterprises, Inc. needed some additional working capital to develop a new product line. It decided to obtain intermediate term financing by giving a second mortgage on its plant and warehouse. Which of the following is true with respect to the mortgages?

a. If Tremont defaults on both mortgages and a bankruptcy proceeding is initiated, the second mortgagee has the status of general creditor.
b. If the second mortgagee proceeds to foreclose on its mortgage, the first mortgagee must be satisfied completely before the second mortgagee is entitled to repayment.
c. Default on payment to the second mortgagee will constitute default on the first mortgage.
d. Tremont can not prepay the second mortgage prior to its maturity without the consent of the first mortgagee.

40 (November 79)

Carter wishes to obtain additional working capital for his construction company. His bankers indicated that they would be willing to lend the company $50,000 if the bank could obtain a first mortgage on the real property belonging to the business. Carter reluctantly acquiesced and mortgaged all his real property to secure repayment of the loan. Unknown to the bank, one portion of the real property was already mortgaged to Johnson for $30,000, but Johnson had neglected to record the mortgage. The bank promptly recorded its mortgage. Which of the following is correct regarding the rights of the parties?

a. Johnson's failure to record makes the mortgage invalid against Carter.
b. The bank's mortgage will have a priority over Johnson's mortgage.
c. Both mortgagees would share the proceeds from any foreclosure on a pro rata basis.
d. The bank will be deemed to have notice of Johnson's mortgage and will take subject to the mortgage.

43 (November 78)

Paxton owned Blackacre, and he obtained a $10,000 loan from a bank secured by a real property mortgage on Blackacre. The mortgage was properly recorded. Paxton subsequently sold Blackacre to Rogers, expressly warranting that there were no mortgages on the property. Rogers was unaware of the bank's interest in the property. Paxton has disappeared, and the bank has demanded payment from Rogers. Rogers has refused, and the bank is seeking to foreclose its mortgage. Which of the following statements is correct?

a. Rogers is personally liable on the mortgage loan.
b. As a bona fide purchaser for value, Rogers will prevail and retain the property free of the mortgage.
c. The bank will prevail in its foreclosure action.
d. The bank must obtain a judgment against Paxton before it can foreclose the mortgage.

21 (November 77)

Miltown borrowed $60,000 from Strauss upon the security of a first mortgage on a business building owned by Miltown. The mortgage has been amortized down to $50,000. Sanchez is buying the building from Miltown for $80,000. Sanchez is paying only the $30,000 excess over and above the mortgage. Sanchez may buy it either "subject to" the mortgage, or he may "assume" the mortgage. Which is a correct statement under these circumstances?

    a.   The financing agreement ultimately decided upon must be recorded in order to be binding upon the parties.

    b.   The financing arrangement is covered by the Uniform Commercial Code if Sanchez takes "subject to" the existing first mortgage.

    c.   Sanchez will acquire <u>no</u> interest in the property if he takes "subject to" instead of "assuming" the mortgage.

    d.   Sanchez would be better advised to take "subject to" the mortgage rather than to "assume" the mortgage.

22 (November 77)

The facts are the same as those stated above in number 21, but the property purchased by Sanchez has declined in value and the mortgage is in default. It has now been amortized to $43,000. The property is sold under foreclosure proceedings and $39,000, net of costs, is received. Which is a correct legal conclusion if Sanchez acquired the property "subject to" the mortgage?

    a.   Sanchez has <u>no</u> further liability after foreclosure.

    b.   Miltown cannot be held personally liable by Strauss for the $4,000 deficiency.

    c.   Sanchez is <u>not</u> liable to Strauss, but is personally liable to Miltown if Miltown pays the deficiency.

    d.   Miltown and Sanchez will have to satisfy the deficiency equally, that is, each owes $2,000.

29 (May 77)

Jane Luft, doing business as Luft Enterprises, owned a tract of land upon which she had intended to build an additional retail outlet. There is an existing first mortgage of $70,000 on the property which is held by the First County National Bank. Luft decided not to expand, and a buyer, Johnson, offered $150,000 for the property. Luft accepted and received a certified check for $80,000 plus a signed statement by Johnson promising to pay the existing mortgage. What are the legal rights of the indicated parties?

    a.   Luft remains liable to First County despite Johnson's promise to pay.

    b.   First County must first proceed against Johnson on the mortgage before it has any rights against Luft.

    c.   The delegation of the debt is invalid if Johnson does <u>not</u> have a credit rating roughly comparable to Luft's.

    d.   The bank is the incidental beneficiary of Johnson's promise to pay the mortgage.

44 (November 76)

A real estate mortgage

    a.   Need not be in writing.

    b.   Creates an intangible personal property right for the mortgagee.

    c.   If properly recorded, gives constructive notice to subsequent purchasers and mortgagees of the recording mortgagee's interest.

    d.   Is <u>not</u> assignable by the mortgagee.

5 (May 74)

Amos purchased a building from Thoms. He paid a small amount of cash and took the building subject to a mortgage given by Thoms to National Bank. Under these circumstances

    a.   Sale of the building to Amos would normally give National Bank an immediate right of action against Thoms.

    b.   Amos became primarily liable on the debt to National Bank.

    c.   Amos incurred <u>no</u> personal liability on the debt.

    d.   Payment of the mortgage debt by Amos would give Amos a right of subrogation against Thoms.

Property

2 (November 93)

On June 1, 1990, Anderson bought a one family house from Beach for $240,000. At the time of the purchase, the house had a market value of $200,000 and the land was valued at $40,000. Anderson assumed the recorded $150,000 mortgage Beach owed Long Bank, gave a $70,000 mortgage to Rogers Loan Co., and paid $20,000 cash. Rogers did not record its mortgage. Rogers did not know about the Long mortgage.

Beach gave Anderson a quitclaim deed that failed to mention a recorded easement on the property held by Dalton, the owner of the adjacent piece of property. Anderson purchased a title insurance policy from Edge Title Insurance Co. Edge's policy neither disclosed nor excepted Dalton's easement.

On August 1, 1992, Anderson borrowed $30,000 from Forrest Finance to have a swimming pool dug. Anderson gave Forrest a $30,000 mortgage on the property. Forrest, knowing about the Long mortgage but not the Rogers mortgage, recorded its mortgage on August 10, 1992. After the digging began, Dalton sued to stop the work claiming violation of the easement. The court decided in Dalton's favor.

At the time of the purchase, Anderson had taken out two fire insurance policies; a $120,000 face value policy with Harvest Fire Insurance Co., and a $60,000 face value policy with Grant Fire Insurance Corp. Both policies contained a standard 80% coinsurance clause.

On December 1, 1992, a fire caused $180,000 damage to the house. At that time, the house had a market value of $250,000. Harvest and Grant refused to honor the policies claiming that the house was underinsured.

Anderson made no mortgage payments after the fire and on June 1, 1993, after the house had been rebuilt, the mortgages were foreclosed. The balances due for principal and accrued interest were as follows: Long, $140,000; Rogers, $65,000; and Forrest, $28,000. At a foreclosure sale, the house and land were sold. After payment of all expenses, $200,000 of the proceeds remained for distribution. As a result of the above events, the following actions took place:

- Anderson sued Harvest and Grant for the face values of the fire insurance policies.
- Anderson sued Beach for failing to mention Dalton's easement in the quitclaim deed.
- Anderson sued Edge for failing to disclose Dalton's easement.
- Long, Rogers, and Forrest all demanded full payment of their mortgages from the proceeds of the foreclosure sale.

The preceding took place in a "Notice-Race" jurisdiction.

Required:

a. Items 61 through 63 relate to Anderson's suit against Harvest and Grant. For each item, select from List I the dollar amount Anderson will receive.

List I

61. What will be the dollar amount of Anderson's total fire insurance recovery?
62. What dollar amount will be payable by Harvest?
63. What dollar amount will be payable by Grant?

A. $0
B. $20,000
C. $48,000
D. $54,000
E. $60,000
F. $80,000
G. $96,000
H. $108,000
I. $120,000
J. $144,000
K. $162,000
L. $180,000

b. Items 64 through 66 relate to Anderson's suit against Beach. For each item, determine whether that statement is True or False.

64. Anderson will win the suit against Beach.
65. A quitclaim deed conveys only the grantor's interest in the property.
66. A warranty deed protects the purchaser against any adverse title claim against the property.

c. **Items 67 through 69** relate to Anderson's suit against Edge. For each item, determine whether the statement is True or False.

67. Anderson will win the suit against Edge.
68. Edge's policy should insure against all title defects of record.
69. Edge's failure to disclose Dalton's easement voids Anderson's contract with Beach.

d. **Items 70 through 72** relate to the demands Long, Rogers, and Forrest have made to have their mortgages satisfied out of the foreclosure proceeds. For each item, select from List II the dollar amount to be paid.

	List II
70. What dollar amount of the foreclosure proceeds will Long receive?	A. $0 B. $28,000
71. What dollar amount of the foreclosure proceeds will Rogers receive?	C. $32,000 D. $65,000
72. What dollar amount of the foreclosure proceeds will Forrest receive?	E. $107,000 F. $135,000 G. $140,000

2 (May 92)

On June 10, 1990, Bond sold real property to Edwards for $100,000. Edwards assumed the $80,000 recorded mortgage Bond had previously given to Fair Bank and gave a $20,000 purchase money mortgage to Heath Finance. Heath did not record this mortgage. On December 15, 1991, Edwards sold the property to Ivor for $115,000. Ivor bought the property subject to the Fair mortgage bud did not know about the Heath mortgage. Ivor borrowed $50,000 from Knox Bank and gave Knox a mortgage on the property. Knox knew of the unrecorded Heath mortgage when its mortgage was recorded. Ivor, Edwards, and Bond defaulted on the mortgages. Fair, Heath, and Knox foreclosed and the property was sold at a judicial foreclosure sale for $60,000. At the time of the sale, the outstanding balance of principal and accrued interest on the Fair mortgage was $75,000. The Heath mortgage balance was $18,000 and the Knox mortgage was $47,500.

Fair, Heath, and Knox all claim that their mortgages have priority and should be satisfied first from the sale proceeds. Bond, Edwards, and Ivor all claim that they are not liable for any deficiency resulting from the sale.

The above transactions took place in a jurisdiction that has a notice-race recording statute and allows foreclosure deficiency judgments.

Required:

a. **Items 61 through 63.** For each mortgage, select from List A the priority of that mortgage. A priority should be selected only once.

	List A
61. Knox Bank.	A. First Priority.
62. Heath Finance.	B. Second Priority.
63. Fair Bank	C. Third Priority.

b. **Items 64 through 66.** For each mortgage, select from List B the reason for its priority. A reason may be selected once, more than once, or not at all.

List B

64. Knox Bank.
65. Heath Finance.
66. Fair Bank.

A. An unrecorded mortgage has priority over any subsequently recorded mortgage.
B. A recorded mortgage has priority over any unrecorded mortgage.
C. The first recorded mortgage has priority over all subsequent mortgages.
D. An unrecorded mortgage has priority over a subsequently recorded mortgage if the subsequent mortgagee knew of the unrecorded mortgage.
E. A purchase money mortgage has priority over a previously recorded mortgage.

Property

c. **Items 67 through 69.** For each mortgage, select from List C the amount of the sale proceeds that each mortgagee would be entitled to receive. An amount may be selected once, more than once, or not at all.

List C

67.	Knox Bank	A.	$0.
68.	Heath Finance.	B.	$12,500.
69.	Fair Bank.	C.	$18,000.
		D.	$20,000.
		E.	$42,000.
		F.	$47,500.
		G.	$60,000.

d. **Items 70 through 72.** Determine whether each party would be liable to pay a mortgage foreclosure deficiency judgment on the Fair Bank mortgage. If the party would be held liable, select from List D the reason for the party's liability. If you determine there is <u>no</u> liability, select <u>D</u>. A reason may be selected once, more than once, or not at all.

List D

70.	Edwards.	A.	Original mortgagor.
71.	Bond.	B.	Assumed the mortgage.
72.	Ivor.	C.	Took subject to the mortgage.
		D.	Not liable.

e. **For items 73 through 75,** determine whether each party would be liable to pay a mortgage foreclosure deficiency judgment on the Heath Finance mortgage. If the party would be held liable, select from List E the reason for that party's liability. If you determine there is <u>no</u> liability, select <u>D</u>. A reason may be selected once, more than once, or not at all.

List E

73.	Edwards	A.	Original mortgagor.
74.	Bond.	B.	Assumed the mortgage.
75.	Ivor.	C.	Took subject to the mortgage.
		D.	Not liable.

f. **For items 76 through 78,** determine whether each party would be liable to pay a mortgage foreclosure deficiency judgment on the Knox Bank mortgage. If the party would be held liable, select from List F the reason for that party's liability. If you determine there is <u>no</u> liability, select <u>D</u>. A reason may be selected once, more than once, or not at all.

List F

76.	Edwards.	A.	Original mortgagor.
77.	Bond.	B.	Assumed the mortgage.
78.	Ivor.	C.	Took subject to the mortgage.
		D.	Not liable.

3 (May 89)

On March 2, 1988, Ash, Bale, and Rangel purchased an office building from Park Corp. as joint tenants with right of survivorship. There was an outstanding note and mortgage on the building, which they assumed. The note and mortgage named Park as the mortgagor (borrower) and Vista Bank as the mortgagee (lender). Vista has consented to the assumption.

Wein, Inc., a tenant in the office building, had entered into a 10-year lease dated May 8, 1985. The lease was silent regarding Wein's right to sublet. The lease provided for Wein to take occupancy on June 1, 1985, and that the monthly rent would be $5,000 for the entire 10-year term. On March 10, 1989, Wein informed Ash, Bale, and

Rangel that it had agreed to sublet its office space to Nord Corp. On March 17,1989, Ash, Bale, and Rangel notified Wein of their refusal to consent to the sublet. The following assertions have been made:

- The sublet from Wein to Nord is void because Ash, Bale, and Rangel did not consent.
- If the sublet is not void, Ash, Bale, and Rangel have the right to hold either Wein or Nord liable for payment of the rent.

On April 4, 1989, Ash transferred his interest in the building to his spouse.

Required: Answer the following, setting forth reasons for any conclusions stated.

a. <u>For this item only</u>, assume that Ash, Bale, and Rangel default on the mortgage note, that Vista forecloses, and a deficiency results. Discuss the personal liability of Ash, Bale, and Rangel to Vista and the personal liability of Park to Vista.

b. Discuss the assertions as to the sublet, indicating whether such assertions are correct and the reasons therefor.

c. <u>For this item only</u>, assume that Ash and Rangel died on April 20, 1989. Discuss the ownership interest(s) in the office building as of April 5, 1989, and April 21, 1989.

a. Ash, Bale, and Rangel will be personally liable to Vista for the deficiency resulting from the foreclosure sale because they became the principal debtors when they assumed the mortgage. Park will remain liable for the deficiency. Although Vista consented to the assumption of the mortgage by Ash, Bale, and Rangel, such assumption does not relieve Park from its obligation to Vista unless Park obtains a release from Vista or there is a novation.

b. The assertion that the sublet from Wein to Nord is void because Ash, Bale, and Rangel must consent to the sublet is incorrect. Unless the lease provides otherwise, a tenant may sublet the premises without the landlord's consent. Since the lease was silent regarding Wein's right to sublet, Wein may sublet to Nord without the consent of Ash, Bale, and Rangel.

The assertion that if the sublet was not void Ash, Bale, and Rangel have the right to hold either Wein or Nord liable for payment of rent is incorrect. In a sublease, the sublessee/subtenant (Nord) has no obligation to pay rent to the landlord (Ash, Bale, and Rangel).

The subtenant (Nord) is liable to the tenant (Wein), but the tenant (Wein) remains solely liable to the landlord (Ash, Bale, and Rangel) for the rent stipulated in the lease.

c. Ash's inter vivos transfer of his 1/3 interest in the office building to his spouse on April 4, 1989 resulted in his spouse obtaining a 1/3 interest in the office building as a tenant in common. Ash's wife did not become a joint tenant with Bale and Rangel because the transfer of a joint tenant's interest to an outside party destroys the joint tenancy nature of the particular interest transferred. Bale and Rangel will remain as joint tenants with each other.

As of April 21, 1989, the office building was owned by Ash's spouse who had a 1/3 interest as tenant in common and Bale who had a 2/3 interest as tenant in common.

Ash's death on April 20, 1989 will have no effect on the ownership of the office building because Ash had already transferred all of his interest to his wife on April 4, 1989.

Rangel's death on April 20, 1989 resulted in his interest being acquired by Bale because of the right of survivorship feature in a joint tenancy. Because there are no surviving joint tenants, Bale will become a tenant in common who owns 2/3 of the office building. Ash's spouse will not acquire any additional interest due to Rangel's death because she was a tenant in common with Rangel.

2 (November 84)

Joe Fine, a clothing manufacturer for the past 30 years, owns a plant on which Muni Bank holds a mortgage. He also leases a warehouse from Jay Co. in which he stores the clothing manufactured in the plant. There are 10 years remaining on the lease term. Fine plans to move his operations to another location and has decided to sell to Bean his interests in the plant and lease.

Fine is contemplating selling the plant to Bean under one of the following conditions:

- Bean taking the plant subject to the mortgage.
- Bean assuming the mortgage on the plant.
- Fine obtaining a duly executed novation from Muni and Bean.

The lease contains a clause prohibiting assignment to third parties. Fine is concerned with this clause as well as his continuing liability to Jay upon the transfer of his interests in the lease to Bean. In this regard, Fine asserts that:

- The clause prohibiting the assignment of the lease is void.
- The prohibition against assignment will not affect his right to sublease.
- He will be released from liability to pay rent upon obtaining Jay's consent either to sublet or to assign.

Required: Answer the following, setting forth reasons for any conclusions stated.

a. In separate paragraphs, discuss Fine's and Bean's liability to Muni under each of the three aforementioned conditions relating to the mortgage, if Bean after purchasing the plant defaults on the mortgage payments, thereby creating a deficiency after a foreclosure sale.

b. In separate paragraphs, comment on Fine's assertions regarding the lease, indicating whether such assertions are correct and the reasons therefor.

a. If Bean purchases the plant subject to the mortgage, Fine will remain liable to Muni on the note and the underlying mortgage. Thus, Fine will be liable to Muni for any deficiency that may exist after a foreclosure sale. By taking the plant subject to the mortgage, Bean avoids liability for any deficiency. Therefore, Bean's potential liability is limited to any equity he may have built up in the plant.

If Bean assumes the mortgage, Fine will continue to be liable to Muni despite the agreement permitting Bean to assume the mortgage. Therefore, any resulting deficiency from a foreclosure sale will be Fine's responsibility. In addition, since Bean assumed the mortgage, he would also be held liable to Muni.

The execution of a novation would release Fine from his liability to Muni on the mortgage and would substitute Bean in his place. In order to have a valid novation involving real property, Muni must agree to it in writing.

b. Fine is incorrect in his assertion that the clause prohibiting the assignment of the lease is void. A clause prohibiting the assignment of a lease will not constitute a disabling restraint sufficient to prevent the free alienation of property and is therefore valid. Fine is bound by the restrictive clause since he consented to it when entering into the lease.

Fine's assertion that the prohibition against assignment will not affect his right to sublease is correct. In the absence of a provision in the lease to the contrary, a tenant has the right to assign the lease or sublet the premises. A prohibition against either will not be a prohibition against both. Therefore, Fine may sublease the warehouse to Bean despite the clause forbidding the assignment of the lease.

Fine's assertion that he will be released from liability under the lease upon obtaining Jay's consent to either sublet or assign is incorrect. Under a sublease or assignment, the original tenant will remain fully liable for the stipulated rent unless the landlord releases the original tenant from that obligation. The fact that the landlord consents to the sublease or assignment will not automatically relieve the original tenant from his obligation to pay rent. Therefore, any rent due pursuant to the lease will continue to be Fine's legal responsibility.

4C (May 80)

Newfeld purchased a parcel of land in New City from Stoneham Realty. His plan was to construct a professional building and parking lot on the property. In order to do this, Newfeld needed financing and approached the New City National Bank for a first mortgage loan. The proposal looked good to New City National and they loaned Newfeld $200,000 to help finance the venture. Newfeld engaged builders who accomplished the construction of the building and the parking lot. After two years of ownership and operation of the building and lot, Newfeld decided to sell. Robbins agreed to purchase Newfeld's interest but indicated she was not willing to assume the existing mortgage. It was finally agreed that the entire property would be transferred to Robbins subject to the New City National's first mortgage. Robbins subsequently defaulted.

Required: Answer the following, setting forth reasons for any conclusions stated.

1. Who is expected to make the payments during the remaining life of the mortgage?
2. What rights does New City Bank have against Robbins and Newfeld upon default?
3. Assume that the bank has to resort to foreclosure and that after the debt, interest, and all expenses have been paid, there is $2,000 remaining. Who is entitled to this amount?

1. Despite the absence of a legal obligation to do so, Robbins is expected to make the remaining mortgage payments. She is the legal owner, subject to the mortgage, and has parted with money sufficient to purchase Newfeld's equity interest. If Robbins defaults, she will lose the money already invested in the purchase. Normally one would default only if the value of the property is less than the mortgage outstanding.

2. New City has no rights against Robbins upon default. Not having assumed the mortgage, Robbins has no personal liability to pay the mortgage. Newfeld remains liable on his original promise; the sale to Robbins does not alter his liability.

3. The $2,000 belongs to Robbins. The mortgagee is not entitled to reap a profit as a result of the foreclosure but is only entitled to complete satisfaction, principal, interest, and expenses. Newfeld is not entitled to anything since he is not the owner, did not satisfy the debt, and has been fully paid for his equity interest by Robbins.

C. Transfer of Real Property by Adverse Possession

41 (November 79)

Dunbar Dairy Farms, Inc., pursuant to an expansion of its operations in Tuberville, purchased from Moncrief a 140-acre farm strategically located in the general area in which Dunbar wished to expand. Unknown to Dunbar, Cranston, an adjoining landowner, had fenced off approximately five acres of the land in question. Cranston installed a well, constructed a storage shed and garage on the fenced-off land, and continuously farmed and occupied the five acres for approximately 22 years prior to Dunbar's purchase. Cranston did this under the mistaken belief that the five acres of land belonged to him. Which of the following is a correct answer in regard to the five acres occupied by Cranston?

   a.   Under the circumstances Cranston has title to the five acres.
   b.   As long as Moncrief had properly recorded a deed which includes the five acres in dispute, Moncrief had good title to the five acres.
   c.   At best, the only right that Cranston could obtain is an easement.
   d.   If Dunbar is unaware of Cranston's presence and Cranston has failed to record, Dunbar can oust him as a trespasser.

24 (May 76)

An individual who has obtained title to land by adverse possession:

   a.   Can convey good title to a subsequent purchaser.
   b.   Must record his interest in the property in order to perfect his interest against the holder of record.
   c.   Must have occupied the property initially with the permission of the owner of record.
   d.   Need not have occupied the land for an uninterrupted period of time as long as the sum total of years he has occupied the land is equal to or greater than the prescribed period.

IV. Principal and Income Allocation

12 (May 95)

Frost's will created a testamentary trust naming Hill as life income beneficiary, with the principal to Brown when Hill dies. The trust was silent on allocation of principal and income. The trust's sole asset was a commercial office building originally valued at $100,000 and having a current market value of $200,000. If the building was sold, which of the following statements would be correct concerning the allocation of the proceeds?

   a.   The entire proceeds would be allocated to principal and retained.
   b.   The entire proceeds would be allocated to income and distributed to Hill.
   c.   One half of the proceeds would be allocated to principal and one half to income.
   d.   One half of the proceeds would be allocated to principal and one half distributed to Brown.

Property

16 (May 94)

Which of the following expenditures resulting from a trust's ownership of commercial real estate should be allocated to the trust's principal?
a. Building management fees.
b. Insurance premiums.
c. Sidewalk assessments.
d. Depreciation.

18 (May 93)

Arno plans to establish a spendthrift trust naming Ford and Sims life income beneficiaries, Trip residuary beneficiary, and Bing as trustee. Arno plans to fund the trust with an office building. Which of the following will be allocated to trust principal?

	Annual property tax	Monthly mortgage principal payment
a.	Yes	Yes
b.	Yes	No
c.	No	Yes
d.	No	No

6 (November 92)

Cox transferred assets into a trust under which Smart is entitled to receive the income for life. After Smart's death, the remaining assets are to be given to Mix. In 1991, the trust received rent of $1,000, stock dividends of $6,000, interest on certificates of deposit of $3,000, municipal bond interest of $4,000, and proceeds of $7,000 from the sale of bonds. Both Smart and Mix are still alive. What amount of the 1991 receipts should be allocated to trust principal?
a. $7,000
b. $8,000
c. $13,000
d. $15,000

10 (November 92)

Which of the following would ordinarily be distributed to a trust income beneficiary?
    I. Royalties.
    II. Stock received in a stock split.
    III. Cash dividends.
    IV. Settlements of claims for damages to trust property.
a. I and II.
b. I and III.
c. II and III.
d. II and IV.

9 (May 91)

Farrel's will created a testamentary trust naming Gordon as life income beneficiary, with the principal going to Hall on Gordon's death. The trust's sole asset was a commercial office building valued at $200,000. The trustee sold the building for $250,000. To what amount of the sale price is Gordon entitled?
a. $0
b. $50,000
c. $200,000
d. $250,000

19 (November 90)

Which of the following expenditures resulting from a trust's ownership of commercial real estate would be allocated to the trust's principal?
a. Sidewalk assessments.
b. Building management fees.
c. Real estate taxes.
d. Electrical repairs.

8 (November 89)

Harper transferred assets into a trust under which Drake is entitled to receive the income for life. Upon Drake's death, the remaining assets are to be paid to Neal. In 1988, the trust received rent of $1,000, royalties of $3,000, cash dividends of $5,000, and proceeds of $7,000 from the sale of stock previously received by the trust as a stock dividend. Both Drake and Neal are still alive. How much of the receipts should be distributed to Drake?
a. $ 4,000.
b. $ 8,000.
c. $ 9,000.
d. $16,000.

11 (May 88)

Rusk properly created an inter vivos trust naming Gold as the trustee. The sole asset of the trust is an office building that is fully rented. Rental receipts exceed expenditures. The trust instrument is silent as to the allocation of items between principal and income. Among the items to be allocated by Gold during the year are insurance proceeds received as a result of fire damage to the building and the mortgage interest payments made during the year. Which of the following items is properly allocable to principal?

	Insurance proceeds on building	Current mortgage interest payments
a.	Yes	No
b.	Yes	Yes
c.	No	Yes
d.	No	No

52 (May 86)

Ryan is the trustee of the Carr Family Trust. The assets of the trust are various income-producing real estate properties. The trust instrument is silent as to the allocation of items between principal and income. Among the items to be allocated by Ryan during the first year were depreciation and the cost of a new roof. Which are properly allocable to income?

	Depreciation	Cost of a new roof
a.	No	No
b.	Yes	No
c.	Yes	Yes
d.	No	Yes

51 (November 81)

The Martin Trust consisted primarily of various income-producing real estate properties. During the year, the trustee incurred various charges. Among the charges were the following: depreciation, principal payments on various mortgages, and a street assessment. Which of the following would be a proper allocation of these items?
a. All to income, except the street assessment.
b. All are to be allocated equally between principal and income.
c. All to principal.
d. All to principal, except depreciation.

427

Property

51 (May 81)

Shepard created an inter vivos trust for the benefit of his children with the remainder to his grandchildren upon the death of his last surviving child. The trust consists of both real and personal property. One of the assets is an apartment building. In administering the trust and allocating the receipts and disbursements, which of the following would be _improper_?

    a.   The allocation of forfeited rental security deposits to income.
    b.   The allocation to principal of the annual service fee of the rental collection agency.
    c.   The allocation to income of the interest on the mortgage on the apartment building.
    d.   The allocation to income of the payment of the insurance premiums on the apartment building.

47 (November 79)

Martin is the trustee of the Baker Trust which has assets in excess of $1 million. Martin has engaged the CPA firm of Hardy & Fox to prepare the annual accounting statement for the allocation of receipts and expenditures between income and principal. The trust indenture provides that "receipts and expenses are to be allocated to income or principal according to law." Which of the following receipts from real property should be allocated to principal?

    a.   An unexpected payment of nine months arrears in rental payments.
    b.   A six-month prepayment of rent.
    c.   Insurance proceeds for the destruction of a garage on one of the properties.
    d.   Interest on a purchase money mortgage arising from the sale of a parcel of the trust's real property.

37 (November 78)

Which of the following receipts should be allocated by a trustee exclusively to income?

    a.   A stock dividend.
    b.   An extraordinary year-end cash dividend.
    c.   A liquidating dividend whether in complete or partial liquidation.
    d.   A stock split.

38 (November 78)

The Unity Trust Company is the trustee of a trust which has large real estate investments. Which of the following receipts or charges should be allocated by the trustee to income?

    a.   Paving assessment for a new street.
    b.   Prepaid rent received from tenants.
    c.   A loss on the sale of one of the rental properties.
    d.   The proceeds from an eminent domain proceeding.

46 (November 76)

The normal types of questions relating to estates and trusts which might be referred from a law firm to a CPA firm would include problems which involve

    a.   The order of distribution under the intestate succession laws.
    b.   Whether an ancillary proceeding is required.
    c.   The amount of property or money to be received by the income beneficiaries as contrasted with the amount to be accumulated for the remainderman.
    d.   Whether a will has been effectively revoked.

7B (May 76)

You have been assigned by a CPA firm to work with the trustees of a large trust in the preparation of the first annual accounting to the court. The income beneficiaries and the remaindermen are in dispute as to the proper allocation of the following items on which the trust indenture is silent:

    (1)   Costs incurred in expanding the garage facilities of an apartment house owned by the trust and held for rental income.
    (2)   Real estate taxes on the apartment house.
    (3)   Cost of casualty insurance premiums on the apartment house.

(4) A two-for-one stock split of common stock held by the trust for investment.

(5) Insurance proceeds received as the result of a partial destruction of an office building which the trust owned and held for rental income.

(6) Costs incurred by the trust in the sale of a tract of land.

(7) Costs incurred to defend title to real property held by the trust.

Required:

1. Explain briefly the nature of a trust, the underlying concepts in the allocation between principal and income, and the importance of such allocations.

2. Indicate the allocations between principal and income to be made for each of the above items.

1. A trust generally involves a transfer of income-producing property (principal) by will, deed, or indenture to a trustee who takes legal title to the property subject to a fiduciary obligation to manage and conserve the property for the benefit of others who are described as beneficiaries. A trust generally provides that the trustee shall invest the trust principal and pay the income therefrom to the income beneficiary and at the termination of the trust transfer the trust principal to the remainderman. The property that composes the principal of the trust may change from time to time as the trustee sells and reinvests the proceeds.

The will or trust agreement can provide the rules for allocation of items between principal and income. In the absence of specific trust provisions, the law of the jurisdiction in which the trust is located will govern. For this purpose, most jurisdictions have adopted the Uniform Principal and Income Act or some variation thereof. Income produced by the investment and management of the trust principal is kept separate for distribution to the income beneficiary. However, ordinary operating expenses incurred by the trust in generating earnings are charged against income. Similarly, expenses incurred in acquiring or protecting the trustee's title to principal are charged against principal. Thus, the allocation between principal and income of a trust is of great importance because it affects the respective benefits derived from the trust by the income beneficiary and the remainderman.

2. (1) Principal

(2) Income

(3) Income

(4) Principal

(5) Principal

(6) Principal

(7) Principal

PART XI -- INSURANCE LAW

TABLE OF CONTENTS

PART XI

INSURANCE LAW

I. Insurable Interest
A. The Principle of Indemnity

59 (May 82)

Tedland Trading Corporation insured its 17 automobiles for both liability and collision. Milsap, one of its salesmen, was in an automobile accident while driving a company car on a sales trip. The facts clearly reveal that the accident was solely the fault of Williams, the driver of the other car. Milsap was seriously injured, and the automobile was declared a total loss. The value of the auto was $3,000. Which of the following is an <u>incorrect</u> statement regarding the rights and liabilities of Tedland, its insurer, Milsap and Williams?

    a. Tedland's insurer must defend Tedland against any claims by Milsap or Williams.

    b. Tedland's insurer has <u>no</u> liability whatsoever since the accident was the result of Williams' negligence.

    c. Milsap has an independent action against Williams for the injuries caused by Williams' negligence.

    d. Tedland's insurer is liable for $3,000, less any deductible, on the collision policy, but will be subrogated to Tedland's rights.

13 (November 78)

Nabor, Inc. purchased a three-year fire insurance policy from the Fidelity Insurance Company covering its factory and warehouse. Which of the following statements is correct as a general rule of insurance law?

    a. The policy will <u>not</u> cover the intentional destruction of the property by a third party.

    b. The policy will <u>not</u> cover the destruction of the property if it is caused by the gross negligence of an employee of Nabor.

    c. If Nabor sells the insured property to a third party and assigns the insurance policy to the buyer, it continues in effect.

    d. If Nabor sells the insured property, but retains the first insurance policy, it will <u>not</u> be able to collect on the policy in the event of its destruction by fire.

28 (May 76)

Marcross Corporation owns a fleet of taxicabs it has insured with the Countrywide Insurance Company against liability and collision. Nabor, one of its drivers, deliberately backed one of the cabs into two other parked cabs in the corporation's garage after a heated dispute with the garage manager. While waiting for a traffic signal, another Marcross cab was hit in the rear by a negligently driven truck. Each cab involved had damages in excess of the minimum deductible.

    a. Marcross can recover against Countrywide for damages to all the cabs less the minimum deductible.

    b. Countrywide has <u>no</u> rights against Nabor.

    c. General creditors of Marcross could insure Marcross' cabs against collision and other types of loss because in the event of bankruptcy the creditors would have to resort to the corporation's property to satisfy their claims.

    d. Marcross must first sue the negligent truck driver, or his principal, for damages to its cab before it can collect against Countrywide.

B. Insurable Interest in Property

60 (November 95)

Which of the following statements correctly describes the requirement of insurable interest relating to property insurance? An insurable interest

a. Must exist when any loss occurs.
b. Must exist when the policy is issued and when any loss occurs.
c. Is created only when the property is owned in fee simple.
d. Is created only when the property is owned by an individual.

60 (May 95)

Which of the following parties has an insurable interest?
      I. A corporate retailer in its inventory.
     II. A partner in the partnership property.

a. I only.
b. II only.
c. Both I and II.
d. Neither I nor II.

57 (November 92)

Daly tried to collect on a property insurance policy covering a house that was damaged by fire. The insurer denied recovery, alleging that Daly had no insurable interest in the house. In which of the following situations will the insurer prevail?

a. The house belongs to a corporation of which Daly is a 50% stockholder.
b. Daly is <u>not</u> the owner of the house but a long-term lessee.
c. The house is held in trust for Daly's mother and, on her death, will pass to Daly.
d. Daly gave an unsecured loan to the owner of the house to improve the house.

60 (November 90)

On February 1, Papco Corp. entered into a contract to purchase an office building from Merit Company for $500,000 with closing scheduled for March 20. On February 2, Papco obtained a $400,000 standard fire insurance policy from Abex Insurance Company. On March 15, the office building sustained a $90,000 fire loss. On March 15, which of the following is correct?

      I. Papco has an insurable interest in the building.
     II. Merit has an insurable interest in the building.

a. I only.
b. II only.
c. Both I and II.
d. Neither I nor II.

60 (November 89)

To recover under a property insurance policy, an insurable interest must exist

	When the policy is purchased	At the time of loss
a.	Yes	Yes
b.	Yes	No
c.	No	Yes
d.	No	No

60 (May 88)

Beal occupies an office building as a tenant under a 25-year lease. Beal also has a mortgagee's (lender's) interest in an office building owned by Hill Corp. In which capacity does Beal have an insurable interest?

	Tenant	Mortgagee
a.	Yes	Yes
b.	Yes	No
c.	No	Yes
d.	No	No

59 (November 87)

With respect to property insurance, the insurable interest requirement
a. Need only be satisfied at the time the policy is issued.
b. Must be satisfied both at the time the policy is issued and at the time of the loss.
c. Will be satisfied only if the insured owns the property in fee simple absolute.
d. Will be satisfied by an insured who possesses a leasehold interest in the property.

59 (November 86)

The earliest time a purchaser of existing goods will acquire an insurable interest in those goods is when
a. The purchaser obtains possession.
b. Title passes to the purchaser.
c. Performance of the contract has been completed or substantially completed.
d. The goods are identified to the contract.

60 (November 85)

West is seeking to collect on a property insurance policy covering certain described property which was destroyed. The insurer has denied recovery based upon West's alleged lack of an insurable interest in the property. In which of the situations described below will the insurance company prevail?
a. West is not the owner of the insured property but a mere long-term lessee.
b. The insured property belongs to a general trade debtor of West and the debt is unsecured.
c. The insured property does not belong to West, but instead to a corporation which he controls.
d. The property has been willed to West's father for life and, upon his father's death, to West as the remainderman.

60 (May 85)

The insurable interest requirement with regard to property insurance
a. May be waived by a writing signed by the insured and insurer.
b. May be satisfied by a person other than the legal owner of the property.
c. Must be satisfied at the time the policy is issued.
d. Must be satisfied by the insured's legal title to the property at the time of loss.

36 (May 83)

The insurable interest in property
a. Can be waived by consent of the parties.
b. Is subject to the incontestability clause.
c. Must be present at the time the loss occurs.
d. Is only available to owners, occupiers, or users of the property.

60 (May 82)

Which of the following is an <u>incorrect</u> statement regarding the insurable interest requirement as it applies to property insurance?

    a.   It is used to determine the amount of recovery to be awarded the insured.

    b.   It need <u>not</u> necessarily be present at the inception of the policy so long as it is present at the time of the loss.

    c.   One of its functions is to prevent recovery by those who have <u>no</u> economic interest in the property insured.

    d.   It can be waived by the parties so long as both are fully competent to contract.

59 (November 81)

A fire insurance policy is one common type of contract. As such it must meet the general requirements necessary to establish a binding contract. In a dispute between the insured and the insurance company, which of the following is correct?

    a.   The contract is always unilateral.

    b.   Insurance contracts are specifically included within the general Statute of Frauds.

    c.   The insured must satisfy the insurable interest requirement.

    d.   The actual delivery of the policy to the insured is a prerequisite to the creation of the insurance contract.

48 (May 81)

Burt owns an office building which is leased to Hansen Corporation under the terms of a long-term lease. Both Burt and Hansen have procured fire insurance covering the building. Which of the following is correct?

    a.   Both Burt and Hansen have separate insurable interests.

    b.   Burt's insurable interest is limited to the book value of the property.

    c.   Hansen has an insurable interest in the building, but only to the extent of the value of any additions or modifications it has made.

    d.   Since Burt has legal title to the building, he is the only party who can insure the building.

14 (May 78)

Wexford Furniture, Inc. is in the retail furniture business and has stores located in principal cities in the United States. Its designers created a unique cocktail table. After obtaining prices and schedules, Wexford ordered 2,000 tables to be made to its design and specifications for sale as a part of its annual spring sales premium campaign. Which of the following represents the earliest time Wexford will have an insurable interest in the tables?

    a.   At the time the goods are in Wexford's possession.

    b.   Upon shipment of conforming goods by the seller.

    c.   When the goods are marketed or otherwise designated by the seller as the goods to which the contract refers.

    d.   At the time the contract is made.

17 (May 78)

Adams Company purchased a factory and warehouse from Martinson for $150,000. Adams obtained a $100,000 real estate mortgage loan from a local bank and was required by the lender to pay for the cost of title insurance covering the bank's interest in the property. In addition, Adams was required to obtain fire insurance sufficient to protect the bank against loss due to fire. The coinsurance factor has been satisfied. Under these circumstances, which of the following is correct?

    a.   Adams can purchase only $50,000 of title insurance since it already obtained a $100,000 title policy for the bank equal to the bank loan.

    b.   The bank could <u>not</u> have independently obtained a fire insurance policy on the property because Adams has legal title.

    c.   If Adams obtained a $150,000 fire insurance policy which covered its interest and the bank's interest in the property and there is an estimated $50,000 of fire loss, the insurer will typically be obligated to pay the owner and the bank the amounts equal to their respective interests as they may appear.

    d.   If Adams obtained a $100,000 fire insurance policy covering the bank's interest and $150,000 covering his own interest, each would obtain these amounts upon total destruction of the property.

20 (May 78)

Peters leased a restaurant from Brady with all furnishings and fixtures for a period of five years with an option to renew for two additional years. Peters made several structural improvements and modifications to the interior of the building. He obtained a fire insurance policy for his own benefit insuring his interest in the property for $25,000. The restaurant was totally destroyed by an accidental fire. Peters seeks recovery from his insurer. Subject to policy limits, which of the following is correct?

    a.   Peters is entitled to recover damages to the extent of the value of his leasehold interest.

    b.   Peters is entitled to recover for lost profits due to the fire even though the policy is silent on the point.

    c.   Peters must first seek redress from the owner before he is entitled to recover.

    d.   Peters will not recover because he lacks the requisite insurable interest in the property.

2 (November 77)

The partnership of Cox & Hayes, CPAs, is a medium-sized accounting firm. The senior staff member, Walton, is the office manager. The office building is owned by the partnership and title is duly recorded in the partnership name. With regard to life and property insurance, which of the following is true?

    a.   Only the partnership, not the partners, has an insurable interest in the lives of the partners.

    b.   The partnership does not have an insurable interest in the life of Walton because he is not a partner.

    c.   Each individual partner has an insurable interest in the partnership property even though title to the property is in the partnership name.

    d.   Only the partnership can insure the firm's office building against property damage.

47 (November 77)

When Wayne died in 1976 his will created a testamentary trust out of the residue of his estate for the benefit of his wife during her lifetime and the remainder to his son, Eric, upon Mrs. Wayne's death. The residue of the estate included rental property subject to a $45,000 first mortgage. Probate of the estate has been completed, and the property deeded to the trustee to hold pursuant to the terms of the will. Carlton, Wayne's attorney and advisor, was named as executor and the Jefferson Trust Company was named as the sole trustee. Which of the following parties does not have an interest in the trust property sufficient to obtain fire insurance on said property?

    a.   The son, Eric.

    b.   Wayne's wife.

    c.   The first mortgagee.

    d.   Eric's wife.

9 (May 77)

Which of the following persons does not have the requisite insurable interest in real property?

    a.   The dominant shareholder of a corporation which holds title to the property.

    b.   The owner of a twenty-year leasehold.

    c.   An unsecured creditor of the owner of the property.

    d.   The remainderman in respect to property which was willed to one person for life and upon that person's death to the remainderman.

40 (November 75)

Which of the following statements best describes the insurable interest requirement?

    a.   It is an historical anachronism and has little or no validity in modern times.

    b.   It is identical for life and property insurance.

    c.   It has been abolished by most modern insurance legislation in respect to fire insurance.

    d.   At a minimum, it must exist at the time of the loss in respect to property insurance.

32 (May 75)

Digital Sales, Inc. leased office space from Franklin Rentals for a five-year period. The lease did not contain any provisions regarding insurance by the lessee. During the term of the lease the office building was gutted by a fire that started in an adjacent building and spread to Franklin's building. In this situation

a. Digital has an implied obligation to insure the portion of the building it leased, to protect its interest in the property and that of the lessor.
b. Digital has an insurable interest in the building, but only to the extent of the value of its leasehold.
c. If the building is fully occupied and leased on long-term leaseholds, Franklin has <u>no</u> insurable interest.
d. If Franklin sold the building, it could nevertheless continue the insurance coverage and collect on the policy because its insurable interest in the building runs from its prior ownership.

6C (November 76)

Anderson loaned the Drum Corporation $60,000. The loan was secured by a first mortgage on Drum's land and the plant thereon. Anderson independently procured a fire insurance policy for $60,000 on the mortgaged property from the Victory Insurance Company. Six years later when the mortgage had been amortized down to $52,000, the plant was totally destroyed by a fire caused by faulty electrical wiring in the rear storage area.

Required: Answer the following, setting forth reasons for any conclusions stated.
1. Anderson seeks recovery of $60,000 from the Victory Insurance Company. How much will it collect?
2. Upon payment by Victory Insurance Company, what rights does Victory have?

1. Anderson's insurable interest equals the extent of the mortgage debt outstanding. Thus, his recovery is limited to the $52,000 debt outstanding plus accrued interest on the debt, but the total recovery cannot exceed $60,000, the maximum coverage under the policy.

2. Upon payment, Victory is subrogated to the rights of Anderson and will succeed to Anderson's right to receive payments under the terms of the mortgage and mortgage bond. If Drum Corporation fails to continue the payments, Victory may foreclose on the mortgage.

C. Insurable Interest in Life

60 (May 90)

Orr is an employee of Vick Corp. Vick relies heavily on Orr's ability to market Vick's products and, for that reason, has acquired a $50,000 insurance policy on Orr's life. Half of the face value of the policy is payable to Vick and the other half is payable to Orr's spouse. Orr dies shortly after the policy is taken out but after leaving Vick's employ. Which of the following statements is correct?
a. Orr's spouse does <u>not</u> have an insurable interest because the policy is owned by Vick.
b. Orr's spouse will be entitled to all of the proceeds of the policy.
c. Vick will <u>not</u> be entitled to any of the proceeds of the policy because Vick is <u>not</u> a creditor or relative of Orr.
d. Vick will be entitled to its share of the proceeds of the policy regardless of whether Orr is employed by Vick at the time of death.

45 (May 81)

On October 15, 1980, Golden made a loan of $100,000 to Phillips and obtained a mortgage for $50,000 on Phillips' home as security for the loan. The home was worth $50,000. The following day Golden, to protect himself further, took out a fire insurance policy on Phillips' home in the sum of $50,000 with himself as beneficiary, and also a policy on Phillips' life in the same sum, with himself as beneficiary. Golden paid the premiums on both policies for one year. On March 1, 1981, Phillips paid his debt to Golden in full and the mortgage was satisfied and cancelled. On April 15, 1981, Phillips' home was completely destroyed by fire, and Phillips, trapped in the house, died in the flames. At this time, the two policies were still in effect, and there had been no change in the beneficiary. On which, if any, policy is Golden entitled to collect?
a. Life insurance policy only.
b. Fire insurance policy only.
c. Both insurance policies.
d. Neither insurance policy.

46 (May 81)

Lincoln loaned Osgood $20,000 and obtained an unsecured negotiable promissory note for that amount. Lincoln wishes to obtain a life insurance policy on Osgood's life as added protection on the loan. With respect to Lincoln's obtaining an insurance policy on Osgood's life, which of the following is true?

    a.   Lincoln has an insurable interest in Osgood's life and may legally assign the insurance policy to a transferee of the note.

    b.   If Osgood consented to Lincoln's insuring him for an amount substantially in excess of the loan, Lincoln would be able to recover the face amount of the policy.

    c.   Lincoln does not have an insurable interest since the note is negotiable.

    d.   The only policy that Lincoln may legally obtain is a term policy.

6 (May 77)

Dey purchases a life insurance policy on Adam's life and names Jones as beneficiary. Who must have an insurable interest for this policy to be valid and at what time?

    a.   Jones at the inception of the policy.

    b.   Jones at the time of death.

    c.   Dey at the inception of the policy.

    d.   Dey at the time of death.

II. Claims and Recovery
A. Coinsurance

(R03)

MNC Corp. bought a building for $300,000. At the same time, MNC purchased a $200,000 fire insurance policy from Building Insurance Co. and a $100,000 fire insurance policy from Property Insurance Co. Each policy contained a standard 80% coinsurance clause. Three years later, when the building had a fair market value of $400,000, the building was totally destroyed in a fire. What amount would MNC recover from the two insurance companies?

    a. $240,000

    b. $300,000

    c. $320,000

    d. $400,000

10 (R00)

A building was purchased for $350,000 and insured under a $300,000 fire insurance policy containing an 80% coinsurance clause. Several years later, the building, having a fair market value of $500,000, sustained fire damage of $40,000. What is the amount recoverable from the insurance company?

    a. $28,000

    b. $30,000

    c. $32,000

    d. $40,000

17 (R99)

In 1992, King bought a building for $250,000. At that time, King took out a $200,000 fire insurance policy with Omni Insurance Co. and a $50,000 fire insurance policy with Safe Insurance Corp. Each policy contained a standard 80% coinsurance clause. In 1996, when the building had a fair market value of $300,000, a fire caused $200,000 in damage. What dollar amount would King recover from Omni?

    a. $100,000

    b. $150,000

    c. $160,000

    d. $200,000

Insurance Law

3 (R97)

Items 1 through 5 are based on the following:

Wolf purchased a factory building for $800,000. At the time of the purchase, Wolf obtained a fire insurance policy with a face value of $400,000 from Acme Fire Insurance Co. At the same time, Wolf obtained another fire insurance policy with a face value of $200,000 from Prevent Fire Insurance Corp. Each policy contained a standard 80% coinsurance clause and a pro rata clause. Two years later, when the building had a fair market value of $1,000,000, a fire caused $600,000 damage.

Required: For **Items 1 through 5**, select the correct answer from List I. An answer may be selected once, more than once, or not at all.

List I	
A $0	H $450,000
B $150,000	I $480,000
C $160,000	J $600,000
D $200,000	K $640,000
E $300,000	L $750,000
F $360,000	M $800,000
G $400,000	

1. What dollar amount of fire insurance coverage should Wolf have obtained when purchasing the building to avoid being considered a coinsurer?
2. What dollar amount of fire insurance coverage should Wolf have at the time of the fire to avoid being considered a coinsurer?
3. What dollar amount should Wolf recover from Acme and Prevent under the fire insurance policies?
4. What dollar amount should Wolf recover under the Acme fire insurance policy?
5. What dollar amount should Wolf recover under the Prevent fire insurance policy?

10 (R96)

Which of the following losses, resulting from a fire, generally may be recovered under a standard fire insurance policy?

	Water damage resulting from extinguishing the fire	Loss of income due to business interruption
a.	Yes	Yes
b.	Yes	No
c.	No	Yes
d.	No	No

59 (May 95)

Clark Corp. owns a warehouse purchased for $150,000 in 1990. The current market value is $200,000. Clark has the warehouse insured for fire loss with Fair Insurance Corp. and Zone Insurance Co. Fair's policy is for $150,000 and Zone's policy is for $75,000. Both policies contain the standard 80% coinsurance clause. If a fire totally destroyed the warehouse, what total dollar amount would Clark receive from Fair and Zone?

a. $225,000
b. $200,000
c. $160,000
d. $150,000

Items 59 and 60 are based on the following:

In 1988, Pod bought a building for $220,000. At that time, Pod purchased a $150,000 fire insurance policy with Owners Insurance Co. and a $50,000 fire insurance policy with Group Insurance Corp. Each policy contained a standard 80% co-insurance clause. In 1992, when the building had a fair market value of $250,000, it was damaged in a fire.

59 (May 93)

How much would Pod recover from Owners if the fire caused $180,000 in damage?

a. $90,000
b. $120,000
c. $135,000
d. $150,000

60 (May 93)

How much would Pod recover from Owners and Group if the fire totally destroyed the building?

a. $160,000
b. $200,000
c. $220,000
d. $250,000

56 (November 92)

Hart owned a building with a fair market value of $400,000. The building was covered by a $300,000 fire insurance policy containing an 80% co-insurance clause. What amount would Hart recover if a fire totally destroyed the building?

a. $0
b. $240,000
c. $256,000
d. $300,000

59 (November 91)

In 1985, Ring purchased a building for $90,000 and insured it with a $90,000 fire insurance policy having a standard 80% coinsurance clause. Ring never increased the amount of the policy. In 1990, the building, worth $120,000, was destroyed by fire. What amount could Ring collect from the insurance company?

a. $0
b. $72,000
c. $90,000
d. $120,000

60 (November 91)

Mason Co. maintained two standard fire insurance policies on one of its warehouses. Both policies included an 80% coinsurance clause and a typical "other insurance" clause. One policy was with Ace Fire Insurance, Inc., for $24,000, and the other was with Thrifty Casualty Insurance Co., for $16,000. At a time when the warehouse was worth $100,000, a fire in the warehouse caused a $40,000 loss. What amounts can Mason recover from Ace and Thrifty, respectively?

a. $0 and $0.
b. $10,000 and $10,000.
c. $12,000 and $8,000.
d. $24,000 and $16,000.

57 (November 90)

One of the primary purposes of including a coinsurance clause in a property insurance policy is to

a. Encourage the policyholder to insure the property for an amount close to its full value.

b. Make the policyholder responsible for the entire loss caused by some covered perils.

c. Cause the policyholder to maintain a minimum amount of liability insurance that will increase with inflation.

d. Require the policyholder to insure the property with only one insurance company.

59 (May 90)

Lawfo Corp. maintains a $200,000 standard fire insurance policy on one of its warehouses. The policy includes an 80% coinsurance clause. At the time the warehouse was originally insured, its value was $250,000. The warehouse now has a value of $300,000. If the warehouse sustains $30,000 of fire damage, Lawfo's insurance recovery will be a maximum of

a. $20,000.

b. $24,000.

c. $25,000.

d. $30,000.

59 (November 89)

McArthur purchased a house for $60,000. The house is insured for $64,000 and the insurance policy has an 80% coinsurance provision. Storms caused $12,000 worth of damage when the house had a fair market value of $120,000. What maximum amount will McArthur recover from the insurance company?

a. $ 8,000.

b. $ 9,000.

c. $ 9,600.

d. $12,000.

59 (May 88)

On April 2, 1987, Ritz Corp. purchased a warehouse that it insured for $500,000. The policy contained a 75% coinsurance clause. On April 25, 1988, a fire caused $900,000 damage to the warehouse. The fair market value of the warehouse was $800,000 on April 2, 1987, and $1 million on April 25, 1988. Ritz is entitled to receive insurance proceeds of, at most,

a. $375,000.

b. $500,000.

c. $600,000.

d. $750,000.

58 (November 87)

In general, the coinsurance feature of property insurance

a. Is fixed at a minimum of 80% by law.

b. Is an additional refinement of the insurable interest requirement.

c. Precludes the insured from insuring for less than the coinsurance percentage.

d. Prevents the insured from insuring for a minimal amount and recovering the full amount of losses.

60 (November 86)

Long Co. owns a warehouse which is insured in the amount of $60,000 against loss by fire. The policy contains an 80% coinsurance clause. A fire totally destroyed the warehouse which was valued at the time of the loss at $150,000. Long is entitled to receive

a. $0, since it failed to meet the coinsurance requirements.

b. $48,000.

c. $60,000.

d. $75,000.

59 (May 85)

The coinsurance clause with regard to property insurance

a.   Prohibits the insured from obtaining an amount of insurance which would be less than the coinsurance percentage multiplied by the fair market value of the property.

b.   Encourages the insured to be more careful in preventing losses since the insured is always at least partially at risk when a loss occurs.

c.   Permits the insured to receive an amount in excess of the policy amount when there has been a total loss and the insured carried the required coverage under the coinsurance clause.

d.   Will result in the insured sharing in partial losses when the insured has failed to carry the required coverage under the coinsurance clause.

37 (May 83)

The underlying rationale which justifies the use of the coinsurance clause in fire insurance is

a.   It provides an insurable interest in the insured if this is not already present.

b.   To require certain minimum coverage in order to obtain full recovery on losses.

c.   It prevents arson by the owner.

d.   It makes the insured more careful in preventing fires since the insured is partially at risk in the event of loss.

56 (November 81)

Carter, Wallace, and Jones are partners. Title to the partnership's office building was in Carter's name. The Carter, Wallace, and Jones partnership procured a $150,000 fire insurance policy on the building from the Amalgamated Insurance Company. The policy contained an 80% coinsurance clause. Subsequently, the building was totally destroyed by fire. The value of the building was $200,000 at the time the policy was issued, and $160,000 at the time of the fire. Under the fire insurance policy, how much can the partnership recover?

a.   Nothing, since it did not have legal title to the building.

b.   The face value of the policy ($150,000).

c.   Eighty percent of the loss ($128,000).

d.   The value at the time of the loss ($160,000).

48 (May 80)

Hazard & Company was the owner of a building valued at $100,000. Since Hazard did not believe that a fire would result in a total loss, it procured two standard fire insurance policies on the property. One was for $24,000 with the Asbestos Fire Insurance Company and the other was for $16,000 with the Safety Fire Insurance Company. Both policies contained standard pro rata and 80% coinsurance clauses. Six months later, at which time the building was still valued at $100,000, a fire occurred which resulted in a loss of $40,000. What is the total amount Hazard can recover on both policies and the respective amount to be paid by Asbestos?

a. $0 and $0.

b. $20,000 and $10,000.

c. $20,000 and $12,000.

d. $40,000 and $20,000.

7 (November 78)

Stein bought an office building valued at $200,000. The fire insurance policy contained a 100% coinsurance clause. Stein insured the building for $120,000.   Subsequently, a fire caused damage of $40,000 to the building. Which of the following is the correct amount Stein will recover?

a. $40,000.

b. $24,000.

c. $13,333.

d.   Nothing because the building was not insured for 100% of its value.

38 (May 74)

Kay owned a building valued at $100,000 when a fire occurred causing $60,000 damage. The loss was insured under an Ace Insurance Company fire insurance policy in the amount of $60,000 which contained an 80% coinsurance clause. Kay's recovery under the policy will be limited to

    a. $60,000.

    b. $48,000.

    c. $45,000.

    d. $36,000.

1(b) (R97)

On April 1, Thorn and Birch negotiated the sale of Thorn's shopping center to Birch for $2.1 million ($2 million for the buildings and $100,000 for the land). The parties orally agreed on the following terms:

- Birch would make a cash down payment of $600,000.
- Birch would give Thorn a $1.5 million first mortgage on the property to secure the balance of the purchase price.
- The contract would contain an anti-assignment clause prohibiting assignment of the contract of sale or the mortgage.
- The contract would contain a "time of the essence" clause requiring that the closing take place on June 1.

No discussion took place regarding any existing mortgages or liens on the property. On April 14, the parties signed a written contract containing the above provisions.

On April 20, Birch took out a $1.5 million fire insurance policy with Acme Fire Insurance Co. on the buildings. The policy contained a standard 80% coinsurance clause.

On April 25, a title insurance report ordered by Birch revealed that there was an existing $500,000 mortgage on the property that had been recorded the previous February. The title report failed to disclose another mortgage for $50,000 that had been given years earlier by a prior owner of the land and had not been recorded. Thorn was aware of the $500,000 mortgage but not the earlier mortgage. The title report also disclosed that there were unpaid property taxes outstanding.

On May 1, Thorn agreed to assign to a third party the prospective mortgage payments Thorn would receive from Birch.

When Birch received the title report and found out about Thorn's assignment of the mortgage payments, Birch accused Thorn of breach of contract for failing to disclose the prior mortgages and for violating the anti-assignment clause in the contract. Birch also insisted on postponing the contract closing date.

Thorn and Birch were able to resolve their differences.

- Birch reduced the mortgage being given to Thorn and assumed the previously recorded mortgage.
- The closing took place on July 1.
- Thorn recorded Birch's mortgage on July 5.
- The previously unrecorded mortgage was recorded on July 10.

On August 1, a fire caused $160,000 damage to the buildings. On that date, the fair market value of the buildings was $2 million. Acme contested payment of the claim, contending that Birch had no insurable interest in the buildings when the policy was taken out. Acme also contended that, even if Birch had an insurable interest, Birch would not be entitled to recover the entire amount of the loss because Birch is a coinsurer.

After the insurance issues were resolved and the buildings repaired, Birch stopped making payments on the mortgages and they were foreclosed. After payment of all foreclosure expenses, there was $1 million available to pay the outstanding mortgages. Thorn's mortgage had a principal and accrued interest balance of $950,000. The mortgage recorded in February had a principal and accrued interest balance of $475,000. The mortgage recorded on July 10 had a principal and accrued interest balance of $60,000.

The above transactions took place in a notice-race jurisdiction.

Required:

1. Determine whether Acme's contentions are correct and give the reasons for your conclusions.

2. Compute the dollar amount to which Birch would be entitled if the policy was valid and show how this amount is arrived at.

3. Determine which mortgage(s) has (have) priority, give the reasons for your decision, and state how the foreclosure proceeds would be distributed.

---

1. Acme's first contention that Birch had no insurable interest in the property when the policy was issued is incorrect. Birch had an insurable interest in the property when the contract was signed, since a contract right is an insurable interest.

Acme's second contention that Birch is a coinsurer is correct. Birch's policy for $1.5 million is less than 80% of the value of the buildings.

2. Birch would recover $150,000 of the loss. This figure is computed by dividing the face value of the policy by 80% of the fair market value of the buildings and multiplying by the amount of the loss.

$$\frac{\text{Face value of policy}}{80\% \text{ of fair market value}} \times \text{amount of loss} = \text{recovery}$$

$$\frac{\$1,500,000}{.80 \times \$2,000,000} \times \$160,000 = \$150,000$$

3. The mortgage recorded in February would have first priority. In a notice-race jurisdiction, the first recorded mortgage has priority unless the holder of a later mortgage has knowledge of the earlier mortgage. Based on the facts presented, no one had notice of the earlier unrecorded mortgage and, consequently, it has no priority despite its being first in time. Accordingly, the February mortgage would be paid in full ($475,000) and the balance of the foreclosure proceeds ($525,000) would be paid to Thorn.

---

3 (May 94)

Items 79 through 84 are based on the following:

On January 12, 1994, Frank, Inc. contracted in writing to purchase a factory building from Henderson for $250,000 cash. Closing took place on March 15, 1994. Henderson had purchased the building in 1990 for $225,000 and had, at that time, taken out a $180,000 fire insurance policy with Summit Insurance Co.

On January 15, 1994, Frank took out a $140,000 fire insurance policy with Unity Insurance Co. and a $70,000 fire insurance policy with Imperial Insurance, Inc.

On March 16, 1994, a fire caused $150,000 damage to the building. At that time the building had a market value of $250,000. All fire insurance policies contain a standard 80% coinsurance clause. The insurance carriers have refused any payment to Frank or Henderson alleging lack of insurable interest and insufficient coverage. Frank and Henderson have sued to collect on the policies.

Required: Items 79 through 84 relate to the suits by Frank and Henderson. For each item, determine whether the statement is True (T) or False (F).

79. Frank had an insurable interest at the time the Unity and Imperial policies were taken out.

80. Henderson had an insurable interest at the time of the fire.

81. Assuming Frank had an insurable interest, Frank's coverage would be insufficient under the Unity and Imperial coinsurance clauses.

82. Assuming Henderson had an insurable interest, Henderson's coverage would be insufficient under the Summit coinsurance clause.

83. Assuming only Frank had an insurable interest, Frank will recover $100,000 from Unity and $50,000 from Imperial.

84. Assuming only Henderson had an insurable interest, Henderson will recover $135,000 from Summit.

5 (November 94)

On May 15, 1993, Strong bought a factory building from Front for $500,000. Strong assumed Front's $300,000 mortgage with Ace Bank, gave a $150,000 mortgage to Lane Finance Co., and paid $50,000 cash.

The Ace mortgage had never been recorded. Lane knew of the Ace mortgage and recorded its mortgage on May 20, 1993.

Strong bought the factory for investment purposes and, on June 1, 1993, entered into a written lease with Apex Mfg. for seven years. On December 1, 1993, Apex subleased the factory to Egan Corp. without Strong's permission. Strong's lease with Apex was silent concerning the right to sublease.

On May 15, 1993, Strong had obtained a fire insurance policy from Range Insurance Co. The policy had a face value of $400,000. Apex and Egan obtained fire insurance policies from Zone Insurance Co. Each policy contained a standard 80% coinsurance clause. On May 1, 1994, when the factory had a fair market value of $600,000, a fire caused $180,000 damage.

Strong made no mortgage payments after the fire and on September 1, 1994, after the factory had been repaired, the mortgages were foreclosed. The balances due for principal and accrued interest were: Ace, $275,000; and Lane, $140,000. At a foreclosure sale, the factory and land were sold. After payment of all expenses, $400,000 of the proceeds remained for distribution.

As a result of the above events, the following actions took place:
- Strong sued Apex for subleasing the factory to Egan without Strong's permission.
- Zone refused to honor the Apex and Egan fire insurance policies claiming neither Apex nor Egan had an insurable interest in the factory.
- Strong sued Range to have Range pay Strong's $180,000 loss. Range refused claiming Strong had insufficient coverage under the coinsurance clause.
- Ace and Lane both demanded full payment of their mortgages from the proceeds of the foreclosure sale.

The preceding took place in a "Notice-Race" jurisdiction.

Required: Answer the following questions and give the reasons for your conclusions.

a. Would Strong succeed in the suit against Apex for subletting the factory to Egan without Strong's permission?

b. Is Zone correct in claiming that neither Apex nor Egan had an insurable interest in the factory at the time of the fire?

c. What amount will Strong be able to recover from Range?

d. What amount of the foreclosure proceeds will Lane recover?

a. Strong will lose its suit against Apex for subletting the factory to Egan without Strong's permission. Unless a lease provides otherwise, a tenant may sublet the premises without the landlord's consent.

b. Zone is incorrect in claiming that neither Apex nor Egan had an insurable interest in the factory. Apex has an insurable interest because it was the original lessee of the factory. Apex has a financial interest both in receiving rent from Egan and its liability to Strong under the original lease. Egan has an insurable interest and a financial interest as tenant in possession.

c. Strong will only recover $150,000 from Range. Strong's recovery is based on the coinsurance formula:

$$\frac{\text{Insurance Carried (policy amount)}}{\text{Insurance required (coinsurance \% x fair market value of the property at the time of the loss)}} \times \frac{\text{The amount of loss}}{} = \text{Recovery}$$

$$\frac{400,000}{.80 \times 600,000} \times 180,000 = \$150,000$$

Strong will be able to recover $150,000 from Range, despite having insufficient coverage.

d. Lane will recover $125,000 of the foreclosure proceeds. Lane's recovery is limited to the amount left after the satisfaction of the Ace mortgage. In a "Notice-Race" jurisdiction, Lane's recorded mortgage will not have priority over Ace's earlier unrecorded mortgage because Lane knew of the Ace mortgage.

4 (May 91)

On February 1, 1988, Tower and Perry, as tenants in common, purchased a two-unit apartment building for $250,000. They made a downpayment of $100,000, and gave a $100,000 first mortgage to Midway Bank and a $50,000 second mortgage to New Bank.

New was aware of Midway's mortgage but, as a result of a clerical error, Midway did not record its mortgage until after New's mortgage was recorded.

At the time of purchase, a $200,000 fire insurance policy was issued by Acme Insurance Co. to Tower and Perry. The policy contained an 80% coinsurance clause and a standard mortgagee provision.

Tower and Perry rented an apartment to Young under a month-to-month oral lease. They rented the other apartment to Zimmer under a three-year written lease.

On December 8, 1989, Perry died leaving a will naming the Dodd Foundation as the sole beneficiary of Perry's estate. The estate was distributed on January 15, 1990. That same date, the ownership of the fire insurance policy was assigned to Tower and Dodd with Acme's consent. On January 21, 1990, a fire caused $180,000 in structural damage to the building. At that time, its market value was $300,000 and the Midway mortgage balance was $80,000 including accrued interest. The New mortgage balance was $40,000 including accrued interest.

The fire made Young's apartment uninhabitable and caused extensive damage to the kitchen, bathrooms, and one bedroom of Zimmer's apartment. On February 1, 1990, Young and Zimmer moved out. The resulting loss of income caused a default on both mortgages.

On April 1, 1990, Acme refused to pay the fire loss claiming that the required insurable interest did not exist at the time of the loss and that the amount of the insurance was insufficient to provide full coverage for the loss. Tower and Dodd are involved in a lawsuit contesting the ownership of the building and the claims they have both made for any fire insurance proceeds.

On June 1, 1990, Midway and New foreclosed their mortgages and are also claiming any fire insurance proceeds that may be paid by Acme.

On July 1, 1990, Tower sued Zimmer for breach of the lease and is seeking to collect the balance of the lease term rent.

The above events took place in a notice-race statute jurisdiction.

Required: Answer the following questions and give the reasons for your conclusions.

a. Who had title to the building on January 21, 1990?

b. Did Tower and/or Dodd have an insurable interest in the building when the fire occurred? If so, when would such an interest have arisen?

c. Does Acme have to pay under the terms of the fire insurance policy? If so, how much?

d. Assuming the fire insurance proceeds will be paid, what would be the order of payment to the various parties and in what amounts?

e. Would Tower succeed in the suit against Zimmer?

a. Tower and Perry owned the property as tenants in common. This form of ownership allows either party to dispose of his or her undivided interest by sale or on death. Any person purchasing or inheriting Perry's interest would become a tenant in common with Tower. Thus, on January 21, 1990, Tower and Dodd are tenants in common, each owning a one-half undivided interest in the house.

b. Both Tower and Dodd have an insurable interest in the house. Tower's interest arose when the property was purchased, continued when the insurance policy was purchased, and still existed at the time of the fire loss.

Dodd's interest arose when Dodd inherited Perry's interest in the house. Acme's consent to the assignment of the policy to Tower and Dodd entitles Dodd to a share of the proceeds of the policy.

c. Acme would have to honor the insurance contract and pay part of the loss. Despite Tower and Perry not maintaining insurance coverage of 80% of the property's market value, the coinsurance clause allows for a percentage of recovery. The formula is as follows:

447

$$\frac{\text{Amount of Coverage}}{\text{Actual Market Value x Coinsurance \%}} \times \text{Amount of Loss}$$

This would allow a recovery as follows:

$$\frac{\$200,000}{\$300,000 \times .8} \times \$180,000 = \$150,000$$

d. The conflict between Midway and New would be resolved in favor of Midway. In a notice-race statute jurisdiction, New's knowledge of Midway's first mortgage would give Midway priority despite New's earlier filing. The insurance proceeds would be distributed as follows:

- $80,000 to Midway representing the balance due on the mortgage including accrued interest. This is due because Midway as a mortgagee is included as a contingent beneficiary in the policy.
- $40,000 to New for the same reasons as above but not paid unless and until Midway is fully paid.
- $30,000 to be divided equally between Tower and Dodd as tenants in common.

e. Tower would not be able to collect rent from Zimmer for the balance of the term of the lease because Zimmer moved as a result of the extensive fire damage to the apartment. The implied warranty of habitability would be considered breached by the landlord and a constructive eviction of Zimmer would be deemed to have taken place because the premises could no longer be used for their intended purpose. Constructive eviction releases both the landlord and the tenant from their obligations under the lease.

5A (November 82)

While auditing the financial statements of Jackson Corporation for the year ended December 31, 1981, Harvey Draper, CPA, desired to verify the balance in the insurance claims receivable account. Draper obtained the following information:

- On November 4, 1981, Jackson's Parksdale plant was damaged by fire. The fire caused $200,000 damage to the plant, which was purchased in 1970 for $600,000. When the plant was purchased, Jackson obtained a loan secured by a mortgage from Second National Bank of Parksdale. At the time of the fire the loan balance, including accrued interest, was $106,000. The plant was insured against fire with Eagle Insurance Company. The policy contained a "standard mortgagee" clause and an 80% coinsurance clause. The face value of the policy was $600,000 and the value of the plant was $1,000,000 at the time of the fire.

- On December 10, 1981, Jackson's Yuma warehouse was totally destroyed by fire. The warehouse was acquired in 1960 for $300,000. At the time of the fire, the warehouse was unencumbered by any mortgage; it was insured against fire with Eagle for $300,000; and it had a value of $500,000. The policy contained an 80% coinsurance clause.

- On December 26, 1981, Jackson's Rye City garage was damaged by fire. At the time of the fire, the garage had a value of $250,000 and was unencumbered by any mortgage. The fire caused $60,000 damage to the garage, which was constructed in 1965 at a cost of $50,000. In 1975, Jackson expanded the capacity of the garage at an additional cost of $50,000. When the garage was constructed in 1965, Jackson insured the garage against fire for $50,000 with Eagle, and this policy was still in force on the date of the fire. When the garage was expanded in 1975, Jackson obtained $100,000 of additional fire insurance coverage from Queen Insurance Company. Each policy contains an 80% coinsurance clause and a standard pro-rata clause.

Required: Answer the following, setting forth reasons for any conclusions stated.
1. How much of the fire loss relating to the Parksdale plant will be recovered from Eagle?
2. How will such recovery be distributed between Second National and Jackson?
3. How much of the fire loss relating to the Yuma warehouse will be recovered from Eagle?
4. How much of the fire loss relating to the Rye City garage will be recovered from the insurance companies?
5. What portion of the amount recoverage in connection with the Rye City garage loss will Queen be obligated to pay?

1. The recoverable loss is determined by reference to the following formula:

$$\frac{\text{Insurance carried}}{\text{Insurance required}} \text{ x the amount of the loss}$$

where the insurance required is defined as the value of the property at the time of the loss multiplied by the coinsurance percentage. Applying the foregoing formula, the amount of the loss recovered is as follows:

$$\frac{\$600,000}{\$1,000,000 \text{ x }.8} \text{ x } \$200,000 = \$150,000.$$

2. The $150,000 will be distributed as follows: $106,000 to Second National and $44,000 to Jackson. This is because Second National's insurable interest equals the extent of its mortgage outstanding, which is limited to debt outstanding plus accrued interest, and is paid first. The remaining $44,000 would then be paid to Jackson.

3. Jackson will recover $300,000--the face amount of the policy. The coinsurance clause does not apply to a total loss.

4. Jackson will recover $45,000. The formula for determination of the total amount recoverable under the 80% coinsurance clause is as follows:

$$\frac{\$150,000}{\$250,000 \text{ x }.8} \text{ x } \$60,000 = \$45,000.$$

5. Jackson will recover $30,000 from Queen. This amount is determined as follows:

$$\frac{\$100,000 \text{ (Queen's coverage)}}{\$150,000 \text{ (Total coverage)}} \text{ x } \$45,000 = \$30,000.$$

B. Other Insurance

60 (November 87)

On May 5, Sly purchased a warehouse for $100,000. Sly immediately insured the warehouse in the amount of $40,000 with Riff Insurance Co. Six months later, Sly obtained additional fire insurance on the warehouse in the amount of $10,000 from Beek Insurance Co. Both policies contained an 80% coinsurance clause. Sly failed to notify Riff of the policy with Beek. Two years later, while both policies were still in effect, a fire caused by Sly's negligence resulted in $20,000 of damage to the warehouse. At the time of the loss, the warehouse had a fair market value of $50,000. Which of the following will prevent Sly from obtaining the full $20,000 from Riff?

a. Sly's negligence in causing the fire.
b. Sly's failure to satisfy the coinsurance clause.
c. Sly's failure to notify Riff of the policy with Beek.
d. Sly's purchase of insurance from Beek.

2 (May 79)

Wilson obtained a fire insurance policy on his dairy farm from the Columbus Insurance Company. The policy was for $80,000 which was the value of the property. The policy was the standard fire insurance policy sold throughout the United States. A fire occurred late one night and caused a $10,000 loss. Which of the following will prevent Wilson from recovering the full amount of his loss from Columbus Insurance?

a. The coinsurance clause.
b. Wilson had a similar policy with another insurance company for $40,000.
c. The fact that 50% of the loss was caused by smoke and water damage.
d. The fact that his negligence was the primary cause of the fire.

38 (November 75)

Margo, Inc. insured its property against fire with two separate insurance companies, Excelsior and Wilberforce. Each carrier insured the property for its full value, and neither insurer was aware that the other had also insured the property. The policies were the standard fire insurance policies used throughout the United States. If the property is totally destroyed by fire, how much will Margo recover?

    a.   Nothing because Margo has engaged in an illegal gambling venture.

    b.   The full amount from both insurers.

    c.   A ratable or pro rata share from each insurer, <u>not</u> to exceed the value of the property insured.

    d.   Only 80% of the value of the property from each insurer because of the standard coinsurance clause.

2 (November 88)

Dunn & Co., CPAs, while performing the 1987 year-end audit of Starr Corp.'s financial statements discovered that certain events during 1987 had resulted in litigation.

Starr had purchased the warehouse on March 1, 1987. The contract between Birk and Starr provided for a closing on September 20,1 987. On July 1, 1987, Birk executed a contract to purchase the warehouse from Starr for $200,000. On September 1, 1987, Birk contacted Starr and demanded that the purchase price be reduced to $190,000 because of a sudden rise in interest rates and declining value of real estate. Starr orally agreed to change the price to $190,000. On September 2, Birk sent Starr a signed memo confirming the reduction in price to $190,000. Starr did not sign the memo or any other agreement reducing the price. On September 15, Starr, by telephone, informed Birk that it would not sell the warehouse for $190,000. Birk refused to pay Starr $200,000 and a closing never occurred.

On October 30, 1987, a fire caused $80,000 damage to the warehouse at a time when its fair market value was $200,000. Starr had obtained a $160,000 fire insurance policy on February 15, 1987, from Pica Casualty Co., covering the warehouse. On April 11, 1987, Starr obtained another fire insurance policy from Drake Insurance Co. covering the warehouse for $40,000. Each policy contained an 80% coinsurance clause and a provision limiting each company's liability to its proportion of all insurance covering the loss. Pica has refused to pay any amount on its policy.

Starr commenced actions against Birk and Pica asserting the following:

-   Birk has breached the contract with Starr because Birk failed to close the transaction and buy the warehouse at a price of $200,000.
-   Starr has an insurable interest in the warehouse covered under the policy with Pica.
-   Starr has met the coinsurance requirement under Pica's policy.
-   Starr is entitled to recover the entire $80,000 from Pica.

Required: Discuss Starr's assertions, indicating whether such assertions are correct and the reasons therefor.

> Starr's first assertion, that Birk has breached the contract with Starr because Birk failed to close the transaction and buy the warehouse at a price of $200,000, is correct. An oral agreement modifying an enforceable existing contract is not enforceable if the modification is within the Statute of Frauds. A contract for the sale of real estate or a modification of such a contract falls within the provisions of the Statute of Frauds and therefore a writing signed by the party to be charged is required. The fact that Birk sent a signed memo to Starr is not effective because it was not signed by Starr. Furthermore, the agreement to reduce the purchase price to $190,000 is not enforceable because Birk did not give any consideration for the modification. Birk had a pre-existing obligation to purchase the warehouse for $200,000 and gave no new consideration for the modification of the price. The fact that Birk may have acted in good faith as a result of the decline in value of real estate and rise in interest rates will not be sufficient to make the oral agreement enforceable against Starr. Therefore, Birk's failure to pay $200,000 as required by the July 1 contract constitutes a breach of that contract.
>
> Starr's second assertion, that it has an insurable interest in the warehouse covered by the Pica policy, is correct. To constitute an insurable interest the element of financial or economic loss to the insured must be present. Furthermore, the insurable interest must be present at the time of the loss but need not be present at the time the policy was issued. Under the facts of this case, Starr had an insurable interest on the date of the loss (October 30) since it owned the warehouse on that date. Whether Starr had an insurable interest on February 15 will not affect Starr's right to recover from Pica.

Starr's third assertion, that it has met the coinsurance requirement under Pica's policy is correct.

Starr's fourth assertion, that Starr is entitled to recover the entire $80,000 from Pica is incorrect. Starr is only entitled to receive $64,000 from Pica calculated as follows:

$$\frac{\$160,000\,(\text{Amount of Insurance Coverage with Pica})}{\$200,000\,(\text{Total Amount of Insurance on Warehouse})} \times \$80,000\,(\text{Amount to be Paid}) = \$64,000$$

Thus, Pica's liability is limited to the amount its policy bears to the amount of insurance on the warehouse.

III. Rights and Defenses of Insurer
A. Defenses of Insurer

55 (November 81)

Jerry's House of Jewelry, Inc. took out an insurance policy with the Old Time Insurance Company which covered the stock of jewelry displayed in the store's windows. Old Time agreed to indemnify Jerry's House for losses due to window smashing and theft of the jewels displayed. The application contained the following provision: "It is hereby warranted that the maximum value of the jewelry displayed shall not exceed $10,000." The insurance policy's coverage was for $8,000. The application was initialed alongside the warranty and attached to the policy. Subsequently, thieves smashed the store window and stole $4,000 worth of jewels. The total value of the display during that week, including the day of the robbery, was $12,000. Which of the following is correct?

a. Jerry's House will recover nothing.

b. Jerry's House will recover $2,000, the loss less the amount in excess of the $10,000 display limitation.

c. Jerry's House will recover the full $4,000 since the warranty will be construed as a mere representation.

d. Jerry's House will recover the full $4,000 since attaching the application to the policy is insufficient to make it a part thereof.

60 (November 81)

Fuller Corporation insured its factory and warehouse against fire with the Safety First Insurance Company. As a part of the bargaining process, in connection with obtaining the policy Fuller was required by Safety First to give in writing certain warranties regarding the insured risk. Fuller did so and they were incorporated into the policy. Which of the following correctly describes the law applicable to such warranties?

a. The warranties given by Fuller will be treated as representations.

b. It was not necessary that the warranties given by Fuller be in writing to be effective.

c. In the event that Fuller does not strictly comply with the warranties it has given, it will be denied recovery in a substantial number of states.

d. In deciding whether the language contained in a policy constitutes a warranty, the courts usually construe ambiguous language in a way which favors the insurance company.

32 (May 76)

The typical fire insurance policy

a. Covers all damages caused by fire whatever the source.

b. Does not cover water damage which results from the fire department extinguishing the blaze.

c. Will not permit recovery for business interruption unless there is a special indorsement.

d. Prohibits the assignment of the policy both before and after a loss.

B. Subrogation

53 (November 80)

Bernard Manufacturing, Inc. owns a three-story building which it recently purchased. The purchase price was $200,000 of which $160,000 was financed by the proceeds of a mortgage loan from the Cattleman Savings and Loan Association. Bernard immediately procured a standard fire insurance policy on the premises for $200,000 from the Magnificent Insurance Company. Cattleman also took out fire insurance of $160,000 on the property from the Reliable Insurance Company of America. The property was subsequently totally destroyed as a result of a fire which started in an adjacent loft and spread to Bernard's building. Insofar as the rights and duties of Bernard, Cattleman, and the insurers are concerned, which of the following is a correct statement?

    a. Cattleman Savings and Loan lacks the requisite insurable interest to collect on its policy.

    b. Bernard Manufacturing can only collect $40,000.

    c. Reliable Insurance Company is subrogated to Cattleman's rights against Bernard upon payment of Cattleman's insurance claim.

    d. The maximum amount that Bernard Manufacturing can collect from Magnificent is $40,000, the value of its insurable interest.

12 (November 79)

Charleston, Inc. had its warehouse destroyed by fire. Charleston's property was insured against fire loss by the Conglomerate Insurance Company. An investigation by Conglomerate revealed that the fire had been caused by a disgruntled employee whom Charleston had suspended for one month due to insubordination. Charleston seeks to hold its insurer liable for the $200,000 loss of its warehouse. Which of the following is correct insofar as the dispute between Charleston and the Conglomerate Insurance Company?

    a. Since the loss was due to the deliberate destruction by one of Charleston's employees, recovery will be denied.

    b. Conglomerate must pay Charleston, but it will be subrogated to Conglomerate's rights against the wrongdoing employee.

    c. The fact that the employee has been suspended for one month precludes recovery against Conglomerate.

    d. Arson is excluded from the coverage of most fire insurance policies, and therefore Conglomerate is <u>not</u> liable.

45 (November 79)

The usual fire insurance policy does <u>not</u>

    a. Have to meet the insurable interest test if this requirement is waived by the parties.

    b. Permit assignment of the policy prior to the loss without the consent of the insurer.

    c. Provide for subrogation of the insurer to the insured's rights upon payment of the amount of the loss covered by the policy.

    d. Cover losses caused by the negligence of the insured's agent.

53 (May 74)

Alphonse, a sole CPA practitioner, obtained a malpractice insurance policy from the Friendly Casualty Company. In regard to this coverage

    a. Issuance of an unqualified opinion by Alphonse when he knows the statements are false does <u>not</u> give Friendly a defense.

    b. The policy would automatically cover the work of a new partnership formed by Alphonse and Borne.

    c. Friendly will <u>not</u> be subrogated to rights against Alphonse for his negligent conduct of an audit.

    d. Coverage includes injury to a client resulting from a slip on a rug negligently left loose in Alphonse's office.

PART XII – PARTNERSHIP*

TABLE OF CONTENTS

*Answers consistent with Revised Uniform Partnership Act (1994) and Revised Uniform Limited Partnership Act (1976) with 1985 amendments.

PART XII

PARTNERSHIP

I. Introduction to Partnership
A. Nature and Formation of Partnership
1. Partnership Defined

6 (R98)

When parties intend to create a partnership that will be recognized under the Uniform Partnership Act, they must agree to

	Conduct a business for profit	Share gross receipts from a business
a.	Yes	Yes
b.	Yes	No
c.	No	Yes
d.	No	No

16 (November 93)

Which of the following requirements must be met to have a valid partnership exist?
  - I. Co-ownership of all property used in a business.
  - II. Co-ownership of a business for profit.
  a. I only.
  b. II only.
  c. Both I and II.
  d. Neither I nor II.

14 (November 91)

A general partnership must
  a. Pay federal income tax.
  b. Have two or more partners.
  c. Have written articles of partnership.
  d. Provide for apportionment of liability for partnership debts.

11 (November 90)

Which of the following is not necessary to create an express partnership?
  a. Execution of a written partnership agreement.
  b. Agreement to share ownership of the partnership.
  c. Intention to conduct a business for profit.
  d. Intention to create a relationship recognized as a partnership.

Partnership

4 (November 89)

A joint venture is a(an)

    a. Association limited to no more than two persons in business for profit.
    b. Enterprise of numerous co-owners in a nonprofit undertaking.
    c. Corporate enterprise for a single undertaking of limited duration.
    d. Association of persons engaged as co-owners in a single undertaking for profit.

58 (May 86)

Noll Corp. and Orr Co. are contemplating entering into an unincorporated joint venture. Such a joint venture

    a. Will be treated as a partnership in most important legal respects.
    b. Must be dissolved upon completion of a single undertaking.
    c. Will be treated as an association for federal income tax purposes and taxed at the prevailing corporate rates.
    d. Must file a certificate of limited partnership with the appropriate state agency.

1 (May 82)

Three independent sole proprietors decided to pool their resources and form a partnership. The business assets and liabilities of each were transferred to the partnership. The partnership commenced business on September 1, 1981, but the parties did not execute a formal partnership agreement until October 15, 1981. Which of the following is correct?

    a. The existing creditors must consent to the transfer of the individual business assets to the partnership.
    b. The partnership began its existence on September 1, 1981.
    c. If the partnership's duration is indefinite, the partnership agreement must be in writing and signed.
    d. In the absence of a partnership agreement specifically covering division of losses among the partners, they will be deemed to share them in accordance with their capital contributions.

23 (November 80)

In the course of your audit of James Fine, doing business as Fine's Apparels, a sole proprietorship, you discovered that in the past year Fine had regularly joined with Charles Walters in the marketing of bathing suits and beach accessories. You are concerned whether Fine and Walters have created a partnership relationship. Which of the following factors is the <u>most</u> important in ascertaining this status?

    a. The fact that a partnership agreement is <u>not</u> in existence.
    b. The fact that each has a separate business of his own which he operates independently.
    c. The fact that Fine and Walters divide the net profits equally on a quarterly basis.
    d. The fact that Fine and Walters did <u>not</u> intend to be partners.

3 (November 74)

Wyatt, Cooper, and Hubble informally agreed to share profits and losses. They agreed that each party would do business under his own name and <u>not</u> disclose the names of the other parties, and would assume liability for his own accounts. All parties lived up to the undertaking. Unfortunately, Cooper overextended himself and, consequently, filed a voluntary petition in bankruptcy. Cooper's business creditors seek to assert rights against Wyatt and Hubble. Under these circumstances

    a. Wyatt and Hubble are partners by estoppel.
    b. Wyatt and Hubble can rely upon the Statute of Frauds to defeat the claims of Cooper's creditors.
    c. Cooper's activities were <u>ultra vires</u>, hence, <u>not</u> binding on Wyatt and Hubble.
    d. Wyatt, Cooper, and Hubble are partners <u>inter se</u> (i.e., among themselves) and, hence, are all liable for Cooper's debts.

2. Partnership Name and Registration Requirements

15 (November 83)

Many states require partnerships to file the partnership name under laws which are generally known as fictitious name statutes. These statutes

a. Require a proper filing as a condition precedent to the valid creation of a partnership.
b. Are designed primarily to provide registration for tax purposes.
c. Are designed to clarify the rights and duties of the members of the partnership.
d. Have little effect on the creation or operation of a partnership other than the imposition of a fine for noncompliance.

3. Entity and Aggregate Characteristics of Partnership

16 (November 95)

Generally, under the Uniform Partnership Act, a partnership has which of the following characteristics?

	Unlimited duration	Obligation for payment of federal income tax
a.	Yes	Yes
b.	Yes	No
c.	No	Yes
d.	No	No

3 (May 83)

For which of the following purposes is a general partnership recognized as an entity by the Uniform Partnership Act?

a. Recognition of the partnership as the employer of its partners.
b. Insulation of the partners from personal liability.
c. Taking of title and ownership of property.
d. Continuity of existence.

20 (November 81)

For which of the following is a partnership recognized as a separate legal entity?

a. The liability for and payment of taxes on partnership gains from the sale of capital assets.
b. In respect to contributions and advances made by partners to the partnership.
c. The recognition of net operating losses.
d. The status of the partnership as an employer for workers' compensation purposes.

5 (November 74)

For federal income tax purposes, a partnership is

a. A taxable entity similar to a trust or an estate.
b. Considered to be a nontaxable entity but which must file an information return.
c. Treated the same as an association for tax purposes.
d. Required to pay a tax upon its profits which in turn must be assumed by its partners.

B. Relationship Among Partners
1. The Partnership Agreement

10 (May 92)

A partnership agreement must be in writing if
a. Any partner contributes more than $500 in capital.
b. The partners reside in different states.
c. The partnership intends to own real estate.
d. The partnership's purpose <u>cannot</u> be completed within one year of formation.

2. Partners' Compensation

18 (November 95)

Which of the following statements is correct regarding the division of profits in a general partnership when the written partnership agreement only provides that losses be divided equally among the partners? Profits are to be divided
a. Based on the partners' ratio of contribution to the partnership.
b. Based on the partners' participation in day to day management.
c. Equally among the partners.
d. Proportionately among the partners.

22 (November 94)

The partnership agreement for Owen Associates, a general partnership, provided that profits be paid to the partners in the ratio of their financial contribution to the partnership. Moore contributed $10,000, Noon contributed $30,000, and Kale contributed $50,000. For the year ended December 31, 1993, Owen had losses of $180,000. What amount of the losses should be allowed to Kale?
a. $40,000
b. $60,000
c. $90,000
d. $100,000

14 (November 90)

Lewis, Clark, and Beal entered into a written agreement to form a partnership. The agreement required that the partners make the following capital contributions: Lewis, $40,000; Clark, $30,000; and Beal, $10,000. It was also agreed that in the event the partnership experienced losses in excess of available capital, Beal would contribute additional capital to the extent of the losses. The partnership agreement was otherwise silent about division of profits and losses. Which of the following statements is correct?
a. Profits are to be divided among the partners in proportion to their relative capital contributions.
b. Profits are to be divided equally among the partners.
c. Losses will be allocated in a manner different from the allocation of profits because the partners contributed different amounts of capital.
d. Beal's obligation to contribute additional capital would have an effect on the allocation of profit or loss to Beal.

6 (November 89)

Gillie, Taft, and Dall are partners in an architectural firm. The partnership agreement is silent about the payment of salaries and the division of profits and losses. Gillie works full-time in the firm, and Taft and Dall each work half-time. Taft invested $120,000 in the firm, and Gillie and Dall invested $60,000 each. Dall is responsible for bringing in 50% of the business, and Gillie and Taft 25% each. How should profits of $120,000 for the year be divided?

a. Gillie $60,000, Taft $30,000, Dall $30,000.
b. Gillie $40,000, Taft $40,000, Dall $40,000.
c. Gillie $30,000, Taft $60,000, Dall $30,000.
d. Gillie $30,000, Taft $30,000, Dall $60,000.

13 (May 88)

X, Y, and Z have capital balances of $30,000, $15,000, and $5,000, respectively, in the XYZ Partnership. The general partnership agreement is silent as to the manner in which partnership losses are to be allocated but does provide that partnership profits are to be allocated as follows: 40% to X, 25% to Y, and 35% to Z. The partners have decided to dissolve and liquidate the partnership. After paying all creditors, the amount available for distribution will be $20,000. X, Y, and Z are individually solvent. Under the circumstances, Z will

a. Receive $7,000.
b. Receive $12,000.
c. Personally have to contribute an additional $5,500.
d. Personally have to contribute an additional $5,000.

21 (November 87)

In the absence of a specific provision in a general partnership agreement, partnership losses will be allocated

a. Equally among the partners irrespective of the allocation of partnership profits.
b. In the same manner as partnership profits.
c. In proportion to the partners' capital contributions.
d. In proportion to the partners' capital contributions and outstanding loan balances.

10 (May 87)

With respect to the following matters, which is correct if a general partnership agreement is silent?

a. A partnership will continue indefinitely unless a majority of the partners votes to dissolve the partnership.
b. Partnership losses are allocated in the same proportion as partnership profits.
c. A partner may assign his interest in the partnership but only with the consent of the other partners.
d. A partner may sell the goodwill of the partnership without the consent of the other partners when the sale is in the best interest of the partnership.

18 (November 81)

Daniels, Beal, and Wade agreed to form the DBW Partnership to engage in the import-export business. They had been life-long friends and had engaged in numerous business dealings with each other. It was orally agreed that Daniels would contribute $20,000, Beal $15,000, and Wade $5,000. It was also orally agreed that in the event the venture proved to be a financial disaster all losses above the amounts of capital contributed would be assumed by Daniels and that he would hold his fellow partners harmless from any additional amounts lost. The partnership was consummated with a handshake and the contribution of the agreed upon capital by the partners. There were no other express agreements.

Under the circumstances, which of the following is correct?

a. Profits are to be divided in accordance with the relative capital contributions of each partner.
b. Profits are to be divided equally.
c. The partnership is a nullity because the agreement is not contained in a signed writing.
d. Profits are to be shared in accordance with the relative time each devotes to partnership business during the year.

4 (November 74)

Webster, Davis, and Polk were general partners in the antique business. Webster contributed his illustrious name, Davis managed the partnership, and Polk contributed the capital. Absent an agreement to the contrary, which of the following provisions would automatically prevail?

    a.   Polk has the majority vote in respect to new business.
    b.   Polk has assumed the responsibility of paying Webster's personal debts upon insolvency of the partnership.
    c.   Webster, Davis, and Polk share profits and losses equally.
    d.   Davis is entitled to a reasonable salary for his services.

C. Partners' Property Rights
1. Rights in Specific Partnership Property

16 (November 91)

In a general partnership, a partner's interest in specific partnership property is

    a.   Transferable to a partner's individual creditors.
    b.   Subject to a partner's liability for alimony.
    c.   Transferable to a partner's estate upon death.
    d.   Subject to a surviving partner's right of survivorship.

7 (November 89)

A partner's interest in specific partnership property is

	Assignable to the partner's individual creditors	Subject to attachment by the partner's individual creditors
a.	Yes	Yes
b.	Yes	No
c.	No	Yes
d.	No	No

16 (November 79)

King, Kline, and Fox were partners in a wholesale business. Kline died and left his wife his share of the business. Kline's wife is entitled to

    a.   The value of Kline's interest in the partnership.
    b.   Kline's share of specific property of the partnership.
    c.   Continue the partnership as a partner with King and Fox.
    d.   Kline's share of the partnership profits until her death.

6 (November 74)

In 1970, Allen, Burton, and Carter became equal partners for the purpose of buying and selling real estate for profit. For convenience, title to all property purchased was taken in the name of Allen. Allen died with partnership real estate and partnership personal property standing in his name valued at $25,000 and $5,000, respectively. The partnership had no debts. Allen's wife claims a dower right in the real property. Allen had bequeathed all his personal property to his children who claim an absolute one-third interest in the $5,000 of personal property. In this situation

    a.   Allen's wife has a valid dower right to all the real property held in her deceased husband's name.
    b.   Partnership property is subject to a right of survivorship in the surviving partners; hence, Allen's wife is entitled only to his share of undistributed partnership profits.
    c.   Allen's children are entitled to one-third of all partnership personal property.
    d.   Allen's estate is entitled to settlement for the value of his partnership interest.

3B (November 82)

While auditing the financial statements of Graham, Phillips, Killian, and Henderson, a real estate partnership, for the year ended December 31, 1981, a CPA uncovers a number of unrelated events which warrant closer analysis:

- Graham died and left her partnership interest to her spouse.

- Phillips owned some real estate prior to the formation of the partnership but never formally transferred legal title to the partnership. The real estate has been used for partnership business since the partnership began its existence, and the partnership has paid all taxes associated with the real estate.

- Killian owes a considerable sum of money to a creditor, Jamison. Jamison has a judgment against Killian and has begun a foreclosure action against certain land owned by the partnership in order to satisfy his claim against Killian.

- Henderson sold some of the partnership real estate for value remitted to the partnership without the approval of the other partners. This sale exceeded Henderson's actual authority but appeared to be a customary sale in the ordinary course of business.

Required: Answer the following, setting forth reasons for any conclusions stated.

1. Graham's spouse is presently seeking to exercise his spousal rights to obtain certain specific property owned by the partnership. Discuss the likely outcome of this matter.

2. Regarding the real estate that is legally in Phillips' name, can the partnership properly reflect this as an asset in the partnership's balance sheet?

3. Will Jamison succeed in his land foreclosure action?

4. If the partnership now wishes to rescind the sale of the real estate by Henderson, can it lawfully do so?

1. Graham's spouse would lose in such an action. One of the principal characteristics of a tenancy in partnership is that upon the death of a partner, that partner's right in specific partnership property vests in the surviving partner or partners. Another characteristic provides that a partner's right in specific partnership property is not subject to dower, courtesy, or allowances to a surviving spouse, heirs, or next of kin.

2. Yes. Despite the fact that legal title to the real estate remains with Phillips, this is not conclusive evidence that the real estate is not a partnership asset. This is a factual question in which the objective intention of the parties may be inferred by examining a variety of factors such as whether the property was improved with partnership funds, whether expenses relating to the assets (such as insurance and taxes) were paid for by the partnership, and so forth. Since the partnership actually paid the real estate taxes, such property may properly be considered a partnership asset and thus included on its balance sheet.

3. No. Jamison may attach Killian's partnership interest in the firm by obtaining a charging order (which would, for example, entitle Jamison to receive Killian's share of the partnership profits) but cannot obtain a fractional interest in any specific item of property.

4. No. The act of every partner for apparently carrying on in the usual course the business of the partnership binds the partnership, unless the partner so acting has in fact no authority and the person with whom he is dealing has knowledge of the lack of authority. The acts of Henderson appeared to be in the usual course of business, and there is no indication that the purchaser knew of Henderson's lack of authority. Accordingly, the partnership is bound.

6C (May 76)

Dowling, a partner of Lazor, Bassett, Dowling & Lamb, died on February 2, 1976. The four partners were equal partners in all respects (i.e., capital accounts, profit and loss sharing, etc.). The partnership agreement was silent on the question of the rights of a deceased partner upon his death. Dowling's Last Will and Testament bequeathed his entire estate to his "beloved wife." His widow is now claiming the right to 25% of all partnership property.

Required:

1. What rights does Dowling's widow have in respect to specific partnership property or against the partnership or surviving partners? Explain.

2. How would a "buy-out" agreement affect you answer to 1? Explain.

1. Mrs. Dowling has no rights to any particular partnership property nor to a share thereof. Pursuant to the Uniform Partnership Act, the surviving partners have a right of survivorship in all partnership property, and such property is not subject to the surviving spouse's share. The property passes according to this law regardless of any provisions contained in a deceased partner's last will and testament.

However, Mrs. Dowling does have the right to compensation for her husband's partnership interest. At a minimum, this would consist of a return of his capital contribution plus accumulated and current profits to the date of death. However, if the partners wish to continue the firm without a "winding up" and under its existing name, then the aspect of goodwill and the fair market value of the decedent's interest becomes more complex. If the problem cannot be solved amicably by negotiation between the remaining partners and the widow, then an independent appraisal or litigation or both would be necessary.

2. A "buy-out" agreement would provide for the automatic continuation of the firm, usually under the original name, despite the legal or technical dissolution caused by death. Also, it would eliminate the requirement and need for a "winding up." Finally, it would solve most of the valuation problems, because the price or method of determining the value of the decedent's partnership interest would be established by specific terms in the agreement.

2. Partner's Interest and Right to Participate in Management--Assignability

19 (November 95)

Which of the following statements best describes the effect of the assignment of an interest in a general partnership?
   a. The assignee becomes a partner.
   b. The assignee is responsible for a proportionate share of past and future partnership debts.
   c. The assignment automatically dissolves the partnership.
   d. The assignment transfers the assignor's interest in partnership profits and surplus.

23 (November 94)

Lark, a partner in DSJ, a general partnership, wishes to withdraw from the partnership and sell Lark's interest to Ward. All of the other partners in DSJ have agreed to admit Ward as a partner and to hold Lark harmless for the past, present, and future liabilities of DSJ. As a result of Lark's withdrawal and Ward's admission to the partnership, Ward
   a. Acquired only the right to receive Ward's share of DSJ profits.
   b. Has the right to participate in DSJ's management.
   c. Is personally liable for partnership liabilities arising before and after being admitted as a partner.
   d. Must contribute cash or property to DSJ to be admitted with the same rights as the other partners.

18 (November 93)

Unless the partnership agreement prohibits it, a partner in a general partnership may validly assign rights to

	Partnership property	Partnership distributions
a.	Yes	Yes
b.	Yes	No
c.	No	Yes
d.	No	No

15 (May 93)

Cobb, Inc., a partner in TLC Partnership, assigns its partnership interest to Bean, who is not made a partner. After the assignment, bean asserts the rights to

      I. Participate in the management of TLC.

      II. Cobb's share of TLC's partnership profits.

Bean is correct as to which of these rights.

    a. I only.

    b. II only.

    c. I and II.

    d. Neither I nor II.

16 (May 89)

Kroll, Inc., a partner in JKL Partnership, assigns its interest in the partnership to Trell, who is not made a partner. After the assignment, Trell asserts the rights to

      I. Receive Kroll's share of JKL's profits and

      II. Inspect JKL's books and records.

Trell is correct as to which of the rights?

    a. I only.

    b. II only.

    c. I and II.

    d. Neither I nor II.

20 (November 87)

Unless otherwise provided for in the partnership agreement, the assignment of a partner's interest in a general partnership will

    a. Result in the termination of the partnership.

    b. Not affect the assigning partner's liability to third parties for obligations existing at the time of the assignment.

    c. Transfer the assigning partner's rights in specific partnership property to the assignee.

    d. Transfer the assigning partner's right to bind the partnership to contracts to the assignee.

9 (May 85)

Unless otherwise provided for, the assignment of a partnership interest will result in the

    a. Dissolution of the partnership.

    b. Assignee obtaining the right to receive the share of the profits to which the assignor would have otherwise been entitled.

    c. Assignee succeeding to the assignor's rights to participate in the management of the partnership.

    d. Vesting of the assignor's right to inspect the partnership books in the assignee.

4 (May 83)

Donovan, a partner of Monroe, Lincoln, and Washington, is considering selling or pledging all or part of his interest in the partnership. The partnership agreement is silent on the matter. Donovan can

    a. Sell part but not all of this partnership interest.

    b. Sell or pledge his entire partnership interest without causing a dissolution.

    c. Pledge his partnership interest, but only with the consent of his fellow partners.

    d. Sell his entire partnership interest and confer partner status upon the purchaser.

Partnership

24 (May 75)

Jack Gordon, a general partner of Visions Unlimited, is retiring. He sold his partnership interest to Don Morrison for $80,000. Gordon assigned to Morrison all his rights, title, and interests in the partnership and named Morrison as his successor partner in Visions. In this situation

 a. The assignment to Morrison dissolves the partnership.

 b. Absent any limitation regarding the assignment of a partner's interest, Gordon is free to assign it at his will.

 c. Morrison is entitled to an equal voice and vote in the management of the partnership, and he is entitled to exercise all the rights and privileges that Gordon had.

 d. Morrison does <u>not</u> have the status of a partner, but he can, upon demand, inspect the partnership accounting records.

25 (May 75)

Morton, a senior staff member of Wilcox & Southern, CPAs, has been offered the opportunity to become a junior partner of the firm. However, to be admitted to the partnership he must contribute $30,000 to the partnership's capital, and he does not have that amount of money. It is estimated that the partnership interest in question is worth at least $100,000. The partnership agreement is silent on assignment of a partner's interest. Morton accepts the offer and becomes a junior partner.

 a. Morton could assign his partnership interest to a bank or other lending institution as security for a loan to acquire his partnership interest.

 b. Morton is personally liable for all debts of the partnership, past and present, unless the partnership agreement provides otherwise.

 c. Since Morton is only a junior partner with very little say in the management of the firm and the selection of client, he has the legal status of a quasi limited partner.

 d. If Morton pledged his partnership interest as security for a loan to acquire his partnership interest, the transaction created a subpartnership between himself and the lending institution.

3 (November 85)

John Nolan, a partner in Nolan, Stein, & Wolf partnership, transferred his interest in the partnership to Simon and withdrew from the partnership. Although the partnership will continue, Stein and Wolf have refused to admit Simon as a partner.

Subsequently, the partnership appointed Ed Lemon as its agent to market its various product lines. Lemon entered into a two-year written agency contract with the partnership which provided that Lemon would receive a 10% sales commission. The agency contract was signed by Lemon and, on behalf of the partnership, by Stein and Wolf.

After six months, Lemon was terminated without cause. Lemon asserts that:

- He is an agent coupled with an interest.

- The agency relationship may not be terminated without cause prior to the expiration of its term.

- He is entitled to damages because of the termination of the agency relationship.

Required: Answer the following, setting forth reasons for any conclusions stated.

 a. Discuss Nolan's property rights in the partnership prior to his withdrawal and the property rights acquired by Simon as a result of his transaction with Nolan.

 b. Discuss the merits of Lemon's assertions.

 a. Nolan's property rights in the partnership prior to the conveyance of his partnership interest consisted of:

- His rights in specific partnership property. This right permitted Nolan to possess any item of partnership property for partnership purposes.

- His interest in the partnership. This interest is classified as personal property and is defined as the partner's share of the profits and surplus (including capital).

- His right to participate in the management of the partnership. This right entitles Nolan to an equal voice in the management and conduct of the partnership business.

Nolan's transfer of his partnership interest to Simon merely entitles Simon to receive Nolan's share of the profits and Nolan's interest in any property distributed by the partnership. Since Stein and Wolf have refused to admit

Simon as a partner, Simon will not be entitled to participate in the management of the partnership or to acquire Nolan's right to possess specific partnership property.

b. Lemon's first assertion that he is an agent coupled with an interest is incorrect. An agency coupled with an interest in the subject matter arises when the agent has an interest in the property that is the subject of the agency. The fact that Lemon entered into a two-year written agency agreement with the partnership that would pay Lemon a commission clearly will not establish an interest in the subject matter of the agency. The mere expectation of profits to be realized or proceeds to be derived from the sale of the partnership's products is not sufficient to create an agency coupled with an interest. As a result, the principal-agency relationship may be terminated at any time.

Lemon's second assertion that the principal-agency relationship may not be terminated without cause prior to the expiration of its term is incorrect. Where a principal-agency relationship is based upon a contract to engage the agent for a specific period of time, the principal may discharge the agent despite the fact such discharge is wrongful. Although the principal does not have the right to discharge the agent, he does have the power to do so. Thus, Lemon may be discharged without cause.

Lemon's third assertion that he is entitled to damages because of the termination of the agency relationship is correct. Where a principal wrongfully discharges its agent, the principal is liable for damages based on breach of contract. Under the facts, Lemon's discharge by the partnership without cause constitutes a breach of contract for which Lemon may recover damages.

5B (May 77)

The Minlow, Richard, and Jones partnership agreement is silent on whether the partners may assign or otherwise transfer all or part of their partnership interests to an outsider. Richard has assigned his partnership interest to Smith, a personal creditor, and as a result the other partners are furious. The have threatened to remove Richard as a partner, not admit Smith as a partner, and bar Smith from access to the firm's books and records.

Required: Answer the following, setting forth reasons for any conclusions stated.

Can Minlow and Jones successfully implement their threats? Discuss the rights of Richard and Smith and the effects of the assignment on the partnership.

Unless there is an express prohibition against the assignment of a partner's partnership interest stated in the partnership agreement, it is assignable. This rule applies whether all or part of the partnership interest is assigned. Probably the most common situation in which a partner assigns his partnership interest is in connection with collateralizing a personal loan. Therefore, barring an express prohibition or a clause requiring the consent of the other partners, Richard may assign his interest.

As a result of the above assignment, Richard remains a partner. Although Richard has assigned his partnership interest he still remains a partner and retains all of the rights, privileges, perquisites, duties, and liabilities he formerly had vis-à-vis the partnership and his fellow partners. The assignee (Smith) has only the right to Richard's share of the profits in the event of a default. He would succeed to Richard's rights, in whole or in part, upon the dissolution and winding up of the partnership or upon its bankruptcy. Smith does not, however, succeed to Richard's right to access to the partnership's books and records.

II. Operation and Termination of Partnership
A. General Partners and Third Parties
1. Nature of Partners' Liability

1 (R97)

Question Number 1 consists of 5 items. Select the **best** answer for each item. **Answer all items.** Your grade will be based on the total number of correct answers.

On March 1, 1995, Grove, Plane, and Range formed Techno Associates, a general partnership. They made capital contributions to the partnership as follows: Grove contributed $125,000; Plane contributed $250,000; and Range contributed $500,000. They prepared and executed a written partnership agreement that provided that profits would be shared equally, that the partnership would last for five years, and that the partnership use a calendar

Partnership

year for accounting purposes. There was no provision as to how losses would be allocated nor was there any provision regarding the continued use of the partnership name in the event of dissolution.

- On April 1, 1996, Range assigned Range's partnership interest to Blank. Blank notified Grove and Plane that Blank wanted to participate in the partnership business and vote on partnership issues.
- On June 10, 1996, a judgment was entered against Techno in a suit for breach of contract.
- On December 31, 1996, Grove resigned from the partnership.
- During the year-end closing, it was established that Techno had incurred an operating loss in 1996 as a result of the judgment. It was also established that Techno, being unable to pay its debts as they became due, was insolvent.
- On May 1, 1997, Techno filed for bankruptcy.

The Uniform Partnership Act applies.

Required:

For **Items 1 through 3**, select the correct answer from List I. An answer may be selected once, more than once, or not at all.

List I
A   No personal liability.
B   Liability limited to the amount contributed to the partnership.
C   Liability limited to the amount in the capital account.
D   Full personal liability for up to one-third of the total amount of the partnership debt.
E   Full personal liability for up to the total amount of the partnership debt.

1. What would be Range's liability for Techno's 1996 operating loss?
2. What would be Blank's liability for Techno's 1996 operating loss?
3. What would be Grove's liability for Techno's 1996 operating loss?

For **Item 4**, select the correct answer from List II.

List II
A   Blank and Plane.
B   Plane and Range.
C   Blank, Plane, and Grove.
D   Grove, Plane, and Range.
E   Blank, Grove, Plane, and Range.

4. As of January 1, 1997, who were the partners in Techno?

For **Item 5**, select the correct answer from List III.

List III
A   Dissolved.
B   Liquidated.
C   Terminated.

5. On May 1, 1997, what was the status of Techno?

17 (November 95)

Which of the following statements is (are) usually correct regarding general partners' liability?

    I.   All general partners are jointly and severally liable for partnership torts.

    II. All general partners are liable only for those partnership obligations they actually authorized.

  a.   I only.

  b.   II only.

  c.   Both I and II.

  d.   Neither I nor II.

21 (November 94)

Which of the following statements is correct concerning liability when a partner in a general partnership commits a tort while engaged in partnership business?

  a.   The partner committing the tort is the only party liable.

  b.   The partnership is the only party liable.

  c.   Each partner is jointly and severally liable.

  d.   Each partner is liable to pay an equal share of any judgment.

12 (November 90)

Eller, Fort, and Owens do business as Venture Associates, a general partnership. Trent Corp. brought a breach of contract suit against Venture and Eller individually. Trent won the suit and filed a judgment against both Venture and Eller. Trent will generally be able to collect the judgment from

  a.   Partnership assets only.

  b.   The personal assets of Eller, Fort, and Owens only.

  c.   Eller's personal assets only after partnership assets are exhausted.

  d.   Eller's personal assets only.

1 (November 85)

Which of the following is a characteristic of an unincorporated association?

  a.   It may only be used for not-for-profit purposes.

  b.   Members who actively manage the association may be held personally liable for contracts they enter into on behalf of the association.

  c.   Certificates representing ownership in the association must be distributed to the members.

  d.   Its duration must be for a limited period of time not to exceed 12 months.

Items 12 and 13 are based on the following information:

Darla, Jack, and Sam have formed a partnership with each agreeing to contribute $100,000. Jack and Sam each contributed $100,000 cash. Darla contributed $75,000 cash and agreed to pay an additional $25,000 two years later. After one year of operations the partnership is insolvent. The liabilities and fair market value of the assets of the partnership are as follows:

Assets

Cash	$ 40,000
Trade accounts receivablee	35,000
Receivable from Darla	25,000
Equipment	100,000
	$200,000

Liabilities

Trade accounts payable	$410,000

Both Jack and Sam are personally insolvent. Darla has a net worth of $750,000.

Partnership

12 (November 84)

If Darla is a general partner, what is her maximum potential liability?
a. $ 95,000.
b. $185,000.
c. $210,000.
d. $235,000.

13 (November 84)

If Darla is a limited partner, what is her maximum potential liability?
a. $0.
b. $ 25,000.
c. $210,000.
d. $235,000.

19 (November 81)

(Additional facts relating to this question are contained in 18 (November 81) on page 459.) If the partnership becomes insolvent and the partnership debts exceed assets by $15,000, which of the following is correct insofar as the rights of partnership creditors are concerned?
a. Daniels is a surety insofar as partnership debts in excess of $40,000 are concerned.
b. Those creditors who were aware of the oral agreement among the partners regarding partnership liability are bound by it.
c. Partnership creditors must first proceed against Daniels and have a judgment returned unsatisfied before proceeding against Beal or Wade.
d. Each partner may be held jointly liable to firm creditors.

15 (November 79)

Jon and Frank Clark are equal partners in the partnership of Clarke & Clarke. Both Jon Clarke and the partnership are bankrupt. Jon Clarke personally has $150,000 of liabilities and $100,000 of assets. The partnership's liabilities are $450,000 and its assets total $250,000. Frank Clarke, the other partner, is solvent with $800,000 of assets and $150,000 of liabilities. What are the rights of the various creditors of Jon Clarke, Frank Clarke, and the partnership?
a. Jon Clarke must divide his assets equally among his personal creditors and firm creditors.
b. Frank Clarke will be liable in full for the $200,000 partnership deficit.
c. Jon Clark's personal creditors can recover the $50,000 deficit owed to them from Frank Clarke.
d. Frank Clarke is liable only for $100,000, his equal share of the partnership deficit.

16 (November 77)

Wilcox & Wyatt, a general partnership, and Wyatt, individually, are insolvent in the bankruptcy sense. Wilcox has sufficient assets to satisfy all her personal creditors as well as the obligations of the firm. Under these circumstances
a. Wilcox will be liable to partnership creditors to the extent that their claims exceed partnership assets.
b. Wilcox has joint and several personal liability for the debts incurred by Wyatt to his personal creditors.
c. Firm creditors can not resort to Wilcox's personal assets beyond her proportionate profit and loss sharing ratio.
d. Wyatt can not escape personal liability to Wilcox for any additional amounts. Wilcox has to pay for and on behalf of firm debts by filing a voluntary petition in bankruptcy and obtaining a discharge.

2 (May 95)

In 1992, Anchor, Chain, and Hook created ACH Associates, a general partnership. The partners orally agreed that they would work full time for the partnership and would distribute profits based on their capital contributions. Anchor contributed $5,000; Chain $10,000; and Hook $15,000.

For the year ended December 31, 1993, ACH Associates had profits of $60,000 that were distributed to the partners. During 1994, ACH Associates was operating at a loss. In September 1994, the partnership dissolved.

In October 1994, Hook contracted in writing with Ace Automobile Co. to purchase a car for the partnership. Hook had previously purchased cars from Ace Automobile Co. for use by ACH Associates partners. ACH Associates did not honor the contract with Ace Automobile Co. and Ace Automobile Co. sued the partnership and the individual partners.

Required: Items 61 through 66 refer to the above facts. For each item, determine whether A or B is correct.

61.   A.   The ACH Associates oral partnership agreement was valid.
     B.   The ACH Associates oral partnership agreement was invalid because the partnership lasted for more than one year.

62.   A.   Anchor, Chain, and Hook jointly owning and conducting a business for profit establishes a partnership relationship.
     B.   Anchor, Chain, and Hook jointly owning income producing property establishes a partnership relationship.

63.   A.   Anchor's share of ACH Associates' 1993 profits was $20,000.
     B.   Hook's share of ACH Associates' 1993 profits was $30,000.

64.   A.   Anchor's capital account would be reduced by 1/3 of any 1994 losses.
     B.   Hook's capital account would be reduced by 1/2 of any 1994 losses.

65.   A.   Ace Automobile Co. would lose a suit brought against ACH Associates because Hook, as a general partner, has no authority to bind the partnership.
     B.   Ace Automobile Co. would win a suit brought against ACH Associates because Hook's authority continues during dissolution.

66.   A.   ACH Associates and Hook would be the only parties liable to pay any judgment recovered by Ace Automobile Co.
     B.   Anchor, Chain, and Hook would be jointly and severally liable to pay any judgment recovered by Ace Automobile Co.

4 (May 94)

Best Aviation Associates is a general partnership engaged in the business of buying, selling and servicing used airplanes. Best's original partners were Martin and Kent. They formed the partnership on January 1, 1992, under an oral partnership agreement which provided that the partners would share profits equally. There was no agreement as to how the partners would share losses. At the time the partnership was formed, Martin contributed $320,000 and Kent contributed $80,000.

On December 1, 1993, Best hired Baker to be a salesperson and to assist in purchasing used aircraft for Best's inventory. On December 15, 1993, Martin instructed Baker to negotiate the purchase of a used airplane from Jackson without disclosing that Baker was acting on Best's behalf. Martin thought that a better price could be negotiated by Baker if Jackson was not aware that the aircraft was being acquired for Best. Baker contracted with Jackson without disclosing that the airplane was being purchased for Best. The agreement provided that Jackson would deliver the airplane to Baker on January 2, 1994, at which time the purchase price was to be paid. On January 2, 1994, Jackson attempted to deliver the used airplane purchased for Best by Baker. Baker, acting on Martin's instructions, refused to accept delivery or pay the purchase price.

On December 20, 1993, Kent assigned Kent's partnership interest in Best to Green. On December 31, 1993, Kent advised Martin of the assignment to Green. On January 11, 1994, Green contacted Martin and demanded to inspect the partnership books and to participate in the management of partnership affairs, including voting on partnership decisions.

On January 13, 1994, it was determined that Best had incurred an operating loss of $160,000 in 1993. Martin demanded that Kent contribute $80,000 to the partnership to account for Kent's share of the loss. Kent refused to contribute.

Partnership

On January 28, 1994, Laco Supplies, Inc., a creditor of Best, sued Best and Martin for unpaid bills totalling $92,000. Best had not paid the bills because of a cash shortfall caused by the 1993 operating loss.

Jackson has taken the following position:

- Baker is responsible for any damages incurred by Jackson as a result of Best's refusal to accept delivery or pay the purchase price.

Martin has taken the following positions:

- Green is not entitled to inspect the partnership books or participate in the management of the partnership.
- Only the partnership is liable for the amounts owed to Laco, or, in the alternative, Martin's personal liability is limited to 50% of the total of the unpaid bills.

Kent has taken the following positions:

- Only Martin is liable for the 1993 operating loss because of the assignment to Green of Kent's partnership interest.
- Any personal liability of the partners for the 1993 operating loss should be allocated between them on the basis of their original capital contributions.

Required:

a. Determine whether Jackson's position is correct and state the reasons for your conclusions.
b. Determine whether Martin's positions are correct and state the reasons for your conclusions.
c. Determine whether Kent's positions are correct and state the reasons for your conclusions.

a. Jackson is correct. Baker, as an agent acting on behalf of an undisclosed principal (Best), is personally liable for any contracts entered into in that capacity.

b. Martin's first position that Green is not entitled to inspect the partnership books or participate in partnership management is correct. Green, as an assignee of Kent's partnership interest, is entitled to receive Kent's share of partnership profits only. Green is not entitled, as an assignee of Kent's partnership interest, to inspect the partnership records or to participate in the management of the partnership.

Martin's second position that only the partnership is responsible for the debt owed Laco is incorrect. Although the partnership is primarily liable for the unpaid bills, both Martin and Kent, as Best's partners, are personally liable for the unpaid amount of the debt. Laco will be entitled to seek recovery against Martin or Kent for the full amount owed.

c. Kent's first position that only Martin is liable for the 1993 operating loss because of the assignment of Kent's partnership interest to Green is incorrect. A partner's assignment of a partnership interest does not terminate that partner's liability for the partnership's losses and debts.

Kent's second position that any personal liability of the partners for the 1993 operating loss should be allocated on the basis of their original capital contributions is incorrect. The 1993 loss will be allocated in the same way that profits were to be allocated between the parties, that is, equally, because Martin and Kent had not agreed on the method for allocating losses between themselves.

2. Contract Liability--Partners' Actual and Apparent Authority

8 (R01)

In a general partnership, which of the following acts must be approved by all the partners?

a. Dissolution of the partnership.
b. Admission of a partner.
c. Authorization of a partnership capital expenditure.
d. Conveyance of real property owned by the partnership.

2 (R97)

Which of the following statements is correct regarding the apparent authority of a partner to bind the partnership in dealings with third parties? The apparent authority

a. Must be derived from the express powers and purposes contained in the partnership agreement.
b. Will be effectively limited by a formal resolution of the partners of which third parties are unaware.
c. May allow a partner to bind the partnership to representations made in connection with the sale of goods.
d. Would permit a partner to submit a claim against the partnership to arbitration.

11 (R96)

Under the Uniform Partnership Act, which of the following statements concerning the powers and duties of partners in a general partnership is (are) correct?

    I. Each partner is an agent of every other partner and acts as both a principal and an agent in any business transaction within the scope of the partnership agreement.
    II. Each partner is subject to joint liability on partnership debts and contracts.

a. I only.
b. II only.
c. Both I and II.
d. Neither I nor II.

12 (November 93)

The apparent authority of a partner to bind the partnership in dealing with third parties

a. Will be effectively limited by a formal resolution of the partners of which third parties are aware.
b. Will be effectively limited by a formal resolution of the partners of which third parties are unaware.
c. Would permit a partner to submit a claim against the partnership to arbitration.
d. Must be derived from the express powers and purposes contained in the partnership agreement.

14 (May 93)

Locke and Vorst were general partners in a kitchen equipment business. On behalf of the partnership, Locke contracted to purchase 15 stoves from Gage. Unknown to Gage, Locke was not authorized by the partnership agreement to make such contracts. Vorst refused to allow the partnership to accept delivery of the stoves and Gage sought to enforce the contract. Gage will

a. Lose, because Locke's action was not authorized by the partnership agreement.
b. Lose, because Locke was not an agent of the partnership.
c. Win, because Locke had express authority to bind the partnership.
d. Win, because Locke had apparent authority to bind the partnership.

15 (November 91)

In a general partnership, the authorization of all partners is required for an individual partner to bind the partnership in a business transaction to

a. Purchase inventory.
b. Hire employees.
c. Sell goodwill.
d. Sign advertising contracts.

13 (November 90)

Acorn and Bean were general partners in a farm machinery business. Acorn contracted, on behalf of the partnership, to purchase 10 tractors from Cobb Corp. Unknown to Cobb, Acorn was not authorized by the partnership agreement to make such contracts. Bean refused to allow the partnership to accept delivery of the tractors and Cobb sought to enforce the contract. Cobb will

a. Lose because Acorn's action was beyond the scope of Acorn's implied authority.
b. Prevail because Acorn had implied authority to bind the partnership.
c. Prevail because Acorn had apparent authority to bind the partnership.
d. Lose because Acorn's express authority was restricted, in writing, by the partnership agreement.

Partnership

15 (May 89)

Cass is a general partner in Omega Company general partnership. Which of the following unauthorized acts by Cass will bind Omega?
- a. Submitting a claim against Omega to arbitration.
- b. Confessing a judgment against Omega.
- c. Selling Omega's goodwill.
- d. Leasing office space for Omega.

16 (November 83)

A general partner of a mercantile partnership
- a. Can by virtue of his acts, impose tort liability upon the other partners.
- b. Has no implied authority if the partnership agreement is contained in a formal and detailed signed writing.
- c. Can have his apparent authority effectively negated by express limitations in the partnership agreement.
- d. Can not be sued individually for a tort he has committed in carrying on partnership business until the partnership has been sued and a judgment returned unsatisfied.

17 (November 83)

Which of the following is a correct statement concerning a partner's power to bind the partnership?
- a. A partner has no authority to bind the partnership after dissolution.
- b. A partner can not bind the partnership based upon apparent authority when the other party to the contract knows that the partner lacks actual authority.
- c. A partner has no authority in carrying on the regular business of the partnership to convey real property held in the partnership name.
- d. A partner, acting outside the scope of the partner's apparent authority, but with express authority to act, can not bind the partnership unless the third party knows of the express authority.

5 (May 83)

In determining the liability of a partnership for the acts of a partner purporting to act for the partnership without the authorization of fellow partners, which of the following actions will bind the partnership?
- a. The renewal of an existing supply contract which the other partners had decided to terminate and which they had specifically voted against.
- b. An assignment of their partnership assets in trust for the benefit of creditors.
- c. A written admission of liability in a lawsuit brought against the partnership.
- d. Signing the partnership name as a surety on a note for the purchase of that partner's summer home.

2 (May 82)

A question has arisen in determining the partnership's liability for actions taken for and on behalf of a partnership, but which were in fact without express or implied authority. Which of the following actions taken by a general partner will bind the partnership?
- a. Renewing an existing supply contract which had previously been negotiated, but which the partners had specifically voted not to renew.
- b. Submitting a claim against the partnership to binding arbitration.
- c. Taking an action which was known by the party with whom he dealt to be in contravention of a restriction on his authority.
- d. Signing the firm name as an accommodation comaker on a promissory note not in furtherance of firm business.

22 (November 81)

Which of the following may a partner not do without the express unanimous assent of the remaining partners?
- a. Assign his entire partnership interest to an outsider.
- b. Dismiss the accounting firm engaged to audit the partnership's accounts.
- c. Submit a long-standing dispute regarding a partnership claim against a recalcitrant customer to arbitration.
- d. Obtain a short-term loan from the partnership's banker to increase the partnership's working capital.

12 (November 77)

A general partner will <u>not</u> be personally liable for which of the following acts or transactions committed or engaged in by one of the other partners or by one of the partnership's employees?

    a.   The gross negligence of one of the partnership's employees while carrying out the partnership business.

    b.   A contract entered into by the majority of the other partners but to which the general partner objects.

    c.   A personal mortgage loan obtained by one of the other partners on his residence to which that partner, without authority, signed the partnership name on the note.

    d.   A contract entered into by the partnership in which the other partners agree among themselves to hold the general partner harmless.

2 (May 91)

Prime Cars Partnership is a general partnership engaged in the business of buying, selling, and servicing used cars. Prime's original partners were Baker and Mathews, who formed the partnership three years ago under a written partnership agreement, which provided that:

- Profits and losses would be allocated 60% to Baker and 40% to Mathews.
- Baker would be responsible for supervising Prime's salespeople and for purchasing used cars for inventory.
- Baker could not, without Mathews' consent, enter into a contract to purchase more than $15,000 worth of used cars at any one time.
- Mathews would be responsible for supervising Prime's service department.

On May 1, 1990, Baker entered into a contract on Prime's behalf with Jaco Auto Wholesalers, Inc. to purchase 11 used cars from Jaco for a total purchase price of $40,000. Baker's agreement with Jaco provided that the cars would be delivered to Prime on September 1. Baker did not advise Mathews of the terms and conditions of the contract with Jaco. Baker had regularly done business with Jaco on behalf of Prime in the past, and on several occasions had purchased $12,000 to $15,000 of used cars from Jaco. Jaco was unaware of the limitation on Baker's authority.

Baker also frequently purchased used cars for Prime from Top Auto Auctions, Ltd., a corporation owned by Baker's friend. Whenever Prime purchased cars from Top, Baker would personally receive up to 5% of the total purchase price from Top as an incentive to do more business with Top. Baker did not tell Mathews about these payments.

On August 1, 1990, Baker and Mathews agreed to admit KYA Auto Restorers, Inc. as a partner in Prime to start up and supervise a body shop facility. KYA made a $25,000 capital contribution and Prime's partnership agreement was amended to provide that Prime's profits and losses would be shared equally by the partners.

On September 1, 1990, Mathews learned of the Jaco contract and refused to accept delivery of the cars. Mathews advised Jaco that Baker had entered into the contract without Mathews' consent as required by their agreement. Jaco has demanded a payment of $10,000 from Prime for Jaco's lost profits under the contract.

Mathews has also learned about the incentive payments made to Baker by Top.

Mathews has taken the following positions:

- Prime is not liable to Jaco because Baker entered into the contract without Mathews' consent.
- In any event, Mathews is not liable to Jaco for more than 40% of Jaco's lost profits because of the original partnership provisions concerning the sharing of profits and losses.
- Baker is liable to Mathews for any liability incurred by Mathews under the Jaco contract.
- Baker is liable to Prime for accepting the incentive payments from Top.

KYA contends that none of its $25,000 capital contribution should be applied to the Jaco liability and that, in any event, KYA does not have any responsibility for the obligation.

Required:

    a.   State whether Mathews' positions are correct and give the reasons for your conclusions.

    b.   State whether KYA's contentions are correct and give the reasons for your conclusions.

a. 1.   Mathews' first position is incorrect. A partner is considered an agent of the partnership in carrying out its usual business. In this case, Baker lacked actual authority to bind Prime to the Jaco contract; however, Baker did have, from Jaco's perspective, apparent authority to do so because of the general character of Prime's business and, more important, because Baker had previously purchased cars from Jaco on Prime's behalf. Jaco was not bound by the limitation on Baker's authority unless Jaco was aware of it.

2.   Mathews' second position is also incorrect. As a general rule, a partner is liable for the debts of the partnership, and a third party is not bound by the profit and loss sharing agreements between partners because the third party is not a party to the partnership agreement. Therefore, Jaco can look to Prime's assets and Mathews' personal assets to satisfy the obligation.

3.   Mathews' third position is correct. A partner is liable to other partners for any liability associated with contracts entered into ostensibly on behalf of the partnership but outside the partner's actual authority. In this case, because Baker violated the agreement with Mathews concerning the $15,000 limitation on used car purchases, Baker will be liable to Mathews for any liability that Mathews may have to Jaco.

4.   Mathews' fourth position is also correct. A partner owes a fiduciary duty (that is, a duty of loyalty) to the partnership and every other partner. A partner may not benefit directly or indirectly at the expense of the partnership. A partner must account to the partnership for any benefits derived from the partnership's business without the consent or knowledge of the other partners. In this case, Baker was not entitled to accept and retain the incentive payments made by Top. Doing so violated Baker's fiduciary duty to Prime and Mathews. Baker must account to Prime for all the incentive payments received.

b.   KYA's contention that its $25,000 capital contribution cannot be used to satisfy Prime's obligation to Jaco is incorrect. A new partner is liable for partnership liabilities that arose prior to the new partner's admission, but the liability is limited to the partner's capital contribution and interest in partnership property. Therefore, KYA's liability is limited to its capital contribution and its interest as a partner in Prime's assets.

3.   Contract Liability--Partnership by Estoppel

22 (November 80)

One of your audit clients, Major Supply, Inc., is seeking a judgment against Danforth on the basis of a representation made by Coleman, in Danforth's presence, that they were in partnership together doing business as the D & C Trading Partnership. Major Supply received an order from Coleman on behalf of D & C and shipped $800 worth of goods to Coleman. Coleman has defaulted on payment of the bill and is insolvent. Danforth denies he is Coleman's partner and that he has any liability for the goods. Insofar as Danforth's liability is concerned, which of the following is correct?

a.   Danforth is not liable if he is not in fact Coleman's partner.

b.   Since Danforth did not make the statement about being Coleman's partner, he is not liable.

c.   If Major Supply gave credit in reliance upon the misrepresentation made by Coleman, Danforth is a partner by estoppel.

d.   Since the "partnership" is operating under a fictitious name (the D & C Partnership) a filing is required and Major Supply's failure to ascertain whether there was in fact such a partnership precludes it from recovering.

1 (November 74)

Charles Norman and Walter Rockwell did business as the Norman and Rockwell Company. This relationship was very informal and neither party considered himself to be a partner of the other. Their stationery was printed with the name of Norman and Rockwell Company. Donald Quirk loaned Rockwell $10,000 for and on behalf of the business. Norman was informed of this but stated to Rockwell, "That's your responsibility; I had nothing to do with it." Rockwell defaulted and Quirk seeks to hold both Norman and Rockwell liable on the debt. Under these circumstances

    a.   Quirk <u>cannot</u> recover against Norman because of Norman's statement to Rockwell, "That's your responsibility; I had nothing to do with it."

    b.   Norman and Rockwell are partners by estoppel.

    c.   Absent a signed partnership agreement, Quirk <u>cannot</u> recover against Norman.

    d.   The fact that neither party considered their relationship to be a partnership precludes recovery against Norman.

5A (May 78)

Millard rented office space in a building owned by Burbank. Millard was in the import-export business and was desperately in need of additional cash. Therefore, he decided to use Burbank's name in conjunction with his own as if they were partners in order to obtain credit from several lenders. He placed a nameplate on his door with the legend "Millard & Burbank" and had the same name listed on the directory in the lobby. In addition, he had business cards and stationery printed with the same title. Finally, he placed an announcement in the local paper that Burbank had joined him in the newly-created partnership of Millard & Burbank. Burbank's rental agent saw the partnership name on the door, saw the listing in the lobby directory, and informed Burbank of the situation. Burbank read the notice in the local paper. In response to this misrepresentation, Burbank told his rental agent to remove the listing in the lobby and to tell Millard to stop the nonsense. These instructions were not followed. In the interim, Millard was negotiating a $10,000 loan with Easy Credit Corporation, one of the other tenants in the office building. Dunlop, one of Easy's officers, had seen the "partnership" nameplate on Millard's door, the listing in the lobby, and the notice in the paper. Therefore, based exclusively upon the credit standing of Burbank, the loan was made. Millard defaulted on the loan and is hopelessly insolvent. Easy demanded payment from Burbank who refused to pay and denied any liability as Millard's partner.

Required: Answer the following, setting forth reasons for any conclusions stated.

    1.   Are Millard and Burbank partners in fact?

    2.   Under what legal theory could Easy prevail?

    1. No. The Uniform Partnership Act provides the criteria for determining whether a partnership exists between two or more parties. Although there are several other factors, such as sharing in losses, joint ownership of property, and exercise of management functions, the most important single factor is whether the parties share in profits. Under the facts of the case presented, there is a total lack of any of the factors necessary to establish the existence of an actual partnership between Millard and Burbank.

    2. Since Millard and Burbank are not in fact partners, the only legal theory upon which Easy might recover is that Burbank is a "partner by estoppel." This theory is contained in § 16(1) of the Uniform Partnership Act:

> When a person, by words spoken or written or by conduct, represents himself, or consents to another representing him to anyone, as a partner in an existing partnership or with one or more persons not actual partners, he is liable to any such person to whom such representation has been made, who has, on the faith of such representation, given credit to the actual or apparent partnership, and if he has made such representation or consented to its being made in a public manner he is liable to such person, whether the representation has or has not been made or communicated to such person so giving credit by or with the knowledge of the apparent partner making the representation or consenting to its being made.

The central issue is apparent from a reading of the facts and the statute. Did Burbank "consent"? There is a split of authority on the question of whether Burbank's inaction constituted consent. It has been held that persons are liable if they have been held out as partners and know that they are being so held out, unless they prevent it, even if to do so they have to take affirmative action. On the other hand, the partnership act takes the position that to be held as a partner, one must consent to the holding out and that consent is a matter of fact to be proven as any other fact. Since "consent" is to be proven as any other fact, it can be inferred from circumstantial evidence, that is, the conduct of one held out taken in light of all the surrounding circumstances. Based upon Burbank's failure to do virtually anything under the circumstances, it would not be surprising if Burbank were held to have consented.

B. Partnership Dissolution and Winding Up

20 (November 95)

Park and Graham entered into a written partnership agreement to operate a retail store. Their agreement was silent as to the duration of the partnership. Park wishes to dissolve the partnership. Which of the following statements is correct?

   a. Park may dissolve the partnership at any time.

   b. Unless Graham consents to a dissolution, Park must apply to a court and obtain a decree ordering the dissolution.

   c. Park may not dissolve the partnership unless Graham consents.

   d. Park may dissolve the partnership only after notice of the proposed dissolution is given to all partnership creditors.

24 (November 94)

The partners of College Assoc., a general partnership, decided to dissolve the partnership and agreed that none of the partners would continue to use the partnership name. Under the Uniform Partnership Act, which of the following events will occur on dissolution of the partnership?

	Each partner's existing liability would be discharged	Each partner's apparent authority would continue
a.	Yes	Yes
b.	Yes	No
c.	No	Yes
d.	No	No

Items 11 and 12 are based on the following:

Downs, Frey, and Vick formed the DFV general partnership to act as manufacturers' representatives. The partners agreed Downs would receive 40% of any partnership profits and Frey and Vick would each receive 30% of such profits. It was also agreed that the partnership would not terminate for five years. After the fourth year, the partners agreed to terminate the partnership. At that time, the partners' capital accounts were as follows: Downs, $20,000; Frey, $15,000; and Vick, $10,000. There also were undistributed losses of $30,000.

11 (May 93)

Which of the following statements about the form of the DFV partnership agreement is correct?

   a. It must be in writing because the partnership was to last for longer than one year.

   b. It must be in writing because partnership profits would not be equally divided.

   c. It could be oral because the partners had explicitly agreed to do business together.

   d. It could be oral because the partnership did not deal in real estate.

12 (May 93)

Vick's share of the undistributed losses will be

   a. $0

   b. $1,000

   c. $9,000

   d. $10,000

Items 12 and 13 are based on the following:

Dowd, Elgar, Frost, and Grant formed a general partnership. Their written partnership agreement provided that the profits would be divided so that Dowd would receive 40%; Elgar, 30%, Frost, 20%, and Grant, 10%. There was no provision for allocating losses. At the end of its first year, the partnership had losses of $200,000. Before allocating losses, the partners' capital account balances were: Dowd, $120,000; Elgar, $100,000; Frost, $75,000; and Grant, $11,000. Grant refuses to make any further contributions to the partnership. Ignore the effects of federal partnership tax law.

12 (May 92)

What would be Grant's share of the partnership losses?
- a. $ 9,000
- b. $20,000
- c. $39,000
- d. $50,000

13 (May 92)

After losses were allocated to the partners' capital accounts and all liabilities were paid, the partnership's sole asset was $106,000 in cash. How much would Elgar receive on dissolution of the partnership?
- a. $37,000
- b. $40,000
- c. $47,500
- d. $50,000

17 (November 91)

On dissolution of a general partnership, distributions will be made on account of:
- I. Partners' capital accounts
- II. Amounts owed partners with respect to profits
- III. Amounts owed partners for loans to the partnership

in the following order
- a. III, I, II.
- b. I, II, III.
- c. II, III, I.
- d. III, II, I.

7 (May 88)

Dill was properly admitted as a partner in the ABC Partnership after purchasing Ard's partnership interest. Ard immediately withdrew from the partnership. The partnership agreement states that the partnership will continue on the withdrawal or admission of a partner. Unless the partners otherwise agree,
- a. Dill's personal liability for partnership debts incurred before Dill was admitted will be limited to Dill's interest in partnership property.
- b. Ard will automatically be released from personal liability for partnership debts incurred before Dill's admission.
- c. Ard will be permitted to recover from the other partners the full amount that Ard has paid on account of partnership debts incurred before Dill's admission.
- d. Dill will be subjected to unlimited personal liability for partnership debts incurred before being admitted.

Items 55 and 56 are based on the following information:

Ted Fein, a partner in the ABC Partnership, wishes to withdraw from the partnership and sell his interest to Gold. All of the other partners in ABC have agreed to admit Gold as a partner and to hold Fein harmless for the past, present, and future liabilities of ABC. A provision in the original partnership agreement states that the partnership will continue upon the death or withdrawal of one or more of the partners.

Partnership

55 (May 86)

As a result of Fein's withdrawal and Gold's admission to the partnership, Gold
a. Is personally liable for partnership liabilities arising before and after his admission as a partner.
b. Has the right to participate in the management of ABC.
c. Acquired only the right to receive Fein's share of the profits of ABC.
d. Must contribute cash or property to ABC in order to be admitted with the same rights as the other partners.

56 (May 86)

The agreement to hold Fein harmless for all past, present, and future liabilities of ABC will
a. Prevent partnership creditors from holding Fein personally liable only as to those liabilities of ABC existing at the time of Fein's withdrawal.
b. Prevent partnership creditors from holding Fein personally liable for the past, present, and future liabilities of ABC.
c. Not affect the rights of partnership creditors to hold Fein personally liable for those liabilities of ABC existing at the time of his withdrawal.
d. Permit Fein to recover from the other partners only amounts he has paid in excess of his proportionate share.

8 (May 85)

Jane White acquired Zelmo's partnership interest in ZBA Partnership. All partners agreed to admit White as a partner. Unless otherwise agreed, White's admission to the partnership will automatically
a. Release Zelmo from personal liability on partnership debts arising prior to the sale of his partnership interest.
b. Release Zelmo from any liability on partnership debts arising subsequent to the sale of his partnership interest.
c. Subject White to unlimited personal liability on partnership debts arising prior to her admission as a partner.
d. Limit White's liability on partnership debts arising prior to her admission as a partner to her interest in partnership property.

10 (May 85)

Long, Pine, and Rice originally contributed $100,000, $60,000, and $20,000, respectively, to form the LPR Partnership. Profits and losses of LPR are to be distributed 1/2 to Long, 1/3 to Pine, and 1/6 to Rice. After operating for one year, LPR's total assets on its books are $244,000, total liabilities to outside creditors are $160,000 and total capital is $84,000. The partners made no withdrawals. LPR has decided to liquidate. If all of the partners are solvent and the assets of LPR are sold for $172,000
a. Rice will personally have to contribute an additional $8,000.
b. Pine will personally have to contribute an additional $4,000.
c. Long, Pine, and Rice will receive $6,000, $4,000, and $2,000, respectively, as a return of capital.
d. Long and Pine will receive $28,000 and $4,000, respectively, and Rice will have to contribute an additional $20,000.

21 (November 81)

Donaldson reached the mandatory retirement age as a partner of the Malcomb and Black partnership. Edwards was chosen by the remaining partners to succeed Donaldson. The remaining partners agreed to assume all of Donaldson's partnership liability and released Donaldson from such liability. Additionally, Edwards expressly assumed full liability for Donaldson's partnership liability incurred prior to retirement. Which of the following is correct?

    a.   Edwards' assumption of Donaldson's liability was a matter of form since as an incoming partner he was liable as a matter of law.

    b.   Firm creditors are <u>not</u> precluded from asserting rights against Donaldson for debts incurred while she was a partner, the agreements of Donaldson and the remaining partners notwithstanding.

    c.   Donaldson has <u>no</u> continuing potential liability to firm creditors as a result of the agreements contained in the retirement plan.

    d.   Since Donaldson obtained a release from firm debts she has <u>no</u> liability for debts incurred while she was a partner.

20 (November 80)

The partnership agreement of one of your clients provides that upon death or withdrawal, a partner shall be entitled to book value of his or her partnership interest as of the close of the year preceding such death or withdrawal and nothing more. It also provides that the partnership shall continue. Regarding this partnership provision, which of the following is a correct statement?

    a.   It is unconscionable on its face.

    b.   It has the legal effect of preventing a dissolution upon the death or withdrawal of a partner.

    c.   It effectively eliminates the legal necessity of a winding up of the partnership upon the death or withdrawal of a partner.

    d.   It is <u>not</u> binding upon the spouse of a deceased partner if the book value figure is less than the fair market value at the date of death.

21 (November 80)

Watson decided to withdraw from the Sterling Enterprises Partnership. Watson found Holmes as a prospective purchaser and his successor as a partner in the partnership. The other partners agreed to admit Holmes as a general partner in Watson's place. As a part of the agreement between Watson and Holmes, Holmes promised to satisfy any prior partnership debts for which Watson might be liable. What potential liability does Holmes or Watson have to firm creditors?

    a.   Holmes has no liability for the obligations arising before he entered the partnership.

    b.   Holmes is liable for the obligations arising before he entered the partnership property.

    c.   Holmes is fully liable to firm creditors for liabilities occurring before and after his entry into the partnership.

    d.   Watson's liability to firm creditors has been extinguished.

8 (November 77)

Concerning the order of distribution for satisfying firm debts upon the dissolution and winding up of a general partnership, which of the following is a correct statement?

    a.   General creditors, including partners who are also general creditors, are ranked first.

    b.   Profits are distributed only after all prior parties, including partners, have had their various claims satisfied.

    c.   Secured obligations are disregarded entirely insofar as the order of distribution.

    d.   Capital contributions by the partners are distributed before unsecured loans by the partners.

10 (November 76)

Grand, a general partner, retired, and the partnership held a testimonial dinner for him and invited ten of the partnership's largest customers to attend. A week later a notice was placed in various trade journals indicating that Grand had retired and was no longer associated with the partnership in any capacity. After the appropriate public notice of Grand's retirement, which of the following <u>best</u> describes his legal status?

    a.   The release of Grand by the remaining partners and the assumption of all past and future debts of the partnership by this via a "hold harmless" clause constitutes a novation.

    b.   Grand has the apparent authority to bind the partnership in contracts he makes with persons who have previously dealt with the partnership and are unaware of his retirement.

    c.   Grand has <u>no</u> liability to past creditors upon his retirement from the partnership if they all have been informed of his withdrawal and his release from liability, and if they do <u>not</u> object within 60 days.

    d.   Grand has the legal status of a limited partner for the three years it takes to pay him the balance of the purchase price of his partnership interest.

Partnership

19 (May 75)

Kimball, Thompson, and Darby formed a partnership. Kimball contributed $25,000 in capital and loaned the partnership $20,000; he performed no services. Thompson contributed $15,000 in capital and part-time services, and Darby contributed only his full-time services. The partnership agreement provided that all profits and losses would be shared equally. Three years after the formation of the partnership, the three partners agreed to dissolve and liquidate the partnership. Firm creditors, other than Kimball, have bona fide claims of $65,000. After all profits and losses have been recorded there are $176,000 of assets to be distributed to creditors and partners. When the assets are distributed

    a.   Darby received nothing since he did <u>not</u> contribute any property.

    b.   Thompson receives $45,333 in total.

    c.   Kimball receives $62,000 in total.

    d.   Each partner receives one-third of the remaining assets after all the firm creditors, including Kimball, have been paid.

4 (November 88)

On January 5, Stein, Rey, and Lusk entered into a written general partnership agreement by which they agreed to operate a stock brokerage firm. The agreement stated that the partnership would continue upon the death or withdrawal of a partner. The agreement also provided that no partner could reduce the firm's commission below 2% without the consent of all of the other partners. On March 10, Rey, without the consent of Stein and Lusk, agreed with King Corp. to reduce the commission to 1 1/2% on a large transaction by King. Rey believed this would entice King to become a regular customer of the firm. King was unaware of any of the terms of the partnership agreement.

On May 15, Stein entered into a contract conveying Stein's partnership interest to Park and withdrew from the partnership. That same day, all of the partners agreed to admit Park as a general partner. Notice of Stein's withdrawal and Park's admission as a partner was properly published in two newspapers. In addition, third parties who had conducted business with the partnership prior to May 15 received written notice of Stein's withdrawal.

Required:

    a.   In separate paragraphs, discuss whether:

        1.   The partnership could recover the 1/2% commission from King.

        2.   The partnership could recover the 1/2% commission from Rey.

    b.   In separate paragraphs, discuss:

        1.   Park's liability for partnership obligations arising both before and after being admitted to the partnership.

        2.   Stein's liability for partnership obligations arising both before and after withdrawing from the partnership.

a.1. The partnership cannot recover the 1/2% commission from King because Rey had the apparent authority to reduce the commission to 1 1/2%. The Uniform Partnership Act states that every partner is an agent of the partnership for the purpose of its business, and the act of every partner for apparently carrying on in the usual way the business of the partnership, binds the partnership, unless the partner so acting has in fact no authority to act for the partnership in the particular matter, and the person with whom the partner is dealing has knowledge of the fact that the partner has no such authority. In determining whether Rey had the apparent authority to bind the partnership, one must examine the circumstances and conduct of the parties and whether King reasonably believed such authority to exist. Because brokerage commissions are generally not uniform, it would be reasonable for King to believe that Rey had the authority to perform the transaction at 1 1/2% commission. Furthermore, King lacked knowledge of the restriction in the partnership agreement that prohibited Rey from reducing a commission below 2% without the other partners' consent. Therefore, King will not be liable for the 1/2% commission.

a.2. The partnership can recover the 1/2% commission from Rey because Rey violated the partnership agreement by reducing the commission to 1 1/2% without the partners' consent. Rey owes a duty to act in accordance with the partnership agreement.

b.1. Under the Uniform Partnership Act, a person admitted as a partner into an existing partnership is liable for all the obligations of the partnership arising before being admitted as thought that person had been a partner when such obligations were incurred, except that this liability may be satisfied only out of partnership property. Thus, Park will not be personally liable for the partnership obligations arising prior to being admitted as a partner but would be liable based upon the extent of partnership interests held. Park will be personally liable for partnership obligations arising after being admitted to the partnership.

b.2. Stein will continue to be personally liable for partnership obligations arising prior to withdrawing from the partnership, unless Stein obtains a release from the existing creditors. Stein will have no liability for partnership obligations arising after actual and constructive notice of withdrawing was properly given. However, Stein may be personally liable for partnership obligations arising after withdrawing but prior to notice being given. Actual notice of Stein's withdrawal was given by written notification to partnership creditors that had conducted business with the partnership prior to May 15. Constructive notice of Stein's withdrawal was given by proper publication in two newspapers to those third parties who had not dealt with the partnership, but may have known of its existence.

5A (May 84)

Hart was a partner in the Hart, Gray & Race partnership. He entered into a contract conveying to Paul his partnership interest. The contract, which was consented to by Gray and Race, provided that Paul would become a partner. All known past and present partnership creditors were given written notice of Hart's withdrawal. Within nine months, the partnership became insolvent. The parties are concerned about their liability for the partnership obligations.

Required: Answer the following, setting forth reasons for any conclusions stated.

1. What effect does Hart's withdrawal have upon his liability with respect to existing debts of the partnership and to debts incurred after his withdrawal?

2. Describe Paul's liability for partnership obligations entered into prior to and after his admission to the partnership.

1. An outgoing partner, such as Hart, continues to have potential liability for partnership debts incurred prior to his withdrawal unless he obtains a release from the existing creditors. Hart has no liability for partnership obligations incurred subsequent to his withdrawal provided that appropriate notice is given to the partnership creditors and other third parties. In this case, actual notice was given to the partnership's creditors in existence at the time of Hart's withdrawal, but constructive notice (i.e., notice by publication) was not given to those third parties who had not dealt with the partnership but may have known of its existence. By giving the appropriate type of notice, Hart would have effectively eliminated third parties' rights to rely on Hart's membership, i.e., his apparent authority in the partnership after his withdrawal. Because constructive notice was not given, creditors or other third parties who deal with the partnership after Hart's withdrawal may not be aware of his withdrawal and he may be liable to them. However, Hart will not be liable to existing creditors who, after receiving actual notice of Hart's withdrawal, dealt with the partnership.

2. The Uniform Partnership Act provides that a person admitted as a partner into an existing partnership is liable for all the obligations of the partnership arising before his admission as though he had been a partner when such obligations were incurred. However, this liability shall be satisfied only out of partnership property. Therefore, Paul has no personal liability as to partnership obligations existing at the time he became a partner but can be held personally responsible for those debts incurred after his admission as a partner.

6C (May 74)

Arms, Balk, and Clee formed a partnership to operate a retail drug and sundries store under the name Drug Shop. Arms and Balk each contributed $25,000, and Clee contributed the store building in which the business was to be carried on. Clee was credited with a contribution of $50,000, the fair value of the property. Clee retained title in his own name. It was agreed that Arms would have the sole right to purchase merchandise on credit. The partners agreed that Balk was to act as manager of the store. The firm hired Dell, a pharmacist, for a five-year term and agreed to pay him a fixed annual salary plus 10% of the profits.

Following are events which occurred subsequent to the formation of the partnership.

Partnership

- Fricke, a supplier of fixtures, indicated to the partners that he would sell fixtures to the firm on credit only if Dell, the pharmacist and a wealthy man, was a partner. Dell, who was present, said that he was a partner, and the sale on credit was made. Dell, however, later notified all others dealing with the firm that he was not a partner.

- Balk ordered merchandise, for resale by the store, on credit from a wholesaler in the firm name.

- Else was admitted as a partner with a 1/5 interest in the partnership and in profits and losses upon payment of $40,000.

- Clee, who was generally known to be a partner in the firm, (a) guaranteed in writing and in the firm name a note executed by a customer in purchasing a car for the customer's own use, and (b) conveyed in his own name the store building to Sweeney.

Required:

1. Prior to admitting Else as a partner, if the partnership agreement was silent about sharing profits and losses, how should the partners share a remaining profit of $30,000 after all payments to Dell? Explain.
2. If the partnership becomes insolvent, may creditors hold Dell liable as a partner? Explain.
3. Can the wholesaler hold the firm to the contract? Explain.
4. Will Else have any liability to creditors of the firm for obligations which arose prior to his admission? Explain.
5. Discuss the liability of the firm on the customer's note in the event of default.
6. Discuss whether Sweeney would obtain good title to the building.

1. The three partners would share the profit equally in the absence of an agreement to the contrary despite the fact that capital contributions were unequal.

2. As a partner by estoppel, Dell would be held liable to Fricke on the obligation because Dell actively held himself out as a partner. He cannot be so held by others who knew that he was not a partner. In spite of the fact that he shared in profits and absent a finding of partnership by estoppel, Dell would not incur partnership liability by virtue of his sharing in profits. While a sharing in profits is evidence of partnership, the Uniform Partnership Act provides that no such inference of partnership shall be drawn if such profits were received in payment as wages of an employee.

3. The wholesaler can hold the firm to the contract unless the wholesaler knew of the restriction on Balk's authority. Balk was acting within his apparent authority as an agent of the partnership in carrying on a normal activity. If the wholesaler knew of the restriction, the firm would not be bound.

4. Under the Uniform Partnership Act, a person admitted as a partner into an existing partnership is liable for all the obligations of the partnership arising before his admission as though he had been a partner when such obligations were incurred, but this liability may only be satisfied out of partnership property, and his liability is limited, therefore, to his share of the partnership property.

5. On the facts given, it seems quite unlikely that the partnership would be liable if the maker of the note defaults. While every partner is an agent of the partnership for the purpose of its business, a partner's act that is not for carrying on the partnership's business in the usual way does not bind the partnership unless authorized by the other partners. Of course, if they had authorized the action, or ratified it, the partnership would be bound. The fact that Clee may have incurred personal liability does not create a partnership obligation.

6. Whether Sweeney obtained good title depends on the circumstances. Where the title to real property of a partnership is in the name of one of the partners, a purchaser for value and in good faith, receiving a conveyance from the partner with record title, obtains the interest of the partnership, provided he had no knowledge of the partnership interest.

III. Limited Partnership
A. Introduction; Formation of Limited Partnership

1 (November 92)

Which of the following statements is correct concerning the similarities between a limited partnership and a corporation?

a. Each is created under a statute and must file a copy of its certificate with the proper state authorities.
b. All corporate stockholders and all partners in a limited partnership have limited liability.
c. Both are recognized for federal income tax purposes as taxable entities.
d. Both are allowed statutorily to have perpetual existence.

11 (May 92)

Which of the following statements is correct with respect to a limited partnership?

a. A limited partner may <u>not</u> be an unsecured creditor of the limited partnership.

b. A general partner may <u>not</u> also be a limited partner at the same time.

c. A general partner may be a secured creditor of the limited partnership.

d. A limited partnership can be formed with limited liability for all partners.

4 (May 91)

Which of the following statements is correct with respect to the differences and similarities between a corporation and a limited partnership?

a. Stockholders may be entitled to vote on corporate matters but limited partners are prohibited from voting on any partnership matters.

b. Stock of a corporation may be subject to the registration requirements of the federal securities laws but limited partnership interests are automatically exempt from those requirements.

c. Directors owe fiduciary duties to the corporation and limited partners owe such duties to the partnership.

d. A corporation and a limited partnership may be created only under a state statute and each must file a copy of its organizational document with the proper governmental body.

7 (May 85)

Which of the following statements is correct regarding a limited partnership?

a. The general partner must make a capital contribution.

b. It can only be created pursuant to a statute providing for the formation of limited partnerships.

c. It can be created with limited liability for all partners.

d. At least one general partner must also be a limited partner.

11 (May 85)

Which of the following is a correct statement concerning the similarities of a limited partnership and a corporation?

a. Both are recognized for federal income tax purposes as taxable entities.

b. Both can only be created pursuant to a statute and each must file a copy of its certificate with the proper state authorities.

c. Both provide insulation from personal liability for all of the owners of the business.

d. Shareholders and limited partners may both participate in the management of the business and retain limited liability.

11 (November 84)

Unless otherwise provided in the limited partnership agreement, which of the following statements is correct?

a. A general partner's capital contribution may <u>not</u> consist of services rendered to the partnership.

b. Upon the death of a limited partner the partnership will be dissolved.

c. A person may own a limited partnership interest in the same partnership in which he is a general partner.

d. Upon the assignment of a limited partner's interest, the assignee will become a substituted limited partner if the consent of two-thirds of all partners is obtained.

14 (November 79)

Dowling is a promoter and has decided to use a limited partnership for conducting a securities investment venture. Which of the following is <u>unnecessary</u> in order to validly create such a limited partnership?

a. All limited partners' capital contributions must be made in cash.

b. There must be a state statute which permits the creation of such a limited partnership.

c. A limited partnership certificate must be signed and sworn to by the participants and filed in the proper office in the state.

d. There must be one or more general partners and one or more limited partners.

Partnership

7 (November 77)

Marshall formed a limited partnership for the purpose of engaging in the export-import business. Marshall obtained additional working capital from Franklin and Lee by selling them each a limited partnership interest. Under these circumstances the limited partnership

a. Will generally be treated as a taxable entity for federal income tax purposes.
b. Will lose its status as a limited partnership if there is ever more than one general partner.
c. Can limit the liability of all partners.
d. Can only be availed of if the state in which it is created has adopted the Uniform Limited Partnership Act or a similar statute.

B. Relationship Among Partners

4 (November 88)

In general, which of the following statements is correct with respect to a limited partnership?

a. A limited partner has the right to obtain from the general partner(s) financial information and tax returns of the limited partnership.
b. A limited partnership can be formed with limited liability for all partners.
c. A limited partner may not also be a general partner at the same time.
d. A limited partner may hire employees on behalf of the partnership.

7 (May 87)

White, Grey, and Fox formed a limited partnership. White is the general partner and Grey and Fox are the limited partners. Each agreed to contribute $200,000. Grey and Fox each contributed $200,000 in cash while White contributed $150,000 in cash and $50,000 worth of services already rendered. After two years, the partnership is insolvent. The fair market value of the assets of the partnership is $150,000 and the liabilities total $275,000. The partners have made no withdrawals. If Fox is insolvent and White and Grey each has a net worth in excess of $300,000, what is White's maximum potential liability in the event of a dissolution of the partnership?

a. $ 62,500.
b. $112,500.
c. $125,000.
d. $175,000.

4 (May 82)

Cavendish is a limited partner of Custer Venture Capital. He is extremely dissatisfied with the performance of the general partners in making investments and managing the portfolio. He is contemplating taking whatever legal action may be appropriate against the general partners. Which of the following rights would Cavendish not be entitled to assert as a limited partner?

a. To have a formal accounting of partnership affairs whenever the circumstances render it just and reasonable.
b. To have the same rights as a general partner to a dissolution and winding up of the partnership.
c. To have reasonable access to the partnership books and to inspect and copy them.
d. To have himself elected as a general partner by a majority vote of the limited partners in number and amount.

20 (May 75)

Bonanza Real Estate Ventures is a limited partnership created pursuant to the law of a state which has adopted the Uniform Limited Partnership Act. It has three general partners and 1,100 limited partners living in various states. The limited partnership interests were offered to the general public at $5,000 per partnership interest. Johnson purchased a limited-partnership interest in the Bonanza Real Estate Ventures. As such, he

    a. <u>Cannot</u> assign his limited-partnership interest to another person without the consent of the general partners.

    b. Is entitled to interest on his capital contribution.

    c. Is a fiduciary vis-à-vis the limited partnership and its partners.

    d. Must include his share of the limited-partnership taxable profits in his taxable income even if he does <u>not</u> withdraw anything.

C. Limited Partners and Third Parties

5 (November 89)

Which of the following statements regarding a limited partner is(are) generally correct?

	The limited partner is subject to personal liability for partnership debts	The limited partner has the right to take part in the control of the partnership
a.	Yes	Yes
b.	Yes	No
c.	No	Yes
d.	No	No

19 (November 87)

In general, which of the following statements is correct with respect to a limited partnership?

    a. A limited partner will be personally liable for partnership debts incurred in the ordinary course of the partnership's business.

    b. A limited partner is unable to participate in the management of the partnership in the same manner as general partners and still retain limited liability.

    c. A limited partner's death or incompetency will cause the partnership to dissolve.

    d. A limited partner is an agent of the partnership and has the authority to bind the partnership to contracts.

18 (November 83)

Vast Ventures is a limited partnership. The partnership agreement does not contain provisions dealing with the assignment of a partnership interest. The rights of the general and limited partners regarding the assignment of their partnership interests are

    a. Determined according to the common law of partnerships as articulated by the courts.

    b. Basically the same with respect to both types of partners.

    c. Basically the same with the exception that the limited partner must be given ten days notice prior to the assignment.

    d. Different in that the assignee of the general partnership interest does not become a substituted partner, whereas the assignee of a limited partnership interest automatically becomes a substituted limited partner.

3 (May 82)

Stanley is a well known retired movie personality who purchased a limited partnership interest in Terrific Movie Productions upon its initial syndication. Terrific has three general partners, who also purchased limited partnership interests, and 1,000 additional limited partners located throughout the United States. Which of the following is correct?

a. If Stanley permits his name to be used in connection with the business and is held out as a participant in the management of the venture, he will be liable as a general partner.
b. The sale of these limited partnership interests would <u>not</u> be subject to SEC registration.
c. This limited partnership may be created with the same informality as a general partner.
d. The general partners are prohibited from also owning limited partnership interests.

24 (November 80)

Ms. Walls is a limited partner of the Amalgamated Limited Partnership. She is insolvent and her debts exceed her assets by $28,000. Goldsmith, one of Walls' largest creditors, is resorting to legal process to obtain the payment of Walls' debt to him. Goldsmith has obtained a charging order against Walls' limited partnership interest for the unsatisfied amount of the debt. As a result of Goldsmith's action, which of the following will happen?

a. The partnership will be dissolved.
b. Walls' partnership interest must be redeemed with partnership property.
c. Goldsmith automatically becomes a substituted limited partner.
d. Goldsmith becomes in effect an assignee of Walls' partnership interest.

11 (November 76)

A limited partner
a. May <u>not</u> withdraw his capital contribution unless there is sufficient limited-partnership property to pay all general creditors.
b. Must <u>not</u> own limited-partnership interests in other competing limited partnerships.
c. Is automatically an agent for the partnership with apparent authority to bind the limited partnership in contract.
d. Has <u>no</u> liability to creditors even if he takes part in the control of the business as long as he is held out as being a limited partner.

4 (May 90)

Smith, Edwards, and Weil formed Sterling Properties Limited Partnership to engage in the business of buying, selling and managing real estate. Smith and Edwards were general partners. Weil was a limited partner entitled to 50% of all profits.

Within a few months of Sterling's formation, it became apparent to Weil that Smith and Edwards' inexperience was likely to result in financial disaster for the partnership. Therefore, Weil became more involved in day-to-day management decisions. Weil met with prospective buyers and sellers of properties; assisted in negotiating partnership loans with its various lenders; and took an active role in dealing with personnel problems. Things continued to deteriorate for Sterling, and the partners began blaming each other for the partnership's problems.

Finally, Smith could no longer deal with the situation, and withdrew from the partnership. Edwards reminded Smith that the Sterling partnership agreement specifically prohibited withdrawal by a general partner without the consent of all the other partners. Smith advised Edwards and Weil that she would take no part in any further partnership undertaking and would not be responsible for partnership debts incurred after this withdrawal.

With Sterling on the verge of collapse, the following situations have occurred:

- Weil demanded the right to inspect and copy the partnership's books and records and Edwards refused to allow Weil to do so, claiming that Weil's status as a limited partner precludes that right.
- Anchor Bank, which made a loan to the partnership prior to Smith's withdrawal, is suing Sterling and each partner individually, including Smith, because the loan is in default. Weil denied any liability based on this limited partner status. Smith denies liability based on her withdrawal.
- Edwards sued Smith for withdrawing from the partnership and is uncertain about the effect of her withdrawal on the partnership.
- Weil wants to assign his partnership interest to Fred Alberts, who wants to become a substitute limited partner. Weil is uncertain about his right to assign this interest to Alberts and, further, the right of Alberts to become a substitute limited partner. Edwards contends that Edwards' consent is necessary for the assignment or the substitution of Alberts as a limited partner and that without this consent any such assignment would cause a dissolution of the partnership. The Sterling partnership agreement and certificate are silent in this regard.

Required: Answer the following questions, setting forth reasons for the conclusions stated.

    a.   Is Weil entitled to inspect and copy the books and records of the partnership?

    b.   Are Weil and/or Smith liable to Anchor Bank?

    c.   Will Edwards prevail in the lawsuit against Smith for withdrawing from the partnership?

    d.   What is the legal implication to the partnership of Smith's withdrawal?

    e.   Can Weil assign his partnership interest to Alberts?

    f.   Can Edwards prevent the assignment to Alberts or the substitution of Alberts as a limited partner?

    g.   What rights does Alberts have as assignee of Weil's partnership interest?

    h.   What effect does an assignment have on the partnership?

    a. Weil is entitled to inspect and copy Sterling's books and records. A limited partner such as Weil has the right to have the partnership books kept at the principal place of business of the partnership and to inspect and copy them at all times.

    b. Generally, limited partners are not liable to partnership creditors except to the extent of their capital contribution. In Weil's case, however, he will probably be liable to Anchor Bank in the same manner as Sterling's general partners because he has taken part in the control of the business of the partnership and, therefore, has lost his limited liability. Smith, as a general partner, would also be personally liable to Anchor because liability was incurred prior to withdrawal.

    c. Edwards will likely prevail in his lawsuit against Smith for withdrawing because the partnership agreement specifically prohibits a withdrawal by a general partner without the consent of the other partners. Therefore, Smith has breached the partnership agreement and will be liable to Edwards for any damages resulting from Smith's withdrawal.

    d. The withdrawal (retirement) of a general partner dissolves the partnership unless the remaining general partners continue the business of the partnership under a right to do so provided in the limited partnership certificate, or unless all partners consent. Therefore, it is possible that Smith's withdrawal will result in Sterling's dissolution.

    e. Weil is free to assign his limited partnership interests to Alberts in the absence of any prohibitions in the Sterling partnership agreement or certificate.

    f. Alberts, however, cannot be a substitute limited partner without the consent of the remaining general partner, Edwards.

    g. Therefore, Alberts, as an assignee of Weil's limited partnership interest, may not exercise any rights of a partner. Alberts is entitled only to any distributions from Sterling to which Weil would have been entitled.

    h. Finally, the assignment by Weil of his partnership interest does not cause a dissolution of the partnership.

3 (May 88)

    Walsh is evaluating two different investment opportunities. One requires an investment of $100,000 to become a limited partner in a limited partnership that owns a shopping center. The other requires an investment of $100,000 to purchase 3% of the voting common stock of a corporation engaged in manufacturing. Walsh is uncertain about the advantages and disadvantages of being a limited partner versus being a shareholder. The issues of most concern to Walsh are:

- The right to transfer a limited partnership interest versus shares of stock.
- The liability as a limited partner versus that of a shareholder for debts incurred by a limited partnership or a corporation.
- The right of a limited partner versus that of a shareholder to participate in daily management.
- The right of a limited partner to receive partnership profits versus the right of a shareholder to receive dividends from a corporation.

Required: Briefly identify and discuss the basic differences and similarities in the formation of a limited partnership and a corporation. Discuss in separate paragraphs the issues raised by Walsh. (Ignore tax and securities laws.)

Partnership

A limited partnership is formed by two or more persons under a state's limited partnership statute, having as members one or more general partners and one or more limited partners. Two or more persons desiring to form a limited partnership must execute a certificate of limited partnership that must be filed in the office of the secretary of state, or other appropriate state or local office. A corporation may be formed only under a state incorporation statute that requires that one or more incorporators sign articles of incorporation which must be filed with the secretary of state.

Unless otherwise provided in the partnership agreement, or other agreements among the partners, a limited partnership interest is assignable in whole or in part. Similarly, in the absence of a restriction in the corporation's organizational documents or other agreements among the shareholders, shares of stock are freely transferable.

A limited partner's liability for partnership debts is generally limited to the partner's investment (capital contribution) in the partnership if the interest is fully paid and non-assessable and the partner does not participate in the daily management of the business. Likewise, a shareholder's liability for a corporation's debts is generally limited to the shareholder's investment (capital contribution) in the corporation.

A limited partner cannot participate in the daily operations of the partnership's business without losing limited liability. A shareholder who is not also an officer or a director cannot participate in the daily operations of the corporation's business. However, a shareholder owning voting stock has the right to vote for a board of directors, which will manage the business affairs of the corporation. The board of directors elects officers to run the daily operations of the corporation.

A limited partner is entitled to receive a share of the partnership's profits in the manner provided in the partnership agreement. On the other hand, whether a shareholder receives dividends is generally within the discretion of the board of directors.

2 (November 86)

Edna Slavin intends to enter into a limited partnership with three of her business associates. Slavin wishes to know the advantages and disadvantages of being a general partner as opposed to a limited partner in a limited partnership. The issues of most concern to Slavin are:

- Her right as a general or limited partner to participate in the daily management of the partnership.
- Her liability as a general partner or limited partner for debts incurred on behalf of or by the partnership.
- Her right as a general or limited partner to assign her partnership interest and substitute a third party as a partner.
- The effect of a clause in the certificate of limited partnership which would permit the partnership to continue after the death of one of the general or limited partners.

Required: Answer the following, setting forth reasons for any conclusions stated.

What are the essential differences in the formation of a general partnership and a limited partnership? Discuss in separate paragraphs the issues raised by Slavin.

Typically, a general partnership is formed by an agreement between or among two or more persons, whether the agreement is written, oral, or implied. No filing of a partnership agreement is necessary in order to legally create the general partnership. In contrast, a limited partnership can only be formed where a state statute permits such formation. In addition, a duly signed certificate of limited partnership must be completed and filed with the appropriate state or local agency. A limited partnership, like a general partnership, is formed by two or more persons. However, unlike a general partnership, the limited partnership must have as members one or more general partners and one or more limited partners.

As a limited partner Slavin would not be able to participate in the daily management of the partnership's business if she wishes to limit her liability to her investment in the partnership. Thus, if Slavin intends to be involved in the daily operations of the partnership and to participate in the control of the partnership, she should consider becoming a general partner since general partners have rights in the management and conduct of the partnership's business.

In her capacity as a limited partner, Slavin's liability would be limited to her investment in the partnership for partnership debts if her interest is fully paid and nonassessable. However, if Slavin were to become a general partner, she would have unlimited liability which would allow partnership creditors to satisfy the debts of the partnership out of Slavin's personal assets.

488

Unless otherwise provided in the partnership agreement, Slavin has the right to assign her limited partnership interest and may also substitute the third party as a limited partner if all the members (except the assignor) consent thereto. Similarly, as a general partner, Slavin may assign her interest in the partnership and the third party may become a general partner if all of the partners consent.

A clause providing for the partnership to continue after the death of a general partner is valid and the partnership will continue. The clause has relatively little if any effect where a limited partner dies since the limited partnership continues upon the death of one of the limited partners, whether or not the clause is contained in the certificate.

5B (May 81)

Lawler is a retired film producer. She had a reputation in the film industry for aggressiveness and shrewdness; she was also considered somewhat overbearing. Cyclone Artistic Film Products, a growing independent producer, obtained the film rights to "Claws," a recent best seller. Cyclone has decided to syndicate the production of "Claws." Therefore, it created a limited partnership, Claws Production, with Harper, Von Hinden and Graham, the three ranking executives of Cyclone, serving as general partners. The three general partners each contributed $50,000 to the partnership capital. One hundred limited partnership interests were offered to the public at $50,000 each. Lawler was offered the opportunity to invest in the venture. Intrigued by the book and restless in her retirement, she decided to purchase 10 limited partnership interests for $500,000. She was the largest purchaser of the limited partnership interests of Claws Productions. All went well initially for the venture, but midway through production, some major problems arose. Lawler, having nothing else to do and having invested a considerable amount of money in the venture, began to take an increasingly active interest in the film's production.

She began to appear frequently on the set and made numerous suggestions on handling the various problems that were encountered. When the production still seemed to be proceeding with difficulty, Lawler volunteered her services to the general partners who as a result of her reputation and financial commitment to "Claws" decided to invite her to join them in their executive deliberations. This she did and her personality insured an active participation.

"Claws" turned out to be a box office disaster and its production costs were considered to be somewhat extraordinary even by Hollywood standards. The limited partnership is bankrupt and the creditors have sued Claws Productions, Harper, Von Hinden, Graham, and Lawler.

Required: Answer the following, setting forth reasons for any conclusions stated.

What are the legal implications of **each** of the above parties as a result of the above facts?

The limited partnership, the general partners, and Lawler are all jointly liable for the debts of Claws Productions. Claws Productions limited partnership is liable and must satisfy the judgment to the extent it has assets. Harper, Von Hinden, and Graham are liable for the unpaid debts of the limited partnership. An interesting problem posed by the fact situation is Lawler's liability. The general rule, in fact the very basis for the existence of the limited partnership, is that the limited partner is not liable beyond its capital contribution. However, a notable exception contained in § 7 of the Uniform Limited Partnership Act applies to the facts presented here:

> A limited partner shall not become liable as a general partner unless, in addition to the exercise of his rights and powers as a limited partner, he takes part in the control of the business.

The statutory language covers the facts stated. Lawler assumed a managerial role vis-à-vis the partnership and in the process became liable as a general partner.

Partnership

6B (May 76)

Fletcher, Dry, Wilbert, and Cox selected the limited partnership as the form of business entity most suitable for their purpose of investing in mineral leases. Fletcher, the general partner, contributed $50,000 in capital. Dry, Wilbert, and Cox each contributed $100,000 capital and are limited partners. Necessary limited-partnership papers were duly prepared and filed clearly indicating that Fletcher was the sole general partner and that the others were limited partners.

Fletcher managed the partnership during the first two years. During the third year, Dry and Wilbert overruled Fletcher as to the type of investments to be made, the extent of the commitments, and the major terms contained in the leases. They also exercised the power to draw checks on the firm's bank account. Finally, Fletcher withdrew and was replaced by Martin, a new and more receptive general partner. Cox did not join his fellow partners in these activities. However, his name was used without qualification and with his general knowledge and consent on the partnership stationery as part of the firm's name.

Required: Discuss the legal liability of Martin, Dry, Wilbert, and Cox, as individuals, to creditors of the partnership.

Martin, Dry, Wilbert, and Cox are all liable as general partners. Martin is an incoming general partner, and, as such, he would have the same liability as a general partner in an ordinary partnership. In effect, the law states that he has unlimited joint and several liability. However, as to obligations incurred prior to his entry into the partnership, his liability cannot exceed his capital contribution.

Dry and Wilbert are liable as general partners because, in addition to the exercise of their rights and powers as limited partners, they also took part in the control of the business.

Cox's liability as a general partner rests upon the doctrine of estoppel or a specific provision under the Uniform Limited Partnership Act. The Act provides that a limited partner whose name appears in the partnership name is liable as a general partner to partnership creditors who extend credit to the partnership without actual knowledge that he is not a general partner. Hence, unless a creditor knows of Cox's true status, Cox has unlimited liability to that creditor.

PART XIII – CORPORATIONS*

TABLE OF CONTENTS

*Answers consistent with Revised Model Business Corporation Act.

CHAPTER X

CORPORATIONS

I. Introduction to Corporations
A. The Law of Corporations

22 (November 95)
Which of the following statements best describes an advantage of the corporate form of doing business?
a. Day to day management is strictly the responsibility of the directors.
b. Ownership is contractually restricted and is <u>not</u> transferable.
c. The operation of the business may continue indefinitely.
d. The business is free from state regulation.

22 (November 78)
Hobson, Jones, Carter, and Wolff are all medical doctors who have worked together for several years. They decided to form a corporation and their attorney created a typical professional corporation for them. Which of the following is correct?
a. Such a corporation will <u>not</u> be recognized for federal tax purposes if one of its goals is to save taxes.
b. The state in which they incorporated must have enacted professional corporation statutes permitting them to do so.
c. Upon incorporation, the doctor-shareholder is insulated from personal liability beyond his capital contribution.
d. The majority of states prohibit the creation of professional corporations by doctors.

B. Incorporation and Admission

9 (R01)
Case Corp. is incorporated in State A. Under the Revised Model Business Corporation Act, which of the following activities engaged in by Case requires that Case obtain a certificate of authority to do business in State B?
a. Maintaining bank accounts in State B.
b. Collecting corporate debts in State B.
c. Hiring employees who are residents of State B.
d. Maintaining an office in State B to conduct intrastate business.

3 (R98)
Under the Revised Model Business Corporation Act, which of the following statements regarding a corporation's bylaws is (are) correct?
    I. A corporation's initial bylaws shall be adopted by either the incorporators or the board of directors.
    II. A corporation's bylaws are contained in the articles of incorporation.
a. I only.
b. II only.
c. Both I and II.
d. Neither I nor II.

Corporations

21 (November 95)

Which of the following facts is (are) generally included in a corporation's articles of incorporation?

	Name of registered agent	Number of authorized shares
a.	Yes	Yes
b.	Yes	No
c.	No	Yes
d.	No	No

11 (May 94)

Under the Revised Model Business Corporation Act, which of the following must be contained in a corporation's articles of incorporation?
   a. Quorum voting requirements.
   b. Names of stockholders.
   c. Provisions for issuance of par and non-par shares.
   d. The number of shares the corporation is authorized to issue.

19 (November 93)

Which of the following provisions must a for-profit corporation include in its Articles of Incorporation to obtain a corporate charter?
   I. Provision for the issuance of voting stock.
   II. Name of the corporation.
   a. I only.
   b. II only.
   c. Both I and II.
   d. Neither I nor II.

16 (May 92)

Generally, a corporation's articles of incorporation must include all of the following except the
   a. Name of the corporation's registered agent.
   b. Name of each incorporator.
   c. Number of authorized shares.
   d. Quorum requirements.

6 (May 90)

In general, which of the following must be contained in articles of incorporation?
   a. Names of the initial officers and their terms of office.
   b. Classes of stock authorized for issuance.
   c. Names of states in which the corporation will be doing business.
   d. Name of the state in which the corporation will maintain its principal place of business.

10 (May 84)

Generally, articles of incorporation must contain all of the following except the
   a. Names of the incorporators.
   b. Name of the corporation.
   c. Number of shares authorized.
   d. Names of initial officers and their terms of office.

12 (May 80)

Golden Enterprises, Inc. entered into a contract with Hidalgo Corporation for the sale of its mineral holdings. The transaction proved to be <u>ultra vires</u>. Which of the following parties, for the reasons stated, may properly assert the <u>ultra vires</u> doctrine?

    a.   Golden Enterprises to avoid performance.
    b.   A shareholder of Golden Enterprises to enjoin the sale.
    c.   Hidalgo Corporation to avoid performance.
    d.   Golden Enterprises to rescind the consummated sale.

14 (May 80)

Destiny Manufacturing, Inc. is incorporated under the laws of Nevada. Its principal place of business is in California and it has permanent sales offices in several other states. Under the circumstances, which of the following is correct?

    a.   California may validly demand that Destiny incorporate under the laws of the state of California.
    b.   Destiny must obtain a certificate of authority to transact business in California and the other states in which it does business.
    c.   Destiny is a foreign corporation in California, but <u>not</u> in the other states.
    d.   California may prevent Destiny from operating as a corporation if the laws of California differ regarding organization and conduct of the corporation's internal affairs.

9 (November 78)

Dexter, Inc. was incorporated in its home state. It expanded substantially and now does 20% of its business in a neighboring state in which it maintains a permanent facility. It has <u>not</u> filed any papers in the neighboring state.

Which of the following statements is correct?

    a.   Since Dexter is a duly-incorporated domestic corporation in its own state, it can transact business anywhere in the United States without further authority as long as its corporate charter so provides.
    b.   As long as Dexter's business activities in the neighboring state do <u>not</u> exceed 25%, it need <u>not</u> obtain permission to do business in the neighboring state.
    c.   Dexter must create a subsidiary corporation in the neighboring state to continue to do business in that state.
    d.   Dexter is a foreign corporation in the neighboring state and as such must obtain a certificate of authority or it will <u>not</u> be permitted to maintain any action or suit in the state with respect to its intrastate business.

10 (November 78)

Which of the following statements is <u>incorrect</u>?

    a.   Dexter has automatically appointed the secretary of state of the neighboring state as its agent for the purpose of service of legal process if it failed to appoint or maintain a registered agent in that state.
    b.   Dexter will be able to maintain an action or suit in the neighboring state if it subsequently obtains a certificate of authority.
    c.   Dexter can <u>not</u> defend against a suit brought against it in the neighboring state's courts.
    d.   The attorney general of the neighboring state can recover all back fees and franchise taxes which would have been imposed plus all penalties for failure to pay same.

37 (November 74)

Weber Corporation was incorporated in the State of Delaware. It does all of its business in several adjoining states. Under the circumstances

    a.   Weber's Delaware corporation was invalid because it does <u>no</u> business there.
    b.   Weber is a domestic corporation in all states based upon full faith and credit.
    c.   Weber will <u>not</u> have to pay corporate income taxes except to Delaware and the United States.
    d.   Weber should either incorporate in the adjoining states where it does business or otherwise qualify to do business therein.

Corporations

C. Preincorporation Transactions--Promoter's Liability

5 (November 85)

Rice is a promoter of a corporation to be known as Dex Corp. On January 1, 1985, Rice signed a nine-month contract with Roe, a CPA, which provided that Roe would perform certain accounting services for Dex. Rice did not disclose to Roe that Dex had not been formed. Prior to the incorporation of Dex on February 1, 1985, Roe rendered accounting services pursuant to the contract. After rendering accounting services for an additional period of six months pursuant to the contract, Roe was discharged without cause by the board of directors of Dex. In the absence of any agreements to the contrary, who will be liable to Roe for breach of contract?

    a.   Both Rice and Dex.

    b.   Rice only.

    c.   Dex only.

    d.   Neither Rice nor Dex.

9 (May 82)

Phillips was the principal promoter of the Waterloo Corporation, a corporation which was to have been incorporated not later than July 31, 1981. Among the many things to be accomplished prior to incorporation were the obtaining of capital, the hiring of key executives and the securing of adequate office space. In this connection, Phillips obtained written subscriptions for $1.4 million of common stock from 17 individuals. He hired himself as the chief executive officer of Waterloo at $200,000 for five years and leased three floors of office space from Downtown Office Space, Inc. The contract with Downtown was made in the name of the corporation. Phillips had indicated orally that the corporation would be coming into existence shortly. The corporation did not come into existence through no fault of Phillips. Which of the following is correct?

    a.   The subscribers have a recognized right to sue for and recover damages.

    b.   Phillips is personally liable on the lease with Downtown.

    c.   Phillips has the right to recover the fair value of his services rendered to the proposed corporation.

    d.   The subscribers were not bound by their subscriptions until the corporation came into existence.

23 (May 81)

Bixler obtained an option on a building he believed was suitable for use by a corporation he and two other men were organizing. After the corporation was successfully promoted, Bixler met with the Board of Directors who agreed to acquire the property for $200,000. Bixler deeded the building to the corporation and the corporation began business in it. Bixler's option contract called for the payment of only $155,000 for the building and he purchased it for that price. When the directors later learned that Bixler paid only $155,000, they demanded the return of Bixler's $45,000 profit. Bixler refused, claiming the building was worth far more than $200,000 both when he secured the option and when he deeded it to the corporation. Which of the following statements correctly applies to Bixler's conduct?

    a.   It was improper for Bixler to contract for the option without first having secured the assent of the Board of Directors.

    b.   If, as Bixler claimed, the building was fairly worth more than $200,000, Bixler is entitled to retain the entire price.

    c.   Even if, as Bixler claimed, the building was fairly worth more than $200,000, Bixler nevertheless must return the $45,000 to the corporation.

    d.   In order for Bixler to be obligated to return any amount to the corporation, the Board of Directors must establish that the building was worth less than $200,000.

38 (November 74)

Walter Thomas as the promoter of Basic Corporation made a contract for and on behalf of Basic with Fair Realty Corporation for the purchase of an office building. Thomas did <u>not</u> disclose that the corporation had <u>not</u> been created. Thomas will <u>not</u> have any liability on the contract

    a.   Because he made it in the name of the corporation.

    b.   If the corporation subsequently adopts the contract.

    c.   If the corporation and Fair Realty enter into a novation regarding the contract.

    d.   If the corporation comes into existence and rejects the contract.

40 (May 74)

(Additional facts relating to the question are contained in 39 (May 74) on page 498.)

Assume that Alpha Corporation was properly formed, and Wentz performed services for the corporation in accordance with his agreement with Korn. If Wentz seeks to recover the compensation agreed upon in his agreement with Korn

    a.   The corporation is probably liable to Wentz for the salary under the agreement if it adopted the agreement.

    b.   The corporation is probably automatically bound by the preincorporation agreement of Korn as its agent.

    c.   Absent express adoption of the agreement by Alpha's board of directors, Wentz may recover for his services to the corporation only from Korn.

    d.   Any obligation Korn undertook under the agreement is terminated if Wentz assumes a position with the corporation at the salary specified in the agreement.

4A (May 78)

Grace Dawson was actively engaged in the promotion of a new corporation to be known as Multifashion Frocks, Inc. On January 3, 1978, she obtained written commitments for the purchase of shares totaling $600,000 from a group of 15 potential investors. She was also assured orally that she would be engaged as the president of the corporation upon the commencement of business. Helen Banks was the principal investor, having subscribed to $300,000 of the shares of Multifashion. Dawson immediately began work on the incorporation of Multifashion, made several contracts for and on its behalf, and made cash expenditures of $1,000 in accomplishing these goals. On February 15, 1978, Banks died and her estate has declined to honor the commitment to purchase the Multifashion shares. At the first shareholders' meeting on April 5, 1978, the day the incorporation came into existence, the shareholders elected a board of directors. With shareholder approval, the board took the following actions:

    1.   Adopted some but not all of the contracts made by Dawson.

    2.   Authorized legal action, if necessary, against the Estate of Banks to enforce Banks' $300,000 commitment.

    3.   Declined to engage Dawson in any capacity (Banks had been her main supporter).

    4.   Agreed to pay Dawson $750 for those cash outlays which were deemed to be directly beneficial to the corporation and rejected the balance.

Required: Answer the following, setting forth reasons for any conclusions stated.

Discuss the legal implications of each of the above actions taken by the board of directors of Multifashion.

In general, preincorporation contracts are not binding upon a newly created corporation prior to their adoption by its board of directors. Overall, one would conclude that the board acted properly and legally with respect to the actions taken. Each item is discussed separately below.

1. The board's action was proper and within its discretion. Care, however, should be taken to avoid an implied adoption by having the corporation avail itself of some or all of the benefits of a contract while purporting to reject the contract. The corporation is not legally bound prior to adoption, because it was not in existence at the time the contract was made. Dawson, on the other hand, has liability on the contracts she made prior to incorporation. Moreover, with respect to the contracts adopted by the corporation, she assumes the status of a surety unless a novation was entered into, releasing Dawson of all liability. The nonexistent principal rule would apply to Dawson unless the contract she made was contingent upon the corporation's adopting it after coming into existence.

2. An exception is made to the general rule of preincorporation actions insofar as stock subscriptions are concerned. Due to necessity and practical considerations, the parties who agree to provide the capital vital to the

corporation's creation are not permitted to withdraw their commitments for six months. The Model Business Corporation Act provides that "a subscription for shares of a corporation to be organized shall be irrevocable for a period of six months, unless provided by the terms of the subscription agreement or unless all of the subscribers consent to the revocation of such subscriptions." Hence, the subscription by Banks is valid and is a bona fide claim against the Estate of Banks.

3. The board of a newly created corporation is, at its inception, free to either adopt or reject preincorporation contracts made on behalf of the corporation. This general rule also applies to the employment contract of a promoter such as Dawson. The rationale for the rule is founded upon the belief that the corporation should not be shackled by commitments that it did not have an opportunity to adequately consider. In addition, promoters as a class have often abused their power and made what have proved to be self-serving contracts. Thus, the board acted properly, and it need not engage Dawson.

4. The only problem that arises is that Dawson was not paid in full. She might be entitled to the full $1,000 under two possible theories. The first is a contract implied in fact (an implied adoption) by the board accepting all the benefits of the $1,000 expenditure. The other theory would be a contract implied in law based upon unjust enrichment. Under this theory, if Dawson can prove that the corporation did receive benefits which were worth $1,000, she can recover the additional $250.

D. Recognition or Disregard of Corporate Form
1. Defective Incorporation

39 (November 74)

The Zebra Corporation is neither de jure nor de facto. As such it
a. Can nevertheless recover on a loan which it made to one of its suppliers.
b. Cannot be held liable for torts committed by its agents.
c. Cannot be treated as a corporation for tax purposes.
d. Can nevertheless validly continue to do business as a corporation without fear of legal action by the state as long as it is solvent and pays taxes.

39 (May 74)

Korn was one of several promoters interested in organizing Alpha Corporation. Korn entered into an employment contract for the services of Wentz. It was mutually understood that Wentz would perform certain duties and that these might be performed on behalf of a corporation yet to be formed. Korn also entered into an agreement with Bates Company for services to be rendered by the corporation at a future date.

The corporation was formed and began operations, but a defective filing prevented compliance with the requirements for legal incorporation.

Failure to comply strictly with all of the filing requirements probably resulted in
a. A de jure corporation.
b. A de facto corporation for some purposes, at least.
c. The formation of a partnership.
d. The unenforceability of all agreements mentioned.

2. Disregarding Corporate Existence--Piercing the Corporate Veil

20 (November 93)

The corporate veil is most likely to be pierced and the shareholders held personally liable if
a. The corporation has elected S corporation status under the Internal Revenue Code.
b. The shareholders have commingled their personal funds with those of the corporation.
c. An ultra vires act has been committed.
d. A partnership incorporates its business solely to limit the liability of its partners.

6 (May 91)

The limited liability of a stockholder in a closely-held corporation may be challenged successfully if the stockholder

  a. Undercapitalized the corporation when it was formed.
  b. Formed the corporation solely to have limited personal liability.
  c. Sold property to the corporation.
  d. Was a corporate officer, director, or employee.

8 (May 84)

For which of the following reasons would the corporate veil most likely be pierced and the shareholders held personally liable?

  a. The corporation is a personal holding company.
  b. The corporation was organized because the shareholders wanted to limit their personal liability.
  c. The corporation and its shareholders do not maintain separate bank accounts and records.
  d. The corporation's sole shareholder is another domestic corporation.

8 (May 82)

A court is most likely to disregard the corporate entity and hold shareholders personally liable when

  a. The owners-officers of the corporation do not treat it as a separate entity.
  b. A parent corporation creates a wholly-owned subsidiary in order to isolate the high risk portion of its business in the subsidiary.
  c. A sole proprietor incorporates his business to limit his liability.
  d. The corporation has elected, under Subchapter S, not to pay any corporate tax on its income but, instead, to have the shareholders pay tax on it.

9 (May 80)

A major characteristic of the corporation is its recognition as a separate legal entity. As such it is capable of withstanding attacks upon its valid existence by various parties who would wish to disregard its existence or "pierce the corporate veil" for their own purposes. The corporation will normally be able to successfully resist such attempts except when

  a. The corporation was created with tax savings in mind.
  b. The corporation was created in order to insulate the assets of its owners from personal liability.
  c. The corporation being attacked is a wholly-owned subsidiary of its parent corporation.
  d. The creation of and transfer of property to the corporation amounts to a fraud upon creditors.

II. Corporate Financial Structure
A. Issuance of Shares

7 (R98)

Under the Revised Model Business Corporation Act, when a corporation's bylaws grant stockholders preemptive rights, which of the following rights is (are) included in that grant?

	The right to purchase a proportionate share of newly-issued stock	The right to a proportionate share of corporate assets remaining on corporate dissolution
a.	Yes	Yes
b.	Yes	No
c.	No	Yes
d.	No	No

17 (November 93)

Which of the following securities are corporate debt securities?

	Convertible bonds	Debenture bonds	Warrants
a.	Yes	Yes	Yes
b.	Yes	No	Yes
c.	Yes	Yes	No
d.	No	Yes	Yes

19 (November 78)

Derek Corporation decided to acquire certain assets belonging to the Mongol Corporation. As consideration for the assets acquired, Derek issued 20,000 shares of its no-par common stock with a stated value of $10 per share. The value of the assets acquired subsequently turned out to be much less than the $200,000 in stock issued. Under the circumstances, which of the following is correct?
   a. It is improper for the board of directors to acquire assets other than cash with no-par stock.
   b. Only the shareholders can have the right to fix the value of the shares of no-par stock exchanged for assets.
   c. In the absence of fraud in the transaction, the judgment of the board of directors as to the value of the consideration received for the shares shall be conclusive.
   d. Unless the board obtained an independent appraisal of the acquired assets' value, it is liable to the extent of the overvaluation.

17 (May 76)

A corporation has the power to create and issue the number of shares of stock stated in its
   a. Articles of incorporation.
   b. By-laws.
   c. Minutes of shareholders' meetings.
   d. Minutes of directors' meetings.

18 (May 76)

Shares of stock without par value may be issued for such consideration (in dollars) as may be fixed by a corporation's
   a. Creditors.
   b. Officers.
   c. Board of directors.
   d. Minority shareholders.

24 (November 75)

Authorized shares means the shares of all classes of stock which a corporation
   a. Has legally outstanding.
   b. Is legally permitted to issue.
   c. Has issued including treasury shares.
   d. Has issued excluding treasury shares.

B. Payment for Shares
1. Stock Subscriptions

15 (November 78)

Watson entered into an agreement to purchase 1,000 shares of the Marvel Corporation, a corporation to be organized in the near future. Watson has since had second thoughts about investing in Marvel. Under the circumstances, which of the following is correct?

a. A written notice of withdrawal of his agreement to purchase the shares will be valid as long as it is received prior to incorporation.

b. A simple transfer of the agreement to another party will entirely eliminate his liability to purchase the shares of stock.

c. Watson may <u>not</u> revoke the agreement for a period of six months in the absence of special circumstances.

d. Watson may avoid liability on his agreement if he can obtain the consent of the majority of other individuals committed to purchase shares to release him.

2. Shareholder Liability for Watered Shares

24 (November 83)

Ambrose purchased 400 shares of $100 par value original issue common stock from Minor Corporation for $25 a share. Ambrose subsequently sold 200 of the shares to Harris at $25 a share. Harris did not have knowledge or notice that Ambrose had not paid par. Ambrose also sold 100 shares of this stock to Gable for $25 a share. At the time of this sale, Gable knew that Ambrose had not paid par for the stock. Minor Corporation became insolvent and the creditors sought to hold all the above parties liable for the $75 unpaid on each of the 400 shares. Under these circumstances

a. The creditors can hold Ambrose liable for $30,000.

b. If $25 a share was a fair value for the stock at the time of issuance, Ambrose will have no liability to the creditors.

c. Since Harris acquired the shares by purchase, he is not liable to the creditors, and his lack of knowledge or notice that Ambrose paid less than par is immaterial.

d. Since Gable acquired the shares by purchase, he is not liable to the creditors, and the fact that he knew Ambrose paid less than par is immaterial.

16 (May 80)

Plimpton subscribed to 1,000 shares of $1 par value common stock of the Billiard Ball Corporation at $10 a share. Plimpton paid $1,000 upon the incorporation and paid an additional $4,000 at a later time. The corporation subsequently became insolvent and is now in bankruptcy. The creditors of the corporation are seeking to hold Plimpton personally liable. Which of the following is a correct statement?

a. Plimpton has <u>no</u> liability directly or indirectly to the creditors of the corporation since he paid the corporation the full par value of the shares.

b. As a result of his failure to pay the full subscription price, Plimpton has unlimited joint and several liability for corporate debts.

c. Plimpton is liable for the remainder of the unpaid subscription price.

d. Had Plimpton transferred his shares to an innocent third party, neither he nor the third party would be liable.

28 (November 75)

Mr. Parker has been issued 100 shares of common stock of Capital, Inc. having a par value of $30 per share. What aggregate consideration must Mr. Parker pay for the shares of stock if he is to escape any contingent liability in connection with these shares in the future?

a. At least $30.

b. At least $3,000.

c. Less than $3,000.

d. Between $30 and $3,000.

34 (November 74)

As the owner of common stock in a corporation, you will <u>not</u> have liability beyond actual investment even if you

a. Paid less than par value for stock you purchased in connection with an original issue.

b. Fail to pay the full amount owed on a subscription contract for no-par stock.

c. Purchased treasury stock for less than par value.

d. Received a dividend distribution which impaired the legal capital of the corporation.

Corporations

C. Dividends, Distributions, and Redemptions

24 (November 95)

Carr Corp. declared a 7% stock dividend on its common stock. The dividend
- a. Must be registered with the SEC pursuant to the Securities Act of 1933.
- b. Is includable in the gross income of the recipient taxpayers in the year of receipt.
- c. Has <u>no</u> effect on Carr's earnings and profits for federal income tax purposes.
- d. Requires a vote of Carr's stockholders.

13 (May 94)

Which of the following rights is a holder of a public corporation's cumulative preferred stock always entitled to?
- a. Conversion of the preferred stock into common stock.
- b. Voting rights.
- c. Dividend carryovers from years in which dividends were <u>not</u> paid, to future years.
- d. Guaranteed dividends.

19 (May 92)

Price owns 2,000 shares of Universal Corp.'s $10 cumulative preferred stock. During its first year of operations, cash dividends of $5 per share were declared on the preferred stock but were never paid. In the second year, dividends on the preferred stock were neither declared nor paid. If Universal is dissolved, which of the following statements is correct?
- a. Universal will be liable to Price as an unsecured creditor for $10,000.
- b. Universal will be liable to Price as a secured creditor for $20,000.
- c. Price will have priority over the claims of Universal's bond owners.
- d. Price will have priority over the claims of Universal's unsecured judgment creditors.

17 (November 90)

All of the following distributions to stockholders are considered asset or capital distributions, <u>except</u>
- a. Liquidating dividends.
- b. Stock splits.
- c. Property distributions.
- d. Cash dividends.

9 (May 90)

Johns owns 400 shares of Abco Corp. cumulative preferred stock. In the absence of any specific contrary provisions in Abco's articles of incorporation, which of the following statements is correct?
- a. Johns is entitled to convert the 400 shares of preferred stock to a like number of shares of common stock.
- b. If Abco declares a cash dividend on its preferred stock, Johns becomes an unsecured creditor of Abco.
- c. If Abco declares a dividend on its common stock, Johns will be entitled to participate with the common stock shareholders in any dividend distribution made after preferred dividends are paid.
- d. Johns will be entitled to vote if dividend payments are in arrears.

15 (May 88)

In general, which of the following statements concerning treasury stock is correct?
- a. A corporation may <u>not</u> reacquire its own stock unless specifically authorized by its articles of incorporation.
- b. On issuance of new stock, a corporation has preemptive rights with regard to its treasury stock.
- c. Treasury stock may be distributed as a stock dividend.
- d. A corporation is entitled to receive cash dividends on its treasury stock.

5 (May 84)

Which of the following statements concerning cumulative preferred stock is correct?

   a.   Upon the dissolution of a corporation the preferred shareholders have priority over unsecured judgment creditors.

   b.   Preferred stock represents a type of debt security similar to corporate debentures.

   c.   If dividends are not declared for any year, they become debts of the corporation for subsequent years.

   d.   Upon the declaration of a cash dividend on the preferred stock, preferred shareholders become unsecured creditors of the corporation.

9 (May 84)

Which of the following statements concerning treasury stock is correct?

   a.   Cash dividends paid on treasury stock are transferred to stated capital.

   b.   A corporation may not purchase its own stock unless specifically authorized by its articles of incorporation.

   c.   A duly appointed trustee may vote treasury stock at a properly called shareholders' meeting.

   d.   Treasury stock may be resold at a price less than par value.

26 (May 81)

Global Trucking Corporation has in its corporate treasury a substantial block of its own common stock, which it acquired several years previously. The stock had been publicly offered at $25 a share and had been reacquired at $15. The board is considering using it in the current year for various purposes. For which of the following purposes may it validly use the treasury stock?

   a.   To pay a stock dividend to its shareholders.

   b.   To sell it to the public without the necessity of a registration under the Securities Act of 1933, since it had been previously registered.

   c.   To vote it at the annual meeting of shareholders.

   d.   To acquire the shares of another publicly-held company without the necessity of a registration under the Securities Act of 1933.

11 (May 77)

A corporation may not redeem its own shares when it

   a.   Is currently solvent but has been insolvent within the past five years.

   b.   Is insolvent or would be rendered insolvent if the redemption were made.

   c.   Has convertible debt that is publicly traded.

   d.   Has mortgages and other secured obligations equal to 50 percent of its stated capital.

15 (May 77)

Randolph Corporation would like to pay cash dividends on its common shares outstanding. Under corporate law, Randolph may not pay these dividends if it is insolvent or would be rendered so by the payment. For this purpose, an insolvent corporation is one which

   a.   Is unable to pay its debts as they become due in the usual course of its business.

   b.   Has an excess of liabilities over assets.

   c.   Has an excess of current liabilities over current assets.

   d.   Has a deficit in earned surplus.

20 (May 76)

The board of directors of a corporation may declare, and the corporation may pay, cash dividends except when the corporation is

   a.   Privately owned.

   b.   Highly leveraged.

   c.   Insolvent.

   d.   In a risky growth industry.

2A (November 80)

The Dexter Corporation has not paid a dividend since 1970 on its 7% noncumulative preferred stock. In the years 1970-1973 the company had net losses which threatened to impair its financial position. Since 1974 the company has had earnings sufficient to pay the preferred stock dividend. In fact, earnings have gradually increased since 1974, and by 1976 Dexter had recouped all losses which occurred in the years 1970-1973. During the years 1974-1979 the profits were credited to retained earnings.

The funds were neither committed to physical plant or equipment nor did the board indicate that it had long range plans calling for such a commitment. Preferred shareholders had complained at board meetings regarding the repeated passing over of preferred dividends. The board's actions were explained on the grounds of pessimism about the company's and the economy's outlook and therefore, the need to build up adequate additional reserves to provide for the possibility of future losses. The board's outlook during the time in question could properly be categorized as one of pessimism and conservatism.

On January 15, 1980, the board decided to pay the 7% dividend on the preferred stock and a large dividend on the common stock. The preferred shareholders were irate. A group of preferred shareholders have commenced a suit seeking an injunction against Dexter and its board of directors prohibiting the payment of dividends on the common stock unless it first pays dividends on the noncumulative preferred for previous years to the extent that the corporation had net earnings available for payment.

Required: Answer the following, setting forth reasons for any conclusions stated.
Will the preferred shareholders prevail?

No. The stock in question was noncumulative preferred. The relationship of the preferred shareholders to the corporation is essentially contractual and the stock certificate is, in fact, the contract. The contract agreed to by the owners of this preferred stock was essentially that if the board of directors passed over the declaration of the preferred dividend in a given year or years, it would not accumulate but would be lost. Whether or not to declare a dividend is within the discretion of the board. Its judgment is not overridden by the courts unless there is dishonesty or a clear abuse of discretion. The fact that there were earnings sufficient to pay preferred dividends after 1973, that the funds were not actually expended for purchase of physical plant or property, or that the earnings were not being accumulated for the purpose of expansion are not sufficient to persuade a court to grant the injunction. Although the board was pessimistic and conservative, that would not be an abuse of their discretion. In conclusion, the law respects the business judgment of directors in determining whether to declare dividends. The board is afforded wide discretion in such matters, and, unless there is an abuse of such discretion, a court will not interfere with its judgment.

III. Corporate Management--Structure and Duties
A. Corporate Management Structure

2 (R97)
Items 1 through 5 are based on the following:

Mill, Web, and Trent own all the outstanding and issued voting common stock of Sack Corp. Mill owns 40%, Web owns 30%, and Trent owns 30%. They also executed a written stockholders agreement in which Mill, Web, and Trent agreed to vote for each other as directors of Sack.

At the initial meeting of the incorporators, Mill, Web, and Trent were elected to the board of directors together with three non-stockholders. At the initial board of directors meeting, Mill, Web, and Trent were appointed as officers of the corporation and given three-year employment contracts.

During its first year of operations, Sack began experiencing financial difficulties, which caused disagreements among Mill, Web, and Trent as to how the business should be operated.

At the next annual stockholders' meeting, Mill was not elected to the board of directors. The new board fired Mill in a management reorganization despite there being two years left on the employment contract. The board, reasonably relying on assurances from Web and Trent regarding financial statements Web and Trent knew to be materially misstated, declared and paid a dividend that caused Sack to become insolvent.

Required: For **Items 1 through 5**, select the correct answer from List I. An answer may be selected once, more than once, or not at all.

	List I
A	Mill only.
B	Web only.
C	Trent only.
D	Mill and Web only.
E	Mill and Trent only.
F	Web and Trent only.
G	Mill, Web, and Trent.
H	Neither Mill, Web, nor Trent.
I	All directors.
J	Sack Corp.

1. According to the stockholders' agreement, what party(ies) must be elected as director(s) of Sack?
2. According to the stockholders' agreement, what party(ies) must be appointed as officer(s) of the corporation?
3. What party(ies) is (are) liable to Mill for Mill's firing?
4. What party(ies) must return the dividend to the corporation?
5. What party(ies) would be liable for declaring the illegal dividend?

23 (November 95)

To which of the following rights is a stockholder of a public corporation entitled?
a. The right to have annual dividends declared and paid.
b. The right to vote for the election of officers.
c. The right to a reasonable inspection of corporate records.
d. The right to have the corporation issue a new class of stock.

2 (November 92)

A stockholder's right to inspect books and records of a corporation will be properly denied if the stockholder
a. Wants to use corporate stockholder records for a personal business.
b. Employs an agent to inspect the books and records.
c. Intends to commence a stockholder's derivative suit.
d. Is investigating management misconduct.

16 (November 90)

A stockholder's right to inspect books and records of a corporation will be properly denied if the purpose of the inspection is to
a. Commence a stockholder's derivative suit.
b. Obtain stockholder names for a retail mailing list.
c. Solicit stockholders to vote for a change in the board of directors.
d. Investigate possible management misconduct.

7 (May 90)

Absent a specific provision in its articles of incorporation, a corporation's board of directors has the power to do all the following, except
a. Repeal the bylaws.
b. Declare dividends.
c. Fix compensation of directors.
d. Amend the articles of incorporation.

Corporations

14 (May 85)

Generally, officers of a corporation

a. Are elected by the shareholders.

b. Are agents and fiduciaries of the corporation, having actual and apparent authority to manage the business.

c. May be removed by the board of directors without cause only if the removal is approved by a majority vote of the shareholders.

d. May declare dividends or other distributions to shareholders as they deem appropriate.

21 (May 76)

Unless otherwise provided by a corporation's articles of incorporation or by-laws, a board of directors may act without a meeting if written consent setting forth the action so taken is signed by

a. A plurality of them.

b. A majority of them.

c. Two-thirds of them.

d. All of them.

2 (May 95)

In 1990, Amber Corp., a closely-held corporation, was formed by Adams, Frank, and Berg as incorporators and stockholders. Adams, Frank, and Berg executed a written voting agreement which provided that they would vote for each other as directors and officers. In 1994, stock in the corporation was offered to the public. This resulted in an additional 300 stockholders. After the offering, Adams holds 25%, Frank holds 15%, and Berg holds 15% of all issued and outstanding stock. Adams, Frank, and Berg have been directors and officers of the corporation since the corporation was formed. Regular meetings of the board of directors and annual stockholders meetings have been held.

Required: **Items 67 through 72** refer to the formation of Amber Corp. and the rights and duties of its stockholders, directors, and officers. For each item, determine whether A, B, or C is correct.

67.   A. Amber Corp. must be formed under a state's general corporation statute.

   B. Amber Corp.'s Articles of Incorporation must include the names of all stockholders.

   C. Amber Corp. must include its corporate bylaws in the incorporation documents filed with the state.

68.   Amber Corp.'s initial bylaws ordinarily would be adopted by its

   A. Stockholders.

   B. Officers.

   C. Directors.

69.   Amber Corp.'s directors are elected by its

   A. Officers.

   B. Outgoing directors.

   C. Stockholders.

70.   Amber Corp.'s officers ordinarily would be elected by its

   A. Stockholders.

   B. Directors.

   C. Outgoing officers.

71.   Amber Corp.'s day-to-day business ordinarily would be operated by its

   A. Directors.

   B. Stockholders.

   C. Officers.

72. A. Adams, Frank, and Berg must be elected as directors because they own 55% of the issued and outstanding stock.
  B. Adams, Frank, and Berg must always be elected as officers because they own 55% of the issued and outstanding stock.
  C. Adams, Frank, and Berg must always vote for each other as directors because they have a voting agreement.

4 (November 86)

Jane Mead, a 7% minority shareholder in Sky Corp. for several years, is unhappy with the way Ed Rice, the president of Sky, has been operating Sky. The Board of Directors of Sky has refused to pursue any of the actions requested by Mead. In addition, Sky is contemplating a proposed merger with King Corp., a conglomerate into which Sky would be merged.

As a result of the foregoing, Mead asserts that she personally has the right to:

- Have Rice removed as president of Sky.
- Obtain payment for her shares in Sky in the event the proposed merger is consummated.

Rice asserts the following:

- That he cannot be removed as president of Sky since he has a three-year written contract with two years remaining, and that such removal can only be made for cause by a majority vote of the shareholders at its annual meeting.
- That Mead would not be entitled to payment in the event the merger is consummated since the articles of incorporation are silent on this point.

Required: Answer the following, setting forth reasons for any conclusions stated. Discuss the assertions of Mead and Rice with regard to whether Rice may be removed as the president of Sky, and whether Mead is entitled to payment for her shares in the event the merger is consummated.

Mead personally does not have the right to remove Rice as president of Sky. However, Rice may be removed as the president of Sky by the board of directors whenever, in its judgment, the best interests of the corporation will be served. However, such removal is without prejudice to the contract rights of the person so removed. Thus, Rice may be removed with or without cause and the vote of the shareholders at its annual meeting is not required for such removal. However, if Rice is removed without cause Sky may be liable to Rice for breach of contract.

Mead is entitled to payment for her shares. A shareholder has the right to dissent from a merger and to obtain payment for her shares in the event that the corporation in which she is a shareholder is a party to a proposed plan of merger. If Mead strictly complies with the statutory requirements as a dissenter, she will be entitled to receive the fair value of her shares (an appraisal remedy). The fact that such a remedy is not provided for in the articles of incorporation is irrelevant where a state statute provides a dissenting shareholder with such a remedy.

B. Duties of Management--Care and Loyalty

12 (R96)

Under the Revised Model Business Corporation Act, a corporate director is authorized to

a. Rely on information provided by the appropriate corporate officer.
b. Serve on the board of directors of a competing business.
c. Sell control of the corporation.
d. Profit from insider information.

5 (May 91)

Davis, a director of Active Corp., is entitled

a. Serve on the board of a competing business.
b. Take sole advantage of a business opportunity that would benefit Active.
c. Rely on information provided by a corporate officer.
d. Unilaterally grant a corporate loan to one of Active's shareholders.

12 (May 85)

Which of the following statements is correct regarding the fiduciary duty?

a. A director's fiduciary duty to the corporation may be discharged by merely disclosing his self-interest.

b. A director owes a fiduciary duty to the shareholders but not to the corporation.

c. A promoter of a corporation to be formed owes no fiduciary duty to anyone, unless the contract engaging the promoter so provides.

d. A majority shareholder as such may owe a fiduciary duty to fellow shareholders.

13 (May 80)

Grandiose secured an option to purchase a tract of land for $100,000. He then organized the Dunbar Corporation and subscribed to 51% of the shares of stock of the corporation for $100,000, which was issued to him in exchange for his three-month promissory note for $100,000. Controlling the board of directors through his share ownership, he had the corporation authorize the purchase of the land from him for $200,000. He made no disclosure to the board or to other shareholders that he was making a $100,000 profit. He promptly paid the corporation for his shares and redeemed his promissory note. A disgruntled shareholder subsequently learned the full details of the transaction and brought suit against Grandiose on the corporation's behalf. Which of the following is a correct statement?

a. Grandiose breached his fiduciary duty to the corporation and must account for the profit he made.

b. The judgment of the board of directors was conclusive under the circumstances.

c. Grandiose is entitled to retain the profit since he controlled the corporation as a result of his share ownership.

d. The giving of the promissory note in exchange for the stock constituted payment for the shares.

2 (November 91)

Frost, Glen, and Bradley own 50%, 40%, and 10%, respectively, of the authorized and issued voting common stock of Xeon Corp. They had a written stockholders' agreement that provided they would vote for each other as directors of the corporation.

At the initial stockholders' meeting, Frost, Glen, Bradley, and three others were elected to a six-person board of directors. The board elected Frost as president of the corporation, Glen as secretary, and Bradley as vice president. Frost and Glen were given two-year contracts with annual salaries of $50,000. Bradley was given a two-year contract for $10,000 per year.

At the end of its first year of operation, Xcon was in financial difficulty. Bradley disagreed with the way Frost and Glen were running the business.

At the annual stockholders' meeting, a new board of directors was elected. Bradley was excluded because Frost and Glen did not vote for Bradley. Without cause, the new board fired Bradley as vice president even though 12 months remained on Bradley's contract.

Despite the corporation's financial difficulties, the new board, relying on the assurances of Frost and Glen and based on fraudulent documentation provided by Frost and Glen, declared and paid a $200,000 dividend. Payment of the dividend caused the corporation to become insolvent.

- Bradley sued Frost and Glen to compel them to follow the written stockholders' agreement and reelect Bradley to the board.

- Bradley sued the corporation to be reinstated as an officer of the corporation, and for breach of the employment contract.

- Bradley sued each member of the board for declaring and paying an unlawful dividend, and demanded its repayment to the corporation.

Required: State whether Bradley would be successful in each of the above suits and give the reasons for your conclusions.

Bradley would be successful in the suit against Frost and Glen for failing to vote Bradley to the board of directors. The stockholders have the right to elect the directors of a corporation. The stockholders have the right to agree among themselves on how they will vote. Therefore, the voting provision of the stockholders' agreement between Bradley, Frost, and Glen is enforceable.

Bradley would be unsuccessful in attempting to be reinstated as vice president. A corporation's board oversees the operations of the business, which includes hiring officers and, at its discretion, dismissing officers with or without cause. Bradley would be successful in collecting some damages for the breach of the employment contract because there was no demonstrated cause for Bradley's dismissal.

Bradley would be successful in having Frost and Glen held personally liable to the corporation for declaring and paying the dividend because payment of a dividend that threatens a corporation's solvency is unlawful. Ordinarily, directors who approve such a dividend would be personally liable for its repayment to the corporation. However, the directors, other than Frost and Glen, in relying on the assurances and information supplied by Frost and Glen, as corporate officers, are protected by the business judgment rule. Therefore, only Frost and Glen would be held personally liable.

4 (May 89)

On May 1, 1987, Cray's board of directors unanimously voted to have Cray reacquire 100,000 shares of its common stock. On May 25, 1987, Cray did so, paying current market price. In determining whether to reacquire the shares, the board of directors relied on reports and financial statements that were negligently prepared by Cray's internal accounting department under the supervision of the treasurer and reviewed by its independent accountants. The reports and financial statements indicated that, as of April 30, 1987, Cray was solvent and there were sufficient funds to reacquire the shares. Subsequently, it was discovered that Cray had become insolvent in March 1987 and continued to be insolvent after the reacquisition of the shares. As a result of the foregoing, Cray experienced liquidity problems and losses during 1987 and 1988.

The board of directors immediately fired the treasurer because of the treasurer's negligence in supervising the preparation of the reports and financial statements. The treasurer had three years remaining on a binding five-year employment agreement which, among other things, prohibited the termination of the treasurer's employment for mere negligence.

Required: Discuss the following assertions, indicating whether such assertions are correct and the reasons therefor.
- It was improper for the board of directors to authorize the reacquisition of Cray's common stock while Cray was insolvent.
- The members of the board of directors are personally liable because they voted to reacquire shares while Cray was insolvent.
- Cray will be liable to the treasurer as a result of his termination by the board of directors.

The assertion that it was improper for the board of directors to authorize the reacquisition of Cray's common stock while Cray was insolvent is correct. A board of directors may authorize and the corporation may reacquire its shares of stock subject to any restriction in the articles of incorporation, except that no reacquisition may be made if, after giving effect thereto, either the corporation would be unable to pay its debts as they become due in the usual course of business or the corporation's total assets would be less than its total liabilities. Because Cray was insolvent before and after the reacquisition of Cray's common stock, it was improper for the board of directors to authorize the reacquisition.

The assertion that the members of Cray's board of directors are personally liable because Cray reacquired its own shares of Cray stock while Cray was insolvent is incorrect. In general, directors who vote or assent to a reacquisition by the corporation of its own shares while the corporation is insolvent will be jointly and severally liable to the corporation. However, the directors will not be liable if they acted in good faith, in a manner they reasonably believed to be in the best interests of the corporation, and with such care as an ordinarily prudent person in a like position would use under similar circumstances. In performing their duties, directors are entitled to rely on information, opinions, reports, or statements, including financial statements and other financial data prepared or presented by one or more officers or employees of the corporation whom the directors reasonably believe to be reliable and competent in the matters presented. The directors may rely on the same information prepared or presented by independent accountants that the directors reasonably believe to be within such person's professional competence. Based on the facts of this case, the directors' reliance on the reports and financial statements prepared by Cray's internal accounting department under the supervision of the treasurer and reviewed by its independent accountants was proper so long as the directors exercised due care, acted in good faith, and acted without knowledge that would cause such reliance to be unwarranted. In addition, the courts are precluded from substituting their business judgment for that of the board of directors if the directors have acted with due care and in good faith.

The assertion that Cray will be liable to the treasurer as a result of his termination by the board of directors is correct. An officer may be removed by the board of directors with or without cause whenever in its judgment the best interests of the corporation will be served by the removal. However, such removal is without prejudice to the contract rights of the person so removed. Thus, the board of directors had the power to remove the treasurer. The treasurer will prevail in a breach of contract action for damages against Cray because the firing violated the employment agreement.

5 (November 84)

Jim Bold is a promoter for a corporation to be formed and known as Wonda Corp. Bold entered into several supply and service agreements with Servco. These agreements were executed in Wonda's name, expressly contingent upon adoption by Wonda, when formed, and were based solely on Wonda's anticipated financial strength. Within two weeks after the signing of the agreements, Wonda was duly formed and operating. Shortly thereafter, Wonda by its board of directors rejected the preincorporation agreements entered into be Bold and Servco, stating that it could obtain more beneficial contracts elsewhere.

During the first year of Wonda's operations certain members of its board of directors were accused of negligence in the performance of their duties. In addition, there were allegations made that these same directors failed to exercise due care by paying cash dividends to shareholders that exceeded the profits and paid-in capital. These directors based their decision upon negligently prepared reports issued by the vice-president of finance indicating that there were sufficient funds to pay cash dividends to shareholders. These incidents caused Wonda severe liquidity problems and huge losses in the following year of operation. White, a shareholder in Wonda, has properly commenced a suit against these directors.

Required: Answer the following, setting forth reasons for any conclusions stated.
   a. Discuss Wonda's and Bold's liability to Servco on the preincorporation agreements.
   b. What are the necessary requirements to properly declare and pay cash dividends?
   c. What defense(s) are available to the directors regarding the charges of negligence in the performance of their duties and the failure to exercise due care in declaring cash dividends?

a. Wonda is not liable to Servco on the preincorporation agreements. A preincorporation agreement made by a promoter does not bind the corporation even though it is made in the corporation's name. The corporation, prior to its formation, lacks the capacity to enter into contracts or to employ agents since it is nonexistent. Furthermore, unless after being formed the corporation adopts or knowingly accepts the benefits under the contract, it will not be held liable. Therefore, Wonda's express rejection of the preincorporation agreement will allow it to avoid liability.

Bold's liability to Servco depends on whether Bold clearly manifested his intent not to be personally bound on the preincorporation agreements. Such manifestation of intent can be shown by the express language or acts of the parties. The facts of the case at hand clearly show that Bold did not intend to be held personally liable on the agreements with Servco, since the contracts were executed in the name of Wonda, contingent upon adoption by Wonda, and were based solely on Wonda's anticipated credit. Therefore, Bold will not be held liable on the agreements with Servco.

Furthermore, a preincorporation agreement that is entered into by a promoter on behalf of a corporation to be formed and that is intended not to bind the promoter is not a contract but is merely a revocable offer to be communicated to the proposed corporation after its formation. Thus, under the facts, neither Bold nor Wonda will enjoy rights or suffer liabilities under the agreement.

b. Cash dividends may be declared and paid if the corporation is solvent and payment of the dividends would not render the corporation insolvent. Furthermore, each state imposes additional restrictions on what funds are legally available to pay dividends. One of the more restrictive tests adopted by many states permits the payment of dividends only out of unrestricted and unreserved earned surplus (retained earnings). The Model Business

Corporation Act as recently amended prohibits distributions if, after giving effect to the distribution, the corporation's total assets would be less than the sum of its total liabilities.

c. The charge of negligence will fail if the directors can establish that they acted in good faith, in a manner reasonably believed to be in the best interests of the corporation and with such care as an ordinary prudent person in a like position would use under similar circumstances. Furthermore, under the business judgment rule, the court will not substitute its judgment for that of the board of directors as long as the directors acted in good faith and with due care.

The allegation that the directors failed to exercise due are by declaring cash dividends to shareholders that exceeded Wonda's profits and paid-in capital is without merit. Generally, if a director votes for or assents to the unlawful payment of dividends, that director will be jointly and severally liable along with all other directors so voting or assenting. However, directors will be relieved of liability if in voting or assenting to the payment of cash dividends they acted in good faith and in reliance upon information, opinions, reports, or statements prepared or presented by an officer or employee of the corporation whom the directors reasonably believe to be reliable and competent in the matters presented. Thus, the directors' reliance on the reports prepared and issued by Wonda's vice-president of finance was proper so long as the directors exercised due care, acted in good faith, and acted without knowledge that would cause reliance on the reports to be unwarranted. The reason for such a rule is to allow directors to use their best business judgment without incurring liability for honest mistakes.

3A (November 82)

William Harrelson is president of the Billings Corporation, a medium-size manufacturer of yogurt. While serving as president, Harrelson learns of an interesting new yogurt product loaded with vitamin additives and with a potentially huge market. He immediately forms another corporation, the Wexler Corporation, to produce and market the new product. In his zeal, however, Harrelson overextends his personal credit and utilizes Billings' credit, along with its plant and employees, as needed, to produce the new product. The new product becomes a big success. As a result, Harrelson's Wexler stock is presently worth millions of dollars.

Required: Answer the following, setting forth reasons for any conclusions stated.

Billings' shareholders contend that Harrelson's actions are improper and seek a remedy against him. Will they succeed and what remedies are available to them?

Yes. The shareholders will succeed. Directors and officers are fiduciaries and consequently must exercise the utmost good faith in respect of their corporation. If a "corporate opportunity" arises, they are required to offer the opportunity to the corporation. Generally a corporate opportunity will be found to exist if

-a director or officer becomes aware of the opportunity in his corporate capacity, or

-the opportunity relates to the business of the corporation.

The facts clearly indicate that such a corporate opportunity did exist, and thus the new yogurt opportunity should have been offered to Billings in the first instance. As a fiduciary, such an offer was necessary prior to exploitation of the opportunity by Harrelson. Moreover, Harrelson's use of corporate credit and personnel was a further violation of his fiduciary obligation. Accordingly, Billings' shareholders will prevail in their action. The remedy will include the holding of the Wexler stock in constructive trust for Billings, as well as possible damages against Harrelson for his personal use of corporate employees and credit.

3C (May 79)

Towne is a prominent financier, the owner of 1% of the shares of Toy, Inc., and one of its directors. He is also the chairman of the board of Unlimited Holdings, Inc., an investment company in which he owns 80% of the stock. Toy needs land upon which to build additional warehouse facilities. The best location in Arthur's opinion from all standpoints, including location, availability, access to transportation, and price, is an eight-acre tract of land owned by Unlimited. Neither Arthur nor Towne wish to create any legal problems in connection with the possible purchase of the land.

Corporations

Required: Answer the following, setting forth reasons for any conclusions stated.
1. What are the legal parameters within which this transaction may be safely consummated?
2. What are the legal ramifications if there were to be a $50,000 payment "on the side" to Towne in order that he use his efforts to "smooth the way" for the proposed acquisition?

1. The Model Business Corporation Act allows such transactions between a corporation and one or more of its directors or another corporation in which the director has a financial interest. The transaction is neither void nor voidable even though the director is present at the board meeting which authorized the transaction or because his vote is counted for such purpose if--
- The fact of such relationship or interest is disclosed or known to the board of directors or committee that authorizes, approves, or ratifies the contract or transaction by a vote or consent sufficient for the purpose without counting the votes or consents of such interested directors; or
- The fact of such relationship or interest is disclosed or known to the shareholders entitled to vote and they authorize, approve, or ratify such contract or transaction by vote or written consent; or
- The contract or transaction is fair and reasonable to the corporation. Common or interested directors may be counted in determining the presence of a quorum at a meeting of the board of directors or a committee thereof that authorizes, approves, or ratifies such contract or transaction.
2. A $50,000 payment to Towne would be a violation of his fiduciary duty to the corporation. In addition, it might be illegal depending upon the criminal law of the jurisdiction. In any case he would be obligated to return the amount to the corporation. Furthermore, the payment would constitute grounds for permitting Toy to treat the transaction as voidable.

4B (May 78)

Duval is the chairman of the board and president of Monolith Industries, Inc. He is also the largest individual shareholder, owning 40 percent of the shares outstanding. The corporation is publicly held, and there is dissenting minority. In addition to his position with Monolith, Duval owns 85 percent of Variance Enterprises, a corporation created under the laws of the Bahamas. During 1977, Carlton, the president of Apex Industries, Inc., approached Duval and suggested that a tax-free merger of Monolith and Apex made good sense to him and that he was prepared to recommend such a course of action to the Apex board and to the shareholders. Duval studied the proposal and decided that Apex was a most desirable candidate for acquisition. Duval informed the president of Variance about the overture, told him it was a real bargain, and suggested that Variance pick it up for cash and notes. Not hearing from Duval or Monolith, Carlton accepted an offer from Variance and the business was sold to Variance. Several dissenting shareholders of Monolith learned the facts surrounding the Variance acquisition and have engaged counsel to represent them. The Variance acquisition of Apex proved to be highly profitable.

Required: Answer the following, setting forth reasons for any conclusions stated.
Discuss the rights of the dissenting Monolith shareholders and the probable outcome of a legal action by them.

Directors and officers of a corporation are fiduciaries in their relationship to the corporation they serve. As such, they can neither directly nor indirectly benefit in their dealings with or for the corporation. They cannot engage in transactions that are in violation of their fiduciary duty to protect and further the best interests of their principal. Making a secret profit or acquiring a personal advantage out of their office is an act which the corporation may seek to have set aside as voidable.

Based upon this general statement of directors' and officers' fiduciary duty, it appears that the dissenting shareholders could sue derivatively on behalf of Monolith. That is, they could institute legal action on behalf of and in the name of Monolith to set aside the Variance-Apex transaction and have the business transferred to Monolith along with the profits earned during the interim. As an alternative, they could seek to recover directly from Duval damages that would be payable to Monolith.

The result seems clear in light of the facts. First, the opportunity came to Duval in his capacity as the chairman of the board and president of Monolith. Next, he did not pursue the matter but instead informed Variance's president of the opportunity to purchase Apex. Duval's conduct appears to be a case of self-dealing, duplicity, secrecy, and perhaps deceit. Taking the law and all the circumstances surrounding the purchase of Apex assets by Variance, Monolith's dissenting shareholders would probably be successful in a derivative shareholder action.

IV. Corporate Management--Special Topics
A. Corporate Litigation

12 (May 94)

Under the Revised Model Business Corporation Act, which of the following statements is correct regarding corporate officers of a public corporation?

   a. An officer may not simultaneously serve as a director.
   b. A corporation may be authorized to indemnify its officers for liability incurred in a suit by stockholders.
   c. Stockholders always have the right to elect a corporation's officers.
   d. An officer of a corporation is required to own at least one share of the corporation's stock.

Items 3 and 4 are based on the following information:

Jane Cox, a shareholder of Mix Corp., has properly commenced a derivative action against Mix's Board of Directors. Cox alleges that the Board breached its fiduciary duty and was negligent by failing to independently verify the financial statements prepared by management upon which Smart & Co., CPAs, issued an unqualified opinion. The financial statements contained inaccurate information which the Board relied upon in committing large sums of money to capital expansion. This resulted in Mix having to borrow money at extremely high interest rates to meet current cash needs. Within a short period of time, the price of Mix Corp. stock declined drastically.

3 (November 85)

Which of the following statements is correct?

   a. The Board is strictly liable, regardless of fault, since it owes a fiduciary duty to both the corporation and the shareholders.
   b. The Board is liable since any negligence of Smart is automatically imputed to the Board.
   c. The Board may avoid liability if it acted in good faith and in a reasonable manner.
   d. The Board may avoid liability in all cases where it can show that it lacked scienter.

4 (November 85)

If the court determines that the Board was negligent and the Board seeks indemnification for its legal fees from Mix, which of the following statements is correct?

   a. The Board may not be indemnified since a presumption that the Board failed to act in good faith arises from the judgment.
   b. The Board may not be indemnified unless Mix's shareholders approve such indemnification.
   c. The Board may be indemnified by Mix only if Mix provides liability insurance for its officers and directors.
   d. The Board may be indemnified by Mix only if the court deems it proper.

10 (May 82)

Fairwell is executive vice president and treasurer of Wonder Corporation. He was named as a party in a shareholder derivative action in connection with certain activities he engaged in as a corporate officer. In the lawsuit, it was determined that he was liable for negligence in performance of his duties. The board would like to indemnify him. The articles of incorporation do not contain any provisions regarding indemnification of officers and directors. Indemnification

   a. Is not permitted since the articles of incorporation do not so provide.
   b. Is permitted only if he is found not to have been grossly negligent.
   c. Can not include attorney's fees since he was found to have been negligent.
   d. May be permitted by court order despite the fact that Fairwell was found to be negligent.

B. Extraordinary Corporate Matters
1. Combinations

11 (R01)

Acorn Corp. wants to acquire the entire business of Trend Corp. Which of the following methods of business combination will best satisfy Acorn's objectives without requiring the approval of the shareholders of either corporation?
   a. A merger of Trend into Acorn, whereby Trend shareholders receive cash or Acorn shares.
   b. A sale of all the assets of Trend, outside the regular course of business, to Acorn, for cash.
   c. An acquisition of all the shares of Trend through a compulsory share exchange for Acorn shares.
   d. A cash tender offer, whereby Acorn acquires at least 90% of Trend's shares, followed by a short-form merger of Trend into Acorn.

6 (R99)

Under the Revised Model Business Corporation Act, a dissenting stockholder's appraisal right generally applies to which of the following corporate actions?

	Consolidations	Short-form Mergers
a.	Yes	Yes
b.	Yes	No
c.	No	Yes
d.	No	No

8 (R98)

Under the Revised Model Business Corporation Act, which of the following actions by a corporation would entitle a stockholder to dissent from the action and obtain payment of the fair value of his/her shares?
   I. An amendment to the articles of incorporation that materially and adversely affects rights in respect of a dissenter's shares because it alters or abolishes a preferential right of the shares.
   II. Consummation of a plan of share exchange to which the corporation is a party as the corporation whose shares will be acquired, if the stockholder is entitled to vote on the plan.
   a. I only.
   b. II only.
   c. Both I and II.
   d. Neither I nor II.

3 (R97)

Which of the following actions may be taken by a corporation's board of directors without stockholder approval?
   a. Purchasing substantially all of the assets of another corporation.
   b. Selling substantially all of the corporation's assets.
   c. Dissolving the corporation.
   d. Amending the articles of incorporation.

25 (November 95)

Which of the following statements is a general requirement for the merger of two corporations?
   a. The merger plan must be approved unanimously by the stockholders of both corporations.
   b. The merger plan must be approved unanimously by the boards of both corporations.
   c. The absorbed corporation must amend its articles of incorporation.
   d. The stockholders of both corporations must be given due notice of a special meeting, including a copy or summary of the merger plan.

25 (November 94)

A parent corporation owned more than 90% of each class of the outstanding stock issued by a subsidiary corporation and decided to merge that subsidiary into itself. Under the Revised Model Business Corporation Act, which of the following actions must be taken?

a. The subsidiary corporation's board of directors must pass a merger resolution.
b. The subsidiary corporation's dissenting stockholders must be given an appraisal remedy.
c. The parent corporation's stockholders must approve the merger.
d. The parent corporation's dissenting stockholders must be given an appraisal remedy.

14 (May 94)

Under the Revised Model Business Corporation Act, a merger of two public corporations usually requires all of the following except

a. A formal plan of merger.
b. An affirmative vote by the holders of a majority of each corporation's voting shares.
c. Receipt of voting stock by all stockholders of the original corporations.
d. Approval by the board of directors of each corporation.

4 (November 92)

Generally, a merger of two corporations requires

a. That a special meeting notice and a copy of the merger plan be given to all stockholders of both corporations.
b. Unanimous approval of the merger plan by the stockholders of both corporations.
c. Unanimous approval of the merger plan by the boards of both corporations.
d. That all liabilities owed by the absorbed corporation be paid before the merger.

20 (May 92)

Which of the following actions may a corporation take without its stockholders' consent?

a. Consolidate with one or more corporations.
b. Merge with one or more corporations.
c. Dissolve voluntarily.
d. Purchase 55% of another corporation's stock.

7 (May 91)

A consolidation of two corporations usually requires all of the following except

a. Approval by the board of directors of each corporation.
b. Receipt of voting stock by all stockholders of the original corporations.
c. Provision for an appraisal buyout of dissenting stockholders.
d. An affirmative vote by the holders of a majority of each corporation's voting shares.

7 (May 84)

Able and Baker are two corporations, the shares of which are publicly traded. Baker plans to merge into Able. Which of the following is a requirement of the merger?

a. The IRS must approve the merger.
b. The common stockholders of Baker must receive common stock of Able.
c. The creditors of Baker must approve the merger.
d. The boards of directors of both Able and Baker must approve the merger.

35 (November 74)

Under which of the following circumstances would a corporation's existence terminate?

a. The death of its sole owner-shareholder.
b. Its becoming insolvent.
c. Its legal consolidation with another corporation.
d. Its reorganization under the federal bankruptcy laws.

Corporations

3 (May 93)

Edwards, a director and a 10% stockholder in National Corp., is dissatisfied with the way National's officers, particularly Olsen, the president, have been operating the corporation. Edwards has made many suggestions that have been rejected by the board of directors, and has made several unsuccessful attempts to have Olsen removed as president.

National and Grand Corp. had been negotiating a merger that Edwards has adamantly opposed. Edwards has blamed Olsen for initiating the negotiation and has urged the board to fire Olsen. National's board refused to fire Olsen. In an attempt to defeat the merger, Edwards approached Jenkins, the president of Queen Corp., and contracted for Queen to purchase several of National's assets. Jenkins knew Edwards was a National director, but had never done business with National. When National learned of the contract, it notified Queen that the contract was invalid.

Edwards filed an objection to the merger before the stockholders' meeting called to consider the merger proposal was held. At the meeting, Edwards voted against the merger proposal.

Despite Edward's efforts, the merger was approved by both corporations. Edwards then orally demanded that National purchase Edward's stock, citing the dissenters' rights provision of the corporation's by-laws, which reflects the Model Business Corporation Act.

National's board has claimed National does not have to purchase Edward's stock.

As a result of the above:

- Edwards initiated a minority stockholder's action to have Olsen removed as president and to force National to purchase Edwards' stock.
- Queen sued National to enforce the contract and/or collect damages.
- Queen sued Edwards to collect damages.

Required: Answer the following questions and give the reasons for your answers.
   a. Will Edwards be successful in a lawsuit to have Olsen removed as president?
   b. Will Edwards be successful in a lawsuit to have National purchase the stock?
   c. 1. Will Queen be successful in a lawsuit against National?
      2. Will Queen be successful in a lawsuit against Edwards?

a. Edwards will not win the suit to have Olsen removed as president. The right to hire and fire officers is held by the board of directors. Individual stockholders, regardless of the size of their holding, have no vote in the selection of officers. Individual stockholders may exert influence in this area by voting for directors at the annual stockholders' meeting.

b. Edwards will lose the suit to have National purchase the stock. A stockholder who dissents from a merger may require the corporation to purchase his or her shares if the statutory requirements are met and would be entitled to the fair value of the stock (appraisal remedy). To compel the purchase, Edwards would have had to file an objection to the merger before the stockholders' meeting at which the merger proposal was considered, vote against the merger proposal, and make a written demand that the corporation purchase the stock at an appraised price. Edwards will lose because the first two requirements were met but Edwards failed to make a written demand that the corporation purchase the stock.

c. 1. Queen will lose its suit against National to enforce the contract, even though Edwards was a National director. Jenkins may have assumed that Edwards was acting as National's agent, but Edwards had no authority to contract with Queen. A director has a fiduciary duty to the stockholders of a corporation but, unless expressly authorized by the board of directors or the officers of the corporation, has no authority to contract on behalf of the corporation. There is no implied agency authority merely by being a director.

2. Queen will win its suit against Edwards because Edwards had no authority to act for National. Edwards will be personally liable for Queen's damages.

4C (November 76)

Rex Corporation, one of your clients, has engaged you to examine its financial statements in connection with a prospective merger or a consolidation with King Corporation. Both methods of acquisition are being considered under applicable corporate statutory law. Rex is the larger of the two corporations and is in reality acquiring King Corporation.

Required: Answer the following, setting forth reasons for any conclusions stated.

1. Discuss the meaning of the terms merger and consolidation as used in corporate law with particular emphasis on the legal difference between the two.

2. What are the major legal procedures which must be met in order to accomplish either a merger or consolidation?

1. The major legal difference between a merger and a consolidation relates to the continued existence of the corporations involved. In the case of a merger of two corporations, one corporation, the acquiring corporation, survives. The acquired corporation, on the other hand, transfers all its assets to the acquiring corporation. Consequently, it is absorbed by the survivor and dissolves. The surviving corporation takes all the assets and assumes all the liabilities of the acquired corporation. When two corporations consolidate, however, both corporate parties to the consolidation transfer their assets to a new corporation and then both dissolve. Liabilities of each of the two consolidating corporations are valid against the new consolidated corporation.

2. The major legal procedures that must be followed in order to accomplish a merger or consolidation under applicable corporate statutory law are essentially these:

(a) Approval of the plan of merger or consolidation must be given by the boards of directors of the two corporations who are parties to the merger or consolidation.

(b) Timely written notice must be given to all shareholders of record. A copy or summary of the plan must accompany the notice to shareholders.

(c) Approval must be given by a majority of the shareholders of each corporation who are entitled to vote on the proposed plan of merger or consolidation. Some states require a higher percentage for approval.

(d) The articles of merger or consolidation must be properly filed by an appropriate officer of each corporation.

2. Dissolution and Liquidation

(R03)

Under the Revised Model Business Corporation Act, which of the following conditions is necessary for a corporation to achieve a successful voluntary dissolution?

a. Successful application to the secretary of state in which the corporation holds its primary place of business.

b. A recommendation of dissolution by the board of directors and approval by a majority of all shareholders entitled to vote.

c. Approval by the board of directors of an amendment to the certificate of incorporation calling for the dissolution of the corporation.

d. Unanimous approval of the board of directors and two-thirds vote of all shareholders entitled to vote on a resolution of voluntary dissolution.

3 (November 92)

Which of the following must take place for a corporation to be voluntarily dissolved?

a. Passage by the board of directors of a resolution to dissolve.

b. Approval by the officers of a resolution to dissolve.

c. Amendment of the certificate of incorporation.

d. Unanimous vote of the stockholders.

Corporations

18 (May 92)

A corporate stockholder is entitled to which of the following rights?

a. Elect officers.
b. Receive annual dividends.
c. Approve dissolution.
d. Prevent corporate borrowing.

6 (May 84)

Which of the following would be grounds for the judicial dissolution of a corporation on the petition of a shareholder?

a. Refusal of the board of directors to declare a dividend.
b. Waste of corporate assets by the board of directors.
c. Loss operations of the corporation for three years.
d. Failure by the corporation to file its federal income tax returns.

APPENDIX

Answers to Objective Questions

Page	Question	Answer
	PART I	
3	6 (May 89)	B
	4 (Nov 86)	A
	1 (Nov 93)	C
4	2 (Nov 93)	C
	1 (May 93)	B
	1 (Nov 91)	D
	2 (Nov 91)	A
	28 (Nov 87)	C
	4 (Nov 83)	C
5	2 (Nov 78)	D
	1 (Nov 76)	B
	21 (Nov 75)	B
	23 (Nov 75)	A
6	1 (R97)	C
7	8 (Nov 95)	B
	4 (Nov 91)	A
	29 (Nov 87)	D
	1 (Nov 83)	A
	18 (Nov 75)	D
10	9 (Nov 95)	C
	2 (May 93)	A
	4 (May 93)	D
	5 (Nov 90)	A
	1 (May 89)	B
11	9 (May 89)	C
	1 (May 81)	B
	3 (Nov 78)	B
	3 (Nov 76)	D
13	2 (R99)	C
	10 (Nov 95)	D
14	10 (Nov 94)	C
	9 (May 94)	B
	3 (May 93)	A
	3 (Nov 91)	C
	5 (Nov 91)	A
	1 (Nov 90)	C
15	2 (May 89)	B
	7 (May 89)	C
	26 (Nov 87)	D
	27 (Nov 87)	D
19	3 (R99)	C
	12 (Nov 95)	B
	12 (Nov 94)	B
20	13 (Nov 94)	D

Page	Question	Answer
	3 (Nov 93)	C
	4 (Nov 93)	A
	5 (Nov 93)	A
	6 (Nov 91)	B
	8 (Nov 91)	C
21	6 (Nov 90)	A
	7 (Nov 90)	B
	8 (Nov 90)	C
	7 (Nov 86)	C
	5 (Nov 84)	B
22	5 (Nov 83)	D
	3 (May 81)	C
	29 (Nov 79)	D
	1 (Nov 77)	C
	4 (Nov 76)	A
24	11 (Nov 95)	D
	13 (Nov 95)	C
	11 (Nov 94)	A
	6 (Nov 93)	A
25	2 (May 92)	C
	3 (May 92)	C
	4 (May 92)	A
	5 (May 92)	C
	7 (Nov 91)	B
	8 (May 89)	C
	8 (May 88)	C
26	2 (May 94)	
	61	C
	62	C
	63	D
	64	D
	65	B
	66	B
28	14 (Nov 95)	D
	15 (Nov 95)	A
29	5 (May 95)	B
	14 (Nov 94)	B
	15 (Nov 94)	C
	10 (May 94)	B
	10 (Nov 93)	B
	6 (May 93)	D
30	9 (May 93)	D
	1 (May 92)	D
	3 (Nov 90)	A
	9 (Nov 90)	B
	1 (May 88)	B

Page	Question	Answer
31	2 (May 88)	B
	3 (May 88)	C
	9 (Nov 86)	A
	10 (Nov 86)	B
	9 (Nov 83)	D
	10 (Nov 83)	C
32	2 (May 81)	D
34	4 (May 95)	D
	7 (May 94)	B
	8 (May 94)	C
	9 (Nov 93)	A
	7 (May 93)	C
35	8 (May 93)	C
	9 (Nov 91)	B
	3 (May 89)	D
	33 (Nov 87)	B
	34 (Nov 87)	B
36	8 (Nov 86)	D
	6 (Nov 83)	C
37	1 (R99)	A
	1 (R98)	B
	1 (R96)	C
	2 (R96)	D
	1 (Nov 95)	C
	2 (Nov 95)	D
38	3 (Nov 95)	B
	5 (Nov 95)	C
	6 (Nov 95)	C
	7 (Nov 95)	A
	2 (May 95)	C
	3 (May 95)	D
39	1 (Nov 94)	A
	2 (Nov 94)	C
	3 (Nov 94)	A
	5 (Nov 94)	D
	6 (Nov 94)	A
40	7 (Nov 94)	B
	1 (May 94)	C
	2 (May 94)	A
	5 (May 94)	D
	6 (May 94)	D
	PART II	
43	6 (May 95)	D
	16 (Nov 94)	B

Page	Question	Answer	Page	Question	Answer	Page	Question	Answer
	11 (Nov 93)	D		16 (Nov 75)	D		36 (Nov 94)	D
	6 (May 92)	C	55	30 (May 75)	C		36 (Nov 93)	A
	11 (Nov 91)	C		13 (May 89)	C		28 (May 93)	B
44	13 (Nov 91)	C		4 (May 88)	A		38 (May 92)	A
	1 (May 85)	D	56	59 (May 86)	A	71	34 (Nov 91)	B
	22 (Nov 84)	C		1 (May 84)	A		38 (May 91)	B
	12 (Nov 81)	A		2 (May 83)	D		38 (Nov 90)	C
	26 (Nov 80)	C		5 (Nov 82)	C		32 (Nov 89)	C
	4 (May 78)	C		31 (May 81)	D		44 (May 88)	A
	5 (May 78)	A	57	10 (May 78)	D	72	15 (Nov 87)	C
45	6 (R01)	C		23 (May 77)	A		36 (May 87)	C
	3 (R00)	A		27 (May 77)	D		38 (Nov 86)	C
	3 (R96)	C	58	2 (Nov 95)			17 (May 86)	C
	9 (May 95)	B		61	B		21 (Nov 85)	D
	30 (May 81)	A		62	A	73	30 (May 85)	D
46	45 (May 79)	C		63	B		39 (Nov 84)	C
	3 (May 78)	D		64	D		28 (May 84)	D
	7 (May 92)	B		65	B		34 (May 83)	C
	3 (May 91)	C	60	7 (May 95)	C		26 (Nov 82)	A
	5 (May 90)	B		17 (Nov 94)	C	74	27 (Nov 82)	D
47	33 (Nov 79)	C		1 (May 90)	C		60 (May 81)	A
	29 (Nov 76)	D		2 (Nov 88)	A		48 (Nov 79)	C
	15 (Nov 75)	D		6 (May 88)	B		47 (May 79)	D
	31 (May 75)	C&D	61	4 (May 87)	D		48 (May 78)	D
	9 (Nov 74)	B		14 (Nov 84)	A	75	14 (May 77)	D
48	4 (R99)	C		2 (May 84)	A		48 (Nov 75)	C
	8 (May 95)	B		29 (Nov 80)	D		35 (May 75)	C
	18 (Nov 94)	A		11 (Nov 74)	B		44 (May 75)	C
	19 (Nov 94)	C		11 (May 89)	B	76	43 (May 74)	A
49	14 (Nov 93)	C	62	3 (May 85)	A		46 (May 74)	C
	4 (May 90)	C		34 (Nov 82)	C			
	3 (Nov 89)	C		50 (Nov 79)	C	**PART III**		
	23 (Nov 87)	B		25 (Nov 76)	B			
	24 (Nov 87)	B	63	13 (Nov 93)	B	81	57 (May 95)	D
	60 (May 86)	D		2 (May 90)	D		50 (Nov 94)	A
50	4 (May 84)	B		2 (Nov 89)	B		42 (May 94)	A
	14 (Nov 83)	A		12 (May 89)	B		50 (Nov 93)	D
	7 (Nov 82)	A		5 (May 87)	A		43 (Nov 88)	C
	29 (May 81)	C	64	12 (Nov 83)	B		34 (May 86)	D
	34 (May 81)	B		13 (Nov 83)	B	82	55 (May 84)	C
51	31 (Nov 79)	B		5 (May 82)	D		33 (Nov 76)	D
	20 (Nov 76)	D		14 (Nov 81)	C		35 (Nov 76)	A
	48 (May 76)	C		15 (Nov 81)	A		11 (Nov 81)	A
	22 (May 75)	D		16 (Nov 81)	D		1 (May 76)	A
52	10 (Nov 74)	B	65	4 (Nov 77)	C		19 (May 78)	A
53	6 (May 87)	D		21 (Nov 76)	B	83	21 (May 92)	B
	15 (Nov 84)	D		45 (May 76)	C		25 (May 89)	A
	3 (May 84)	A		27 (May 75)	A		15 (Nov 86)	D
	6 (May 82)	A&B	66	14 (Nov 74)	B		7 (Nov 85)	D
	7 (May 82)	C	69	5 (R01)	C		27 (Nov 83)	C
54	27 (Nov 80)	A		16 (R01)	D	84	6 (May 83)	B
	40 (May 79)	B	70	33 (Nov 95)	A		2 (Nov 82)	B
	22 (Nov 76)	D		34 (Nov 95)	B		7 (Nov 79)	D

Page	Question	Answer
	27 (Nov 78)	D
85	16 (May 88)	C
	7 (Nov 81)	C
	3 (May 76)	D
	13 (Nov 92)	C
	10 (Nov 88)	B
86	3 (Nov 82)	C
	10 (May 81)	B
	17 (Nov 74)	D
	33 (May 74)	A
	24 (May 89)	A
87	19 (Nov 84)	D
	28 (Nov 83)	D
	4 (Nov 81)	D
	8 (May 76)	A
	10 (May 76)	A
88	6 (May 75)	D
	18 (R01)	D
	41 (Nov 95)	B
	51 (Nov 83)	B
	38 (May 83)	A
89	18 (May 81)	D
	8 (Nov 75)	B
	39 (May 75)	B
90	21 (May 89)	C
91	22 (May 89)	D
	11 (Nov 92)	B
	12 (May 90)	B
	17 (May 88)	A
	1 (May 86)	A
92	9 (May 83)	D
	6 (May 76)	D
	18 (Nov 74)	B
	46 (Nov 89)	A
93	53 (Nov 84)	D
	53 (Nov 83)	B
	4 (Nov 82)	D
	35 (May 79)	C
94	36 (May 78)	D
	1 (Nov 75)	C
	14 (May 90)	D
	23 (May 89)	D
95	34 (May 74)	A
	16 (May 91)	A
	46 (May 90)	C
	41 (May 85)	B
	8 (May 83)	D
	15 (Nov 80)	A
96	5 (Nov 79)	B
	9 (Nov 79)	B
97	22 (May 92)	B
	11 (May 91)	C
	13 (May 90)	C

Page	Question	Answer
98	9 (Nov 89)	C
	11 (Nov 88)	C
	12 (Nov 88)	A
	11 (May 87)	C
	15 (May 87)	D
99	16 (May 87)	A
	12 (Nov 86)	A
	24 (Nov 86)	A
	2 (May 86)	C
	6 (Nov 85)	C
100	11 (Nov 85)	D
	18 (Nov 84)	D
	29 (Nov 83)	B
	1 (Nov 82)	A
	15 (May 82)	A
101	15 (May 78)	B
	4 (May 76)	D
104	12 (Nov 92)	B
	11 (May 90)	A
	17 (May 85)	C
105	26 (Nov 83)	B
	3 (Nov 79)	A
	22 (Nov 74)	B
	9 (May 79)	A
106	21 (Nov 90)	A
	7 (May 75)	D
	54 (May 92)	C
107	53 (May 84)	C
	6 (Nov 82)	D
	45 (Nov 82)	B
	25 (May 74)	C
108	20 (May 95)	A
	10 (Nov 89)	A
	13 (Nov 85)	A
109	12 (May 82)	A
	36 (Nov 76)	B
	7 (May 76)	B
	19 (Nov 74)	A
	24 (May 92)	D
	1 (Nov 87)	D
110	22 (Nov 83)	C
	13 (May 79)	B
	18 (May 88)	B
	51 (May 82)	D
111	34 (Nov 76)	C
	30 (May 74)	D
	23 (May 92)	B
	12 (R01)	C
	21 (Nov 93)	A
112	21 (May 93)	C
	15 (Nov 92)	C
	17 (May 90)	B
	11 (Nov 89)	B

Page	Question	Answer
	13 (Nov 86)	C
	4 (May 86)	D
113	25 (May 92)	D
	22 (Nov 90)	D
	26 (May 89)	B
	19 (May 88)	A
	14 (Nov 86)	D
114	5 (May 86)	A
	20 (Nov 84)	C
	11 (May 84)	C
	10 (May 83)	B
115	13 (Nov 88)	D
	2 (Nov 87)	D
	18 (May 87)	A
	8 (Nov 82)	A
	12 (May 79)	B
116	35 (May 77)	C
	16 (May 95)	B
	23 (Nov 93)	B
	28 (May 92)	B
	21 (Nov 91)	A
117	22 (Nov 91)	B
	21 (May 91)	C
	21 (May 90)	C
	14 (Nov 89)	D
	15 (Nov 89)	C
	30 (May 89)	C
118	25 (May 88)	C
	5 (Nov 87)	A
	19 (Nov 86)	D
	20 (Nov 86)	A
119	21 (Nov 86)	C
	8 (May 86)	B
	10 (Nov 85)	C
	19 (May 85)	D
	9 (Nov 82)	A
	10 (Nov 82)	B
120	9 (Nov 81)	D
	2 (Nov 79)	A
	34 (May 77)	B
	14 (May 76)	B
	1 (May 75)	A
122	17 (May 95)	A
	29 (May 92)	C
	23 (May 90)	B
123	16 (Nov 88)	D
	22 (May 87)	C
	12 (May 84)	D
	14 (May 83)	C
	3 (Nov 81)	C
124	5 (R00)	C
	20 (May 91)	D
	23 (Nov 90)	C

Page	Question	Answer	Page	Question	Answer	Page	Question	Answer
	28 (May 89)	C		8 (Nov 79)	D	152	16 (May 78)	B
	4 (Nov 87)	A		11 (Nov 79)	A		21 (Nov 92)	C
125	10 (May 86)	B		5 (Nov 76)	D		33 (May 92)	D
	15 (Nov 85)	C	138	3 (Nov 75)	B		34 (May 92)	C
	23 (May 85)	B		41 (May 75)	D	153	19 (May 90)	A
	15 (May 83)	C		21 (May 88)	D		24 (May 90)	D
	14 (May 82)	D		40 (Nov 87)	D		17 (Nov 89)	A
126	18 (May 95)	B		55 (Nov 84)	C		17 (Nov 85)	A
	24 (Nov 93)	B	139	50 (Nov 83)	A		18 (Nov 85)	B
	22 (Nov 92)	C		27 (May 80)	D	154	26 (May 85)	C
	23 (Nov 92)	C		33 (May 79)	C		25 (Nov 84)	D
127	30 (May 92)	A		38 (May 78)	D		17 (May 83)	D
	23 (Nov 91)	C		43 (May 77)	B		12 (Nov 82)	B
	16 (Nov 89)	B		42 (May 78)	No		4 (May 75)	A
	12 (May 86)	C			Correct	155	19 (May 95)	A
128	25 (May 85)	C			Answer		25 (Nov 92)	A
	23 (Nov 84)	C					25 (Nov 86)	A
	16 (May 83)	B	143	1 (R98)			13 (May 81)	C
	41 (May 83)	D		1	J	156	32 (Nov 78)	D
	49 (Nov 82)	B		2	C		21 (May 78)	C
129	12 (May 81)	A		3	D		10 (May 75)	B
	4 (Nov 79)	D		4	E		13 (R01)	A
	33 (May 77)	A		5	G	157	26 (Nov 93)	A
	6 (Nov 76)	C		6	E		25 (Nov 90)	B
	24 (Nov 74)	D		7	E		24 (Nov 84)	D
130	16 (Nov 92)	D		8	H		19 (May 83)	D
	26 (May 92)	D		9	K		35 (May 74)	C
	15 (May 90)	C		10	A	159	47 (Nov 95)	B
	20 (May 90)	A		21 (May 95)	B		55 (Nov 94)	D
	16 (Nov 86)	A		22 (May 95)	C		19 (Nov 89)	C
131	9 (Nov 85)	D		24 (Nov 92)	A		35 (May 89)	B
	12 (May 83)	D		24 (Nov 91)	D		51 (Nov 88)	D
	20 (May 88)	D	145	22 (May 90)	C	160	27 (May 85)	D
	26 (May 78)	D		18 (Nov 89)	B		21 (Nov 82)	A
132	27 (May 89)	D		33 (May 89)	D		43 (May 75)	A
	13 (May 87)	B		21 (May 87)	A		22 (May 74)	B
133	6 (May 86)	A		18 (May 83)	A	161	23 (May 95)	A
	33 (May 81)	C		11 (Nov 82)	B		24 (May 95)	D
	25 (Nov 80)	C	146	5 (Nov 81)	C		25 (Nov 91)	C
	13 (May 78)	A		44 (May 78)	D	162	23 (May 91)	A
134	17 (Nov 92)	D		3 (Nov 77)	D		51 (May 91)	A
135	12 (Nov 89)	C		36 (May 75)	B		34 (May 89)	D
	14 (Nov 88)	C	147	37 (May 75)	C		37 (Nov 76)	D
	18 (May 90)	A		23 (Nov 74)	A	165	9 (R99)	A
	21 (Nov 84)	D	150	25 (May 90)	D		25 (May 93)	A
	9 (R00)	C		24 (May 88)	A		24 (May 91)	B
136	46 (May 94)	A		13 (May 84)	C		13 (Nov 80)	C
	17 (May 91)	B		8 (May 79)	B		22 (May 78)	A
	40 (May 90)	C		18 (Nov 88)	D	166	5 (Nov 77)	B
	29 (May 89)	C	151	23 (May 88)	D		32 (May 92)	C
	47 (Nov 86)	D		20 (May 85)	A		35 (May 92)	D
137	46 (Nov 85)	D		21 (May 85)	D		48 (May 90)	D
	13 (May 83)	D		22 (May 85)	C	167	25 (May 87)	D
				13 (Nov 82)	A			

Page	Question	Answer	Page	Question	Answer	Page	Question	Answer
	18 (Nov 86)	A		36 (May 81)	D		23 (May 94)	D
	20 (May 83)	B	181	31 (May 77)	B		(R03)	B
	13 (May 82)	C		16 (May 76)	C	195	27 (Nov 93)	D
	2 (May 76)	D		10 (May 74)	C		28 (Nov 93)	B
	11 (R97)	D		29 (Nov 95)	D		29 (Nov 93)	D
168	25 (May 95)	B		24 (May 84)	C		30 (Nov 92)	A
	22 (Nov 93)	D	182	44 (May 80)	B		30 (May 91)	D
	22 (May 93)	A		30 (May 77)	B		29 (Nov 90)	D
	19 (Nov 92)	D		28 (Nov 74)	C	196	25 (Nov 89)	B
	15 (May 91)	D		25 (May 94)	B		32 (May 88)	D
169	22 (May 88)	B		26 (May 87)	A		22 (May 83)	D
	7 (May 86)	C	183	27 (May 87)	B		16 (Nov 82)	A
	2 (Nov 81)	C		24 (Nov 82)	C		18 (May 82)	A
				25 (Nov 82)	B		6 (R00)	A
PART IV				24 (Nov 81)	C	197	34 (Nov 94)	C
				29 (Nov 81)	D		27 (Nov 89)	A
173	22 (Nov 82)	A	184	1 (May 79)	C		28 (Nov 88)	C
	17 (Nov 77)	D		20 (Nov 78)	D		27 (Nov 90)	B
	11 (May 76)	C		24 (Nov 76)	C		28 (Nov 84)	D
	12 (Nov 75)	C		15 (May 76)	D		41 (May 81)	D
	27 (Nov 74)	C		(R03)	B	198	30 (Nov 93)	D
174	11 (May 74)	B	185	28 (Nov 95)	D		37 (Nov 92)	B
	24 (May 94)	B		31 (Nov 94)	A		38 (Nov 92)	D
	26 (Nov 90)	D		25 (Nov 93)	C		39 (Nov 92)	C
	25 (Nov 81)	D		26 (Nov 92)	B		33 (May 91)	C
	27 (Nov 81)	D		28 (Nov 92)	C	199	34 (May 91)	A
175	39 (May 80)	B		26 (Nov 91)	B		34 (May 87)	A
	27 (Nov 76)	D	186	27 (May 91)	B		18 (May 84)	A
	20 (Nov 74)	B		21 (Nov 88)	C		44 (May 81)	C
	25 (Nov 78)	B		29 (May 87)	A		3 (May 80)	A
	18 (Nov 77)	A		32 (Nov 85)	B		2 (May 94)	
176	26 (Nov 76)	C	187	22 (May 84)	D		70	F
	19 (Nov 74)	A		23 (May 84)	C		71	T
	30 (Nov 95)	C		26 (May 83)	C		72	F
	20 (Nov 89)	B		20 (Nov 82)	D	201	28 (Nov 90)	C
	21 (Nov 89)	A		25 (May 82)	D		42 (May 81)	C
177	28 (Nov 86)	C		41 (May 80)	B		2 (R98)	
	27 (May 83)	A	188	7 (May 79)	D		1	A
	26 (Nov 81)	B		21 (Nov 78)	D		2	F
	35 (May 81)	B		24 (Nov 78)	C		3	H
	38 (May 81)	C		32 (May 77)	B		4	F
178	36 (May 80)	D		31 (Nov 76)	C		5	B
	42 (May 80)	A		25 (Nov 74)	B	203	28 (May 95)	D
	5 (May 79)	A					29 (May 95)	C
	32 (Nov 76)	D	**PART V**				30 (May 95)	A
	12 (May 76)	B					39 (Nov 93)	A
	26 (Nov 74)	D	193	13 (R96)	B	204	30 (Nov 91)	B
179	30 (Nov 94)	D		26 (Nov 95)	B		42 (Nov 91)	D
	19 (Nov 77)	B		27 (Nov 95)	A		43 (Nov 91)	C
180	13 (May 74)	D		26 (Nov 94)	C		44 (Nov 91)	C
	26 (May 95)	A	194	28 (Nov 94)	A		45 (Nov 91)	B
	15 (Nov 82)	B		21 (May 94)	A		34 (Nov 90)	A
	23 (May 82)	A		22 (May 94)	D	205	28 (Nov 89)	D

Page	Question	Answer	Page	Question	Answer	Page	Question	Answer
	23 (Nov 88)	D		**PART VI**			37 (Nov 89)	A
206	20 (May 82)	C					44 (May 89)	C
	22 (May 82)	B	223	6 (R96)	A		45 (May 89)	C
	43 (May 81)	B		30 (May 93)	C		39 (May 88)	C
	3 (Nov 95)			34 (Nov 86)	B	234	45 (May 87)	B
	71	A		28 (Nov 79)	B		22 (May 86)	B
	72	B	224	41 (Nov 94)	B		40 (Nov 80)	D
	73	B		43 (Nov 94)	B		3 (Nov 95)	
	74	C		31 (May 94)	A		76	A
	75	A		32 (May 94)	D		77	B
207	2 (May 93)			33 (May 94)	D		78	B
	61	Y		29 (May 93)	B		79	B
	62	N	225	39 (May 92)	A		80	D
	63	Y		40 (May 92)	D	235	2 (Nov 92)	
	64	N		36 (Nov 91)	B		61	Y
	65	N		37 (Nov 91)	D		62	Y
	66	B		40 (May 91)	D		63	N
	67	E		41 (May 91)	C		64	Y
	68	A	226	39 (Nov 90)	B		65	Y
	69	D		29 (May 90)	C		66	Y
	70	C		40 (May 89)	D		67	Y
210	12 (R97)	D		41 (May 89)	B		68	Y
211	33 (Nov 94)	A		37 (May 88)	A		69	Y
	31 (Nov 93)	B		8 (Nov 87)	C		70	N
	31 (May 91)	A	227	41 (May 87)	B		71	N
	30 (Nov 90)	D		32 (Nov 86)	D		72	Y
	32 (Nov 90)	D		43 (May 79)	B		73	N
	33 (Nov 90)	C		3 (May 77)	C		74	N
212	22 (Nov 89)	B	229	42 (Nov 94)	D		75	Y
	25 (Nov 88)	D		33 (May 93)	A	237	52 (Nov 94)	A
	26 (Nov 88)	A		34 (May 93)	B		32 (May 90)	C
	27 (Nov 88)	B		43 (May 92)	B		4 (May 77)	D
	33 (May 87)	B		35 (Nov 91)	B	238	48 (Nov 94)	C
213	16 (May 84)	B	230	45 (May 91)	C		24 (May 86)	D
	17 (Nov 82)	C		39 (Nov 89)	A		31 (Nov 82)	C
	35 (May 80)	C		42 (May 88)	B		48 (May 79)	B
216	34 (May 95)	D		42 (Nov 84)	B		6 (May 78)	C
	35 (May 95)	D		(R03)	D	239	30 (May 76)	A
217	37 (Nov 94)	B		44 (Nov 94)	D		(R03)	C
	32 (Nov 93)	C	231	37 (May 94)	B		39 (May 94)	A
	33 (Nov 93)	A		40 (May 94)	B		37 (Nov 93)	D
	34 (Nov 93)	D		40 (Nov 93)	A		5 (May 93)	B
218	31 (Nov 92)	A		43 (Nov 93)	D	240	32 (Nov 88)	B
	32 (Nov 92)	D		44 (Nov 93)	B		20 (May 86)	D
	29 (Nov 89)	B		45 (Nov 93)	C	241	15 (R01)	C
	26 (Nov 85)	B	232	35 (May 93)	B		45 (Nov 94)	B
	24 (May 83)	D		40 (Nov 91)	A	242	46 (Nov 94)	A
	19 (Nov 82)	B		43 (Nov 90)	D		47 (Nov 94)	A
219	27 (Nov 94)	B		44 (Nov 90)	C		34 (May 94)	B
	40 (May 81)	B		45 (Nov 90)	A		35 (May 94)	A
				33 (May 90)	A		41 (Nov 93)	C
				37 (May 90)	D	243	31 (May 93)	A
			233	35 (Nov 89)	B		32 (May 93)	B

Page	Question	Answer	Page	Question	Answer	Page	Question	Answer
	41 (May 92)	C		32 (Nov 91)	C		36 (May 84)	D
	42 (May 92)	B		36 (May 91)	D		37 (May 84)	B
	39 (Nov 91)	D	256	36 (Nov 90)	B	269	35 (Nov 82)	B
	42 (May 91)	C		26 (May 90)	B		37 (Nov 82)	C
244	40 (Nov 90)	A		37 (May 89)	D	270	37 (May 82)	D
	30 (May 90)	A		43 (May 88)	C		38 (Nov 88)	D
	31 (May 90)	B		37 (May 87)	A		36 (May 85)	D
	33 (Nov 88)	D		39 (Nov 86)	A	271	43 (May 82)	C
	38 (May 88)	A	257	18 (May 86)	D		46 (Nov 80)	B
245	40 (May 88)	C		22 (Nov 85)	C		42 (May 76)	C
	12 (Nov 87)	B		32 (Nov 95)	B		2 (May 74)	C
	39 (May 87)	A		36 (May 95)	D		8 (R00)	B
	40 (May 87)	C		35 (Nov 94)	B	272	44 (May 95)	D
	33 (Nov 86)	C	258	37 (May 92)	D		46 (Nov 90)	D
246	35 (Nov 86)	C		33 (Nov 91)	A		49 (May 89)	A
	41 (Nov 80)	C		37 (Nov 90)	D		37 (Nov 88)	C
247	21 (Nov 79)	A		31 (Nov 89)	C	273	41 (Nov 82)	C
	12 (Nov 78)	D		36 (May 89)	C		40 (May 93)	A
	43 (Nov 75)	C		45 (May 88)	B		34 (Nov 92)	A
248	45 (Nov 74)	D	259	16 (May 86)	D	274	46 (Nov 91)	A
	48 (Nov 74)	D		4 (R97)	A		47 (Nov 91)	C
	8 (May 78)	D		35 (Nov 95)	C		46 (May 88)	D
	17 (Nov 76)	D		36 (Nov 95)	A		43 (Nov 86)	B
	42 (Nov 75)	A	260	37 (Nov 95)	A	275	34 (May 85)	C
249	45 (Nov 75)	C		39 (Nov 95)	A		40 (Nov 81)	D
	47 (Nov 75)	B		40 (Nov 95)	D		3 (Nov 80)	D
	1 (May 80)	C&D		37 (May 95)	C		43 (May 95)	A
250	35 (Nov 79)	B		38 (May 95)	A	276	48 (May 89)	B
	12 (May 78)	D	261	39 (May 95)	B		48 (Nov 87)	B
	45 (Nov 77)	A		40 (May 95)	B		7 (Nov 80)	C
	32 (Nov 81)	C		38 (Nov 94)	B	277	19 (May 77)	D
	44 (Nov 74)	B		27 (May 94)	B		39 (May 76)	D
251	34 (Nov 83)	A		28 (May 94)	B	280	44 (Nov 86)	D
	31 (Nov 81)	A		29 (May 94)	A		2(a) (R96)	
	18 (Nov 80)	C	262	40 (Nov 94)	B		1	A
	27 (May 82)	C					2	A
252	5 (May 80)	A		**PART VII**			3	D
	37 (Nov 79)	D					4	B
	32 (May 83)	A	265	(R03)	A		5	E
	34 (Nov 81)	B		14 (R99)	C	281	45 (May 95)	C
	41 (Nov 77)	C		41 (May 95)	A		41 (May 93)	D
253	46 (Nov 74)	D		42 (May 95)	A		36 (Nov 92)	D
	46 (Nov 77)	B	266	33 (Nov 92)	B	282	47 (Nov 87)	C
	42 (Nov 74)	B		40 (Nov 89)	C		60 (Nov 82)	A
	43 (Nov 74)	A		46 (May 89)	A		35 (Nov 81)	B
254	35 (Nov 83)	B		59 (May 89)	B	283	21 (May 80)	B
	47 (Nov 74)	C		36 (Nov 88)	A		46 (Nov 78)	B
	37 (Nov 83)	A		47 (May 88)	D		50 (Nov 78)	A
	28 (May 82)	C	267	26 (May 86)	B	284	25 (May 77)	C
255	31 (Nov 95)	A		36 (Nov 85)	C		7 (May 74)	C
	26 (May 94)	A		33 (May 85)	A		16 (May 74)	B
	26 (May 93)	B	268	46 (Nov 84)	C		46 (May 92)	D
	36 (May 92)	C		47 (Nov 84)	A	285	49 (Nov 90)	B

Page	Question	Answer	Page	Question	Answer	Page	Question	Answer
	41 (May 90)	D		43 (Nov 81)	A	317	43 (Nov 92)	D
286	41 (Nov 86)	D		32 (May 79)	A		49 (May 92)	A
	37 (Nov 85)	C		1 (May 74)	D		47 (May 91)	C
	48 (May 95)	B	304	50 (May 95)	C		42 (Nov 88)	B
287	41 (May 84)	C	305	42 (May 93)	D		49 (May 88)	A
	42 (May 82)	B		28 (May 86)	C		40 (May 85)	C
	3 (May 94)			41 (May 82)	C	318	46 (May 84)	C
	73	F	306	38 (Nov 82)	C		47 (Nov 83)	C
	74	C		34 (Nov 77)	D		44 (May 83)	D
	75	D	307	36 (May 76)	C		45 (May 83)	B
	76	D		9 (May 74)	D		47 (Nov 81)	B
	77	A		3 (Nov 94)		319	25 (Nov 77)	C
	78	G		76	B			
288	17 (R01)	C		77	G		**PART VIII**	
	39 (Nov 85)	B		78	E			
289	28 (May 79)	A		79	F	323	48 (Nov 95)	B
	18 (May 77)	A		80	I		56 (Nov 93)	B
	48 (May 88)	D		81	D		54 (May 87)	B
	42 (Nov 85)	B		82	E		43 (May 78)	C
290	40 (May 76)	C		83	A		46 (May 77)	C
	36 (May 82)	B		84	H	324	47 (May 77)	A
	36 (Nov 77)	B		85	A		48 (May 77)	D
	47 (May 95)	A		86	B		6 (Nov 75)	A
291	40 (Nov 88)	D		87	J		12 (Nov 76)	C
	1 (Nov 80)	A		88	I		19 (R01)	A
	46 (May 95)	B	309	41 (Nov 92)	D	325	51 (Nov 89)	D
	38 (May 90)	A		41 (Nov 89)	C		11 (Nov 80)	D
	41 (Nov 85)	A		43 (May 93)	C		34 (May 79)	C
292	42 (Nov 78)	C		6 (Nov 80)	D		44 (May 79)	C
294	49 (Nov 83)	A	310	27 (Nov 77)	B	326	50 (May 84)	A
295	36 (May 93)	A		39 (Nov 77)	A		19 (May 87)	C
	37 (May 93)	C		34 (May 76)	B	327	47 (May 82)	D
	38 (May 93)	B	311	9 (Nov 80)	B		14 (R97)	B
	39 (May 93)	D		3 (May 74)	B		45 (May 90)	C
296	48 (Nov 90)	A	312	15 (May 80)	D		58 (Nov 81)	B
	51 (May 89)	A		30 (May 80)	B		15 (R99)	C
	29 (May 79)	B		30 (May 79)	D	328	12 (R98)	A
	35 (Nov 77)	A	313	19 (May 80)	A		45 (Nov 95)	B
300	49 (Nov 91)	D		47 (Nov 78)	D		46 (Nov 95)	C
	39 (May 90)	C		43 (Nov 77)	C		54 (Nov 94)	D
	44 (Nov 89)	C		39 (Nov 88)	A		45 (May 94)	D
301	38 (Nov 81)	B	314	8 (Nov 80)	C		49 (Nov 93)	C
	42 (Nov 81)	A	315	20 (R01)	C	329	55 (Nov 93)	A
	25 (May 79)	D		16 (R99)	D		51 (May 92)	C
	35 (May 76)	C		5 (R97)	C		52 (May 92)	C
302	49 (May 95)	B		15 (R97)	D		53 (May 92)	D
	40 (Nov 92)	D		15 (R96)	C		44 (May 90)	D
	47 (May 92)	D	316	59 (Nov 95)	D	330	48 (Nov 89)	A
	50 (Nov 87)	C		58 (May 95)	D		49 (Nov 89)	D
	52 (Nov 84)	A		46 (Nov 93)	B		46 (Nov 88)	D
	44 (May 84)	D		47 (Nov 93)	D		39 (Nov 87)	B
303	43 (Nov 82)	C		44 (May 93)	D		55 (May 87)	B
	38 (May 82)	D		42 (Nov 92)	A		45 (Nov 85)	C

Page	Question	Answer
331	49 (May 84)	D
	17 (May 81)	D
	33 (May 80)	A
	39 (May 79)	C
335	56 (Nov 94)	C
	48 (Nov 85)	B
	56 (Nov 84)	C
	9 (Nov 76)	B
	23 (May 74)	C
337	36 (May 86)	A
	13 (Nov 79)	C
	38 (May 79)	A
	29 (May 74)	D
338	47 (May 94)	B
	47 (May 90)	B
	47 (May 84)	D
339	11 (R98)	A
	50 (Nov 95)	A
	57 (Nov 93)	D
	56 (May 92)	A
340	59 (May 92)	B
	52 (Nov 89)	A
	43 (May 85)	C
	58 (Nov 83)	C
	34 (May 80)	C
	39 (May 78)	A
341	52 (May 87)	A
	53 (May 87)	B
	51 (May 84)	B
	38 (May 80)	C
342	13 (Nov 89)	A
	17 (Nov 86)	C
	54 (May 84)	B
	59 (Nov 83)	B
343	13 (R97)	D
	60 (May 92)	A
	43 (May 90)	A
	45 (Nov 88)	A
	32 (May 80)	C
344	37 (May 79)	A
	2 (Nov 75)	B
345	51 (Nov 94)	D
	55 (May 92)	B
346	47 (Nov 88)	D
	50 (May 88)	D
	54 (Nov 84)	C
	54 (Nov 83)	A
	43 (Nov 95)	B
347	51 (Nov 93)	A
	52 (Nov 93)	C
	48 (May 91)	C
	14 (May 81)	C
	16 (May 81)	D

Page	Question	Answer
348	35 (Nov 78)	D
	36 (Nov 78)	B
	7 (Nov 75)	A
349	43 (May 94)	A
	42 (May 90)	C
350	52 (Nov 83)	B
	50 (May 91)	A
	55 (May 89)	D
	56 (May 89)	B
	57 (May 89)	C
	58 (May 89)	B
351	39 (May 83)	A
	47 (Nov 82)	C
352	40 (May 78)	C
	45 (May 77)	A
	34 (May 75)	B
	44 (Nov 95)	D
	53 (Nov 94)	D
353	44 (May 94)	D
	54 (Nov 93)	D
	57 (May 92)	A
	45 (Nov 89)	A
	46 (Nov 86)	B
	42 (May 85)	C
354	37 (May 80)	B
	40 (May 75)	A

PART IX

Page	Question	Answer
359	45 (May 75)	A
	38 (Nov 80)	A
	18 (May 79)	A
	35 (Nov 75)	D
	37 (Nov 75)	D
360	57 (Nov 94)	C
	48 (May 94)	C
	58 (Nov 93)	D
	46 (May 93)	C
	45 (Nov 92)	B
361	46 (Nov 92)	D
	57 (May 91)	C
	50 (Nov 89)	A
	53 (Nov 88)	A
	42 (Nov 87)	D
	58 (May 87)	A
362	44 (May 85)	C
	45 (May 85)	C
	50 (May 83)	B
	52 (Nov 82)	B
	54 (Nov 82)	B
	47 (May 75)	C
363	2(b) (R96)	
	6	E

Page	Question	Answer
	7	I
	8	H
	9	G
	10	C
364	53 (Nov 89)	C
	58 (Nov 84)	D
	37 (Nov 80)	C
	26 (Nov 77)	C
365	50 (May 94)	B
	48 (May 93)	D
	47 (May 83)	C
	49 (May 78)	A
	28 (Nov 77)	A
366	47 (Nov 92)	D
	48 (Nov 92)	A
	60 (May 89)	A
	59 (May 87)	B
	56 (Nov 82)	C
367	33 (Nov 80)	D
	36 (Nov 75)	A
	58 (Nov 94)	D
	59 (Nov 93)	B
	47 (May 93)	C
368	60 (May 91)	C
	48 (May 85)	A
	50 (May 85)	D
	57 (May 84)	A
	51 (May 83)	B
369	58 (Nov 82)	C
	48 (May 82)	C
	46 (Nov 81)	D
	25 (Nov 79)	D
370	34 (Nov 75)	A
	39 (Nov 75)	C
373	60 (Nov 94)	A
	54 (May 94)	A
	55 (May 94)	C
	53 (Nov 93)	C
374	50 (May 93)	A
	50 (Nov 92)	A
	44 (Nov 87)	B
	57 (May 87)	C
	50 (Nov 85)	D
375	47 (May 85)	B
	57 (Nov 84)	C
	52 (May 83)	D
	50 (May 78)	D
376	52 (May 94)	C
	60 (Nov 93)	D
	32 (May 91)	D
	59 (May 91)	D
377	43 (Nov 87)	C
	39 (May 86)	B

Page	Question	Answer
	22 (Nov 77)	A
	29 (May 77)	A
	44 (Nov 76)	C
	5 (May 74)	C
420	2 (Nov 93)	
	61	K
	62	H
	63	D
	64	F
	65	T
	66	T
	67	T
	68	T
	69	F
	70	G
	71	C
	72	B
421	2 (May 92)	
	61	C
	62	B
	63	A
	64	D
	65	D
	66	C
	67	A
	68	A
	69	G
	70	B
	71	A
	72	D
	73	A
	74	D
	75	D
	76	D
	77	D
	78	A
425	41 (Nov 79)	A
	24 (May 76)	A
	12 (May 95)	A
426	16 (May 94)	C
	18 (May 93)	C
	6 (Nov 92)	C
	10 (Nov 92)	B
	9 (May 91)	A
427	19 (Nov 90)	A
	8 (Nov 89)	C
	11 (May 88)	A
	52 (May 86)	B
	51 (Nov 81)	D
428	51 (May 81)	B
	47 (Nov 79)	C
	37 (Nov 78)	B
	38 (Nov 78)	B

Page	Question	Answer
	46 (Nov 76)	C

PART XI

Page	Question	Answer
433	59 (May 82)	B
	13 (Nov 78)	D
	28 (May 76)	A
434	60 (Nov 95)	A
	60 (May 95)	C
	57 (Nov 92)	D
	60 (Nov 90)	C
	60 (Nov 89)	C
435	60 (May 88)	A
	59 (Nov 87)	D
	59 (Nov 86)	D
	60 (Nov 85)	B
	60 (May 85)	B
	36 (May 83)	C
436	60 (May 82)	D
	59 (Nov 81)	C
	48 (May 81)	A
	14 (May 78)	C
	17 (May 78)	C
437	20 (May 78)	A
	2 (Nov 77)	C
	47 (Nov 77)	D
	9 (May 77)	C
	40 (Nov 75)	D
	32 (May 75)	B
438	60 (May 90)	D
	45 (May 81)	A
439	46 (May 81)	A
	6 (May 77)	C
	(R03)	B
	10 (R00)	B
	17 (R99)	C
440	3 (R97)	
	1	K
	2	M
	3	H
	4	E
	5	B
	10 (R96)	B
	59 (May 95)	B
441	59 (May 93)	C
	60 (May 93)	B
	56 (Nov 92)	D
	59 (Nov 91)	C
	60 (Nov 91)	C
442	57 (Nov 90)	A
	59 (May 90)	C
	59 (Nov 89)	A
	59 (May 88)	B

Page	Question	Answer
	58 (Nov 87)	D
	60 (Nov 86)	C
443	59 (May 85)	D
	37 (May 83)	B
	56 (Nov 81)	B
	48 (May 80)	C
	7 (Nov 78)	B
444	38 (May 74)	C
445	3 (May 94)	
	79	T
	80	F
	81	F
	82	T
	83	T
	84	T
449	60 (Nov 87)	D
	2 (May 79)	B
450	38 (Nov 75)	C
451	55 (Nov 81)	A
	60 (Nov 81)	C
	32 (May 76)	C
452	53 (Nov 80)	C
	12 (Nov 79)	B
	45 (Nov 79)	B
	53 (May 74)	C

PART XII

Page	Question	Answer
455	6 (R98)	B
	16 (Nov 93)	B
	14 (Nov 91)	B
	11 (Nov 90)	A
456	4 (Nov 89)	D
	58 (May 86)	A
	1 (May 82)	B
	23 (Nov 80)	C
	3 (Nov 74)	D
457	15 (Nov 83)	D
	16 (Nov 95)	D
	3 (May 83)	C
	20 (Nov 81)	D
	5 (Nov 74)	B
458	10 (May 92)	D
	18 (Nov 95)	C
	22 (Nov 94)	D
	14 (Nov 90)	B
459	6 (Nov 89)	B
	13 (May 88)	C
	21 (Nov 87)	B
	10 (May 87)	B
	18 (Nov 81)	B
460	4 (Nov 74)	C
	16 (Nov 91)	D

Page	Question	Answer
	7 (Nov 89)	D
	16 (Nov 79)	A
	6 (Nov 74)	D
462	19 (Nov 95)	D
	23 (Nov 94)	B
	18 (Nov 93)	C
463	15 (May 93)	B
	16 (May 89)	A
	20 (Nov 87)	B
	9 (May 85)	B
	4 (May 83)	B
464	24 (May 75)	B
	25 (May 75)	A
465	1 (R97)	
	1	E
	2	A
	3	E
	4	B
	5	A
467	17 (Nov 95)	A
	21 (Nov 94)	C
	12 (Nov 90)	C
	1 (Nov 85)	B
	12 (Nov 84)	D
	13 (Nov 84)	B
468	19 (Nov 81)	D
	15 (Nov 79)	B
	16 (Nov 77)	A
	2 (May 95)	
	61	A
	62	A
	63	B
	64	B
	65	B
	66	B
470	8 (R01)	B
471	2 (R97)	C
	11 (R96)	C
	12 (Nov 93)	A
	14 (May 93)	D
	15 (Nov 91)	C
	13 (Nov 90)	C
472	15 (May 89)	D
	16 (Nov 83)	A
	17 (Nov 83)	B
	5 (May 83)	A
	2 (May 82)	A
	22 (Nov 81)	C
473	12 (Nov 77)	C
474	22 (Nov 80)	C
	1 (Nov 74)	B
476	20 (Nov 95)	A
	24 (Nov 94)	C

Page	Question	Answer
	11 (May 93)	A
	12 (May 93)	C
477	12 (May 92)	B
	13 (May 92)	A
	17 (Nov 91)	A
	7 (May 88)	A
	55 (May 86)	B
	56 (May 86)	C
478	8 (May 85)	D
	10 (May 85)	A
	21 (Nov 81)	B
479	20 (Nov 80)	C
	21 (Nov 80)	C
	8 (Nov 77)	B
	10 (Nov 76)	B
480	19 (May 75)	C
482	1 (Nov 92)	A
483	11 (May 92)	C
	4 (May 91)	D
	7 (May 85)	B
	11 (May 85)	B
	11 (Nov 84)	C
	14 (Nov 79)	A
484	7 (Nov 77)	D
	4 (Nov 88)	A
	7 (May 87)	C
	4 (May 82)	D
485	20 (May 75)	D
	5 (Nov 89)	D
	19 (Nov 87)	B
	18 (Nov 83)	B
	3 (May 82)	A
486	24 (Nov 80)	D
	11 (Nov 76)	A

PART XIII

Page	Question	Answer
493	22 (Nov 95)	C
	22 (Nov 78)	B
	9 (R01)	D
	3 (R98)	A
494	21 (Nov 95)	A
	11 (May 94)	D
	19 (Nov 93)	C
	16 (May 92)	D
	6 (May 90)	B
	10 (May 84)	D
495	12 (May 80)	B
	14 (May 80)	B
	9 (Nov 78)	D
	10 (Nov 78)	C
	37 (Nov 74)	D
496	5 (Nov 85)	A

Page	Question	Answer
	9 (May 82)	B
	23 (May 81)	C
497	38 (Nov 74)	C
	40 (May 74)	A
498	39 (Nov 74)	A
	39 (May 74)	B
	20 (Nov 93)	B
499	6 (May 91)	A
	8 (May 84)	C
	8 (May 82)	A
	9 (May 80)	D
	7 (R98)	B
500	17 (Nov 93)	C
	19 (Nov 78)	C
	17 (May 76)	A
	18 (May 76)	C
	24 (Nov 75)	B
	15 (Nov 78)	C
501	24 (Nov 83)	A
	16 (May 80)	C
	28 (Nov 75)	B
	34 (Nov 74)	C
502	24 (Nov 95)	C
	13 (May 94)	C
	19 (May 92)	A
	17 (Nov 90)	B
	9 (May 90)	B
	15 (May 88)	C
503	5 (May 84)	D
	9 (May 84)	D
	26 (May 81)	A
	11 (May 77)	B
	15 (May 77)	A
	20 (May 76)	C
504	2 (R97)	
	1	G
	2	H
	3	J
	4	F
	5	F
505	23 (Nov 95)	C
	2 (Nov 92)	A
	16 (Nov 90)	B
	7 (May 90)	D
506	14 (May 85)	B
	21 (May 76)	D
	2 (May 95)	
	67	A
	68	C
	69	C
	70	B
	71	C
	72	C

Page	Question	Answer	Page	Question	Answer	Page	Question	Answer
507	12 (R96)	A	514	11 (R01)	D		20 (May 92)	D
	5 (May 91)	C		6 (R99)	A		7 (May 91)	B
508	12 (May 85)	D		8 (R98)	C		7 (May 84)	D
	13 (May 80)	A		3 (R97)	A		35 (Nov 74)	C
513	12 (May 94)	B		25 (Nov 95)	D	517	(R03)	B
	3 (Nov 85)	C	515	25 (Nov 94)	B		3 (Nov 92)	A
	4 (Nov 85)	D		14 (May 94)	C	518	18 (May 92)	C
	10 (May 82)	D		4 (Nov 92)	A		6 (May 84)	B